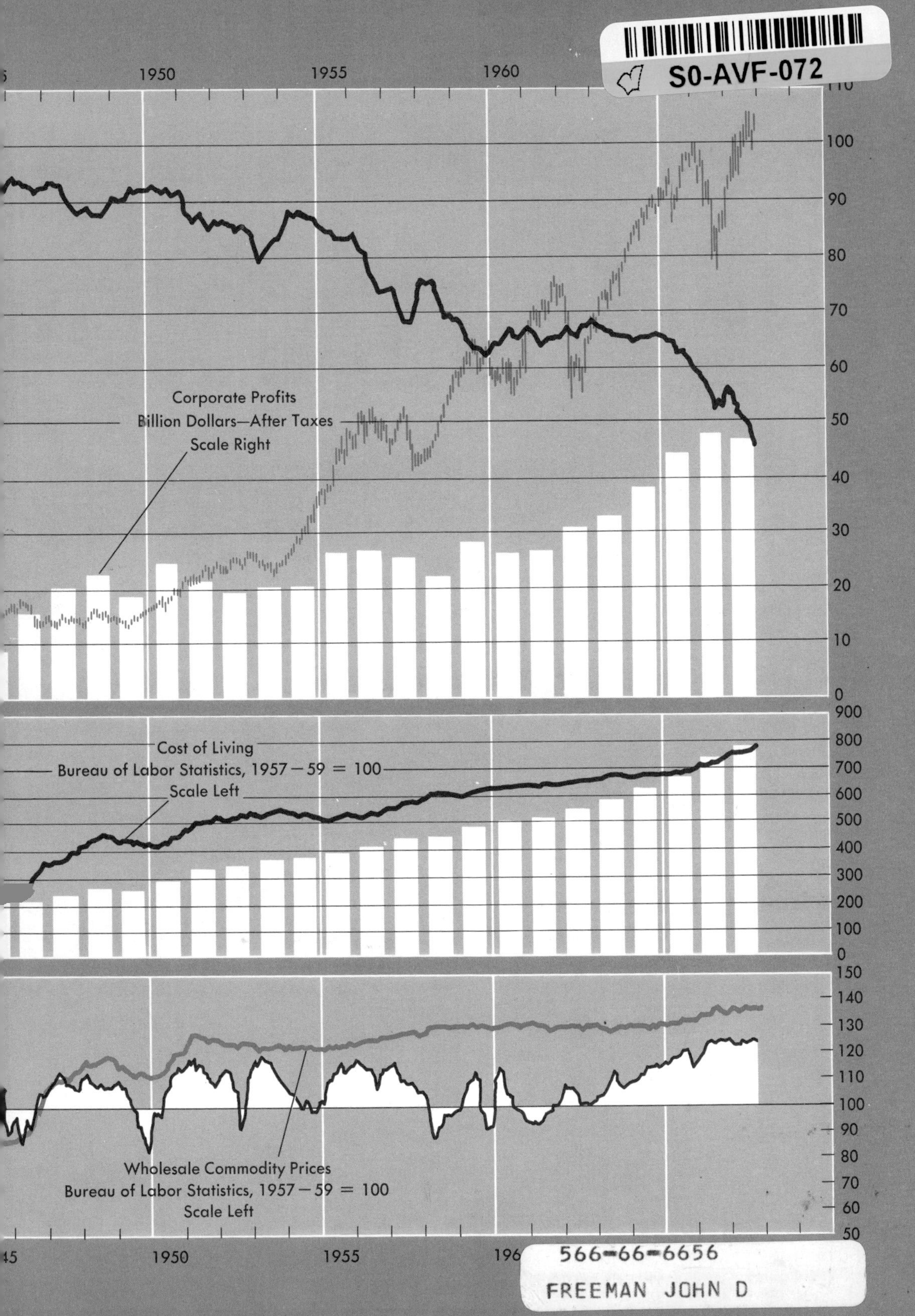

1950
1955
1960
Corporate Profits
Billion Dollars—After Taxes
Scale Right
110
100
90
80
70
60
50
40
30
20
10
0
Cost of Living
Bureau of Labor Statistics, 1957 — 59 = 100
Scale Left
900
800
700
600
500
400
300
200
100
0
Wholesale Commodity Prices
Bureau of Labor Statistics, 1957 — 59 = 100
Scale Left
150
140
130
120
110
100
90
80
70
60
50
45
1950
1955

INTRODUCTION TO MODERN BUSINESS

Prentice-Hall, Inc., Englewood Cliffs, New Jersey

VERNON A. MUSSELMAN
Professor of Business Education
University of Kentucky

EUGENE H. HUGHES
Lecturer in Business Administration
and Labor Arbitrator
Sacramento, California

INTRODUCTION TO MODERN BUSINESS

Analysis and Interpretation

FIFTH EDITION

INTRODUCTION TO MODERN BUSINESS

Fifth Edition

MUSSELMAN/HUGHES

Library of Congress Catalog Card No. 69-10304

Printed in the United States of America. Designed by Mel Haber.

Current printing (last digit)

10 9 8 7 6 5 4

PRENTICE-HALL INTERNATIONAL, Inc., London

PRENTICE-HALL OF AUSTRALIA Pty. Ltd., Sydney

PRENTICE-HALL OF CANADA, Ltd., Toronto

PRENTICE-HALL OF INDIA Private Ltd., New Delhi

PRENTICE-HALL OF JAPAN, Inc., Tokyo

Preface

Since business plays such an important and multifaceted role in our capitalistic society, the study of business and its environment can prove to be a vital part of any student's formal education. Business is a broad and complex subject because it combines many related and unrelated activities—the various roles of business organizations, the relationship of business to government, the interdisciplinary approach to the management of the firm. Too, within each business there are functional operations to be understood, including problems of production, marketing, personnel, finance, and transportation. Further, laws made at several levels greatly influence business. Indeed, the closer we look at the role of business today, the broader and more complex does it seem to become.

Introduction to Modern Business: Analysis and Interpretation, Fifth Edition, is a major revision of the 1964 publication. It updates statistical and economic data, and highlights new laws and regulations as well as other significant phenomena affecting, or soon to affect, the functional areas of business. Because the authors have continued to probe rather deeply into the various subject areas whose study relies heavily on a knowledge of the behavioral sciences, the treatment and coverage of these areas remains superior to the "once-over-lightly" approach common to many introductory business texts (for example, three chapters are devoted to business and its environment; the organization of the enterprise is heavily emphasized in four chapters; all phases of marketing are covered in the six chapters devoted to this functional field).

Although no single introductory text could possibly include all facets of business, with the guidance of many users of previous editions we have again tried to account for all the essential elements required for a complete and up-to-date first course. To this end we have brought in much new information on current practices, as well as trends in electronic data processing and computer technology, as well as on the aforementioned behavioral areas of business management. We have also expanded the variety of interesting and helpful features which have proved so popular as aids to more enjoyable learning. The time-tested literary style, however, remains the same: a simple, straightforward delivery that tends to make the reader feel that he is actually "sitting in on" every discussion.

Because this book, though written as an introductory text, is a study in considerable depth of many phases of business, it may be used as a first- or second-year college text; as the basic text for elementary business courses in schools of business, engineering, or technology; or in liberal-arts programs. And, because it is in some respects more advanced than its predecessors, it should appeal more than ever to today's collegian, who in certain ways is better equipped than was his counterpart just a few years ago, and thus is better qualified to understand advanced concepts and to engage in more extensive analysis and interpretation of basic data.

Once again the authors are indebted to friends far too numerous to list in detail. A special debt of gratitude is due the following persons: Edgar M. Bowers, Jr., District Manager, and Edward Corona, Claims Unit Supervisor, Bureau of Old Age and Survivors Insurance, Department of Health, Education, and Welfare, Houston; Philip F. Finnegan, Actuarial Director, Prudential Insurance Co. of America, Southwestern Home Office, Houston; Conrad H. Collier, Director of Public Relations and Advertising, Tenneco, Inc., Houston; Dwight E. Smith, Advertising Dept., Continental Oil Co., Houston; Robert W. Sterling, M. C. Horsey & Co., Salisbury, Md.; Allen O. Felix, New York Stock Exchange; John Dunsmore, *The Wall Street Journal;* Richard H. Kaufman, Associate Economist, *World Business,* The Chase Manhattan Bank; Stanley M. Rice, Vice-President, United Business Service, Boston; and Merrill Lynch, Pierce, Fenner & Smith, Inc., New York and Houston.

We also wish to express appreciation to our colleagues for their suggestions toward improving the manuscript: Dr. Z. S. Dickerson, Professor of Business, Madison College, Harrisonburg, Va.; Dr. Russell Johnston, Professor of Business, Virginia Commonwealth University, Richmond, Va.; Edward Carlisle, Head, Data Processing Center, Owens, Potter, and Hisle, Certified Public Accountants, Lexington, Ky.; and Professors Jerome M. Peschke, Truman Barber, Frank M. Allen, and Louis L. Irwin, of the College of Business Administration, University of Houston.

We acknowledge the cooperation of Donald A. Schaefer, Assistant Vice-President, Prentice-Hall, Inc.; Marvin R. Warshaw, College Division Art and Design Director; Mel Haber, the College Division artist who designed this edition; and James Bacci, our College Division production editor. Finally, we are indebted to our editor, George A. Rowland, for his painstaking effort to make this book more readable.

VERNON A. MUSSELMAN

EUGENE H. HUGHES

Contents

PART 1
BUSINESS AND ITS ENVIRONMENT

PART 4
OPERATIONS OF THE ENTERPRISE

PART 6
MARKETING MANAGEMENT

PART 1
BUSINESS AND ITS ENVIRONMENT

American Business and Our Economic System

1

This is a study of American business that encompasses its past, present, and future. Basically, business is an art, a science, and a social institution. It is an art in that it requires the development of certain tastes and the achievement of special skills. For instance, the experienced buyer and the veteran salesman are both artists of sorts. It is a science because it is based on well-established principles and practices. The social and behavioral scientists, especially, consider business, which reflects various individual and group behavior patterns, to be within their purview. And it is a social institution since it exerts a broad influence on people's work, and in fact on their entire lives, operating as it does in an economic environment.

Anything as varied and changing as business will of course pose many problems, particularly to the neophyte businessman—and these problems can best be solved by those who are adequately prepared to deal with them. This book about business is designed to help the student confidently and capably to face the challenges—and, hardly less important, to take advantage of the opportunities—that lie before him in his chosen profession.

You will find that this book covers many areas of the broad field that is business. One of these areas to which you will be introduced first is economics, because business and economics are mutually complementary. (Indeed, because of the many close interrelationships between business and economics, you as a business administration student will pursue more than one course in economics as part of your preparation for a career.) This chapter will introduce you to a formal study of business and to the relationships between business and the economic system in which it operates.

One might be tempted to say, in trying by way of prologue briefly to describe what business is about, merely that it is concerned with the production and distribution of goods and services—with clothes, automobiles, housing, land investments, banking, insurance, and so on. But this would be a gross oversimplification, for it would leave out much of the excitement inherent in this fascinating and rewarding aspect of human endeavor.

WHAT IS BUSINESS?

Modern business, as we have rather broadly hinted, is so complex that you might easily spend a lifetime studying it. Indeed, it is the sum total of all the enterprises that play a part in the manufacturing and marketing of goods and services to consumers. However, for practical purposes, we shall simplify matters and use the term *business* as it is commonly used—to denote just three things: *production, distribution,* and *business services.*

Production

This element of business begins on the farms and in the forests and mines from which come the raw materials used in making the products of all types and sizes of manufacturing enterprises. Because most other types of business activity are in some way dependent upon manufacturing, it has often been said that manufacturing is the cornerstone of American business.

Distribution

Distribution, also a vital part of modern business, is the phase with which you are probably most familiar. Every article you buy has been distributed from its source of origin to the place where you purchase it. (You normally buy it from the retailer, who in turn secured it from a wholesaler, though this is not always the case.) In addition to wholesalers and retailers, transportation companies and advertising agencies play vital roles in today's distribution processes.

Business Services

The third major area of business is that of business services. This category includes hotels, dry-cleaners, hair-dressers, appliance repairmen, communication, utilities, banks, and insurance. Even many businesses commonly thought of as selling merchandise deal as much in services as they do in goods. The florist, for example, sells flowers; but he also arranges and delivers them, and plans floral layouts for weddings, etc. And the ubiquitous gas station is frequently referred to as a "service station."

CLASSIFICATION OF BUSINESS ORGANIZATIONS

For our purposes, commercial business organizations may be grouped into nine principal divisions of activity:

1. Agriculture
2. Production of raw materials
3. Manufacturing
4. Construction
5. Wholesale and retail trade
6. Transportation and communication
7. Finance, insurance, and real-estate
8. Service enterprises
9. Government

Agriculture

Among the specialized types of American farms and ranches, the largest number are engaged in raising livestock. Next in number are dairy farms, followed in order by farms raising grains and other field crops, vegetables, poultry, and fruits. The gross farm income has averaged approximately $35 billion per year for the past decade, and the total annual net income for agriculture has averaged nearly $14 billion.

American farmers, although constituting less than 2 percent of those who are engaged in agriculture, still manage to produce about one-sixth of the world's agricultural products. In 1820, the average American farmer could grow enough food and fiber to supply only four people; today he can provide enough to meet the food and fiber needs of 42 persons. He can do this because he has been able to take advantage of the world's finest and most sophisticated farm machinery, a wide selection of sure-fire fertilizers, and highly effective insecticides.

But the national agricultural labor force is constantly decreasing. In 1850, almost two-thirds of those gainfully employed worked on farms. Today, only 6 percent are employed on farms, and it has been estimated that by 1975 this number will drop to about 4 percent.

Production of Raw Materials

This activity includes mining, quarrying, forestry, and fishing. These industries provide the *raw materials* from which a wide variety of commodities are produced. Together with agriculture, they constitute the basic industries of our economy; for without them our factories and stores would stand idle. Raw (or unprocessed) materials originate from the country's natural resources.

Manufacturing

Across the country, thousands of factories are engaged in producing millions of consumer items, and manufacturing employs almost one-fourth of the active American labor force. Without manufacturing, few raw materials would be in usable form and there would be few consumer goods to be marketed.

Table 1.1 shows the total number of persons employed from 1930 to 1964 in the nine selected industries we are discussing here. You will observe that the largest number are employed by manufacturing enterprises.

TABLE 1.1

EMPLOYEES IN NINE SELECTED INDUSTRIES, 1930–1964 (IN MILLIONS)

Industry	1930	1940	1950	1960	1964	Percentage Change by 1975
Manufacturing	9.4	10.8	14.9	16.4	17.3	+14
Wholesale and Retail Trade	6.0	6.9	9.6	11.7	12.1	+33
Government	3.1	4.2	6.0	8.5	9.6	+54
Services	3.0	3.4	5.0	6.7	8.6	+43
Agriculture	12.5	10.9	9.9	7.1	4.8	−21
Transportation and Public Utilities	3.7	3.0	3.9	3.9	3.9	+12
Contract Construction	1.3	1.3	2.3	2.8	3.1	+37
Finance	1.4	1.4	1.8	2.5	3.0	+26
Mining	1.0	.9	.9	.7	.6	−2

Source: U.S. Dept. of Labor.

As you study the figures in Table 1.1 you will note the rapid increases that have taken place in certain categories, and the decreases in others. At present the greatest employment growth is occurring in the area of government and in the service types of businesses.

Construction

The construction industry, by utilizing the finished products of many other industries in the building of our highways, homes, hospitals, schools, office buildings, factories, and other structures, contributes immensely to the annual increase in our national wealth.

Construction activity is one of the prime factors considered when judging trends in the national economy. It is basic because it represents a significant factor both in labor employment and in the use and consumption of a variety of products such as lumber, brick, steel, copper, glass, and cement.

In 1968, construction provided employment to more than 3½ million persons, and construction expenditures amounted to approximately $100 billion.

Wholesale and Retail Trade

There are far more retail stores than wholesale establishments in the United States, and many more persons are employed in retail than in wholesale trade. Together, these two activities provide employment for one-fifth of our working population—the second highest employed by those industries listed in Table 1.1.

Trade constitutes the heart of our distribution system, serving as the principal connecting link between producer and consumer. In a later section of this text we shall look more closely at the distributive functions of American business.

Transportation and Communication

The function of these business activities is to aid other types of business. For example, our transportation system carries raw materials to factories, and manufactured goods to wholesalers and retailers. In fact, American business as we know it would collapse were it not for our highly developed system of transportation. Similarly, our modern techniques of communication —telephone, telegraph, radio, and television—make it possible to carry out important business transactions with speed and efficiency. Although the number of transportation and communication businesses is not great, they render an important service in today's economy.

Finance, Insurance, and Real-Estate

Here again we have a group of businesses whose primary function is to facilitate the conduct of other businesses. Without banks and investment companies modern business could not function, because these financial institutions make it possible for businesses to exchange goods. Most business carried on in this country is done on credit. When payments are made, they are usually in the form of some type of commercial paper handled (and frequently issued) by banks.

Most construction in America is financed by savings-and-loan institutions and by insurance companies. Insurance companies also invest huge sums in government securities and in corporate stock and bonds, thereby undergirding to a great degree the entire business structure.

Service Enterprises

In addition to the businesses that create and sell merchandise, there are many that provide services. Dry-cleaners, repairmen, barbers, beauticians, hotels, motels, and theater managers, directors of sports organizations, and the like, all render services. They are just as much businessmen (or business institutions) as are those who deal in products, and the services they render constitute an essential segment of today's economy. In fact, as the per capita income increases, the percentage of total income spent for services increases. The percentage of the consumer dollar now being spent for services is the largest it has ever been in the history of American business. It probably represents the most significant trend in consumer spending today.

Government

The federal government, which engages in many different types of business, is the largest purchaser of business goods and services, and the largest employer of labor in this country. The government's labor force is now three times what it was in 1930, with total government employment approximating 10 million persons. When you exclude military personnel, this represents approximately one-sixth of the nonfarm workers.

Besides purchasing and hiring, the government takes an active role in attempts to stabilize business in periods of recession, subsidizes important business activities, and regulates and controls numerous business functions.

BUSINESS FURNISHES EMPLOYMENT

Business furnishes employment to more people today than does any other segment of our economy. The percentage of persons employed in nine major lines of work is shown in Table 1.2.

TABLE 1.2
OCCUPATIONAL EMPLOYMENT

Occupation	%	
Managers and Proprietors	10.6	Business occupations = 32% of the total
Clerical	14.7	
Sales	6.6	
Skilled	12.8	
Semiskilled	18.0	
Professional and Technical	11.2	
Farm owners and Managers	4.2	
Service Occupations	9.2	
Laborers	12.7	
(Farm, 3.9%)		
(Household Workers, 3.3%)		

When you leave college, you will be concerned at the outset with what we might call "initial employment." You will possess certain qualities and skills that you know will be valuable to some employer, and you will be interested first of all in finding employment where you can put them to use. But you will also want to find a position that affords both opportunities to "learn the business," and a chance to earn promotions.

Modern business provides a wide variety of such jobs, with numerous opportunities to advance. If you make good, you will soon be given greater responsibilities. You may even be made a supervisor over other employees. Later, as you increase in knowledge and experience, you may become an assistant manager, and in turn a department head.

If you possess true administrative ability, you can just about decide for yourself how far you will go in the business world. There are many top-level jobs in every large business organization, and they go to the people who have the ability to handle them. Let us assume, for example, that after you graduate from college, you take a job as an accountant. Later on, you probably can specialize as a cost accountant, auditor, or tax specialist. From there you might become head of the accounting department, treasurer, comptroller, office manager, or assistant budget officer. Some years later, the position of vice-president in charge of one of the major divisions of your company may be offered to you.

OUR ECONOMIC SYSTEM

We have just reviewed briefly the American business system. Business operates within a much larger scheme called our economic system. The economic system in America is a competitive one. Goods and services are produced by entrepreneurs with reasonable freedom from governmental controls. Profit serves as the reward for an individual's being willing to risk his time, effort, and capital in a business venture. The name generally applied to our economic system is *capitalism.*

The men who founded our country felt that a competitive economic system, financed by private capital, was the one most compatible with the American way of life. And their confidence and judgment have been validated by its outstanding achievements. It has been under capitalism that our industrial production and national wealth have prospered so tremendously.

Some people call capitalism a free-enterprise system. But it is not entirely free due to various governmental regulations and controls. A more appropriate label is that of *private enterprise,* for it is based solidly on the right and privilege of individual citizens to the private ownership of property. And growing out of one's legal ownership of property is his right to risk his property in a business venture.

Wants vs. Scarcity

Scarcities in natural and human resources limit man's ability to satisfy all his needs and wants. *The presence of unlimited wants in the face of scarcity is the primary economic problem of every society.* The fact of scarcity—limited resources—has always plagued mankind. Its very existence serves to challenge man's ingenuity and spur him to increase his economic competence and efficiency.

Solving the problem of how to utilize scarce resources to satisfy unlimited wants involves the establishment of an economic system. *Economics is a study of the ways and means by which a society allocates its limited resources in the production and distribution of goods and services.* This study also includes an analysis of people's activities in connection with producing, saving, and spending.

In addition to individual needs, mankind has a group of collective wants, such as those of education, highways, national defense, and a variety of social welfare benefits. Some of our economic goals here in America are: high wages, stable prices, a high return on investments, increased leisure time, conservation of natural resources, increased production of goods, protection by the government, freedom from government regulation, greater cooperation among management and labor groups. The full significance of some of these objectives may not be clear to you at this point, but they will surely take on meaning as you progress through this book. Yes, some of these objectives are in conflict with one another, but they do illustrate the economic goals of various individuals and groups.

The Basic Economic Questions

The people of any nation must answer some very fundamental questions regarding their economic system. They must decide in what ways they will utilize their national resources to satisfy man's economic wants. They must decide how to work together to bring about the greatest good to the largest number of individuals. The basic questions that must be answered before a nation's economic pattern may be developed are:

1. What goods are to be produced—what capital goods, what consumer goods? Who determines what goods are to be produced?
2. How shall these goods be produced—how do we organize our resources to produce them?
3. Who shall receive and use the goods and services that are produced? How shall they be distributed? Who shall buy them, and at what price?

The way these questions are answered determines the relative roles of private and governmental leadership. As they are answered and as they are implemented, a nation's economic goals become established. And a method of achieving those goals can be developed.

In democratic countries, economic decisions are made by millions of individuals. In socialistic countries, where the major industries are owned collectively (by the government), economic decisions are made by "the people's government." In authoritarian or communistic societies, economic decisions are made by a dictator and his few trusted advisers. Later in this chapter you will see that in America the economic organizational pattern is based on private enterprise and free markets. The Soviet Union, on the other hand, practices a controlled, centrally planned economy. There, the nation's rulers decide the type of transportation facilities to be used in any location, the amount and kinds of consumer goods to be manufactured, and even the types of work different individuals are to perform.

THE FOUNDATIONS OF CAPITALISM

There are certain factors that are essential to any private-enterprise economic system. They are sometimes called the foundations of capitalism. In a very real sense they constitute the democratic foundations of our economic system. A political democracy and a private-enterprise economy complement and supplement each other. Free enterprise assumes that the individual is the best-qualified judge of his own interests. And an economic system that sponsors this philosophy makes it possible for individuals to pursue those interests that achieve the most not only for the individual, but also for the welfare of society.

These economic rights are intimately related to other freedoms that characterize American democracy—social and political freedoms. Without the right of private enterprise, we could not be sure of a free press. No single freedom stands alone, and no one freedom alone can make a free society. Every type of freedom is interrelated with, and interdependent upon, all other freedoms. The economic foundations of the private-enterprise system truly constitute one of the foundation blocks of our democratic way of life.

Right to Property Ownership

Private enterprise is built around the use of private property. By *private enterprise* we mean the system under which individuals are free to carry on business with their own capital, experience, and desire to succeed, without the aid of the government or other subsidizing agencies. Under private enterprise, land, buildings, and factories are owned by private individuals or groups of individuals. Our right to own property is guaranteed by the Fifth and Fourteenth Amendments to the Constitution. In fact, the preservation of this right is an essential function of our government. Many laws have been enacted to protect our ownership rights to property against theft, confiscation, and embezzlement.

The right of ownership of property includes the right to control its use, to sell it, or to give it to another. Most of the property in this country—farms, homes, factories—is owned by individuals, not by the government.

The right to ownership serves as an incentive to care for, to preserve, and to improve the wealth of the nation. Most of us take better care of our personal possessions than we do of the property of others. This right also encourages individuals to acquire more property. A person's awareness that he may retain the earnings of his labor serves as an incentive for him to try to increase the amount he owns. As a result, not only does he profit personally, but society in general gains as well. The right of property ownership is fundamental to a free-enterprise economy.

The Profit Incentive

The individual's opportunity to gain from his ownership and use of property encourages him to go into business. And in attempting to improve his own economic position, he renders valuable services to others. The hope of making a profit is the chief incentive for venturing into a business operation. *Profit* is the return to the property-owner in excess of his cost of operations—that is, the amount by which his income exceeds his costs and expenses.

An *entrepreneur* is a person who assumes the risk and management of a private enterprise. He faces the possibility of losing money, of course, instead of making a profit. Since he risks his time, money, and effort, many argue that he should be allowed to make as large a profit as he can. Others feel that he should be restricted to making only a fair and reasonable profit. Just what constitutes a "fair and reasonable" profit, however, is difficult to decide—many factors enter into the picture. At any rate, the entrepreneur is entitled to an interest return on his investment. He should enjoy a margin of profit to cover possible losses in future years, and a reward for his efficiency and ingenuity in management.

The opportunity to try to make a profit is one of the foundations of our private-enterprise system, and the danger of suffering a loss is one of the risks assumed by every entrepreneur.

The Opportunity To Compete

Private enterprise under the capitalistic system inevitably leads to competition. *Competition* is the practice of trying to get something that is being sought by others under similar circumstances at the same time. The ground-rules and ethics of competitive practices are set up by the members of society. From many angles, competition is good for both businessmen and consumers. Self-interest encourages businessmen to ask high prices; but when many competitors are bidding for the same business, price reductions ultimately enter the picture. In addition, the aggressive characteristics of one dealer may make him more efficient than another; thus, under competition, managerial practices tend to be kept on a high plane of efficiency.

Competition operates in the market in many ways. To begin with, producers compete with one another for the best raw materials at the lowest prices. They also compete for the best factory locations and for the most efficient and productive workers. Wholesale and retail establishments also vie with one another for qualified employees and for the most desirable locations.

Some industrial firms compete principally with rival business enterprises that manufacture identical or similar products. Tool-makers are an example of this type of competition, for they must manufacture products to meet specifications. They attempt to meet or beat their competitors by making a better-quality or a better-designed product, and by giving better service. Similarly, a radio station competes with both newspapers and television stations for advertising.

Competition also prevails among firms that produce or sell different but related products. Manufacturers of one line of toys are competing with producers of other toys and games for a share of the recreation market.

Probably the most active area of competition among entrepreneurs is that of price, for they engage in a ceaseless attempt to gain a price advantage over their competitors through effecting lower costs or increasing the efficiency of management.

Competition among entrepreneurs usually benefits consumers in several ways. It leads to better service, for example. In an attempt to gain a service advantage over a competitor, a business owner may air-condition his place of business, extend credit to his customers, deliver merchandise to their homes. Competition also leads to better products for the consumer, and tends to eliminate inefficient entrepreneurs. The businessman who cannot meet the competition—who fails to provide better service or to produce a better product or a cheaper one—soon goes out of business.

Freedom of Choice and Contract

Freedom of choice is the right of every person in a free-enterprise society. Each of us is free to decide whether to become an entrepreneur or to work for someone else. We have the privilege of choosing whether to manufacture goods ourselves or to distribute goods that others have produced. We can choose the type of goods we will produce or sell, and we can make our own decisions regarding our place of residence and employment.

We also enjoy freedom of choice as consumers in a private-enterprise system. We have the right to decide whether to buy, where and when and how much to buy, and whether the product or service is worth the price being asked.

Another privilege enjoyed by members of a free society is *freedom of contract,* which is simply the right of every entrepreneur, worker, property-owner, and consumer to bargain with one another. This freedom includes the right to exchange goods and services on terms that are acceptable to all parties concerned.

A SYSTEM OF "FREE MARKETS"

Under a private-enterprise economy goods are exchanged in the market place. Persons who own goods offer to sell them through competitive bidding at the highest price the goods will bring. At the same time, those who wish to buy these same goods hope to secure them at the lowest possible price. In order for a sale to be completed, the seller and buyer must reach an agreement on the price of the good. A *market* then may be defined as *a place where sellers and buyers exchange goods (or services) for an agreed-upon price.*

The existence of a free market means that an entrepreneur may purchase his merchandise, his fixed assets, and his labor at a fair price. It also means that he may borrow needed capital at a fair price. But it also means that the persons he employs receive a fair price for their services. And Mr. Consumer can get full value for the dollars he spends for the commodities he buys.

When the market system is free of external controls, it serves as the nerve-center of business, ordering that certain types of goods be produced and distributed. But nowhere is a market completely free of "imposed" restrictions. Were it entirely free, some person or company might gain an upper hand and, through unfair practices, drive competitors out of business. After securing a monopoly of the market, prices might be raised to unreasonably high levels, to the detriment of the best interests of society. So you will see, as you progress through this book, that governments have imposed certain controls on the American market system. But basically, the functioning of American capitalism depends primarily on the theory of making economic decisions through "free markets."

The free-market system offers several advantages. In the first place, it ensures that goods will be produced efficiently. It also rewards workers for outstanding performance, and thereby provides an incentive for them to do their best. Furthermore, it makes for flexibility, for every transaction is registered, and it immediately effects specific adjustments in the economy.

The Law of Supply and Demand

In a system of free markets the ideal situation is that of maintaining a balance between the supply and the demand for any commodity.

When a new product is produced, a market for it must be created. At first, the price for the article is relatively high because only a few are available. As the demand for the new product increases, however, the number produced is increased to meet it, and the unit cost is reduced. And as the unit price decreases, more people can afford to purchase the good, so the demand increases further. The demand will vary according to the price; under a system of free markets, there will be a balance between the supply and the demand at any given price.

The choices people make when they buy goods create a greater demand for certain products than for others. This demand signals the production of more goods like, or at least similar to, those "chosen." Decisions to buy these goods are not only votes for them, but votes against other goods. This is called "voting in the market place." Consumers, by deciding how to spend their income, decide how our resources are to be used, and which factories and stores are to survive and prosper and which to fail.

APPRAISING OUR ECONOMIC ACHIEVEMENTS

How would you set about determining whether an economic system had done well or poorly? This is usually measured in terms of production growth and the equity with which the fruits of production are shared by the people of the nation. Let us examine America's economic system—capitalism—to see how well it has fulfilled these two objectives.

Our Economic Growth

There are several measures of economic growth, but the most commonly used one is the *gross national product.*

The Gross National Product. By *gross national product* (GNP) we mean *the total market value of all the finished goods produced and services rendered in the economy in one year.* In a way, this serves as an index of the degree to which our output is growing (measured in terms of market value). It is the most comprehensive measure we have of what we produce. The GNP increased from $504 billion in 1960 to $785 billion in 1967. This represents an increase of better than 40 percent.

Investment in Plant and Equipment. The economist uses the term *capital* to refer to industry's productive equipment. By reinvesting profits in new plants and equipment, we increase the amount invested in these business assets which are essential to all basic manufacturing operations. Continuous capital improvements and expansion are essential to increased industrial production. The recent history of American industry has been a record of rapidly expanding investments in new buildings and equipment—an index of growth in our ability to produce.

Productivity. *Productivity* means *output achieved in relation to input*—the amount of materials and labor consumed to produce goods and services. Increased output makes for higher wages, shorter hours, lower prices, and a greater return to the business owner. There are two ways of measuring productivity: by means of the average hourly output per worker, and in terms of national income per man-hour (one man times one hour equals one man-hour).

The average worker today produces approximately six times as much as the average worker produced a hundred years ago. This ratio is based on dollar value in terms of constant (not fluctuating) purchasing power. The output per man-hour increased by one-fifth during the five-year period from 1960 to 1965.

One of the important results of increased expenditures for plants, equipment, and research is a greater output per man-hour of labor. Over the past

50 years, output per man-hour has advanced at approximately 2.3 percent per year. During the period since World War II, the rate has risen 3.1 percent per annum. Much of this increase has resulted from spectacular growth rates in agriculture.

The Bureau of Labor Statistics forecasts a continuing growth rate only slightly lower than the average for the post-war years. Projections of current productivity growth rates suggest that by 1970, output per hour in manufacturing may be 85 percent greater than in the years right after the war.

Personal Income

The *total national income* differs from the GNP in that it represents the amount left after subtracting the costs of maintaining the nation's productive capacity. *National personal income* represents the total earnings of all the people in the form of wages or salaries, profits, interest, dividends, and royalties. This amount has continually increased from year to year. In 1946 it was $181 billion, had risen to $306 billion by 1953, to $417 billion in 1960, and to almost $650 billion in 1967.

But any increase in the size of the employed working force would result in a corresponding increase in their total earnings. What is most important is the degree to which the income per worker has been increased.

Growth in Per Capita Income. *Per capita income* is an average figure computed by dividing the total national income by the total population. *Real income* is income that has been adjusted to account for fluctuations in prices and in the buying power of the dollar. Our *real per capita* income has increased during the past century at a rate varying between 2 and 3 percent per year. It approximately tripled between 1910 and 1950, while the population increased by only 66 percent. In 1930 the per capita income was $1,030; in 1950 it was $1,670 (measured in dollars of 1954 purchasing power). This was an increase of 62 percent for the 20-year period.

To interpret statistics on personal income, one must keep in mind whether the data are in current dollars or in dollars that are adjusted for changes in purchasing power.

Distribution of Income. Average family income rose to $7,436 in 1966, a gain of $554 per family unit or 8 percent over 1965. We can calculate the average income per person, but how many persons receive this average figure? How is the national income distributed; how is it shared by the population as a whole? There has been a significant shifting of more and more persons into the middle-income brackets—people who are earning enough to buy more than the basic essentials of life. With few exceptions, income per consumer unit in terms of real purchasing power has increased steadily throughout the post-war period.

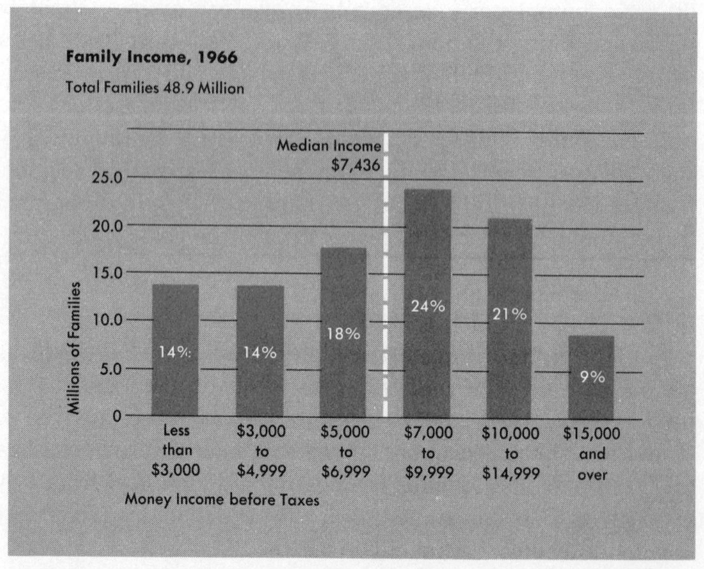

Distribution of per capita personal income.

Upward Shift in Distribution of Income. As the average annual family income increases, the number of families whose income places them in the lower income brackets decreases. Accompanying this shift there is a marked increase in the number whose income places them in the upper brackets.

The effect of these changes can be seen in the bar graph above, which shows the percentage of units and of income in the different income categories in 1966. The largest concentration of units is found in the $7,000 to $10,000 income class, which contains approximately 24 percent of all consumer units. Of particular interest is the growing percentage in the income intervals above $10,000, where 30 percent, or almost one-third, of all units were found in 1966.

THE CHANGING FUNCTIONS OF AMERICAN BUSINESS

Business in America has never been static—each generation has witnessed rapid strides forward. The past generation saw the large corporation become the dominant force in American capitalism. Today we are seeing several transformations occurring simultaneously—the exceedingly strong influence of organized labor, the decentralization and diversification of business operations, the separation of ownership and control, and the increasing recognition of the social responsibility of big business.

The Extent of Corporate Bigness

There are various ways of comparing large and small business—the number of enterprises, the gross value of assets, the number of persons employed, and the amount of sales, gross income, or net income.

Our immediate concern has to do with the degree to which corporate bigness sets the tone for the private-investment sector of the national economy. There are about the same number of partnerships as corporations, and proprietorships outnumber corporations by more than six to one. Yet the total profits before taxes for all corporate business in the United States is almost twice as much as that for all nonincorporated businesses (proprietorships and partnerships combined).[1] Corporations employ almost as many people as the rest of the economy combined, including federal, state, and local governments.

We are living in not only a corporate society, but a society of large corporations. It is the activities of the corporate giants in industry that we watch with the greatest concern and interest. To bear out this contention, one has only to observe the news featured in the business section of such periodicals as *Business Week* or *Time.* Most of the space and stories are devoted to big business—mergers of already huge corporations, labor negotiations in the giant industries such as steel or automotive, changes in the executive officers of the major corporations, fluctuations on the stock markets. Only infrequently is some unique accomplishment of an individual proprietor given recognition.

The problems of an economy dominated by large corporations differ in type and magnitude from those of an economy made up predominantly of small business enterprises. At this point, we are merely noting that the pattern of business in the United States is being set by large corporations. The details of the corporate form of organization, and its operational structure, are discussed in later chapters.

The Growing Influence of Organized Labor

The history of organized labor in the United States is a record of the increasing importance of labor's role in determining economic policy. Labor unions, with their 17 million members, constitute a tremendous influence in both business and politics. They maintain effective lobbies in both houses of Congress, endorse candidates for public office, and contribute liberally to the treasuries of their favorite political parties. They have funds available to support hundreds of thousands of their members during prolonged

[1] The U.S. Treasury Dept. estimated the number of businesses in 1964 to be 9.2 million proprietorships, 922,000 partnerships, and 1.4 million corporations. *Source: Statistical Abstract of the U.S.*, 1967, p. 484.

strikes—strikes which, in the transportation, automotive, steel, or coal industries, at least, attract widespread public attention and create interest on a national scale.

The internal government of some of our largest unions has on a number of recent occasions been the subject of court action. The question of anti-monopoly labor legislation is continually being raised. The degree to which labor should share in profits has not yet been settled. Whether labor should be guaranteed a minimum number of weeks of work or given an annual wage is still being debated at important collective-bargaining sessions.

Like large corporate businesses, large, powerful labor unions give rise to large and important economic problems which are difficult to solve. Whether they will be solved during the present generation remains to be seen.

Decentralization and Diversification

Businesses that *decentralize* are businesses that locate their factories and offices in different places instead of concentrating them at one site. The modern trend is to decentralize because adjacent properties and buildings generally are too expensive, particularly when a business's headquarters are located in a big city. Also, in the case of a serious riot or a bombing attack, an entire business might be wiped out if it is concentrated in one place.

Businesses that *diversify* are those that launch out into new areas of manufacturing or service. Companies that once made only radios have found it economically wise to manufacture washers, dryers, and refrigerators as well. They have done this either by creating and producing their own new lines of goods and building new facilities, or by buying out manufacturers of the goods they are interested in.

Often a healthy business will buy out one that is suffering losses, in order to acquire its line of products. In the bargain, the surplus funds of the healthy business aid the weak one, and the latter's losses provide a tax credit for the former.

Separation of Ownership and Control

The owner-entrepreneur of the small-business, proprietorship-partnership era has yielded, as has already been noted, to the corporation. Since anyone may buy shares in a corporation, the ownership of today's business is widely held. For example, there are more than 3 million persons who own stock in American Telephone and Telegraph. But the management of financial assets and the determination of sales policy fares best when it is entrusted to only a few persons. Thus the corporate form of business organization has led to the separation of ownership and control in our American business enterprises.

Not only is this true, but today the leading investors in stocks are the trustees of pension funds, mutual funds, investment banks, and insurance companies. These groups vote for their stockholders; thus even the right to vote has been transferred from the real owners to these investing groups.

This separation of ownership from control has given impetus to the growth of what might be called *professional management*. Professional managers are specialists who are employed to operate and manage business enterprises. The idea men who develop the operational plans and procedures for getting jobs done make up what is termed *middle management*. Those who make policy decisions and supply the executive leadership to business organizations constitute the highest level of professional management. We shall look more fully at the types, organizational structures, and functioning of management in later chapters.

The Social Responsibility of Big Business

The making of a profit has always been considered legitimate, for a business institution's very existence depends on its making a profit. Likewise, the idea of service is an accepted function of business. A business makes a profit for itself by rendering a service for others. In addition, a business is supposed to serve society *well*—that is, it should provide well-paying jobs for its employees, and yield a profit to its owners commensurate with the risks involved.

All this worked fairly well, with no serious problems, under the owner-entrepreneur business system. But under the corporate form of business organization—especially large corporations—the best interests of all facets of society are sometimes difficult to serve. A firm's economic responsibility may come in conflict with its social responsibility. This situation is perhaps best illustrated by the dependence of a local community on a single large corporation located there. Should the management decide that survival necessitates a move to a new community where tax or labor advantages exist, serious problems will arise for the community. Many citizens, perhaps a goodly number of whom own stock in the firm, will lose their jobs, and the tax loss will seriously affect the community's economy.

All this points up the complexity of the social responsibility of a corporate economic society, and reflects the changing nature of American business in today's economy. It has given rise to new and unsolved problems in our kaleidoscopic society—problems in which ownership, labor, and government all have tremendous stakes.

The Increased Role of Government

The government has always had a stake in American business. It is supported by taxes and taxes are paid to the government by businesses. Businesses pay taxes on the property they own and on the profits they earn. In a sense, then, whatever is good for business is good for the government.

The United States government has never taken a *laissez-faire* attitude toward business, although in the early years of our country its influence upon the economic system might have been appropriately described by the phrase, "the working of the invisible hand of government." Then, as the economy grew and businesses became large and complex, the activity of the federal government in the affairs of business increased. At first the government exercised largely the functions of supervision, inspection, and minor regulation, but with the passing of the years its regulatory aspects were intensified. In recent years its influence in many instances might best be described by the word "control."

Perhaps one of the most notable instances of government interference in business in recent history occurred in April, 1962. President Kennedy became quite irritated over certain price increases that had been instituted by the steel industry, and the possible inflationary effect these increases might have on the economy. He immediately sent a message to the presidents of twelve major steel companies, asking them not to raise the price of steel. He threatened to withdraw from the market any government purchases of steel from those companies that raised their prices. The result was that impending price increases were cancelled, and those which had already been put into effect were rolled back to their previous levels. Since that date there have been frequent occurrences of price regulation and rollbacks. President Johnson caused the aluminum industry to roll back its price increases during the spring of 1966.

It seems to have become standard policy for the federal government to use its powers to encourage capital spending when it has felt business has needed to be spurred, and to discourage it when the economy has appeared to be expanding too rapidly. During the fall of 1966 the rules regarding depreciation allowances and writeoffs were tightened in an effort to curtail plant expansion and cool off the apparent overheated boom in the economy. Under President Johnson, wage negotiation teams were called to Washington on numerous occasions to carry on their dealings under the close scrutiny of the administrative branch of the federal government. Guidelines for wage and price increases have become commonplace, and prices are no longer determined strictly through competitive bidding in the market place. It very well may be that this increased role of the government in business represents one of the most significant changes on the American business scene today.

THE NEW ECONOMICS

We have just seen some of the ways that the role of the federal government in the business affairs of the nation has taken on special significance in recent years. One of the foremost advocates of the increased role of government in business was John Maynard Keynes. Lord Keynes, writing in the 1930's, was one of the first to show that government not only has the ability but also the responsibility to exercise its influence to increase a nation's production, employment, and income. He held that this could be accomplished without destroying the basic freedoms of private enterprise or restricting competition, arguing that the government can go a long way toward maintaining continuing prosperity through: tax increases and reductions, the easing and tightening of credit, and the exercising of restraint in budgetary matters. His idea was to use these activities on the part of government to supplement and complement those of the private sector of the economy, particularly in the areas of capital and consumer spending, investment, and production. He argued that the government should furnish the incentive, but that private businesses and consumers should decide whether to spend, and when, where, and for what to spend.

Classical Economic Theory. Keynesian economic theory differed radically in its basic concepts from those of earlier economists. Prior to Keynes, the leading economists presumed that the economy was held in balance by certain natural forces that counterbalanced one another. The French economist Jean Baptist Say, for example, advanced the theory that a nation's production facilities would just naturally create enough income to purchase the goods manufactured. He argued that any excess in demand would correct itself automatically. And Adam Smith argued that if wages rose too rapidly, business would dismiss workers to cut down on labor costs, and that this reduction would continue until a point was reached where business would again hire more workers.

The New Theory. Keynes showed that economic history did not bear out these theories, but actually refuted them. He pointed out that for many years the economic cycle had fluctuated from boom to bust, and that prosperity based on inflation invariably lead to deflation, recession, and depression. Keynes reasoned that if employers reacted to decreased demand by laying off workers and/or reducing wages, the end result could only be one of less income to buy fewer goods, thus decreasing demand and curtailing production. He advocated that "the remedy for the trade cycle is not to be found in abolishing booms and keeping us permanently in semi-slump; but in abolishing slumps and thus keeping us permanently in a quasi-boom." His formula for bringing this about was to maintain a constant high level of total demand—demand for investment, as well as for consumption. His plan called for the government to come to the aid of the private sector of the economy whenever that sector fell off.

The key elements in the Keynesian theory are:

1. If left to make its own adjustments in wages and prices, a market economy might come into balance but it would not necessarily balance out at the full employment level.
2. The level of employment essentially depends on the amount of income that business and consumers combined spend for goods.
3. If and when consumers withold money from spending, and if at the same time industry curtails capital-expansion investment, the economy may settle into a low employment level.
4. To correct low economic levels, government must increase the purchasing power in the money system. It might do this by loosening credit, by decreasing taxes, or by increasing its own spending.

Keynes stated that the economy should be evaluated in its totality, not piecemeal; that all the many forces at work in the total economic structure—production, prices, income, profits, interest, etc.—should be measured and considered as a whole. He looked upon money as a means to an end, not as the end itself; money was to be used to achieve economic objectives rather than to be treated as a valuable possession.

The economists who have advised our presidents since the establishment of the Council of Economic Advisers by Congress in 1946 have for the most part been followers of Keynesian economic theory. The economic policies of our federal government during the past decades have frequently been referred to as "the new economics."

SUMMARY

Business is the sum total of all enterprises engaged in supplying goods and services to consumers. Business may be broken down into three major divisions: production, distribution, and business services.

Business furnishes employment to more persons than does any other area of economic activity. It not only provides a variety of types of work, but furnishes employment at both entering and advancement levels.

The scarcity of resources to meet the unlimited wants of mankind is the most basic problem in any economy. It forces every nation to economize in using its resources. Deciding how to organize to use resources to produce goods leads the people of every nation to develop some kind of economic system.

In the United States the basic decision-making process rests with the people. The economic system which they developed is called *capitalism.* It is essentially a private-enterprise economy resting squarely on the individual's right to private ownership of property. Other basic tenets of capitalism are profit motivation, competition, and freedom of choice and contract. Together these factors form a basis for the political and social freedoms we enjoy in this country.

The heart of a private-enterprise economy is its system of free markets. This means that goods and services are exchanged in the open market through competitive bidding. *Supply and demand* are kept in balance through the system of pricing; when the price becomes too high, persons refuse to buy goods, thus signaling a reduction in the supply. Decision-making in buying, called "voting in the market place," is the means by which each person plays a significant role in helping to decide how a nation's resources are to be used.

An economic system is appraised in terms of how much it can produce efficiently, and the degree to which the entire population share in the distribution of that which is produced. The capitalistic economic system ranks high, since it supports one of the highest standards of living found anywhere.

The basic functions of the American economy have undergone some significant changes, resulting in corporate bigness and dominance, increased influence of organized labor, decentralization and diversification of industry, absentee ownership, the growing social responsibility of big business, and the increased role of the government in business activities.

Economic theories have changed in recent years, giving emphasis to a greater role of government in business. The father of this new economic theory was John Maynard Keynes. Today most of the leading public and private economists follow the theories advanced so forcefully by Lord Keynes.

VOCABULARY REVIEW QUIZ

Match the following vocabulary terms with the statements on the next page.

a. Capitalism
b. Competition
c. Decentralization
d. Distribution
e. Diversification
f. Economics
g. Entrepreneur
h. Freedom of choice
i. Free market
j. Gross national product
k. Market
l. National personal income
m. Private enterprise
n. Production
o. Productivity
p. Professional managers
q. Profit
r. Raw materials
s. Real income

1. The process of removing materials from forests and mines and the growing of crops on farms PRODUCTION
2. The movement of articles from their points of origin to the places where they are purchased DISTRIBUTION
3. Unprocessed materials taken from the land or oceans
4. The name generally used to refer to the American economic system
5. An economic system based on the legal right of individuals to own and use property
6. The study of the manner in which the people of a state or nation utilize resources to satisfy their wants
7. A monetary return to the business owner in excess of the cost of operating his business
8. A person who assumes the risk of losing his property by investing it in a business in the hope of earning a profit
9. Attempts to gain things that are also sought by others
10. The privilege of deciding where and how one wishes to earn a living
11. A place where goods are bought and sold
12. The exchange of goods, money, or services through competitive bidding
13. The total market value of all goods and services produced in a period of one year
14. The output of goods and services achieved in relation to the input of material and labor required to produce them
15. The total earnings of all the people, counting wages, profits, interest, dividends, and royalties
16. The amount of a person's income stated in terms of the amount of goods and services it will buy
17. The scattering of a company's plants by building them in different geographical locations DECENTRALIZATION
18. Broadening the scope of a company's operations by producing several different lines of goods DIVERSIFICATION
19. Specialists who are hired to operate and manage business enterprises PRO. MANAGERS

QUESTIONS FOR REVIEW STUDY

1. What are the main classifications of business organizations? Which ones are increasing in relative importance and which are decreasing?
2. Why is the business field so important in supplying employment to the American working force?
3. What does the word "capitalism" mean to you?
4. What are the prime economic problems that confront the people of any nation?
5. Why is the right of property ownership such a key factor in a capitalistic economic system?

6. How does a private-enterprise economy contribute to democracy in government?
7. What are the chief risks and rewards that are of the most concern for entrepreneurs?
8. In how many different ways do business enterprises compete with one another? In what way or ways might a business compete with itself?
9. How many freedoms do you enjoy as an American citizen? Which ones are directly related to the capitalistic economic way of life?
10. What are the requirements of a "free market"? What are its advantages?
11. How can the accomplishments of any nation's economic system be evaluated?
12. What is the distinction between production and productivity? Which one is the better index of economic achievement?
13. In what ways do corporations dominate the American business scene?
14. Why have decentralization and diversification become so important to American industries?
15. What are the essential elements of the Keynesian economic theory?

PROBLEMS AND PROJECTS

1. How would you describe a capitalistic economic system?
2. Examine the current issue of a news magazine for a report of some important happening in the business world. Write a two-paragraph summary of the article. Indicate what you think is the most important statement in the article.
3. For each of the following types of business, name one important way in which it is strongly affected by some governmental regulation: building contractor, department store, drive-in restaurant, meat-packing plant, public utility, real-estate developer.
4. Assume that you wish to assess the current trend in the American economy. Name six factors that you consider important in indicating this trend. (Example: freight carloadings)
5. The average family income in the United States has been increasing continually in recent decades. Name at least three ways that this has affected the manner in which Americans spend their income.

A BUSINESS CASE

Case 1-1 Company Relationship to the Community

A manufacturer of small office appliances has been in operation in the northeast part of the United States for 42 years. Most of its highly skilled labor and supervisory personnel, who have been with the company for many years, are between 40 and 50 years of age, and own their homes. Much of its production machinery is obsolete and should be replaced with modern equipment. But the company's sales have leveled off, and its profits are slowly decreasing.

The company is housed in an old building, which it does not own, that is too small and badly needs major renovation. The company knows, however, that the building is available for purchase, and also that the land on which it is located is large enough to accommodate both expansion and employee parking.

Both the skilled and unskilled labor is organized—all of the nonsupervisory personnel belong to some type of union. The labor force has been stable, and the turnover rate is low, for there is a surplus of unskilled labor in the community. The economic life of the community is to a significant degree tied to the production of this factory.

Recently, the board of directors of the company has considered closing the factory, since it represents only a very small part of the total corporation's operations. The major considerations supporting this suggestion are the large capital outlay that would be needed to modernize the company operation, and the forecast for the future, which indicates a decreasing demand for the types of appliances now being manufactured. The chief argument against closing is the economic effect it would have on both its employees in the community, and the total life of the community.

1. What are the chief problems facing the corporate board of directors?
2. Does a corporation have any responsibility to the community where its plant has been located for several years? If so, in what way?
3. What is the stake of the city government and the community in the continuance of this enterprise? How can the people of the community hold this enterprise?

Government Regulation and Taxation

2

Government influence over and regulation of business have increased steadily since this nation was founded. During the early history of our country, the authority of the federal government was rather heavily restricted. But with the passage of time, the authority of centralized government has been expanded to the point where all business is influenced in a host of ways by federal, state, and local government.

In the minds of many, the control of business by government is a very thorny subject. "What," they ask, "is the legal basis for the public regulation of private business in the United States? What should be the regulatory role of the federal government as compared with that of the 50 state governments, which themselves are sovereign powers having the right to impose controls? Is it good for the nation to have the federal government not only regulate business, but compete with it?" (Two familiar examples of such competition are the generating of electric power under the Tennessee Valley Authority, and the sale of "GI" life insurance to veterans.)

Everyone agrees that labor, capital, natural resources, managerial skills, and technological know-how are indispensable in maintaining the high productive capacity needed to sustain this nation. But opinions differ widely as to the amount of government intervention required to provide these necessities for the over-all good of society as well as for the benefit of a particular line of business. Students of government, and well-informed businessmen alike, give divided counsel on this subject. Meanwhile, government participation in and control of business and industry continue to increase (they have in fact reached a scale that could not even have been anticipated only a generation or two ago), and our taxes keep rising with no relief in sight.

The subject of taxation, like that of government regulation, is of exceptional interest to businessmen, for the increasing costs of government at all levels have imposed upon the business enterprise an increasingly heavy tax burden. There is no disputing the fact that in order for the government to finance its operations it must obtain vast sums of money by means of public taxes. The question is: What sort of taxes are most equitable, and who should pay them?

All in all, in this chapter we shall try to do five things: (1) explore the functions of our federal and state governments as related to our economy; (2) analyze the reasons for government controls over business; (3) discuss the nature of those controls, and of related laws; (4) analyze the various kinds of taxes that are levied on businesses and individuals; and (5) measure the effect of these taxes on our business system.

THE ROLE AND FUNCTIONS OF GOVERNMENT

Businessmen are keenly interested in the present role of government in their field because they know they are much affected by it. And they are alert to signs of further governmental encroachment into their territory, aware that the regulation of business has increased steadily since the nation's founding. But the point of emphasis here is not that businessmen are alarmed by government regulations (true though that may be). It is that businessmen realize that in order to safeguard their interests, they must be familiar with the *over-all* direction in which government is moving, and either move with it or try to change it.

What is Government? *Government* is often defined as *the center of political authority that has the power to govern the people.* Aristotle regarded government as the most efficient and practical means of providing "the good life" for the citizenry. For our purposes, let us look at government both as a source of authority and as the political framework that provides for the enforcement of such authority.

Government is made up of those individuals who, whether elected to do so by the citizenry or appointed to it by elected officers, are expected to carry out the will of the majority. We can have either good and efficient government or its opposite, depending on the judgment and the intensity of interest which we as voters are willing to display. The point is that government will as a rule be only as good as we insist that it be.

Government Functions

We do not live and work in an economic system which operates in a vacuum, but in one in which government plays a dominant role. Thus, we ask ourselves the question: What are the functions of government? Government is generally considered to perform four basic functions, though they are not always sharply distinguished. The first is what is called the *police function.* Second is the *control and directive function* over the private economy. Third, every government is expected to provide for its citizens a program of *positive social services.* The fourth is the *function of transferring income.* Let us examine these functions in somewhat greater detail as a background for the remaining portion of this chapter.

The Police Function. This function of government involves the maintenance of public order, with all that this implies. The state and its agencies, and the federal government together with its agencies, are responsible for carrying on the activities necessary for this purpose. Legislatures, courts, and executive officials, together with police officers, are charged with maintaining public order—with providing a continuous stream of government services to protect the property, health, welfare, and life of citizens.

Many of the more common controls over business are based on the police powers of government. *Police powers* (which are limited in the USA by the Fourteenth Amendment) are those that government bodies use to protect the property, life, and well-being of the citizens they are responsible for. For example, city zoning, building and sanitary codes, and health regulations are police powers.

The Control and Directive Function. This function concerns the control and direction of private economy along such lines as are considered socially desirable. Over the years, at the national level, our government has built up, beginning with the establishment of the Interstate Commerce Commission in 1887, a group of federal agencies to give direction to business in a manner prescribed by law. The Federal Trade Commission, the Federal Power Commission, and the Federal Communication Commission are examples of types of government agencies charged with control and direction of business. Oddly enough, once these controls are set up, business seems to adjust, and those being regulated generally admit the value and necessity for such controls. The early feeling of banks toward the Federal Reserve System as compared with their present attitude illustrates this point.

The Social Service Functions. As we have said, government is expected to provide its citizens with a program of social services. This seems to be what most people want. A wide variety of such services are rendered today by local, city, and state governments—and to a great degree by the federal government. These services are constantly increasing in number. For example, there is a need at the local level to clean and light streets, provide libraries and recreational facilities, build hospitals, furnish police and fire protection, and supply water and disposal of sewage. Many states have accepted the responsibility for providing employment service. Federal social security benefits, patent protection, and postal service are illustrative of social-service functions performed by the federal government.

The Function of Transferring Income. This fourth function involves the transfer of money through an activity of the government. Such transfers take place largely through payments to groups of citizens on pensions or receiving insurance payments. Expenditures for unemployment relief and drought-stricken and flood areas are in essence a transfer of money income from one group of citizens to another. Many persons are critical of this function, particularly because of the kind of programs in which it is carried on. Such criticism is based chiefly on the belief that social programs will eventually lead to complete socialism in the United States.

In the material already covered, many illustrations of these various functions are to be found. The remainder of this chapter is an endeavor to discuss more fully the manner in which these government functions are being used to regulate such activities as monopolies, patents, copyrights, trademarks, prices, and other activities.

GOVERNMENT AND PUBLIC POLICY

The extent to which governments attempt to regulate business activities is largely a matter of public policy determined by what the public seems to want. The doctrine of *laissez faire* ("to let alone"), which prevailed in this country from about 1780 to 1870, characterized our private-enterprise system as one under which the government did not interfere in the conduct of business. Of course, the concept of "let alone" was never completely maintained because there have always been certain laws affecting business: tariffs, banking laws, patents.

More and more of the activities of business have expanded, but not without increasing regulation and control by government. This trend toward more control has been presumed to be in the interest of public policy. Consequently, the alternatives of public policy offered by our political parties have rarely allowed choices between complete government domination on the one hand and complete business control of the economy on the other.

The Meaning of Public Policy

What is the meaning of *public policy*? A precise definition has not yet been formulated by our courts. As used here, however, it may be said to be *the community conscience in the form of a statement, or interpretation of a statement, that carries with it the weight of government to matters of public morals, welfare, safety, or public health.*

How is public policy determined? The implementation of statutory public policy is probably the point between government and business where this contact is most direct. When Congress enacts legislation and the President has approved it, the impact on business may not be felt immediately. Much depends on the way in which the statute is interpreted and enforced. In the end, however, no significant statutory public policy can be fully implemented until the law has been tested in the courts. Hence, it can be said that the public-policy process culminates in the federal courts, where the judge must decide if there is a conflict between public and private rights.

A distinctive feature of the American economy is the existence of a comparatively few large corporations which are able to control the major share of the output of certain products and to exercise discretionary power over the supply and price structures. In the interest of public policy the question is frequently raised: "Are certain American corporations becoming too big?" Economists argue correctly that certain technical economies go hand-in-hand with any increase in size and scale of operation, but can a situation be justified which sees one business become so powerful that it can control prices and limit product supply, and thus practically nullify the all-out efforts of its smaller competitors to survive? At this point the courts must determine what is in the best interest of public policy that is consistent with the law of the land.

Attitudes Toward Government Controls

During the past century both government and business have grown tremendously, and they are bound to grow more. Both are striving for the same result—greater social well-being—and to this end, both are increasingly sharing more responsibilities for the nation's broad social problems. Yet, despite this spirit of cooperation, businessmen and others are constantly criticizing our government for increasing its influence over business.

The public seems to fall into two groups which differ widely in their attitude toward the role of government in its relations with business. One group complains of the evils of "too much government in business," because of the restraining effects on the activities of certain concerns. Many people in this group would advocate having a free economy wherein price is allowed to seek its own level because of the absence of controls. The amount of control which this group would sanction would be limited. Certainly, this group would not look with favor on antitrust laws, since they are by their nature highly restrictive. Try to picture what would happen if there were no controls over monopolies, or if advertisers were unrestricted in their claims about their products. And suppose railroad, bus lines, telephone companies, and public utilities were free to set whatever rates they wished!

The second group is inclined to be more liberal in their position. They view government as an instrument of aid and assistance to business, and as a means of restraining business when necessary. According to this group, unless we recognize the right of private property, the sacredness of contracts, and the need to punish those who violate the law, business transactions could not be carried on safely, and our personal rights would be in jeopardy.

The difficulty is in deciding how much regulation is needed and over which businesses. Owners of small businesses normally do not complain when restraints are placed only on "big" business. Conversely, managers of large companies are not inclined to raise objections to controls over small firms.

Source of Controls. The federal government derives its authority to act from the Constitution of the United States. This document recognizes, among other things, the right of private property and the sacredness of contracts. It sets up two broad levels of government: federal, and state. All powers and duties that are not specifically delegated to the federal level are left to the several states. (The interpretation of this point has never ceased to cause heated debates between various states and the several branches of federal authority.)

The powers of government may be extended in two ways: through legislative action by passage of laws or amendments to the Constitution, and through the processes of judicial interpretation of existing laws. In fact, it has been through judicial interpretation of the Constitution that the powers of the federal government to control business have been established without specific laws.

Regulatory Powers of Congress

In addition to the broad powers granted to Congress, the Constitution provides certain specific powers. Among these are the following:

Collect taxes
Levy duties
Designate roads
Coin money
Pay debts of the U.S.
Grant patents and copyrights
Regulate trade between the states
Establish post offices
Establish systems of courts
Patrol coastal waters
Provide for national defense
Fix standards of weights and measurements
Make laws to enforce private contracts

The power to regulate trade between the states carries with it direct control over such activities as public utilities, telephone and telegraph systems, railroads, bus lines, pipelines, airlines, stock exchanges, and national banks.

Reasons for Government Control of Business

In the kind of economy we live in, it is often asserted by some that government control over business and industry should be totally eliminated. Perhaps enough has been said thus far to indicate that this is unlikely, for there is no sacredness in private enterprise *per se.* Actually, the guiding principle should be as follows: *Whatever activity that is needed in the best interest of the public should be performed by a government agency when: (1) there is a strong expectation that it will be better performed by a government than by a private individual or agency, or (2) when private enterprise is not willing to or cannot perform such an activity.* In applying this guiding principle, there is no hard-and-fast line that determines when an activity should be performed by government or when it can be more satisfactorily provided by a private agency. The final choice is a matter of judgment, weighing all the facts, and not one of abstract principle.

In light of the foregoing principle, here are some of the reasons that have been suggested for government control of business:

1. *To protect the welfare of the individual and to promote higher standards of public health, safety, morals, and well-being.* Most communities have established health and sanitary regulations that must be observed by restaurants, food stores, and other kinds of eating establishments. Without these regulations, some businesses might become careless and fail to apply proper precautions in the handling of food and equipment. Other laws have been enacted to protect the health of workers in offices and factories.

Local zoning laws help protect the value of residential property by restricting the areas in which industrial plants and other commercial enterprises may be established. Finally, traffic laws have been passed to safeguard human lives.

2. *To prevent monopolies and combinations of business that tend to restrain trade or promote unfair practices.* A *monopoly* exists when a

firm exercises control over the supply of a commodity or service in such a manner as to give the organization either complete or dominant control over the price. If business interests were completely free of restraint, they would tend to take over competing firms in order to control selling prices or to dominate the sources of supply. The unrestrained monopoly that would inevitably grow out of such practices would undoubtedly prove detrimental to the public interest. (The subject of monopolies will be discussed at greater length in this chapter.)

3. *To conserve our natural resources.* The government is apparently the only agency in a position to protect our natural resources from willful destruction. Soil and water conservation, power-development projects, and reforestation programs are among the methods our federal government uses to conserve our natural resources.

4. *To maintain an expanding and prosperous economy.* Among the most common economic controls exercised by government are those over banks, building-and-loan societies, trust companies, investment companies, investment funds, and stock exchanges. Farm prices, wages, hours of employment, and personal credit are also subject to controls, on the grounds that wise regulation will prevent recessions and depressions. Our government is dedicated to promoting and maintaining conditions that will help to sustain high employment, full production, and peak consumption.

5. *To protect the public against abusive practices.* Government control is needed to prohibit certain abusive business practices, such as usury, false advertising, and reduction in standards. At the state and local level, legislation in the form of sanitary codes and zoning laws helps to protect the health and welfare of the public.

REGULATING BUSINESS ENTERPRISE

American public policy has long supported the principle that freedom to engage in a business of one's own should be guaranteed. Obviously one purpose of public policy is to regulate unfair competition and prohibit illegal monopolies.

Competition and Monopoly

Traditionally, our economic system is characterized by the presence of *competition,* which we defined in an earlier chapter as "the practice of trying to get something that is being sought by others under similar circumstances at the same time." Since we believe in a competitive economy because it promotes efficiency, it is interesting to note the types of facts which designate competition and the kinds of economic controls found in a competitive market.

Economists generally recognize three characteristic types of markets: the *competitive,* the *oligopolistic,* and the *monopolistic.*[1]

The *competitive market* involves many buyers and sellers, each free to deal with others after evaluating the quality of the goods or services and the price. While quality and price are each subject to negotiation and bargaining, the market price is determined by the relation between supply and demand.

The *oligopolistic market* arises when a few concerns are so powerful that they are not subject to the normal market influences, but instead are capable of influencing the market themselves. Illustrations of oligopoly include the steel, automobile, and cigarette industries, and flour millers. Oligopolistic control may also be accomplished through intercorporation agreements.

At the opposite end of the competitive market we find the *monopolistic market,* which exists when either the buyer or the seller controls the market. Until after World War II, when other aluminum companies were started, the Aluminum Company of America exercised a monopolistic control over the market. As a result, Alcoa was subjected by the government to numerous suits for monopolistic practices.

The type of competition that helps consumers is the one wherein the producer can lower his costs by more efficient operation, increase production to the limit, and then be willing to reduce his price below that of his competitors. It is this kind of competition that keeps competitors on their toes. But achieving this accomplishment does not make for an easy life. Hence, it is not surprising that producers would undertake to reduce competition by engaging in monopolistic practices rather than spend more money on promotion and reduce quality. It is easy to understand that, whether open or concealed, the existence of agreements among companies to eliminate competition can be far more beneficial to the producer than to the consumer.

One way in which the government has been able to protect consumers and help maintain competition has been to make it illegal to create monopolistic conditions. However, the chief difficulty in controlling or eliminating monopolies is that there is always disagreement over whether a particular business under indictment is really a monopoly—whether it has actually restrained trade unfairly.

Antitrust Laws and Competition

Even to begin to discuss fully the evolution of all state and federal laws affecting business and competition would require at least a cumbersome

[1] Another method by which competition is controlled and monopoly created is by a public grant. For example, a franchise given to a railway company for a city transportation system gives the firm a monopoly.

textbook. Therefore, an effort will be made here to mention only some of the more common legislative acts pertaining to this subject.

The Sherman Antitrust Act. Back in 1787, Thomas Jefferson advocated that an antimonopoly provision be written into the new Constitution. But it was not until Congress passed the Sherman Antitrust Act in 1890 that the federal government began to acquire power to combat monopolies. This late-arrived and somewhat underpowered act has since been strengthened and expanded by the passage of the Clayton Antitrust Act of 1914, and the Federal Trade Commission Act, passed the same year.

The chief devices used prior to 1890 to limit competition or restrict trade were: (1) price conspiracies—resulting in discrimination in price, (2) trust agreements to produce combinations—resulting in monopolies, and (3) the formation of corporations to acquire the stock of smaller competing companies.

It is not surprising to find that the three main prohibitions of the law were aimed specifically at these restraints. The main provisions of the Sherman Antitrust Act are Sections 1, 2, and 3, which are quoted in part as follows:

> Section 1. Every contract, combination in the form of trust or otherwise, or conspiracy, in restraint of trade or commerce among the several states, or with foreign nations is hereby declared to be illegal. . . .
>
> Section 2. Every person who shall monopolize or attempt to monopolize or combine or conspire with any other person or persons, to monopolize any part of the trade or commerce among the several states, or with foreign nations, shall be deemed guilty of a misdemeanor. . . .
>
> Section 3. Every contract, combination in the form of trust or otherwise, or conspiracy, in restraint of trade or commerce in any Territory of the United States or of the District of Columbia, or in restraint of trade or commerce between any such Territory and another, or between any such Territory or Territories and any State or States or the District of Columbia, or with foreign nations, or between the District of Columbia and any State or States or foreign nations, is hereby declared illegal. . . .

The fourth section provides that the several district courts of the United States shall be given jurisdiction to prevent and restrain violations of the act and shall have jurisdiction of the criminal and seizure sanctions.

In the many years since the enactment of the original Antitrust Act, the courts by their decisions have established the rule that the Act applies not only to interstate trade, but also to *persons* who are shown to affect interstate commerce. This means that the Act is broader than might originally have been interpreted. Retail stores locally owned but selling goods or liquor produced out-of-state, including in foreign countries, are subject to the Act. Prior to 1955, violators of the Sherman Act could be fined $5,000, or sent to prison for one year, or both. In 1955, Congress raised the maximum fine to $50,000.

At this point you may well ask why Congress passed antitrust legislation in the first place. Early English common law, from which our own legal system was derived, originally held that *all* restraints of trade were illegal. In the United States, common law during our early history distinguished between reasonable and unreasonable restraints, with only the latter being illegal. The courts even held that reasonable restraints of trade were valid where there was no intent to raise prices.

During the period from 1870 to 1890, many corporations engaged in devious business practices designed to gain market power. The more unscrupulous of these became increasingly distasteful to alert, business-oriented people who recognized that they were blatantly contrary to public policy. Under increasing public pressure, Congress finally enacted the Sherman Act.

The Addyston Pipe Case (1899) was one of the first tried under Section 1 of the Act.[2] This case involved six manufacturers who controlled about 30 percent of all cast-iron pipe production. These companies divided their sales territories and fixed prices on their pipe. The court ruled that this action was an effort to destroy competition. Evidence showed that the prices under the six-company agreements were one-third higher than they might have been under independent competition.

In 1911 the Supreme Court rendered decisions under the Sherman Act against two of the largest industrial companies in the nation at that time—Standard Oil of New Jersey and the American Tobacco Co. The ruling against Standard required that there be a breakup of the company into many smaller organizations. By this plan, each owner of one share of stock in Standard received shares in some 33 separate corporations, in addition to his stock ownership in the parent company. Similarly, in the American Tobacco case, the Court directed that the company, which controlled more than 95 percent of cigarette production, be broken up into three independent companies. Thus in both the Standard Oil and the American Tobacco cases the companies were ordered to dissolve their monopolistic mergers.

In 1903 a special Antitrust Division was created in the Department of Justice to investigate and prosecute alleged violations of the Sherman Act. Today the division has six field offices and a total of about 300 lawyers and 30 economists engaged full-time. The Division conducts investigations and secures evidence resulting from complaints, which number about 100 per

[2] *Addyston Pipe and Steel Co. v. U.S.*, 175 U.S. 211 (1899).

month. Complaints (price-fixing is the most common complaint) come mostly from individuals and federal and state agencies. Civil cases are more common than criminal cases.

The first state to enact antimonopoly laws was Kansas, in 1899. Since then, more than 40 other states have passed similar legislation.

The Clayton Act and the Federal Trade Commission Act. Between 1890 and 1914, considerable dissatisfaction and unrest were expressed over the ineffectiveness of the Sherman Act. Despite this Act, monopolies and trust agreements continued to flourish. The Supreme Court established the so-called "rule of reason" in evaluating the legality of what constituted a combination. By this rule, the Court gave a very broad and liberal interpretation of the Sherman Act. As a result, many mergers were authorized that otherwise could not have been approved under a less liberal interpretation. (By *merger* is meant the uniting of two or more companies into a single entity.[3] Thus by merging, it was possible to create a monopoly instead of by the use of a trust agreement. Such companies as Nabisco (National Biscuit Co.), U.S. Steel, and American Can were among the several that were formed by mergers of several smaller companies. Today, they are among our largest and most prosperous corporations.

In 1914 the Clayton Act was passed to accomplish two broad purposes: to strengthen the Sherman Act by declaring it unlawful for a company to acquire stock in a competing company in order to gain a monopoly or to set up interlocking directorates, and to forbid persons engaged in interstate commerce to "discriminate in price between different purchasers of commodities . . . where the effect of such discrimination may be to lessen substantially competition or tend to operate a monopoly in any line of commerce."

The Clayton Act did not forbid price differentials resulting from real differences in the quantity or quality of goods. Nor did it forbid the purchase of corporation stock by another company as an investment, provided the purchase did not reduce or eliminate competition. Since the Clayton Act was passed, further controls over stock purchased by corporation officials

[3] The distinctions between "merger" and "acquisition" are not sharp. A *merger* is an agreement among independent firms to join to form a new, larger one. The component firms pool their executive talents to conform to a prearranged plan. Very often, the new firm bears a new name perhaps derived from a combination of component company names. *Acquisition* means the outright purchase of assets of a company, or of sufficient interest in it, to gain control of it. The acquiring firm takes the initiative and determines how the new firm is to be operated and by what name it is to be known.

Firms often merge in order to acquire a greater distribution of risk. Too, diversification of product offerings frequently brings about production economies. Very few of the nation's largest corporations achieved their present stature without combining with several formerly independent firms. Working out the numerous problems involved in a merger often requires the services of bankers, management consultants, attorneys, investment brokers, and certified public accountants.

have been established under the supervision of the Securities and Exchange Commission.

Although hundreds of cases have been tried under the Sherman and Clayton Acts, involving many of the largest firms in America, probably the most complex and far-reaching decision involved the du Pont-General Motors Corp., decided by the Supreme Court against du Pont in 1957.[4] An order was issued in 1961 by the Court, finding du Pont engaged in restraint of trade, and ordering it to divest itself of its 63 million shares of General Motors' stock. The company was allowed 34 months, dated from May 1, 1962, to dispose of its stock to the public.

Recognizing that there were still loopholes in the existing laws, Congress adopted the Federal Trade Commission Act to supplement both the Sherman and Clayton Acts. This act spelled out unfair business practices more specifically, and also established the Federal Trade Commission to enforce the laws.

Regulating Prices

Controlling prices, otherwise known as "price-fixing," is another device that government uses to regulate business. Federal controls to maintain reasonable prices for goods and services were first applied to railroad freight and passenger rates, and to public utilities. Subsequently, similar regulations were extended to banking and insurance. Most of these so-called regulations have specified the maximum rate of interest that could be charged and the maximum investment return that could be made.

The Robinson-Patman Act. As we have seen, the Clayton Act was passed to prohibit price discrimination and exclusive agreements involving the sale of goods, wares, machinery, and other commodities for consumption in the United States. Section 2 of the act prohibited price discrimination against small firms where such discrimination substantially interfered with competition, except when price differentials were due to differences in

[4] *United States v. E. I. du Pont de Nemours & Co., et al., Vol. 353, U.S. 586.* Governmental interest in this case actually began in 1917, when du Pont acquired General Motors stock. A total of 63 million shares were bought over the years. These shares are carried on the du Pont books at a value of $1.2 billion, but at current market prices they are considered to be worth about $3.4 billion. The trial of this case began in 1952. In 1954, Federal Judge Walter J. LaBuy dismissed the government's charges, finding there had been no conspiracy to restrain trade and no "reasonable probability" of it. The government appealed to the U.S. Supreme Court. In 1955, and again in 1957, the Court ruled there was a "reasonable probability" of restraint. The case then was sent back to Judge LaBuy for a means to satisfy the Supreme Court's decision. But in 1959, Judge LaBuy refused to order divestiture of the stock on the grounds it would be punitive. Instead, he suggested other ways to eliminate du Pont's influence on General Motors, but the Supreme Court said "No," and in May, 1961, ordered complete divesture as the only satisfactory means. Tax legislation was then passed by Congress, stipulating that any tax gains to the stockholders in this case be subject to capital gains, which carries a comparatively low rate of tax.

quality, quantity, or grade. Many independent merchants, however, complained that this section of the Clayton Act gave chain stores an unfair advantage in getting quantity discounts from suppliers.

In 1936, the Robinson-Patman Act amended the Clayton Act, making it unlawful for any person to discriminate in price among purchasers if the effect of such discrimination might be to lessen competition, to create a monopoly, or to injure, prevent, or destroy competition. This law is actually designed to protect one buyer from another. For example, if a seller makes any allowance to one buyer, he must make the same concession to all other buyers. The offer or the accepting of a discount in excess of the permissible limit constitutes a criminal offense. As it turned out, the real targets of this act were the chain stores.

A special provision of the Robinson-Patman Act prohibits the payment of brokerage fees to a purchaser or his agent, except for services actually rendered. In 1947, the Great Atlantic & Pacific Tea Co. was found guilty of violating this law.[5] The Atlantic Commission Co., a subsidiary of A&P, obtained part of its income from brokerage fees on sales to independent wholesalers and retailers, as well as from distributing produce to the parent company. The court held that this practice strengthened the competitive price position of the A&P against other independent stores who were also customers of the commission company but at the same time were competitors of A&P.[6]

Although Congress presumably intended the Robinson-Patman Act to prevent large organizations from receiving special discounts for big orders, this act in its final form does allow large-quantity buyers to receive increased discounts over those permitted to small firms. Such price differentials are permissible when the orders are based on actual differences in costs, including such factors as costs of selling, costs of manufacturing, and delivery expenses. The Federal Trade Commission, which is directed by the act to administer these provisions, has the difficult task of determining which cost differences are proper.

The Celler-Kefauver Antimerger Act. From the very beginning, the purpose of antitrust legislation was to preserve competition. But the vagueness of the laws, and some court inconsistencies in enforcing them, left businessmen in a quandary. In 1950, Congress amended Section 7 of the Clayton Act to eliminate a loophole. Under the Clayton Act of 1914, intercorporate stock purchases were prohibited where the effect might be to re-

[5] *United States v. New York Great Atlantic & Pacific Tea Company*, 67 Fed. Sup. 626. Decision affirmed by Circuit Court of Appeals in 1948. This case has since established an important precedent in the matter of paying brokerage fees.

[6] The chief force pushing for passage of the Robinson-Patman Act was the United States Wholesale Grocers' Assn. The original bill was written by the general counsel of that organization. Despite the bill's protective measures, the independents have continued to decline in numbers and the chain stores have gained in strength.

duce competition between two or more corporations. At the same time, this provision had been weakened by court decisions so that it no longer prohibited acquisition of assets, although the same result accomplished by acquiring stock was forbidden. Thus, the purpose of the Celler-Kefauver Act was an attempt to tighten the stock-acquisition ban. It also prohibited the acquisition of assets of competitors where the effect was to substantially reduce competition. Consequently, companies who are major competitors cannot merge under *any* circumstances. If Company A is a giant, it cannot acquire Company B no matter how small that company's share of the market is. Thirdly, companies cannot merge if the consolidation would result in a control of 30 percent or more of the market.

The Antimerger Act also amended the Clayton Act by giving both the Federal Trade Commission and the Justice Department jurisdiction over merger cases. Businessmen are constantly asking for clarification of antitrust laws. Apparently, clarification should be even more widely sought: between 1950 and 1965, for instance, the number of suits initiated by the Justice Department involving antitrust cases more than doubled. As the laws stand now, small companies have no way to grow and diversify in an industry dominated by giant corporations who may have taken the merger route.

Patents, Copyrights, and Trade-Marks

If you invent a mechanical device or develop a formula for a marketable product, federal statutes provide that you have the right to apply for a patent. Patents have an obvious importance to businessmen, since they provide the holder with a government-approved monopoly—at least for a limited time.

Patents. In the United States a *patent* is in the nature of a contract between the inventor and the government, granting him exclusive right to own, use, and dispose of his article for 17 years, after which this protection expires and cannot be renewed. The holder is also protected against infringements abroad, since the United States is a member of the International Convention for the Protection of Industrial Property, which is an agreement on patent regulations among the member nations.[7] The United States Patent Office in Washington, D.C., is the federal authority that grants patents. The

[7] Prompted by a backlog of more than 200,000 patent applications, President Johnson appointed a commission to recommend revisions of the patent law. As this book was being written, a bitter battle appeared to be shaping up over the Commission's recommendations. Some of the proposed changes were: (1) to make a patent valid for 20 years after its earliest filing, instead of 17; (2) to allow assignees as well as inventors to file for patents—a move to protect the interest of employers of inventors; (3) to hold that a patent claim held invalid by a court would free the patent, and that no one thereafter would have to pay royalties; and (4) to provide that imports into the U.S. of any unlicensed product made abroad by a process patented in the U.S. would be considered a patent infringement. This would strengthen the validity of U.S. patents used abroad without a license.

first patent granted in the United States was under the Patent Law of 1790. Over the years it has been the feeling that even though patents take considerable time to acquire, they protect more than discourage inventions.

The 1952 Patent Act established three requirements, or "tests," that every invention must meet (or pass) before a patent will be granted on it: (1) it has to be new, (2) it has to be useful, and (3) it has to be more than an "obvious" improvement over previous inventions of a similar or related nature. Sometimes these points are difficult to prove—and, in fact, it is virtually impossible for the average layman to obtain a patent without the services of a patent attorney.

Copyrights. A *copyright* is a form of permission granted by the federal government to an author or publisher, giving him the exclusive authority to own, sell, or otherwise use his written works. Such items as books, songs, poems, plays, and even photographs may be copyrighted. (See the copyright in the front of this book, for an example.) A copyright may be obtained by sending a fee of $6 and a copyright "form" (obtainable through the U.S. Copyright Office), along with two true copies of the legitimate work, to the Copyright Office of the Library of Congress in Washington, D.C. A copyright is good for 28 years and may be renewed for 28 more.

Trade-marks. Most large businesses and some smaller ones use a *trade-mark*—a distinctive symbol, title, or mark readily identified with the product or name of the business. By registering it with the Patent Office you are granted the exclusive right to use it for 20 years, and the registration may be renewed for another 20 years. (Applicants must submit a written application, five copies of specimens, and a fee of $35.) However, registration does not automatically protect the owner from involvement in law suits, for although once the trade-mark has been registered the Patent Office is empowered to deny the registration of infringing trade-marks, the owner himself has to initiate legal action to restrain the use by another who has unlawfully adopted his trade-mark.

The major benefits derived from registering a trade-mark are as follows: (1) registration is *prima facie* ("on first appearance") evidence of the registrant's exclusive right to use the mark; (2) it is a record that others can review before presenting their trade-mark to be registered; (3) it provides federal court jurisdiction in infringement cases; and (4) it allows the owner to secure an automatic embargo on foreign goods, imported into this country, that infringe on that trade-mark.

Licenses and Permits

Another method of regulating businesses and professions is by means of the licenses and permits issued by most towns, cities, and states. In principle, licenses and permits are intended as a means of protecting the life, health, and safety of the public. More recently, however, these devices have become important revenue-producers, and are often used chiefly for that purpose.

GOVERNMENT AIDS TO BUSINESS

From this discussion you may have received the impression that government is interested only in regulating business and industry. Such, however, is not the case, for government, particularly at the federal level, provides many special aids to business. At one time government aid was limited to such activities as providing weather reports, patent protection, foreign trade opportunities, and regulations to prevent monopolies in restraint of trade. But since the economic depression of the 1930's, federal agencies of many kinds have been established to help business.

In recent years billions of dollars have been spent on the development of ports and navigable streams. Merchant shipping has received funds for ship construction. Dams, bridges, airports, and highway construction have been paid for with federal funds, and medical and scientific research projects have been sponsored by federal agencies. Another example is price supports for agriculture. And the strengthening of banking and credit systems under the Federal Reserve Act of 1913 has proved beneficial to business as well as to the nation in general. Even small business has received special attention since 1940, through a number of federal laws which culminated in the establishment of the Small Business Administration (SBA) as a permanent agency. (The SBA is discussed in greater length in Chapter 5.)

The SBA performs various helpful services to business. To mention several: it issues a monthly Products List Circular containing a brief digest of patented machines, devices, or processes that are available for use by small firms; it lends money to small business enterprises; and it publishes special bulletins and technical aids (referred to in the chapter on small business).

By far the most prolific source of business information furnished for businessmen home and abroad is the *Department of Commerce.* Since it maintains 37 regional field-offices, the Department collects an enormous amount of information about international business opportunities, and so can even supply directories of foreign buyers for American businessmen who want to sell abroad. Through its Bureau of Standards, the Department has helped to standardize materials according to type and size. Such items as woven wire, ceramic tile, and pipe have become more standardized as a result of this bureau's efforts. The thousands of reports which flow into the Department weekly and monthly are a wellspring of information for many organizations and individuals preparing projects and reports. On the physical sciences side, the Department conducts coastal and geodetic surveys. On the marketing sciences side, the Department's Bureau of Standards helps to facilitate business transactions by establishing commodity weights, measures, and standards. And its Bureau of the Census is the official census-taker for this country, including among its reports tabulations of monthly retail sales according to kinds of stores.

From the *Department of Agriculture* you can obtain (for instance) monthly reports on crop-growing conditions, and information on commodity standards. This Department administers price-support and production-adjustment programs for the farmer. It competes with private enterprise by making loans to farmers, often on better terms than are usually available from banks. Then, too, the Department sells crop insurance at premiums below those of private agencies because most of the administrative expenses are financed by Congressional appropriations.

The *Food and Drug Administration,* which is under the recently established Health, Education and Welfare Department, performs a regulatory function in promoting purity in food and drug products and requiring informative labeling of food, drugs, and cosmetics. Whereas the Federal Trade Commission Act prohibits false advertising, the Federal Food, Drug, and Cosmetic Act prohibits adulteration and misbranding. The sale of untruthfully labeled food and drugs by means of false advertising is a form of unfair competition, which explains the reason for so much federal interest.

TAXATION AND THE BUSINESS ENTERPRISE

One characteristic of government is its power to tax. State and local governments (which need money to pay their bills, too) get the dollars to pay for their expenditures primarily from taxes, with a substantial portion coming from business. The taxing power of the federal government is provided for in Article I, Section 8, of the Constitution. This article specifically states that Congress shall have the power to collect revenues, to pay debts, and to provide for the common defense and general welfare. Because the so-called "general welfare" clause has been so broadly interpreted by Congress and various of the Presidents, the federal government consistently finds itself in need of increasingly larger sums of money. The usual reply to one's question: "When might we expect the tax burden to be lightened?" is "Relief will come when government expenditures are substantially reduced." Most businessmen know all too well that these expenditures cannot possibly be reduced to any appreciable extent as long as the public continues to look to the government for the services that tend not only to perpetuate themselves but to multiply rapidly.

Classes of Taxes

Before we engage in a discussion of the classes of taxes, let us offer a simple definition: *taxes* are compulsory contributions made by persons or corporations from their wealth to defray the costs of government. Government tax revenues are the result of compulsory levies; individuals and businesses have no choice but to pay.

In terms of their economic effects on individuals, taxes are generally divided into three major types: regressive, progressive, and proportional. A *regressive* tax (such as a sales tax) is one that takes a larger fraction from low incomes than it does from high. This is because the lower one's income is, the more of it he must spend on the necessities of life, and the less he can save or invest—and the necessities are more heavily taxed than are savings and investments. This is one of the reasons why labor unions generally object to city and state sales taxes. Another example of a regressive tax is the excise tax on cigarettes, liquors, and cosmetics.

A tax is *progressive* if its rate increases as the tax base increases. A progressive tax may take a higher percentage from high incomes than from low. For example, a personal income tax that is graduated to take more and more out of each extra dollar of income is progressive. Such a tax claims not only a large, absolute amount, but also a larger fraction or percentage of the tax base as the base increases. We have only to examine the federal income tax to verify this point.

A tax is *proportional* when its rate remains the same, regardless of the size of the tax base. For example, a tariff duty, levied either as a percentage of the value (*ad valorem*) or as a specific amount per unit of the imported good (a specific duty), illustrates proportional taxation. A better understanding of the distinctions among progressive, regressive, and proportional taxes and the reasons for their existence will be gained when we discuss certain principles of taxation.

Judging the Merits of Taxes

What makes a tax fair and equitable? To answer this question, we must inquire into the criteria which may be used in judging the relative merits and drawbacks of various taxes. First, let us consider the merits of a tax on its effectiveness in raising revenue. If a tax is broadly based (that is, imposed upon the mass of a nation's citizenry), it is considered a more productive revenue producer than a narrowly based levy. Also, a tax that is difficult to evade tends to be a more efficient revenue-producer. Taxes that discourage production and income may cause revenue losses.

Another frequently applied criterion is the equity or fairness of a tax. In judging fairness in taxation, two ideas seem to have general acceptance:

the *benefit principle* and the *ability-to-pay principle.* Unfortunately, what seems fair to one person may represent gross injustice to another.

The Benefit Principle. Advocates of this principle contend that those who benefit from government services should pay for them. No one could argue very long that this is not a logical concept. The federal tax on gasoline, for example, is used to build highways which in turn are used by those who drive automobiles. Thus, by the use of the excise tax on gasoline it is possible to apply the benefit principle. Of course, the application of this principle does have its limitations. Suppose public school taxes were levied only on parents, on the basis of the number of children they have in school. The local banker would probably experience no difficulty in paying his taxes, but how about the poor family with six school-age children? Obviously, the well-to-do could afford to pay the school taxes, whereas the poor could not. Generally speaking, however, there is considerable merit in the benefit principle when judging a tax.

The Ability-to-pay Principle. Taxation based on this principle sounds even better to many people than that based on the benefit principle. But what measures one's ability to pay? Net money income received during a given year is probably the most widely accepted criterion. Others prefer gross income as the basis. But even after the measure of ability to pay has been agreed upon, there still remain the problems of determining the acceptable tax rate that correctly measures ability to pay, and whether the tax rate should be proportional or progressive.

Income taxes are broadly based and are set up on the basis of the government's estimates of the people's ability to pay what is asked of them. For example, a man with a $15,000 income may be asked to pay twice as much as one earning $7,500. Such a proportional tax considers the wealthy man's greater ability to pay more, and the dollar amount demanded in taxes is therefore adjusted to the size of the income. In the final analysis, tax-paying ability generally increases as income rises, and the best example of the ability-to-pay principle is the progressive income tax.

It is said that most tax systems combine regressive and progressive characteristics in an effort to extract as much revenue as possible. It has also been observed that the final "incidence" (or resting place) of a tax may be far from the man who turns the money over to the government. Obviously it is this final incidence of the tax that is most important. The best system, then, becomes a matter of one's personal opinion, rather than of the application of scientific determination. On the other hand, it cannot be denied that taxes do nothing to increase demand for taxed commodities or businesses. But taxes do tend to raise costs, and thereby to reduce supply—and thus, lower supply pushes up prices.

Characteristics of Specific Taxes

In light of the principles we have discussed, how does our present system of taxation stand up? Let us try to find out by examining several specific taxes imposed on business, industry, and individuals.

From the proportionment of the tax dollars collected by the federal government, as shown in the following illustration, you can quickly see that the individual and corporate income taxes produce more revenue than all other federal taxes combined.

The Sources of the United States Tax Dollar
(Fiscal Year 1968 Estimate)

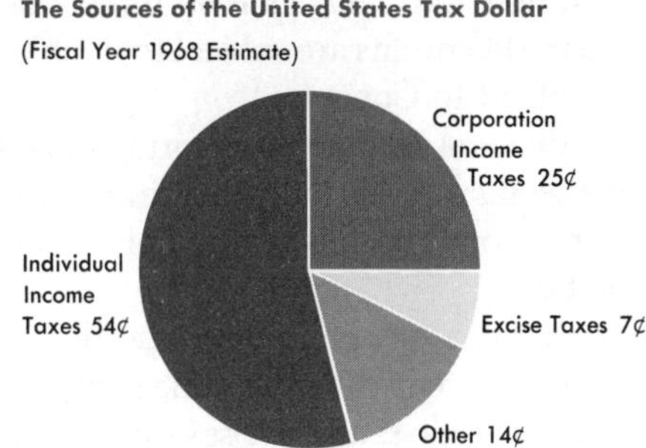

Source: Bureau of the Budget and U.S. Treasury Department.

The Federal Income Tax. We have already seen that the federal income tax, established in 1913 by the Sixteenth Amendment, is the primary revenue producer for the federal government. Table 2.1 shows a comparison of federal tax collections by source for selected years since 1949, during which period individual income taxes and taxes on corporate profits have been climbing steadily, whereas collections on excise and customs have not.

TABLE 2.1

FEDERAL TAX COLLECTIONS BY SOURCE FOR SELECTED FISCAL YEARS, 1949–1967[1] (IN MILLIONS OF DOLLARS)

Source	1949	1959	1965	1966[2]	1967
Income and Profits Taxes	$29,605	$58,826	$79,792	$92,090	$97,640
Individual Income	18,052	40,735	53,661	61,225	62,540
Corporation Income and Profits	11,554	18,092	26,131	30,835	35,100
Excise Taxes	7,579	10,760	14,793	13,407	13,557
Estate and Gift Taxes	797	1,353	2,746	3,089	3,331
Employment Taxes	2,476	8,854	17,104	20,256	24,583
Customs Taxes	384	948	1,478	1,811	1,880

[1] Estimated for 1967.
[2] Data for 1966 preliminary.

Source: U.S. Treasury Dept.

Income-tax rates are progressive, and the tax is broadly based. Few persons on a regular payroll "get around" the laws concerning paying an income tax; every person residing in the United States, adult or minor, who has an annual gross income of a prescribed amount (for 1968, $600 or more, and if 65 years of age or over, $1,200 or more) must file a tax return. (Because of its many deductions and exemptions, it is hardly surprising that the administration of the law involves considerable litigation.)

Probably the most outstanding virtue of the income tax is that it is based on the ability-to-pay principle. Secondly, generally the incidence is on the taxpayer; the tax cannot be shifted. (The corporate income tax is levied first on the profits of the corporation and then again on those who receive dividends. In this respect, corporation profits are subject to double taxation. This is a constant source of complaint to Congress.)

At the federal level, individual income taxes furnish slightly more than half of the tax dollar. At the state level, individual income taxes furnish a little more than 14 percent of total receipts. A total of 35 states have some form of individual income taxes.

The corporation income tax imposes no direct burden on the costs of doing business, and therefore does not have the same direct deterrent effect on employment and production as do sales-, excise-, and payroll taxes. However, the rate of business investments depends largely on profits after taxes. A tax that reduces profits (which reflect the yield of investment) is bound to have an adverse effect by slowing down company growth.

High income taxes are often accused of destroying a man's incentive. In fact, some person may tell you that an increase in his salary would not help him at all because it would place him in a higher tax bracket. This criticism is rarely valid, for even in the highest income-tax brackets, the taxpayer has some part of the added income left.

The General Property Tax. Real and Personal property taxes remain the chief source of revenue for local and state governments. (Although the terms "real property" and "personal property" are rather fully defined in the chapter dealing with our legal environment, it will be helpful here to repeat briefly that real property is considered that which is attached to the soil, and personal property is thought of as movable things, tangible or intangible.) The value of property is determined by an assessment procedure which often produces a value that bears little apparent relationship to the price of the property, either at the time of assessment or later. For example: in some states, once a house is assessed its official value will remain the same for years, although there may be changes in the neighborhood and/or in the market value. In fact, the current standards and practices utilized in determining assessed valuation have been very much criticized.

TABLE 2.2

SOCIAL SECURITY TAX RATES, PERCENTAGE OF COVERED EARNINGS FOR OASDI AND HOSPITAL INSURANCE

Year	Total Rate Paid by Employer and Employee alike (percentage)	Total Rate Paid by Self-employed persons (percentage)	Hospital Insurance Payment (included in total percentage rate)
1967–68	4.40	6.40	0.6
1969–70	4.80	6.90	.6
1971–72	5.20	7.50	.6
1973–75	5.65	7.65	.65
1976–79	5.70	7.70	.7
1980–86	5.80	7.80	.8
1987 and after	5.90	7.90	.9

1967 and 1968, for an employee earning $6,600, shows that the tax paid by him and his employer would amount to $290.40 for each, or a total of $580.80 for both. For 1969 and 1970, the employee and his employer each pay 4.80 percent of $7,800 or $374.40. A self-employed person pays 6.90 percent of $7,800 or $538.20. In 1971, employee and his employer will each pay 5.20 percent of $7,800 or $405.60. A self-employed person will pay 7.50 percent of $7,800 or $585.00. Note that these payments cover the cost of Medicare.

Coverage. Social security is available to practically all classes of occupations. For most of these, coverage is compulsory. Under the 1965 amendment, clergymen could elect to be covered. In 1968 those clergymen who did not elect social security under the old law are covered unless they declare they are opposed to being included because of religious principle or conscience. The clergyman reports his income and makes his tax payment as if he were self-employed, even though he may be working as an employee. Self-employed medical doctors and medical interns are eligible for benefits. Policemen and firemen, who are under a retirement plan, and federal employees who are covered by a federal retirement system, are not covered. Starting in 1968 persons who served in the Armed Forces have increased social security protection. Beginning with January, 1968, an additional $100 is counted for each month in which the individual is on active duty. However, no additional social security taxes are deducted from a person's military pay. Under the 1967 amendment additional benefits are provided disabled survivors.

Approximately 118 million workers have been assigned social security numbers. Of this total, slightly over 80 million are under the program and about 17 million persons are receiving benefits.

OASDI Covering Requirements. Any person electing to retire at the approved age who has contributed for the required number of quarters may draw benefits. The length of time required to qualify depends upon one's date of birth. Each worker receives social security credit up to four quarters in a year. The total number of credits necessary for retirement benefits is shown below.

A Worker (Male or Female) Who Reaches Age 62 or Dies In:	*Will Need Credits For No More Than The Following Years of Covered Employment:*
1968	4¼
1969	4½
1970	4¾
1975	6
1979	7
1983	8
1987	9
1991 or later	10 or 40 quarters

To become eligible for disability benefits, the worker must have credit for five out of the last 10 years of employment before he becomes disabled. No one is fully insured with credit for less than one and one-half years of work, and no one needs more than 10 years of work to be fully insured.

Under the 1967 amendment new benefits for disabled survivors such as a widow, widower, or divorced wife of a worker who was insured under social security at death, are provided.

OASDI Monthly Benefits. The amount of social security cash benefits one may receive will depend on one's average earnings and at what age benefits are started. Using the information in Table 2.3 as a guide, you can see that average monthly earnings of $350 after 1950 would give the insured worker at age 65 $140.40 a month for the remainder of his life. At age 65 his wife will also receive benefits that are equal to half of her husband's benefits—$70.20. Rapid calculation should tell you that the two incomes will total $210.60 per month. A smaller amount of monthly cash benefits may be received at age 62. These lesser amounts for age 62 are not shown in Table 2.3 for the worker and his wife.

Starting with 1968, the new amendment raised from $1,500 to $1,680, the amount of total earnings per year from other employment a social security beneficiary may receive without any of his benefits being reduced. But if a person's total outside income from gainful employment exceeds $1,680, $1.00 may be withheld from his social security computed on his earnings for each $2.00 between $1,680 and $2,880; $1.00 in benefits may be withheld for each $1.00 of earnings above $2,880. Regardless of one's total earnings, no benefits will be withheld for any month in which one neither earns over $140

TABLE 2.3
EXAMPLES OF MONTHLY SOCIAL SECURITY BENEFITS

Average Monthly Earnings After 1950	Worker's Monthly Benefits 65 or Older	Worker and Wife, Age 65	Survivors	
			Widow 62 or Over	Widow Under 62 With One Child
$ 75	$ 55.00	$ 82.50	$ 55.00	$ 82.50
150	88.50	132.60	73.00	132.60
250	115.00	172.50	94.90	172.60
350	140.40	210.60	115.90	210.60
450	165.00	247.50	136.20	247.60
550	189.90	284.90	156.70	285.00
650	218.00	323.00	179.90	327.00

in wages nor performs substantial services as self-employed. At age 72 or older, no monthly benefits may be withheld regardless of how much one may earn in any single year.

Unemployment Insurance. In addition to old-age and survivors' insurance, the Social Security Act provides for unemployment insurance to be administered by each state. Although the Act does not establish a federal unemployment insurance program, it does provide financial aid to the states that have established acceptable programs of their own.

To cover the cost of insurance benefits, the law imposes upon each employer of one or more persons a federal tax equal to 3.1 percent of the wages and salaries, based on the first $3,000 of each employee's annual pay. According to the act, all employers are authorized to deduct the amount of the tax paid to the state from that levied by the federal government. As a result, the proceeds, or 2.7 percent of the employer's payroll tax authorized by federal law, goes to the state fund, and the remaining .4 percent of the employer's payroll is retained by the federal government to pay administrative costs of the program. The obvious intent of the law is to induce all states to enact an acceptable unemployment insurance plan. Tax contributions are deposited in the Unemployment Insurance Trust Fund, which invests in federal securities and which is administered by the United States Treasury. Each state has its own account in the Fund, from which it may draw benefit payments and into which its tax collections are deposited. Interest accumulations are credited to the state's account.

The amount of unemployment benefits paid by the various states is usually about half the worker's regular weekly wages. The length of time that payments are made varies by state; the average is from three to six months. Every state now has an approved unemployment insurance program and collects taxes from business and industry for this purpose.

Federal Grants-in-Aid for Health and Welfare

The principal benefits of the social security program are in the form of old-age pension and unemployment compensation. But the third part of the Act provides for grants-in-aid to the states for designated programs in health and welfare, and for assistance to the needy and aged, to the blind, and to dependent children and incapacitated persons. To participate in federal grants, the states are required to establish health and welfare programs for these purposes. Grants are generally allotted on the basis of the financial needs of the state, its population, and the severity of its health problems. Federal grants are often equal to two-thirds of the total money appropriated by the state. No special federal taxes are levied to support these federal grants to states.

Medicare

A few pages ago we mentioned medicare which was established by Congress in 1966. This is a broad program of hospital and medical insurance for persons 65 and older provided through Social Security. The 1967 amendment to the Social Security Act also expanded these benefits.

Medicare is a two-part program. The first part is the hospital insurance portion financed by a special 0.6 percent tax paid by employees, employers, and self-employed. This tax is based on the first $7,800 of yearly earnings. The tax rate is 0.6 percent which is expected to remain through 1972. (See Table 2.2) The hospital insurance part covers hospital care, post-hospital service in a qualified nursing home or other facility, and home health services including nursing costs.

The second part is medical insurance which helps to pay doctor bills. This part is a voluntary program for persons 65 and over, who pay a monthly rate of $4.00. The plan covers the cost of physician's services in the home, and at the hospital, clinic, or the doctor's office. In addition, the plan pays for special health "services" including X rays, laboratory tests, ambulance service, rental of equipment, and artificial legs, arms, and eyes.

Of the 20 million persons over 65, more than 90 percent have enrolled in the second part of the medical program.

Effects of Taxation on Business

The power of the federal and state governments to tax has always had an important effect upon business. In fact, every tax is in some measure "regulatory," since in one way or another it attaches more of an economic impediment to the activity taxed than it does to similar activities not taxed. The Supreme Court has held as a matter of course that Congress may use its powers to tax both as a penalty and as a sanction in the regulation of commerce. Interpreted in this way, the protective tariff is a tax levied mainly for the purpose of excluding foreign competition; only its secondary purpose is to raise revenue. However interpreted or applied, the tariff serves in a dual capacity, providing protection to one party and restricting another.

Another effect of taxation is on the choice of form of business ownership. Tax laws definitely favor the sole proprietorship and partnership over the corporation. The corporate income tax, as we mentioned earlier, entails a highly controversial problem—"double taxation." Over the years, Congress has done little about this inequity, although many groups have appealed for corrective action. In 1958 Congress did enact legislation to allow certain small corporations to be taxed as partnerships, but nothing was done to give relief to those holding shares in large corporations.

Taxes also influence the choice of a business location. Several southern states have offered new industries special tax concessions—such as lower property taxes for a given number of years, or reduced corporation fees. Concessions of this type have been partly responsible for the movement of industry to the South and West.

Taxation allowances for depletion of such natural resources as oil and gas wells play an important part in the financing of extractive industries. If the existing 27½ percent depletion allowance were reduced substantially, oil companies would be forced to cut their exploration programs in search for new deposits.

The relatively large increases scheduled by the Social Security Act of 1967 (particularly the base increase from $6,600 to $7,800) will for many employers add an additional tax burden which can be reduced only by substituting equipment for employees in order to cut the social security taxes paid by the employer. For example, a firm engaged in petroleum refining finds that a new machine calculated to last 10 years and do the work of 10 men will reduce its annual social security tax by as much as $5,000 annually, as compared with the amount paid prior to the tax increase. Even if the company has in the past considered such equipment much too expensive in spite of its labor-saving potential, the $5,000 tax-saving inducement is almost certain to make the investment seem not only worthwhile but imperative especially since the social security tax will continue to increase during the next two decades. In very large manufacturing industries, where it is possible to use more labor-saving equipment, this effect on labor-capital ratios can be significant. On the other hand, in some industries this tax inducement may be only modest. For example, bankers estimate that a machine capable of replacing 10 employees and having a 10-year depreciation period would offer them a tax inducement of only about $1,000. All told, however, as salaries increase, the social security tax savings earned by substituting machines for manpower definitely will become increasingly significant.

Let us end this part of the discussion with a few brief observations. The ability-to-pay principle of taxation is more evident in the American tax structure than is the benefit principle. Taxes on corporate and personal incomes, and inheritance taxes, rely heavily on the ability-to-pay principle; they are the outstanding examples of a progressive tax. General sales-, excise-, and property taxes are fertile sources of revenue as regressive taxes. The general sales tax is broadly based and, like the excise tax, its incidence is primarily on the consumer. Whereas personal income taxes are not likely to be shifted, sales and excise taxes can be shifted by the business involved in collecting the tax.

The Need for Further Tax Revision

You will recall that when we began our discussion of taxes, we asked the question: "When might we expect the tax burden to be lightened?" We know that any reduction in taxes must come about by a reduction in government spending. But since this spending seems to be increasing each year, the hope for reducing taxes in any substantial amount is nil. The one possibility left is to study our tax system continually for the purpose of improving the system. The best tax system is a matter of personal opinion, rather than of scientific determination; in practice, taxes will reflect a compromise of many conflicting points of view and political pressures.

In recent years there have been several revisions to our tax system. The Revenue Acts of 1962, 1964, and 1965 resulting in the following revisions:

1. Reduction of the standard tax rate on corporate profits from 52 to 48 percent
2. Elimination of most of the federal excise taxes, except those on tobacco, alcoholic beverages, and highway use (many federal excise taxes were levied to support World War II)
3. Reduction in federal income-tax rates; also, the provision for special allowances entirely exempting some low-income persons from income-tax payments
4. Allowances for accelerated charge-offs of capital equipment resulting in lower business taxes on profits
5. Allowance of a credit equal to a percentage (7 percent in most cases) of certain kinds of investment expenditures against business income tax

As a result of these changes, several discriminations were removed—but the need for continued study of the national tax structure still exists. Since World War II, taxation increasingly has been regarded at the federal level as a fiscal device to control the national economy. The theory behind using taxes to control the national economy is rather simple: If the economy shows increasing inflationary strains, such as rapidly rising prices, then taxes are raised; if the economy seems to be slumping or running well below its potential as based on previous records, taxes are reduced to release more purchasing power. This type of fiscal manipulation obviously requires federal legislation and is for the short-run period. The question then arises: How can we reduce taxes and pay our costs of government, which keep increasing? The usual answer given by advocates of tax reductions is that lower tax rates will stimulate private enterprise to increase business activity, and more taxes will be paid than before the tax cut. Unfortunately, claims of this nature cannot always be proven in advance.

The next major breakthrough in the federal government's tax policy may well take the form of the turning back to the states of a portion of the federal income taxes. Presumably, the monies from these federal grants to the states would come out of the rising total of taxes the Treasury Department collects during periods of high prosperity. During periods of depression this tax policy might be altered. In any case, such grants would be automatic and unconditional—no strings attached.

Tax Avoidance and Loopholes

Finally, we turn to the matter of tax avoidance—that is, of reducing taxes by ethical means, specifically by finding and taking advantage of "loopholes" in the tax laws and court decisions. (Of course, you can avoid paying a a gasoline tax by simply not driving your car, and you can avoid the state and federal tax on cigarettes by not smoking, but these are really neither loopholes nor acts of avoidance involving the use of legal means to reduce the effective tax.)

One "loophole" used as a means of tax avoidance (not to be confused with tax evasion, which is illegal) is investments in corporations, land, or buildings, whereby it is possible to obtain capital gains from the sale of the asset after it has been held over six months. Another loophole is ownership of a farm or a racing stable which can legally be claimed as part of your business expense and which therefore can be used to reduce your personal income tax. Then, too, loopholes can occur when an individual works out an agreement with an employer (usually a corporation he owns) to be paid salaries, earned in one year, over several years. This enables the individual either to reduce his income tax or to qualify for a lower *surtax—a special tax, over and above the normal income tax, imposed on the amount by which the net income exceeds a specified sum.*

Some tax loopholes permit large amounts of income either to go untaxed or to be taxed at lower levels. For example, many corporation executives are granted stock options which permit them to buy shares at prices below those of the market. They are allowed to sell the shares after they have advanced in price, and need pay only at a moderate capital-gains tax rate rather than the higher normal rate. Corporate executives often take generous retirement benefits, financed by their corporation, in lieu of additional current salary payments, since the retirement benefits are taxable only when received by which time the individual presumably has dropped into a lower tax-rate.

If the tax loopholes are numerous enough, high tax-rates do not really hurt high-income receivers very much. Since about three-fourths of all federal revenue comes from personal and corporation income taxes, if existing loopholes were closed, rates on all income levels could be cut without revenue loss. Some authorities are recommending tax reforms as an alternative to a surtax.

SUMMARY

Government's role in the affairs of business has grown steadily over the years. This is not accidental because for years more businesses have become overly dependent on government, with the result that it wields increasing influence over them. Alert business managers avoid as much government interference as is possible, while taking the fullest advantage they can of the environment that government has created for their protection.

The federal government derives its authority to direct and control business activities from the Constitution, which provides two broad levels of government: federal and state. All powers and duties that are not specifically delegated to the federal level are left to the several states.

The right to regulate business at either the state or federal level comes from police power, which is the authority the government has to enact laws to protect the health, safety, morals, and welfare of the people.

American public policy has long supported the principle that freedom to engage in a business of one's own should be guaranteed. Therefore, one purpose of public policy is to regulate unfair competition and prohibit illegal monopolies. In one way or another, the Sherman Antitrust Act, the Clayton Act, the Federal Trade Commission Act, and the Robinson-Patman Act are designed to accomplish this objective.

The subject of controlling business monopolies is a highly controversial one, partly because the federal government has not followed a consistent and comprehensive policy in dealing with them: it has both restrained and promoted monopolies. Control over monopolies is enforced mainly through the provisions of the Sherman Act and its amendments. By prohibiting corporation mergers, this Act has restrained the elimination of competition.

Another method of regulating business is by the use of licenses and permits. These are authorized mainly at the local and state levels. The federal government confers exclusive control of certain artistic productions and trade labels in the form of copyrights and trade-marks.

Congress also derives its taxing powers from the Constitution. Some taxes are levied for revenue, some serve as a control measure, and some are for protective reasons. Property taxes are the main source of revenue for many local governments. States rely largely on retail sales- and use-taxes. Excise taxes are primarily levied by the federal government. Both the states and the federal government use the income tax.

The Social Security Act is another example of federal participation. The taxing provisions of this program require contributions from both employers and employees.

What features make a good tax? The first goal of a tax is to raise revenue. To raise huge sums, a tax must reach the largest possible number of citizens—and a broadly-based income tax or general sales tax does this. Also, a tax should be designed so that the taxpayer cannot avoid it.

Taxes may be designed to apply the benefit principle, or they may be based on the ability-to-pay principle. For this latter principle, progressive rates, which rise with growing income, are used. The personal income tax is an example of a progressive tax. A tax is regressive if the proportion of income taken by tax declines as income increases. The sales tax is an example of a regressive tax because it takes a larger proportion of income from people of low income than from those in high-income brackets. The reason for the distinction between progressive and regressive taxes is to be found in the principle of ability-to-pay.

The largest revenue producer on the lower levels of government (local and state) is the tax on real estate; almost half of all local revenue depends on the property tax. More states are beginning to levy a general sales tax or a selective sales tax. The federal government has made extensive use of the excise tax imposed on specific items sold at retail—such as jewelry, furs, household appliances, musical instruments, luggage, distilled spirits, and many other items.

VOCABULARY REVIEW QUIZ

Match the following vocabulary terms with the statements on the next page.

a. Competition
b. Competitive market
c. Copyright
d. Estate tax
e. Government
f. Incorporation tax
g. Merger
h. Monopolistic market
i. Oligopolistic market
j. Patent
k. Police power
l. Public policy
m. Regressive tax
n. Trade-mark

1. The center of political authority having the power to govern the people
2. Powers used by government to protect the property, life, and well-being of its citizens
3. Community conscience in the form of a statement that carries the weight of government
4. A state of trying to get something that is being sought by others under similar circumstances at the same time
5. A market involving many buyers and sellers, each free to deal with others after evaluating the quality of the goods or services and the price
6. A market wherein a few concerns are so powerful that they are not subject to the normal market influences, but instead are capable of influencing the market themselves
7. A situation wherein either the buyer or the seller controls or dominates the market
8. The uniting of two or more companies into a single entity under a new firm name
9. A contract between the inventor and the federal government, granting him exclusive right to own, use, and dispose of his article for a period of 17 years
10. Authority conferred by the federal government to a person, giving him the exclusive use of his own written works
11. An assessment levied against the entire estate of the deceased
12. A tax levied for the privilege of doing business in a certain state
13. Taxes that take a larger proportion of income from people of low incomes than from those in high-income brackets
14. A distinctive symbol, title, or mark readily identified with a product or business name

QUESTIONS FOR REVIEW STUDY

1. What do you feel are the reasons for government control and regulation of business?
2. What are the main functions of government, and how are they related to business?
3. What is meant by the term "public policy" as it is related to government control of business?
4. From what source does the federal government derive its power to regulate business activities?
5. What is the purpose of the Sherman Antitrust Act?
6. Trace the government legislation concerning monopolies and restraint of trade from the Sherman Antitrust Act through the Celler-Kefauver Antimerger Act.
7. Why are some monopolies legal while others are not? Discuss several examples.
8. Explain the difference in protection provided by a patent, a copyright, and a trade-mark.

9. How does a progressive tax differ from a regressive and proportional tax?
10. Of the various taxes discussed in this chapter, which ones are based on the ability-to-pay principle and which on the benefit principle?
11. Discuss the meaning of the statement, "Every tax is in some measure regulatory."
12. Of the several kinds of taxes discussed in this chapter—income, sales, excise, estate, value-added, and social security—which ones in your opinion are the most equitable to the taxpayer?

PROBLEMS AND PROJECTS

1. Assume you have been asked to explain to a group of foreign businessmen visiting your campus the different ways the federal government is able to help businessmen. Prepare this report, using specific illustrations.
2. Assume that because of a substantial increase in government spending for military purposes, the cost-of-living index has jumped 50 percent, resulting in increased inflation and a public demand for either a new tax, or additional taxes. Two proposals (see below) have been made. Which do you consider the more equitable, which the less desirable? Explain your position in writing.
   (a) Levy a constitutional amendment for a national sales tax
   (b) Increase the income tax on personal incomes below $9,000, but make no change on corporation income taxes
3. Using library resources or other reference materials, write a 600-to 800-word report on Medicare.

A BUSINESS CASE

Case 2-1 The Union Jack Oil Company

The Union Jack Oil Co., a large, integrated (meaning "both producing and distributing") dealer in petroleum products, operating in three states, has been cited by the Antitrust Division of the Department of Justice and charged with violating the Sherman Antitrust Act. This charge grew out of a complaint by the lessee of a company service station.

In addition to its production and refinery operations, the corporation owns a chain of 400 service stations, operated under lease agreements as a voluntary chain called Pay Less Petroleum Co. In addition, the company owns and operates 15 stations under the name Union Jack Oil Co. These stations are often used to make marketing studies of consumer buying habits, and for the training of supervisors.

Each franchise agreement that accompanies the lease of a Pay Less station requires the lessee to buy his cash register, two display cases, grease guns, a kit of tools, and tire repair equipment from the company at the time the lease is signed. The company allows the lessee 90 days' credit, without interest, to pay for these assets. The lease stipulates that should the lease agreement be canceled, the company will repurchase these assets from the lessee at a price agreeable to both parties. The lease also requires the lessee to buy all gasoline, lubricating oil, batteries, tires, and accessories from the lessor unless the lease is canceled by agreement of both parties.

After operating a station three years under this agreement, Robert Janks decided to cancel his lease. The company refused to repurchase his equipment, and he filed a written complaint with the Department of Justice.

1. In your opinion, was there a violation of the Sherman Antitrust Act?
2. Is the Union Jack Co., as a lessor, subject to interstate regulations?
3. Why is or is not the lessee entitled to relief in this case? Explain your answer.

Legal Environment and Business Ethics

3

Almost since the beginning of civilization, societies have relied on law to help them enforce and mediate relationships among men and between men and their governments. The laws of a society furnish its framework, so to speak, because they reflect the moral standards, the religious beliefs, the economic practices, and often the actual philosophy of those in the society. Thus, a fully developed legal system is composed of more than mere basic legal principles, codes, and standards of conduct.

We have implied that the law prescribes the conduct of business. Business administration consists mainly of making decisions, and the many decisions involved in virtually every business transaction have legal implications. It is unwise to try to make such decisions without having gained a working knowledge of one's legal rights and obligations, of individual recourse, and of the rules of conduct, for when business disputes arise—and they often do—they have to be settled by the due processes of law, not by force or any other illegal means.

To anyone contemplating a career in business, a basic knowledge of legal terms and principles is highly important. Indeed, the whole field of business administration will be better understood even if you have an understanding only of the legal background that is relevant to your particular business interest. This should at least help you to avoid common legal blunders when signing a contract, forming a partnership, buying real-estate —in fact, when engaging in any of a host of business activities. It should also help you to determine when you need legal counsel: sooner or later you may be involved with a court of law, and at that point you would do well to recall the old saying, "A man who serves as his own lawyer has a fool for a client."

This chapter is also concerned with the subject of business ethics, which is a much broader field than law. There are some business practices which, although not in direct violation of law, are not necessarily in harmony with established standards of conduct. The regulation of these practices is left to groups which voluntarily band together for their own protective welfare. They adopt a code of ethics which is the standard of behavior they have agreed to follow. Several of these codes are discussed in this chapter because they are so closely identified with business law. (While these codes are not the same as law, and also do not have the weight of law, very often the amount of public disapproval that is aroused when they are violated can be as effective as law itself.) Many businessmen believe that if business cannot discipline the unethical in its midst, this task will be taken over by the states or even by the federal government.

THE NATURE AND PURPOSE OF LAW

Before exploring the relationship of law to business, let's review briefly the nature of law, its classifications, and some of its history.

What Is Law?

Law may be defined as *a body of rules, statutes, legal codes, and regulations that are enforceable by a court.* Blackstone, in his *Commentaries on the Laws of England,* states that law is "a rule of civil conduct prescribed by the supreme power of a state, commanding what is right and prohibiting what is wrong." Law is not an end to itself; rather, it is an instrument to obtain social justice. Laws that are applied to the more common business transactions come under the heading of *business law.*

Some laws provide protection against criminals and some against violations of public health, safety, and morals. Laws pertaining to compulsory vaccination, food inspection, or safety devices to prevent accidents when using machines, are intended to protect the individual from public-health and safety violations. Some laws serve to protect the rights and duties of certain individuals. Examples of these rights and duties include, for instance: the duty of a seller to furnish the buyer with the kind of goods promised, and the right of the buyer to demand what has been promised; the right of lawful freedom of movement, and the duty not to restrain this freedom unlawfully. Too, there are laws that provide procedures involving the use of such negotiable instruments as checks and notes. And still other laws seek to enforce the expressed intention of a party to a contract. In short, if your rights are interfered with or your duties ignored, you may seek recourse by turning to the law for protection, relief, or recovery.

Classification of Laws

Over the years our laws have been developed under a legal system which includes both *civil law,* derived from legislative statutes, and *common law,* which consists of precedents based on court decisions. The broad scope of the law gives rise to several classifications. The two major categories of law are *substantive law* and *procedural law.*

Substantive Law. Substantive law is that part of the law which defines, creates, and regulates the individual's legal rights. Laws pertaining to contracts, property, sales, crimes, and the constitution are classified as substantive law.

Substantive law may be further subdivided into *public law* and *private law. Public law* deals with the relation of the government to the individual and with the creation and operation of governments. Within the scope of public law, we find such subcategories as *constitutional law,* which deals with the legal principles of the constitution; *administrative law,* which is concerned with the mechanics by which governments carry out their legal functions; and *criminal law,* which defines conduct deemed a crime against the government.[1]

Laws which are concerned with the rights and liabilities between private individuals, partnerships, corporations, and other organizations are called *private laws.* In addition, there are private laws having to do with wrongs of a noncontractual nature known as *torts.*[2] Examples of torts include

[1] Crimes are classified as either *felonies* or *misdemeanors.* A *felony* is a criminal offense punishable by imprisonment in a state penitentiary in excess of one year, or by death. A *misdemeanor* is also considered a criminal offense, but not so severe as a felony. It carries either a fine or imprisonment, or both. Imprisonment for conviction of a misdemeanor is generally not in a state penitentiary but in a city or county jail, and generally for less than one year.

[2] A *tort* is a civil (private) wrong (other than a breach of contract) that may result in legal action. A tort is also a violation of a private duty which may result in damages to the injured party. Damage then is an essential element of the tort. Both slander and libel are examples of torts. Slander consists of publication or communication of defamatory spoken words or gestures. Libel is a wrong against an individual in the form of written defamation, or in print, picture, or some other visual form.

false arrest, false imprisonment, deceit, slander, and libel. Some understanding of the law of torts is important to the businessman because he needs to know which civil conduct, apart from any considerations of contracts, society denounces as socially undesirable or unreasonable, and for which torts monetary liability in the form of damages may be court-imposed.

Procedural Law. This classification of the law, sometimes referred to as *adjective law,* has to do with the procedural machinery required to enforce personal rights and duties. Included under procedural law are such matters as court pleadings, court jurisdiction, decrees, evidence, and administrative decisions. Procedural or adjective law is the body of rules that regulate the conduct of a lawsuit.

The Historical Development of Law

Over a period of centuries our Western civilization has developed under two systems of law. Most of the civilized world now lives under one or the other of these two systems. The older system is the Roman or Civil law, which was founded in the Roman Empire. Continental Europe and most of the countries colonized by the European nations live under Roman or Civil law. The English-speaking countries and the nations colonized by them live under the English or Common law system. Whereas common law is largely nonlegislative in character, civil law is based on written statutes and codes dating back to the time of Justinian. Let us turn to the sources of our present legal system.

Legal Sources. In the United States, there are two main sources of law. One is the unwritten body of principles known as *common law,* which is based mainly on court decisions—decisions which become precedents to be followed in cases of a similar nature. (This is known as the doctrine of *stare decisis.* By this doctrine the judge, in effect, makes law in the sense that the principles he enunciates may be followed by other judges.) The source of most of our laws pertaining to contracts, property, and agency relationships is common law.

The other source of law is *statutory law.* This is written law consisting of formal declarations or enactments (statutes) by various governmental bodies and agencies. These statutes, together with the federal and state constitutions, constitute what is commonly known as *law by enactment.*

Constitutional law is regarded as superior to statutory law, and statutory law is considered higher than common law. Hence, common law applies only to those instances where there are no written laws applicable to the situation. On the other hand, such organizations as corporations, partnerships, and trusts are forms of ownership subject to statutory laws, as are many other activities in business.

Under the Constitution of the United States, each state has the right to enact its own laws. State laws pertaining to many areas of business are often lacking in uniformity, which makes trade between states confusing. To bring about greater uniformity, the National Commission of Uniform State Laws has over the years recommended model laws to the states. One of these was the Uniform Limited Partnership Act proposed by this national commission at various times to the several states.

Other uniform codes that have been adopted by the several states include the Uniform Partnership Act, the Uniform Negotiable Instruments Act, the Uniform Sales Act, the Uniform Bills of Lading Act, the Uniform Warehouse Receipts Act, the Uniform Conditional Sales Act, and the Uniform Stock Transfer Act.

During the last two decades, however, there has been a trend toward the adoption of a uniform code applicable to many kinds of business transactions replacing some of the existing codes in order to accomplish uniformity throughout all the states. The code that embraces the major areas of commercial law is the Uniform Commercial Code (UCC) and generally referred to as "the code." It is the result of a project sponsored by the National Conference of Commissioners on Uniform State Laws and by the American Law Institute.

The first edition of the code was published in 1952. Supplement No. 1, amending certain sections of the 1952 edition, was published in January, 1955. Subsequent revisions were made and finally, in 1957, the official edition of the code was completed. A total of 47 states, the District of Columbia, and the Virgin Islands have adopted the code in part of in total. Since the UCC embraces the major areas of commercial law, it expressly provides that in the states where adopted, it will replace the various Uniform Acts, including those mentioned above. These acts presumably are superseded by and incorporated into the UCC. From all indications, the code is destined to be adopted by all the states and territories.

Specifically, the UCC regulates many kinds of business transactions, including sales and bulk sales, commercial paper (negotiable instruments), warehouse receipts, bills of lading, secured interests in personal property, chattel mortgages, conditional sales, and rights of parties in defaults.[3] Unfortunately, because it would be too space-consuming due to its comprehensiveness, we cannot give a detailed analysis of every aspect of the UCC. Nor is it possible here to make an analytical comparison between the code and the various Uniform Acts. However, various parts of the UCC will be discussed later in this chapter.

[3] The purposes of the UCC are (1) to simplify, clarify, and modernize laws governing commercial transactions, (2) to permit expansion of commercial practices through custom, usage, and agreement of the parties, and (3) to make uniform the laws among the states and legal jurisdictions.

The Court System

A *court* is a tribunal created by government for the purpose of hearing and deciding on matters properly brought before it. It may give redress to the injured by enforcing some kind of punishment against the wrongdoer. It may direct compliance with the law, or prevent wrongs from occurring. There are various levels of courts in both the federal and state systems. Jurisdiction and organization of courts are regulated by constitutional and statutory provisions.

The Constitution of the United States, while ordaining the Supreme Court, provides considerable discretion to Congress to establish and administer the judicial power through legislation. The federal system of courts is provided for by Article III, Section 1: "The judicial power of the United States shall be vested in one Supreme Court, and such inferior courts as the Congress may from time to time ordain and establish." The Supreme Court is the only federal court established by the Constitution and not by Congress. Congress, however, determines the number of justices. The federal system of courts, as shown on the following chart, reveals the relationship of the Supreme Court to other courts in the federal judicial system.

State Courts. The state system of courts is similar to the federal system. Most states have a State Supreme Court or Supreme Court of Errors,

The Federal Courts System of the United States

UNITED STATES SUPREME COURT
(9 Judges)

UNITED STATES COURTS OF APPEALS
(11 Judicial districts)

Reviews decisions of lower courts. May sustain or set aside orders by federal commissions and agencies.

UNITED STATES DISTRICT COURTS

Composed of 88 districts in 50 states, Puerto Rico, District of Columbia, Guam, Canal zone, and Virgin Islands. These are courts of original jurisdiction.

U.S. COURT OF CLAIMS	U.S. CUSTOMS COURT	U.S. COURT OF CUSTOMS AND PATENT APPEALS	U.S. TAX COURT
Hears claims against the federal government. Judgments payable by federal appropriations.	Hears cases concerning custom rates and duties. Rules on regulations involving revenues received.	Reviews decisions of Customs Court, patents, trade-marks.	Conducts trials to settle tax controversies involving federal taxes.

which is followed in rank order by a Superior Court, which is the highest state trial court with general jurisdiction. Some states refer to the Superior Court as their Circuit Court or District Court. A total of 16 states have an intermediate Appellate Court in between the State Supreme Court and the Superior Court. The County Court is the lowest level that has jurisdiction in both civil and criminal cases. In cities it is customary to have Municipal Courts presided over by a municipal justice or magistrate. The lowest-level state court is the Justice of the Peace or Police Magistrate who handles petty offenses and traffic violations. Recorded testimony is seldom taken in the Justice of the Peace court.

Remedies at Law and at Equity

Through the system of courts, society provides redress (justice) to any person who believes he has suffered from a legal wrong. The alleged injured person, the *plaintiff*, is the one who brings the action against the accused, known as the *defendant*.

The American system of jurisprudence operates under a dual system of remedies obtained from the courts. One is known as *remedies at law* and the other as *remedies at equity*.

Equity, derived from the Latin *aequitas*, means "equality" or "justice." In general, remedies from courts of law provide only two forms of redress—namely, the restoring of real or personal property to one from whom it has been unjustly withheld, and the awarding of money damages. Since the remedies are limited and because common law has not provided protective or preventive remedies, equity courts were developed to supplement the restricted remedies at law. Equity courts may issue an injunction, which is simply a court order directing a particular party to perform an act or to refrain from continuing a certain act. Thus, an order directing that a party carry out a contract provision is an example of equity remedy. A court of equity may order a written instrument changed if the evidence is clear and compelling that the instrument failed to reflect an agreement between the parties because of an error in preparing the contract.

In a court of law, either party has the right to have the issues of fact determined by a jury, which is the fact-finding body, although the judge decides the issues of law. But in a court of equity, the right to trial by jury does not exist. The judge makes the decision and, therefore, determines the fact as well as law.

MODERN BUSINESS AND THE LAW

You will discover that almost every business transaction in some way involves a contract. Even if you only agree to rent office space, buy an automobile, or purchase raw materials, a contract is involved.

Business Contracts

A *contract* is a binding agreement between two or more competent parties in the form required by law, for a lawful purpose, and supported by consideration; and, if not performed by one party, it is enforceable by the other party. Notice that this definition mentions the following elements, which must exist in order that an agreement be enforceable as a contract: *mutual assent, competent parties, consideration, lawful purpose,* and *required form.*

Mutual Assent. When you make an offer and someone accepts it, both parties have freely and intentionally expressed assent on the same thing. For mutual assent to exist, then, one person, known as the offerer, must make a definite offer; the one to whom the offer is made, known as the *offeree,* must accept it exactly as it is made. Advertisements and price quotations on merchandise that is displayed are not offers. Instead, they *invite* offers. But if you offer to sell your fountain pen to Smith for three dollars and Smith accepts by handing you the money, then a contract results. The minds of the parties are then said to have met in mutual assent, having mutually agreed on the same thing.

Competent Parties. The law regards a competent person as one who may make contracts that are enforceable against him. Not all persons are considered competent to make a binding contract. According to common law, any person, male or female, under 21, is considered a minor, and is regarded as incompetent to make a contract binding himself. Insane persons, convicts, aliens, and drunkards are also not considered competent to make an enforceable contract. If you ever make a contract with a person in one of these categories, you will find that it is not binding on him unless he wishes to perform. But you, the competent party, cannot void the contract.

In most states, a minor may be held for a contract made for certain necessities, such as food, clothing, shelter, medical care, and education. If you furnish necessities to a minor under contract, you are entitled to collect only the reasonable value of these items.

Consideration. Ordinarily, a promise is not binding unless it is supported by consideration, which is something of value given for a promise. In other words, it is what you give in exchange for a promise. Consideration may consist of money, goods, services, or even another promise to do or not to do something that you have a legal right to do. For example, A agrees to buy an automobile from B for $500 provided B will deliver it within 24 hours. The consideration is the money exchanged for the automobile. Consideration need not be equal to the exact value of the promise. For example, if a merchant agrees to sell you a $100 watch for $15, the amount of the consideration is considered adequate even though the watch is actually worth far more than the price you agree to pay.

Consideration is not required in all contracts. For example, promises or offers of subscriptions for charitable, educational, or religious purposes are generally enforceable without consideration. Under the UCC, consideration is not required to discharge in writing a claim for breach of a commercial contract, or to change a contract for the sale of goods.[4]

Lawful Purpose. Before you make a contract, you must be sure that the transaction is lawful. An unlawful contract, such as an agreement to commit a crime, or a wagering or gambling agreement, is not enforceable. A contract that requires the payment of interest in excess of the maximum rate established by state law is not enforceable, either. However, the contract to pay the principle is. Any interest that is charged beyond the contract or maximum rate is known as *usury.*

The effect of usury on contracts is determined by state law. The least stringent provides only for forfeiture of excessive interest. Other states provide for forfeiture of two or more times the excessive interest. Some states impose a criminal penalty in addition to voiding the contract.

Agreements in restraint of trade are also considered unlawful. One example is an agreement that prevents you from carrying on your trade or profession. An agreement to control prices or to limit production by an act involving restraint of trade is considered an unlawful contract.

Required Form. For practical purposes, important contracts should be in writing: it is easy to prove the terms of the agreement when it is spelled out on paper and signed. Generally, a contract is valid whether it is written or oral—though an important exception to the general rule that a written contract is not required is the requirement that conveyances of land and negotiable instruments must be in writing.

The most common contract provisions are contained in the Statute of Frauds, a statute adopted in England in 1677 and since been adopted in various forms by the different states. In general, the Statute of Frauds in most states requires that the following types of contract must be in written form such as a note, memorandum, or formal document signed by the person against whom the contract is to be enforced:

1. Any contract by which a person agrees to answer for an obligation of another. For example, A promises to pay B certain debts contracted by C in case C fails to pay.
2. An agreement consisting of a special promise made upon a consideration of marriage. For example, if a person agrees to

[4] Uniform Commercial Code, Sec. 1-107 and Sec. 2-209 (1).

pay a sum of money to another in consideration of marriage, the agreement must be in writing. Engagement contract need not be in writing to be enforceable.

3. An agreement for which performance cannot be executed within one year.
4. Agreements to hold an administrator or executor liable out of his own property for debts of the estate. No administrator of an estate can be held liable for debts of the estate unless he agrees in writing to pay the debts.
5. An agreement for the sale of real estate. However, the statute applies only to agreements between the owner and the purchaser or their agents, and not to any other related agreements such as an agreement to pay for the examination of the title to the property to be sold. Leases for less than one year need not be in writing.

Section 2-201 of the UCC provides a modification of the Statutes of Frauds concerning a contract for the sale of goods for $500 or more. The UCC uses the $500 figure but makes changes in the wording and application as follows:

> Except as otherwise provided in this section, a contract for the sale of goods for the price of $500 or more is not enforceable by way of action or defense unless there is some writing sufficient to indicate that a contract for sale has been made between the parties and signed by the party against whom enforcement is sought or by his authorized agent or broker. A writing is not insufficient because it omits or incorrectly states a term agreed upon, but the contract is not enforceable under this paragraph beyond the quantity of goods shown in such writing.

In business a great many contracts are made so casually and so frequently that they need not be in writing. The following agreement illustrates a typical contract containing the essentials needed to make the agreement binding on both parties.

Remedies for Breach of Contract. For many reasons not all contracts, whether written or oral, are carried out. When a contract is *breached* (broken), the injured party may select from among several remedies. ("Injured" and "remedies" look like colloquial terms, but are part of the legal vocabulary.) For example, he can avoid carrying out his part of the agreement, acting in effect as though there had been no contract. The right of the injured party to cancel or rescind a contract is known as the *right of rescission.*

Or the injured party may bring an action for damages. Even if he has not sustained an actual loss from the breach, he is still entitled to a judgment for

AGREEMENT

THIS AGREEMENT, made this 15th day of December, 19 , between Edward Z. Sax, hereafter called the party of the first part, and Ingo J. Lem, hereafter called the party of the second part, both of Reno, Nevada, witnesseth:

That said party of the first part agrees to deliver to the premises of the second party, 3593 Yale Road, Reno, Nevada, one hundred (100) bales of clean, baled alfalfa hay, standard size bale and weight, between the first and fifth day of the month for each of the next twenty-four months (24), beginning January, 19 .

It is agreed that the price each month shall be determined by the prevailing price of baled alfalfa hay paid by the Valley Farm Cooperative on the last business day of the previous month of business, which said second party agrees to pay.

The party of the first part further agrees and stipulates to pay the cost of transportation and to bear all risks involved in hauling the baled hay to the premises of the party of the second part.

Payment by the party of the second part to the party of the first part shall be made by check or draft on or before the 10th day of each calendar month for all hay delivered that month.

Edward Z. Sax
Ingo J. Lem

Signed and delivered
in the presence of

Velma D. Greenwood
William R. Roberts

An agreement or contract.

a nominal sum, such as one dollar. This is known as *nominal damages*. On the other hand, if the injured party has sustained an actual loss, he is entitled to *compensatory damages*—a sum that will, as far as possible, compensate him for that loss.

A third remedy is for the injured party to ask for "performance of the contract." If the payment of damages would not actually compensate him for his real loss, the court will sometimes grant him special relief by ordering the defaulting party to perform the agreement. As a rule, damages in excess of actual loss (for the purpose of punishing the defendant) cannot be recovered for breach of contract. Such damages are called *punitive damages* or *exemplary damages*.

Ordinarily, a court does not compel specific performance if there is some other adequate remedy at law; or if the agreement is illegal, immoral, or fraudulent; or if the court cannot supervise performance; or if it is established that specific performance would cause undue hardship on the defaulting party.

Statute of Limitations. Each state provides that after a certain number of years have elapsed, a contract claim is barred. Under the statute of limitations, there is a time within which an action or suit at law may be instituted, but the lapsing of which "outlaws" the claim. The period of limitation is computed from the time the right to sue arises, and the length of the period varies according to the nature of the claim. The statute of limitations does not discharge the contract; it merely supplies a defense to a claim for breach of contract, that defense being that no legal action was taken during the prescribed period. In any case, the defendant must plead the statute in defense in order to defeat any action brought against him. A new promise, in writing, to pay a debt (principal or interest) barred by the statute of limitations, will revive the whole debt and start the statute running again.

Notice in Table 3.1 that the statute of limitations enacted by each of the 50 states applies to civil actions. *Civil actions* are charges against one individual by another to redress a wrong committed against the one by the other. Action to recover a debt established by a promissory note, or a damage suit to obtain money for injuries resulting from an accident, are illustrations of a civil action. The figures listed in each column in the table indicate the number of years within which a court action to recover must be commenced. (This table is presented merely as an illustration; it should not be used as an actual reference, since these time limits are subject to change at any session of a state legislature.)

The Law of Agency

The Nature of Agency Relationship. One of the most common legal business relationships is between a principal and his agent. An agreement between two parties by which one is vested with authority to represent the other in business transactions with third parties is known as a *contract of agency*. The party who represents another is the *agent*. The *principal* is the party the agent represents.

Any person who has the right to act for himself may delegate his per-

TABLE
3.1

STATUTES OF LIMITATIONS FOR CIVIL ACTIONS (O MEANS ORAL; W MEANS WRITTEN)

State	Promissory Notes (years)	Open Accounts (years)	Instruments and Contracts Under Seal (years)	Ordinary Contracts (years)	Domestic Judgments in Courts of Record (years)
Alabama	6	3	10	6	20
Alaska	6	6	10	6	10
Arizona	6	3	6	6-W—3-O	5
Arkansas	5	3	5	5-W—3-O	10
California	4	4	4	4-W—2-O	10
Colorado	6	6	6	6	20
Connecticut	6	6	17	6-W—3-O	21
Delaware	6	3	No limit	3	No Limit
Dist. of Columbia	3	3	12	3	12
Florida	5	3	20	5-W—3-O	20
Georgia	6	4	20	6-W—4-O	7
Hawaii	6	6	6	6-W—4-O	10
Idaho	5	4	5	5-W—4-O	6
Illinois	10	5	10	10-W—5-O	20
Indiana	10	6	20	20-W—6-O	20
Iowa	10	5	10	10-W—5-O	20
Kansas	3	3	5	5-W—3-O	
Kentucky	15	5	15	15-W—5-O	15
Louisiana	5	3	10	10	10
Maine	6	6	20	6	20
Maryland	3	3	12	3	12
Massachusetts	6	6	20	6	20
Michigan	6	6	6	6	10
Minnesota	6	6	6	6	10
Mississippi	6	3	6	6-W—3-O	7
Missouri	10	5	10	10	10
Montana	8	5	8	8-W—5-O	10
Nebraska	5	4	5	5-W—4-O	
Nevada	6	4	6	6-W—4-O	6
New Hampshire	6	6	20	6	20
New Jersey	6	6	16	6	20
New Mexico	6	4	6	6-W—4-O	7
New York	6	6	6	6	20
North Carolina	3	3	10	3	10
North Dakota	6	6	6	6	10
Ohio	15	6	15	15-W—6-O	21
Oklahoma	5	3	5	5-W—3-O	
Oregon	6	6	10	6	10
Pennsylvania	6	6	20	6	20
Rhode Island	6	6	20	6	20
South Carolina	6	6	20	6	10
South Dakota	6	6	20	6	20
Tennessee	6	6	6	6	10
Texas	4	2	4	4-W—2-O	10
Utah	6	4	6	6-W—4-O	8
Vermont	6	6	8	6	8
Virginia	5	3	10	5-W—3-O	20
Washington	6	3	6	6-W—3-O	6
West Virginia	10	5	10	10-W—5-O	10
Wisconsin	6	6	10	6	20
Wyoming	10	8	10	10-W—8-O	5

formance to an agent. Acts of a personal nature, however, such as voting, holding public office, or serving on juries, may not be delegated to others.

How Agency is Created. The usual way of creating an agency is by express authorization. (A simple example is one person appointing another to act as his agent.) Authorization may be either verbal or in writing. A formal written appointment is called a *power of attorney,* an example of which is shown in the form of a proxy in Chapter 4. The fourth section of the Statute of Frauds requires that a contract creating agency be in writing when the period of performance necessitates more than one year from the date of the contract.

Agency may also be created by the conduct of the principal. For example, if you knowingly, and without objection, permit another to act as your agent, the law will find this to be an expression of authorization to the agent and you will not be allowed to deny that the agent was in fact authorized. This is sometimes known as *agency by implication.*

A third method of creating agency is by *estoppel.* This happens when a third party believes, because of the words and deeds of the principal, that another is his agent. If the agent is not in fact authorized as an agent, but the principal has represented him to be one, the law will *estop* (stop) the principal from asserting this false information by creating an *agency by estoppel.*

A principal has the same obligations to his agent that an employer generally has to an employee. For example, the principal is obliged to reimburse the agent for legitimate expenses and to carry out the agreement that created the agency. If you appoint an agent for a year and then wrongfully discharge him in three months, he is entitled to damages for the loss of time. On the other hand, by mutual agreement it is possible to terminate the relationship on or before the completion of the task. Among other methods of terminating an ordinary agency are (1) the death of either party, (2) the insanity of either party, and (3) war involving the country of the principal and agent.

THE LAW AND YOUR PROPERTY

The term *property* refers to the rights you have to use, enjoy, and dispose of anything that is subject to ownership. Historically, the original division of property into *real* and *personal property* was part of the English feudal system, which dealt primarily with land as the main source of wealth. Roman law termed property "movable" instead of personal and "immovable" instead of real. In modern law, the distinction between real and personal property is not always clear, though it is a good rule-of-thumb to observe the movable/immovable concept in making the distinction.

Classes of Property

The Constitution of the United States provides that no one can be deprived of his property rights without due process of law. In law the word "property" is not restricted to the material object itself—"property" is both the right and the interest, whether real or personal.

In addition to the rights in land, buildings and fixtures, mineral deposits, and bodies of water on the land, *real property* is also anything that is attached to the soil (such as grass, trees, bushes, and fences) and must be conveyed by a formal instrument recorded in a public office. The Uniform Aeronautics Act, which has been adopted by 21 states, provides that the owner of land owns even the space above it, subject to the right of aircraft use that does not interfere with the use of the land below and does not make such use dangerous to persons or property lawfully on the land. But how far an owner's rights extend above the land is as yet undetermined by law. Generally, all property that is not real is classed as *personal property,* which consists of things temporary and movable and not of a freehold nature (that is, not an estate of inheritance or an estate for life).

Forms of Real Property Ownership. Real property held by a person in his own right, without any other person being joined with him, is known as an *estate in severalty.* Real property held by more than one person is said to be co-owned. The forms of co-ownership of property generally recognized in this country (although no single state recognizes them all) are *joint tenancy, tenancy in common, tenancy by entirety,* and *community property.* The basic distinguishing characteristic between joint tenancy and tenancy in common is right of survivorship.

A *joint tenancy* is ownership held by two or more persons jointly with equal rights to share in its enjoyment during their lives. In joint tenancy, after the death of one owner, his interest passes to the surviving joint tenant or tenants (owners) until only one joint tenant survives. Upon the death of the only remaining tenant, the estate passes to his heirs. The use of joint tenancy in some states has been abused because of the tendency to avoid probate proceedings upon the death of a joint tenant. A joint-tenancy relationship may be severed by sale or conveyance of the interest of any joint tenant, or by partition or agreement.

Tenancy in common is property ownership in which two or more persons have, or are entitled to have, undivided possession of a common property *without* right of survivorship. If one owner dies, his interest passes to his heirs rather then to the other owner or owners. During his lifetime, each tenant is entitled to possession and use of the entire property. In general, a tenancy in common can be terminated only by consent of the parties or by partition—a division of property held jointly. In some states, if a deed is

POWER OF ATTORNEY

THE STATE OF TEXAS,
COUNTY OF GALVESTON } KNOW ALL MEN BY THESE PRESENTS:

THAT I, WILLIAM H. LOCK

of the County of Galveston and State of Texas

ha s this day Made, Constituted and Appointed and by these presents do Make, Constitute and Appoint ROBERT WESTON CALLAWAY

of Galveston , in the County of Galveston and State of Texas, true and lawful Attorney for me and in my name , place and stead, to

DEMISE AND RENT MY ONE STORY BRICK GARAGE BUILDING LOCATED UPON LOT SEVEN IN BLOCK ELEVEN IN THE CITY OF GALVESTON TO SUCH TENANTS AS MY SAID ATTORNEY SHALL SELECT FOR THE HIGHEST REASONABLE RENTAL OBTAINABLE AND TO MAKE, EXECUTE AND DELIVER A GOOD AND SUFFICIENT LEASE THEREFOR FOR A TERM NOT TO EXCEED TWO YEARS;

TO COLLECT THE RENTS AND PROFITS THEREFROM AND TO DEPOSIT THE SAME TO MY ACCOUNT IN THE THIRD NATIONAL BANK OF GALVESTON, WHEN COLLECTED AND RECEIVED;

TO KEEP AND MAINTAIN SAID BUILDING IN GOOD REPAIR AND CONDITION DURING THE TERM OF SAID LEASE AND TO DRAW CHECKS AGAINST MY ACCOUNT AT SAID BANK IN PAYMENT OF SUCH REPAIRS AND IN PAYMENT OF HIS COMPENSATION AS HEREINAFTER SPECIFIED.

IN CONSIDERATION OF SAID SERVICES PERFORMED BY SAID ATTORNEY, HE SHALL RECEIVE THE SUM OF $30.00 PER MONTH DURING THE TERM OF SUCH LEASE.

hereby giving and granting to said Attorney full power and authority to do and perfôrm any and all acts and things whatsoever requisite and necessary to be done in and about the premises, as fully to all intents and purposes, as I might or could do if personally present, with full power of substitution and revocation, hereby ratifying and confirming all that the said Attorney or his substitute shall lawfully do in the premises by virtue hereof.

IN TESTIMONY WHEREOF, I have hereunto set my hand and seal at, Galveston, Texas this 12th day of June A. D. 19

WITNESSES: William H. Lock (SEAL)
Fuller Greenwood (SEAL)
Carol Griffin (SEAL)

This formal written document, in which an agent is appointed, is called a *power of attorney.*

made out to X and Y without any statement as to the nature of ownership, the presumption is that the parties are tenants in common.

Tenancy by entirety is property ownership that may be held only by husband and wife. In other words, it is dependent upon the marital status. This tenancy is endowed by the right of survivorship: upon the death of one spouse the entire property goes to the surviving spouse. Also, neither tenant alone can transfer his interest to a third party. Tenancy by entirety may be terminated only by joint agreement, and becomes a tenancy in common upon divorce.

Several western and southwestern states provide for a community system between husband and wife known as *community property.*[5] Under this law, all real and personal property acquired by the husband and wife during the marriage, except that acquired by will, gift, or descent, shall be jointly owned. Some statutes provide for the right of survivorship; others provide that the half of the property belonging to the deceased spouse shall descend to the heirs of the decedant. In community-property states, husband and wife may each file a separate state income-tax return, each reporting only half of the community income. (The federal income-tax law also permits the filing of separate returns.)

Forms of Personal Property Ownership. Whereas real property consists of an interest in land and things attached to the soil, personal property is restricted to movable goods such as furniture, stocks, bonds, automobiles, jewels, and clothing. Intangible goods such as monetary claims and debts are personal property, too. *Chattels personal* consist of both tangible and intangible personal property. This is quite different from *chattels real,* which are interests in real-estate limited to their duration. It is important to understand how these chattels are different, and the manner in which personal and real property differs, since the methods of acquiring or transferring ownership are different.

How Property May be Acquired. You may acquire real and personal property in different ways. One common way is by gift and another is by inheritance (descent), or by *legacy,* which is by means of a will—a written instrument. Or you may acquire personal property by *accession*—that is, by an increase in something you already own. Crops grown on your land or animals born to your herd belong to you by right of accession. Then, too, you may acquire personal property by intellectual achievement. For example, as an author or inventor you may obtain exclusive right to your production for a limited time by obtaining a copyright or a patent. Or, you may acquire real property by outright purchase, in which case the seller conveys a deed to you.

Deeds. A *deed* is an instrument, in writing and requiring a notary public's seal, by which an owner or *grantor* conveys or transfers his interest in land to the buyer, who is called the *grantee.* Unlike a contract, no con-

[5] States currently having community-property laws are Arizona, California, Idaho, Louisiana, Nevada, New Mexico, Oklahoma, Texas, Hawaii, and Washington.

sideration is needed to make it valid. A deed is required to transfer title to land even when it is a gift and no money is exchanged.

In terms of the interest conveyed, there are two types of deeds: (1) the *quitclaim deed*, which merely transfers whatever interest the grantor may have in the property; and (2) the *warranty deed*, which warrants or guarantees that the owner has the right to convey title to the land. A warranty deed also warrants the title by guaranteeing that the property is free of debt unless otherwise stated. Actually, title to real property does not pass until the deed has been delivered. Since it is an instrument under seal, it must be recorded in the county where the property is located. The accompanying warranty deed is ready to be recorded.

Apart from the protection provided by recording the deed, a buyer may protect himself by requiring the seller to furnish an *abstract of title*. This is a summarized report based on the county records of all conveyances which affect said land, as well as a statement of all liens, charges, and encumbrances affecting the title to the land. A purchaser of land should request that he be furnished an abstract of title brought up-to-date.

Leases. When you start your own business, you may find it more practical to lease real property than own it. Your agreement with the landlord to use the property is a *lease*. You are the *lessee* and your landlord is the *lessor*. A lease for longer than a year must, according to the Statute of Frauds, be in writing to be enforceable. The ground on which Radio City is located in New York City is leased for 99 years. A lease is an example of chattels real.

The more formal types of leases, such as the one shown on page 85, usually contain the following information:

1. Date of agreement
2. Names of landlord and tenant
3. Description of property
4. Length of lease
5. Manner of payment of rent
6. Responsibility for repairs
7. Liability for injury to third party
8. Right to sublet or assign

Mortgages. Property may be pledged as security for a loan in which case the owner gives the lender a claim against the property by offering a mortgage. Mortgages against real estate are known as *real estate mortgages*. Mortgages on tangible personal property are known as *chattel mortgages*. Mortgages must be in writing and executed under seal, and should be recorded in the county in which the property is located. The parties to a mortgage are the *mortgagor* (debtor)—the one who gives the property as security for the loan, and the *mortgagee* (creditor)—the person to whom property is given as security for the loan. In other words, the mortgagor is the borrower

The State of Texas,
County of HARRIS

Know All Men by These Presents:

That JAMES GREEN, a widower not since remarried

of the County of HARRIS State of TEXAS for and in consideration of the sum of Ten Thousand ($10,000)--- DOLLARS

to be paid, and secured to be paid, by the grantee

hereinafter named --- as follows:

The sum of one thousand ($1,000) dollars to be paid on the delivery of this instrument, the receipt of which is hereby acknowledged, and the further sum of seventy-five ($75.00) dollars the first day of each and every month thereafter until the purchase price has been paid in full. All of said sums except the first payment of one thousand ($1,000) dollars are to be represented by promissory notes in the amount of seventy-five ($75.00) dollars and to bear interest at the rate of six (6) per cent per annum from date until paid,

have Granted, Sold and Conveyed, and by these presents do^es^ Grant, Sell and Convey, unto the said WALTER H. JENSEN

of the County of HARRIS State of TEXAS all that certain

TRACE OR PARCEL OF LAND DESCRIBED AS FOLLOWS, TO-WIT:

Lot Three (3) Block Six (6) in the OPAL Addition, City of South Houston, in the County of Harris and State of Texas.

TO HAVE AND TO HOLD the above described premises, together with all and singular the rights and appurtenances thereto in anywise belonging unto the said Grantee, his

heirs and assigns forever and he do^es^ hereby bind

heirs, executors and administrators, to Warrant and Forever Defend, all and singular the said premises unto the said grantee, his

heirs and assigns, against every person whomsoever lawfully claiming, or to claim the same, or any part thereof.

But it is expressly agreed and stipulated that the Vendor's Lien is retained against the above described property, premises and improvements, until the above described note , and all interest thereon are fully paid according to face and tenor, effect and reading, when this deed shall become absolute.

WITNESS this hand at, South Houston
this 25th day of November 19

Witness at request of Grantor:

Leeder Greenwood
Carol Griffin

James Green
Walter H. Jensen

A warranty deed used to convey title to real property. This type of deed may also contain certain statements, usually by the grantor, that other things will be done or are true.

and the mortgagee is the lender. If the debt is not paid, the mortgagee has the right to foreclose and sell the property to pay off the debt.

The Law of Negotiable Instruments

No one knows for certain when negotiable instruments were first used, though it is common knowledge that "commercial paper" (legal documents used in making loans) appeared on the business scene at least as early as the Middle Ages. The law at that time, commonly known as "the law of merchant," was eventually assimilated by English common law, and finally became part of our legal structure when the colonies adopted the English system. In succeeding years the several states enacted statutes pertaining to "commercial paper," which term eventually was changed to "negotiable instruments."

The term *negotiable* comes from the three Latin words *neg, otius,* and *able,* and when joined together as one means *not able to be leisurely.* The connotation is that if anything is not performed at leisure, it is done quickly. When applied to a legal instrument, this means that it has a ready or quick transferability from one person to another. Under early English common law, commercial paper was not easily transferable mainly because the credit standing of the person desiring the transfer was often questionable. Further, even if that person possessed a good credit rating, it was risky for him to use commercial paper because the law permitted the maker of the document to take legal action against any transferees who did not meet its terms.

A *negotiable instrument* is a written contract evidencing rights to receive money, which rights by negotiation may be transferred from one party to another by indorsement. The instrument need not be on any particular kind of material to be legal, nor must it necessarily be written with a certain instrument. It may be in ink, pencil, crayon; it may be printed, hand-written, typewritten, engraved.

In 1896 the Uniform Negotiable Instruments Act brought all the common laws and state laws together that dealt with negotiable instruments. This Act was adopted *in toto* by most of the states. More recently, the aforementioned UCC, dealing with commercial paper and negotiable instruments, has rapidly been replacing the Negotiable Instruments Act in most states.

The requirements to which a negotiable instrument must adhere are in the following sections of the UCC and may be summarized thusly:

UCC Section 3-104: Form of Instrument. A negotiable instrument must be in writing, must be payable in money, and must be signed by the person putting it into circulation (the maker or drawer); and the promise to pay must be unconditional.

The State of Texas,
County of } **Know All Men by These Presents:**

Made this 2nd day of MARCH , A. D. 19 , by and between

Smithson R. Conway---, known herein as LESSOR,

and Rollo J. Jenkins---

---, known herein as LESSEE,

(The terms "Lessor" and "Lessee" shall be construed in the singular or plural number according as they respectively represent one or more than one person.)

WITNESSETH, That the said Lessor does by these presents Lease and Demise unto the said Lessee the following described property, to-wit: Lying and being situated in the County of WALLER , State of Texas, and being A single family dwelling located at 1301 First Street in the town of Hempstead, con-six (6) rooms and bath.

for the term of twelve (12) months beginning the 2nd day of MARCH A. D. 196- and ending the 1st day of MARCH, 19 , paying therefor the sum of Twelve hundred ($1200)-------------------------------------- DOLLARS, payable monthly installments the second day of each month in advance.

upon the conditions and covenants following:

First. That Lessee will well and PUNCTUALLY pay said rents in manner and form as hereinbefore specified, and quietly deliver up said premises on the day of the expiration of this lease, in as good condition as the same were in when received, reasonable wear and tear thereof excepted.

Second. That the said premises shall be used for Family residence by the lessee and his immediate family.

and for no other purpose.

Third. That Lessee will not sub-let said premises, or any part thereof, to any person or persons whatsoever, without the consent of said Lessor, IN WRITING, thereto first obtained.

Fourth. That on failure to pay the rent in advance, as aforesaid, or to comply with any of the foregoing obligations, or in violation of any of the foregoing covenants, the Lessor may declare this lease forfeited at Lessor's discretion and Lessor or Lessor's agent or attorney shall have the power to enter and hold, occupy and repossess the entire premises hereinbefore described, as before the execution of these presents.

IN TESTIMONY WHEREOF, The parties to this agreement have hereunto set their hands in duplicate, the day and year above written.

Smithson R. Conway, LESSOR

Rollo J. Jenkins, LESSEE

A lease for a period of one year.

UCC Section 3-105: When Promise or Order Unconditional. This section provides that mere expressions of intention by a maker to pay his note, or a request of a drawee to pay a bill, are unconditional, and such intentions and wording will not create a negotiable instrument. A promise or order is not unconditional if the instrument states that it is subject to or governed by any other agreement, or stipulates that it is to be paid only out of a particular fund.

UCC Section 3-106: Sum Certain. The sum payable must be a sum certain in amount even though it is to be paid with a stated interest or by stated installments, or with a stated discount.

UCC Section 3-107: Money. An instrument is payable in money if the medium of exchange in which it is payable is money at the time the instrument is made.

UCC Section 3-108: Payable on Demand. Instruments payable on demand include those payable at sight or on presentation, and those in which no time for payment is stated.

UCC Section 3-109: Definite Time. An instrument is payable at a definite time which can be on or before a stated date or at a fixed period after a stated date, or at a fixed period after sight.

UCC Section 3-110: Payable to Order. For an instrument to be negotiable, it must be payable to order when by its terms it is payable to the order or assigns of any person specified with reasonable certainty, or to him or his order. Also, the instrument may be payable to the order of the maker or drawer, or the drawee, or to a payee who is not maker, drawer, or drawee. A distinction should be made between instruments payable "to bearer" and those payable "to order." Instruments (such as checks) payable to bearer on the face are transferred the same as money. Title passes by simple delivery, and an innocent transferee gains title even though the transferor had no title. But an instrument payable "to order" requires the indorsement of the payee before it may be negotiated. If it is lost or stolen before indorsed, legal title will not pass.

It is plain to see from this summary that certain legal instruments—leases, wills, mortgages, and sales tickets, for example—do not possess all the requirements of a negotiable instrument and therefore are not negotiable. (Our most commonly used negotiable instruments—checks, drafts, and promissory notes—will be discussed again in Chapters 17 and 24.)

Words of Negotiability. In preparing a negotiable instrument, the words "order" and "bearer" are precise terms that should be used if negotiability is intended. An instrument is payable "to order" when it is drawn to the order of a specified person or his order. For example, an instrument payable "to the order of Smith" or "to Smith or order" is negotiable. But an instrument "payable to Smith" is not negotiable because the words "order of" are missing.

An instrument may be drawn to the order of two or more payees. This makes the instrument negotiable and payable to either party. For example, an instrument payable "to A *or* B" is in the alternative and so is payable to either A or B and may be indorsed by either party. An instrument payable "to A *and* B" is not in the alternative and may be negotiated only by both of them, which means that both A and B must indorse in order to negotiate.

How Negotiable Instruments are Transferred. Transfer of these commercial papers from one person to another is by the simple process of *indorsement* (by way of a signature), which should appear on the back of the instrument. The person to whom the instrument is transferred is the *indorsee.* This person is also the "holder in due course," which means that he must be either in possession of the instrument properly indorsed, or be the bearer of the instrument, having been named as the payee. A *holder in due course* is one who acquires the instrument under the following conditions: (1) it must be complete and regular on its face; (2) the holder must have given consideration (value) for the paper; (3) it must be accepted in good faith; and (4) the instrument must be accepted without notice of defects in the title, or defense against payment. If you accept a bank check by indorsement under the above conditions, you are a holder in due course, and the legal owner of the check.

Forms of Indorsement. Commercial law recognizes four principal kinds of indorsements which may be used to transfer ownership of a negotiable instrument. They are: (1) blank, (2) special, (3) restrictive, and (4) qualified. Let us see how each of these forms of indorsement appears in everyday practice.

When the indorser merely signs his name, he is using a *blank indorsement.* This is the most common form used to endorse checks, drafts, and promissory notes. When you indorse a check in blank, you transfer ownership of the instrument, you warrant that it is genuine and valid, that you had title to it, and that you accept a liability to pay the amount of the instrument if it is not honored by the drawee bank.

It is not wise business procedure to indorse a check in blank except at the time it is negotiated. If it is indorsed in blank and is lost or stolen, it may be negotiated by the finder or thief. By using an indorsement that restricts a check to certain purposes, or by indicating the name of the indorsee, you can avoid this danger.

A *special indorsement* consists of your signature and words specifying the person to whom you make the instrument payable. The language of this indorsement may read "Pay to order of Jack Johnson," followed by your own

Blank Indorsement

Jim Right

Special Indorsement

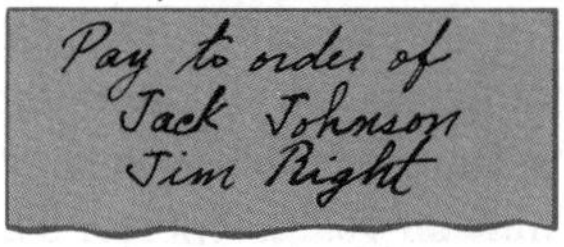

Pay to order of
Jack Johnson
Jim Right

Restrictive Indorsement

For deposit only
Jim Right

Qualified Indorsement

Without recourse
Jim Right

signature. This special indorsement is sometimes called an *indorsement in full.* As in the case of the blank indorsement, a special indorsement transfers title to the instrument and imposes a liability upon the indorser to pay the amount of the instrument.

A *restrictive indorsement* prevents further negotiations of the instrument to any other person except for collection or deposit. If you hold several checks that you want to deposit in a bank to the credit of your account, you may indorse each check by writing "For deposit only," or "For collection only," or "For deposit to the account of James John." Actually, a restrictive indorsement restricts further negotiation of the instrument. It is an excellent safeguard.

A fourth way to indorse a check, although it is not commonly used, is by means of a *qualified indorsement,* which qualifies or limits the obligation that ordinarily exists when you indorse an instrument. It does not affect the passage of title, but it limits the indorser's liability to the extent of the qualification. In fact, it does not release you from all liability, but you are released if the drawee bank refuses to make payment. Thus, if you want to transfer a check or note by qualified indorsement, you indorse it by writing the words "Without recourse," followed by your signature. Qualified indorsements may be used by attorneys and trustees when representing another person while at the same time not wishing to accept the normal responsibility of an indorser. This form of indorsement is most often used when the qualified indorser is the one who admits to having no personal interest in the transactions, as in the case of an attorney who merely indorses to his principal a check made payable to him by a third party. Since the indorser is not a party to the transaction, he is not in a position where he should be required to guarantee payment of the instrument.

The Law of Sales

Buying and selling goods are two of the most common business transactions. The sale of goods is an agreement whereby the seller, for a consideration, transfers title and possession of the goods to the buyer. The seller is known as the *vendor* and the buyer as the *vendee.* A bill of sale may be used to transfer title to personal property, and a deed, as we have said, is used to transfer real property. The law of sales is an outgrowth of common law; it was codified by the enactment of the Uniform Sales Act by several states. The more recent Uniform Commercial Code, which includes articles on sales, is the prevailing legal source. Our discussion shall deal primarily with two broad topics: *title transfer* and *sales warranties*.

When Does Title Pass? A sales transaction may give the buyer the privilege of returning the goods. This is known as a *sale on approval.* Section 2-326 of the UCC provides that in the absence of a contrary agreement, title and risk of loss remain with the seller under a sale on approval. If there is approval by the buyer, then title transfers. One way to indicate approval is by keeping the article beyond the time fixed, or, if no time was agreed upon, beyond a reasonable time.

Title to goods sold "FOB" (free on board) at a named place, according to UCC Section 2-319, passes to the buyer when goods are delivered at the point of named place. The seller bears the risk of leaving them at the designated place.

UCC Section 2-328 provides that when goods are sold at auction, title passes to the buyer when the auctioneer announces by the fall of the hammer or in any other customary manner that the auction is completed as to that lot. Each lot is a separate transaction, and title to each passes independent of other lots sold.

Many articles of personal property are sold on an installment plan. Under the UCC, possession of the goods is transferred to the buyer, but title remains with the seller, as security, until the full purchase price is paid. When the final installment is paid, the title then passes to the buyer.

In a cash sale, the title does not pass until the price is paid, and if the seller accepts a check, the title ordinarily does not pass until the check is cashed. If the check does not clear the bank, the seller can retake the goods unless they have been resold to an innocent third party.

When goods are sold "COD" (cash on delivery), a device by which the seller appoints the common carrier as his agent to collect the purchase price of the goods as a condition of delivery, title passes to the buyer subject to delivery. However, the seller has the right to instruct the carrier to retain possession until payment is made in full. The risk of loss of goods in transit is on the buyer.

It is not uncommon for a manufacturer or distributor to send goods to a dealer for sale to the public with the understanding that the manufacturer or distributor himself is to remain the owner of the goods and that the dealer is acting only as his agent. The agent is often called the *consignee* because he is the one to whom the goods are consigned; the owner who sends the goods is called the *consignor*. Understanding the role of the parties under this arrangement is important because fire and theft insurance on goods on consignment are the responsibility of the consignor.

Sales Warranties. A seller may make a guarantee with respect to the goods he sells. If the goods are not as guaranteed, he may be held liable for a breach of warranty. Thus, we may define a *warranty* as an affirmation of fact or promise, stated or implied by one contracting party to another, that certain facts about the goods or services are as promised or implied. It is a guarantee that a seller makes or implies, usually to induce the potential customer to buy.

The law recognizes two kinds of warranties: *express* and *implied.* An *express warranty* is any statement of material fact issued by the seller, made either orally or in writing, which becomes part of the sales agreement. This statement may be about the quality, condition, or title of the goods. The seller may say: "This article is pure silk," or "This knife is made of stainless steel."

An *implied warranty* is one that was not made by the seller but is implied by the law. For instance, in the absence of the parties' expressed intent to the contrary, it is implied by the law that a seller has the right to sell his goods and that he has title to the goods at the time of sale. Another implied warranty is that the goods will prove fit for the purpose for which they are purchased. On this point, Section 2-315 of the UCC states: "Where the seller at the time of contracting has reason to know any particular purpose for which the goods are required and that the buyer is relying on the seller's skill or judgment to select or furnish suitable goods, there is unless excluded or modified under the next section an implied warranty that the goods shall be fit for such purpose."

Breach of Warranty. According to the UCC, when it is established that breach of warranty exists, the buyer may seek to exercise his rights to recover through the process of any one of these four actions: (1) retain the goods but claim a deduction from the original price; (2) reject the nonconforming goods delivered by the seller; (3) return the goods and request a refund if money has been paid; or (4) refuse to accept the goods and bring an action against the seller to recover damages sustained.

Bailments

During the normal course of business there are times when one person (called "the bailor") gives possession and control of personal property to another person (called "the bailee") with the understanding that the bailee is to hold the property in behalf of the bailor. The delivery of property—such as goods, money, or other valuables—to another person for some special purpose, with the understanding that the property is to be returned to the owner when the purpose has been fulfilled, is a *bailment.* The person who has title to the property is the *bailor,* and the person to whom the owner delivers possession of the property is the *bailee*. The bailor always remains the owner of the chattel; although he may part with possession, he does not give up the title.

The law provides that ordinary and reasonable care must be exercised by the bailee while in possession of the property. The failure of the bailee to return the property at the termination of the bailment gives the bailor the right to seek recovery.

Such common carriers as railroads, airlines, and bus companies have a bailment relationship with those who entrust their baggage with the carrier. Also, a bailment relation arises when goods are stored in a warehouse. And, the hotelkeeper is given a lien on the baggage of his *guests* for the agreed charges as a bailee.

Bankruptcy

Another important aspect of our legal environment in business has to do with the application of bankruptcy laws. Congress, using its constitutional power, enacted the first Bankruptcy Act in 1898, which was designed to establish a uniform system of bankruptcy. The National Bankruptcy Act, as amended in 1938 by the Chandler Act, even provides plans for corporation reorganization in situations wherein one is adjudged to be bankrupt. State laws prevail where the individual or business is not subject to interstate trade legislation.

Under Section I (4) of the Bankruptcy Act, the term *bankrupt* is defined to include "a person against whom an involuntary petition or an application to revoke a discharge has been filed, or who has filed a voluntary petition, or who has been adjudged a bankrupt." Any insolvent business or individual, with the exception of municipal corporations, railroads, insurance companies, banks, and building-and-loan associations, can now resort to bankruptcy and thus discharge all liabilities to creditors. According to the Bankruptcy Act, a person or corporation is insolvent "whenever the aggregate of his property . . . shall not, at a fair evaluation, be sufficient to pay his debts."

Bankruptcy may be either voluntary or involuntary. *Voluntary bankruptcy,* which is the more common, occurs when a person or corporation files with a federal court a petition claiming he is unable to pay his debts because his liabilities exceed his assets. By this action, the debtor expresses a desire to be adjudged a bankrupt and asserts he is willing to make his assets available for equitable distribution among his creditors under the supervision of the court. If approved by the court, he is discharged from his debts and is free to begin anew.

Involuntary bankruptcy occurs when the creditors of an insolvent person or business (except a wage-earner receiving less than $1,500 yearly, a farmer, or any corporation that cannot declare itself a voluntary bankrupt) may seek to have that business or person declared bankrupt. To do this, the creditors must prove that the debtor committed one or more of the acts of bankruptcy as defined in the law.

The acts may be summarized as follows: (1) removing or concealing assets; (2) transferring while insolvent a portion of his property to one or more creditors; (3) allowing any creditor to obtain a lien upon his property and failing to discharge the lien within 30 days; (4) admitting in writing his inability to pay his debts; (5) making a general assignment of his property for the benefit of creditors; and (6) while insolvent, accepting or permitting the appointment of a receiver or trustee to take charge of the property.

When a petition of involuntary bankruptcy is filed in the federal court, the judge appoints a receiver. An investigation is conducted by the court to determine if the debtor is actually insolvent and if he is guilty of violating one of the acts of bankruptcy. If there has been a violation, the court takes over the supervision of the assets by appointing a referee in bankruptcy, who notifies the creditors to file and prove their claims. The creditors then meet and elect a trustee in bankruptcy, who is charged with the task of liquidating the business or estate. This same procedure applies to both voluntary and involuntary bankruptcy after the court has declared the defendant bankrupt.

The Bankruptcy Act permits payment to creditors under certain priority: (1) administrative costs, including certain expenses of creditors, fees, trustee's expenses, etc.; (2) wages due to employees not to exceed $600 earned within three months before the date of commencement of proceedings; (3) reasonable expenses of creditors who oppose the confirmation of an arrangement or wage-earner plan, or through whose efforts conviction of an offense under the act is obtained; (4) taxes due to the municipality, state, county, or the federal government; (5) debts due anyone according to the priority under state and federal laws.

BUSINESS ETHICS

Since the beginning of recorded history—and probably since before that—people have lived by rules of some kind. At first these rules were simple, because human wants were simple. Then societies became more complex, resulting in more complicated laws. And as societies developed more formal rules, they also turned to moral codes. These were often closely identified with their religion. The fourth chapter of the first book of the Bible poses this question: "Am I my brother's keeper?" And the Golden Rule, with its simple statement, "Do unto others as you would have them do unto you," has remained over the centuries a basic moral code. But some persons are not willing to accept the social responsibilities that go with living with a moral code. Often these persons believe in a code for others but not for themselves—a position which, to the dislike of everyone, forces the enactment and enforcement of more and more laws. And there is already a surplus of critics who strongly argue that business needs fewer governmental controls—not more.

One of the heartening signs of our times is the increasing interest of businessmen in the ethical implications of their work. We are living in an age when traditional values and mores are being examined and reviewed with increasing regularity. This is not a society in search for more rules of conduct applicable to business and living. We already have rules (laws) to go by that the vast majority of us agree are adequate. What is missing in our total business conduct is the unwillingness of some groups in business and industry to improve and police their own ethical conduct. It is the purpose of this part of the chapter to focus attention upon the problems of business ethics.

What Is Ethics?

The term *ethics* comes from a Greek word meaning "custom." In a broader sense, it is a body of social rules of conduct that may guide men in attaining their goals. Ethics generally is concerned with the creation and application of judgments of right and wrong. When it is applied to business dealings, we call it business ethics.

Implicit in ethical rules is the concept of *equity,* a term that is commonly used in law as well. The emperor Justinian said that equity means "to live honestly, to harm nobody, and to render every man his due." Equity constitutes both the basis of ethics and a system of jurisprudence. In the courts, equity implies fairness, justice, and honest dealings.

Although most businessmen strive to be honest, some seem to have one set of standards for their personal lives and another for use in business. In fact, a corporation executive may actually disclaim personal responsibility for unethical acts committed by his company. It was this tendency that led Congress to pass the Federal Trade Commission Act, outlawing unfair trade practices.

Is Ethics Broader Than Law?

The concept of ethics includes more than the legal technicalities of punishing a person who commits an unlawful act. We take pride in the belief that our civilization has advanced to the point where as mature individuals we know right from wrong. Yet the lack of ethical conduct on the part of some individuals makes you wonder what potential tragedy lies ahead. What happened to some ancient civilizations could well be a lesson to be observed now.

A genuinely ethical man does not seek to justify his conduct by the plea that he has kept within the law, for an act may be lawful and yet highly unethical. Since ethics carries with it the broad idea of "what should be," it demands the existence of sound moral character. Ethical rules differ from legal rules chiefly because the former are not enforced by public authority, whereas legal rules are. If business transactions were conducted on a high ethical plane, there would be no need for business law.

Making Business More Professional

One attempt that has been made to foster a sense of ethical responsibility in business has been the creation of professional standards for particular business groups. Those who advocate this development point out the high ethical standards that have been achieved by such professions as law, medicine, dentistry, teaching, engineering, and accounting. They ask why businessmen should not strive to achieve the same level of responsibility.

In order to transform any day-by-day practice engaged in by countless individuals, into a genuine profession, certain basic requirements must be established and enforced. The following seem to be the commonly accepted requirements for establishing a profession:

1. The existence of a body of specialized knowledge that can be mastered
2. A set of rules for membership in the professional group
3. A code of ethics to govern the conduct of the members in their occupational pursuits
4. Provisions for enforcing the code
5. Penalties for noncompliance with the code
6. Standards to increase the educational level of the membership

Developing a sense of common identity among the members of a professional group is a gradual process that sometimes takes many years to complete. Moreover, public acceptance of a new profession is usually slow in developing. Nevertheless, several business groups have been making a sincere effort to establish professional status, and some of them, notably the accounting profession, have made outstanding progress.

The Accounting Profession. Like the practices of law and medicine, the history of accounting reaches back over the centuries. As a profession, however, with its own code of ethics, accounting is only about 65 years old. In the beginning, those who practiced accounting were first known as a society. In 1896, New York State passed the first law establishing the Certified Public Accountant (CPA) designation, and this occupation began to take on the characteristics of a profession. This was also the beginning of public recognition of a code of ethics for the accounting profession.

The code of ethics that the Certified Public Accountant is expected to observe is strongly enforced by the members of this profession. The CPA serves both large and small enterprises. Each public accounting engagement is a separate and distinct assignment. The work varies with the type and size of the business, kind of record, and the amount of services required. Hence, the fee charged for the accountant's services is contingent upon the amount of work involved. Members of the profession are not permitted to advertise except by means of modest "cards" announcing the formation of a firm or the election of partners.

The CPA is forbidden to violate the confidential relations between himself and his client by revealing facts about his client's business. His professional judgment must not be influenced in any way by the personal interest of his client. Moreover, he must not allow his name to be associated with business forecasts in a manner which would suggest that he guarantees the forecast. Few professions have taken their code of ethics more seriously than have the Certified Public Accountants.

Other business groups are striving for heightened professional status, however. And some have made encouraging progress—particularly the insurance, advertising, banking, and public-relations groups.

Ethics in Business Practices

An increasing number of businessmen recognize the need for raising the standards that govern their moral obligations to others. One of the purposes of the Better Business Bureau, for example, is to encourage a better understanding of our economic system and to build public confidence in business by helping to establish codes of ethics for business groups to adopt and follow. Local bureaus have helped to demonstrate to businessmen in each community the value of voluntary compliance with an ethical code or standard. Many trade associations have developed their own codes of ethics. And industry has taken the lead in developing ethical standards of operation ranging from advertising to personnel administration. All this means that businessmen themselves are seeking a way to conduct their own activities within the framework of moral and social obligations. But despite these efforts, the pressure of competition and conflicting interests sometimes leads to unethical practices in business.

Conflict of Interest. Today one of the most talked-about ethical business problems is known as the "conflict of interest" issue. This is a situation wherein executives divide their loyalties between the firm they work for and another company in which they are stockholders. For example, the president of Company A approves, without regard to price, the purchase of a large order of supplies from Firm B, a company in which he holds shares. He is aware that his purchase will result in a substantial personal monetary gain.

What is wrong with this practice? Is it a violation of any law? In most cases it is not a direct legal violation, but it may become one if it can be established that Company A was acting in restraint of trade by circumventing competitive bidding practices. Besides the fact that a conflict of interest may eventually bring about a charge of monopoly, perhaps the more serious result is that when people read about this practice, they become convinced that our entire system of buying and selling is shot through with dishonesty. They tend to lose confidence in business and demand more governmental intervention.

Recognizing this problem, many large companies are opposed even to a hint of conflict of interest. When it becomes known that it exists within a firm, company officials make an effort to stop it. It is well known that conflicts of interest do not make for good public relations.

Ethics in Insurance. The ethical standards of the insurance business extend far beyond state laws. This high level of ethical behavior is the direct result of the self-discipline exerted by individual companies and by associations of companies, and by their attempts to establish patterns of conduct that will be binding on the entire group.

For example, the Life Insurance Assn. of America has been organized for the primary purpose of increasing the public's understanding of the values of life insurance. The Insurance Executives Assn., which is made up of executives from all types of insurance companies, has several objectives: to carry on research, to provide a forum for discussion, to establish high standards of business ethics, and to encourage conformity to these standards.

One of the oldest and most important associations in insurance is the National Board of Fire Underwriters, which was established in 1866. The purposes of this organization are to promote principles of sound underwriting, to gather statistics, to distribute information to the public, to help standardize policy forms and rules, and to encourage safe methods of construction and fire prevention.

To further these objectives, the National Board of Fire Underwriters has set up five regional trade associations: the Western Underwriters Assn., the Western Insurance Bureau, the Eastern Underwriters Assn., the Southeastern Underwriters Assn., and the Board of Fire Underwriters of the

Pacific. These associations seek to enforce fair trade practices, to decrease fire waste, to furnish advisory services to communities, to reduce fire losses, and to cooperate with governmental authorities in the enforcement of regulations.

The National Assn. of Insurance Agents has adopted a code of ethics setting forth the members' responsibilities to the public, to the companies, and to the members of the association. In a similar manner, the Insurance Brokers' Assn. of the State of New York, Inc., has adopted a Code of Professional Standards that covers many phases of conduct.

One of the most significant educational achievements in life insurance education has been the formation of the American College of Life Underwriters, chartered in 1927 by Congress. The organization's purpose is to raise the ethical and educational standards of those engaged in selling and underwriting life insurance. The American College prepares annually a series of five examinations over a wide range of subjects in life insurance and related business fields. Those successfully completing these tests and meeting other requirements are awarded the designation CLU (Chartered Life Underwriter), which shows that the recipient is qualified to render a high type of service in the sale of life insurance. Although the American College conducts no classes, it does suggest outlines of study and arranges with universities and colleges to conduct certain courses preparatory to these examinations. The American College also suggests a study program and gives examinations in life insurance agency management.

A similar educational function is performed by the American Institute for Property and Liability Underwriters in the field of property and casualty insurance. It awards the designation of Chartered Property Casualty Underwriter (CPCU) to those who successfully complete a series of examinations in the field of property and casualty insurance and who also meet other requirements. These individuals are principally agents, brokers, and employees of insurers.

Ethics in Advertising. Since the days of the patent-medicine show, the consumer has been plagued by persons who seek to sell their goods through the use of misleading information in advertising. By the use of mass advertising media, great quantities of goods are distributed by American producers all over the world. Because of the volume of advertising used, it has become almost impossible to detect and apprehend those who use deceptive practices in advertisements. To detect such deception has become both a costly and difficult problem for the advertising industry and for the government.

There was a time when advertisers themselves were not in agreement as to what represented deception. One of the first concerted efforts to attack the problem of standards and dishonest advertising was made by *Printers'*

Ink, a nationally known magazine devoted to advertising and marketing. This magazine developed a model statute which any state could adopt to regulate and control those who used false and deceptive statements in advertising. To date, 44 states and the District of Columbia have enacted legislation based on the *Printers' Ink* code, making it a misdemeanor to use an assertion or statement of fact which is untrue, deceptive, or misleading in advertising.

In 1917, when the leading advertising agencies formed the American Association of Advertising Agencies (the "4A's"), one of the first things this group did was to adopt a code of ethical obligations to the public, to advertisers, and to publishers who accept paid advertising. But despite the pressure from this code, advertising agencies sometimes still make exaggerated claims about their products. This may be due to a tendency of the agency to draw a thin line between that which is regarded as ethical and that which is not. On occasion, an agency may surrender to pressures from a client to make a statement or claim that is only a half-truth. Responsible advertising men know they must recognize these pressures, and be willing to accept their responsibility to tell the truth to the public regardless of the advertising medium used. If they do not, the public will demand stronger governmental controls.

Another effective self-regulating procedure is the work done by newspaper and magazine publishers who may have a code not to accept advertisements that do not meet the prevailing standards of accuracy and ethics. The *New York Times*, for example, has for years maintained a strong censorship by declining to take ads making questionable claims. When Hadacol, a patent medicine, was popular, the *Milwaukee Journal* declined to take several thousands of dollars in advertising, presumably because it would have been in poor taste for the newspaper to publicize this product.

Ethics in the Community. No doubt you have heard of the Better Business Bureaus, which have been established in more than 125 cities by privately-owned business firms to promote ethical conduct in their communities. Specifically, a Better Business Bureau concerns itself with the morals of the business community. For example, it acts as a watchdog in detecting and investigating cases of unethical practices reported to it. Local bureaus scrutinize advertisements in local newspapers and magazines for misleading statements or misrepresentation of fact about products or services intended to divert trade from responsible firms.

While these bureaus have no legal authority, they can and do bring pressures on unethical firms by public exposure. If unsuccessful, the local bureau will contact the appropriate local enforcement agency. The extent to which a bureau is successful depends in part on how well it is financed by local firms. Collectively, these local bureaus annually handle over half a million inquiries, review more than 2 million advertisements, and make investigations of approximately 50,000 complaints.

Society itself is composed of different groups, each of which has responsibilities to others. For example, business management is responsible for seeing that stockholders, customers, and the general public are treated fairly. It is also necessary that we, as consumers, practice the same ethical standards we expect of business. Your authors strongly believe that every consumer has an ethical responsibility to deal fairly with the seller. Failure of the community to demand ethical practices will inevitably result in the enactment of more controls by government over everyone.

SUMMARY

Public laws are concerned in part with the relationship of government to persons and groups. These laws are classified as constitutional, administrative, and criminal. Criminal laws cover treason, felonies, and misdemeanors.

Private laws cover rights and liability among private individuals, partnerships, corporations, and other groups. Law suits that seek to enforce these rules are civil actions. These actions may seek money damages, injunctions to prohibit actions, or specific performance.

Many business transactions are based on agreements known as contracts. Some contracts are unenforceable because they lack the basic contractual elements, which are: offer and acceptance, competent parties, lawful form and purpose, and consideration.

Real property is the term applied to an interest in land, buildings, or anything attached to the soil. Personal property is the right in movable, tangible, or intangible property including furniture, jewelry, stocks, books, and patents.

A negotiable instrument is a contractual obligation which calls for the payment of money through the medium of commercial paper (in lieu of money) that can be transferred to others by indorsement. Examples of negotiable instruments are checks, notes, drafts or bills of exchange, and certificates of deposit. To be negotiable, an instrument must conform to a code adopted by the state—either the Uniform Commercial Code or the Uniform Negotiable Instruments Act. The UCC has replaced the UNIA in most of the states.

A sale or contract to sell is a transfer of title to tangible personal property in consideration of payment of money, an exchange of other property, or the performance of services. A sale differs from a bailment in that in a sale the title to the goods passes to the vendee; in a bailment it does not.

Ethics is related to law, but it is a much broader field because it includes more than the punishment of the individual. An act may be lawful and yet unethical because it violates a moral consideration involving the difference between right and wrong. In recent years an increasing amount of regulatory legislation has come about as a result of the business community's inability to govern itself.

VOCABULARY REVIEW QUIZ

Match the following vocabulary terms with the statements below.

a. Abstract of title
b. Adjective law
c. Agent
d. Bailment
e. Consideration
f. Contract
g. Deed
h. Joint tenancy
i. Negotiable instrument
j. Nominal damages
k. Principal
l. Real property
m. Statutory law
n. Substantive law
o. Tenancy in common

1. That part of the law which defines, creates, and regulates the individual's legal rights
2. That which has to do with the procedural machinery required to enforce personal rights and duties
3. A binding agreement between two or more competent parties in the form required by law, for a lawful purpose and supported by consideration
4. Something of value given in exchange for a promise
5. A judgment granted for a nominal sum
6. The one whom an agent represents
7. Property that includes land, buildings, and things attached to the soil
8. Ownership in land held jointly by two or more persons with the right of survivorship
9. An instrument in writing under seal by which a grantor conveys his interest in land to the grantee
10. A written contract evidencing the right to receive money, which right may be transferred from one party to another by indorsement
11. The delivery of property for safekeeping or for some specified purpose
12. Written laws consisting of statutes enacted by various governmental bodies
13. One who serves as a business representative for another
14. Ownership of property in which two or more persons have an undivided interest without the right of survivorship
15. A summarized report based on the county records of all transactions affecting the title to land

QUESTIONS FOR REVIEW STUDY

1. How does statutory law differ from common law?
2. In its broadest sense, what is the general purpose of law?
3. Which class of law governs business transactions?
4. What is the difference between public law and private law?
5. Which is superior: constitutional law or statutory law?
6. Why is the Uniform Commercial Code so important to business?
7. Explain what is meant by "consideration" in a contract.
8. What remedies does a businessman have under breach of contract?
9. How is the Statute of Frauds applied to a business situation?
10. What is the difference between an agent and a principal?
11. Distinguish real property from personal property.
12. Explain how joint tenancy differs from tenancy in common.
13. How is a mortgage used in business?
14. Describe two ethical problems caused by conflict of interest.
15. What are the legal requirements for an instrument to be negotiable?

PROBLEMS AND PROJECTS

1. Smith offered in writing to buy Jack's home. Jack accepted the offer, but Smith failed to make a down-payment at the agreed time. Later, Jack sold the property to Black. Smith immediately claimed a breach-of-contract violation. Is Smith right? What are the reasons for your answer?

2. Hix held a note payable to himself. It was stolen by Max, who forged Hix's name on the indorsement and then sold the note to Mooney, who was not aware of the theft or forgery. Mooney then transferred the note to Lee for value received. When the note became due, the maker refused to pay it. Lee sued Mooney. Can Lee recover? Explain your reasons.

3. Haley purchased a set of book-ends from a local department store. The salesman described them as made of real marble. They were also described on the sales ticket as marble. After Haley took them home he discovered they were made of much less expensive material but to look like marble. Haley returned the book-ends but the store refused to refund his money. Is Haley entitled to recover his purchase price? What is your reasoning?

4. Professor Sims ordered a book through the mail from a Chicago publishing company. He asked that it be delivered COD by parcel post to his home. After two months, when Sims failed to receive the book, he made inquiry of the publisher and was told the book had been mailed to him five weeks ago. The book was not insured by the sender. Who is liable for its loss? Why?

A BUSINESS CASE

Case 3-1 Miles v. Sax

The object of this action is to determine whether the plaintiff or the defendant is responsible for the loss of an order of building materials. Miles sold the defendant an order of building materials amounting to $3,800. The order included several hundred squares of cedar shingles, 20 rolls of tar paper, and three kegs of nails. The defendant personally selected and approved the shipment on a visit to the plaintiff's lumber yard.

The day before the shipment was to be made, a flood carried the material away, damaging most of it. The defendant had counted on receiving the materials, and because he did not, he suffered considerable damages caused by the delay in a building project he had contracted to complete. His loss amounted to $1,500. Miles brought an action against Sax to recover the price of the materials.

1. Can Miles recover from Sax the price of the materials?
2. What is the basis for your opinion?

PART 2

ORGANIZATION OF THE ENTERPRISE

Legal Forms of Business Ownership

4

One of the first and most crucial questions which anyone starting a business must ask himself is: Which is the best form of ownership for *me* to use? Each of the several legal forms of business ownership has its peculiarities, and because of this the future of an undertaking may very well depend on the appropriateness of the form selected for carrying it out. Unfortunately, many a new owner is not fully aware of why it is so important to make the proper choice.

If you were planning to set up a business, some of the other important questions facing you would be: How difficult is it to organize the enterprise, and what formalities are necessary? What is the approximate cost to meet the legal requirements, including legal fees, state levies, and filing costs? How can additional capital be obtained? How easily can ownership be transferred? Will it be possible for the owners to participate actively in the management of the business? How easy is it to change from one form of ownership to another after the business has been organized?

The various forms of business ownership discussed in this chapter are the means by which private property used in business may be acquired and disposed of at will. Let us examine these forms of legal ownership, presented in the following succession in order to throw more light on the above questions:

1. Sole proprietorship
2. General partnership
3. Limited partnership
4. Corporation
5. Joint-stock company
6. Business trust
7. Joint venture—syndicate
8. Co-operative

These forms of ownership are determined by statutory or common law. They are classified as legal structures, either as corporate or noncorporate entities. Sole proprietorships and general partnerships have common-law origin. They are noncorporate, which means that they are easily established and can operate anywhere. In contrast, the corporation is of statutory origin, which means that the corporate laws of the various states prescribe procedures for its formation, scope of operation, and legal control.

THE MODERN BUSINESS FIRM

In its time the family, the clan, the tribe, and the community each was the basic societal unit involving business and industry. Today the business firm—the sole proprietorship, the partnership, the corporation, and the like—is the basic business unit in our society. As we begin this discussion of the modern business firm, it is important that we keep in mind that the personification of the business firm is its own basic unit, management. When we talk about one aspect or another of the "behavior" of a firm, then, we will in fact be discussing an activity based on a managerial decision—and perhaps we will be relating the actual behavior of the management itself as it oversees or participates in the execution of its orders.

The Essential Nature of the Firm

What distinguishes the business firm from other economic and social units in modern society? In the first place, whereas the business firm usually does business essentially to make money, such other units as families, clans, tribes, and communal groups generally do not. Another distinguishing characteristic of the modern firm is its attitude of social responsibility toward other segments of society. Today's business managers are mindful of the social power that business leaders wield in a community. When advice is sought of a business leader while he is fulfilling his alternate role as a leading citizen, he often finds it difficult to speak and act as a dutiful citizen without having his words and deeds reflect upon the reputation, and therefore the future status, of the firm for which he works or which perhaps he owns. Other distinguishing characteristics of the modern business firm are private ownership, the ability to use human and physical resources to produce goods for sale in organized markets, and the ability to be subjected to managerial motivation—which is the subject of our next discussion.

The Motivation of Business Firms

Motivation, from our present point of view, may be thought of as *that form of mental and emotional stimulation which creates the desire within persons in an organization to achieve certain results.* It is triggered by a maze of interacting factors that combine to create certain tensions and drives which in turn develop into incentives. Different people are motivated by different incentives. Money, for example, is an effective incentive only in terms of how much it means to the individual. Some persons are to a large extent self-motivating. For example, a person working for himself provides his own variety of motivational stimuli, which may include the desire to be creative, and the need to be respected, or to be recognized as an individual. But most persons are not self-motivating. Most employees (wage-earners and salaried persons), for instance, more often than not have to look to one or more "bosses" in the firm for direction—for motivation.

The usual answer to the question "What motivates firms to do what they do?" is "Profit." But although the profit motive is a powerful force in stimulating business activity, it is not the only one. The desire to render a vital and meaningful service can be very effective as a motive, too. Indeed, many more managerial decisions are based on the service objective than one might imagine. Or a firm may be motivated to achieve community prestige or favor. Every firm wants to have influence and a good image in the community in which it operates, and so certain business decisions are made to achieve this goal. Whatever his goal, the effective manager is one who can get results by motivating others; and he can encourage and develop this motivation through his own methods of leadership.

SOLE PROPRIETORSHIPS

A business owned and operated by one person is known as a *sole proprietorship* (sometimes called *individual proprietorship*). This form was used by the ancient Egyptians, Phoenicians, Greeks, and Romans. In addition to being the oldest of the several legal forms, it is the most widely used in the United States. It is particularly popular in real-estate, retail, wholesale, and service-type establishments. The private owner or manager is called in economic language an *entrepreneur;* the function of making policy decisions in business is known to practitioners and students of business activity as *entrepreneurship.*

Though you as a manager will have to solve such problems as obtaining the necessary capital and locating the proper site for your venture, you will encounter no general legal requirements in organizing a sole proprietorship except in making contractual agreements. (Of course the business must be lawful.) The owner runs his business to suit himself, since there are no stockholders to whom he must report. Legally, the proprietor and the firm are the same, and so the owner is taxed as an individual and not as a business.

Management Advantages of Sole Proprietorship

Among the management advantages of the sole proprietorship are these:

1. Simple to start
2. Owner receives all profits
3. Owner has freedom to manage
4. Few legal restrictions
5. Easy to dissolve the firm
6. Owner, not business, is taxed

Management Disadvantages of Sole Proprietorship

Although the advantages of sole proprietorship are several, it also has some disadvantages:

1. Unlimited liability of owner for debts
2. Difficult to raise capital
3. Over-all direction may become a burden on owner when business grows
4. Limited opportunity for employees since organization is not permanent
5. Uncertainty of duration: death, imprisonment, or insanity automatically terminate the firm

The individual owner is legally liable for all the debts of his firm; not only his original capital investment, but also his personal and real property may be attached by creditors. (In only a few states is a person's home exempt.) Moreover, he is limited almost entirely by the amount of money he possesses or the amount he is able to borrow from friends, banks, or relatives when starting the firm. And, unlike most other forms of ownership, this one ceases to exist when the owner dies; this limits the degree of permanence for the employees. Lastly, the typical proprietor may have to be an expert in many phases of business, for his problems of management are numerous and he may have no responsible person to help him. It is obvious that the small proprietorship is, by its nature, well suited to small-scale business because of its common-law origin, its simple legal structure, and its ease of operation as compared with that of other forms. Indeed, its advantages so far outweigh its disadvantages that the majority of American businesses are sole proprietorships.

PARTNERSHIPS

The Uniform Partnership Act, which has been adopted by most states, defines a *partnership* as "an association of two or more persons to carry on as co-owners of a business for profit." Although most partnerships are operated for profit, a nonprofit organization established as a partnership is also legal. The partnership was actually devised to overcome certain weaknesses inherent in the proprietorship. It has distinct advantages and disadvantages that are not found in the proprietorship form. The authority for its creation rests in the common-law right of voluntary association. Consequently, there can be no partnership relation between individuals unless there is an expressed intention on the part of both that a partnership is to exist.

Types of Partnerships

The law recognizes two distinct types of partnerships: *general* and *limited.* In a *general partnership,* all partners participate actively in the operation of the business, sharing all the responsibilities, including unlimited liability. The distinctive feature of the *limited partnership* is the limited liability of one or more partners. But there must always be at least one partner in a limited partnership who is subject to unlimited personal liability. The number of limited partners is not restricted by law, provided there is at least one general partner in the firm. The withdrawal of a limited partner does not necessarily dissolve the firm, but when a general partner withdraws, the partnership must be terminated.

A limited-partnership agreement must be drawn up in accordance with the laws of the state in which the firm is to operate, and a copy of the agreement must usually be filed with the appropriate state official. Limited partners exercise no voice in the active management of the business, but they do share in the profits according to the agreement. As a rule, they are prohibited from withdrawing their capital except under unusual circumstances. (In general, this point is covered in Section 16 of the Uniform Partnership Act.)

If no agreement is set up specifying that certain members of the firm are limited partners, all partners are considered to be general partners. Hence, when a partnership is formed and announced to the public, it is common practice to state in the announcement which members are general and which are limited partners.

Five states—Michigan, New Jersey, Ohio, Pennsylvania, and Virginia—have statutes permitting the formation of *limited-partnership associations,* an arrangement in which the liability of *all* partners is limited. This is more like a corporation than a partnership, however, because the partners elect a board of directors and authorize them to manage the association. The limited-partnership association is not widely used as a form of ownership.

Kinds of Partners

Common and statutory law recognize various types of partners. For example, an owner who takes an active role in the business but who does not want to reveal his identity to the public is known as a *secret partner.* A *silent partner,* on the other hand, takes no active part in the business even though he may be known to the public as a partner. A *dormant partner* is one who plays no active role and at the same time remains unknown to the public as a partner. A *nominal partner* is not actually one of the owners of the business, but he suggests to others by his words or actions that he is a partner. Under certain circumstances, the other partners may be obligated by the acts of a nominal partner and may become liable for his share of the debts.

A general partner who has been with the partnership for a long time and who owns a large share of the business is called a *senior partner. Junior partners* are those who have been with the business a relatively short time and who are not expected to assume great responsibility for major decisions.

Forming a Partnership

If you decide that a general partnership is the best form of ownership for the business you are planning to set up, you will find it fairly simple to organize. As with the individual proprietorship, few legal steps are necessary. The proposed business must be a lawful one, of course, and all that is required is an oral or written agreement between the partners. This agreement is known as the *Articles of Partnership* (sometimes referred to as *Copartnership Articles*).

As in any undertaking that involves more than one person, many questions are likely to arise after a partnership has been formed. Consequently, it is wise to have the partnership agreement drawn up in advance by an attorney who is familiar with partnership law. Although no two written agreements are absolutely identical, the following points are usually covered in most agreements:

1. Firm name
2. Names of partners
3. Addresses of partners
4. Location of business
5. General nature of business
6. Duration of the agreement
7. Amount of each partner's capital
8. Salaries or drawing accounts of partners
9. Distribution of profits or losses
10. Procedure for admitting new partners
11. Procedure for dissolving partnership
12. Each individual's duties and authority

Some states require that a written agreement be drawn up if the general partnership is to last more than one year. If it is organized to engage in the business of buying or selling real-estate, the agreement need not be in writing. But if by the terms of the partnership agreement one partner is to receive an interest in real-estate now owned by another partner, then the agreement must be in written form.

A general partnership is automatically dissolved if one partner dies, withdraws, or is declared insane, or if the firm claims bankruptcy. Because of these limitations, banks are often reluctant to extend long-term credit to general partnerships. Perhaps the most serious disadvantage is the joint and unlimited personal liability of each general partner for the debts of the firm. Unless limited by agreement, each partner is liable for the whole amount of the partnership debts, regardless of the size of his investment. If one partner lacks the personal wealth to assume his full share of the loss or debts, the other partners are required to make good on the deficit. In fact, all acts by the partners in the name of the general partnership are binding on all other partners, even though the action may be unknown to them at the time.

Management Advantages and Disadvantages of the General Partnership

The advantages of the general partnership may be summarized as follows:

1. Firm can operate in any state
2. Better credit standing than sole proprietorship
3. Allows for specialization of managerial skills as well as pooling of partners' knowledge
4. Ease of dissolution
5. Freedom from tax on business income; partnership is taxed as an individual
6. Few legal restrictions
7. Can provide for larger capital resources than sole proprietorship

While the partnership has many of the advantages of the sole proprietorship, plus the advantage of pooling the resources and abilities of two or more persons, it also has certain disadvantages. These disadvantages are:

1. Restricted transfer of ownership
2. Difficulty in withdrawing investment
3. Partnership friction may terminate the agreement
4. Duration of partnership limited to lives of partners
5. Unlimited liability of partners for debts of business

Most general partnerships in this country are probably very informal organizations operating on limited funds and without a formal written agreement. On the contrary, a formal agreement is required in the formation of a limited partnership. The agreement must be filed with an appropriate public official—often the county clerk—and must state who the general partners are and who are limited partners. Interestingly, despite the apparent desirability of both the general and limited partnership, neither is used as extensively as the corporation or sole proprietorship.

Types of Business Adaptable to Partnerships

There seems to be no clear-cut method of deciding in advance which kinds of business are best adapted to the general or limited partnership. Any small or medium-sized firm could conceivably operate as a partnership. Some partnerships have as many as 100 partners.

There are, however, certain instances where partnerships seem to be advantageous. For example, in the professions of law, dentistry, medicine, and accountancy, partnerships work out particularly well. By sharing office and clerical expenses, the partners effect considerable savings. Stock-brokerage firms, investment banks, and consulting agencies can also operate efficiently as partnerships. The brokerage firm of Merrill Lynch, Pierce, Fenner & Smith once had more than 70 partners before it became a corporation in 1959. Cluett, Peabody & Co., Montgomery Ward, and Proctor & Gamble all started as partnerships, too, and only eventually became corporations. Limited partnerships are commonly used for financing theatrical enterprises in order to avoid the double taxation inherent in corporations.

CORPORATIONS

The modern corporation has come to be the dominant and most important form of economic organization in American life. It is the symbol of our capitalistic economy and so-called "big business." For many years it has been the principal means by which large amounts of capital have been collected to operate thousands of industrial plants. Today, American corporations control huge amounts of wealth, employ millions of workers, produce substantial amounts of goods, and wield tremendous influence in the social and political spheres in America.

The Economic Importance of Corporations

Table 4.1 shows a comparison of total dollar income of corporations as compared with that of other forms of ownership. In terms of total income, the corporate form produces more economic wealth than all other forms of business ownership. Undoubtedly the reasons for its dominance are its unique characteristics that help to distinguish it from partnerships and proprietorships. Statistics show that about half of all gainfully employed Americans, excluding farm workers, are on corporation payrolls, and that slightly more than one out of every eleven businesses is a corporation. Corporations do about three times as much business as do partnerships and proprietorships combined. This is largely a consequence of the larger size of the average corporation compared with other forms of ownership.

Four of the biggest and best-known American corporations are American Telephone & Telegraph (the world's largest organization engaged in the telephone business), General Motors (the world's largest manufacturer of automobiles), Standard Oil (New Jersey), and United States Steel. Standard Oil of New Jersey has approximately 750,000 common stock holders, General Motors has almost 1.5 million, and American Telephone & Telegraph has over 3 million.

TABLE 4.1

ANNUAL INCOME BY LEGAL FORMS OF OWNERSHIP, 1965

Sources of Income	In Billions	Percentage
Income from:		
Corporations, Including Mutual Institutions	$317.5	56.8
Sole Proprietorships and Partnerships	106.3	19.0
Other Forms of Private Ownership Operated for Profit	37.3	6.7
Government Enterprises	7.4	1.3
General Government	67.7	12.1
Miscellaneous Groups, Nonprofit	18.3	3.3
Other Income not Included in Above Sources	4.3	.8
Total	$558.8	100.0

Source: U.S. Dept. of Commerce, *Survey of Current Business,* July, 1966, p. 15. (Totals rounded to next highest number.)

Today it is almost impossible for one person to obtain the needed capital to start an automobile factory, a steel plant, or an oil refinery. But by organizing a corporation it is possible to obtain funds from many thousands of persons through the sale of corporate stock.

As we have seen, the individual proprietorship and the partnership are common in retailing and agricultural enterprises. But the corporation is more prevalent in manufacturing, mining, transportation, finance, insurance, banking, and communications. Let us analyze more closely the structure of a corporation to see if we can discover why this form of ownership has become dominant in American business.

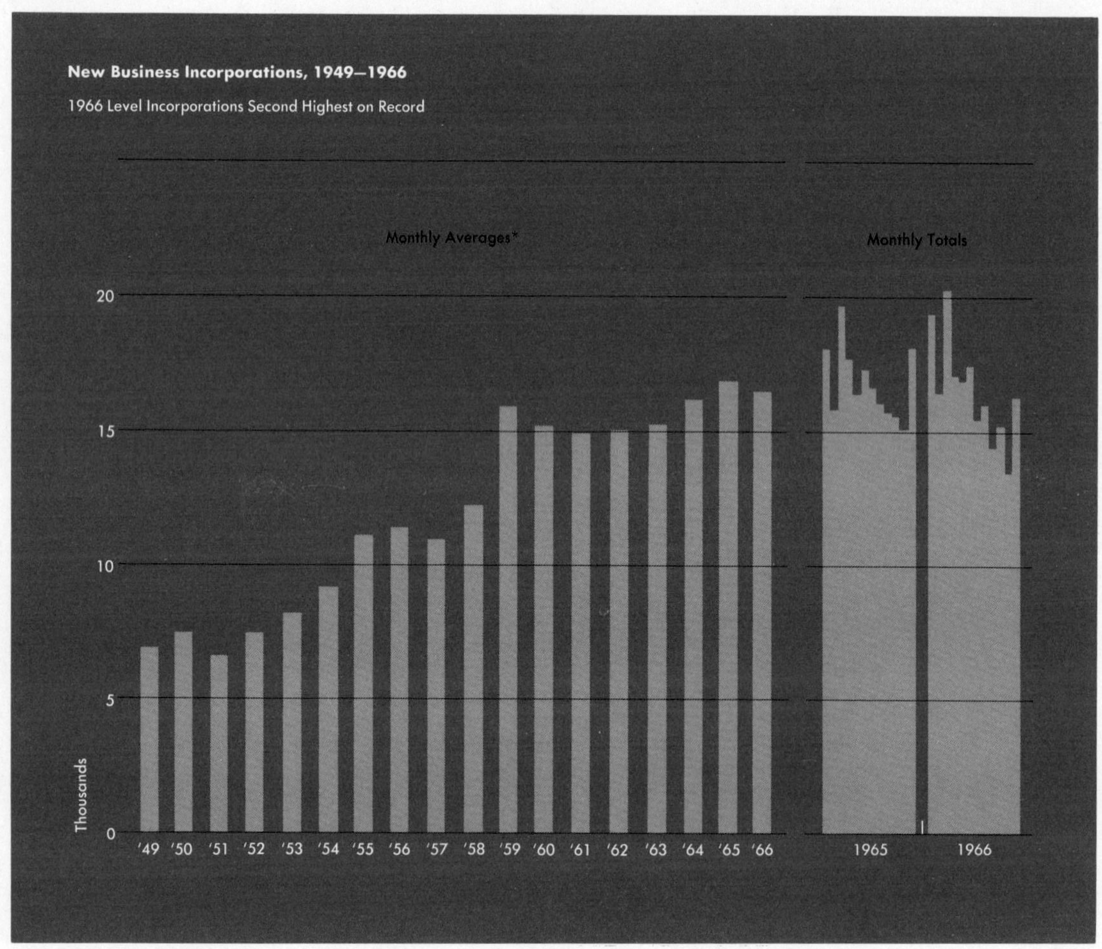

Source: Small Business Administration, 1966 Annual Report, 1966.

What Is a Corporation?

A corporation is created by state governments through the enactment of legislation called *corporation laws.* These laws differ widely in stringency and interpretation among the various states. For example, certain states have more lenient laws than others with respect to incorporation requirements and taxation. (In this case, for instance, Delaware is considered a lenient state and New York a strict one.)

A definition often used to describe a corporation originally appeared in an opinion handed down in 1819 by Chief Justice Marshall on the famous *Dartmouth College* case. According to Chief Justice Marshall's definition, a corporation is an "intangible reality"—an artificial but legal "person" which can in spite of its Twilight Zone sort of semi-existence be held responsible for many of the things a real person can. Fortunately, the term *corporation* has since been defined by the Supreme Court as "an association of individuals united for some common purpose, and permitted by law to use a common name, and to change its members without dissolution of the association." By abandoning the fictitious-person concept, the Court attempted to make the actual persons running the corporation more accountable for their acts. According to this view, a corporation consists of real people, not a legal person separate from others in it. But regardless of which definition you use, a corporation has the right to buy, sell, own, manage, mortgage, and otherwise dispose of real and personal property which it possesses, and it may sue and be sued.

Types of Corporations

A corporation may be organized for *profit* or *nonprofit* purposes. The typical corporation is organized to make profits for its owners. A nonprofit corporation uses its gains (income) that may result from its operation to promote the purposes for which it was conceived. Religious and charitable organizations often incorporate as nonprofit enterprises.

From the standpoint of ownership, a corporation may be either a stock or non-stock corporation. A *stock corporation* may be defined as one issuing capital stock, representing shares of ownership, which provide a means of distributing the profits to the shareholders. Some state statutes make provision for chartering a private corporation "not for pecuniary profit." Corporations of this kind have no capital stock and issue no shares and are called *non-stock corporations.* Certificates of membership are issued to the members as evidence of their affiliation, but this certificate is in no sense of the word a share in the corporation. A *foreign corporation* is one organized under the laws of one state but doing business in other states. A company doing business in the United States but chartered by a foreign government is known (in the United States) as an *alien corporation.*

Public and Private Corporations. A *public corporation* is one organized for a nonprofit purpose by a city, county, or state, or by the federal government. The Federal Deposit Insurance Corp. (described in Chapter 17) and the Tennessee Valley Authority are familiar examples of public corporations.[1]

A *private corporation* is one that is established and operated by private individuals either for profit or nonprofit purposes. Typical examples of private corporations operated for stockholders' profit are the Ford Motor Co., the Union Pacific Railroad, and the Cities Service Co. Hospitals and charitable institutions are also classed as private corporations without stock ownership.

Open and Close Corporations. If the stock can be bought by the public on one of several security-exchange markets or in an over-the-counter market, it is known as an *open corporation.* A *close corporation,* on the other hand, does not offer its stock to the public; instead, the stock is owned by the incorporators, or by members of a single family. Many businesses begin as close corporations with only a few stockholders, each of whom is active in the company management. Then, as the business grows and new capital is required, the corporation directors decide to "go public" by selling shares to others. Usually this change is made only in order to raise rather large sums of outside capital, however. For years the Ford Motor Co. was a close corporation; not until 1954 was the stock first offered to the public.

Organizing a Corporation

Let's assume you have decided that the corporate form offers you more advantages than any other form of ownership. How do you go about setting up a private corporation?

First, you must obtain a charter from one of the 50 states. Unlike the proprietorship and general partnership, a private corporation must meet the legal requirements of the state in which it is to be incorporated. (Although state laws vary rather widely, they all follow a general pattern.)[2]

[1] The Texas Business Corporation Act classifies corporations as public (municipal bodies), and private corporations. Private corporations are further divided into profit and nonprofit. Some interesting changes in terminology (not mentioned in earlier laws) are in this act. For example, the word "shares" replaces the term "stock," the title "Articles of Incorporation" replaces the word "charter," and "capital surplus" takes the place of the term "capital." In the new Texas law, owners of stock are called "shareholders" instead of "stockholders." (Many corporations chartered by other states use the terms "shareholder" and "stockholder" interchangeably.)

[2] In determining the jurisdiction of the federal courts over corporations, the United States Supreme Court has held that a corporation is a citizen of the state under whose laws it is incorporated.

Steps Involved in Incorporation. Here are the actual steps that must be followed:

1. Secure the necessary application forms from the appropriate official of the state in which your concern plans to do business.
2. Complete the papers and file them with the state official.
3. Pay the required fees to the state authority.

The application must bear the signatures of at least three petitioners of adult age who desire to form the corporation—these are known as the *incorporators*. The application must be notarized, and accompanied by the required financial information. In general, an application must furnish the following facts about the proposed business:

1. Name and address of the proposed corporation
2. Names and addresses of the incorporators
3. Proposed duration of the organization, which may be either perpetual or for a limited number of years
4. Kind of business in which corporation is to engage
5. Names and addresses of the officers and directors
6. Address of the principal business office
7. Amount of capital to be authorized. The amount of capital is officially known as the *authorized capital stock*, which is divided into shares of ownership ranging in value from $1 to $1,000. Some states require a minimum of $1,000 in capital stock; all require at least $500.
8. Maximum number of shares, called *authorized stock*, to be issued, and whether these shares are to be par or no-par value, and with or without voting rights.[3] Shares are in the form of stock certificates, which are numbered serially and recorded when issued on the books of the company. To be valid, they must bear the officers' signatures.
9. Name and address of each subscriber to certificates, and statement showing the total number of shares paid for by each subscriber

The information entered on the application should be carefully worded, in order to permit as much freedom as possible in determining the furture activities and objectives of the company.

It is easier and less expensive to set up a corporation in some states than in others. Delaware, Maryland, New Jersey, Arizona, Nevada, South Dakota, Maine, Florida, and Texas are popular states in which to incorporate. They

[3] The terms *par* and *no-par value* are explained in Chapter 16.

demand smaller incorporation fees, impose lower taxes, and offer more liberal provisions in their corporation laws.

The Corporation Charter

After you have paid your filing fees and organization taxes and have fulfilled any other necessary conditions, your application is (hopefully) approved. Now the secretary of state issues your corporation charter and mails a copy to the county clerk of the county in which the principal office of the newly-formed corporation is to be located. (This procedure varies slightly in different states.) The following items illustrate what a typical charter might contain:

1. Title of corporation
2. Name of state granting corporation charter
3. Descriptive statement of purpose of corporation
4. Location of corporation's general office
5. Term of years for which corporation is incorporated
6. Number of directors, including minimum and maximum
7. Names of directors and their addresses
8. Amount of capital stock fully subscribed and paid up
9. Notarization by notary public in the county in which corporation is to maintain its general office

By-laws of a Corporation

Now your corporation is in business, and you call the first meeting of the shareholders. The meeting begins with a vote on the proposed by-laws, which serve as the general rules for operating the business and list the duties of the officers, the amount of stock that must be represented at the stockholders' meeting in order to constitute a quorum, and any other rules that are needed to conduct the corporation's affairs.

Corporation Officers. The officers of the corporation carry on the active management of the company. The by-laws usually specify that they are to be chosen by the board of directors. The president is normally the highest-ranking officer, although some firms regard the chairman of the board as top man. Other officers are vice-president, secretary, treasurer, and sometimes a comptroller. It is the practice in some companies to name several vice-presidents, each responsible for a specific operation such as production, sales, or personnel.

The corporate secretary keeps the corporation seal, signs all corporation documents, and records the minutes of meetings held by the directors and

TEXAS EASTERN *Transmission Corporation*

P. O. BOX 2521  HOUSTON, TEXAS 77001

NOTICE OF ANNUAL MEETING OF STOCKHOLDERS

TO BE HELD APRIL 24, 1967

NOTICE IS HEREBY GIVEN that the Annual Meeting of Stockholders of Texas Eastern Transmission Corporation will be held at the office of the Company in the State of Delaware, 100 West Tenth Street, in the City of Wilmington, Delaware, on Monday, April 24, 1967, at 11:00 a.m. Eastern Standard Time to consider and act upon the following matters:

1. The election of a Board of Directors;
2. The amendment of the Certificate of Incorporation to increase the authorized Common Stock to 40,000,000 shares from 30,000,000 shares and to authorize a new class of 3,000,000 shares of Second Preferred Stock, par value $5 per share; and
3. The transaction of such other business as may properly come before said meeting or any adjournment thereof.

Information regarding the matters to be acted upon at this meeting is contained in the accompanying Proxy Statement.

The close of business on March 15, 1967, has been fixed as the record date for the determination of stockholders entitled to notice of and to vote at this Annual Meeting or any adjournment thereof.

Please specify your choice on the enclosed proxy and then date, sign and mail it in the enclosed envelope for which you will need no postage. A prompt response will be helpful and appreciated.

By order of the Board of Directors,

D. E. McCRAVY
Secretary

Houston, Texas
March 22, 1967

Courtesy Texas Eastern Transmission Corporation

Notice of annual meeting of stockholders.

stockholders. The treasurer is the chief financial officer and often is responsible for the entire accounting operation. In a very large company, the comptroller may be authorized to take over some of the accounting and finance duties from the treasurer.

Legal Responsibilities of Directors. The boards of directors of American business corporations function in several ways. (As you might expect, in family-owned corporations, the board of directors is an often-ignored formality.) In many corporations having their stock listed on an exchange, with hundreds of thousands (sometimes millions) of shares outstanding, the boards of directors are almost complete strangers to most of the shareholders. Very often these directors have leading positions in other companies, professions, or public service. They are chosen because it is believed they can bring business and/or add a certain amount of prestige to the organization. Some boards meet often and deal with many and detailed topics. Others meet infrequently and concern themselves with establishing only broad policies to guide the business.

Corporation laws of the various states rarely take into account these variations; in the eyes of the law, boards in general are alike, and are to be so treated. (As you may imagine, to some businessmen this view seems unrealistic and impractical.) For this reason, it is important that every businessman who serves as a corporate director be aware of what the law actually requires of him. Otherwise, his sense of propriety, upon which he often depends as his guide in many areas, may unwittingly lead him into a law violation.

The legal responsibilities of the board of directors may be summarized as follows:

1. The directors manage the company in the interests of the shareholders. To do this legally the board must be entrusted by law with the necessary powers of business management.
2. As company management, board members must exercise reasonable business judgment—at least the same degree of prudence that reasonable men would exercise in conducting their own affairs.
3. The board may delegate extensive decision-making authority to officers and other employees of the company, but the board must supervise and evaluate their performance. Directors are not liable for honest mistakes in judgment made without carelessness.

Directors' Meetings. The board of directors, the officers, and the stockholders are required by law to meet at least once each year. They may meet more frequently if the by-laws specify they should. The corporate secretary notifies the stockholders by mail of the time, date, place of meeting, and any specific resolutions to be voted on. If there are several thousand stockholders, it is unlikely that they will be present at any one meeting. In fact, it is common practice to enclose a proxy form (see sample one below) with the notice of the meeting. By signing and returning the form, the stockholder can submit his vote in lieu of attending the meeting in person.

Legally, a *proxy* is a power of attorney that transfers to a third party the stockholder's right to vote; it does not, however, transfer his legal title of ownership of his shares. The proxy is usually valid only for a given meeting; it does not transfer the voting right indefinitely. A stockholder who cannot attend the meeting is not obliged to return the proxy, but he loses his vote (for that occasion) if he does not. When the stockholder returns his proxy,

PRENTICE-HALL, INC.

PROXY SOLICITED ON BEHALF OF THE MANAGEMENT

The undersigned stockholder of PRENTICE-HALL, INC. hereby appoints PAUL R. ANDREWS, FRANK J. DUNNIGAN and Z. A. POOL, III, and each of them, to act as agents and proxies of the undersigned with power of substitution and revocation, at the annual meeting of stockholders of such Corporation to be held at its office, 229 South State Street, Dover, Delaware, on May 5, 1967 at 10:00 A.M., Eastern Daylight Time, or at any adjournment thereof, with authority to vote all shares of stock registered in the name of the undersigned:

1. For the election of Directors.
2. To ratify the appointment of Haskins & Sells as auditors for the Corporation for the year 1967. **FOR □ AGAINST □**

and at their discretion upon such other matters as may come before the meeting.

Management favors a vote "FOR" proposal 2.

Unless a contrary choice is specified above, this proxy will be voted "FOR" proposal 2.

(Continued, and to be SIGNED, on other side)

The undersigned hereby acknowledges receipt of the Notice of Annual Meeting of Stockholders and the Proxy Statement relating to such Annual Meeting, both dated March 31, 1967.

Dated ...., 1967 ....

....(Seal)
Signature

IMPORTANT: In signing this proxy please sign your name in the same way as it is stenciled on this Proxy. When signing as attorney, executor, administrator, trustee or guardian, please give your full title as such.

Courtesy Prentice-Hall, Inc.

Most stockholders vote by proxy using a form similar to the one above.

he may simply sign it and give no specific instructions on how his vote is to be cast. In this case, management simply assumes that he is willing to have his vote cast in the affirmative on all the issues stated on the proxy.[4]

[4] One of the most celebrated proxy battles in U.S. business history occurred in 1954, when the late Robert R. Young, millionaire president of the Chesapeake & Ohio Railway, succeeded in gaining control of the New York Central Railroad from William White, company president. Mr. Young used company funds to buy 800,000 shares of New York Central stock, and then arranged for the sale of this stock to two friends, the oil-rich Clint W. Murchison and Sid W. Richardson of Texas. Mr. Young's proxy statement read: "Dear Fellow Shareholders: Put us to work to make your stock more valuable. We have bought stock with a present market value of $25 million in the faith that we can." Before the contest, Young declared he would not ask the railroad to pay the cost of the proxy contest. After he won, he submitted his bill for $1,308,733.71, which the directors approved for payment. William White spent more than a half-million dollars of company funds too, only to lose the election. Robert Young died in 1958, still president of the railroad company.

The Board's Relationship to Company Officers. Many companies point out that it is difficult, if not impossible, to distinguish the boundaries between the functions of the board and the corporate officers. Nevertheless, it is a widely accepted principle that boards of directors concern themself with basic policy (as opposed to operating policy), with matters of importance (as opposed to routine matters), and with planning (rather than with how to implement a decision that has already been made).

The relationship between directors and officers is (ideally) one of trust and confidence. This is what the law calls a *fiduciary relationship.* The significance of being a fiduciary is that neither party is allowed to take advantage of the fiduciary relationship for personal gain. If he does, he is legally liable and accountable to the corporation for whatever profit he has made or caused the corporation to lose.

Classes of Corporate Stock

Several kinds of stock are issued by modern corporations, but almost all of them may be classified as either *common* or *preferred stock.* In Chapter 16 we shall look closely at both these classes of stock; here we shall simply note their general characteristics as they relate to the ownership and control of the corporation.

Common Stock. Common stock is the least complicated and most frequently issued corporation stock. Holders of common stock are in much the same position as the partners in a partnership. They participate in the management of the business and share in the profits or losses, if any. Their liability is limited to the value of their stock; consequently, the most any common stockholder can lose is the value or amount of his investment. Dividends may be paid from profits after all interest on funded obligations, including mortgages, and dividend payments to preferred stockholders, have been paid. Likewise, common stockholders share in the liquidation of the corporation after bondholders and creditors have been paid.

Preferred Stock. As the name implies, this class of stock guarantees to its owner certain priorities or preferences not available to common stockholders. These preferences may pertain to the granting of dividends, to the distribution of the assets after dissolution, or to voting rights.

The dividend rate, expressed either as a percentage or in dollars and cents, is printed on the face of the preferred-stock certificate. A $5 preferred stock is one on which the company is to pay $5 a year. Nevertheless, there is no guarantee that the dividend will be paid unless it is earned and declared by the board of directors. As a rule, preferred stock does not provide the right to vote, whereas common stock usually does provide that right.

N61799

CERTIFICATE FOR LESS THAN 100 SHARES

Number 00000

Shares One

COMMON STOCK

PAR VALUE $5

INCORPORATED UNDER THE LAWS OF THE STATE OF DELAWARE

TENNECO INC.

THIS CERTIFICATE IS TRANSFERABLE IN HOUSTON, NEW YORK, CHICAGO OR LOS ANGELES

This Certifies that ---------- JOHN Q. PUBLIC ---------- is the owner of

ONE (1)

SEE REVERSE FOR CERTAIN DEFINITIONS

FULLY PAID AND NON-ASSESSABLE SHARES OF THE COMMON STOCK

of Tenneco Inc. transferable on the books of the Corporation in person or by duly authorized attorney upon surrender of this certificate properly endorsed. This certificate and the shares represented hereby are issued and shall be held subject to all the provisions of the Certificate of Incorporation of the Corporation (copies of which are on file with the Transfer Agent), to all of which the holder by acceptance hereof assents. This certificate is not valid unless countersigned by the Transfer Agent and registered by the Registrar.

Witness the signatures of the duly authorized officers.

Dated

CERTIFICATE OF STOCK

SPECIMEN SECRETARY

SPECIMEN CHAIRMAN OF THE BOARD

REGISTERED: FIRST NATIONAL CITY BANK, REGISTRAR BY AUTHORIZED OFFICER

COUNTERSIGNED: CHEMICAL BANK NEW YORK TRUST COMPANY, TRANSFER AGENT BY AUTHORIZED SIGNATURE

AMERICAN BANK NOTE COMPANY

Courtesy Tenneco Inc.

A stock certificate typical of the kind issued to stockholders of an open corporation. On the following page is an illustration of the reverse side of the certificate. When a person sells his shares, he fills out this assignment form and transfers ownership to another person by indorsement.

The Stockholder's Ledger. Immediately after a stock certificate is issued to a stockholder, the company opens an account for him known as the *stockholder's ledger.* These ledgers differ in form from one company to another, but they usually contain the following information: (1) name and address of stockholder, (2) number of shares of stock issued, (3) date shares were acquired or sold, and (4) the stock certificate number shown on the certificate. The facts recorded in this ledger determine if the stockholder is entitled to the dividend paid to those who owned stock prior to a certain date. Usually the corporation secretary is responsible for maintaining this record, but in large corporations with thousands of stockholders, this and other records are maintained by a transfer agent, which is usually a bank employed for this purpose.

TENNECO INC.

The following abbreviations, when used in the inscription on the face of this certificate, shall be construed as though they were written out in full according to applicable laws or regulations:

TEN COM — as tenants in common

TEN ENT — as tenants by the entireties

JT TEN — as joint tenants with right of survivorship and not as tenants in common

UNIF GIFT MIN ACT — .... Custodian ....
(Cust) (Minor)
under Uniform Gifts to Minors
Act............
(State)

Additional abbreviations may also be used though not in the above list.

THE CORPORATION WILL FURNISH WITHOUT CHARGE TO EACH STOCKHOLDER WHO SO REQUESTS THE DESIGNATIONS, PREFERENCES AND RELATIVE, PARTICIPATING, OPTIONAL OR OTHER SPECIAL RIGHTS OF EACH CLASS OF STOCK OR SERIES THEREOF OF THE CORPORATION, AND THE QUALIFICATIONS, LIMITATIONS OR RESTRICTIONS OF SUCH PREFERENCES AND/OR RIGHTS. SUCH REQUEST MAY BE MADE TO THE CORPORATION OR THE TRANSFER AGENT.

For value received, ________ *hereby sell, assign and transfer unto*

PLEASE INSERT SOCIAL SECURITY OR OTHER IDENTIFYING NUMBER OF ASSIGNEE

PLEASE PRINT OR TYPEWRITE NAME AND ADDRESS OF ASSIGNEE

Shares of the capital stock represented by the within Certificate, and do hereby irrevocably constitute and appoint

Attorney to transfer the said stock on the books of the within named Corporation with full power of substitution in the premises.

Dated, ________

NOTICE: THE SIGNATURE TO THIS ASSIGNMENT MUST CORRESPOND WITH THE NAME AS WRITTEN UPON THE FACE OF THE CERTIFICATE IN EVERY PARTICULAR, WITHOUT ALTERATION OR ENLARGEMENT, OR ANY CHANGE WHATEVER.

THIS SPACE MUST NOT BE COVERED IN ANY WAY

Corporation Bonds. If a corporation needs additional funds and does not wish to issue more stock, it may sell bonds. A *bond* is a certificate of indebtedness given as evidence of debt to the bondholder. In some respects, a bond is a kind of promissory note, except that it ordinarily extends over a longer period of time than the usual promissory note. When bonds are sold by a corporation, they become a part of its capital structure. (Since financing by the sale of bonds is a method of borrowing money, this subject is dealt with more fully in Chapter 16.)

Corporate Ownership and Policy Formulation

Corporations whose stock is held by the public impose pressures on managers which are different from those that proprietorships and partnerships must face. This is because in the first case the owners and managers are two separate and distinct groups possessing different responsibilities. For this reason, it is important to note the differences between corporate managers and owners.

Who Are the Stockholders? Every firm has an owner or owners. In individual proprietorships and partnerships, with some exceptions in the case of large partnerships, the owners are the managers. But in large corporations (and in most small ones) the owners, who are the stockholders, frequently are not the managers. Hence, there is a separation between ownership and management in most corporations.

It is estimated that today there are over 20 million people who, through owning stock, have direct ownership in one or more of our great corporations. These people come from every walk of life. Other millions of people have an indirect ownership in corporations through insurance policies, banks, pension funds, profit-sharing funds, and mutual funds. (Banks, insurance companies, and savings-and-loan firms generally choose to hold preferred stocks or bonds; mutual funds, private pension funds, and profit-sharing funds favor owning large blocks of common stock.)

Most shareholders are not active participants in the business they have invested in, but have turned this responsibility over to professional managers of one kind or another. But even when these managers gain virtual managerial control over the corporation, they still must be concerned with what the stockholders want, since angry owners may take any of several courses of retaliative action that could prove most embarrassing to the managers.

What Do the Stockholders Own? It is commonly accepted that stockholders are the owners of the company in which they hold stock. But what do they actually own? Are these stockholders really the owners of corporate property? Or do they simply own pieces of paper, in the form of stock certificates, whose value is determined day-by-day in the stock markets?

From a purely legal standpoint, stockholders do not own property in the sense in which we normally think of property ownership. For one thing, they

Courtesy General Motors Corp.

An annual meeting of stockholders at which time the corporate officers give an oral report of the corporation's achievements and future plans. Stockholders may ask questions about the affairs of the corporation.

do not possess title to the company property, and therefore cannot control its use, as can the single proprietor. Property is owned by the corporation, and not by the stockholders. Although it is true that, in the case of business failure and liquidation, stockholders have a direct claim on corporate property, their claims are subordinate to those of creditors, preferred stockholders, and bondholders.

Looking at it realistically, "owing a share of stock" is just what the phrase implies: having a fractional interest in the total entity called the corporation. But this claim is not for a fixed amount payable at any time, because indeed its value does fluctuate. From this viewpoint, then, on any given date, stockholders own merely an unapportioned share of the corporation's net worth on that day.

Rights of the Stockholders. Stockholders have certain legal rights which for discussion purposes may be classified as group rights and individual rights. *Group rights* are those rights that stockholders have when assembled at regular and special meetings. *Individual rights* are those that each stockholder has without any reference to other stockholders. Stockholder common-law group rights are:

1. To elect directors
2. To adopt and amend the by-laws
3. To change the charter upon the consent of the state
4. To sell or otherwise dispose of corporation assets
5. To dissolve the corporation

In the absence of any restrictions by state law or the corporate charter, each holder of stock has, among others, these individual rights:

1. To buy and sell stock registered in his name
2. To receive dividends in proportion to the number of shares owned, provided each dividend has been duly declared by the board of directors
3. To share in the distribution of assets on a *pro rata* (proportional) basis if and when the directors decide to dissolve the firm
4. To subscribe to additional stock before shares are offered to the public, unless this right is waived (The right to additional shares is called the *pre-emptive right.* The pre-emptive right has frequently been limited by state law and by charter provisions.)
5. To review and inspect company records
6. To vote at regular stockholder's meetings
7. To receive stock certificates
8. To sue officers and directors for misuse of power or for fraud

Corporation Management

We have seen that the real control of most corporations is in the hands of their professional managers, and that as a rule stockholders are not particularly interested in bothering with the company's affairs as long as profits are paid in the form of dividends. The trend, in fact, is for a team of managers to run the business, supplanting the one-man management so characteristic of earlier days. Today we hear little of men like the Carnegies, Astors, Vanderbilts, and Morgans, and a great deal about the idea of "management teams" in virtually all our larger publicly-owned corporations such as the Great Atlantic & Pacific Tea Co., Montgomery Ward & Co., and the Coca-Cola Co. Such autocrats as the late table-pounding George Washington Hill, of the American Tobacco Co., and the rambunctious Sewell Avery, former president of Montgomery Ward, are rare among the management of today's corporations.

Advantages of the Corporate Form of Ownership

You can see that a corporation offers certain advantages over other forms of business ownership, but that it is not entirely suitable for all types of business enterprises. In discussing the partnership, we found that the personal liability of general partners extends to the debts incurred by the firm, and this amount may be far in excess of their original investment. We also discovered that the ownership of a partnership cannot be transferred unless the firm is first dissolved. For all practical purposes, however, the life of a corporation is perpetual. Each stockholder's share in the ownership may be transferred at will simply by the sale of stock; there is no need to get the approval of other stockholders before the transfer is made.

The corporation is usually in a position to employ specialists to do specific types of work. This is particularly true when the corporation is large, with many kinds of specialized work to be done.

A corporation may be able to attract a large number of investors as stockholders, who in turn may advertise the business and encourage others to buy its products. This advantage is not possible in the individual proprietorship. The advantages of the corporation may be summarized as follows:

Advantages of the Corporate Form of Ownership

1. Life of corporation is almost perpetual
2. Limited stockholder's liability
3. Easy to transfer ownership
4. Easy to expand
5. More permanent
6. Investors need not manage
7. Adaptable to both small and large businesses
8. Permits use of management specialists

Disadvantages of a Corporation

From the viewpoint of a business manager, the corporation has two main drawbacks. In the first place, forming a corporation is far more complicated than starting either a proprietorship or a partnership. As we saw earlier, definite legal steps must be taken to obtain a charter. Moreover, if you want to sell the stock on a national market, you must first obtain approval from the Federal Securities and Exchange Commission. All these requirements involve legal procedures and consume a great amount of time.

A more serious disadvantage is the heavy tax burden imposed upon corporations. For example, the federal government taxes a corporation on its profits. Then, when these profits are distributed to stockholders as dividends, another tax must be paid by the stockholder as a part of his personal income tax.[5] But this tax disadvantage is not always as serious as it may seem. Such cowboy stars as Gene Autry and Roy Rogers have organized their own corporations to license manufacturers who want to use their names on products. In return, the stars receive either shares in the corporation or a cash royalty, neither of which is taxable as personal income because the money goes to the star's company and is taxable at a lower corporate rate.

Many states levy taxes on corporations. For example, a corporation doing business within the boundaries of a state must pay an annual franchise tax or license tax for the privilege of doing business. Corporations also pay real-estate and property taxes similar to those levied on individuals. Other examples of state taxes not generally required of the sole proprietorship or partnership are a filing fee, which is payable on application for a charter, and an organization tax based on the amount of authorized capital stock. Some states tax such corporations as railroads, gas transmission lines, and insurance companies.

A third disadvantage is the growing federal and state regulation of corporations. This is a matter of increasing concern to many executives. You will recall that many of these regulations were discussed in the chapter on government regulation and taxation (Chapter 2).

These and other disadvantages may be summarized as follows:

Disadvantages of the Corporate Forms of Ownership

1. Subject to special taxation
2. More difficult and expensive to organize than other forms
3. Charter restrictions may limit activities
4. Subject to state and federal controls
5. Tendency for impersonal relationships between management and employees, and management and customers, in large corporations
6. Subject to higher tax on business income

Corporate Mergers and Combinations

There are many reasons why firms combine. One is that some corporations manufacturing one product find that it is not only more profitable to make others, but that diversification adds "safety." Another is that many owners find that their businesses must expand or die—they cannot remain static and continue to be competitive. Yet another is that when a smaller company and a large one combine, much-needed capital can be obtained

[5] Under the Technical Amendments Act of 1958, a corporation can be taxed as a partnership if only one class of stock is owned by not more than 10 stockholders, who must consent to this method of taxation by an election. The effect of such tax treatment is to levy income taxes on the stockholders as partners, with no income tax payable by the corporation.

through the substitution of the credit-rate of the larger for that of the smaller. And still another is that operating costs can be reduced by eliminating duplicate facilities. In short, then: the economic and other advantages of stepping up to a larger-scale operation can be very significant.

Merger. Experience has shown that in most cases it is more economical as well as quicker to attain large-scale operation by merging with one or more other companies than by trying to expand alone and from within. A *merger* may be defined as *the joining of two or more business firms so that they may be operated as one company.* When two firms merge, one acquires sufficient stock in the other for purposes of control of the management. Usually, a large company buys out and legally absorbs the smaller company. The stockholders of each corporation must approve the merger, usually by a two-thirds majority vote. The working out of the details of a merger through negotiation may take many months.

The stock price proposed by the offering corporation to the shareholders of the other company is the *tender price offer.* (The stockholder has the right to agree or refuse to tender his shares at the proposed price.) The "tender offer" is growing in popularity partly because it is far cheaper than a proxy fight, and less time-consuming for all parties involved. The costs of it are limited to advertising expenses, legal fees, and interest charges on standby financing, where it is necessary. A proxy contest, by contrast, can require tremendous outlays for publicity, mailing charges, and for presenting arguments before the Securities and Exchange Commission.

A merger designed to consolidate several firms producing the same product or engaged in the same type of business is called a *horizontal merger.* Should two motel chains merge, for instance, this would be a horizontal merger or *combination.* A *vertical merger,* on the other hand, brings under one corporate ownership a control over unlike plants, engaged in various stages of production from raw materials to the end product. A third type of merger or combination is the *conglomerate* or *circular merger,* which unites firms producing diverse and unrelated product lines. Many conglomerate mergers reflect normal corporate desires to spread risks, to find use for idle capital funds, and to add new products which can be expected to be sold because of the company's marketing knowledge. On the other hand, some of these mergers reflect little more than a drive to obtain greater economic power. An example of a conglomerate is Litton Industries, which by late 1967 had acquired through merger all or part of 55 companies, including firms engaged in shipbuilding, engineering, book publishing, food handling, and computer and office-machine manufacturing. Between 1954 and 1967, these mergers helped boost its total sales from $3 million annually to $1.5 billion.

Amalgamation takes place when there is the fusing of corporate ownership of two or more enterprises into a new corporation requiring the liquidation or dissolution of the formerly existing corporation.

THE HOLDING COMPANY

The holding company is a type of corporation which merits some attention. In principle, any corporation which owns stock in other corporations is a holding company. However, in a strict legal sense, the term is generally used to identify only those corporations which own enough of the voting stock in one or more other corporations (called *subsidiaries*) to control them. Some holding companies own all the voting stock of their subsidiaries, but even those that own less than half can take advantage of the system of management-secured proxies and thus still maintain effective control over the board of directors of the subsidiary.

For many years holding companies have been popular in the public-utilities field, and today many telephone, gas, electric, and transportation companies are controlled by large holding companies. The American Telephone & Telegraph Co., for example, owns all the stock in 10 associate telephone companies, and from 6 to 25 percent of the stock in other companies. There is no doubt that in the past the main purpose of the holding company has been not to improve managerial efficiency, but to gain a monopoly in order to exercise control over vast resources, thereby obtaining economic advantages. In the mid-1920's, abuses by certain public-utility holding companies resulted in higher utility prices for consumers, and financial losses to the investors.

To curtail the growth of holding companies and eliminate the many abuses that existed in the operation of public-utility holding companies, Congress in 1935 enacted the Public Utility Holding Company Act. This legislation has been called "a specialized antitrust act" because its purpose is to prevent economic concentration of power in the public-utilities field. One important provision of the Act requires holding companies to register with the Securities and Exchange Commission, to file with the commission certain basic data, and to submit annually such information as the commission may request. Interlocking directorates with banking companies are prohibited, and intercompany borrowing is illegal. Since this Act was passed, many utility companies have gradually emerged from the layers of pyramided holding-company organizations.

JOINT-STOCK COMPANIES

With the expansion of business that started with the explorations of Marco Polo and reached its peak with the establishment of our American colonies, a new type of business organization developed. During these centuries, individual businessmen, even partnerships, were unable to raise the necessary venture capital. So joint-stock companies were organized to meet the need for large concentrations of capital. The East India Company, chartered in 1600, was the first large-scale English joint-stock company. In 1606 the English established the London Company, which was created to finance the Jamestown colony, and in 1623 the Dutch West India Company was organized to promote the Hudson Valley.

The *joint-stock company* is a voluntary association of persons operating under articles of agreement and with the capital divided into transferable shares. Shares may be readily bought and sold, with almost no restrictions by the states. Owners of the stock do not participate in the management, but they do elect directors who have the authority and responsibility for directing the business. The company is bound by the decisions the directors make. The life of the company is continuous and not affected by the death of any stockholders.

The joint-stock company is usually subject to the same regulations as a corporation, although in a few states it has the same status as a general partnership. For purposes of federal income tax, it is considered to be a corporation. However, suit must be brought against the members individually or as a group. Ownership of property is in the name of the trustees, who hold title to the property on behalf of the shareholders.

The joint-stock company has several advantages, among which are these: (1) it is inexpensive to organize; (2) death of a shareholder does not terminate the agreement; and (3) ownership certificates are transferable.

The main disadvantage, the unlimited liability of its members, has been known to discourage prospective investors.

Many of the joint-stock companies that were founded during the early years of our nation's history have in recent years been changed to corporations to gain the benefits of the corporate form. Presently, the joint-stock company is not popular in the United States.

BUSINESS TRUSTS

Although less popular than some other forms of business ownership, the business trust offers the advantages of a corporation and eliminates the disadvantages of a partnership. The owners of real property deed it to trustees for purposes of management, receiving in return a proportionate share in the income. The owners are not liable for the debts of the trust. The agreement describes the nature of the business, terms of control, its duration, and capitalization. Such trusts are often called a *common-law trust* or a *Massachusetts trust.*

A board of trustees, similar to a board of directors for a corporation, is chosen. The board elects officers, makes policies, declares dividends, and otherwise runs the business. The board may issue trust certificates to shareholders which are transferable in the open market. Bonds may also be issued and traded.

The parties to a trust are: (1) the *trustor* (often called the grantor or donor) who is the person placing the property in trust; (2) the *trustees*—those who are designated to hold legal title to the property and manage it; and (3) the *beneficiary*—the one for whose benefit the trust is established.

The business trust principle is frequently used in the investment field, especially where the holding and trading of real estate is prohibited to corporations by state law. Oftentimes a trust may invest a significant portion of its funds in bonds or fixed-income securities acceptable under the "legal list" prepared by the state of residency. It is common practice for most states now to follow the "prudent man" rule, under which the trust company is held to the same degree of responsibility in exercising judgment as that exercised by a prudent man in making his own investments. The advantages and disadvantages of the business trust may be summarized as follows:

Advantages of the Business Trust

1. Its formation is simple and inexpensive.
2. It insures freedom from personal liability by the stockholders, unless they have the right to change trustees.
3. It is practically free from government control.
4. It provides for the aggregation of large capital with flexibility of management.

Disadvantages of the Business Trust

1. It is taxed by the federal government and by some states as though it were a corporation.
2. There is the possibility of unlimited liability for shareholders if they have agreed to the right to change trustees.
3. The securities of a business trust may not be as easily marketed as those of a corporation, chiefly because most people do not understand this type of organization.
4. There may be certain specific time limitations on the life of the trust.

JOINT VENTURES OR UNDERWRITING SYNDICATES

The joint venture is one of the oldest forms of partnership types, originating with the trading ventures of the 1600's and 1700's by European and British businessmen. These individuals would pool their resources and sponsor trading missions to China, India, and other foreign countries. After the venture was completed and the profits distributed among the partners, the organization was dissolved. It was common practice when organizing such a venture to prepare a partnership agreement which would include the purpose of the trip, the names of the partners, their respective obligations, and the date of sailing. There was also a statement that if a partner died during the trip, this would not terminate the agreement.

The joint-venture type of ownership used in modern business is very similar to that found in foreign countries. It is used today in such undertakings as real-estate developments and large-scale construction jobs, and when large blocks of securities are sold to the public. It is usually limited to a general undertaking.[6]

When used in the sale of stocks and bonds, the joint venture is often called an *underwriting syndicate,* which is a group of investment banks or security dealers who join together temporarily to sell a new issue of securities. Upon completion of the sale of these securities, the syndicate is dissolved until another situation develops. Ofttimes the syndicate may buy an entire issue and resell the shares to the general public. Members of the syndicate receive their profits from the difference in price paid for the securities and the price at which they are sold to the public. This is commonly referred to as "the spread." (Should the shares drop in price before they are sold, the syndicate members would, of course, make less profit.) The underwriting syndicate differs slightly from the usual joint venture in that syndicate members have a limited liability.

CO-OPERATIVES

The *co-operative* is a special form of business ownership that differs from all other forms we have discussed so far. In this type of organization, the capital is supplied by individuals who buy shares similar to those of a corporation. Each shareholder has one vote in the management of the business, regardless of the number of shares he owns. Surplus earnings are distributed to the shareholders in the form of dividends, which are usually based on the volume of the shareholder's purchases from the co-operative. The primary motive behind co-operatives is to supply goods and services at a cost lower than they could be obtained from businesses that are operated by the owner for profit. Small co-operatives appoint a manager to direct the business, whereas larger concerns elect a board of directors to make policies, and appoint an operating manager.

[6] See also Chapter 24 for a discussion of joint ventures in international business operations.

There are co-operatives in many areas of business, including retailing, telephone service, agriculture, and money-lending. In marketing there are three major kinds of co-operatives: the *consumer* co-operative, the *agricultural marketing* co-operative, and the *agricultural purchasing* co-operative.

The Consumer Co-operative

The *consumer co-operative* is a retail store established by a group of consumers to make it possible for them to purchase goods at the wholesale cost. In other words, the objective is to eliminate the profit made by the ordinary retailer. Such stores are rare in the United States, and it is unlikely that their number will increase substantially in the future.

The Agricultural Co-operative

Agricultural marketing co-operatives are associations operated by the growers or producers of a single product or a group of closely related products. The Sunkist Growers, Inc., for example, market oranges and lemons, and Land-O-Lakes Creameries, Inc., markets dairy and poultry products. These middlemen are important agencies in the marketing of several kinds of farm products.

A second type of co-operative association that serves farmers is the *agricultural purchasing co-operative.* These associations purchase and resell to both members and nonmembers such commodities as fertilizer, seeds, gasoline, feeds, and farm machinery. Dividends, in cash or stock, are distributed on the basis of the patronage of members. Each member has an equal voice in controlling the affairs of the association.

Advantages and Disadvantages of the Co-operative. Co-operatives enjoy a tax advantage over other forms of business ownership. For example, farmers' co-operatives are exempt from corporate income tax, provided they meet the requirements of federal and state laws. In consumer co-operatives, the so-called "patronage dividends" paid to members who make purchases from the co-operatives are usually deductible before net earnings subject to income taxes are determined. These dividends are regarded as a refund to members in return for their patronage, rather than as a part of what might otherwise be known as profits. Other advantages co-operatives enjoy are the low cost of organizing, and the lower annual franchise tax, which is less than on some other forms of ownership. Also, a co-operative is usually able to obtain more favorable prices for its members by regulating the flow of goods from the source.

Like other forms of business ownership, co-operatives have certain disadvantages. For example, there is a lack of freedom on the part of the producer members to sell their produce in any market or at any time they desire. Another disadvantage is the absence of the profit incentive common to other forms of ownership. Finally, from the standpoint of successful operation, the tendency to pay low salaries has often meant inability to employ the most competent managers.

SUMMARY

Business is based on rights associated with the ownership of property. In order to have legal status, a business firm must adopt a form of ownership that is recognized in the eyes of the law. In all states the law recognizes the sole proprietorship, partnership, and corporation as acceptable forms of ownership. Since there are advantages and disadvantages to each of these forms, business owners must decide which form to adopt. Other forms of ownership, not recognized alike in all states, are the joint-stock company, the business trust, the joint venture, and the co-operative association.

In general, sole proprietorships and partnerships are relatively easy to organize, and are permitted considerable freedom of operation. On the other hand, both forms necesarily subject the owners to substantial amounts of risk; both have the inherent disadvantages of unlimited liability and limited life.

Proprietorships and partnerships predominate in small-scale businesses. Although both forms appear in all businesses, except where excluded by law in the case of commercial banks and public utilities, they are more common to retail and service enterprises. As a business increases in size, the most common transition is to corporate form.

The corporation grew from the need for a form of ownership that would combine flexibility of operation with capital-raising advantages. Among the characteristics of the corporation are these: (1) the corporation is a legal entity, separate and distinct from its owners, the stockholders; (2) it can own, buy and sell property, and be sued; (3) it exists for many purposes, but its powers are derived from and limited by its charter, which is granted by the state; (4) it may be established for profit or nonprofit, and the sale of its stock may be open to the public, or restricted.

There are, however, disadvantages to the corporate form. For one thing, it is more difficult to start because of legal requirements. Also, a heavier tax burden is imposed on corporations than on other forms. And it is subject to more governmental control than other forms of ownership. But, despite these disadvantages, the corporation has become a symbol of "big" business, and the fact that ownership can be divided into small fractional amounts has proven attractive to investors. Hence, it is easy to understand why the corporation has become the dominant legal form.

The joint-stock company is comparable in many respects to the limited partnership. In contrast to the limited partnership, however, its shares may be transferred freely, and the shareholders are subject to unlimited liability. The transferability feature of the joint-stock company is a feature of the business corporation, while the unlimited liability characteristic is similar to the general partnership.

The joint venture is a temporary partnership formed for a single project and terminated upon its completion. A typical example is the underwriting syndicate used by security dealers to sell or buy an issue of stocks and bonds; the syndicate is dissolved upon the sale of the entire issue. In contrast to the usual unlimited liability incumbent upon participants in most joint ventures, the partners in the syndicate have only limited liability.

Although less popular than some other forms of business ownership, the business trust gives the advantages of a corporation and eliminates the disadvantages of a partnership. A trust is evidenced by a trust agreement which expresses the purpose, duration, capital investment, and management control arrangements. Perhaps the significant advantage is freedom of owners from liability of debts of the trust.

The co-operative is more popular as a business organization than either the trust or joint-stock company. The low cost of organizing a co-operative as compared with the corporation or joint-stock company is an advantage. Co-operative managers sometimes have difficulty maintaining the loyalty of members, who complain that they lack the freedom to sell their produce at any time they desire.

VOCABULARY REVIEW QUIZ

Match the following vocabulary terms with the statements on the next page.

a. Agricultural purchasing co-operative
b. Articles of partnership
c. Close corporation
d. Consumer co-operative
e. Dormant partner
f. Entrepreneur
g. Fiduciary relationship
h. General Partner
i. Grantor
j. Holding company
k. Joint-stock company
l. Limited partnership
m. Non-stock corporation
n. Open corporation
o. Private corporation
p. Partnership
q. Pre-emptive rights
r. Proxy
s. Public corporation
t. Secret partner
u. Silent partner
v. Alien corporation
w. Trustee
x. Underwriting syndicate
y. Limited liability

1. A relationship of trust and confidence between officers and directors of the company
2. A corporation whose stock may be bought by the public as an investment
3. A corporation which does not open its stock for sale to the general public
4. The person placing property in trust on behalf of the beneficiary
5. An association operated by growers or producers that buys and resells farm commodities to its members and nonmembers
6. A business chartered by a foreign country but doing business in the United States
7. A written agreement among partners
8. A member of a partnership who takes no part and also remains unknown to the public
9. An owner who takes an active role in the business but who does not want to reveal his identity
10. One who owns or manages a business
11. A partner who takes no active part in the business even though he may be known as a partner
12. A corporation operated by private persons for either profit or nonprofit purposes
13. An association of two or more persons to carry on as co-owners of the business for profit
14. A partnership in which one or more partners have limited liability, but in which at least one partner must have unlimited liability
15. One who is designated to hold legal title to property and manage it for the benefit of the beneficiary as directed by the agreement
16. A form of business ownership combining the features of a corporation and a partnership, of which the latter group does not enjoy the advantages of limited liability
17. A retail establishment owned by consumers who by virtue of their ownership may buy goods from the retail firm at wholesale cost
18. One corporation which exists to control other corporations through stock ownership
19. A private corporation, similar to a co-operative, for which no stock is issued to the owners
20. One who acts in place of another by having the power of attorney
21. A group of persons organized to a specific purpose such as the sale of stock through an investment bank or security dealer
22. A business organized for a nonprofit purpose by government
23. The right of the stockholder to buy additional shares of stock in a particular company
24. All partners who have unlimited liability and who share in full the firm's responsibilities
25. A term meaning that an owner's loss is restricted to the amount of his investment in a business

QUESTIONS FOR REVIEW STUDY

1. Why are so many small businesses organized as partnerships?
2. Under what set of conditions might it be better for a sole proprietorship to change to a partnership form of ownership?
3. What are the advantages and disadvantages of the general partnership as compared with the limited partnership?
4. Why is it important to have a written partnership agreement?
5. What limitations common to the proprietorship does the general partnership attempt to overcome?
6. What is usually covered in the general partnership agreement?
7. Explain the popularity of the corporation as a form of ownership.
8. How does common stock differ from preferred stock?
9. What points are usually contained in the application for a corporation charter?
10. How does the liability of a general partner differ from a corporate stockholder?
11. Why are most large businesses corporations?
12. What is the difference between an open and a close corporation?
13. Does a joint venture stockholder have any personal liability?
14. How does an underwriting syndicate work?
15. Why is the selection of the form of ownership so important when starting a business?

PROBLEMS AND PROJECTS

1. Five businessmen have each agreed to invest $100,000 to form a corporation for the purpose of buying out companies that have been mismanaged or are having financial difficulties. Since the five businessmen have other responsibilities, they have agreed to appoint a manager to investigate various projects for their consideration. Which form of legal ownership would be the most appropriate for this venture? Give reasons for your choice.

2. Four persons are equal owners in a general partnership. After a few months of operation, one partner—the top executive in the business—proves to be incompetent. When confronted by the other partners about his mistakes, and asked if he would sell his partnership interest, he replies, "I may have made an error, but I refuse to sell my share in the partnership." Two of the partners, who are still unhappy about the situation, wish to dissolve the partnership and organize a corporation. This is obviously a move to force the incompetent partner to sell. Suppose he refuses to sell and another partner proposes to sell his interest instead:

   a. How would this second proposal affect the partnership agreement if it were carried out?
   b. Do you believe that the partnership should suggest that the first partner agree with the others to form a corporation?

c. If this were done, would this affect the first partner's relationship to others when a corporation is formed?

3. James Ace desires to put a large sum aside for the benefit of his crippled daughter. He wants the money invested in stocks and bonds to produce an income. Which form of legal ownership would you recommend as an effective way to accomplish his purpose?

A BUSINESS CASE

Case 4-1 The Acme Engineering Company

Robert Reilly is the owner of the Acme Engineering Co., a sole proprietorship that has been in operation for seven years in a city of a million people. After graduating from college with a degree in mechanical engineering, Reilly worked for three years in the engineering department of a large corporation. Finally, he decided to start his own company. During the past seven years his firm has rendered consulting engineering services for the construction of more than 40 large buildings. In addition to his consulting business, Reilly is also the agent for a well-known conveyor-belt manufacturing company, and has a dealership for Kamron mechanical-lift forks, which are considered a very reliable item.

Last year, Reilly's company made a net profit, after taxes, of $47,000. That was the third consecutive year in which the firm enjoyed a 10 percent growth in total revenue. In fact, the company is now at the stage where it cannot take on any additional projects of any consequence until at least two more engineers are employed. But engineers are difficult to find, and very often do not want to work in a sole proprietorship because it does not provide them an opportunity to invest in the company. Mr. Reilly has been aware of this situation for several years, having lost two of his best engineers for this reason. However, he is uncertain as to what to do about it.

A few days ago, one of the largest producers of electronic and mechanical valves and switches used in industrial plants offered Reilly an exclusive dealership for the entire state. Reilly estimates that this would require the construction of a fireproof warehouse and about 6,000 square feet of additional engineering and office space. And it would entail adding at least two engineers immediately.

Fortunately, Reilly has no immediate space problem because he recently constructed a warehouse and office building on a 10-acre tract near a freeway. However, he estimates that in another year, the company will need additional warehouse space and a new loading dock, all of which will require an additional expenditure of $200,000—and the company cannot finance this. The most recent audit report shows the following:

BALANCE SHEET

Acme Engineering Company, March 31, 19___

Assets		Liabilities	
Cash	$ 50,000	Accounts Payable	$175,000
Accounts Receivable	600,000	Notes Payable	15,000
Factory Inventory	60,000	Mortgage on Building	160,000
Building and Office Furniture	62,000	Capital and Surplus	442,000
	$772,000		$772,000

Since Reilly does not have the additional capital to build the new facilities, it has been proposed that he borrow the money on a long-term loan. However, capital is tight and interest rates are high—well above the 5 percent mortgage on his office building. A local banker has suggested the possibility of incorporating.

Reilly's attorney estimates it would cost $1,000 to form a corporation, and about $300 to form a partnership. In either case, it seems possible that Reilly can obtain additional capital. Actually, the pressing need for expansion seems to depend on whether he takes over the new product-line or continues with only the present line.

1. What should Reilly do?
2. How would changing the existing form of legal ownership help Reilly?
3. Which form of ownership offers greater possibilities for raising capital five years from now?

A BUSINESS CASE

Case 4-2 Norman Brothers and Rose

Over the past five decades Norman Brothers and Rose, general contractors operating as a general partnership, have built a fine reputation as a heavy-industry construction firm. W. J. Rose, one of the original founders, retired completely from the business two years ago, selling his share of the partnership to the Norman brothers. Both of the brothers plan to retire soon, and would like to see the firm continued, but wish to take no active part in its operations because they realize the various risks they will run if they remain as general partners after they retire. They want to retain a financial interest, but with a minimum of financial responsibility. A number of very competent engineers work for the company, and it is likely that these individuals would choose to remain with it if it were continued, and that they can provide new leadership for it.

1. What is the main problem in this case?
2. What is the best way to solve the problem? State reasons to support your solution.

Small Business Enterprise

5

There are at least two ways to approach success in today's business world. The first choice of most businessmen (if they can't buy out or inherit a business, or marry into an owner's family) is to work their way up the managerial ranks of a well-established company. The second way, which we shall concentrate on in this chapter, is to go into business for themselves.

Fortunately, the United States provides the kind of business climate wherein it is possible for a person with a simple idea, a few hundred dollars, and a strong will to work hard to start a business of his own, and succeed. Our business history is replete with many one-man success stories: the names Ford, Macy, Firestone, Walgreen, and Penney are only five of what must be thousands of individuals whose names at one time or another meant little to the American business community, but today literally are houshold words. They are the names of individuals who began their long-established business empires on the proverbial shoestring. And business history has a way of repeating itself, for many of our present-day industrial giants—automobile companies, air and steamship lines, steel and oil companies, retail and wholesale chains, and all kinds of manufacturing companies—were begun on quite a small scale, too.

The fact that thousands of men and women, many of them working at a good job for a well-established firm, annually venture forth on their own to become their own boss, is indicative of the attractiveness and flexibility of the American business milieu. It is also a tribute to the rugged individualism that is still (in spite of the influences of conformity) a dominant American trait. Of course, as you might expect, some of these ventures fail, and much money, time, and effort are lost. (It is for this very reason that in recent years there have been many studies made to determine the causes of business failures, especially among the small firms.) But the fear of failure, even if failure has already been realized, does not keep many Americans from persisting in their efforts to make entrepreneurship work for themselves.

Although big business bathes in the limelight of publicity much more often than does small business, and thus seems all the more prominent, from the standpoint of numbers, big firms are definitely in the minority. Not the least important reason for this is that whereas big business in the United States is less than a century old, small business was operating successfully long before the Declaration of Independence was even thought of. So it would seem that small business is here to stay.

In the light of this pleasant forecast, let us familiarize ourselves with some of the myriad problems associated with operating a small firm, and in so doing arm ourselves with insight—which, roughly translated, means with facts about what it takes to be successful in owning your own business.

WHAT IS SMALL BUSINESS?

The term "small business," though used as freely as if it had a universal definition, actually means different things to different people. Most people use the word to describe the corner drugstore, service station, hardware store, barber shop, and the like. This concept is accurate enough for general purposes, for most small concerns are, it is true, conducted on a modest scale. But in defining "small business," the federal government through the Small Business Administration (SBA), an agency you will read more about in another chapter, stands by certain criteria:

> *Manufacturing*—small if average employment in the preceding four calendar quarters did not exceed 250 employees, including those employed by any affiliate companies; and large if average employment was more than 1,000
>
> *Wholesaling*—small if yearly sales are not over $5 million

Retailing and Service—small if annual sales or receipts are not over $1 million

In 1965, the SBA altered several size standards to allow firms to be classified as small in order to become eligible to bid on government contracts for various products. For example, the size standard for small producers of artificial leather, oilcloth, and other impregnated and coated fabrics, was raised from 500 to 1,000 employees.

A slightly different concept is used by the Committee for Economic Development (CED) to determine, qualitatively rather than quantitatively, criteria to distinguish small firms from large ones. According to CED, any small business is characterized by at least two of the following characteristics:

1. *Management is independent.* Generally the managers are the owners.
2. *Capital is furnished by an individual owner or small group.*
3. *The area of operation is local.* Employees and owners reside in one home community. (Markets served need not be local.)
4. *Size within the industry is relative.* The business is small when compared to the biggest units in its field. The size of the top bracket varies widely, so that what might seem large in one field would definitely be small in another.[1]

In the opinion of the authors, the criteria used by the CED are preferable because they are more comprehensive and less arbitrary. But no matter which criteria we use, it is evident that small business consists of a variety of enterprises operated on a small scale with limited capital and few workers.

Characteristics of Small Firms

Several characteristics clearly distinguish small firms from big business: *management, capital requirements, local operation,* and *enterprise.*

Management. The management of small firms is generally independent.[2] Since the manager is the owner, he is in a position to make his own decisions. Unlike a partner in a partnership or a stockholder in a corporation, he assumes total responsibility for what happens within the business. As a

[1] The Research and Policy Committee of the Committee for Economic Development, *Meeting the Special Problems of Small Business,* policy report of the Committee for Economic Development, New York, June, 1947, p. 14.

[2] The term "management" as used here refers to the person who actually owns and manages the establishment. This term has other meanings that are discussed in other chapters.

In 1920, the Pitney-Bowes Postage Meter Co. began operations at this location (*left*) in Stamford, Conn., with 60 employees. Today Pitney-Bowes, Inc., employs over 5,000—2,200 in this modern, 10-acre plant (*right*) in Stamford.

small-scale operator, he is both investor and employer; this gives him far more freedom to act than if he were merely an employee.

Capital Requirements. Seldom is the initial capital needed to start a firm raised by a stock-selling campaign. Instead, the source is more often the owner's savings, or funds from relatives and friends (who are likely to invest only a small amount). As the firm prospers and there is need for more capital, the business may become a partnership or corporation—in which case the original owner no longer may have the freedom he previously enjoyed to manage affairs without considering others.

Local Operation. The typical small business is a local operation. Both the employer and his employees—if he has any—live in the same community, and almost all the income is derived from local sales. This does not necessarily mean that all small firms serve only local markets. Small importing and exporting firms, canning factories, manufacturing plants, and packing plants are examples of small businesses that serve extensive, sometimes nationwide, areas.

Enterprise. Every type of small business requires some degree of enterprise on the part of the owner. This entails a willingness to take risk, whether it be in pioneering a new idea or developing an already established product. The small businessman is continually confronted with new and difficult problems. Some of these problems can be solved quickly and easily,

but others require singlemindedness and an obstinate refusal to give up even when the situation looks impossible. One who lacks enterprise or drive may find it very difficult being the owner of a small business.

In view of its size, many people assume that a small business is easy to operate and that there are few managerial or administrative problems. This assumption is erroneous; practically all the managerial problems common to big business exist (even if in a small way) in small concerns, including those involving marketing, management, taxes, financing, and research. And even office management and public relations are important to the small as well as the large firm.

Essential characteristics of the small business and the big business are compared below:

Small Business	*Big Business*
Generally owner is manager	Usually non-owners are managers
Ordinarily a local operation	More often a regional or national operation
Simple organizational structure	Frequently a complex organizational structure
Very often a sole proprietorship	Generally a corporation
Owner acquainted with all employees	Owners seldom know many employees
High percentage of business failures	Low percentage of business failures
Owner performs most management functions	Management specialists commonly used

According to the SBA, there are approximately 4.75 million small firms in the United States, excluding farm units. One-fifth of all the small firms are in the two most populated states—New York and California. About 30 percent are in Pennsylvania, Illinois, Texas, Ohio, Michigan, and New Jersey.[3] During the past decade, small business has fared better than the most optimistic had anticipated. In 1966, net profits after taxes of small manufacturing corporations reached the highest level since 1950.

Approximately one out of every two persons gainfully employed in this country either owns, manages, or is employed in a small establishment. The largest single group of small firms are retail stores including food, eating, and drinking establishments. Real-estate, insurance, and finance companies rank second in total number of small units, while wholesalers and brokers of various kinds are in third place. Next are general-merchandise stores, followed by laundries and dry-cleaning firms. About 75 percent of all small firms have three or fewer employees. Only 1 percent employ as many as from 50 to 100 persons.

One of the best-known examples of small financial institutions is the country bank—a commercial bank of relatively small size found in small towns. Other financial firms classified as "small" are personal-loan companies, pawnbrokers, auto finance houses, and building-and-loan associations. It is evident from the above statistics that small firms are contributing substantially to the total economy, especially in service-type enterprises.

Self-Employment vs. Salaried Employment

Statistics would indicate that most individuals decide in favor of salaried employment and against self-employment (entrepreneurship). The minority who prefer self-employment do so because of several advantages.

Advantages of Self-Employment. 1. The entrepreneur enjoys a high degree of independence and security generally not found in working for someone else. This is largely psychological in nature, but it is a very compelling advantage.

2. An entrepreneur is free to try out his own ideas and to exercise all of his managerial talents. Because big business is often bureaucratic, employees cannot exercise full creative imagination, so many have the urge to get into business for themselves.

3. The owner reaps all the financial gains. Once the business is on a paying basis, its owner enjoys both financial and occupational security. The fact that many firms fail does not deter the confident young man or woman from business ownership.

[3] Small Business Administration, 1965 Annual Report, August 9, 1966, p. 3.

4. Business ownership provides opportunity for achieving more recognition socially and politically than is generally afforded an employee of a firm. There is a recognized prestige in being a successful businessman.

Disadvantages of Business Ownership. Attractive as it may seem to be self-employed, there are certain disadvantages or negative aspects, among which are the following:

1. Business income is typically less regular than the paychecks of a salaried employee. This may be due in part to the fact that a business owner is subject to more risks than an employee. And errors in business judgments, or changes in economic conditions, may reduce the owner's income.
2. Owning your own business entails making all the decisions as well as carrying a heavy burden of responsibility for meeting payrolls and other expenses. Usually, the proprietor has no one with whom he can share these responsibilities. Furthermore, these responsibilities may be distasteful after a certain length of time.
3. In the beginning of a new venture, longer hours of employment are often necessary. This is normally not the case for an employee.
4. Small businesses as well as large ones are subject to various regulations and restrictions imposed by local, state, and national governments. These restrictions may make operating problems difficult to solve for the inexperienced owner. Taxation often bears heavily on the beginning small enterprise. To persons not temperamentally equipped for the role of entrepreneur, these burdens are an undesirable aspect of such a career in business ownership.

Advantages of a Salaried Position. There are several advantages to being an employee of a successful business, such as:

1. There is little financial responsibility and virtually no business risk.
2. Working hours are regular and often shorter than those of the owner.
3. In the beginning the employee's monthly income may be larger than the owner's. (This advantage, however, is usually lost as the business prospers.)
4. Salaried employees enjoy such benefits as overtime pay and paid vacations, and often also medical care, hospitalization, and unemployment compensation.

Disadvantages of Salaried Employment. While being a dependent employee carries with it advantages, it also entails certain disadvantages. Several of these are:

1. Security of the job and employment opportunities may fluctuate with changes in economic conditions. During the depression of the 1930's,

many companies reduced the number of employees at all levels of employment. In more recent years some large concerns, in an effort to cut expenses, have discharged highly-paid executives and replaced them with younger men at lower salaries.

2. In addition to being subject to discharge without cause, an employee is likewise subject to transfer from one geographical area to another at the discretion of his employer. Such transfers may be made on short notice and without time to make the necessary family plans. To decline the transfer may limit his future advancement in the organization.

3. High-level executives in many concerns carry heavy responsibilities. In fact, many executives have been known to drive themselves to work at a harder pace than if they were self-employed.

4. There is a salary limitation in many career fields. In some cases an employee may earn more than the owner during a lifetime of earnings, but, assuming the business grows, there is no ceiling upon the owner's earnings.

When choosing between business ownership and employee status, it is important to weigh advantages against disadvantages. Neither status is a guarantee of success, security, and happiness for the individual who is not properly qualified for the career of his choice.

Buy an Established Business, or Start a New One?

What about the road to business ownership? The prospective businessman may follow one of two routes to ownership of his own establishment: he may (1) buy an established business, or (2) start a new one.

Advantages of Buying an Established Business. One of the important advantages of buying a going concern in a good location is that the choice of location has been proven wise. When one wants to start a new business, costly research must first be done to measure traffic at or near the sight of the proposed location. Even at that, though, the wisdom of the choice of site does not become apparent until after the business has been in operation for a while.

A second advantage to buying a going operation is that to some extent at least the uncertainty of its success in the future is reduced. The actual operating record of an existing business is far superior to an evaluation of a firm not yet in existence.

A third advantage to buying a going concern is that the business may be available at a bargain price. The owner may wish to retire and, in order to make a quick sale, sacrifice it by lowering the price. Or the price may be reduced to settle an estate. Of course, in any case the value of the business must be carefully verified to make certain it is a bargain.

A fourth advantage that may accrue with the buying of an established firm is the elimination of time, effort, and costs related to the starting of a new one. The seller has already accumulated an inventory of stock and has assembled the needed personnel (who, if competent, can be an asset to the new owner).

Advantages of Starting a New Business. For various reasons some persons prefer to start a completely new enterprise rather than buy one already established. Some of the advantages of doing this should be considered.

First, starting from scratch allows the owner to choose his own location, employees, brand of merchandise, and kind of equipment. Furthermore, a loyal clientele can be cultivated without assuming any ill-will of an existing business.

Secondly, upon examination one may find that, due to the inefficient management of existing concerns, the market is not adequately served by existing companies and that there is a need for a new, aggressive, and efficient enterprise.

Thirdly, often it is possible to start on quite a small scale, with little capital. It is a mistake to assume that all new businesses must start on a large scale; the facts show that many do not.

The arguments on this subject may be summarized as follows:

Established Firm	*New Firm*
Less time needed to begin operation	Can build to meet needs of new business
Old location may be better than new one	New location may be better than old
Maintaining old equipment may cost less	Can start with new stock and equipment
Can begin with a corps of customers	Possible to select customers
No delay in waiting for stock or equipment to operate	New firm gives greater freedom to organize
May take advantage of reputation	Not bound by old firm's policies and practices

The Mortality of Small Businesses

In every kind of business there is an element of risk, but as a class, small business is apparently subject to more failures than large concerns. From 1959 to 1967, nine out of 10 concerns failing had liabilities of less than \$100,000, with six out of these nine firms having liabilities of less than \$25,000. Although not all business withdrawals are caused by failures (some

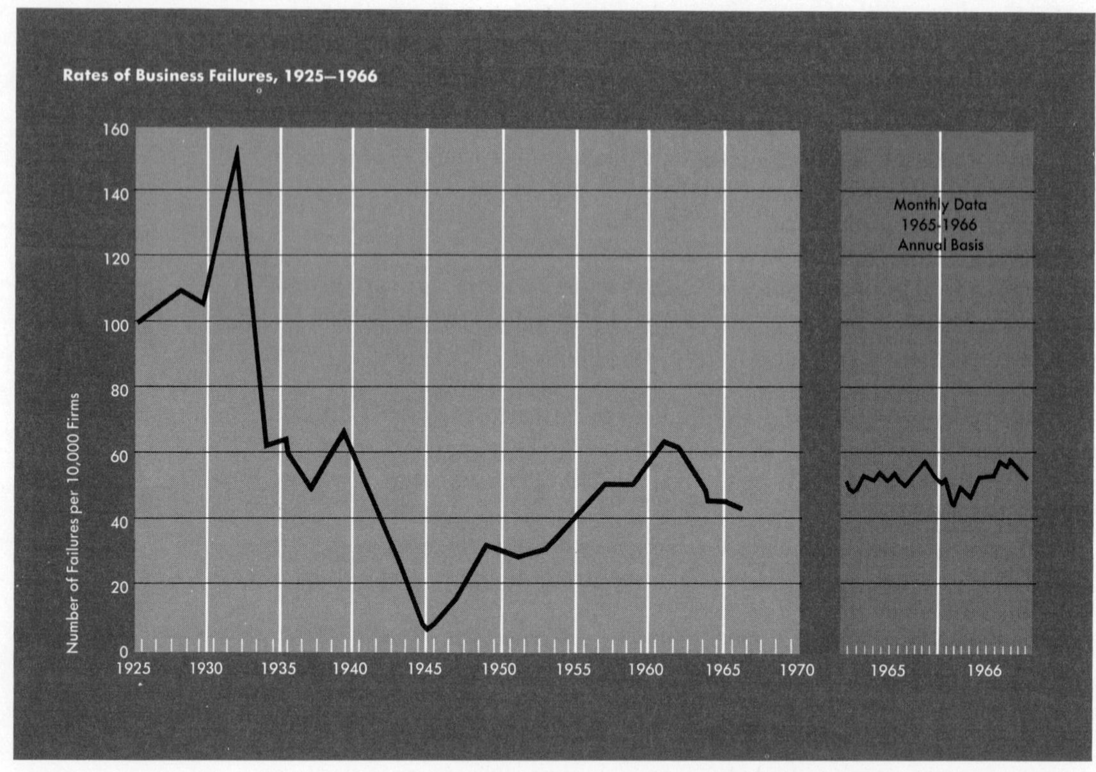

Source: Small Business Administration, 1966 Annual Report, 1966.

concerns are abandoned because of the ill health or death of the owner), most of them are, and we shall discuss the reasons for these shortly.

The Number of Business Failures. As shown by the accompanying chart prepared by the Small Business Administration, failure rates increased almost annually from 1925 to 1932. After an extremely low rate of failure during World War II, the rate again rose gradually but leveled off in 1949 and 1950. Although it has risen again through 1961, the rate of failure since is still well below the peak in 1932.

Another view of business failures, covering several classes of business, is shown in Table 5.1. This table also reflects an increase in failures for five fields from 1955 through 1966. According to these data, business mortality is highest among retail concerns, and lowest for commercial service-type enterprises.

As a rule—and as the accompanying pie graph shows—the majority of small firms that fail do so during their first five years. In 1966 the figure for

TABLE 5.1

TOTAL ANNUAL U.S. BUSINESS FAILURES BY FIELDS FOR SELECTED YEARS

Business Fields	1966	1965	1964	1960	1955
Commercial Service	1,368	1,299	1,226	1,367	860
Construction	2,510	2,513	2,388	2,607	1,404
Mining and Manufacturing	1,852	2,097	2,465	2,612	2,202
Retail Trade	6,076	6,250	6,873	7,386	5,339
Wholesale Trade	1,255	1,355	1,392	1,473	1,164
Total	13,061	13,514	13,501	15,445	10,969

Sources: Dun & Bradstreet, Inc., *The Failure Record through 1961,* p. 9; "Business Failures," *Dun's Review and Modern Industry,* Vol. 87 (February, 1966), p. 11; *op. cit.,* Vol. 89 (February, 1967), p. 15.

under-age-five failures was 56 percent. This would seem to indicate that if a small firm can survive its first five years, it has a better-than-average chance of continuing until at least its tenth anniversary party is over.

Although business failures are no more an indication that all businesses are failing than divorce rates indicate that all marriages will end up in the divorce courts, there are some fields that carry more risk than others. In retailing, for example, as shown by the following statistics, the rate of failure per 10,000 concerns was highest in infants' and children's wear stores, second highest for sporting goods stores, and lowest for grocery, meat, and produce markets.[4]

[4] *The Failure Record through 1963* (New York: Dun & Bradstreet, Inc., undated pamphlet), p. 6.

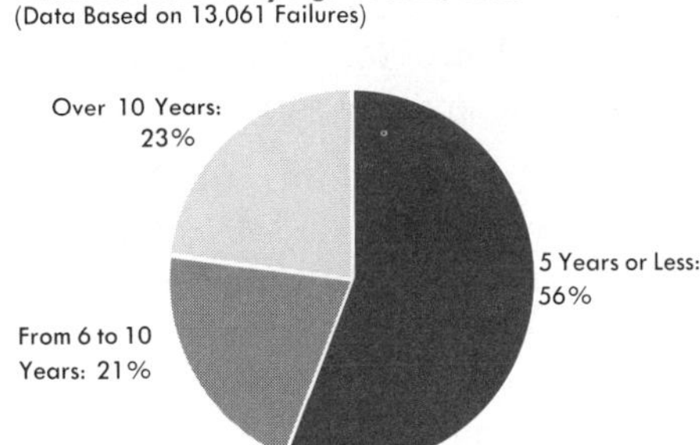

Sources: Dept. of Commerce; Dun & Bradstreet, Inc.

Line of Retailing	Failure Rate Per 10,000 Concerns
Infants' and Children's wear	120
Sporting Goods	108
Men's wear	76
Shoes	57
Drugs	37
Automobiles	31
Groceries, Meats, and Produce	21

In manufacturing industries, furniture makers rank highest in failures, followed by transportation equipment and electrical machinery manufacturers. In this category of business, stone, clay, and glass manufacturers are lowest in rate of failures per 10,000.

Many failures ultimately involve court proceedings, which frequently end in a loss to creditors. When a firm owes more debts than it can pay, and there is little or no possibility that the firm can obtain sufficient funds from the sale of its assets to cover these debts, it is considered *insolvent.* The owner can then seek legal relief from paying his debts by petitioning the court to be declared brankrupt. The term *bankrupt* implies that one is unable to pay his just debts, and therefore has been adjudged a bankrupt under federal bankruptcy laws. (The topic of bankruptcy was discussed in Chapter 3, as you no doubt recall.)

Causes of Business Failure

The decision to start one's own business should be made only in the light of a thorough understanding of the risks involved and of the reasons why so many businesses fail. We have already observed that business mortality is heaviest among concerns in business five years or less. We also know from available statistics that a business that has operated for over 10 years has a slightly higher failure percentage than one that has been going from six to 10 years. Considering the number of forces that can conspire to cause a business to fail, it is a wonder that so many survive at all.

Mismanagement as a Cause of Failure. Aside from the relatively few failures caused by fraud, poor health, disaster, and marital difficulties, the most important single reason for business failure is lack of managerial skills. This conclusion is supported by constant studies conducted by Dun & Bradstreet. The following data have been extracted from a report which appeared in one of their business publications.[5]

[5] "Business Failures," *Dun's Review and Modern Industry,* Vol. 90, No. 3 (September, 1967), p. 13.

CAUSES OF U.S. BUSINESS FAILURES IN 1967

Neglect		3.8%
Fraud		1.6
Inexperience, incompetence		92.9
Inadequate sales	40.5%	
Heavy operating expenses	13.2	
Accounts receivable difficulties	10.2	
Inventory difficulties	6.0	
Excessive filed assets	4.5	
Poor location	3.3	
Competitive weakness	23.4	
Other	4.1	
Disaster		1.1
Reason unknown		1.4
Total number of failures	13,555	

Note: Classification in this report is based on opinions shown on credit reports and other information. Since some failures are attributed to a combination of causes, percentages do not equal 100 percent (see inset column).

SOME PROBLEMS OF OWNING AND OPERATING YOUR OWN BUSINESS

Starting a business of your own is both challenging and risky. However, neither challenge nor risk has ever held back a really ambitious person, because the ambitious invariably believe that challenges are there to be met, that nothing is certain except death and taxes anyway, and that the only thing anyone can know for sure about the future is that it will be different from the present. Whatever your attitude toward risk and challenge, should you ever decide that you want to own your own business, you should satisfactorily be able to answer the following questions before you commit yourself:

1. Have I selected the right kind of business? Am I qualified to operate it?
2. Is the business I have chosen already crowded? Is competition unusually strong?
3. Do I have sufficient capital to start and to carry me through any unforeseen difficulties?
4. Have I selected the best possible location?
5. Have I made the right choice of legal form of ownership?
6. Would it be better for me to buy an established business instead of starting a new one?

Why Go into Business for Yourself?

One of the first decisions you must make is to determine whether by temperament, ability, and education you are suited to own your own business. This is the time when snap judgments should be avoided and an honest appraisal made. One who is inclined to worry about responsibilities, or who has difficulty in making decisions, is not likely to be happy as a proprietor. Furthermore, anyone who is not willing to work long hours and make the necessary personal sacrifices during the early years of a new business should beware starting one.

Some persons want to own their own business because they are convinced that they will be more successful working for themselves than for someone else. Owning your own business does permit more freedom than employees ordinarily have.

Another important satisfaction is that the harder you work in your own business, the more profits you are likely to receive. But again, you should be realistic, for the percentage of profit in most small business is low, and competition is keen. Some owners frankly admit that they could make more money if they worked a little harder, but they do not regard the extra money as being worth the effort.

Choosing the Right Business

This is often the most difficult decision to make when you are thinking about starting your own business, for the fact is that you cannot be sure whether you have made the right choice until you have actually had some experience in the business you have chosen. At the very least, however, you should have some liking for the kind of activity at which you will be spending your time. And the qualifications required by the business should be in line with your own qualifications and your likes and dislikes.

Probably the best procedure at the outset is to prepare a list of different kinds of businesses. Then select several from the list and make a careful examination of the important factors involved in each. Regardless of how extensive your analysis is, you must ultimately come to some specific conclusions concerning such factors as the amount of capital the business will require, the amount of risk involved, the kind of personal qualifications needed, how well your own qualifications meet these requirements, and finally your own ability to manage. A natural tendency of some persons who want to go into business for themselves is to be overly optimistic about their own ability and the opportunities the venture offers them.

Determining Your Capital Needs

Records show that most small firms start with inadequate capital. In fact, you will recall that earlier in this chapter we mentioned that lack of sufficient capital is a prime cause of business failure.

Speaking very broadly, *capital* means purchasing power. It includes not only the funds invested by the owner but also funds made available by creditors. Thus, for a business requiring initial capital of $12,000, the owner may have $7,000 of his own, plus a bank loan of $3,000 and credit amounting to $2,000 from one or more wholesalers or manufacturers.

Capital invested in machinery, buildings, land, and fixtures is classified as *fixed capital. Working capital* represents funds invested in such items as supplies, materials, rent, and wages. Good planning requires that the owner be able to distinguish between these kinds of capital in estimating capital needs. It is also important that the small businessman realize that a reasonable period, usually a minimum of six months, normally will be required before his income will be sufficient to cover his expenses. Thus he must include in his estimated needs a minimum salary to provide for his living during this period.

Capital requirements for one kind of business may easily differ from those for another. For example, according to Dun & Bradstreet estimates, the minimum capital needed to start a beauty shop ranges from $2,000 to $3,000. For a small retail furniture store the range is from $15,000 to $18,000; for a drugstore from $15,000 to $25,000. A retail store's largest single investment is probably in merchandise. Service-type firms, such as radio and television repair shops, do not need large stock inventories because they are primarily engaged in selling repair service, although many do carry a small stock of saleable goods. It is also true that firms selling on credit need more initial capital than noncredit businesses.

Sources of Capital

Students and young businessmen often ask what are the chief sources of capital available to those desiring to go into business for themselves. Before identifying these sources, it seems appropriate to point out that business capital is of two types: *equity* and *borrowed.*[6] *Equity capital* is money invested in the business which no one is legally obligated to return or pay interest on. In other words, there is no stated time within which it must be returned to the investor. If the owner wishes to retrieve his investment, he must either sell his stock or wait until the firm has been liquidated. *Borrowed capital* is money acquired through a loan on which the borrower is expected to return the principal together with interest at some specified date.

Major Sources of Funds. Generally speaking, the most common sources of capital for small business (you may think of several others) are as follows:

[6] Equity and borrowed capital are discussed more fully in Chapters 16 and 17.

Sources of Small Business Capital

Personal savings	Credit from wholesalers
Friends and relatives	Money from partners
Sale of stock	Retained earnings
Commercial loans	Small Business Administration

Small firms just starting often differ somewhat from existing small firms in the sources of capital they are likely to tap. For the new firm, the most common source is personal savings; usually at least half must come from this source because more often than not it is often impossible to obtain funds from any other. Credit (for the most part short-term, to be sure) from suppliers and wholesalers and from banks is also a significant source of capital for new firms.

Sources of capital for an *expanding* business range from retained earnings and sale of capital stock, to government agencies. In 1958, Congress passed the Small Business Investment Company Act, providing for the establishment of privately-owned capital banks as a source of long-term loans and equity capital to small business. These companies are licensed and regulated by the Small Business Administration.

Selecting the Proper Location

It is absolutely vital to some businesses to be properly located; to other businesses location matters little. To illustrate, the site chosen for a drugstore can make or break it. In contrast, the location of a plumbing shop or of a building contractor's headquarters is of relatively minor importance. Some firms obviously need to be where customers can easily reach them. For example, retail outlets that depend on drop-in customers usually do best on streets where pedestrain traffic is heavy. A location that offers adequate automobile parking is a definite advantage.

It is also important to know what other kinds of businesses surround you. Do other stores in the block attract the kind of trade you want? For instance, if you are starting a men's shoe store, you probably would not locate in a block that contained only a beauty shop, a women's apparel store, and a gasoline station, because these stores would not necessarily attract the kind of patronage to make your store a success. Men's shoe stores tend to do better in larger shopping centers, where there is a variety of retail establishments that men patronize, such as restaurants, barber shops, and hardware and clothing stores.

In other cases, firms that make most of their sales by mail, or that sell their goods through traveling salesmen, are less concerned with location than those that must be close to transportation facilities for the convenience of employees and customers. Banks require a downtown or shopping-district location. Doctors prefer a location near a hospital or medical clinic. Small wholesalers try to locate near the center of the trading area they will serve, yet remain accessible to highways and railroads.

Choosing the Form of Ownership

In Chapter 4 we discovered several different forms of business ownership developed to meet the needs of all kinds of business enterprises, both large and small. The problem: select the best adapted to the situation.

The simplicity of the sole proprietorship makes this form well adapted to small enterprises, but under certain conditions the partnership and corporate organizations are also satisfactory forms of operation for small-scale ventures. You will have to decide as early as you can which form to use. Here are some helpful questions to ask yourself:

How large is my business going to be? Your answer should help you determine how much working capital you will need. Should you take in a partner to obtain the required initial capital? If you need more than one partner, would it be better to form a corporation?

How much business risk am I as the owner willing to assume in starting the venture? You know from the preceding chapter that the sole proprietorship and partnership forms of ownership involve unlimited liability. This is the reason so many small businesses incorporate.

What about my tax position? The sole proprietorship and partnership offer you a favorable tax position. They avoid the double tax of business profits involved in the corporation income tax and the stockholders' tax levied on dividends. The proprietorship and partnership pay no annual franchise tax, nor any stock transfer taxes. The proprietor and the partners pay a personal income tax on taxable income, including net business profits, at individual tax rates, which generally are lower than for corporations.

These are some of the considerations that you need to take into account in choosing the proper form of ownership. In the final analysis, the form you select should be the one that provides you with the most advantages.

Factors in Business Success

To be successful, the modern independent enterpriser must have more than just a desire to work for himself. He must be proficient in business procedures and management practices, for as an owner, he is faced with a multitude of problems, many of which were unknown a generation or two ago. For example, he needs a working knowledge of government restrictions. And, if the business grows, there are ever more tax problems and labor laws to confront him. Not the least important, he must constantly adjust to the moves of the competition, lest he be left to rust, as it were, in their dust.

Evidence of Business Opportunity. An important prerequisite for the small-business owner's success is evidence that his business will provide needed goods and services. This means that he must investigate the existence of a real (not merely an apparent) business opportunity; he must analyze how much of a market exists and at what prices his goods or services can be sold, and determine the possible extent of market expansion. It is important to know the elasticity of the demand, and at what price sales will continue to be profitable. Only when the results of his investigation show the outlook to be favorable can he be assured of the existence of a real business opportunity.

Managerial Ability. A second prerequisite for the successful operation of a small business is the owner's managerial ability. This includes his skill in handling employees and in creating favorable public relations and satisfactory employee relations. In large concerns, it is the professional manager rather than the owner who carries this management responsibility, but in small firms the owner or manager makes all the business decisions.

Managerial ability requires both a background of satisfactory business experience, preferably in a management capacity, and formal training in business administration. From experience the owner learns how to control expenses, and ways to solve personnel problems. And with training he acquires knowledge of tax angles, labor law, insurance needs, and accounting procedures.

Modern Business Methods. A third prerequisite for success in small business, closely related to managerial ability, is the use of modern business methods, including the use of research to solve problems. Many small-business owners feel that the use of research is precluded by the high cost. Actually, the reverse is often true. Failure to use research or to take advantage of modern business practices may cost the owner more in the long run than if he used a more scientific approach to solve his business problems. The small-business owner can keep abreast of modern developments by using information available to him from such sources as private research organizations, trade associations, trade literature, and governmental agencies.

Ratio Analysis. Every small business should make use of certain financial management tools which help determine precisely what the firm's working capital should be, how funds are being used, and what profits are being realized from them. One of these tools is *ratio analysis.* A *ratio* is a mathematical measure expressing a relationship between two items. It may be expressed as a percentage. For example, a baseball player who hits safely one out of three trips to the plate has a batting ratio of 1 to 3. Expressed as a percentage it is .333. By the use of a ratio it is possible to evaluate certain facts about a firm's financial resources.

Actually, it is possible to compute at least a dozen useful ratios from a financial statement. Each tells something different about the firm's financial condition. Richard Sanzo, a well-known financial analyst of small business, has suggested a number of ratios as having great usefulness for analyzing the financial needs of small firms: current assets to current liabilities, current liabilities to tangible net worth, net profits to tangible net worth, net sales to inventory, total debt to tangible net worth, and stock turnover ratio.[7] In this chapter we shall discuss only the *stock turnover ratio.* Several others are discussed in Chapter 8, which deals with accounting.

Stock Turnover Ratio. The number of times a firm sells its complete stock inventory during a given period is its *stock turnover ratio.* Assume that you own a small retail clothing store whose stock cost $5,000. If you sell this entire stock in three months and replace it with a second order of $5,000 worth, and subsequently repeat this operation enough times to sell your complete stock four times during a given year, your stock turnover ratio is 4. (Since a store rarely sells all its stock in a given period, computing the turnover rate is more complicated than this illustration would make it appear.)

One method of computing your stock turnover ratio is to divide the cost of goods sold by the average of the opening and closing inventories. Assuming the cost of goods sold is $40,000 and the average of your initial and ending inventories is $5,000, the turnover ratio would be calculated as follows:

$$\frac{\text{Cost of goods sold}}{\text{Merchandise inventory average}} = \frac{\$40{,}000}{\$\ 5{,}000} = 8$$

Your stock turnover ratio in the above example is 8. This means you have sold your complete stock eight times during the year. A high stock turnover commonly indicates that a satisfactory volume of sales is being maintained. A more rapid turnover might change a losing concern into one with average or better-than-average profits. It may also indicate that you have not overbought and that you have an effective inventory control and an accurate sales record. These would be reasonable assumptions in most cases.

To compute stock turnover it is necessary to keep all figures at either cost or selling-price levels. If the average inventory is computed at cost, you must divide that average into the cost of goods sold, rather than into net sales. But if net sales are used, then you should figure the average inventory at the selling price.

[7] Richard Sanzo, *Ratio Analysis for Small Business* (Washington, D.C.: Small Business Administration, 1957), p. 6. This booklet contains a comprehensive survey and discussion of ratio analysis.

Stock turnover ratios vary according to the kind of goods. The ratio is much lower for slow-moving goods, such as pianos, furniture, and farm equipment. It is high for such merchandise as groceries, meats, gasoline service stations, and women's specialty shops. According to Dun & Bradstreet, the average ratio of stock turnover for an independent grocery and meat market was 19.9 per year, but only 3.6 for a retail hardware store. For furniture stores with 50 percent or more installment sales, the ratio was 4.5.

What is the significance of ratios for small business? When the stock turnover ratio is high it means that capital is used more efficiently and that smaller fixed charges are incurred, markdowns are fewer, the cost of handling the goods is reduced, storage-space needs are reduced, and stocks are likely to be kept fresher. When merchants keep their stock turning, they are able to take advantage of special offers and be ready to buy new merchandise. Finally, all other factors being equal, net profit is increased, and less capital is needed.

How to Increase Stock Turnover. By taking the following actions, it is possible to increase stock turnover: (1) price merchandise so that it will sell rapidly and with a minimum markdown; (2) study the market and buy goods that are salable; (3) avoid replacing slow-moving merchandise that is carried for prestige; (4) avoid carrying too many brands of the same goods; (5) maintain appealing advertising displays (for larger businesses that can afford it, media advertising is an even more effective sales aid); and (6) maintain an efficient sales staff.

Franchising and Small Business

One way to go into business for yourself is by obtaining a *franchise*. This term is broadly defined as an exclusive arrangement, usually between a manufacturer and a private distributor, allowing the latter the right to sell an established product or service in a specified geographical area. The parties to a franchise agreement are the *franchisee* and the *franchiser*. The company (manufacturer or operating company) with whom you make the agreement to sell their product or service is the *franchiser*, sometimes called *licenser*. The franchisee is the independent businessman (partnership or a corporation) who agrees to establish the outlet.

With such high national prosperity, franchising is increasing in popularity. For many years the Walgreen and Rexall drug companies granted franchises to independent druggists, mostly in smaller communities. Many of the Howard Johnson restaurants are franchise owned. Other popular franchise operations are car-washing stations, motels, dance studios, slenderizing salons, ice-cream stores, food drive-in establishments, coin-operated laundries, and business accounting services. In some instances only $1,000 capital is needed to start to operate a franchise, but many require as much as

$10,000 starting capital. A few eat up as much as $50,000 just to get them going, but these are firms requiring more expensive buildings and grounds. Of course, not all franchises work out satisfactorily—sometimes even the most promising. One must be aware that the glitter of some well-nigh irresistible propositions intimating pie-in-the-sky profits the first year is in reality the glitter of fool's gold.

Benefits Derived by the Franchisee. The franchiser generally agrees to provide some or all of the following benefits. (1) His firm will help you find a suitable location, which may require some research. (2) He will help you design the structure, and aid you in setting up your inventory control and accounting procedures. (3) He will help plan your advertising and promotion, and give you long-term financing to buy equipment. (4) Some franchisers give the franchisee special training in the operation of the business. More often than not, if the franchiser's directions are followed, the business has good possibilities of succeeding: franchising is uniquely suited to small firms.

One of the fastest-growing franchise businesses is the Memphis-based Holiday Inns of America. Its approximately 800 inns with over 100,000 rooms top Hilton Hotels, Hilton International, and the Sheraton Hotel chain combined. Currently there are more than 660 franchised inns, and over 125 owned by the company. A franchise costs about $10,000, or $100 a room, depending upon the size of the inn. In addition to the initial cost, franchisees pay either 15¢ a day per room, or 3 percent of gross rooms revenue, plus 8¢ a day for national advertising, and $2.50 a room a month for use of the computerized reservation system. Additional capital, beyond that invested by the franchisee himself, to cover the total cost of building construction, is borrowed by the franchisee from the franchiser, at prevailing interest rates.

One service provided by the franchiser is the computerized room reservations system involving 85,000 leased telephone miles. Another is the opportunity for each prospective innkeeper to go to a five-to-seven-week training school in order to prepare to manage the inn. Four times a year the franchiser sends a representative to inspect each inn.

THE SMALL BUSINESS ADMINISTRATION

As an instrument of the federal government, the SBA is the first peacetime agency created on a permanent basis to help owners of small businesses. The general aims of the SBA are as follows:

1. To help small-business owners gain access to capital and credit
2. To help small business obtain a fair share of government contracts

3. To enable small business to receive managerial, production, and technical counsel
4. To make disaster loans to persons whose homes or businesses have been damaged or destroyed by floods, storms, and other disasters; and aid small concerns that have suffered economic loss caused by draught or excessive rainfall in their areas

Financial Assistance

While most SBA loans are small—some are of less than $1,000—it is possible to borrow up to $350,000. These loans may be for as long as 10 years. The maximum interest rate is 5.5 percent. A bank may set a higher rate on its share of a participation loan and on SBA's share of a guaranteed loan until the agency actually provides its share.

The SBA Small Loan Plan. The SBA offers a small loan plan tailored to the needs of small retail, service, and other firms. Under this plan, the agency will lend up to $15,000 for as long as six years. Good character of an applicant and his past record for meeting debts are the two main requirements for a loan. As security, SBA will accept whatever worthwhile collateral is available. The SBA also helps finance small firms through the medium of small-business investment companies (SBIC's). These are privately owned but SBA-licensed companies which furnish small firms long-term financing and equity capital so that they can develop and promote new products, or expand or modernize the business. The SBA has licensed more than 700 SBIC's. A list of these companies is available from SBA field offices in most of the nation's major cities.

Management and Technical Publications

The SBA distributes a wide range of management and technical publications to established or prospective owners of small businesses. These publications include several series available without charge from SBA offices and several obtainable from the Superintendent of Documents, Washington, D.C.

Free Series of Publications. These include five types of leaflets:

1. *Management Aids for Small Manufacturers:* typical subject, "Getting Facts for Better Sales Decisions."
2. *Technical Aids for Small Manufacturers:* typical subject, "Designing for Higher Profits."
3. *Small Business Bibliographies:* typical subject, "Furniture Retailing."
4. *Management Research Summaries:* typical subject, "Accounting Practices in Small Firms."

5. *Small Marketers Aids:* typical subject, "Remodeling for Better Retailing."

The College Graduate and Small Business

What opportunities does small business offer to young men and women with a college education? You have already seen how significant a role small business plays in our nation. Small business is "typically American." And with the growing number of new enterprises started annually, it has become one of the main sources of employment for college-trained men and women.

Small business provides an opportunity for persons to go into business for themselves on a small scale, in keeping with the amount of capital they have available. It offers ambitious young men and women the satisfaction of being their own employers, subject only to their individual limitations. The harder the owner of a small firm works, the greater are his benefits. If you like to pioneer, small business is a natural for you. If you like to carry through to a successful completion even if it means working overtime, perhaps you should be in business for yourself.

Small Business and the Future

There are 5 million small firms in this country, and new enterprises are being launched at the rate of about 15,000 a year. At the same time, only about 13,500 small firms are closing their doors each year. These figures indicate that the number of opportunities in small business will stay on the increase for young college graduates.

The long-time trend in American business has been favorable to small business, especially in terms of the number of new firms and growing opportunities. As each new industry develops, although it may be dominated by a few large corporations, new opportunities are created for small establishments, resulting in many new establishments. The point of emphasis is that the study of small business is justifiably a subject of importance for business students. Like big business, small business is subject to economic fluctuations, but in spite of the ups and downs, it has stood the test and is stronger now than ever before. If carefully planned and properly financed, a new small business can be reasonably sure of continuation, provided modern management methods are applied.

SUMMARY

The widespread notion that owning your own business is an easy and profitable way to earn a living has prompted many young persons to start one for themselves. But no matter what their inspiration may be, far too many persons plunge into business on their own without first making a careful review and analysis of all the prevailing conditions. Consequently, the rate of failure is higher in small business than it is in "big" business. Some of the more common reasons for failure are: lack of managerial experience by the owner, personal neglect of the business, poor location, and inadequate capital.

The characteristics of the small firm differ from those of large concerns. Management of a small establishment is more independent. Most small firms serve primarily a local or limited market, leaving national markets to be supplied by large corporations. Capital requirements are much less for small organizations than for large ones. Then, too, the small firm seldom sells stock to raise funds; instead, the capital comes from friends, relatives, the owner's personal savings, or banks or other kinds of loan agencies.

By far the majority of small firms are single proprietorships or partnerships. Only a few start as corporations, which are more difficult and costly to organize.

Large firms generally have complex organizational structures, whereas the small ones depend on simple organization. The recent trend toward the application of modern research methods in order to find better ways to apply more efficient business methods is increasing. There is also more emphasis being placed on labor-saving devices as a means of reducing operating costs.

Finally, there is an increased interest on the part of the federal government to make small businesses more substantial enterprises.

VOCABULARY REVIEW QUIZ

Match the following vocabulary terms with the statements below.

a. Bankrupt
b. Borrowed capital
c. Fixed capital
d. Franchise
e. Franchisee
f. Franchiser
g. Insolvent
h. Personal savings
i. Ratio
j. Small business
k. Stock turnover ratio
l. Working capital

1. The state of a person or business that is unable to pay its debts due to lack of means
2. A business or person adjudged by a court to be without sufficient funds to pay its (or his) creditors
3. Funds supplied the business to pay for materials, supplies, rent, wages, and other expenses

4. Funds invested by an owner in business to buy assets including buildings, land, and machines
5. Funds obtained by a loan that requires repayment of principal at a specified date
6. The exclusive right to sell an established product or service in a specified geographical area
7. A businessman operating under an exclusive agreement to sell a product or service in a given territory
8. The firm that grants you the exclusive right to sell its product or service
9. A source of capital common to small business enterprises
10. The number of times a business sells its complete stock during a given period
11. A mathematical measure expressing a relationship between two items
12. A business independently owned, operated on a limited scale, and locally operated

QUESTIONS FOR REVIEW STUDY

1. Compare the definition of small business advocated by the Committee for Economic Development with the definition used by the Small Business Administration.
2. What are the characteristics that distinguish small business from big business?
3. Why is small business considered to be such an important segment of the economy?
4. If you had to make a choice whether to go into business for yourself or to work in a large corporation, what factors would you consider important in making this decision?
5. Explain the advantages of buying an established firm with those of starting a new one.
6. What are some of the causes of business failures?
7. What is meant by the statement, "It is possible that firms just starting may differ somewhat from existing small firms in the sources of capital which they are likely to use"?
8. What effect, if any, does the "stock turnover ratio" have on the capital needs of a business?
9. Explain at least five ways to increase stock turnover. Why are these important to the owner of a small business?
10. Explain a franchise and describe what the franchiser generally has agreed to do.

PROBLEMS AND PROJECTS

1. Using data obtained from the SBA or from your college library, prepare a 300-word report on the subject of the Small Business Investment Company Act as a source of capital for small business enterprises.

2. Prepare an outline in detail of how you would study a particular type of business to determine if it is one you would like to start. Refer to your local community library and to your college library as sources of information.

3. Ever since Robert Jay graduated from high school five years ago he has worked in a local furniture store. During this time he has saved $1,900. Recently he inherited $15,000 from his grandfather. Now he is considering going into business for himself, and has asked you for some advice. Prepare a list of things you think Jay should do that will help him decide whether to buy an established firm or start from the beginning. Also, since Jay thinks he would like to own an automobile parts store, state some sources of information about such stores.

A BUSINESS CASE

Case 5-1 The Casey Hardware Store Has a Credit Problem

Robert Casey, a retired high-school chemistry teacher, and his wife operate a neighborhood hardware store near the university campus in Lincoln, Neb. His closest competitor is about two miles distant. During the three years he has owned the store, Casey has built up a good volume of trade. Most of his customers live nearby, including a few university students, and some military personnel assigned to the Air Force base about six miles away.

About 14 months ago, Casey decided to sell on credit, hoping that this would increase his volume. He consulted the manager of the local retail credit association, who advised him to put a limit of $50 on credit sales at any one time. The manager also urged him to join the association, but Casey decided it was too expensive.

Robert Casey describes his credit policy as follows:

> We grant credit up to $50 during any given month. We take references from customers and when a person opens up an account, we call these references only if we cannot get satisfactory information from the customer's employer.
>
> When military personnel ask for credit, we call the Commanding Officer for enlisted personnel but we do not inquire about officers because we have always heard that officers are gentlemen, and, this being the case, they should be honest and pay their debts.
>
> On the matter of students, we give credit up to $10 at one time. We get the student's full name and make him show his student identification card. We call the Dean of Men for male students and the Dean of Women for women students.

Approximately nine weeks ago, a certain Col. Henry House came into the store and purchased on credit a $79 electric-power lawnmower. He was in uniform when he opened the account, and he showed his officer's identification card. At the time of the purchase, he agreed to pay $25 down, with the balance to be paid in three monthly installments due on the tenth day of each month. He was aware of the $2 monthly carrying charge when he signed a conditional sales contract. After putting the lawnmower into his customer's car, Casey observed that the Colonel had a Colorado automobile license.

A second payment was due in 30 days, and so Casey mailed a statement to Col. House. The envelope carried the store's return address and, since it did not come back, Casey was certain the statement was received. A third payment was due the next month, and when that became overdue, Casey telephoned three times in an effort to talk with the Colonel, each time being told that the Colonel was not at home. On the last occasion, Casey left a message reminding Col. House that he was two months delinquent, and asking him to call the store. Casey waited another week, without any contact from Col. House.

An in-person visit to the Colonel's residence found him in the yard using a hedge trimmer. It was obvious that he had just cut his lawn. Casey politely asked for the two payments. The Colonel became angry and began to use abusive language, stating that the mower was no good, that it never had worked properly, and that $25 was all it was worth. He told Casey that he was not going to pay any more. At this point, Casey reminded him that the article was sold under a conditional sales contract. Colonel House replied, "That may be true, but you just try and take this mower off my premises and I'll call the police and have you arrested for trespassing."

Casey then left without his payments and the mower.

1. What are Casey's problems in this case?
2. What is your opinion of Casey's credit policy?
3. What action should Casey take about the debt owed by Col. House on the lawnmower? Comment fully.

Management and Executive Leadership

6

In the preceding chapter we explored the place of the small business enterprise in our economy, and noted its characteristics. We also observed the causes for business failures, and compared the advantages and disadvantages of owning a small business with those of being an employee. From these analyses, there emerges the need to recognize that, regardless of the size of the firm, the main decisions concerning it are made either by its owner or by a group of persons who are referred to as its "management." So, at this point, we focus our attention on the subject of business management and executive leadership.

It is the managers of a business who are responsible for seeing that the public receives the firm's goods and/or services at the proper time, in the correct amount, and at a price it is able and willing to pay. In carrying out these responsibilities, management performs certain activities commonly referred to as "functions." This chapter concentrates on the functions of management, the areas of managerial authority, qualities of executive leadership, and career opportunities in the field of management.

MANAGEMENT: WHAT IT IS AND WHAT IT DOES

Over the years the term "management" has acquired several different meanings. Some writers describe it rather than define it. Some restrict its use to specific activities within the firm, such as the work of the personnel manager, the office manager, or the marketing management. Others define it by noting what management does—the management functions. The economic literature of the eighteenth and nineteenth centuries made little use of the word; writers more often used such terms as "proprietor," "entrepreneur," or "capitalist" to identify a person or persons engaged in commerce, trade, or manufacturing. Let us note several definitions taken at random, and see what they have in common.

Louis A. Allen, a management consultant, defines *management* as "a body of systematized knowledge, based on general principles which are verifiable in terms of business practice."[1] Claude S. George, Jr., defines management as "The function that deals with getting things done through others."[2] A more recent definition by Professors Koontz and O'Donnell states, "Management is defined here as the accomplishment of desired objectives, by establishing an environment favorable to performance by people operating in organized groups."[3]

Some writers see management as a function or a process. Others look upon it as a body of knowledge based on certain general principles. It is worthy of note that, despite the diversity of opinions expressed in the above quotations, the majority of the writers strongly imply that management involves activities designed to accomplish a purpose. As far as the business world is concerned, these activities are involved in achieving a profit.

For the purpose of this discussion, we are defining management as *the task of planning, organizing and staffing, and controlling the work of others in order to achieve one or more objectives.* This definition implies that management is a process of actions that involve several distinct functions which managers perform. This chapter concentrates on the study of these functions.

Management as an Art and as a Science

Management is often referred to as an art because it deals with the application of both knowledge and skill used to achieve an objective. And since it involves the use of certain principles (management techniques), it is

[1] Louis A. Allen, *Management and Organization* (New York: McGraw-Hill Book Co., 1958), p. 5.

[2] Claude S. George Jr., *Management in Industry* (Englewood Cliffs, N.J.: Prentice-Hall, Inc., 1959), p. 6.

[3] Harold Koontz and Cyril O'Donnell, *Principles of Management,* 2nd ed. (New York: McGraw-Hill Book Co., 1964), p. 1.

also called a science. As a *science*, then, management includes the orderly application of pertinent facts to specific management problems. Some examples of the types of problems in which scientific methods may be used include employee testing, production cost analysis, market analysis, and systems of inventory control.

It is also important to note that, as an *art*, management has played a significant role in the programs of modern business. There are many decisions to be made in business concerning which not all the facts are available, and the effectiveness of which often depend on extemporaneous value judgments. The art of management involves the ability of the manager to make these important decisions and to take action *despite* the fact all the factors are not present (and indeed perhaps cannot be obtained). Thus management an an art has become very much a matter of knowing when and to what extent one should exercise his powers of leadership. It goes without saying, perhaps, that though it is much more difficult to practice management as an art than as a science, there is no doubt that management will always be—to the wonderment of those involved in decision-making—a mixture of both an art and a science.

Areas of Managerial Authority

In our study of what management is and does, it is important to understand that managerial authority and responsibility breaks down into two broad areas: *administration* and *execution*. The distinction between these two areas may be clearly seen in the accompanying diagram. The board of directors, company president, and vice-presidents are members of *administration*, or *administrative, general*, or *top management*, as they are sometimes called. These are the officers concerned chiefly with the activities so vital to the success of any business venture—planning, organizing, staffing, and controlling.

Executive management or *execution* is concerned with carrying out specific projects. In this area are departmental executives, such as the sales manager, office manager, and traffic manager, who have the responsibility of carrying out plans established by administration. The principal function of executive management is that of control.

Some companies use the term "executive" to identify top management. They tell their first-line supervisors that they are members of the management team, which is true. Such a distinction, however, is not too logical, simply because management is the function of executive leadership throughout the organization.

Perhaps a fuller understanding of the areas of management authority and execution may be attained by envisioning *levels* of management (though

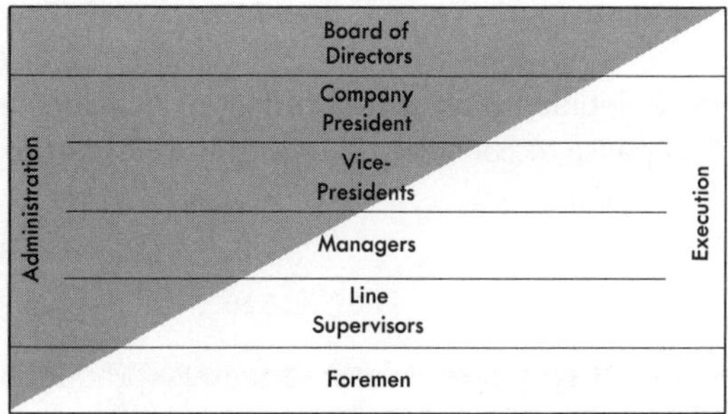

Areas of management authority and execution.

admittedly in some organizations it is difficult to identify more than one level). In large firms there are usually three levels: (1) top management, (2) middle management, and (3) operating management. The following chart illustrates the manager's role for each of these levels of management. The arrows show the flow of communications from one level to another.

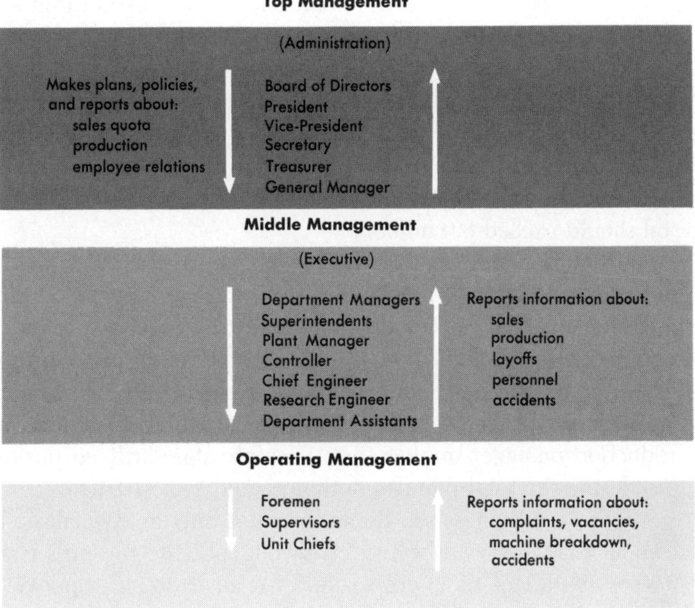

Levels of management authority and execution (Arrows show flow of communications)

THE BACKGROUND OF MODERN MANAGEMENT

Before we take a more detailed look at the subject of management and executive leadership, let us pause to consider their origins as far as the American business scene is concerned.

The Rise of a Managerial Class

The Industrial Revolution greatly accelerated factory production, and at the same time helped to create a managerial class. A further significant factor caused by the Industrial Revolution in many instances was the change from the sole proprietorship to the corporation form of ownership in order to overcome certain limitations imposed by private control of property. Not only did the corporation offer industry a means of raising more capital, but large corporations created a need for substantial increases in the number of hired managers who had no ownership in the business. While the major stockholders could at best hold only a few top positions, the middle and lower ranks of management were filled by professional managers who made up this managerial class. So long as stockholders received a reasonable return on their investment, these professional managers experienced little or no difficulty in obtaining sufficient proxy votes to remain in control. As Peter Drucker has observed, we now talk about the "responsibilities of management" rather than the "responsibilities of capital."[4]

Over the years the manager's responsibilities have grown with the expansion of medium- and large-size businesses. The number of managers in the United States has increased fourfold since 1900. In 1900 there were 1.6 million managers in the total work-force. By 1930 this number had increased to 3.6 million, and 30 years later the total reached 7.0 million. By 1975 the total should exceed 8.0 million.

Although almost every business has managers, or at least a managerial job to be done, there is no standardized managerial position that is common to all businesses. A president of one company may devote much of his time to engineering (a field he knows best); another may spend some of his time in finance or marketing. Some managers concentrate on promoting mergers. The widespread use of such titles as sales manager, general manager, and production manager implies that these are standardized positions, and yet, considering the total picture, nothing could be less true.

Today's managers see themselves not only as specialists, but as generalists, in that they can be moved throughout the business from one job to another as part of their preparation for an eventual top-level position. Indeed, the degree of skill with which management discharges its responsibilities today may well determine the destiny of the American business system.

[4] Peter F. Drucker, *The Practice of Management* (New York: Harper & Bros., 1954), p. 3.

This would seem sufficient reason for placing at least as much stress on the selection and education of managers as on that of others preparing for professional careers.

The Scientific Management Movement

Although people had for hundreds of years talked about how to improve their work, few persons ever really examined human work systematically until Frederick W. Taylor began his studies about 1885. It is quite true that Henri Fayol (a Frenchman who managed a coal mine a few years before Taylor became interested in managers) analyzed the process of management, and is generally credited with giving us the basic management principles upon which Taylor developed his theories of scientific management. However, in the USA, Taylor is generally given credit for being the father of scientific management. The fact that he did most of his work in shops probably accounts for the concentration of scientific management in industrial plants.

Contributions of Taylor. Taylor recognized that labor-saving machinery, job specialization, mass production, and large-scale distribution were all worthless unless those who managed were able to keep pace with technical improvements. He recognized too the need to systematize management and to assign parts of a job to those best placed in the organization to perform them, and the need to analyze the work to be done. Managers, Taylor declared, should concern themselves with such work as setting up and enforcing standards and finding ways to improve methods and promote cooperation. Today, his conclusions seem rather commonplace.

Born in Philadelphia in 1856 of a fairly well-to-do family, Taylor was urged by his parents to study law, but because poor eyesight forced him to give up this objective, he took a job as a laborer with the Midvale Steel Co. In a short time he was promoted to clerk, then to machinist, gang boss, and finally chief engineer. During this same period he became interested in experiments involving work accomplishment, including the "science of shoveling." During the next several years he conducted added experiments involving the analysis of pig-iron handling. Out of this research came recommendations that, used in steel mills, increased productivity from 12½ to 47½ tons per man per day, and raised average daily earnings from $1.15 to $1.85 per man.

After leaving Midvale Steel, Taylor joined the Bethlehem Steel Co., where he spent considerable time testing many of the scientific methods he had written about previously. His philosophy was that by increasing productivity through the application of scientific principles to managerial tasks it would be possible to pay higher wages to workers and higher profits to owners while decreasing the individual employee's workload.

Among the several basic principles of scientific management advocated by Taylor were:[5]

1. All managers must be trained to use scientific principles replacing the rule-of-thumb methods to solve problems.
2. Managers should select and then train and develop workmen rather than let them choose their own work habits.
3. Managers should cooperate with workmen so as to insure that all work would be done in accordance with scientific principles.
4. There must be an almost equal division of work responsibility between management and workmen.

But Taylor was not the only person to contribute to scientific methods in management. Among his associates who also made significant contributions were Frank G. Gilbreth and his wife Dr. Lillian M. Gilbreth, Henry L. Gantt, Harrington Emerson, and Carl Barth. The Gilbreths initiated early studies in the field of motion-and-time analysis through the use of motion pictures. Both Gantt and Barth were associates of Taylor and worked with him on several of his experiments. Gantt's major contribution was the promotion of graphic techniques for analyzing data for managerial control. The Gantt charts, widely used in the United States and Europe, have probably done more than anything else to make him famous. Gantt charts plot activities and time along a horizontal scale. Planned activities can then be compared with the time schedule along a horizontal scale to determine whether the actual performance is according to the schedule. The important point about the Gantt chart is that it presents facts according to time. This system can be designed to plan and control product production activities by single machines, groups of machines, or even whole departments. The chart can also be used for other activities, such as personnel recruitment, purchasing, and transportation.

Unfortunately, in spite of the many contributions which Frederick W. Taylor and his colleagues made to management as a science, they did not develop a systematic body of knowledge. A likely reason is that they lacked an adequate conceptual framework, since various concepts of management had not yet been developed sufficiently to formulate definite management processes.

GENERAL MANAGEMENT FUNCTIONS

Now, to return to our study: We have already mentioned briefly the functions performed by management in its attempts to attain the common

[5] Frederick Winslow Taylor, *The Principles of Scientific Management* (New York: Harper & Bros., 1911), pp. 36–37.

business goals of maximum profits, good customer service, and recognized public responsibility. Although here and there you will find these functions given different names and described in various ways, for the purposes of this discussion, they are (to repeat): *planning, organizing* and *staffing, coordinating,* and *controlling.* Because they are such important functions, we will now consider them in more detail.

Planning

Planning is that function of management concerned with the preparation of future business activities. This general function involves the following activities:

1. Determining company objectives of both short- and long-range duration
2. Formulating business policies, procedures, and programs
3. Preparing methods for exercising financial controls, including the use of budgets and unit control procedures

Planning is one of the most important of the managerial functions. It involves the formulation of what is to be done, who is to do it, where it is to be accomplished, and in what manner the results will be appraised. For example, a firm may decide to double production within the next two years by building two new factories. Top management must first decide where the new plants will be built and how much will be spent. Second, if funds are not available, management must decide how to obtain them. It may even be necessary to evaluate which methods of raising funds will be best. After such decisions have been made, a work schedule must be developed to show when production can begin. Too, there will be time-lags involved in the procurement of materials and labor, and this factor must also be taken into account in the long-range planning.

Planning is equally important in day-by-day activities, such as departmental planning by both middle management and operating personnel. In other words, whether it be for a long or short duration, planning is a continuous function. The chart on page 178 shows how planning is related to business operations.

Organizing and Staffing

The second of the general functions of management is that of organizing and staffing. *Organizing,* which basically involves preparation for putting plans into action, requires the defining and delegating of authority and responsibility, the making up of procedures, and the establishing of relationships for the purpose of enabling people to work most effectively together in

Determining Company Objectives by Operational Planning

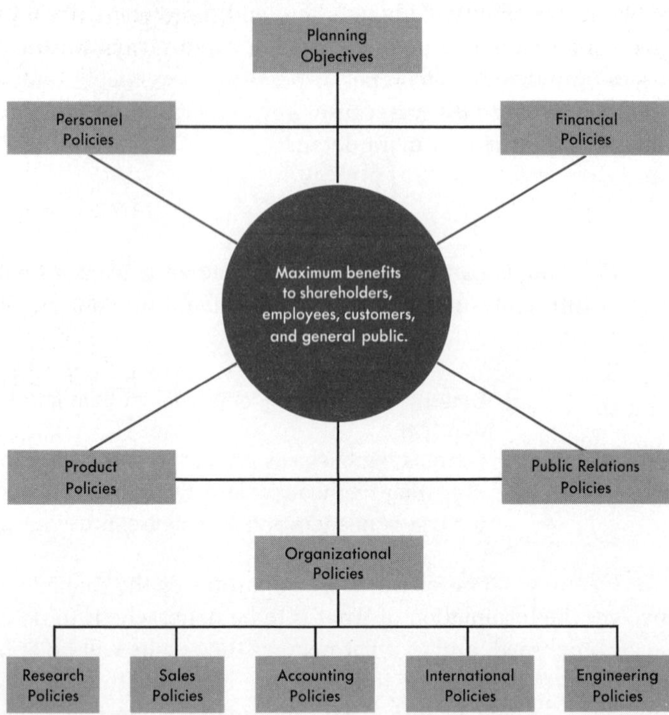

Planning is a management function which, if properly used, affects the entire organization and brings maximum benefits to shareholders, employees, customers, and the public.

accomplishing objectives. More specifically, organizing involves deciding to whom each employee will report, and exactly what work each individual in the enterprise shall perform.

How much organizing is needed by the one-man business? Since in this case the proprietor is the only one who performs managerial tasks, he needs to delegate no authority; the organizing process is not nearly as essential to him as it is to large firms with many managers, subordinate managers, and different departments. But suppose that at a later time he should decide to enlarge his business, requiring additional personnel. At that time he may find it necessary to assign some of his duties to a subordinate or two—and to establish an organizational structure.

Organizing is really a means by which the manager seeks to bring order out of chaos, remove conflicts over work assignments, and create a suitable climate to produce teamwork. Organizing should be regarded not as an end in itself, but as an important tool for accomplishing the firm's objectives.

Staffing, a function which managers at all levels perform, involves the selection, development (training and promotion), and retirement of subordinate managers. When the board of directors hires a president, it undertakes a staffing function; a manufacturing vice-president discharges this function by employing subordinate managers under his direction; and a plant superintendent likewise is engaged in staffing when he selects his foreman. (For a discussion on the techniques of personnel selection and development, see Chapter 11.)

Coordinating

The third general function of management is *coordinating*, which may be defined as *the process of reaching agreement on plans and procedures by interchanging information.* An activity concerned with the integration of all the different factors of the business at all levels, coordination is best accomplished by the coordinator during the early stages of planning and policy-making.

Perhaps an illustration or two will serve to explain more precisely what coordination is. Consider, for example, what might develop if in creating a new product the production department did not first discuss the product with the sales department or those in charge of warehousing and transporting this product. A production man thinks mainly of unit costs and not of other elements such as marketing, advertising, warehousing, or transportation. A foreman must see to it that schedules of production have been coordinated with the department responsible for ordering in advance the necessary materials. Failure to coordinate on the part of either can bring on a host of problems. The company president must also see that coordination takes place at the top level, among his executives who are responsible for finance, production, and distribution.

Group meetings are an effective technique for achieving a high degree of coordination. Such meetings are a planned effort to bring into personal contact those persons especially concerned with a subject under consideration. Typewritten communications, such as letters, bulletins, and memoranda are often used to achieve coordination.

Although methods of achieving coordination are more often largely a matter of using horizontal rather than vertical levels of organization, it is possible to achieve coordination in both directions within the organization. An example of horizontal and vertical coordination is shown by the chart on page 180.

Controlling

The fourth general function of management is controlling. This function is often misunderstood and misapplied because of the lack of a precise

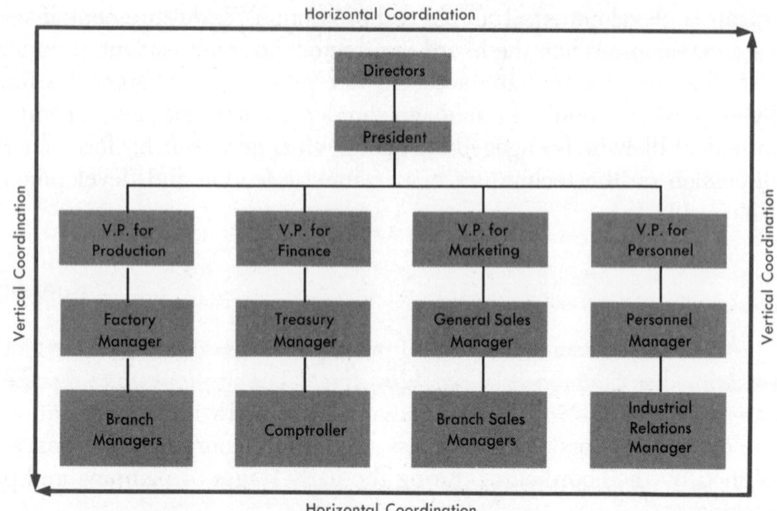

An organization chart showing the concept of horizontal and vertical coordination within five levels of company management.

definition. *Controlling* as used here means *guiding something in the direction in which it is intended to go.* You can see that this is not the same as the giving of orders or commands, which is the meaning sometimes given to this function.

The need for controls springs from the inherent imperfection of things and people. In business, control involves appraisal of results, followed by any remedial action if necessary when results are below par. Generally, five distinct operations are involved in applying the control function:

1. Enacting controls for the purpose of exercising general supervision
2. Setting up controls to accomplish regular or periodic inspection
3. Providing controls to determine if work is being performed according to standards and schedules
4. Using controls to ascertain what corrective action is needed
5. Applying controls to measure the general efficiency of a given unit

Control techniques are essentially the same for office procedures, cash, product quality, product quantity, and unit cost. (When adopting control techniques and systems, one must always assume that authority has been granted to apply such techniques, otherwise it is unreasonable to hold anyone responsible for the outcome.) One widely used, albeit somewhat misunderstood, device for managerial control is the *budget.* It has sometimes been assumed that the budget is the solution to all fiscal problems, when it is in reality only effective to the point to which the budget officer is willing to enforce it. (More about budgets is discussed in Chapter 8.)

To conclude: In this discussion we have identified and discussed four general management functions which are the same for all firms regardless of size. It must be recognized that the general functions of management are performed at all levels of management (top, middle, and operating), but that, naturally, the magnitude and complexity of these functions decreases with descending levels of management.

QUALITIES OF EXECUTIVE LEADERSHIP

Now that you are familiar with the functions of business management and the areas of an organization in which these functions are performed, let us turn to the role of the executive—what he is and does, and what sort of qualities make him an executive.

What Is an "Executive"?

An *executive* is a person who is responsible for the work performed by others under his supervision; he is the medium through which orders flow from administration to workers. Thus he must be ambitious and know how to get along with people.

As a supervisor of his group, the executive translates company policies and also makes decisions. As a decision-maker, he must possess understanding and ability to use three basic skills, which we will call *technical, human,* and *conceptual.* While interrelated, they may be examined separately.

Technical skills are those requiring an understanding of, and proficiency in, a specific kind of activity involving procedures, techniques, and processes. The technical skills of an accountant, engineer, or surgeon are examples of specialized knowledge and ability one must have to be successful in his particular field.

Human skills represent the executive's ability to work effectively with others as part of a group. This involves having a sense of feeling for other persons, and an appreciation of their rights. This skill is demonstrated in the way the individual recognizes his subordinates, equals, and superiors, and in his relations with them in planning and carrying out the purposes of the organization.

Conceptual skills involve the executive's ability to see the whole enterprise, how the various functions of an organization are dependent on one another, and what happens when changes occur in any one part. These skills are useful in decision-making: one must be able to conceive the nature of a problem before deciding how to solve it. One effective method of developing conceptual skills is to expose the individual to hypothetical situations (business cases) requiring sufficient analysis to make a decision. At the college level, in the preparation of prospective executives, the case method is indeed widely used.

How well an executive may succeed on the job depends largely on his ability to apply these three skills—assuming also that he has developed the ability to express himself effectively. The executive should speak with the vocabulary and grammar of the "educated," for if he does not, he is immediately downgraded by his associates.

Managerial Leadership

There are varying degrees of leadership in business. A foreman, for example, is a leader to a lesser degree than a plant manager. The president's job may require more leadership activities than that of the chairman of the board. And line managers have more opportunity to demonstrate leadership than do most staff officers. Whatever its level, however, all management has the responsibility for motivating those under its direction—a task often referred to as the "leadership function." But in business, leadership is more than just taking initiative, and planning and organizing. It is also maintaining a satisfactory relationship with one's followers, who can in many instances either make or break their leader.

The question of whether leaders are born or developed has long been controversial. Some argue that inherited qualities are more important to the achievement of leadership positions than are acquired qualifications. Others contend that it is possible to develop leadership abilities through environmental and educational experiences. There seems to be a common belief that executive skill is a God-given attribute and that some have it in abundance while others seem to have little. But between these two extremes there are a greater number of individuals who are gifted to a more moderate degree, and for them education and self-development provide opportunities for developing leadership qualities.

Some studies of leadership stress that the attainment of desired goals requires the use of power and influence on the part of the leader to achieve collaboration between workers and management. In contrast are other explanations of leadership that stress a less power-motivated approach to harmonious group relations. In these, emphasis is given to minimizing personal conflicts, and on the creation of mutual confidence between leaders and followers. Studies of this subject will continue to be made, and our knowledge of this topic undoubtedly will expand, but the theories we have mentioned here will suffice for our present purposes.

At this point, let us turn our attention to a discussion of those quality traits that seem to have a bearing on executive leadership.

Qualities of a Good Executive

The quality traits that make for executive leadership are of two kinds: *managerial* and *personal*. Keep in mind that neither kind alone is adequate to make a person a competent executive. (As you read the lists below, you may find yourself comparing your own qualifications.)

Managerial Traits. The managerial traits generally considered essential for a competent executive include the following:

1. A philosophy of management: an understanding of how the management process operates and why
2. An understanding of the impact of social, economic, and political forces that normally influence business policy
3. A broad background in the conceptual skill of decision-making
4. An appreciation of the firm's responsibilities to the community welfare
5. A knowledge of the importance of maintaining good human relations with all other members of the firm
6. An appreciation of the need for constant managerial training and education

Personal Traits. The following personal traits are considered essential to a good executive:

1. Ability to lead others
2. Willingness to work effectively with others
3. Willingness to listen to others and maintain an open mind until all facts are known
4. Desire to accept responsibility
5. A dynamic approach to both old and new ideas
6. Maintenance of high moral and ethical standards
7. Ability to communicate effectively in writing and speech
8. Possession of emotional stability at all times, regardless of outside pressures

In applying his personal qualities and abilities to the actual operation of a business, the executive observes the following procedures and approaches:

1. He devotes his attention to broad problems and assigns minor ones to subordinates.
2. He is willing to delegate duties that can be performed by others.

3. He bases his decisions on facts rather than on prejudices or guesswork.
4. He respects the opinions of others and invites suggestions.
5. He communicates his decisions to all who need to be familiar with them.
6. He praises those who deserve commendation but censures constructively those who commit willful errors.
7. He uses the services of others trained in special fields in which he may not be fully qualified.
8. He is careful to train an "understudy" and requires his subordinates to do likewise.
9. He keeps himself informed on all company activities.

The Balance of Executive Qualities

In a survey conducted by the placement officer of a large midwestern university, 97 companies were asked to rank the characteristics of men hired five years ago who had subsequently made outstanding progress in their jobs. The attributes were ranked in the following order: ability to work with others, ability to get things done, mental ability, initiative, leadership, hard work, and good judgment.

Although mental ability received only half as many votes as the ability to work with others, it is interesting that the scholarship records of the men described revealed that about three-fourths had achieved an above-average record in college, about one-fourth had achieved an average record, and none was below average. Clearly there is a relationship between the ability to get along with others and the ability to get along in business, but it is also apparent that there is a relationship between scholarship and success on the job.

THE EDUCATION OF AMERICAN EXECUTIVES

Some useful insights about the education of practicing executives are provided by several surveys. A (1964) study of 1,000 top officers of the 600 largest United States nonfinancial corporations by Dr. Mabel Newcomer dealt with the educational, social, and cultural backgrounds of these individuals.[6] The results of this study, when compared with an earlier (1955) study by Dr. Newcomer, revealed many interesting facts.[7] In her study

[6] Mabel Newcomer, *The Big Business Executive 1964* (New York: Scientific American, 1964), pp. 2–10.

[7] Mabel Newcomer, *The Big Business Executive 1955* (New York: Columbia University Press), p. 68.

covering from 1900 to 1950, Dr. Newcomer found that whereas in 1900 71 percent of all executives had not more than an elementary school education, by 1964 only about 12 percent had only an elementary school education. The percentage of executives with degrees in science and engineering increased nearly five times—from 7 percent in 1900 to 20 percent in 1950, and then abruptly to 33 percent in 1964. As of 1964, 91 percent of the country's big-business executives had some college education—a percentage 10 times greater than that for all males of a corresponding age in the total population. Engineering, the natural sciences, business administration, economics, law, and accounting are the most common educational fields in which the big-business executives in 1964 had received college educations. Further, a study by *Fortune* magazine concluded that 85 percent of the college graduates who were among the 1,700 top-management executives surveyed had majored in law, business, science, engineering, or economics. One-fourth of these without college degrees reported having completed some undergraduate work.[8]

A conclusion reached in all these studies is that executives are better educated than the population in general. Moreover, a college education has become ever more important as a qualification for initial employment in business and industry.

What Is Appropriate Education for Executives?

Writers on the subject of executive education frequently have lauded a broad liberal-arts education as the ideal preparation for executive positions. On the other hand, recruiters from industry visit college placement offices in search of young graduates who have one or more specialties such as a major in marketing, accounting, finance, management, or advertising. And in other fields they ask for majors in chemical engineering, physics, or psychology.

The trend in collegiate business education is to stress as much broad preparation in basic liberal arts (science, economics, mathematics, English history, etc.) as possible, and at the same time not neglect the study of business administration subjects in the functional areas including accounting, finance, marketing, management, and transportation. Education for business involves more than executive development; other essential courses include communications, business law, international business, and quantitative analysis.

Getting the Degree Comes First. At the present time many large companies require as a prerequisite to consideration for employment a bachelor's degree, preferably in business administration. Some firms employ

[8] *Fortune*, Vol. 60, No. 5 (November, 1959), p. 139.

graduates of liberal-arts colleges, but too often these people come out second-best in their search for employment in business. Lawrence A. Appley, retired president of the American Management Assn., predicts that within 15 years the man who aspires to top-management positions will be at a serious disadvantage without an M.B.A. (Master of Business Administration degree).

Having a college degree—even the "right" one for your career field—may not automatically guarantee you an executive position, but it will help your chances for one, because it is proof of your intelligence, interest, and persistence. Businessmen know that college is a proving-ground which eliminates the incapable, the disinterested, and the easily discouraged. And anyway, unless you're very lucky, real business advancement comes only when you have acquired a wide variety of experience, and have mastered the professional skills we have been discussing.

Collegiate Management Courses. College courses in commerce and business are relatively new. Some universities began to offer business administration programs 50 years ago, but most of the specialized courses in management have developed during the past two decades. Among the many courses offered by colleges now are those in principles of personnel management (sometimes called personnel administration), office management, business organization, supervisory training, employment techniques, job evaluation, and industrial relations. In most cases, these courses are offered after the student has completed at least two years of liberal-arts education with emphasis on the humanities.

If you are interested in more specialized subjects, you may choose courses in industrial management, including time-and-motion study, plant layout, materials handling, and production control. Or you may want to concentrate on legislative controls, in such courses as labor law, and collective bargaining.

What can you expect to receive from courses in management? The most important thing you will acquire is an understanding of the principles that underlie the organization, operation, and control of an enterprise. From president to supervisor, mastery of the principles and techniques of the emerging profession of management has become a matter of vital concern. Students of business and aspirants to business leadership cannot prepare themselves adequately unless they become thoroughly familiar with the new and changing concepts of management and organization provided by courses in management.

Whether you intend to have your own business or become a manager in some enterprise, you will find formal college training very valuable. An important part of your study, in addition to management courses, should be in the field of business administration. In all your studies, remember that

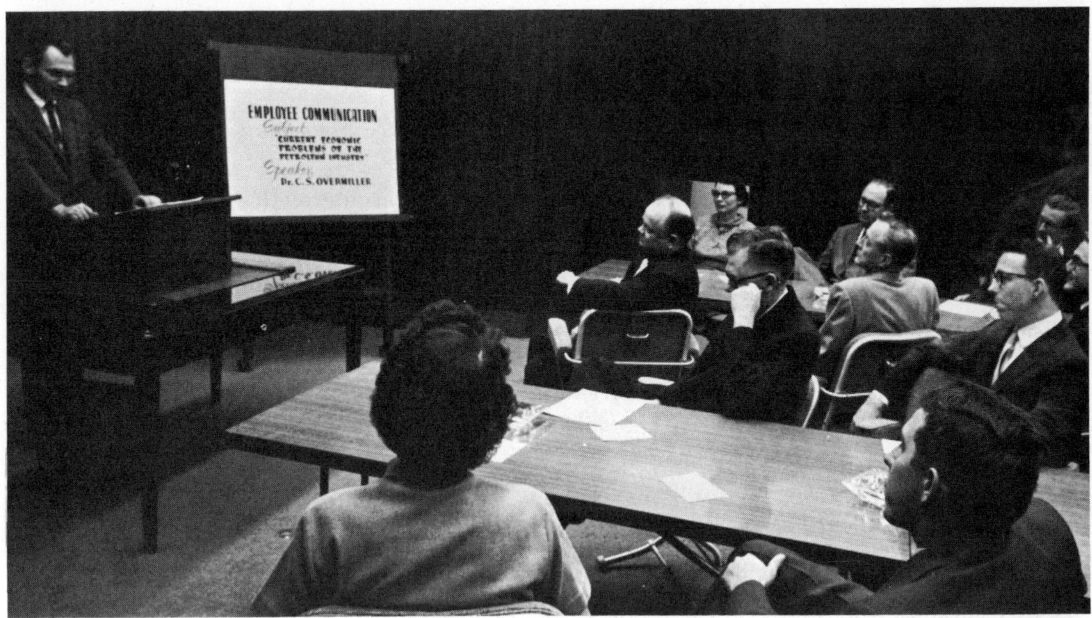

Courtesy Humble Oil & Refining Co.

A group of line executives studying how to improve employee communications within their organization.

education will serve to open the door to opportunities, but will not guarantee you success. That depends on how you use it.

Special Executive-Development Courses. You will find that in many companies education does not stop when employment starts. A substantial number of companies are sending their executives to university-sponsored, "on-campus" integrated programs that take a broad approach to executive development. Such programs are generally known as *executive-development programs,* since they are for men holding executive positions. The duration of these programs varies from two weeks to several months, and the cost ranges from $500 to $2,000. Usually, no college credit is granted.

Programs of this kind are intended to broaden the executive's concepts of managerial functions and acquaint him with all phases of company operations. Many schools use the case method of instruction, or combinations of the lecture, role playing, seminar, and other techniques. Regular faculty members and specialists from industry and other universities comprise the teaching staff. A few companies conduct executive-development programs for their own personnel on the company premises. While the nature of these programs is similar to university-sponsored programs, there is likely to be more emphasis on the company's policies and procedures, without regard to what other firms are doing to solve management problems.

OPPORTUNITIES IN MANAGEMENT

The role and importance of business management is a natural outgrowth of the business and industrial development that has transpired during the past half-century. In America we have the only system in the world which utilizes a large number of professional, trained college graduates as managers. It is to the business manager that we must look for leadership and direction which is so important in coordinating the work of company personnel and executing the policies of the business organization.

The Growing Need for Managers

The function of the manager as a decision-maker is not confined to a single industry or to a particular type of work. On the contrary, managers with broad training are needed wherever there are people working together toward a specific goal. There is a scarcity of persons qualified for managerial positions in business, industry, government, and nonprofit agencies.

Business management is one of the largest fields of employment. Above the foreman or supervisory level, there are a substantial number of positions in middle management. These include such positions as office manager, personnel manager, sales manager, department manager, traffic manager, and superintendent.

In industrial production, there is also a field of managerial occupation generally described as *industrial management,* which includes various kinds of administrative assignments. Here you will find plant managers, industrial-relations supervisors, training directors, job analysts, and employment managers. In smaller companies, several of these positions require experience and training in management and business administration.

Tremendous expansion of the federal government has created a need for additional employees in managerial positions. Outside of business there are many opportunities for managers in hospitals, trade associations, chambers of commerce, and educational nonprofit foundations. In all these fields there is a scarcity of qualified candidates.

SUMMARY

The strength of every enterprise is its management. Managers of business bear a heavy responsibility in satisfying the needs of customers, employees, and owners. Thus, the role of management is to direct, coordinate, and control the various elements of the business firm.

Since 1900, the number of managers has grown about fourfold. This increase has been largely responsible for increases in the efficiency and production of American business and industry.

Recognizing that management might profit from the use of scientific methods, Frederick W. Taylor and his associates were the first Americans to approach some of management's problems—particularly production—scientifically. Taylor experimented with various work techniques in an effort to eliminate waste motions and increase output. He advocated the principle of planning for production before its execution. Another contribution made by Taylor and his associates was the development of motion and time study techniques in analyzing a task.

A manager is a person who gets things done by working with people and other resources. In order to reach the desired objective, he performs certain managerial functions, including: (1) planning, (2) organizing and staffing, (3) coordinating, and (4) controlling. A key activity of all managers in planning. This requires both imagination and analytical ability. The purpose of planning is to develop a blueprint for future action and decision-making. Organizing involves the assigning of tasks to the proper persons. In organizing, the manager must find ways of getting the necessary work done and at the same time make certain that it follows a plan. On the other hand, coordination is the process of reaching agreement on the plans and requirements under consideration. This involves an integration of different factors concerning procedures, people, policies, and plans. This management function can take place at all levels of management. The control function is the process of assuring that performance corresponds with plans and procedures.

The one factor that probably influences most the destiny of a business is the quality of its executive leadership. Executives are members of the management team charged with the responsibility of executing policies, plans, and decisions, while the level of administrative management determines policies. Among the desirable characteristics of an executive are: dynamic personality, ability to work effectively with others, ability to make competent decisions, possession of a strong personal sense of responsibility, high moral character and ethical standards, and a knowledge of the forces that motivate others.

The ability to climb to the level of executive status is based partly on educational preparation and partly on personal qualifications. Various types of management courses are taught at the college level for those seeking a career in management. A broad collegiate education is a good foundation for advanced courses in business administration and business management.

VOCABULARY REVIEW QUIZ

Match the following vocabulary terms with the statements below.

a. Controlling
b. Conceptual skills
c. Coordinating
d. Executive management
e. Executive development program
f. Human skills
g. Industrial management
h. Management
i. Organizing
j. Planning
k. Personal traits
l. Technical skills

1. A process of action that involves several distinct functions performed by managers
2. That part of the organization concerned with carrying out specific projects
3. That function of management concerned with determining company objectives, formulating business policies, and planning methods of control
4. Guiding an activity or group in the desired direction by exercising a management function
5. Skills possessed by an executive which permit him to see the whole enterprise
6. Those skills which enable an executive to work with others in a personalized way
7. A field of management that includes various kinds of administrative assignments involving industrial production
8. That function of management that involves those activities to be performed and the grouping of these activities by departments with assignments to managers
9. That function of management by which it is possible to reach agreement on plans and procedures
10. Skills requiring an understanding of, and a proficiency in, specific kinds of activities using procedures, techniques, and processes
11. Educational programs for executives, intended to broaden their knowledge of management functions
12. The name of a group of traits which includes leadership and the desire to accept responsibility

QUESTIONS FOR REVIEW STUDY

1. Explain what is meant by the term "management."
2. How does administration differ from execution or executive management?
3. Distinguish between management as an art and as a science.
4. Describe the factors that brought about the rise of the factory system.
5. What were some of the contributions to management theories made by Frederick W. Taylor and others in the scientific management movement?

6. How does the planning function of management differ from the organizing function?
7. Compare the management function called coordinating with the function called control.
8. How does horizontal coordination differ from vertical coordination?
9. Describe the managerial and personal traits of a good executive.
10. What are the differences among human, technical, and conceptual skills?
11. How does the education of an executive today differ from that of a decade ago?
12. Do you feel that the practice of business management meets the standards of a profession? Why?

PROBLEMS AND PROJECTS

1. It has sometimes been said that planning is looking ahead and control is looking back. Write a 200-word paragraph giving your interpretation of this saying and showing how it is related to the subject of management.
2. Write a report explaining what brought about the rise of a managerial class in the United States.
3. Managing is working with people. Discuss in approximately 200 words what you believe are the 10 most important qualities an executive should possess.
4. Using reference materials, write a report on Frederick W. Taylor's principles of scientific management, showing how these principles prepared the way for the specialization demonstrated by modern business.

A BUSINESS CASE

Case 6-1 The Western Electronics Company

The Western Electronics Co. is an established manufacturer of electric relays, condensers, semiconductor devices, industrial electronic systems, and nuclear fuel elements. The company began on a small scale in 1940 as a supplier of radio parts. When World War II started, the company received numerous government contracts, and by the end of the war had increased from 35 to 275 employees.

The adjustment from the war to the post-war period was made with no loss of business; in fact, despite new competition, the firm continued to grow. In 1966 one of the two founders retired and died suddenly from a heart attack. Soon the other founder, a Mr. Abbott, who owned a controlling interest, announced that he would like to sell his majority interest and retire. In 1967 the Keith Electronics Corp. purchased 55 percent of the stock, with the understanding that the present executives above the supervisory level would be assured continued employment. Abbott was to retire in six months.

Immediately after the Keith Corp. took over the firm, a team of executives came in to study Western's operation. The study revealed some startling developments, at least from the viewpoint of Keith Electronics. There was no organization chart showing the chain of command. Supplies used in manufacturing were bought by the comptroller and not by the purchasing agent. (The comptroller formerly was the purchasing agent, and when he was promoted to comptroller he continued to approve orders for materials. The new purchasing agent approved everything else.) The executive with the title of "purchasing agent" did little more than serve as the office manager for plant operations. The vice-president of the company came up from the ranks, having formerly been the chief plant engineer. He continued to serve in this capacity after being promoted to vice-president, although he was made vice-president in charge of marketing. The president of Western Electronics held very close control over the firm, virtually requiring that all decisions be approved by him whenever the expenditure involved any amount over $1,000.

The only top-management executive who seemed to have any authority was the president's nephew, who was the company treasurer. For one thing, he was allowed to sign all checks. He also was authorized to promote foremen and other executives whose annual salaries were not above $10,000. The record, however, showed that during the previous year he had fired three foremen and hired four new supervisors, all without presidential approval.

When questioned about the company's operation, the president made the following statement:

> Our company has always made money. I believe we made money because I watched everything closely. Furthermore, I did not feel that I could turn the business of planning, controlling, staffing, and so on, over to different managers because they were not qualified. So, I performed these functions myself. In this way, I could make certain they were done correctly.

The Keith Electronics investigators made this reply to the outgoing president:

> The fact that Western Electronics has enjoyed some success does not necessarily prove anything. Who knows but what the company might have been twice as successful in terms of operation and profits with better-organized management.

1. Were any management principles violated in this case?
2. Do you agree with the Keith Electronics investigators in their remarks to the outgoing president?
3. What are your recommendations?

Internal Organization Structure

7

In earlier chapters we discussed the legal forms of business ownership, including the sole proprietorship, the partnership, and the corporation. There, the emphasis was primarily on legal relationships and on requirements for obtaining capital. We also spent a considerable amount of time discussing the role of business management—what it is and what it does. As we noted in those earlier chapters, there has been a trend toward the separation of business ownership and management, especially in medium-size and large concerns. The result has been that managerial functions—planning, organizing and staffing, coordinating, and controlling—are today characteristically being performed in all but the smallest firms at various levels of management.

In this chapter we turn our attention to the subject of internal organization structure—to the study of various types of formal organization plans that managers may set up, and principles that they may apply.

THE NATURE AND DEVELOPMENT OF ORGANIZATION

Although there are differences of opinion as to the precise nature of organization, there is no disputing the fact that the proper organizational structure is the backbone of the successful enterprise, the foundation upon which the entire business is built. Let us take a look now at the subject of internal organization structure in all its various aspects.

WHAT IS ORGANIZATION?

The term *organization* is known to have several definitions. One (of Webster's) is "the executive structure of a business." This definition indicates that organization is the framework by means of which the work of a business, managerial and otherwise, is performed; that it provides the required channels, points of origin, and flow of management direction and controls. "Organization" also denotes a creative process. All the parts of a business do not come into existence spontaneously; they are the result of managerial efforts to carry out a predetermined course of action—and thus, of organization. (You can see from these two definitions that there is a definite relationship between organization and management.) Too, "organization" is often used to refer to the total business enterprise, including facilities, materials, money, and manpower. (This final definition implies the "team" concept, according to which each member is assigned specific duties, and under the terms of which all members work effectively together within a framework of superior and subordinate relationships.)

All these things considered, it should go without saying that modern business cannot function long without organization.

How Is Organization Developed?

In the small business operated entirely by one person, the owner has no real need for a complicated organization. Since he does everything himself, there is no one to whom he can delegate any authority or responsibility. As owner, manager, and chief executive, he is the sum total of the organization. But with the addition of employees, a greater organization becomes necessary. Working relationships among employees need to be established, as well as arrangements for coordinating decisions and for assigning the workload. Naturally, the larger the firm, the more complex its organizational setup tends to become; the limited capacity of each executive is but one factor that makes the need for better organization imperative.

To help improve organizational efficiency, an executive can reduce his workload by delegating certain of his lesser tasks to the next lower level. But this may itself cause complications, for each time new employees are added, another level of executive personnel may eventually be needed.

As the firm continues to grow, it becomes necessary to separate operations into divisions, departments, or sections (these terms are often used interchangeably), each under the supervision of a person with administrative authority and responsibility. It is not enough in most situations simply to divide the work and to establish an authority hierarchy; ultimately, some kind of over-all organization plan or pattern is needed. Though some companies begin without a clearly defined plan, they eventually see the need for one of a specific type. (Later in this chapter we shall discuss in detail four of the most widely used organizational plans: line, functional, line-and-staff, and committee. As we analyze them, you will see the advantages and disadvantages of each.)

Human Behavior and the Organization

Because people are a primary resource of business firms, a knowledge of how people behave is important to the solution of many types of management problems. To be an effective manager requires an understanding of the interactions between persons who are members of subgroups and those belonging to higher levels of the organization, and also between them and the organization as a whole. As an organizer and supervisor, the manager must be able to accurately predict employee behavior. (The term "employee" is broadly used to mean anyone working in the firm, regardless of his task.) All types of factors must be taken into consideration in making business decisions, and the behavior of people affects them all.

If you have ever participated in the activities of a student group—a club, fraternity, or sorority—you may have observed some problem situation that developed as a result of individual conflicts within the group. The group leader who understands human behavior usually can prevent the development of such situations. For obvious reasons the business manager also needs to understand the behavior of people—both as individuals and as members of groups.

The study of individual behavior is generally considered to belong to the psychologist, and group behavior to the sociologist and cultural anthropologist, although there is some overlap among these disciplines. Very often we use the term "behavioral sciences" in referring to these areas of study.It is the role of the behavioral scientist to study how people behave and why, and what is the relationship between human behavior and the total environment. Many firms either sponsor or run programs by means of which their employees can study human behavior. Some of these programs include college courses in the behavioral sciences—an area which has been gaining new emphasis in business administration courses, too.

CONCEPTS OF ORGANIZATIONAL PLANNING

As we have already suggested, when trying to get a new organization started (especially for a new business), it is not enough in most instances merely to divide the work: the matter of who makes decisions, and to whom they are to be referred, must also be clarified. This means that a workable internal structure must be set up. In choosing such a structure (which if properly established will be based on a logical organizational plan), one choice must be made as to whether this plan will involve centralization of management or decentralization of management, and another regarding the size of the enterprise. We shall discuss these choices now.

Centralized and Decentralized Organizations

One of the more important questions that a company must answer as it grows is whether to continue management that is centralized in one person, or to decentralize management by delegating some of its authority to subordinates.

In a *centralized management organization*, as shown in the chart on page 197 (top), major decisions are made by a few top executives; subordinates exercise little (if any) initiative in decision-making. Even where there are multiple plants, most decisions are made at the company headquarters rather than at the local plants. Chain department and grocery stores frequently adopt a centralized management scheme. Centralized management in these organizations assumes that the responsibility for buying, advertising, marketing, accounting, and other functions will be conducted at one location even though there are many operating branches.

A *decentralized management organization* represents a systematic effort to delegate to lower levels all authority except that which can only be exercised at the highest level. Decentralization of responsibility is not a matter of primary concern simply because work must be assigned to the levels where it is to be performed. The key question is: How *much* authority should be given to those who do the work? The answer is: Give them as much authority as they are capable of carrying within the broad policies made at a higher level. In general, this is the concept practiced by such companies as General Motors, Ford, General Electric, Prudential Life, American Brake Shoe, and J. C. Penney. Notice in the chart on page 197 (bottom), which shows the structure of authority of a decentralized organization, that the president delegates to each plant manager the responsibility for making decisions concerning production and sales in his own area of authority.

Decentralization takes place at different rates in different levels and for different reasons in different companies. For example, some firms decentralize their managerial functions because they know that conditions vary from

Centralized Management Organization

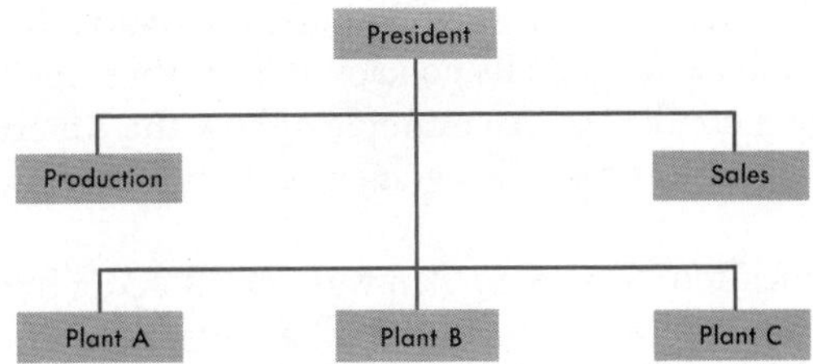

plant to plant, and that the officials at each plant know their own operation better than other officials and are thus prepared to make the best decisions affecting that operation. Then again, when a company has a strong management team at the local level, top management may decide to decentralize by giving that team as much authority as possible in order to allow headquarters personnel more time to devote to long-range planning. Although decentralization generally works best in those firms having extensive decentralized operations on a product division basic, even under such favorable circumstances some companies find lack of managerial talent a limiting factor in their plans for the decentralization of management.

Let us summarize what we have said about decentralization and add a further observation. Decentralization places responsibility and authority in field offices where the action occurs, allowing top-management functions of planning and financing to be performed where they should be in the central office, and lesser managerial functions to be delegated to lower levels of management. Decentralization also tends to give local managers greater incentive (they virtually hold full sway over their own activities), and thus serves as a boon to greater product and market emphasis.

The Size of the Enterprise

Both the scope and the detail of planning increase with the size of the operation. And an expanding business may even be faced with planning for a

Decentralized Management Organization

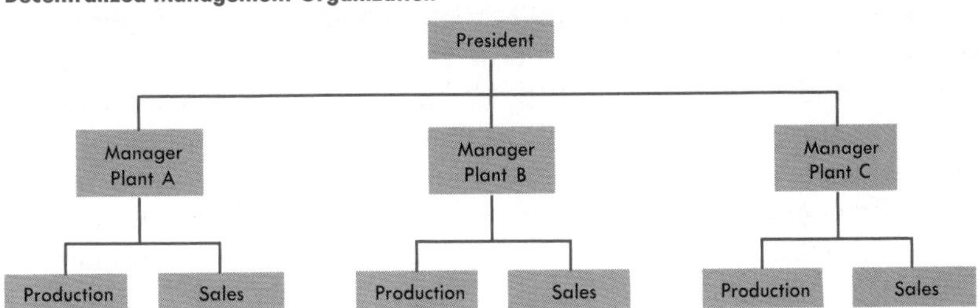

radically different form of organization, whose peculiar problems are best taken into account well in advance. A growing business invariably needs to include in its plans a possible change in its policies in more than one direction in order to meet changing conditions. An example of how the American Can Co. reorganized its top-level internal management structure is shown in the chart on page 199.

Prior to its reorganization, American Can was considered a fragmented federation of almost autonomous divisions which had experienced difficulty keeping pace with changes in the packaging industry. As you can see from the accompanying diagram, the company changed to a highly centralized managerial structure with almost complete control vested in a strong headquarters group. Headquarters staffs were enlarged to do more of the work formerly handled by divisional staffs in areas such as accounting, advertising, taxes, and law. Under the new plan, interlocking committees keep key officers in close touch with all departmental decisions. A company-wide accounting system replaced divisional systems that were considered incompatible. All purchasing was transferred to headquarters. And, finally, marketing and product-planning operations were centralized, allowing headquarters to take a broader look at the total enterprise.

FORMAL AND INFORMAL ORGANIZATIONS

Taking a note from social psychologists, who have long recognized the role of formal and informal organization structure in group behavior, management, in designing an organization's structure, usually gives consideration to the need for either a formal or informal arrangement of management functions. In business parlance, the *formal organization* is a system of well-defined jobs, each bearing a definite measure of authority, responsibility, and accountability. The formal structure is created to deal with routine and recurring activities. It provides a framework for creating such human-relations phenomena as leadership, job incentive, and job status. This is because the formal organization provides relatively fixed areas within which people can develop their own abilities without encroachment on the part of other employees.

None of the concepts common to formal organization apply to the *informal organization,* in which personal relationships are based more on emotions and attitudes than on procedures and company rules. In the informal organization, people work together because of their personal likes and dislikes. There is no organized effort to control group behavior even as it relates to the group's final objective. And lines of authority, if there are any, are less clear-cut; at first glance it may even be difficult to determine who is actually in charge.

How Canco Pulled Itself Together

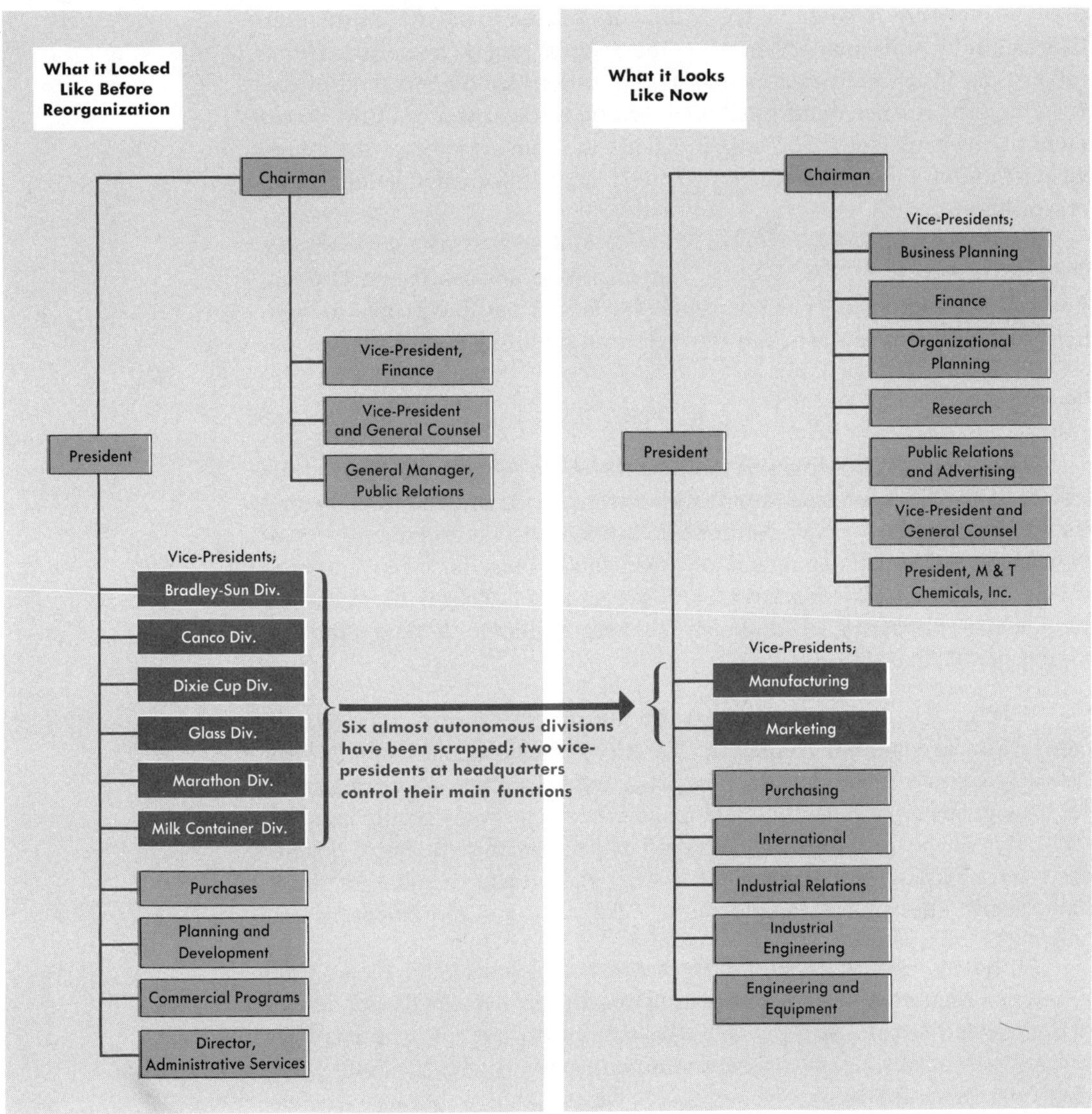

Courtesy Business Week Magazine (McGraw-Hill, Inc.)

This chart indicates how the organization structure of a large corporation may be changed by the process of shifting from a decentralized to a centralized operation involving the company president and chairman of the board of directors.

Source: *Business Week*, September 17, 1966.

Often the informal organization can be discovered by asking, "Who does the boss turn to when he has a difficult decision to make?" More often than not, in the informal organization the decision will be made by a clique rather than by an individual acting as the leader. Another method of discovering the presence of informal organization is the existence of the "communications grapevine." Sometimes called "the rumor factory," the grapevine is one of the most common expressions of informal relations in an organization.

Informal organization is much more common to small and even medium-size firms than to large ones. The small business usually starts on an informal plan out of sheer circumstance because it has few people to organize, few problems to solve, and few activities requiring coordination.

Understanding Organization Structure

Before any business organization can be made to work effectively, various of its activities must be grouped into proper units of responsibility, and the relationships between these units determined. In determining these relationships, certain fundamentals of organization must be taken into consideration. These fundamentals include an understanding of the following terminology: (1) policy, (2) authority, (3) responsibility, (4) accountability, (5) delegation, and (6) principles.

Policy. The term *policy* has several meanings. It is often used to indicate an ethical connotation, such as "Honesty is the best policy." In its business sense, policy means an oral or written statement that serves as a guide for management decisions. Although policies are issued only by top management, it is the people at lower levels who make policies work. Some policies are referred to as "working policies," since they relate to rules governing such specific operations as employment, sick leaves, and retirement.

Authority. The term *authority* has a twofold meaning. First, it denotes the right to make decisions as part of the executive function of planning; and second, it represents the power to direct subordinates, requiring their obedience to perform certain duties. (Authority also implies the right *not* to act or decide.) Some people have authority because of their knowledge of a subject. In a corporation, authority is passed from its source, the stockholders, to a trusted and competent board of directors. They in turn delegate authority to the topmost company officers, starting with the president or chairman of the board. Ultimately, all rights and powers of management rest with ownership. But ownership must necessarily delegate its authority to those in managerial positions.

Responsibility. *Responsibility* may be defined as the individual's obligation to carry out duties assigned to him. Embodied in this definition are three characteristics: *obedience, dependability,* and *compliance.*

Responsibility and authority can never exist in isolation; they must inevitably go hand-in-hand. Imagine what would happen if an executive were given the responsibility to plan the manufacture of a new product without being given the authority to select the materials, obtain the equipment, and employ the people to produce the product. (The relationship between authority and responsibility will be covered more fully later in this chapter, in our discussion of organization charts.)

Accountability. By *accountability* is meant the liability of a subordinate for the proper discharge of his duties. In substance, to be accountable is to be answerable for one's conduct in satisfactorily fulfilling an assignment. Accountability is always *upward* because a person is always accountable to the superior who has delegated responsibility and authority to him. (The flow of authority and responsibility is *downward* because both are delegated to subordinates by a higher authority.)

Delegation. We noted previously that authority and power go hand-in-hand. Like authority, power (in the business world, at least) is not assumed—that is, unilaterally claimed as an inherent right or by virtue of seizure. It is delegated. *Delegation* is the investment of one person with the power to act for another. The primary purpose of delegation is to make organization possible. Since no one person in an organization can do all the tasks, authority must be delegated to subordinates who will make decisions within the area of their assigned duties. Delegation is considered an art of management that is generally not well practiced; studies show that a principal reason for failure of managers is their inability to delegate authority.[1]

Principles. The successful manager usually has the ability, based on experience, to apply general ideas or concepts to his work. He often states these in the form of "laws" or "principles." A *principle,* according to Webster, is "a settled rule of action; a governing law of conduct." A principle emphasizes the idea of a basic truth, unvarying and general in its application to a given consideration. In the study of business, there are certain truths that are accepted or professed as fundamental, and are used as guides. For example, we refer to principles of accounting, or principles of economics. In this chapter we are concerned with principles of organization—and this requires that you understand the meaning of the term "principle."

[1] F. J. Gaudet, "The Mystery of Executive Talent," *Business Week,* May 21, 1955, pp. 43–46.

PRINCIPLES OF ORGANIZATION

Before turning our attention to an analysis of the various types of formal organization plans, we should consider some of the principles that underlie all types of organization structure. It is widely assumed that the designing of a company organization structure requires little more than the balancing of an assortment of rectangles on an organization chart. This is a seriously naïve fallacy. There are certain accepted principles of organization to be observed, chief among which are the following:

1. *Every organization should have an objective.* The performance of all parts of the organization should be directed toward the achievement of the same objective. This is known as *unity of objective;* it is necessary in order to develop effective teamwork within an organization. A distinction should be made, however, between the organization's objectives and the individual goals of the people (executives, supervisors, and workers) who make up the organization. The individual worker's goal is not the same as the organization's objective. For example, the objective of raising additional operating funds may be assigned to the chief finance officer. The employees through their local union may vote to have as their objective a 10 percent hourly wage increase. The two goals are different and would be achieved differently.

2. *There must be clear lines of authority and accompanying responsibility, beginning at the top and descending to the lowest level.* A good organizational structure provides for delegation of authority from (let us say) the president to the vice-president, to the general manager, to the supervisor or foreman, and finally to the workers. Thus, authority stems from the highest executive level and is progressively delegated downward. The president of the firm may, for example, assign to his manufacturing vice-president the responsibility of buying raw materials and new equipment, and of hiring new employees. At the same time the vice-president must have the authority to determine what prices he will pay for these items.

3. *The number of levels of authority should be held to a minimum.* Each time a new management level is created, another link is introduced into the chain of command. And the longer the chain, the more time it takes for instructions to pass down to the lower levels, and for information to travel up to the top level. The number of levels depends upon whether the firm is to be centralized or decentralized. Where there are too many levels of authority, splintered authority exists. This being the case, a problem cannot be solved or a decision made without pooling the authority delegations of two or more managers. In many day-by-day operations there are cases of splintered authority, and probably most managerial conferences are held because of the need to pool authority before making a decision.

4. *No one in the organization should have more than one supervisor.*

This is known as the "unity of command" principle of organization. This principle is based on the theory that each subordinate should report to only one superior. This principle is useful in the clarification of authority-responsibility relationships because whenever a manager lacks total control to hold his subordinates responsible, his position becomes one of confusion and frustration, and in fact it eventually may be undermined.

5. *There is a limit to the number of positions one person should supervise directly.* This is called the "span of control" principle. Application of this concept in developing the organization structure is of importance in that it places some kind of limit on the number of subordinate persons who can be satisfactorily managed by a single executive. While the span of control is rarely uniform throughout an organization, authorities generally agree that from six to eight persons should be the maximum permissible limit. Where the operations of a concern have been decentralized, however, with operating units that are nearly autonomous, it is possible for top-level executives to supervise as many as 12 positions.

6. *The organization structure should be flexible enough to permit changes with a minimum of disruption.* Since change is inevitable in any business, the ideal organization structure is one that permits an executive to make changes without destroying the continuity of the business or the efficiency of the employees. Good organization structure must not be fitted to a straitjacket.

LINE, STAFF, AND FUNCTIONAL RELATIONSHIPS

In addition to being classed as either formal or informal arrangements of activities, business organizations often are placed in one of three categories or patterns of formal authority relationship structures. These are identified as line, staff, and functional relationships. Some writers identify "line" and "staff" structures in terms of the kind of work performed therein. Others emphasize the nature of the authority relationships these create among individuals in the firm. Both of these identifications usually are seen as belonging to formal organizational structures, though there is no reason why they cannot be applied to informal ones as well.

There is probably no area of organization which causes more difficulties than that of line-, staff-, and functional relationships. Suppose we approach our consideration of this subject by examining first the nature of and the differences among these relationships.

Definitions

Line Relations. When there is a recognized chain of command existing between the superior and the subordinate, a *line relationship* (see the chart on page 205) is said to exist. In this situation, the subordinate accepts the responsibility to receive and carry out orders of the person to whom he is responsible. You can see by the chart that the line of authority between the superior and subordinate is a direct one. In the line structure chart (as in the others) the chain of command is indicated by a solid line connecting the various levels that constitute the organizational hierarchy. This solid line relationship may also be looked upon as a chain of communication, and of accountability.

Staff Relations. In contrast to what "line" denotes (authority relations among organizational components), *staff* refers to advisory and service relationships. A *staff relationship* can be seen in (for instance) the work of the specialized counsel to management; he acts at their request to help in preparing plans, studying problems, and making recommendations based on facts which he and other staff members obtain.

Actually, both line and staff authority may be exercised by the same individual. For instance, the personnel manager exercises line authority in that he has command over his subordinates in his department, and staff authority by means of his advisory or service relationships with individuals outside his department.

Functional Relations. Some firms make use of *functional relationships* as well as those we have described. Where functional relations exist, a staff specialist has authority over his particular function (consequently, the term "functional"), no matter where in the organization it is performed. Perhaps this concept of functional relation can best be understood if functional authority is regarded as a small slice of the total authority of the line manager. For example, a personnel manager exercises functional authority when he is assigned responsibility for all matters pertaining to personnel problems in the plant. In a similar manner the production manager, the sales manager, and the plant superintendent all exercise plant-wide authority within their respective areas of operation.

The accompanying illustration depicts the functional structure. In this example, each employee has three supervisors or managers, each responsible for different areas of operation.

You are likely to find more staff positions in a big business than in a small one, because increasing size inevitably brings with it a need for more specialized information upon which decisions are made. And the special worth of staff executives is that they have concentrated their attention on the intricacies of one particular phase of the operation. Line positions are to be found in both large and small organizations.

We will have more to say about how the line, line-and-staff, and functional organization plans actually operate as we study now the several kinds

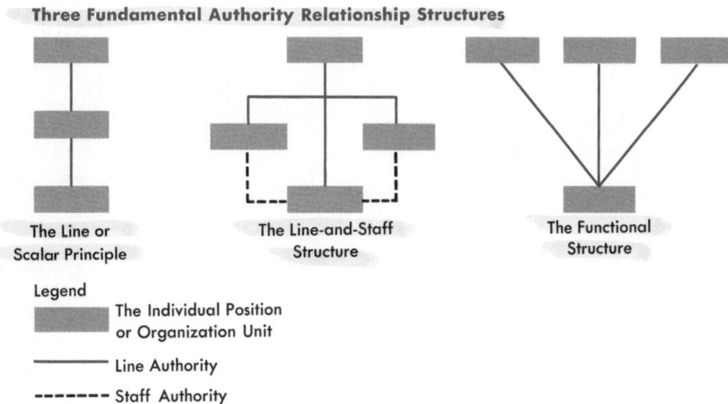

of formal organization plans and note (as shown by an organization chart) how they are structured.

TYPES OF FORMAL ORGANIZATION PLANS

Actually, a number of types of internal management organization plans exist, none of which is solely identified with any particular kind of business. Indeed, some of each type are found in every field of business. The three primary types of internal structures (whose names probably seem rather familiar) are the *line*, the *line-and-staff*, and the *functional*; the fourth is the *committee* plan. In actual practice, no one of these plans is used in its pure form; the realities of business life always dictate that certain modifications be made to enable the organization to adapt to its environment.

The Line Organization Plan

The line organization is the oldest and simplest plan involving formal organization. In this plan, subordinates do not act without first receiving a delegation of authority from the top commander to the lower ranks; the direct chain-of-command concept is its dominant characteristic. In the line organization, department heads or section executives on the same level of authority are "self-contained," which means that the head of a department has charge only of activities directly under his jurisdiction. In turn, he is responsible only to the person directly above him.

The accompanying diagram will show you how the line organization plan is used in a bank. Notice that the line of authority begins at the top with the directors, who are elected by the stockholders, and extends downward through the chairman of the board, the executive committee, and the president, who in turn exercises authority over six departments. By virtue of his

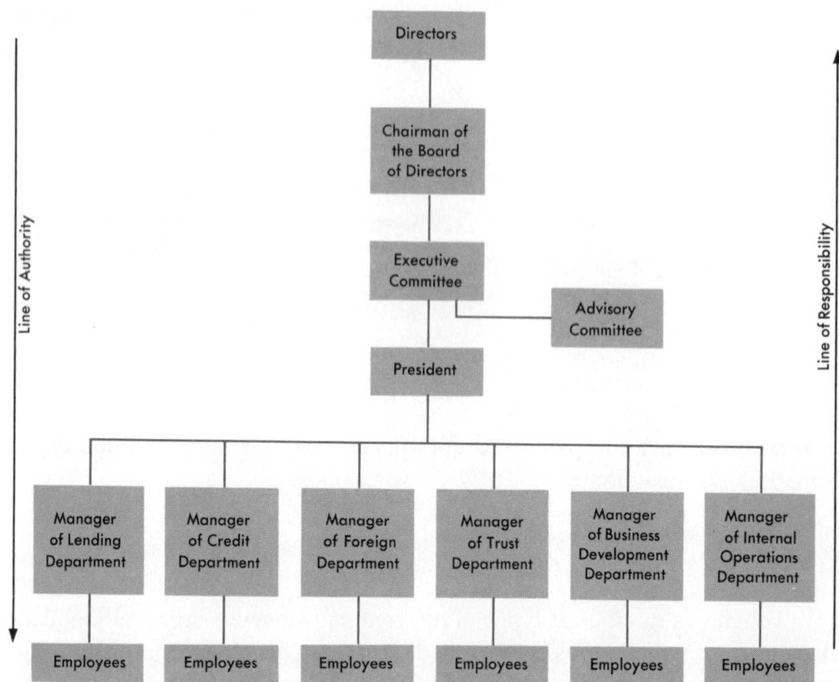

A line organization plan of a medium-sized bank. In this plan the department head must perform highly specialized functions and at the same time direct or supervise his subordinates.

authority, the president can delegate responsibility and authority to others within the chain of command. Notice, too, that the employees within each department are responsible to only one boss, and that each manager is also responsible to only one boss. Authority and responsibility are greatest at the top and taper off at successively lower levels of management. All authority is delegated directly along a straightforward chain of command.

The line organization resembles the chain of command used in a military organization, in that commands go down from the highest officer. Although modern armies are far too complex to follow this plan in precise detail, the military has always recognized the importance of the chain-of-command principle. This plan is also identified as the *scalar* principle (previously mentioned), which in the line organization involves the principle of tapering authority. Where there are two individuals working in a supervisor-subordinate relationship, there is a scalar chain which is an instrument of delegation, the vehicle that implements the flow of authority previously described.

As a formal organization, the line plan has certain advantages and disadvantages which may be summarized as follows:

Advantages of the Line Organization Plan

1. The plan is simple and easy for employees and management to understand.
2. It allows for definite designation of authority and responsibility for each position.
3. Each worker is responsible only to one boss, who is the immediate source of authority.
4. The plan makes for direct communications upward and downward along the chain of authority.

Disadvantages of the Line Organization Plan

1. Each supervisor has responsibility for several duties and cannot become an expert in all of them.
2. The plan overburdens top executives with day-by-day administrative details, to the point where they have little time to devote to planning.
3. The plan fails to provide a specialized staff for more highly specialized manage ment activities.
4. As a business grows and the chain of command increases, more and more time is needed to execute orders.

The line organization plan is more likely to be used in medium-sized or smaller businesses where there is desired a high degree of centralized control for quick decision-making. Certainly, there can be no quibbling as to who gives orders and whether they should be obeyed.

The Line-and-Staff Organization Plan

The line-and-staff organization plan is similar to the line organization in that line executives make the major decisions. But since the work in a large enterprise is often so much more complex than a line executive can handle, specialists are added to advise line personnel. Consequently, these specialists serving as staff executives are considered to be unusually well trained in technical matters.

As shown in the chart at the top of page 208, the lines of authority are shown by solid lines, while staff relationships are indicated by broken lines. Observe how the line of authority runs from the president down to the three vice-presidents and continues through the plant engineer, the personnel manager, and the production manager. This illustration demonstrates the

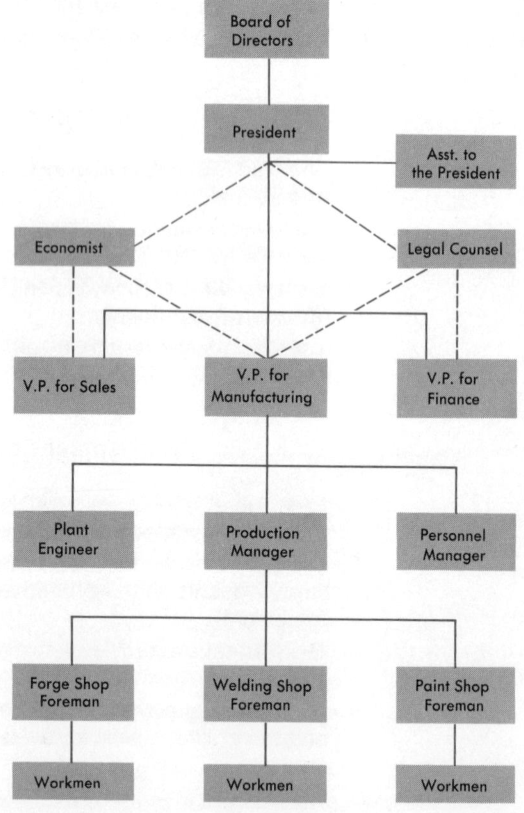

A line-and-staff organization plan. Solid lines show lines of authority; broken lines show staff functions. The positions of Assistant to the President, Economist, and Legal Counsel are filled by staff officers who serve in an advisory capacity to the top-ranking officers of the firm.

"unity of command" previously discussed on page 203. Both the president and the three operating vice-presidents are at liberty to call on the company economist and legal counsel for advice. In both the line and functional plans, this consulting service is not available as such.

Examples of staff executives and the corresponding line executives they generally advise are shown in the chart at the top of page 209.

Widespread use of staff in American business is a product of the twentieth century beginning with the Depression of 1929. The emphasis on the need for internal control and planning, coupled with increased government regulations and problems of taxation and accounting, created the requirement of staff assistance. The growth of "big" business since that time has accelerated the need for more staff specialists.

Staff Executives	Line Executive Being Advised
Research Director	Advises president, vice-president, general manager, and perhaps the production manager
Legal Counsel	Advises president and other top-ranking officers
Economist	Makes studies for and advises president and other high-level line officers
Controller	Makes analysis and furnishes advice and recommendations to high-level line officers
Advertising Manager	Furnishes top-line officers with information and advice regarding advertising and marketing problems
Chief Engineer	Advises high-level line officers on matters of a technical and engineering nature

Among the advantages of the line-and-staff organization plan are these:

Advantages of the Line-and-Staff Organization Plan

1. It provides for line authority with flexibility to use staff specialists who can operate across various department lines.
2. It allows for highly qualified technical specialists to advise line executives.
3. No matter where an employee works in a service, staff, research, or production department, he rarely reports to more than one person.

The disadvantages of this plan may be summarized as follows:

Disadvantages of the Line-and-Staff Organization Plan

1. Decisions may be slowed up by line executives who are waiting for staff personnel to furnish technical information.
2. Staff personnel may attempt to become line officers and assert administrative control, resulting in confusion and misunderstanding.
3. The use of staff specialists increases company overhead costs.

The Functional Organization Plan

As we indicated earlier in this chapter (in the discussion of functional relations), it is possible to assign authority and responsibility in a different pattern from that of the line-and-staff structure. This may be accomplished by giving a manager power over specified processes or functions. He will thus supervise employees in several different departments, but only on matters concerning a specific functional area. In the organization chart of the functional organization plan shown below, you will observe that each employee has five different supervisors, each representing a functional area of the total organization. Although the practice of having more than one "boss" for each employee is at variance with the important organizational principle of "unity of command" discussed earlier in this chapter, many firms do not hesitate to follow it.

The pure functional plan was originally conceived by Frederick W. Taylor, who (as we reveal elsewhere in this book) was a pioneer in the development of scientific management about the end of the nineteenth century. The plan was originated to correct certain weaknesses in the line plan structure as it was used at the shop foreman level. Taylor had experienced difficulty in finding good supervisors who could carry out their duties as foremen under the line plan of organization. So he conceived the idea of dividing up shop foremen's responsibilities on the basis of the kinds of functions they performed. This resulted in each foreman having charge of a specific kind of work.

Under Taylor's organization plan, each executive or supervisor has authority and responsibility for a narrow slice of the total operation. It then becomes necessary for that individual to become a specialist in his particular field. For instance, the personnel manager handles only matters pertaining to personnel, and the production superintendent is concerned only with handling problems involving production—he is not responsible for what happens to the personnel of the plant.

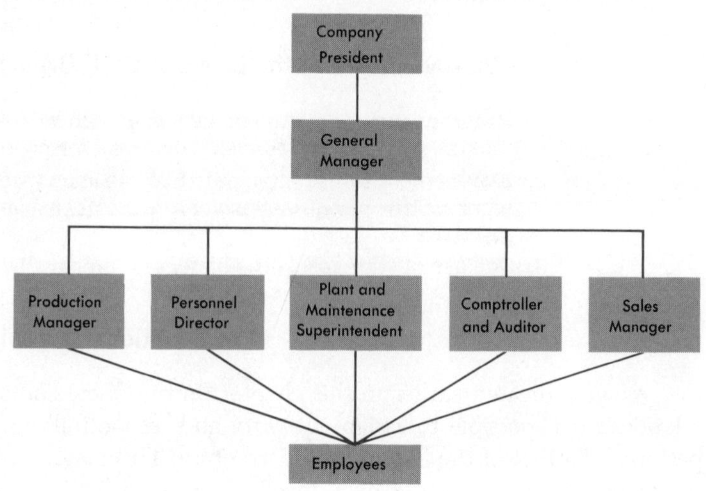

A functional organization plan of a manufacturing business.

The functional plan works well for small businesses which can be organized into functional departments. But as a business grows, the tendency is to change over to a line-and staff plan of organization in order to have the advantage of staff specialists. In the following illustration you will see that the workmen are responsible to several supervisors, each of whom is expert in a highly specialized kind of work in his own department. Even the personnel function is performed by a personnel director, rather than by the worker's immediate supervisor.

In this plan every person, except for those at the top levels, reports to several different supervisors. Each supervisor is a specialist in his field, with authority to supervise his particular function in the entire organization. Notice that there are five different specialists who supervise the workmen.

How well does the functional plan work? Here are some of its advantages and disadvantages:

Advantages of the Functional Organization Plan

1. Each supervisor works exclusively in his specialty. This means he can grow with the firm.
2. Activities of the business are divided into functions and assigned to specialists. Each specialist spends his time performing only one type of duty.
3. Expert advice is available to each individual worker.

Disadvantages of the Functional Organization Plan

1. Workers have more than one boss because separation of functions results in each supervisor having authority over his particular function. This can be in conflict with the "unity of command" principle.
2. Since employees report to more than one supervisor, discipline tends to break down because there are just too many bosses.
3. Overlapping of authority among supervisors often promotes conflict and encourages buck-passing.
4. With so much emphasis on specialization, supervisors seldom have an opportunity to become broadly trained outside their field.

The Committee Organization Plan

Management by executive committee is a form of organization not commonly used in American business.[2] The *committee organization plan* is a

[2] Since 1921, E. I. du Pont de Nemours & Co., one of the world's largest manufacturing companies, has used the committee management plan of organization for many of its important problems.

modification of the line-and-staff plan, with the functional duties carried out by committee members rather than by individual staff officers. These committees do not necessarily replace line-and-staff personnel, however; instead, they bring together the ideas of various groups for further study. For example, the president may appoint a budget committee to study the firm's financial needs before the next budget is prepared, and the committee will then report its findings to the line officials.

The advantages and disadvantages of this plan are as follows:

Advantages of the Committee Organization Plan

1. It combines the judgments of several officials when decisions are being made.
2. Committees act in a less personal way than do individuals when discussing the "pros" and "cons" of an issue.
3. Committees usually are composed of specialists who can devote more time to important problems than can most line officers.

Disadvantages of the Committee Organization Plan

1. Committees often take longer to reach a decision than does a single individual.
2. An original idea often has to be compromised and modified before committee approval can be won.
3. If an aggressive person dominates the committee, the other members may be unduly influenced by him in rendering their final decision.
4. Final decisions of the committee may not be entirely acceptable to everyone on the committee.

ORGANIZATION CHARTS AND MANUALS

Organization Charts

As we discussed each of the formal organization plans in the preceding pages, we presented a diagram to help you understand how the parts of the plan are related. Such a diagram is called an *organization chart.* Every organization can be charted, for a chart merely shows how departments or units are tied together along the lines of authority. As a blueprint showing the structural composition of the business, a chart indicates not only the lines of control, but also the job titles of those persons who hold positions of responsibility.

Because charts are so effective in developing coordination among departments, many executives display them prominently in their offices and work areas. Too, as a business grows, the use of charts can become progressively more important. (For instance, a chart can perform a valuable service merely by allowing an executive to see the entire organization in a simple perspective as it changes. And, since a chart maps lines of authority, sometimes it may show inconsistencies and complexities that will lead to their correction.) A recent survey of organization charting made by the American Management Assn. showed that 67 of the 118 companies studied stated that one of the purposes of organization charting is to fix responsibility and authority and to establish the chain of command. Twenty firms stated that charting helped to improve communications.[3]

Making Organization Charts. Organization charts may take one of several different forms. Most companies use a pyramid-type chart with rectangular boxes connected by lines. The boxes may be linked together with solid lines to show line relationships. Sometimes lines of different colors may also be used to show positions. Broken lines often are used to indicate staff relationships. The lines connecting the boxes represent the flow of responsibility from the bottom upward, and the flow of authority from the top downward.

Limitations of Charts. Although charts are revealing and useful to company management, they are subject to serious limitations. For one thing, a chart does not reflect the many informal and informational relationships. It fails to depict (with the possible exception of the top position) how much authority actually exists at any point in the organization. Finally, charts easily become out-of-date because from time to time company executives are transferred, promoted, or retired, or die.

Another form of organization chart follows. (The chart shown on page 206 is more common than this chart.)

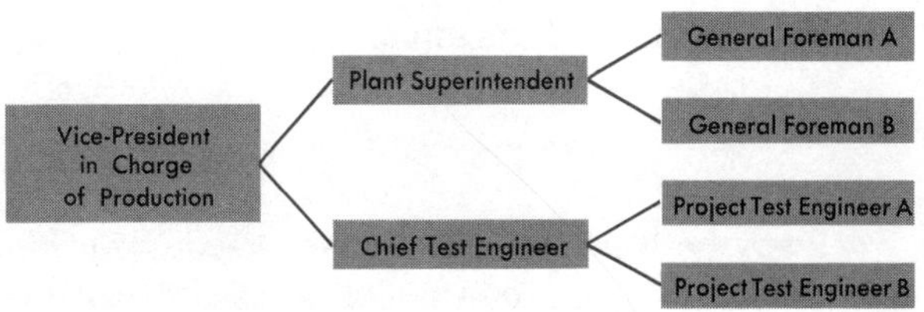

Organization Manuals

Manuals serve several purposes. They can help promote an understanding of a company organization. They spell out functions, duties, authority,

[3] K. K. White, *Understanding the Company Organization Chart,* AMA Research Study No. 56 (New York: American Management Assn., 1963), p. 14.

and responsibility for each department. They may also present detailed job descriptions.

The *office manual* is a collection of written rules and procedures dealing mainly with those working in the offices performing clerical and technical service. Some office manuals also contain information about employee benefits, sick-leave policy, vacations, retirement benefits, and working hours. Some even serve as a guide for employees in areas where they can supervise themselves.

The *training manual* describes company policies concerning employee training programs and how they are administered. It may also outline the duties and responsibilities of those working in the training programs, as well as stipulate the necessity for executive cooperation in releasing employees for training. Airlines have training manuals spelling out the kinds of training to be given to new pilots and other flying personnel, and delineating the nature of refresher training for the more experienced personnel.

In a highly decentralized company having many divisions or units it is often considered necessary to publish a *procedure manual,* which is a compilation of rules and procedures for performing certain kinds of tasks. As a rule, these are office tasks rather than scientific assignments. For instance, if the comptroller's office issues to the field staff a budget procedure, this becomes part of the procedure manual and is distributed throughout the organization.

Preparing manuals. If ever you are called on to prepare an organization manual, here are a few guides that may prove useful. Keep all the information concise and simply stated, and make sure the sequence of topics follows some logical order. Avoid ambiguous terms and lengthy descriptions; they detract from the clarity and effectiveness of the material. A loose-leaf manual is generally more satisfactory than a bound manual, because it is possible to substitute new pages for obsolete or altered sheets. The manual should be kept up-to-date by the insertion of all changes in procedures, personnel, and policy information.

SUMMARY

Every business—small or large—needs some kind of planned organization. Internal organization makes it possible to bring together a group of people to work effectively under a central authority.

A sound and effective organization structure is based on certain fundamental principles, such as unity of command, span of control, proper organization, balance, and flexibility. For example, in a good organization no one should have more than one immediate supervisor, the levels of authority should be held to a minimum, and the organization should provide for top-executive planning.

In planning organization, it is essential to provide for the delegation of authority and responsibility. Each employee has a certain amount of responsibility, which increases with his rank and work assignment. Authority commonly originates at the top and flows downward to the lower levels of command. Authority and responsibility go hand-in-hand; one cannot be isolated from the other.

There are four basic organization plans. In the line plan, authority passes in a direct line from the top downward. Employees are responsible to only one boss. Throughout the organization, each supervisor or executive is in complete charge of the specific activities assigned him. A characteristic of the line plan is the manner in which authority is delegated along the straightforward chain of command.

The functional plan differs from the line plan. For one thing, it allows for the use of specialists. And, since workmen are responsible to various specialists, each workman reports to more than one foreman in a completely functionalized structure. It is probable that no completely functionalized organization has ever been developed.

The line-and-staff plan combines the various features of the line plan and the functional plan of organization.

In the line-and-staff plan, the line officers are supplemented by experts or staff assistants who serve in an advisory capacity. In the functional plan, the distinction between line and staff tends to disappear, because the executives exercise direct authority over line personnel in respective areas of specialization. In the committee plan, groups of officers are provided to assist the line executive in making decisions.

Organization charts and manuals provide a valuable means of communication within the firm and enable both employees and executives to recognize lines of authority, responsibilities, and duties.

VOCABULARY REVIEW QUIZ

Match the following vocabulary terms with the statements below.

a. Authority
b. Accountability
c. Centralized management organization
d. Decentralized management organization
e. Delegation
f. Formal organization
g. Informal organization
h. Line relationship
i. Line organization
j. Organization
k. Organization chart
l. Office manual
m. Policy
n. Principle
o. Procedure manual
p. Responsibility
q. Staff relationship
r. Training manual

1. The total enterprise, including facilities, materials, and people, and the manner in which they are arranged by positions based on work assignments
2. A system of well-defined jobs or activities to be performed on various levels of authority
3. Groups of persons in an organizational unit existing in the absence of written rules of conduct or established formal procedures
4. A form of organization that provides for major decision-making by a few executives at the top of the organization
5. An oral or written statement setting forth the determined course of action to be followed in a given situation or many similar situations
6. A systematic effort to delegate to the lower levels all authority except that which can only be exercised at the highest level of organization
7. The power to direct subordinates, requiring their obedience to perform certain functions
8. The individual's obligation to carry out all duties assigned to him
9. To be answerable for one's conduct in fulfilling satisfactorily an assignment
10. To invest one person with the power to act for another
11. A law governing the conduct of employees
12. A recognized chain of command existing between the superior and the subordinate in an organization
13. The oldest and simplest plan of formal organization
14. The giving of advice or rendering of a service often needed by the line executive in making a decision
15. A compilation of written company policies concerning employee training programs and how they are administered
16. A collection of written procedures and rules dealing mainly with those working in offices performing clerical and technical service
17. A diagram to help you understand how the parts of an organization are related
18. A compilation of rules and procedures for performing certain kinds of tasks

QUESTIONS FOR REVIEW STUDY

1. How would you define the term "organization structure"?
2. What meaning would the behavioral scientist give to the term "organization"?
3. Why do organization problems increase with the size of the organization?
4. How do formal and informal organizations differ from one another?
5. Differentiate between centralized and decentralized organization. Which one provides the greater amount of management control?
6. Distinguish between authority and responsibility.
7. How important is the function of policy formulation by management?
8. Explain the difference between "unity of command" and "unity of objective."
9. Contrast the work of line personnel with staff personnel. Which would you rather be? Give reasons for your answer.

10. Compare the advantages and disadvantages of the line organization plan with those of the functional organization plan. Which plan tends to be in conflict with the "unity of command" principle?
11. What purposes does an organization chart serve and in what ways does it differ from an organization manual?
12. What are some of the disadvantages of the committee organization?

PROBLEMS AND PROJECTS

1. The Hixon Corp., manufacturers of home lawnmowers, employs a total of 85 employees. Of these 20 are salesmen, 12 work in the office, six work in the warehouse, and the remaining 47 are engaged in production. Mr. Hixon, the president and majority stockholder, has been in charge of virtually all activities, with virtually all employees reporting to him. He has finally conceded that this is not the most efficient method of operation. You are to construct an organization chart for him that will completely revamp the internal structure of this family-owned corporation.
2. Using outside reading assignments, give a definition and illustration for each of the following terms: span-of-control principle, staff executive, line executive, first-line supervisor, and procedure manual.
3. List several ways in which the owner of a medium-sized business might improve the internal organization structure of his business.

A BUSINESS CASE

Case 7-1 The Thwarted Vice-President

Lawrence Fry, president of the Lone Tree Chemical Co., a well-established, medium-sized chemical company, was authorized by the board of directors to employ Harold Foster to fill the new position of vice-president for personnel. Foster was recently graduated with a Master of Business Administration degree. He was highly recommended. He was employed because the management felt its personnel relations, union relations, and general management relations were very unsatisfactory. Too, the board decided it was better to go outside the company to find a qualified person than to take someone from within the organization. After all, one of the reasons for creating this new position was to fill it with a person who had some new ideas; most of the company officers had been with the firm for many years.

Foster was told that he had a free hand and that he was expected to make many proposals. With this in mind, his first project was to recommend a complete reorganization of the company along functional lines and following the functional organization plan. After seven months of study the new plan, including an organization chart, was presented to the directors, who approved it but took no action to set a date for its implementation. Foster was told that this would be determined later.

Foster's second project was to draw up a new set of company policies involving recruitment, promotion, job placement, employee separation, and training. He established new guidelines to clarify relations with the union. He proposed a profit-sharing plan. He developed, as part of the new organization structure (and to bring order out of chaos), a series of guidelines concerning the assignment of authority and responsibility. Finally, he recommended that the company conduct a series of short supervisory courses in the plant for all first-line supervisors.

Every one of Foster's recommendations was accepted by the board of directors, and on the strength of this he believed they would be implemented in due time. But actually there had been no change in company policies, practices, and attitudes, despite the 18 months Foster worked so hard to reorganize the entire company. The organization was still operating exactly as it was when Foster first arrived; nothing had been carried out.

Recently, toward the middle of his second year with the firm, Foster received a telephone call from a well-known manufacturing firm, inviting him to confer with the company president. The outcome of this interview was a job offer from one of the largest chemical companies in nearby Louisiana. It was a good offer and provided a substantially higher salary, and a stock option plan.

After several days of consideration, Foster is on the verge of making two decisions. The first is not to accept this offer because implementation of his proposals might yet be possible, and a big promotion might then ensue. The second is not to give in to the indifference and opposition he encounters in the company; not to simply become passive and innocuous in a comfortable and well-paid job. But, on the other hand, he wonders: "If I remain with the company, how can I convince the directors that my proposals should be implemented immediately? And if I can't do this, should I resign?"

Stymied, Foster has turned to you for advice, because you are a trusted friend.

1. What advice would you offer Foster about this situation?
2. Should Foster appeal directly to the board of directors and demand a decision?
3. Should he go to the company president and threaten to resign?

PART 3
TOOLS FOR MANAGERIAL CONTROLS

Accounting and Budgets

8

The success of any business enterprise depends in large measure on having accurate data for management to use in decision-making. (Over the years, the lack of accurate accounting records has been one of the principal causes of business failure.)

Accounting consists of recording, analyzing, and interpreting the results of a firm's daily business transactions. Accounting records are concerned with the buying and selling of goods; of the purchase, depreciation, and disposal of fixed assets; of the receipt and disbursement of cash; and of money due from customers and owed to creditors.

In this chapter we shall study about the function of accounting, the various types of accounting data reported by the accounting department, and the use of financial reports by management. We shall also consider the role of budgeting in business management.

THE FUNCTION OF ACCOUNTING IN BUSINESS MANAGEMENT

The function of accounting in modern-day business management can best be illustrated by discussing the need for accounting data, and by explaining the various ways in which different persons utilize accounting reports.

Need for Accounting Data

Imagine you have just inherited your father's business. Unfortunately, although you had been with him in his store many times (even worked there, in fact, as a sales clerk on Saturdays and during rush periods), your father never discussed the financial affairs of his business with you. But rather than close the store or sell it, you choose to operate it for a while, at least until you can decide upon the most prudent course of action to follow. What are some of the cold financial facts you must know about this business to keep it going?

To begin with, there is a sizable weekly payroll. And, in addition to the amount to be paid in salaries, you must know the number of deductions to make for each employee, and the amount of each deduction. Then, there are the federal income and social-security tax deductions, and those for group hospital and insurance protection. Are there any employees buying savings bonds through a payroll deduction plan? Does the business have a private pension plan to which the employees contribute? Too, there is the state income tax to be withheld, and the local payroll tax.

There are other matters. How about the cash balance shown on the bank statement? The checkbook stub record shows several checks outstanding. Is there enough money in the bank to pay the salaries and also the unpaid bills that are in one of the desk drawers? Other bills, too, will undoubtedly arrive on the first of the month. On which are discounts allowable? Will there be enough money coming in from customers to meet current obligations?

In the midst of wondering about all these things, you discover that many of the customers' accounts are long past due. It would really be helpful if you knew which ones had already been mailed statements, and what efforts had been made to collect on accounts that are past due. Would it be advisable to place some of these, together with the past due notes, in the hands of an attorney or a collection agency? Should you continue to sell on credit to customers who already owe large amounts? Have they always paid up?

There are periodic reports that must be made to the government, too—quarterly payments of social security taxes; payment of income taxes withheld; payment of property taxes, state unemployment taxes, state and municipal sales taxes. Where does one get the information needed for all these reports?

The problems continue to mount. *Inventory,* or stock control, has to be considered. Which items are in greatest demand by your customers? Is there an adequate supply on hand? Are there up-to-date records of merchandise stored in the warehouse? In what quantities should items be ordered? Do the records show any departmental breakdown on sales? Which goods have been on hand so long that they should be sold out and discontinued?

These are but a few of the many typical business questions concerning accounting data that you, as the management, will have to answer—and their answers are to be found only in the accounting records. So it should be clear, even from the brief and incomprehensive example given here, that the need for accounting data is crucial.

Groups Interested in Accounting Data

Several groups are directly concerned with the financial records and reports of any business enterprise: *owners, creditors, governments,* and *labor unions.*

Owners. We have already seen the degree to which the owner of a retail business is concerned with accounting records. This same dependency upon accounting data exists for all sizes and types of business enterprises, and in all forms of business organizations—proprietorships, partnerships, and corporations. Owners need accounting information to make decisions leading to remedial action, or for the improvement of business operations.

In the case of the corporation, there are two groups of persons interested in accounting reports: stockholders and management. Stockholders depend on the interpretation of financial reports as their chief means of checking on the effectiveness with which the business is being run. (*Prospective* purchasers of new issues of stock are also interested in the firm's financial reports.) And much of the work of the accounting department is aimed at assisting management in operating the business: buying merchandise, borrowing money, investing surplus funds, raising capital, and distributing profits.

Creditors. Accounting reports normally prepared at the close of the business year are the most reliable source of information on the financial condition of any business. If a business wants credit with a bank, the loan department of the bank analyzes the firm's financial statements in considering whether or not to grant the loan.

How does a *creditor* (a person to whom the business owes money) measure a business firm's ability to pay? He can use any of the "three C's" of credit—character, capacity, or capital— but chances are he will look closely at the firm's capital as revealed in its accounting reports. Financial reports may, of course, reveal a firm's capacity as well as its capital, but creditors usually have more confidence in an actual statement of capital. Credit losses are usually high in cases where adequate accounting data are not available.

Financial statements also serve as the basis for a firm's financial rating by such agencies as Dun & Bradstreet and banks making loans to the business. Persons who invest in stocks and bonds almost invariably review a firm's financial reports when they are considering purchasing its securities.

Governments. Various government agencies have a great interest in the accounting records of a business enterprise. For tax purposes, both federal and state laws require private businesses to file financial statements. State and federal income taxes are calculated from the amount of profit a business earns. Moreover, contributions by business for the Federal Old Age and Survivors Insurance Program, and to the state and federal unemployment compensation programs, are based on a firm's payroll records. Computation of state sales taxes and federal excise taxes also require that accurate accounting records be kept by private business.

Accounting records such as time cards and payroll analyses enable the government to determine whether a business is complying with minimum-wage laws and governmental regulations pertaining to working hours and overtime payments. All corporations whose stock is listed on the nation-wide stock exchange are required to file reports of their financial operations with the Securities and Exchange Commission quarterly, and prior to offering new capital stock to the public.[1] When the federal government is purchasing goods on a cost-plus contract, it requires detailed accounting reports from the vendor, covering production operations and costs.

Labor Unions. Financial information reflected by a firm's income and expense statements is the basis for demands made by labor during collective-bargaining sessions. Demands for wage increases and added fringe benefits usually are accompanied by arguments and data based on the firm's profits. Labor unions give more attention to a company's financial statements today than ever before. Union officials often know as much about the factors that affect a firm's profits as does the firm's management. Increases in rates of productivity, reductions in unit costs, and trends in profits are among the factors that union management studies carefully.

In a close corporation, financial statements may not be readily available to labor union leaders, and this of course puts labor at a disadvantage when negotiating for wage increases. However, corporations that have stock listed on the exchange are required to publish financial reports, and labor unions do have access to this information.

[1] The provisions of the Securities and Exchange Act are discussed in Chapter 16.

HOW DATA ARE REPORTED BY THE ACCOUNTING DEPARTMENT

We have seen that the prime function of accounting is to furnish management with information it can use in making financial decisions. Many such decisions are necessary in the day-by-day operation of a business and in planning for the future. Management, whether it be the owner-manager of a small business or the management of a large corporation, is interested in having information regarding:

1. Total net income earned during a given period
2. Factors that influence the amount of profit
3. Total value of the assets owned, and changes taking place in them
4. Amount of liabilities and net worth.

The Accounting Period

Profits and losses are generally computed for a given period of time, such as one month, six months, or one year. This is known as the *accounting period.* For tax-paying purposes, the accounting period is one year. A year other than the calender year may also be used for accounting, however, and this is called the *fiscal year.* At the conclusion of this period, financial reports and other records are prepared for the owner. For example, a business which normally is at its peak of sales in December through February, then experiences a drop for the next few months, may start its fiscal year on April 1 and end it on March 31. Hence, the accounting period may be based on either a period beginning with January 1 and ending on December 31, or some other 12-month period. Most government units use as their fiscal year the period from July 1 to June 30. When a period shorter than a year (such as a month or a quarter) is used as the accounting period, this is known as the company's *fiscal period.*

Types and Amounts of Income

The chief purpose of a privately owned business is to make a profit. By selling goods at a *profit*—that is, a price greater than their cost—*income* is produced. Income is the increase in the owner's proprietorship interest resulting from business transactions. *Gross profit* is profit made on the sale of goods before expenses are deducted. *Net income* (often used as a synonym for *net profit*) is the amount of income after subtracting expenses. Income earned from the normal course of business operations—the sale of goods or services—is called *operating income.* Income derived from sources other than the principal operation of the business is called *nonoperating income.*

Examples of nonoperating income are interest earned on notes owned by the business, and profit made by selling a piece of equipment at a figure exceeding its depreciated value. The depreciated value of a fixed asset is its *book value.*

Expenses

Some business transactions result directly in a decrease in a proprietor's equity in a business. These decreases are called *expenses,* and normally result from paying for services such as rent, salaries, and utilities. Expenses are generally classified as administrative expenses and selling expenses. Administrative expenses include such items as rent, the cost of utility services, and salaries of office personnel. Selling expenses include salaries, commissions, and traveling expenses for salesmen, and the cost of advertising and delivering the merchandise sold.

The Cost of Goods Sold

In addition to showing income and expenses, statements of operations give the cost of merchandise sold. This is in reality a statement of the *cost price* of the merchandise represented by sales. It is determined by adjusting the total of merchandise purchased by the net change in merchandise inventory during the period. For example, suppose a business had $13,000 in goods on hand at the beginning of the accounting period, had purchased $57,800 worth during the period, and had an inventory of $11,900 on hand at the end of the period. Then the goods which were sold cost the business $58,900 [$57,800 + $1,100 (difference in inventories)]. Another way of showing this same calculation is as follows:

Beginning Inventory	$13,000
plus Purchases	57,800
Total Goods Available for Sale	70,800
minus Ending Inventory	11,900
Cost Price of Goods Sold	$58,900

The Income Statement

The *income statement* is one of the most important statements prepared by the accounting department. It reports the various elements just discussed: income from sales, cost of goods sold, net profit from operations, and financial income. A simplified version of such a statement would appear as follows:

THE HARTFORD COMPANY

Income Statement January 1, 19__ to March 31, 19__

Income from Sales:		
Net Sales		$95,000
Cost of Goods Sold:		
Cost Price of Merchandise Sold*		58,900
Gross Profit on Sales		$36,100
Expenses:		
Administrative Expenses	$13,385	
Selling Expenses	14,715	
Total Operating Expenses		28,100
Net Income		$ 8,000

* Supporting Schedule
Cost of Goods Sold

Beginning Inventory	$13,000
Purchases	57,800
Merchandise Available for Sale	70,800
Ending Inventory	11,900
Cost of Goods Sold	$58,900

The income statement is important to stockholders and prospective stockholders because it gives a comparison of present accomplishments with those of previous fiscal periods. Most corporations, in their periodic reports to stockholders, compare earnings during the past quarter with those of the corresponding quarter of the previous year. In some cases, reports are included showing the accumulations for all quarters so far during the current fiscal year. For example, at the end of the third quarter, results may be given for both the three-month period and the nine-month period.

Accounting for Cash and Receivables

The inflow and outflow of cash is important to a business operation. The inflow is known as *cash receipts* and the outflow is called *cash disbursements*. Because most businesses operate on the *accrual*[2] basis, a business enterprise may find its cash balance decreasing even though its operations are profitable. *Cash control* is also important; management must plan to have money on hand as it is needed to make the necessary payments as they fall due.

Accounting records of cash inflow and outflow and the balance of cash

[2] Some income and expense items belong to one fiscal period but are actually not paid or received until a future period. Under the *accrual* method an attempt is made to record these in the period to which they belong, rather than in the one in which the cash actually changes hands.

on hand reveal the liquidity of a company's resources. Accounting also helps assure the safe and proper handling of an organization's cash assets, preserving their availability and protecting against their being wasted, misused, or embezzled.

The cash forecast. The purpose of the *cash forecast* is to present an estimate of the amount of cash to be received during a given period of time, the amount needed to meet anticipated disbursements, and the cash balance expected to be on hand at the end of that period. Here, much as in the estimating of income, it is desirable to prepare cash forecasts for the entire accounting period as well as for shorter periods. The cash record for past fiscal periods, anticipated receipts from operations (both cash sales and short-term credit operations), interest to be received and paid, and estimated expenses all have a bearing on the cash forecast.

Receivables. *Short-term receivables* (amounts due from customers) are closely related to cash, for every business hopes to collect on its credit sales as accounts come due. However, regardless of the care exercised in granting credit, every business suffers some losses on its credit customers. It is the responsibility of the accounting department to estimate these losses and set up appropriate reserves for them. (Records of past experience are important here.) In addition, one of the usual practices is to age the accounts, applying the greatest loss against those longest overdue. Such a computation might appear as follows:

Age analysis of accounts receivable June 30, 19__

Age in Months	Amount of Receivables	Percentage Loss Expected	Amount of Anticipated Loss
0–1	$25,500	0.2	$ 51.00
1–2	5,400	1.0	54.00
2–3	1,700	4.5	76.50
3–6	1,020	20.0	204.00
Over 6	680	50.0	340.00
Totals	$34,300		$725.50

This analysis shows an expected loss of $725.50 from inability to collect on receivables. This, therefore, is the amount of reserve to be set up.

Accounting for Inventories

To operators of a retail store the term *merchandise inventory* refers to a listing of various goods that were bought for resale. Businesses may inventory other articles also, such as supplies or fixed assets. Manufacturing enterprises, of course, must inventory their raw materials and the goods in process but not yet completed. The three chief concerns relating to inventories are their *cost*, the keeping of accurate *records*, and the exercising of adequate *control* to prevent merchandise from being taken for nonbusiness use.

The starting point for pricing inventory items is their *invoice cost*. From this figure discounts allowed are deducted, then correct amounts are added for such factors as transportation, handling, and storage.

Some businesses attempt to keep a *perpetual inventory* of goods on hand—that is, a complete, up-to-date count of the number of each item on hand at all times. You perhaps have noticed price-tags on articles in a furniture store; usually the number of units of that item still in stock is recorded on the back of these tags. You have also noticed sales clerks in hardware and clothing stores recording item code numbers on their sales slips. These records make it easier for office clerks to keep accurate records of the quantity of items sold and remaining in stock.

The third problem, control, is relatively easy to deal with in retail stores. However, in manufacturing operations where expensive raw materials are used, it is more difficult. Usually, some scheme of checking out materials is used whereby the person receiving them signs for them, or a record is kept of the quantity of material furnished each worker and the amount he uses. An actual count of goods on hand is made periodically, even when perpetual inventory records are maintained.

In all these instances, an accounting staff prepares the records system and keeps daily records as business is transacted. It also prepares internal audits from time to time to verify the accuracy of its records.

Accounting for Payables

The amount of money owed by a business constitutes its *payables*. Sums owed on open account are called *accounts payable*, while debts evidenced by written documents are *notes payable* or *mortgages payable*.

The accounting department must devise some plan for paying invoices within the discount period. Furthermore, care must be exercised that credit is not overextended. Therefore, payables must be controlled so that the cash on hand will be adequate not only to pay all debts, but to do so within the discount period allowed.

The Statement of Financial Position

Earlier we saw a statement of income earned during an accounting period. Another equally important and valuable report is the statement of financial status called the *balance sheet*—a statement of the financial condition of a business on a specific date. The completion of only one new business transaction would entail making minor changes in this report. A balance sheet is like a physician's report on the physical condition of a patient: the picture may change in a relatively short time, but the report is quite accurate at the time it is prepared.

The balance sheet is in reality a statement of assets and equities, the latter showing the equity of the creditors in the assets and also the equity of the owner or owners. It shows the present balances in cash, receivables, inventory, and payables.

Divisions of Balance Sheet

1. *Assets:* items of value owned by the business
2. *Liabilities:* debts owed by the business; equity of the creditors
3. *Proprietorship:* the owners' equity in the business

Assets = Liabilities + Proprietorship

A simplified balance sheet might appear as follows:

TABLE 8.2

THE HARTFORD COMPANY

Statement of Financial Position — March 31, 19__

ASSETS			LIABILITIES		
Cash	$21,600		Accounts Payable	$11,200	
Receivables	80,600		Notes Payable	2,000	
Merchandise on Hand	11,900		Accrued Liabilities	800	
Fixed Assets	57,700		Total Liabilities		$ 14,000
Other Assets	2,200		OWNER'S EQUITY		
			Owners' Investment		160,000
Total Assets		$174,000	Total Equities		$174,000

USE OF ACCOUNTING REPORTS BY MANAGEMENT

Regardless of how accurately records are kept or how complete summary statements are, the value of most accounting data lies in their analysis and interpretation. In a small business, the bookkeeper prepares the financial statements and the owner interprets them. In a large business, however, accountants prepare the statements and the chief accountant and administrative officers interpret them.

Appraising the Results of Operations

Comparative Statements. One of the ways in which accountants prepare financial reports for interpretation by the officers of a business is through the use of *comparative statements.* Figures for the current year are shown side-by-side with those of the previous year or two; thus the current statement may be compared directly with the past record. This comparison shows clearly and succinctly trends in business operations. Comparative statements are used for both the balance sheet and income statement.

A comparative balance sheet is shown on this page. Notice that each breakdown shows a comparison with the preceding quarter. The trend may be seen for each type of asset as well as for the totals of assets. Comparisons are also shown for liabilities and ownership.

The term *current assets* refers to items owned by the business that will be converted into cash within a reasonably short time. Prepaid expenses include such items as insurance premiums that have been paid in advance, and supplies that will be consumed within a relatively short time. *Fixed assets*

THE HARTFORD COMPANY

Statement of Financial Position

			March 31 Current Quarter	December 31 Previous Quarter
ASSETS				
Current Assets:				
Cash			$ 21,600	$ 19,000
Accounts Receivable			74,100	70,500
Notes Receivable			6,500	5,600
Merchandise Inventory			11,900	13,000
Prepaid Expenses			2,200	2,000
Total Current Assets			$116,300	$110,100
Fixed Assets:	Current	Previous		
Equipment (Cost)	$15,600	$15,600		
Less Allowance for Depreciation	(3,000)	(2,600)		
Buildings (Cost)	56,700	56,700		
Less Allowance for Depreciation	(11,600)	(10,800)		
Total Fixed Assets			$ 57,700	$ 58,900
Total Assets			$174,000	$169,000
LIABILITIES				
Current Liabilities:				
Accounts Payable			$ 11,200	$ 12,500
Notes Payable			2,000	3,000
Accrued Liabilities			800	1,500
Total Liabilities			$ 14,000	$ 17,000
OWNERSHIP				
Mr. Alton Hartford, Capital			$160,000	$152,000
Total Liabilities and Capital			$174,000	$169,000

refers to items, representing major capital investments, that will be used for a long period of time. Most businesses consider items that extend beyond one year as fixed items. The same distinction is made between current and fixed liabilities.

The term *accrued liabilities* usually refers to items in connection with services which have been received or rendered but not yet paid for. An example of an accrued liability would be interest earned on a note payable but not yet paid because the note is not yet due. Another example of an accrued liability would be wages for labor rendered but not yet paid for because the payroll usually covers a whole week and the accounting period ended in the middle of the week. Taxes payable is yet another example of an accrued liability.

Use of Percentages. Another statistical tool management uses to interpret financial reports is *percentages.* For example, various items in the income statement, such as cost of goods sold, administrative expenses, and selling expenses, are shown both in dollar figures and percentages of income from sales. Such percentages are included in the following income statement.

THE HARTFORD COMPANY

Income Statement Jan. 1, 19— to March 31, 19—

			Percentage
Income from Sales:			
Net Income from Sales		$95,000	(100.0)
Cost of Goods Sold:			
Cost of Goods Sold		58,900	(62.0)
Gross Profit on Sales		$36,100	(38.0)
Operating Expenses:			
Administrative Expenses	$13,385		(14.1)
Selling Expenses	14,715		(15.5)
Total Operating Expenses		28,100	(29.6)
Net Profit from Operations		$ 8,000	(8.4)

Even a quick glance at the above statement shows that the cost price of the merchandise sold was 62 percent of the selling price, making the gross profit 38 percent of the selling price. Both the relative amounts and percentages of the administrative and selling expenses are clear. The net profit of $8,000 represents a profit rate of 8.4 percent of sales.

The two methods of interpretation we have just explained—comparison by fiscal periods, and use of percentages—may be combined in a single report to management. These methods were presented separately here for the sake of simplification and clarity.

Sometimes the income-and-expense statement is broken down according to departments. In this way, management can see at a glance how the various departments compare with one another in total sales, costs, and profits during the period covered by the statement.

Use of Ratios in Statement Interpretation

Businessmen and prospective stock purchasers frequently interpret financial statements through the use of ratios. We shall explain three ratios commonly used by modern business management: the *current ratio,* the *working capital ratio,* and *inventory turnover.*

The Current Ratio. One of the most commonly used ratios utilized in preparing financial statements is the *current ratio.* It is found by dividing the amount of current assets by the total of current liabilities. This ratio gives management an indication of the solvency of the business, and of the firm's ability to pay its debts. What constitutes a desirable current ratio depends on the nature and type of business. In a business where the turnover of merchandise is slow (for example, a jewelry store), there will be a greater need for cash and a larger current ratio than in a business where the turnover is rapid (as it is in a supermarket). A department store might have one current ratio and a public utility quite a different one.

In the balance sheet report of the Hartford Co. shown on page 231, the current ratio improved from 6.5 to 8.3.

$$\frac{110{,}100}{17{,}000} = 6.5 \qquad \frac{116{,}300}{14{,}000} = 8.3$$

A recent study of 278 retail department stores revealed that their average current ratio was 3.5; the current ratio for 168 retail furniture stores was 4.0; for 67 retail hardware stores it was 5.97; and for 66 independent retail groceries it was 1.5.

Working Capital. Working capital is closely related to the current ratio, since it is the same information stated in terms of dollars rather than as a ratio. It is the excess (in dollars) of current assets over current liabilities. Working capital indicates a firm's ability to meet its operating expenses and to purchase additional merchandise for resale. If a firm has enough capital on hand, it can take advantage of attractive buying propositions that it would otherwise have to pass up. The working capital of The Hartford Co. is $93,100 for the first year ($110,100–$17,000), and for the second year, $102,300 ($116,300–$14,000).

Stock Turnover Ratio. Businessmen feel it undesirable to have large sums of money tied up in merchandise stock. When the merchandise manager discovers that inventories are too large, he determines which goods are not moving, and makes plans for selling them.

We discussed inventory or stock turnover in Chapter 5, in connection with determining capital needs. We pointed out that the usual method of calculating stock turnover is to divide the average inventory into the total sales, using the cost price of the goods sold. The average inventory may be found by adding the beginning and ending inventories together and dividing by 2. Using the figures appearing on the income statement for The Hartford Co. shown on page 227, we would calculate as follows:

$$\frac{\text{Beginning Inventory} + \text{Ending Inventory}}{2} = \text{Average Inventory}$$

$$\frac{\$13{,}000 + \$11{,}900}{2} = \frac{\$24{,}900}{2} \text{ or } \$12{,}450$$

$$\frac{\text{Cost of Goods Sold}}{\text{Average Inventory}} = \frac{\$58{,}900}{\$12{,}450} = 4.7$$

The inventory or stock turnover ratio is 4.7.

A recent study of a number of retail stores showed that the average stock turnover for selected types of retail businesses were:

	Inventory Turnover Ratio
Department Stores (278)	5.2
Furniture Stores (168)	4.5
Hardware Stores (67)	3.6
Independent Groceries (66)	20.9

A study of selected ratios for 1968 for several different types of retail businesses showed that the average current ratios and the average inventory turnover for the year were as follows (the number of stores included is shown in parentheses):

	Current Ratio	Inventory Turnover
Automobile dealers (128)	1.9	8.8
Building Materials (96)	2.5	7.7
Clothing—Men's and Women's (75)	3.0	4.4
Department Stores (202)	3.4	5.4
Farm and Garden Supplies (88)	2.7	9.3
Furniture (175)	3.2	4.8
Groceries and Meats (156)	2.0	16.6
Hardware (99)	3.6	3.4
Jewelers (63)	2.9	2.9
Lumber Yards (140)	3.7	5.0
Paint, Glass, and Wallpaper (39)	4.6	4.8
Women's Specialty Shops (208)	2.5	6.7

These ratios have been discussed here as illustrations of the ways in which ratios are used in interpreting financial reports. Accountants use other ratios also, such as the ratio of net profit to sales and the ratio of inventory to accounts and notes receivable—but since we are illustrating how ratios are used, and are not trying to give a comprehensive treatment of them, we shall not discuss them here.

THE USE OF BUDGETING

We have observed from time to time that planning is one of the most significant aspects of business management. Much of the financial planning of business is based on budgets. A *budget* may be defined as a financial plan showing anticipated income and outlays for a given period of time. Budgets are usually prepared for both individual departments and the business as a whole. If the expenditures for any one department equal the amount appropriated, we say that its budget is *balanced.* When the expenditures exceed the amount budgeted, we say that the department has operated at a *deficit.*

Purposes of Budgets

A well-prepared budget helps management in several ways. Perhaps its primary function is to serve as a guide in planning financial operations. A second purpose is to establish limits for departmental expenditures. Although budgets are at best only estimates, they are usually accepted as the limits within which a department is to operate. If there must be an overexpenditure in one area, an attempt is made to curtail expenses in other areas.

Another important purpose of a carefully prepared budget is to encourage administrative officials to make a careful analysis of all existing operations. On the basis of their analysis, present practices may be justified and even expanded, eliminated, or restricted. Budgets are also used for control purposes—an activity that is discussed more fully on page 237.

Types of Budgets

Perhaps the most important budget to be prepared—certainly the first one—is the *sales budget.* This is an estimate of the total anticipated sales during the budgetary period. One method of preparation commonly used is to have each salesman estimate the sales increase he can effect in the territory he serves. As a rule, these estimates are broken down by principal lines, or in some cases by individual items.

Another approach to the preparation of the sales budget is to begin with a line graph of sales for recent years. This is projected for the budgetary period. Any factor or new development must be taken into account that is expected to increase or decrease future sales as compared with past performance. In this way, management can make a fairly accurate forecast of total sales and sales by products, and can then go on to determine the expected gross income.

In this same manner—that is, comparing past performance with anticipated operations and interpreting these in terms of new developments, such as changes in equipment installations or office procedures—budgets are prepared for production operations, raw materials and supplies, sales expenses, advertising, labor, plant expansion, and any other activity that requires an important expenditure.

Steps in Budgeting

The first step in budgeting is to make preliminary plans for the period ahead. All the important phases of the business operation must be studied, with the records of past performance as the starting point. Finally, estimates for the budgeting period are prepared.

The second phase is the planning and maintenance of records of expenditures during the budgetary period. These records should be broken down into several budget categories. They must be accurate, up-to-date, and relatively easy to interpret. Records of this sort enable management to make

CASH BUDGET

Item	Monthly Average for 1968	1969 January	1969 February	1969 March
Receipts:				
Accounts Receivable Collections	$11,000	$11,000	$11,500	$11,400
Disbursements:				
Accounts Payable Paid	$ 2,200	$ 2,400	$ 2,700	$ 2,900
Direct Labor	2,100	2,300	2,600	2,600
Indirect Labor	750	750	750	750
Variable Manufacturing Expenses	1,100	1,200	1,300	1,400
Insurance and Taxes	150	150	150	150
General and Administrative Expenses	2,700	2,700	2,700	2,700
Selling Expense	600	600	700	700
Total Disbursements	$ 9,600	$10,100	$10,900	$11,200
Initial Cash		$ 6,200	$ 7,100	$ 7,700
Cash Change Resulting From Operations		900	600	200
Cumulative Cash	6,200 December 31	7,100	7,700	7,900
Desired Level of Cash		5,400	6,200	6,000
Cash Excess		$ 1,700	$ 1,500	$ 1,900

comparisons from time to time to see how actual expenses are falling into line with the estimates that were prepared.

The third step is to study any departure from the original estimates. In some cases, management may decide to alter the budget. Such a situation might be created by unusual capital costs, such as building enlargement or modification that had not been anticipated, or by the unavoidable replacement of heavy equipment that suddenly becomes obsolete. However, in most cases management will take steps to bring expenditures into line with the original estimates.

Budgets are generally prepared in the accounting department from data furnished it by the heads of other departments. In some cases this procedure is reversed; the respective department heads prepare their departmental budgets from data supplied them by the accounting department.

BUDGETARY CONTROL

If there is to be a fully effective cost-reduction program in the administration of an office, constant pressure must be applied by means of a continuing cost-control program. And budgets are the tools that management uses for control purposes. When they are well prepared and based realistically on past performances, they serve to reveal weaknesses in office organization, make it easier to fix responsibility, make possible comparisons that show trends in office performance, and help to maintain balance among the divisions of the office organization.

Budgetary control helps shape over-all plans, set performance standards, and coordinate activities into a unified whole. It is achieved through the use of forms that show at a glance both the budget estimates and up-to-date records based on actual performance. If there should be any deviations from the budgetary plan, they are called to the attention of management through the budget committee. For example, if materials or supplies are being consumed at an abnormal rate, out of proportion to the amount of goods being produced, immediate attention is given to improving the materials-control procedures. And if sales of a particular product are declining rapidly, or if sales are falling off in a given territory, immediate conferences and investigations are held to correct this situation.

Budgetary control includes the development and use of three basic budgets: *income, cash,* and *capital.*

The *income budget* includes estimates of both gross and net income. The *gross income* estimate is premised on forecasts of sales. The *net income* estimates result from subtracting anticipated expenses from the estimated gross income. The preparation of this budget requires perception and analysis of factors outside the business itself. The trends for the industry as a whole and the general economy of the region play an important role. Even the best and most accurate forecasts may prove invalid because of unforeseen price competition or research developments. Or a sudden shortage of essential raw materials may curtail operations severely.

Earlier in this chapter we mentioned the *cash budget* or forecast. It represents a combination of the financial position of a business at the beginning of the fiscal period, and the expected results of operations during the period. Basically it states two things: the cash available for the period, and an itemized list of expected demands for funds.

The *capital budget* indicates how the sums allotted for capital expenditures are to be allocated to the major departments. Like all budgets, the estimates for capital expenditures must be kept flexible. Changes in market operations may cause changes in plans for expansion. Labor difficulties, even those of suppliers, may force a delay into a future fiscal period. Also, the use of surplus funds in terms of what they could earn by employing them in a variety of ways might become an important consideration.

The income and capital budgets are primarily the responsibility of the operating departments, but the cash budget is solely a financial function. The income and capital budgets represent a coordinated plan of action to achieve company objectives. But the cash budget is a reflection of the anticipated results of those plans.

Notice that although budgetary estimates and performance records focus attention on areas where action is needed, the actual control over funds, materials, expenses, etc., must be exerted by individuals. The budget as a control tool is no better than the knowledge and understanding of the persons who prepare it or of those who live with it. Management should create a climate that stimulates interest in budgets, and a desire to utilize them as guides against which to measures actual performance.

RELATION OF ACCOUNTING TO ECONOMICS, STATISTICS, AND LAW

Just as economics is concerned with the distribution of wealth and society's attempts to produce and develop greater quantities of goods, so accounting is concerned with man's efforts to develop his business so that it will produce additional profits.

Whereas in economics emphasis is placed on economic functions as they relate to society, accounting is the concern of business ownership, who use it to show the nature and degree of changes that take place in the property of a particular business enterprise. Whereas economics is primarily applied to "economizing" the natural resources of communities and nations, accounting is intended to enhance efficiency of operation for an individual or business firm. Accounting is actually one form of applied economics.

Accounting and statistics are similar in purpose but different in scope.

Both are designed to present numerical data objectively and in a clear, understandable form. *Accounting* deals mainly with financial data that are related to business transactions and their effects on business operations. *Statistics,* however, refers to the collection, interpretation, and presentation of all types of quantitative data, not just those stated in monetary terms. "Statistics" is the broader term and includes all that is encompassed in the term "accounting."

Accounting practices are influenced by legal restriction. For example, if a business is incorporated, the law requires that certain records and reports be kept. Therefore, regardless of the number of shareholders, records must be kept, reflecting the equity of the owners (shareholders) as well as amounts due creditors (including bondholders). A business may maintain any kind of records considered desirable, provided accounting practices are in accord with standard accounting procedures and comply with existing state and federal laws.

CAREER OPPORTUNITIES IN ACCOUNTING

No matter which area of business you choose to follow as your specialty, you should certainly study accounting for at least two semesters. You will find it of great value in understanding the financial condition and operation of any business. In addition, a mastery of the basic principles of accounting will make your study of economics, finance, and business management far more meaningful. As you advance to junior executive and executive positions in business, you will find yourself using your knowledge of accounting principles and applications over and over again.

Fields of Accounting

Accounting practice may be divided into three areas: *private, public,* and *governmental.*

In *private* business, the accountant usually starts as a junior accountant or clerk. In proprietorships, partnerships, corporations, schools, and hospitals, accountants may serve as business managers, financial managers, comptrollers, treasurers, auditors, cost analysts, credit managers, and tax specialists.

The *public* accountant offers his services to the general public for the purpose of installing accounting systems, preparing income-tax returns, or auditing accounting records.

The accountant in *governmental* service takes an examination administered by a civil service commission or a state merit system. Then he is assigned to some governmental agency or bureau. As a government employee, you might work as an accountant, a cost analyst, an auditor, or an income-tax specialist.

Specialization in Accounting

In addition to the three main fields of accounting, you will find more highly specialized areas. Specialization in accounting, just as in any other field, usually leads to higher salaries. If you decide to specialize in accounting, you may choose among several important fields:

1. Systems installation
2. Cost accounting
3. Governmental accounting
4. Research
5. Teaching
6. Property appraisal
7. Budgetary control
8. Auditing (manufacturers, retailers, eleemosynary institutions, governments)
9. Taxation (income, estate, social security, sales, property)
10. Management consultant

At present and in the immediate future, you will probably find the greatest opportunities in the last four areas listed. We can illustrate a combination of areas of specialization and the general fields of accounting with the following chart:

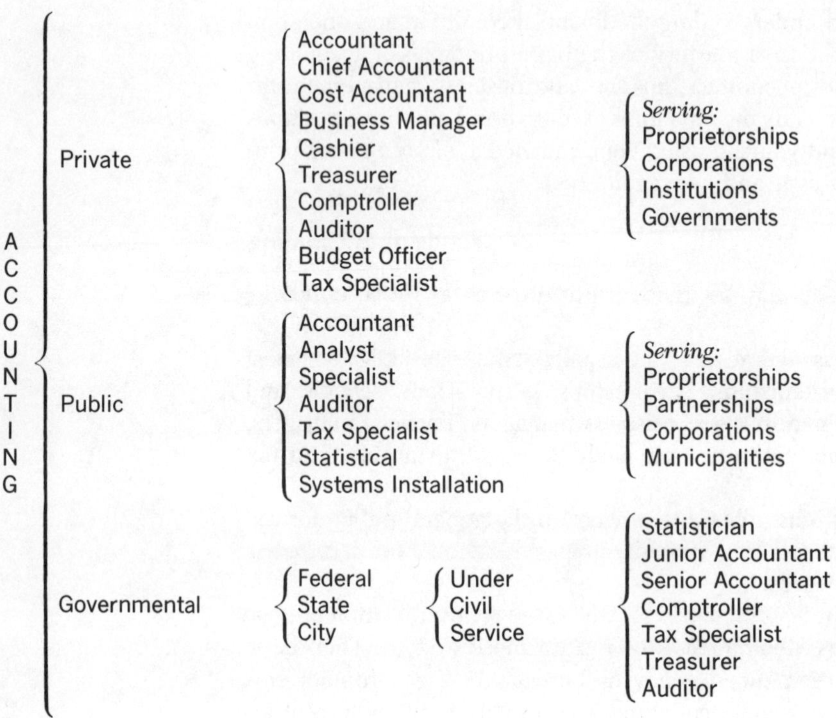

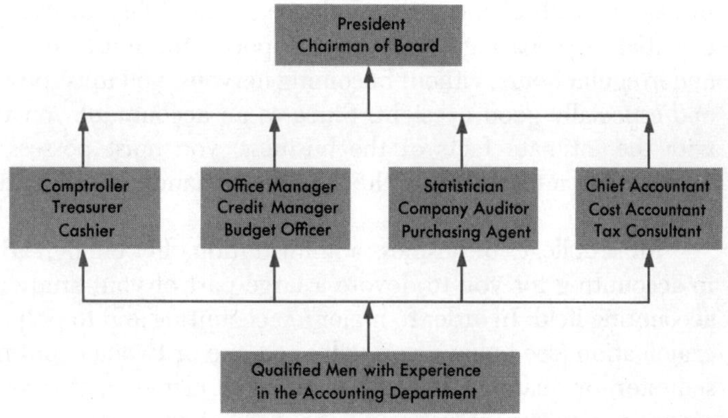

Promotional opportunities for accountants.

Employment and Promotional Opportunities

If you decide to concentrate in accounting, chances are you will find opportunities for employment immediately upon graduation from college. Later on, if you possess desirable executive qualities, your training will serve as an excellent stepping-stone to executive positions. One advantage of a career in accounting is that you can find suitable positions in all areas of the country. If you succeed in this type of work, and if you have broad training and experience, you will be eligible for promotions within the accounting department or in other departments of the business organization.

Some of the positions in accounting toward which increased experience will lead you are: chief accountant, cost accountant, company auditor, tax consultant, treasurer, and comptroller. Positions outside the accounting department for which you may become eligible are: cashier, purchasing agent, sales analyst, budget officer, office manager, credit manager, vice-president, and president. Most business organizations prefer to start young men and women who have had accounting training as assistants to experienced or senior accountants, and to advance them according to their ability and their value to the company. Promotional opportunities are summarized in the chart at the top of this page.

Personal Qualifications and Preparation

To be a success as an accountant, you should like to work with details, enjoy studying mathematical records, and have a knack for comparing names and numbers quickly and accurately. If you are thinking of becoming a public accountant, you will need in addition a pleasing personality, and tact in dealing with clients and employees. The ability to use good English is essential in preparing final written reports. You must be able to work long and irregular hours without becoming nervous; you must possess good health and especially good eyesight. Since as an accountant you will be working with the intimate facts of the business, you must possess a high degree of personal integrity and the ability to handle confidential information properly.

Most colleges of business administration offer enough advanced courses in accounting for you to devote a large part of your study program to the accounting field. In order to major in accounting and to prepare for the CPA examination (see below), you will need one or two accounting courses each semester, or quarter, after you have taken elementary accounting. For this reason, you will want to begin your study of accounting as early as possible. Specialized courses include accounting systems, cost accounting, corporation accounting, auditing, income taxation, petroleum or mine accounting, government accounting, and CPA problems.

In addition to specialized training in accounting, you will also need a knowledge of business law, especially the details of contracts and negotiable instruments. You would also do well to take several courses in economics, management, finance, quantitative analysis, marketing, and communication. Of course, you will find practical experience an invaluable part of your equipment in preparing for accounting work.

The *Certified Public Accountant* is among the top members of his profession. Before you can lay claim to the title of CPA, you must meet certain requirements in education and experience, and pass a state proficiency examination. Requirements vary from state to state, but in general a candidate must meet the following qualifications:

1. He must be a United States citizen
2. He must be at least 21 years of age
3. He must sit for and pass the CPA examination given in the state in which he wishes to be certified
4. He must have practical experience in the field of accounting
5. He must be a high-school graduate and, in some states, a graduate of some recognized college of business administration

The examinations are relatively uniform, since most states use those prepared by the American Institute of Accountants. The candidate is examined in business law, auditing, accounting theory, and accounting practice. It is not necessary for you to have a CPA certificate to practice private accounting, but without it you cannot practice as a public accountant and certify accounting statements.

SUMMARY

The function of the accounting department is to furnish data pertaining to finances and operations of the business. The chief statement that shows the financial condition of the business is the balance sheet, which is a report of the assets, liabilities, and owners' equity in the business. The results of operations are shown by the income statement.

In addition to company managers and owners, certain other groups of persons are interested in the accounting reports of a business enterprise. Chief among these are the creditors, prospective purchasers of company stock, and the government.

Some of the important accounting ratios of interest to management are the current ratio, the working capital ratio, and the stock turnover.

Budgeting is an important management function that is dependent upon data prepared by the accounting department. Some budgets are prepared by that department, while others are prepared in other departments from accounting and other statistical data supplied to the heads of those departments. There are several different types of budgets normally prepared by a business enterprise, but budgetary control is centered around the income, cash, and capital budgets.

Accountancy is an excellent career choice for persons who like to work with figures. It offers employment opportunities at beginning positions and is also rich in opportunities for promotion. Accountants are needed by every medium-size and large business enterprise, by service institutions, and by the government. The CPA certificate is the ultimate objective of persons who make accounting their life work.

VOCABULARY REVIEW QUIZ

Match the following vocabulary terms with the statements below.

a. Assets
b. Balance sheet
c. Book value
d. Budget
e. Cash forecast
f. Current assets
g. Current ratio
h. Fiscal period
i. Fixed assets
j. Gross profit
k. Income statement
l. Liabilities
m. Merchandise inventory
n. Proprietorship
o. Working capital

1. The period for which accounting records are summarized and financial reports issued

2. The amount of profit earned before the expenses of the business are deducted

3. The depreciated value of a fixed asset as carried on the accounting records
4. The financial statement that reports detailed information regarding the amount of sales, the costs, and the expenses
5. An estimate of the amount of cash that will be on hand at stated times in the future
6. A listing of all the goods on hand that were bought for the purpose of resale
7. An accounting statement that reports on the financial condition or status of the business on a given date
8. Those items of value that are owned by the business
9. The persons or firms to whom the business owes money
10. Those items of value owned by the business that will be converted into cash within a relatively short time
11. The amount of the equity of the owners of a business
12. The ratio of current assets to current liabilities
13. Items in which a business has made capital investments with the intention of keeping its money so invested for a period exceeding one year
14. The amount by which the total of the current assets is larger than the total of the current liabilities
15. An estimate of amounts a business expects to receive and spend

QUESTIONS FOR REVIEW STUDY

1. What is the function of the accounting department in relation to management?
2. In what way is the interest in the accounting statements on the part of the owners, the creditors, and the government similar?
3. What are the three main sections of an income statement?
4. What information is shown on the balance sheet?
5. What is the purpose of aging the accounts receivable?
6. What is the difference between a current asset and a fixed asset?
7. What is similar and what is different between current ratio and working capital?
8. For what purposes is the ''working'' capital of a business used?
9. What is the significance of a small inventory turnover ratio?
10. Which is the better index of the solvency of a business: working capital or fixed capital? Why?
11. Why are budgets prepared, and how are they used by business management?
12. What are some of the different types of specialization available to accountants?

PROBLEMS AND PROJECTS

1. (a) Arrange the following figures, shown by a bank on its financial statement, in the form of a balance sheet. Cash on Hand and in Other Banks, $23,500,000; United States Government Bonds, $14,000,000; State and Municipal Securities, $10,000,000; Federal Reserve Bank Stock, $150,000;

Loans and Discounts, $86,000,000; Building and Equipment, $1,950,000; Deposits, $122,685,000; Dividends Payable, $160,000; Taxes Payable, $450,000; Accrued Expenses Payable, $695,000; Capital Stock, $2,500,000; Capital Surplus, $2,500,000; Undivided Profits, $6,610,000. (b) If there are 4,500 shares of stock outstanding, what is the book value of each share?

2. The Income Statement of the Jake Wagner Co. shows the following data:

Net sales	$142,000	Administrative expenses	$17,040
Cost of sales	85,200	Selling expenses	28,400
Gross profit	56,800	Net operating profit	11,360

What is the percentage of net sales for each of the items?

3. There are several common ratios used by business executives in the appraisal of their financial reports. Here are three ratios:

(1) *Current ratio:* current assets divided by current liabilities
(2) *Working capital:* current assets minus current liabilities
(3) *Inventory turnover:* sales divided by average inventory (both at cost prices)

Find these three ratios using the following financial data:

Current assets	$134,400
Current liabilities	42,000
Average inventory	11,800
Sales (cost price)	106,200
Expenses	42,000

4. The Accounts Receivable for the Jones Sales Corp. totaled $42,550 with $28,650 current (less than 30 days old); $7,300 was from 30 to 60 days old; $3,200 was 60 to 90 days old; $2,200 was between three and six months old, and the balance was more than six months past-due. Using as percentages for expected losses those used in the illustration given in the chapter, prepare a similar table calculating the anticipated bad-debt losses.

A BUSINESS CASE

Case 8-1 Allocation of Profits

The Strange Co. has made a profit of $200,000 for the current year. If the entire net income for the year were paid out as dividends, the stockholders would receive a return on their investment of 15 percent for the year.

The company must modernize and enlarge its plant facility, at a cost of $1,250,000. The company president has recommended that only a 5 percent dividend be declared, and that the remainder of the profits earned be allocated to plant expansion.

Assume that you are a member of the Board of Directors. What are some of the factors that would have a bearing on your decision in this case?

Research, Statistics, and Decision Making

9

"Decision making" is in essence choosing one thing, proposition, or course of action in preference to all its alternatives. In the business world, a great investment in time, money, effort, personnel, materials, and so on may be involved in a decision. The extent to which these things *are* involved, as well as the total effect of their involvement, depends on the business level at which the decision is made.

Perhaps the most important difference between high-level and low-level decisions is the extent to which they can affect the future of a firm. This is particularly true of "bad" (ill-timed or otherwise unwise) decisions. A mistake made in a routine low-level operation is usually of minor importance because more often than not it is caught promptly and corrected. Also, even if it is not immediately compensated for, its consequences cannot be very damaging to the firm. But a high-level error in judgment may have far-reaching detrimental effects, especially if—as sometimes happens—corrective steps are not swiftly taken in reaction to it.

One of the elements that distinguishes business management from the lower-level positions in business is the responsibility for decision making. Business executives must live with their decisions, so naturally they keep abreast of any new developments that result from new policy decisions. In other words, decision making is a continuous process; earlier decisions are modified, as well as new ones just being made. And this constant vigilance of results requires all kinds of data, for the wisest decisions far more often than not are based upon and evaluated in terms of a variety of types of business information. The scientific process of seeking new information, applying it to problem situations, and interpreting interrelationships in groups of data, is called *research*. Research is carried on in a variety of ways and is utilized by business management in the areas of product design, packaging, consumer wants, and marketing techniques. Some decisions are based on interpretation of numerical data regarding past performance. For example, an analysis of sales for previous years gives some indication of what might be expected this year. The science of working with this sort of numerical data is known as *statistics*. Essential in certain types of decision making, statistics is also one of the most valuable all-around tools used by business management. Statistical data are most useful when presented in a form that is easy to read and interpret—and thus the wide usage of the chart, the graph, and (though to a lesser extent) the table. Indeed, pictorial methods of presenting statistical data are quite common to business, to government, and to a vast array of business periodicals.

In this chapter we shall study the processes used in making business decisions, and the ways in which research and statistics are used in business operation and management. We shall also study about useful sources of business information, methods of statistical measurement used in business analysis and research, and various graphic methods of presenting statistical information.

WHAT IS DECISION MAKING?

For purposes of our discussion, the definition of *decision making* will be narrowed somewhat (eliminating "things" and "propositions") to mean *the process of choosing a specific procedure or course of action from among several possible alternatives.* Decisions fall into one of three classes: *policy decisions, administrative decisions,* and *ad hoc decisions.*

Policy decisions determine such matters as the organizational and financial structures of the business, the degree of automation to be employed, and whether the finished products are to be marketed through wholesalers, through retailers, or direct to consumers.

Administrative decisions determine how policy is to be carried out. For example, after the policy decision has been made as to the size of the advertising budget, administrative decisions choose the advertising media and decide the nature and type of advertising to be used. Policy decisions set forth the basic principles that are to govern the over-all business operation. Administrative decisions translate company policies into courses of action.

Ad hoc decisions are those that must be made to cover specific situations as they arise. The decision made in each instance applies to that particular problem situation, under the specific circumstances that prevail at that time, and it may never arise again.

PROCEDURES FOLLOWED IN DECISION MAKING

A business's objectives determine its areas of decision. For example, assume that the demand for a certain factory's products dictates an enlargement of production facilities. The objective is to construct new facilities. The first basic decision that must be made is whether to build an addition to the present plant or to construct a new plant. If the latter is decided on, many other decisions will need to be reached regarding size, design, location, equipment, etc. In each of these decisions many alternatives may be feasible, but specific choices from among them must be made.

Defining the Problem and Suggesting Solutions. A clear-cut definition of the problem, and an immediate identification of several plausible alternative courses of action toward its solution, is the first step. (Since the two activities are practically concurrent, and since no firm course of action need be decided on yet, these two steps may be regarded as one.) It is most desirable to define the problem in such a manner that quantitative measurement methods can be applied in its solution; usually the best decisions are reached when they are supported by numerical data analyses. Frequently there are several practicable alternative courses of action which it is obvious may be taken, and it may even be decided to pursue more than one alternative. In some cases these alternatives may be followed separately, while in others they may be combined.

Gathering Pertinent Data. The second step is obtaining data—facts, observations, and experiences—that bear directly upon the problem. Data may take a variety of forms; but if numerical data can be assembled, this should be done. Often, data outside the business operation itself may have an important bearing on the problem at hand. Secondary sources generally report data covering a much wider scope than that from company records alone. This larger picture may be as important as, or even more important than, in-house data. Certainly all information available that relates to the problem to be solved and the decision to be made should be utilized. The

Economic Almanac and the *Statistical Abstract of the United States* collect data from many primary sources; they serve as useful secondary sources of information on almost every aspect of business operation faced by American business enterprises.

Analyzing the Data. The data collected must be *classified* into "groups" of related information. Actually, this step is one of organizing the information so that it may be studied. After the data are classified, the relative importance of each "group" must be decided on. The proper study and interpretation of data will go a long way in determining its usefulness in decision making by persons responsible for formulating policy.

Presenting the Data. The chief purpose in analyzing and interpreting data is to select the information most pertinent to the problem's solution. Closely associated is the choice of the method of presenting data to management. (These methods are discussed later in this chapter.)

Choosing a Course of Action. After all alternatives are evaluated, a course of action must be decided on—for here, too, the proof of the pudding is in the eating. Only the actual tryout of the chosen course of action proves the wisdom of the decision made. Of course, decision making is not an independent function of management. Decisions are always made in the context of one or more of the true management activities: planning, organizing, staffing, directing, controlling, or innovating.

METHODS OF COLLECTING DATA

There are several different methods used in collecting data when doing research, but the most common ones are observation and the survey method. Experimentation, which is the chief research method used in science, is also used to some degree in business. It may be used for evaluating advertising techniques or for measuring relationships among working environmental factors, attitudes, and production accomplishments.

The Observation Method

In the *observation method,* the researcher studies the behavior of people while they are shopping or at work. It is used by drugstores and retail establishments, for example, in the study of customer buying habits and preferences. It is especially valuable in determining desirable locations for retail stores, for the observer can take an accurate check on the number of cars passing selected locations, or the number of people walking past during specified periods of the day.

Observation is the basic method employed in job analysis and in time-and-motion study, where motion pictures are often used to supplement direct observation. The chief advantage of the observation method is its accuracy and objectivity: it collects facts rather than opinions.

The Survey Method

In the *survey method*, the researcher gathers his information through the use of questionnaires or uniform interview forms—by asking people questions. This research method is often used in gathering information related to marketing. Purchasers are asked about their buying habits, income level, size of family. Businessmen are surveyed regarding plans for plant expansion, intentions of opening new territories, employment practices. Researchers using the survey method may be interested either in factual data or in people's opinions.

One common survey technique is the mail *questionnaire*. This is especially useful when information is wanted from a large geographical area. The questionnaires are mailed either to a sample of the public at large or to a selected group of individuals. Although the percentage of returns is never large, this device is still the most economical way to cover a wide area.

When designing questionnaires, one should keep both the form and the questions short. Naturally, in order to yield helpful information, questions should relate to the kinds of factual information that the persons being surveyed would be expected to know. Questions should be very carefully worded so as not to suggest certain answers. Both questionnaires and interview forms should be pre-tested before the final copy for the instrument is decided upon. And, one should avoid surveying persons for information that is already available elsewhere.

The *interview* is another commonly used survey technique. In recent years the telephone has been used extensively for collecting information on consumer preferences and on radio and television listening habits. The telephone is also used to locate potential customers for special types of services, such as photographs or home repairs.

Face-to-face interviews are used to gather information in both homes and offices. Naturally, this type of interview is more costly than either the telephone interview or the mail questionnaire, and largely for this reason is used most often with a select group of people. Advertising agencies use the personal interview to check on reader attention and reaction to magazine advertisements.

One of the problems of interviewing is that the interviewer, try as he may not to, injects his personality into the questioning to some extent. Because of this, when several different interviewers are used, variations appear in the data collected. Add to this the fact that supervision of the actual interviews is impossible, and you see why coaching sessions for prospective interviewers are considered a vital necessity.

RESEARCH AND DEVELOPMENT

There has been considerable emphasis placed on research and development for many years, and the amount of money thus spent continues to grow. The total amount spent for research and development in 1967 was over $21 billion, or 3½ times as much as was spent a decade earlier. Approximately two-thirds of the funds for research and development are furnished by the federal government. In 1955 the government furnished slightly over 50 percent of research money, and between 1960 and 1967 about two-thirds of it. The federal government spent approximately $16 billion for research in fiscal 1967, but there are some indications that this is beginning to level off. This means that private industry will need to increase its contributions in this field if we are to avoid reaching a plateau in research-and-development spending.

Although the government supplies a large share of the funds we have been discussing, the work they support is largely carried out in industrial laboratories: in 1968, for instance, more than three times as much research money was spent in industry's laboratories as in governmental labs. Universities and university research centers rank third in the amount of money spent for research.

Product Research

Product research is largely concerned with the improvement of present products and the development of new ones. It is for the most part experimental research carried on in research laboratories. Most large businesses maintain research labs devoted to the discovery, development, and testing of new materials and products.

A considerable percentage of the funds supplied by the federal government was channelled into research concerned with the military and space programs. It contributes heavily to experimentation in the biological and physical sciences, and in aeronautics, in both state and private universities. It also subsidizes most of the research and development done by private businesses in the aircraft and electronics industries.

Market Research

Market research includes all studies of marketing for both products and services. Concerned with analyzing marketing methods and consumer buying habits, its purpose is to secure information useful in increasing company sales (and thus in improving sales position in relation to the total potential market). It is most essential in those areas where competition is keenest, for it helps a company to remain successful by keeping abreast of consumer preferences regarding its product lines. Although some companies carry on thier own market research, many employ advertising agencies to perform this service.

FORECASTING

Many decisions are based on estimates of what is likely to happen in the future. Such decisions are made almost daily by both businessmen and economists employed by governments. These estimates of future economic conditions or trends, based on thorough analyses of the past and present, are called *forecasts*. Both *short-term* and *long-range* forecasts are used.

Types of Forecasts

There are many different types of forecasts undertaken by business management, but most of them can be classified as forecasts regarding *supply, control,* and *demand. Supply forecasts* are concerned with the purchase and use of resources which represent cost factors to the company. Forecasts designed to aid in *control* may relate either to materials or financing. *Demand forecasts* are those anticipating the amount of future sales.

Supply Forecasts. The establishment of production schedules must be preceded by forecasts of both the supply and cost of labor. Two factors relating to available labor and scheduling are the need for overtime work and the efficient use of expensive machinery.

The demand for raw materials and supplies must be forecast as accurately as possible. If shortages of materials or difficulties in delivery due to possible labor strikes against suppliers are likely, orders must be placed well in advance. The forecast of market costs of materials plays a significant role here. If a rising market is anticipated, early purchasing will be ordered and a large inventory maintained. If a falling market is forecast, inventories will be maintained at a minimal figure.

Control Forecasts. In the preceding chapter the use of budgets for control purposes was discussed and illustrated. The cash forecast and controls on expenses are essential. If interest rates are likely to rise, management will favor long-term loans, while a forecast of future decreases in the cost of borrowed funds would dictate borrowing for short periods of time.

Demand Forecasts. Sales budgets are actually forecasts of the consumer demand for company products. Estimates of income must be based on forecasts of the market demand.

Sales budgets are greatly affected by forecasts of the economic trend for business in general. Also, the outlook of the particular industry must be studied; the past sales record must be interpreted in the light of current and future company policies that might increase sales volume—development of new products, diversification of product lines, expansion of territory, increase in advertising, etc. Other factors must also be considered, such as changes in consumer income or tastes, the strength of competitors, or the marketing of substitute products.

Techniques of Forecasting

The method to be used in forecasting will depend somewhat on the purpose of the forecast and the way it is to be used. There are many methods (such as opinion polling and econometrics, which you would study in a full course in statistical method), but here we shall discuss only three of those most commonly used: *trend analysis, correlation,* and *composite estimate.*

Trend Analysis. Forecasting by trend analysis is actually an interpretation of the historical sequence of the past, applying it to the immediate future. It assumes that the rate of growth or change that has persisted in the past will continue. Historical data are plotted on a graph and a trend line is established. Frequently a straight line is extended for the future. However, if certain known factors indicate that the future rate will increase, the line may be curved upward. As a general rule, there may be several future projections, depending on the length of the historical period selected. Excellent examples of forecasting by trend analysis are the line graphs of population growth and production shown in earlier chapters of this book. The accuracy of forecasting by historical sequence or trend analysis depends on good judgment in interpreting those changing factors that may keep history from repeating.

Correlation. Correlation is simply a matter of establishing a pattern of relationship between two or more variables. The closer or greater the relationship, the higher the degree of correlation. This relationship may be either positive or negative. For example, as the total volume of manufacturing increases, the number of gainfully employed workers grows larger. In other words, there is a direct relationship between the volume of production and the number of workers employed. This is a positive relationship, because as one increases, so does the other. So we call it a *positive* correlation.

However, as the amount of money available for investment increases, the earning power of money (usually expressed in terms of interest rates) decreases. When the money supply is plentiful, increased competition among lending institutions forces interest rates down. On the other hand, when money becomes more scarce, the competitive bidding among people who want to borrow money brings about higher interest rates. In other words, the availability of money has a direct effect on prevailing interest rates; there is obviously some kind of relationship between the two. Since one decreases as the other increases, the correlation is *negative.*

In the same way, a decrease in the number of bushels of corn produced would probably cause an increase in the price of corn, other things being equal. Here again there is a definite relationship between the two and therefore a degree of correlation; and again the correlation is negative, because as one increases the other decreases.

When using correlation for forecasting purposes, one must keep in mind that a relationship that has been present in the past may not continue to exist in the same ratio. Unusual weather conditions, international tension, or labor-management troubles may disturb the relationship. Correlation forecasting is most useful when one factor in the relationship always occurs prior to the second factor. For example, the demand for most consumer products in any given area varies in direct proportion to the population change. An unusual increase in the number of houses being constructed due to the influx of new industries would signal an increased demand for products sold at retail. In such situations, statistical correlations may be established and rather accurate forecasts made.

Composite Estimate. The composite estimate is largely used in forecasting future sales volume. Each district manager is asked to report his best estimate of the future demand for his territory. (It is assumed that he knows more about the potential market for his area than anyone else, and that he will present an accurate forecast.) The total of all district estimates becomes the prediction of total sales for a given future period, such as six or 12 months. This total is then checked against the judgment of the person at the head of the sales department for the whole organization.

The Forecasting Process

Forecasting changes in business activity involves more than statistical analysis. It includes an understanding of why changes have occurred in the past, for the historical record serves as the basis for future projections. Another important aspect is that of choosing the items to be measured. Some factors bear directly upon a particular problem, whereas others may be only indirectly related to it. For example, the U.S. Department of Commerce in determining the gross national product uses a carefully selected group of factors.

After these steps have been taken, it is necessary to decide upon the measuring devices to be employed—trend analysis, cyclical fluctuations, index numbers, etc. Then, all data that seem to have a bearing upon the forecast projection must be interpreted in terms of anticipated alterations in future events or planned courses of action. For example, when forecasting the gross national product for 1966, anticipated changes in government purchases was closely tied to the federal government's intentions regarding Great Society programs. However, when forecasting the GNP for 1967, the degree of change in the government sector was more closely related to the degree of escalation of the war in Vietnam.

The Prudential Insurance Company's *Annual Economic Forecast* for 1968, which is based on seven major components, is shown below. Supporting graphs are also shown for four of the seven components on which the GNP estimate is based. You will note that in only one of the seven components, foreign trade, was a decrease anticipated. In all other components significant increases were forecast.

GNP COMPONENTS (IN BILLIONS)

	1967	1968
Government		
Federal Government Spending	$ 90.5	$100.0
State and Local Outlays	86.5	95.0
Business		
New Plant and Equipment	82.5	87.5
Inventory Investment	2.7	5.5
Consumers		
Housing Outlays	24.3	28.0
Consumer Spending for Durables, Nondurables and Services	493.0	527.0
Foreign Trade	5.5	5.0
Total GNP	$785.0	$848.0

SOURCES OF BUSINESS INFORMATION

There are many sources of data that are extremely helpful to business management. We have just discussed research, which is categorized as a *primary source* since it gathers data not previously available. *Secondary sources* are those that report information assembled from primary sources. The Bureau of Labor Statistics of the U.S. Department of Labor, and the Bureau of the Census of the Department of Commerce collect and publish

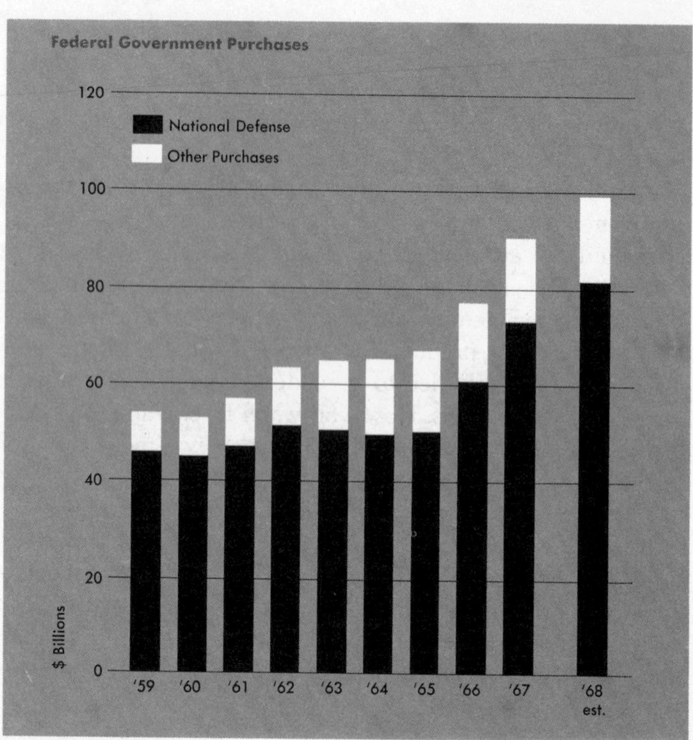
Federal Government Purchases
National Defense
Other Purchases
120
100
80
60
40
20
0
$ Billions
'59
'60
'61
'62
'63
'64
'65
'66
'67
'68
est.

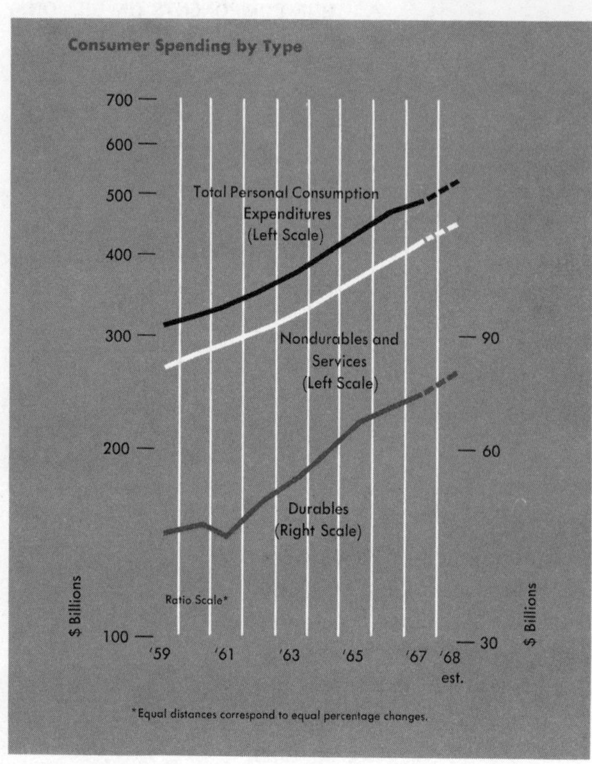
Consumer Spending by Type
700
600
500
400
300
200
100
90
60
30
Total Personal Consumption
Expenditures
(Left Scale)
Nondurables and
Services
(Left Scale)
Durables
(Right Scale)
Ratio Scale*
$ Billions
$ Billions
'59
'61
'63
'65
'67
'68
est.
*Equal distances correspond to equal percentage changes.

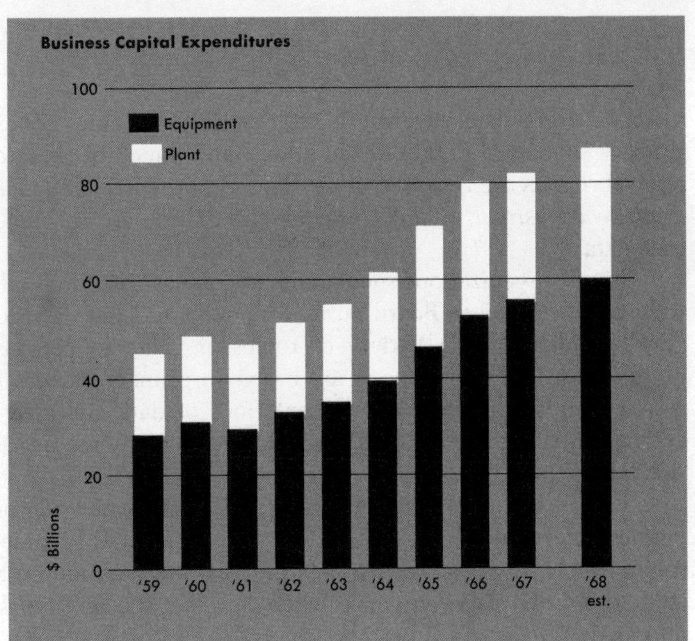
Business Capital Expenditures
Equipment
Plant
100
80
60
40
20
0
$ Billions
'59
'60
'61
'62
'63
'64
'65
'66
'67
'68
est.

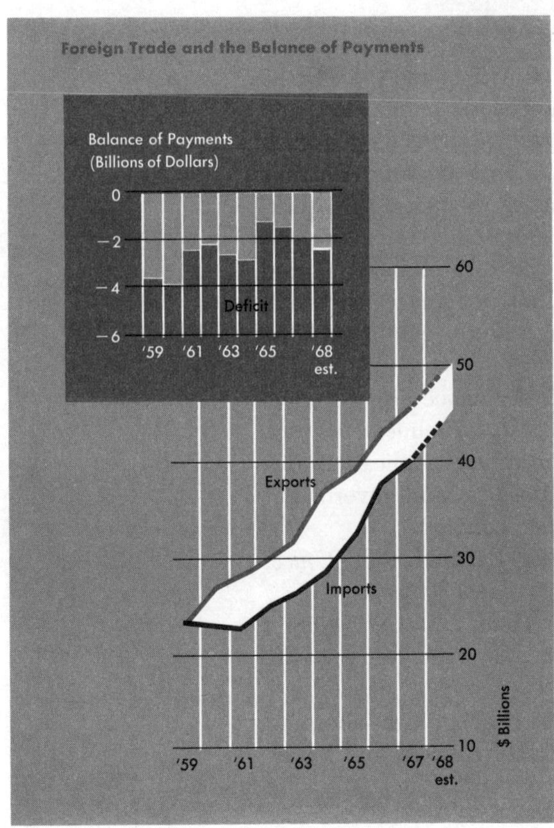
Foreign Trade and the Balance of Payments
Balance of Payments
(Billions of Dollars)
0
−2
−4
−6
Deficit
'59
'61
'63
'65
'68
est.
Exports
Imports
60
50
40
30
20
10
$ Billions
'59
'61
'63
'65
'67
'68
est.

in report form data covering a wide variety of topics. Their reports are primary sources of data. On the other hand, much of these data from the original reports are repeated or condensed in the *Economic Almanac* or the *Statistical Abstract of the United States.* These are secondary sources of such data.

Private organizations such as the Brookings Institute and the National Industrial Conference Board publish reports and issue statistical charts and graphs dealing with a variety of topics of value to persons engaged in business. Most of their reports are based on primary sources, but some are merely graphic and succinct presentations of data collected originally by another agency such as the Department of Commerce or Department of Labor.

Since both private and governmental agencies provide much valuable business information, you, as a business student, should become familiar with some of them. Every student who is studying business administration should learn the best places to look when seeking specific types of business information.

Business Periodicals

Many general and specialized periodicals are of interest and value to the businessman and the business student. Among the general publications are: *Business Week* (issued weekly), *The Prentice-Hall Report on Business* (issued weekly), *Fortune* (issued monthly), and *The Economic Almanac* (issued annually). Some representative publications on the principal specialized areas of business are listed below:

Advertising. Among the periodicals that discuss research being carried on in the field of advertising, and that report news about agencies, methods, and trends, are: *Advertising Age, Broadcasting, Editor and Publisher, Printer's Ink,* and *Tide.*

Finance. The leading periodicals in the field of finance are: *Banking, Barron's National Business and Financial Weekly, Financial World, Moody's Stock Survey,* and *The Wall Street Journal.* These publications discuss economic trends, new financial policies of business and government agencies, and the over-all financial condition of the economy.

Information handling. Publications in this field include *The Office, Office Appliances and Administrative Management,* and *Systems.*

Insurance. Best's Insurance News, Insurance Field, and *The National Underwriter* are among the best sources of current news and trends in the field of insurance.

Labor relations. Three important publications dealing with labor and labor-management relations are *Labor, Monthly Labor Review,* and *Industrial and Labor Relations Review.*

Management. Fortune, Business Week, Modern Management, Nation's Business, and *Business Review and Forecast* contain current information about processes, new equipment, and automation in production.

Marketing. Excellent sources of information about current marketing trends, and reports on marketing management, are provided by *Industrial Marketing, Purchasing, Sales Management,* and *Journal of Marketing.*

Personnel management. The leading periodicals of interest to persons in personnel and industrial relations work include: *Personnel, Personnel Administration, and Personnel Psychology.* These publications contain articles dealing with employment practices, fringe benefits, employee training, and wage negotiations.

Retailing. Some of the periodicals of interest to those engaged in retailing are *Department Store Economist, Chain Store Age,* and *Women's Wear Daily.* They deal with current fashion trends, store management, and consumer-research reports.

Governmental Publications

The federal government is the leading collector and publisher of statistical data and reports. In addition to the data that governmental agencies accumulate for their own use, they make a great deal of information available to business executives through published reports. The Federal Reserve Board, the Treasury Department, the Department of Labor, and the Department of Commerce are all vitally interested in assembling and distributing business and financial data. Many reports are published by the Bureau of the Census and the Bureau of Foreign and Domestic Commerce, both of which are in the Department of Commerce. In fact, governmental publications have become so numerous that an index of all bulletins, reports, and documents issued by the various branches is printed each month. Called the *Monthly Catalogue of Useful Documents,* it is issued by the United States Superintendent of Documents.

Here are some of the regularly issued governmental publications:

Publications of the United States Bureau of the Census

Census of the United States. Published every 10 years. In addition to statistics on population, with which you are probably familiar, census reports cover unemployment, business, manufacturing, distribution, agriculture, and state and local governments.

Census of Manufactures. Published biennially. Contains detailed statistical reports for different industries, such as textiles, paper products, and food products. Includes statistics for the various industries in each of the 50 states.

Census of Business. Covers, on an area basis, retail trade, wholesale trade, service businesses, construction, and distribution of manufacturer's sales.

Statistical Abstract of the United States. Published annually. Contains a summary of statistics of the industrial, social, political, and economic organizations of the United States.

Other Publications

Foreign Commerce Yearbook. Series of annual compilations of foreign economic statistics. (*Foreign Commerce Yearbook* alternates each year between statistics on the United States and foreign countries.)

Domestic Commerce. Published monthly. Includes articles on business trends, census releases, and reports of important legislation affecting markets and prices.

Survey of Current Business. Published monthly. Presents articles and statistics on current business situations for the major fields of activity in trade and industry. Summarizes data relating to trends in economic conditions. A supplement to this periodical is published weekly.

Foreign Commerce Weekly. A series of reports and discussions on world trade and commerce.

Market Research Sources. Published biennially. A guide to sources of information on domestic marketing. Lists recent publications on marketing.

Consumer Market Data Handbook and *Industrial Market Data Handbook.* Published every 10 years. Present statistical data on general consumer market, farm market, and industrial market upon which the public can base economical marketing or sales operations.

Monthly Labor Review. Published by the Bureau of Labor Statistics. Deals with trends and status of employment and unemployment, labor legislation and court decisions, wages, retail prices, and wholesale prices.

Federal Reserve Bulletin. Published monthly by the Federal Reserve Board. Presents articles pertaining to business conditions and has approximately 55 pages of statistical tables dealing with finance, industrial production, construction, employment, and costs of living.

USING MEASURES TO SUMMARIZE DATA

The thousands of items of information that the researcher collects must be tabulated and analyzed before they can be put to use. In recent years, machine methods of tabulation have greatly reduced the time required for this step. After all the data have been tabulated, the experienced statistician is ready to analyze them. Actually, he has planned, or helped to plan, the whole research project beforehand. Thorough preparation in systematic planning will make his analysis easier. It is in the analysis and summarization of data that the statistician draws on his knowledge and experience in fitting the facts together into an orderly and meaningful picture. Usually, data are grouped together so that some type of measure may be used.

Statistical Averages

Perhaps the most frequent use of statistical data is some form of average. The most commonly used forms of average are the *mean*, the *median*, and the *mode*.

The Mean. The *mean* is sometimes called the *arithmetic mean* or *arithmetic average*. It is calculated simply by adding a group of numbers and dividing the total by the number of items in the group. It is the most commonly used average in business.

Let's assume that you are the manufacturer of a line of electrical appliances. You are interested not only in knowing your total sales and your total profit for each month, quarter, or year, but also in how the current figures compare with those for previous periods. You might discover, for example, that although your total sales for all products are lower this year than they were last year, still the sales of one product (Product *N* in the following table) have been unusually good. As a basis for comparison, you might gather together sales data for the last five years as follows:

Year	Total Sales of All Company Products	Sales of Product *N*
Current year	$6,300,000	$320,000
Last year	6,600,000	300,000
2 years ago	5,900,000	280,000
3 years ago	6,000,000	275,000
4 years ago	6,300,000	260,000
5 years ago	6,200,000	235,000
5-year average	$6,200,000	$270,000

With these figures, you can compare this year's record with other years during the past five-year period and also with the average for the period. Here are some of the pertinent facts that such a comparison would bring home to you:

1. Total sales for this year are below those of last year.
2. Total sales for this year were exceeded only once during the previous five-year period—last year.

3. Total sales for this year exceed the yearly average for the five-year period by $100,000.
4. This year's sales of Product *N* were the greatest of any year during the five-year period.
5. This year's sales of Product *N* exceed the average by $50,000.

If you had compared this year's record with that of last year only, you would have an entirely different picture from that shown by a comparison with the five-year period. This year's sales, when compared with last year's, fell off, but when compared with the five-year period this year's total sales are good. When we examine the record for Product *N* sales, we see that this year's increase is about the same as that for any other previous year—$20,000 seems to be the normal increase.

When the record of Product *N* sales is compared with the total sales, we see that whereas the total sales have fluctuated from year to year the sales for Product *N* have shown a continuous increase. With this information, management is in a position to determine why the sales of Product *N* varies so greatly from that of the total sales. By making a similar analysis of other products, management may be able to determine the cause of the fluctuation of the total sales and which products should be dropped from the line of goods handled.

The Median. Another type of average that is sometimes used in business is the *median.* This is determined by arranging a series of numbers in ascending or descending order; the middle number is the median number in the series. In other words, there are as many numbers in the series that are smaller than the median as there are numbers that are larger. Here is how we would find the median if we used the same series of numbers that we used in solving for the arithmetic mean:

	Total Sales	
	$6,600,000	
	6,300,000	The median number in this series is $6,200,000, which is exactly the same as the arithmetic mean.
Median	6,200,000	
	6,000,000	
	5,900,000	

	Sale of Product X	
	$300,000	
	280,000	In this case, the median number is $275,000, whereas the arithmetic mean was $270,000.
Median	275,000	
	260,000	
	215,000	

In these two cases, both the mean and the median are meaningful—either one could,be used. On the other hand, here is an example involving the costs of five different possible plant sites, any one of which would meet the needs of the business:

	$147,000
	32,000
Median	27,000
	21,000
	18,000
	5) $245,000 $49,000 . . . . *arithmetic mean*

In this case, the median ($27,000) would be far more meaningful than the arithmetic mean ($49,000). None of the properties is valued at $49,000; only one exceeds that amount, and it exceeds the mean by a considerable sum. However, one piece of property is actually valued at the median price of $27,000, and there are as many pieces of property priced higher than $27,000 as there are lower. In this illustration, you can see that there is a tendency for the prices to be grouped about the median, whereas there is no tendency for them to be grouped about the mean.

The Mode. A third measurement of averages that is sometimes used is called the *mode.* This is the point of greatest concentration—in other words, the figure that occurs the greatest number of times in a series. Let us consider the hourly wages paid to a group of men who are performing similar work but who, because of differences in seniority and skill, receive different wage rates. The wage distribution is as follows:

Hourly Wage	Number Earning That Wage	Calculation of Arithmetic Mean
$2.20	2	(2.20 × 2) = $ 4.40
2.10	6	(2.10 × 6) = 12.60
2.05	10	. . . . 20.50
2.00 . . median	12	. . . . 24.00
1.90 . . mode	14	. . . . 26.60
1.75	8	. . . . 14.00
1.70	4	. . . . 6.80
	56	56) $108.90 (1.94 . . . arithmetic mean

In this example, we found the arithmetic mean by multiplying the hourly wages by the number of men earning each wage; then we added all these figures together and divided by the total number of wage-earners. The arithmetic mean turns out to be $1.94, the median is $2.00, and the mode—that is, the point of greatest concentration—is $1.90.

You can see from these examples that different types of averages show different values. The value of an average lies in the degree to which it conveys a real meaning to the data. If the distribution of data is relatively concentrated about the average, the *mean* is significant. When the data are distributed over a wide range, the *median* may be more meaningful. At least the median indicates that in the distribution, there are as many cases falling above the median as below it. There are times when it is important to know which figure occurs most frequently, and the *mode* gives this information.

Index Numbers

In many situations, figures that show relationships are much more significant than absolute figures would be. One of the most common ways to show relationships is by means of index numbers. An *index number* indicates the changes that have occurred in groups of related data on different dates or for different periods of time. Index numbers are used in business probably more frequently than any other statistical device. They are used to measure a variety of business activities, such as agricultural and mineral production, manufacturing, wholesale and retail trade, employment, construction, finance, and general business activity.

A common use of index numbers is in relation to the cost of living. In fact, perhaps the best-known index is the *Consumer Price Index*. This index, prepared and published by the federal government, is in effect a method of showing from one month to another the average price of selected articles considered to be basic in determining the cost of living of American families. In order to show comparisons, a base period is chosen and assigned a value of 100. The data for other years is shown as a percentage of this base period. In Table 9.1 the period from 1957 to 1959 is the base period.

The Consumer Price Index measures the average change in prices of goods and services purchased by city wage-earner and clerical-worker families, and by single persons living alone. The weights used in calculating the index are based on studies of actual expenditures by wage-earners and clerical workers. The quantities and qualities of the items in the "market basket" remain the same between consecutive pricing periods, so that the index measures the *effect of price change only* on the cost of living of these families. The index does *not* measure changes in the total amount families spend for living expenses.

Table 9.1 shows the trend in consumer prices for selected commodity groups, 1951 to 1966. Alaska and Hawaii were included for the first time in 1964.

Let us take an example in relation to the cost of living to show how the index numbers are calculated. The year 1958 is frequently chosen as a base year—or the period 1957 to 1959 inclusive may be used as the base.

TABLE 9.1

CONSUMER PRICE INDEX, 1951–1966 (1957–1959 = 100)

Year	All Items	Food[1]	Housing	Apparel and Upkeep[2]	Transportation	Health and Recreation
1951	90.5	95.4	88.2	98.2	84.0	(NA)*
1952	92.5	97.1	89.9	97.2	89.6	(NA)*
1953	93.2	95.6	92.3	96.5	92.1	89.7
1954	93.6	95.4	93.4	96.3	90.8	90.7
1955	93.3	94.0	94.1	95.9	89.7	91.4
1956	94.7	94.7	95.5	97.8	91.3	93.6
1957	98.0	97.8	98.5	99.5	96.5	97.0
1958	100.7	101.9	100.2	99.8	99.7	100.3
1959	101.5	100.3	101.3	100.6	103.8	102.8
1960	103.1	101.4	103.1	102.2	103.8	105.4
1961	104.2	102.6	103.9	103.0	105.0	107.3
1962	105.4	103.6	104.8	103.6	107.2	109.4
1963	106.7	105.1	106.0	104.8	107.8	111.4
1964	108.1	106.4	107.2	105.7	109.3	113.6
1965	109.9	108.8	108.5	106.8	111.1	115.6
1966	112.0	113.9	109.6	108.2	111.4	117.6

* (NA) = Not Available.

[1] Beginning 1953, includes restaurant meals and other food bought and eaten away from home.

[2] Formerly apparel; redefined in 1964 to include laundry, drycleaning, and other apparel upkeep services.

Source: U.S. Dept. of Labor, Bureau of Labor Statistics, *Monthly Labor Review*, and unpublished data.

In figuring index numbers, the base period is assigned a value of 100. In our example we shall assign a value of 100 to the base period 1957 to 1959, since this was used as the base in Table 9.1. The calculation would be made as follows:

Item	Average Yearly Cost, 1957–1959	Index Number	Cost for 1966	Index Number
Food	$1,750	100	$1,995	114
Housing	1,386	100	1,511	109
Apparel	584	100	631	108
Transportation	568	100	630	111
Health and Recreation	314	100	370	118
Other Living Expenses	1,004	100	1,124	112
Total	$5,606	100	$6,261	112

The index number in each case was found by dividing the figure for the year to be compared (1966) by the figure for the base year.

For food $\dfrac{\$1{,}995}{\$1{,}750} = 114$

For housing $\dfrac{\$1{,}511}{\$1{,}386} = 109$

Another way to state this would be in terms of proportion, as follows:

For food $\dfrac{\$1{,}750}{100} = \dfrac{1{,}995}{x}$ $\quad 1{,}750x = 199{,}500$ $\quad x = 114$

For housing $\dfrac{\$1{,}386}{100} = \dfrac{1{,}511}{x}$ $\quad 1{,}386x = 151{,}100$ $\quad x = 109$

The cost-of-living index has become extremely important in recent years. Many labor agreements provide for automatic adjustments in wage rates as the cost-of-living index fluctuates. Likewise, management considers this when deciding on increments (increases) for salaried workers; in addition to merit raises, a cost-of-living adjustment is also included. Other important indices are the wholesale price index and the index of industrial production.

PRESENTATION OF STATISTICAL DATA

In most organizations, top management does not want to be burdened with masses of unorganized data or to waste valuable time in attempting to interpret them. After the data have been collected, tabulated, and organized, they should be presented clearly and concisely. The devices most commonly used for presenting data are numerical tables, charts, maps, and graphs. There are several kinds of graphs; the ones you will meet most often are line, bar, and circle graphs. Although most data may be presented in various ways, usually one method of presentation is more effective than the others. Just to show you why this is true, in the following paragraphs we shall present data in several different ways.

Line Graphs

The *line graph* is one of the most commonly used types of graph. It is especially useful when the variations to be presented are a time series. The time factor is nearly always plotted horizontally, and the variation data, vertically. The points plotted are then connected by either solid or dotted lines. When it is desired to illustrate several series on the same graph, different-colored lines are drawn. Economic trends, and growth factors such as population increases or increased sales volume, are common examples of

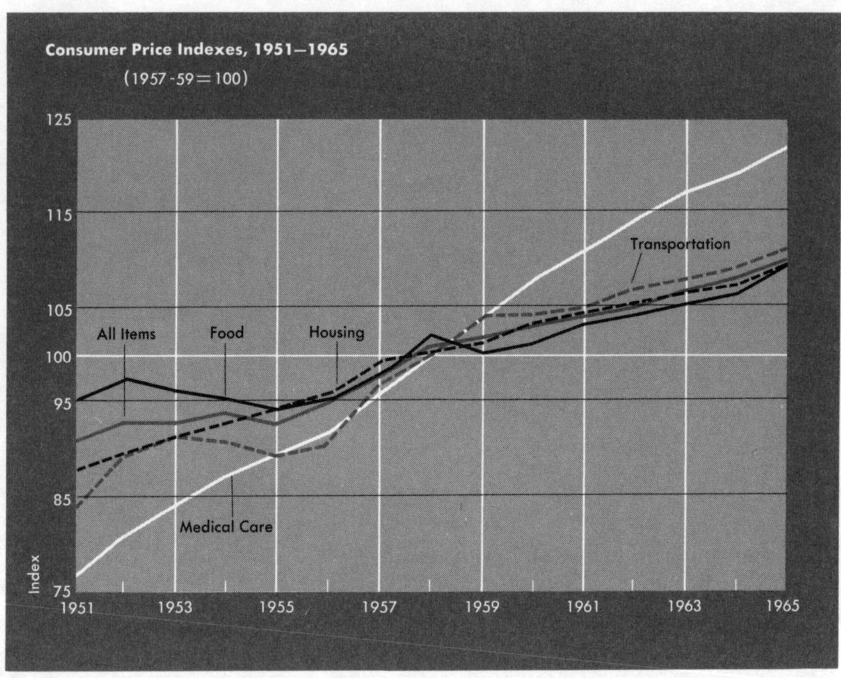

After a chart prepared by Dept. of Commerce, Bureau of the Census. Data from Dept. of Labor, Bureau of Labor Statistics.

the sort of data that can be illustrated in an easy-to-understand fashion by means of line graphs.

In order to illustrate the differences between a numerical table and a line graph, the data shown in Table 9.1 is reproduced here in the form of a line graph. Although you can see the relationships much more readily in the chart (that is, the graph), for comparative purposes, exact figures are easier to obtain quickly from the table.

Other examples of line graphs are shown in a number of places in this book. Note for example the graph on labor union membership on page 336 and that for the cost of living adjustments on page 358.

Bar Graphs

In *bar graphs,* which are also widely used, the bars may be drawn either vertically or horizontally. The horizontal bar graph is useful in comparing different data for the same time interval; the vertical bar graph is excellent for comparing data for different time intervals. Bar graphs are easy to interpret, for the lengths of the bars show the relative quantities. Sometimes

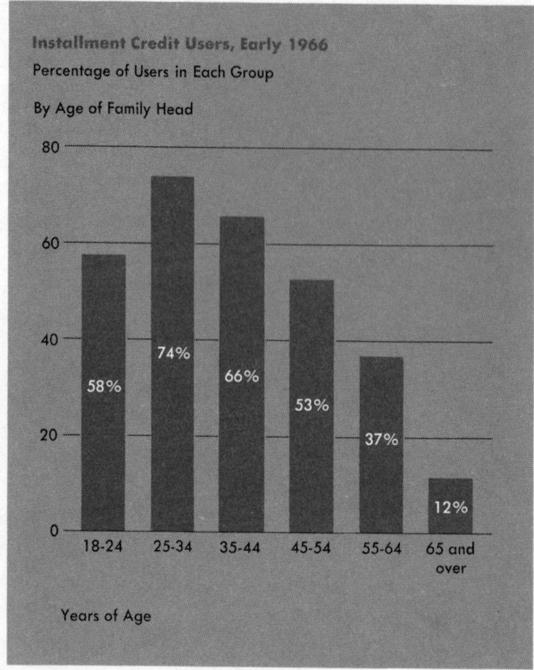

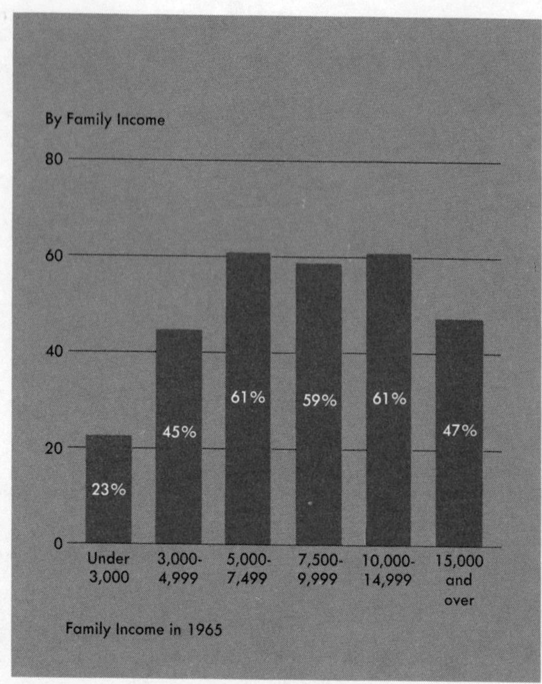

Source: Survey Research Center, University of Michigan

two sets of bars are shown side-by-side, with different shadings used to distinguish them. In another variation, different shadings are introduced to show a breakdown of the total figures being presented.

Interesting data on the uses of installment credit are shown in the accompanying bar graphs. Other examples of bar graphs are shown in the section on forecasting on pages 256 and 257.

Circular Graphs

The simplest type of statistical graph is the *circular graph* or *pie graph,* which is especially valuable for presenting a breakdown of items expressed in dollar values or as percentages. The complete circle represents 100 percent, and each segment shows a percentage of the whole. Circle graphs frequently are used to show the distribution of the tax dollar—both the sources of income and the items of expenditure. They may also be used to show the breakdown of a company's sales dollar.

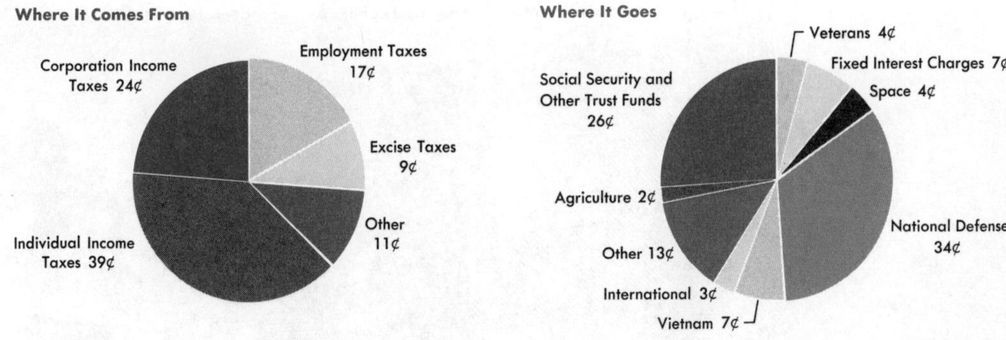

The Federal Government Dollar: 1967. [For year ending June 30. Based on estimated federal administrative budget and trust-fund receipts and expenditures.]

Source: After a chart prepared by Dept. of Commerce, Bureau of the Census. Data from Executive Office of the President, Bureau of the Budget.

Statistical Maps

Sometimes you may find it appropriate to present statistical data pertaining to one state, to an area of several states, or to the country as a whole, on a map of the geographical area being discussed. For example, on an outline map of the United States you can enter the figures for each state, or else use symbols to represent the numbers. Another method is to group the states into three or four divisions; by shading the states in each group differently, you can readily suggest the comparisons that the observer is to make.

RESEARCH AND STATISTICS AS A CAREER

In recent years there has been increasing recognition, both in business and government, of economic problems that can best be studied through statistical procedures. As a result, there has been a marked growth in the use and application of statistics.

The present demand for statisticians and statistical workers is greater than the supply. Graduates of collegiate schools of business administration who are trained in statistics experience little or no difficulty in securing desirable positions. There is also a shortage of individuals who are qualified to teach statistics in colleges and universities. Probably the supply of statisticians will be insufficient to meet the demand during the next half-century, because the field of statistics is not sufficiently glamorous to attract large numbers of individuals.

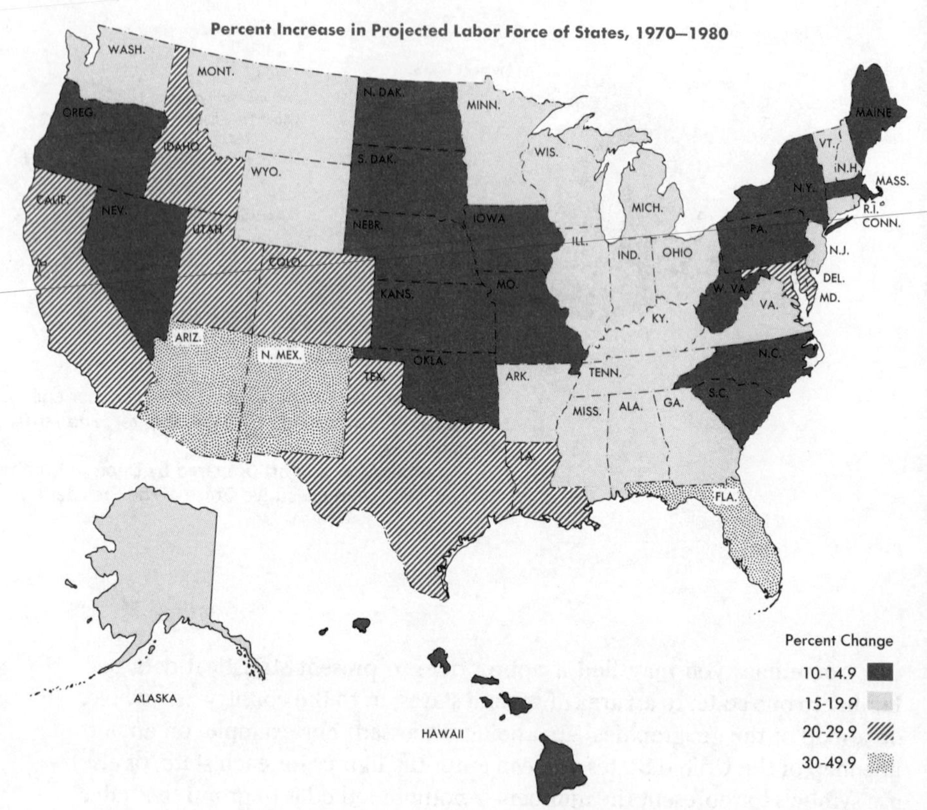

Monthly Labor Review, October, 1966.

Manufacturers, retailers, and advertising agencies spend millions of dollars each year to determine consumers' preferences, habits, opinions, and attitudes as a basis for making business decisions; both sampling and polling methods are used extensively. Statisticians with training and experience in scientific sampling find the fields of advertising and market research an important source of employment. Moreover, there is a shortage of actuaries in the field of insurance.

Your initial employment in the field of statistics might be as a statistical clerk, statistical draftsman, assistant statistician, or statistical analyst. It might be work in some related field, such as that of computer, accountant, tabulating-machine operator, or research assistant. There are also secretarial positions that require a knowledge of statistics. The statistician's salary is not unusually high, but employment is steady in this field, and increases in salary are commensurate with the increasing value of the statistician to the growth and development of the business.

Positions in governmental agencies under civil-service tenure vary from junior statistical clerk to principal statistician. Promotions to other fields are also common; you may become head of the department of accounting or finance, director of statistical research, or administrative consultant. Advancement depends on native ability, breadth of training, and experience.

Qualifications and Preparation

It is obvious from what we have said so far that statistical work is largely mathematical. Measurement of data must be accurate and orderly, and the statistical worker must like to work with figures. Artistic ability and originality are necessary in order to determine the types of charts or graphs that should be used. A certain amount of manual dexterity is essential, because the statistical worker is frequently called on to prepare charts and graphs requiring lettering and other drafting techniques. He must be able to operate calculating machines and to perform moderately complex statistical computations. He must develop a knack for reading and understanding charts and tables, and learn to distinguish between essential and unimportant data. Above all, he must possess the kind of mind that is apt at visualizing relative values from masses of data.

Statistics is a tool in research. It is necessary to know how to gather data and present them in such a way that the results will be reliable, valid, and objective. To be reliable, the results must be dependable; to be valid, the material must be accurate; and to be objective, the results must be free from personal judgments.

SUMMARY

Decision-making is practiced at every level of management, from the top executives to the supervisor. Almost every phase of business from production to sales must be planned in advance. This calls for schedules in production, budgets for financial planning, and sales forecasts. The steps in decision-making are very similar to those used in the scientific method of problem-solving.

Research aids in making business decisions because they must be based on the interpretation of facts and on projections of historical trends into the future. Experimental research characterizes research laboratories. Observational research is used in the factory through job analyses and time-and-motion studies. It is also useful for determining desirable locations for retail enterprises. The survey technique is most common in market research.

There are many useful sources of business information. Both private organizations and the federal government publish many books and periodicals which are very helpful to business management. The various statistical reports of the Bureau of the Census, *Economic Almanac,* and *Statistical Abstract of the United States* are considered standard works. There are special periodicals for almost every area of specialization in business—accounting, personnel, advertising, industrial management, and sales.

Both business and government economists employ a variety of measures such as the mean, median, mode, and index numbers. Almost every business publication and economic report makes use of statistical tables, charts, and graphs of all types. The most commonly used graphs are the line graph, bar graph, and circle graph.

There is a growing demand for research and statistical workers in business and government. Statistics is an attractive field for young people who are accurate in working with figures and who enjoy doing research or the preparation of statistical reports.

VOCABULARY REVIEW QUIZ

Match the following vocabulary terms with the statements below.

a. *Ad hoc* decision
b. Administrative decision
c. Composite estimate
d. Consumer Price Index
e. Correlation
f. Decision-making
g. Demand forecast
h. Index number
i. Mean
j. Median
k. Mode
l. Observation
m. Primary source
n. Product research
o. Research
p. Supply forecast
q. Survey method
r. Trend analysis

1. The scientific process of analyzing problem situations and drawing conclusions based on facts
2. The reaching of a conclusion as the basis for establishing a course of action
3. A decision having to do with the choice of procedures in implementing policy
4. A decision made in a specific case that may not occur again
5. A research method in which events are watched and recorded as they occur
6. The collection of data through the use of the questionnaire or interview
7. Research concerned with the development of new and improved goods
8. An estimate of the future need for different types of raw materials
9. An estimate of the future sales during a given period of time
10. An interpretation of past performance records as the basis for making estimates for the future
11. The degree of relationship between two or more variables
12. The combining of district estimates to secure the total forecast

M 13. The original source of business information

L 14. The arithmetic average of a group of related numbers

K 15. The point of greatest concentration as measured by the figure that occurs most frequently in a series of numbers

H 16. A figure used to indicate the degree of change that has taken place in relation to a base period

J 17. The middle number in a series of related figures

D 18. An index prepared by the federal government showing how the average price of selected cost-of-living factors compared with a selected base year or period

QUESTIONS FOR REVIEW STUDY

1. What are the steps followed in the scientific method of problem-solving?
2. What is the role of research in connection with decision-making by business management?
3. Describe a problem situation wherein the observation method would be suitable for collecting data.
4. What are the relative advantages and weaknesses of the questionnaire and interview?
5. What types of research are supported most liberally by the federal government?
6. What is the relationship between forecasting and control?
7. In using a trend analysis for forecasting future sales, under what circumstances would you change your forecast from the course of action suggested by just extending the historical line-graph?
8. Give an example showing how correlation is used in forecasting.
9. Describe the nature of the contents of a recent issue of *Survey of Current Business.*
10. Describe a situation in which the median would be more meaningful than the mean.
11. At what rate per year has the Consumer Price Index increased during the past decade? What items are included in calculating the index?
12. What types of data are ideally suited for being shown in the form of a line graph? In a bar graph? In a circle graph?
13. When would a statistical table be preferred over a graphic presentation?

PROBLEMS AND PROJECTS

1. Decide which types of graphs would be most suitable for depicting the following kinds of data:
   - (a) total income for five consecutive years
   - (b) comparison of sales for four districts during a given year
   - (c) breakdown of the income dollar by cost factors and profit
   - (d) trends in three cost-of-living items for a period of 10 years

2. The Arthur Fuller Co. has five departments with sales for one quarter as shown below. Compute the percentage of the total sales accounted for by each department and show this information as a circle graph.

Clothing	$150,000	Appliances	$75,000
Furniture	125,000	Household supplies	50,000
Cosmetics and jewelry	100,000		

3. Justify the practice of the federal government in furnishing money to private industry for experimental research.
4. Examine a recent volume of *Statistical Abstract of the United States.* Name eight specific types of information available there that would be of interest and value to various department chairmen of a chain of retail stores doing business in all sections of the United States.
5. Select an article from a recent issue of *Fortune* magazine. (a) Prepare a two- or three-paragraph condensation of the article. (b) What types of persons (those in what positions) would be most interested in reading the article? (c) Are the statistical data reported (if any) primary or secondary data?

A BUSINESS CASE

Case 9-1 An Interview Study for Paying Salesmen

The Harvey & Son Co., which processes and packages a variety of foodstuffs, employs 35 salesmen, whom it pays on a straight salary basis. The company has been awarding three small prizes to the three sales leaders each month. However, the management has observed that all salesmen sell about an equal volume of goods and that their sales are fairly constant from month to month.

The vice-president in charge of sales has recommended that the company change to a scheme of paying only commissions. The salesmen are asking for a combination plan of salaries plus commissions. As a research assistant to the president, you have been asked to make an interview survey of other similar companies to determine their practices and how well they are working.

What information would you seek in your interview study?

Information Management: Electronic Data Processing

10

We have already seen that decision-making by management is based on information, or data. Traditionally, information was recorded by pen, typewriter, or calculator, and records were stored in file cabinets or on microfilm. Today, information systems are much more complex, for the same information is used in many different departments of a typical business enterprise. Ordinarily, the same information is duplicated several times and filed in several different places.

As you might imagine, it requires many people to provide management with the various kinds of records information needed to transact today's business. Recent studies indicate that at the present time we need one office worker for every three employees in business.

Records and reports are becoming increasingly more complex, as well as more essential, in today's fast-paced business world. Therefore, the mechanization and automatization of records handling is a business "must." Many businesses are large enough to warrant their own installations of high-speed electronic equipment. Others can obtain the services of such equipment and specially trained personnel on a lease-time or contract basis.

DATA PROCESSING

Most persons who use the term data processing probably have in mind the handling of large amounts of numerical information by machine at a very rapid rate. However, *data processing* in its simplest terms includes *any* process of information handling. When a clerk prepares invoices for payment, he is processing data. When the bookkeeper in a bank sorts checks, he is processing data. When a typist prepares statements of account to send to a physician's patients, he, too, is processing data.

We can process information by hand or by machine. In every office a great deal of information is processed by hand. In fact, most data must be processed by hand to a certain degree in order to prepare it in the proper form to be processed by machine. Today we handle most accounting and statistical data by machine, and machines now process information at terrific speeds. A typical office force can now provide management personnel with information that was not even available to them a generation ago.

What Is "Data Processing"?

Perhaps the meaning of the term "data processing" can best be explained by using as an illustration the handling of a typical business transaction. Let us consider, for example, what happens when goods are ordered, the shipment is received, and payment is made.

Every purchase order describes and states the amount of the items wanted, and lists the item cost and the total cost of the goods ordered. This latter figure is arrived at by multiplying the price per unit by the number of units. (This figure may, however, differ from the total cost of purchase: other changes may be added.) So *computation* is a "must" operation.

After the order form is prepared, it is sent to the company from which the goods are to be purchased. This operation can be called *communication*. At a later date there will be other instances of communicating information—such as when the goods are shipped by the seller, and when a check is issued in payment for the shipment.

There are several records to be made in connection with the transaction we are using as our illustration: a record of the order, of the receipt of merchandise, of the obligation to pay for the goods, and of the payment which is made later. So the process of *recording* is another essential operation in the proper handling of a business transaction. And records do not just float around; they must lodge somewhere, so they are usually filed according to some prearranged plan. When records are systematically arranged in specially prepared storage cabinets, we usually call this *filing*. But when data are recorded by a computer, the term *storage* is commonly used. So the filing or storing of information is another operational function in handling data.

And before they are stored, most records are classified according to the nature of the transaction involved. It is easier and faster to record information by machine if it is stated numerically than if words are used. So the goods to be ordered in our illustration need to be classified—assigned an identification number. This is usually called *coding*, and it speeds up the operation when working with large quantities of data.

If you were responsible for paying for merchandise purchased, how would you know to do this on or before the particular day that the invoice falls due? One way would be to write yourself a note on your desk calendar pad. You might actually make the note on the sixth of the month, but you would write it on the page of the calendar pad that is dated the sixteenth, the date the bill is to be paid. A better way might be to file the invoice in a bellows file under the date of the sixteenth, and then on the sixteenth issue your check. In fact, however, you would at the same time have to prepare checks to pay *all* the invoices previously filed in the bellows file as due on that day. So it is clear that, using the bellows file system when preparing several invoices for filing, you would arrange them in order according to their due dates. This is called *sorting*, and it is another important function in data processing. (Note that whereas in our illustration we sorted invoices and prepared them for filing by hand, in electronic data processing, cards would be sorted rapidly by machine.)

The final phase of data processing is vital because it is important to know how many invoices are paid each day, and the total amount spent in order to pay them. A list of all invoices paid on a particular date, the amount of each invoice, and the total paid would constitute a summary of this group of business transactions. Thus, *summarizing* is yet another essential function when handling large quantities of data.

The seven operations we have discussed here—coding, computing, communicating, recording, sorting, storing, and summarizing—make up the basic elements involved in data processing. We might define *data processing* then as *that group of operations performed in handling units of business data from the original entry to the final entry.* So we see that data processing serves the accounting, statistical, and reporting needs of business management. The term *electronic data processing*, on the other hand, is more restrictive; it refers to the handling of business data through the use of electronic computers. A *data processing system* would be the total method used to carry out the seven basic elements of data processing to accomplish the accounting, statistical, and reporting functions of business management.

Advantages of Data Processing

Electronic computers process data so rapidly that they provide reports to management that otherwise would not be available. And the information is more complete, more accurate, and more immediately available than when done by hand or by the use of simple machines. By operating the computer center during the night, management may have reports that are as up-to-date as the close of business operations the previous day. And without the aid of computers, management might not be able to have these reports at all.

The IBM 2020 processor unit,[1] which is the heart of the IBM System 360, performs arithmetic calculations, and gives instructions to the card-handling machines attached to it, telling them which cards to read, which new cards should be punched, and what should be printed. Its instructions are stored in a memory unit with 4,000 positions that can be increased to 8,000 or 16,000 positions. The IBM 2560 Multi-Function Card Machine can read cards at speeds of up to 500 per minute, or punch cards at the rate of 160 columns per second. And the IBM 1403 Printer has an output of 600 alphameric[2] lines per minute, and greater speeds when the data is all numeric.

Automatic machines can do a complete accounting job, and automatic electric typewriters can prepare the finished accounts from punched cards. These (computing) machines can handle as many as five separate accounts simultaneously—and the limits of their versatility have not yet been reached. New electronic typing calculators combine the electric typewriter with a high-speed electronic computer. They are used to process material in which mathematical calculations are part of the typing operation. Any typist can type in the correct information and numbers, and these machines automatically calculate and then type out the answer.

Electronic data-processing machines are used in the following activities: payroll, inventory, expense accounting, sales statistics, accounts receivable, computation of commissions and dividends, property accounting and invoicing. In addition to speeding up operations, the use of electronic machines in processing information also saves time and money through the elimination of duplicated effort.

The typical sales-order entry can serve to illustrate this point. As a rule, an order for goods is originated by a salesman who writes out a sales order and mails or telegraphs it to the home office. When this order is received, a production order is typed. It repeats the name and address of the purchaser and most of the other information written on the sales order by the salesman in the field. A copy of much of this information is included in the report that

[1] The 2075 computer processor operates at even greater speeds.

[2] "Alphameric" means that both alphabetical and numerical characters are used.

goes to the accounting office, and it is typed out again in the billing and shipping departments.

Actually, less than 10 percent of the information typed on the sales invoice and on the bill of lading is new information— that is, different from that first typed when the production order was prepared. With electronic data-processing equipment, as much as 80 percent of the information on the sales invoice is written automatically from a magnetic or punched tape. A separate record is prepared on tape for each regular customer, bearing his name and address and all other information needed for any sales invoices issued to him. This information is typed only once, and thereafter is reproduced automatically through the use of the tape. New information, such as the purchase order number, date of order, quantity ordered, unit price, and total amount, are added to the tape by the machine operator.

WHAT IS A COMPUTER?

A *computer* may be defined simply as *a calculator that operates at very rapid speeds.* Perhaps the work of the computer may be best illustrated by comparing it with an adding or calculating machine. As with these simpler machines, the three basic elements involved are the *input, processor,* and *output units.* But the similarity stops there because in the simpler machines the keyboard inevitably is the means of putting information or data into the machine; the internal machinery is largely composed of gears, racks, and counting-wheels; and the output is achieved through some type of simple printing mechanism; the report usually being printed on a paper tape of limited further use.

There are two types of computers—the analogue computer and the digital computer.

The *analogue* computer is used to construct models or scaled-down conceptions of design problems. It is very adaptable to alterations in data fed into the computer, but its solutions are only in approximate (not exact) figures. Its chief function is in structural design calculations for seeing how new models might work. The *digital computer* is widely used in business and yields exact figures in its calculations. Computers of both types are manufactured in a wide variety of sizes by dozens of companies.

The Input Unit

The *input unit* feeds data into the computer system. Unlike the adding machine or the acounting machine, data fed into a computer must be placed on some type of medium that can be handled *automatically* and at rapid speeds. The most commonly used input media are punched cards, magnetic tape, and punched paper tape. The card reader converts holes in the cards into electrical impulses and transmits the information to the memory unit of the computer, ready for processing. Similarly, the tape reader performs this same function when the data are first recorded (on paper tape instead of cards, of course). The important factor here is that this "reading" of data by the card or tape reader is done independently of human attention. Using magnetic tape, the IBM 360 computer can read at speeds of up to 340,000 characters per second.

The Optical Scanner. Instead of punched cards or paper tape, the *optical scanner* may be used as the input medium. The optical scanner reads each character from some input medium, and in turn translates it into electrical impulses. These impulses are then transmitted to the computer for processing. Scanning devices are programmed to read and evaluate certain numerals, characters, and symbols. Rays of light scan a field on a document, form an internal image, and compare it with an image that has been pro-

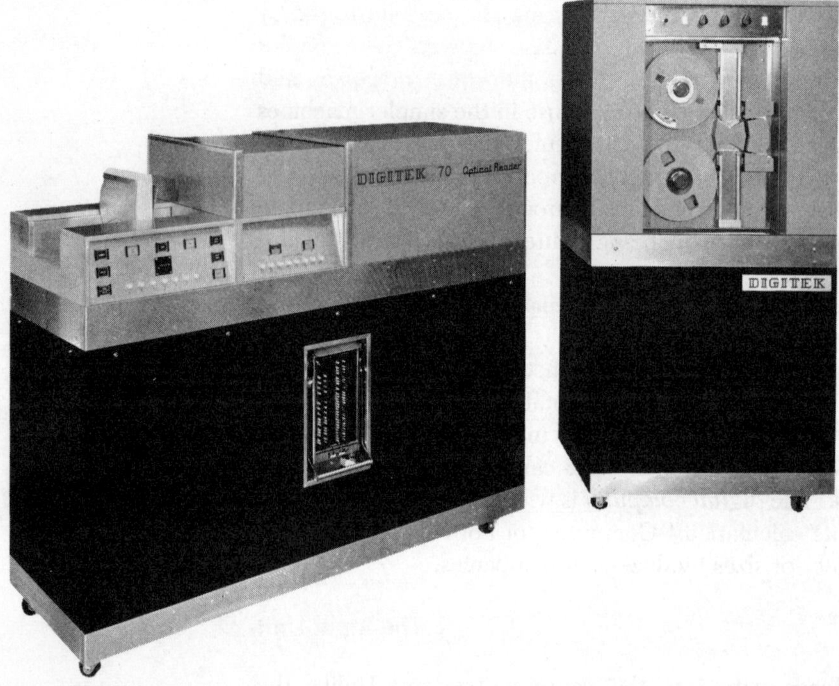

Courtesy Optical Scanner Corp.

Digitek Optical Reader can read pencil-marked data from source documents at a basic speed of 2,500 sheets an hour, and transfers this information directly to magnetic tape.

grammed into the scanner's memory component. If it finds the corresponding image, it accepts it and moves on to the next figure. If it cannot find a corresponding image, it rejects the figure. The optical scanner makes possible the use of journal records, adding-machine tapes, and accounting-machine tapes as input media, instead of the usual punched card or punched tape. And, special "sensing" marking pencils may be used on specially prepared forms for reading by optical scanners. The optical scanner represents the coming thing in data processing. The Internal Revenue Service and the Social Security Administration are already using scanners to collect employee earnings data which employers submit quarterly. Most systems will be converting to optical scanners, thus avoiding the dependence on the card-punch operator.

The Processor Unit

In a computer the *processor unit* includes a control panel (usually called a *console*), a calculator which performs all kinds of arithmetic functions, and a memory or storage element. The console is undoubtedly the most familiar part of the computer since it is frequently pictured in books and on television. It is the panel where the operator pushes the control buttons.

The arithmetic component performs many different types of computations using addition, subtraction, multiplication, and division. It performs at electronic speeds and can operate from original data (the results of earlier computations). It may work with data currently being fed into the computer, with information previously stored in the memory component, or with both.

The Binary Number System. Digital computers operate by opening and closing electrical circuits. The circuit is either open, permitting the electrical impulse to go through, or it is closed. Therefore the binary number system is used instead of the more familiar decimal system. A comparison might be made to an electric light bulb—it is either on or off. Similarly, within the computer, transistors are held in either a conducting or nonconducting state, and specific voltage potentials are either present or absent. These binary modes of operation are signals to the computer in much the same way that light or the absence of light is a signal to a person. Since an electric current can only indicate either an "on" or "off" situation, only two symbols are registered by the computer—either a zero (for the off position) or a 1 (for the on position). In any single position of binary notation, the zero represents the absence of any assigned value and the 1 represents the presence of an assigned value.[3]

The memory component might consist of a drum-type element, discs,

[3] IBM, *General Information Manual,* p. 18.

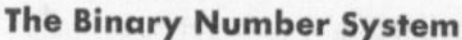

The Binary Number System

Unlike the decimal system, which employs the digits "0" through "9," the Binary System employs only two digits, "0" and "1."

64	32	16	8	4	2	1...value of each position
0	0	1	0	1	0	1 equals 21

The lowest-order position in the binary system is called the 1-bit, and can have only two conditions, "0" or "1." The next position is called the 2-bit; the next, the 4-bit; the next, the 8-bit; etc.... each of which can have one of two conditions, "0" or "1."

Another example:

64	32	16	8	4	2	1...value of each bit
1	0	1	0	0	1	1 equals 83

This is just another way of writing the quantity "83," sixty-four ones, plus sixteen ones, plus two ones, plus one one, equals eighty-three units.

or magnetic cores. Actually, these memory components serve as an electronic filing-cabinet. They have the capacity for storing huge amounts of information in a small space, and this information may be read out of storage *automatically* and at electronic speeds.

The Program. The control panel merely controls the mechanical operations of the machinery. The instructions to the machine telling it what to do are in the form of a program. The person who writes these directions is called a *programmer*. A *program* consists of a set of coded instructions that inform the computer as to which data are to be picked up to be used, where the data is stored, what mathematical computations are to be performed, the order in which each operation is to be done, and what is to be done with the output. This "program" is first written out by hand or on a typewriter. Then it is transferred to cards or tape so that it may be fed into the computer.

Programs must be written in a language that the machine "understands." Each step is written out in a carefully prepared sequence. There are several languages used when preparing programs. One common language is called Common Business Oriented Language (COBOL) and another is called Formula Translation (FORTRAN). COBOL resembles English and may be used by different types of computers. It utilizes the numerals zero through nine, the 26 letters of the alphabet, and a dozen or so special characters such as the dollar sign, the asterisk, parentheses, etc.

The Output Unit

After information has been processed, it is printed out in the form of a report—this is called *output.* The equipment used is in the form of a high-speed printer, and several printers can be placed on the line with the central processor simultaneously. Each printer is capable of printing approximately a thousand lines of numeric data per minute, and somewhat fewer lines of alphabetic-numeric data.

In connection with a printed report, the output may take the form of a punched tape or a punched card, depending on the type of output. This is the case when it is desirable to process the data further by the use of computers, or to repeat the operation at a later date.

The Use of Computers Has Increased Rapidly. The first computer, known as UNIVAC, was developed by Remington-Rand, Inc.,[4] and installed

[4] The Sperry Corp. and Remington-Rand, Inc., were merged and the current corporate title of the company is The Sperry-Rand Corp.

Courtesy UNIVAC Division of Sperry Rand Corporation

High speed UNIVAC 490 Real-Time computing system manufactured by the Sperry Rand Corporation's UNIVAC Division. This is the installation at the Keydata Corporation, Cambridge, Mass., one of the nation's first on-line, real-time, and time-sharing computing centers.

in 1953 for use by the U.S. Bureau of the Census. In this same year, UNIVAC computers were delivered to the Atomic Energy Commission, to the General Electric Co., and to the DuPont chemical company. Today, General Electric uses more than 200 computers, and DuPont has almost 100. Indeed, it would be difficult to find a major business in America that does not utilize the services of computers.

DuPont estimates that approximately 5,000 of its employees are involved in some phase of data handling. Of this number, 800 persons operate the data-processing machines, and another 800 do programming, systems analysis, and related tasks.

The United States government is the largest customer/user of data-processing equipment. Direct government expenditures for data processing amounted to over $800 million in the year ending June 30, 1966. The Bureau of the Budget estimates that this will increase to somewhere between $2.5 billion and $3 billion by 1970.

BUSINESS APPLICATIONS OF DATA PROCESSING

As one example of how computers serve business management, consider the General Electric Appliance Park operation in Louisville, Ky. Here, in a single location, are grouped together what might have been built in several widely separated communities. In one large building, washing machines and dryers are manufactured; in another, electric refrigerators are produced; and in still another, stoves are made. And small appliances, such as disposal units, dehumidifiers, and mixers, are fabricated under their own roof, too. In fact, seven major operations are carried on, each in a separate building.

In one central office at the Park there is a computing center, and smaller installations of electronic equipment are located in several of the other buildings. By having all these manufacturing operations located in close proximity to one another, all may utilize the services of the computer center. By having a small office crew operate the computers during the night, an up-to-date inventory can be ready for use by management the following morning. Here is dramatic proof of what we have already said: that the speed of the computer makes possible the preparation of reports which otherwise would take so long to prepare that they would be of little or no value when finally ready.

As another example, the REA Express has a data processing operation which is called "Projex." It is an electronic computer system used to speed up its receipting and accounting procedures. REA Express moves approximately 100 million pieces of freight a year. These shipments originate and terminate in their more than 8,000 offices located throughout the nation. Each office sends its receipting documents to a "feeder city"—a transmitting point in its area. This city transmits shipment data to designated central *receiving stations.* The receiving stations prepare *machine-printed and punched delivery cards* and make them available to their "satellite" cities, pending arrival of the actual shipments. Thus each office is served by a transmitting city for outbound shipments, and a receiving station for inbound traffic. The advantages to the public are: lower costs resulting from increased efficiency; improved service to the shipping public; and a better utilization of the work force employed by the company.

The Treasury Department provides us with another illustration. The National Computer Center in Martinsburg, W. Va., the hub of the Internal Revenue Service automatic data-processing system, began computer processing of tax data from their Southeast Regional Service Center in Chamblee, Ga., in 1961. The Chamblee center was the first of seven regional service centers to be established to convert individual and corporate income tax data to a magnetic tape format. The reels of tape containing this data were sent to Martinsburg as the initial step in establishing a national master file of all taxpayers. Since 1961, additional regional offices have been added, on a carefully phased schedule, to the computer network. By January 1, 1968, all individual and corporate tax accounts of the nation's taxpayers were being processed on the computers at Martinsburg from data received from seven regional service centers. The computers check the arithmetic computations, verify the validity of the deductions taken, and make sure that all taxable income has been reported on one's return.

By having data on all taxpayers in the national master file at Martinsburg, IRS can easily check on their failure to file returns, and can ascertain whether a taxpayer owes anything for a prior year before paying him a refund claimed on his current year's return. In cases where tax credit from prior years has been forgotten or overlooked, IRS can remind the taxpayer of his good fortune. It can also match information relative to wages, dividends, and interest on taxpayers' returns with information received from employers and financial institutions reporting to the Service. In fact, businesses can now file their tax returns on magnetic tape, provided they use tape that is compatible with IRS equipment. The IRS is already receiving some 25 million taped returns a year. Most of these are No. 1099 (dividend-payment) or W-2 (tax-withholding) report forms.

In addition to the Internal Revenue Service and the Bureau of the Census, nearly all areas of the federal government use electronic computers for data processing. The Defense Department is one of the largest users, having almost a thousand computers in use today—this number is increasing each year.

Use by Banks. The banking field is very greatly dependent upon data-processing by computers. There are approximately 30 million checks written and processed daily in this country. These checks are sorted and cleared many different times, first by the banks where they are originally deposited, then by one or more clearing houses, and finally by the banks where the persons who wrote the checks maintain their accounts.

To facilitate sorting, identification numbers are printed in magnetic ink in the lower lefthand corner of the checks. It is anticipated by the leadership in the banking field that by 1975 all checks will be sorted electronically through the use of these magnetic ink characters. Even today some banks require their customers to use specially printed personalized checks bearing their account number and identification in magnetic ink.

The computer has enabled banks to update their method of figuring service charges on their customer accounts. Formerly they used the minimum balance during the month. Now they are able to use the average daily balance.

Another recent data-processing development used by banks is that of input units in branch banks being wired in to the central computer at the main bank. This is called *on-line processing*. Deposits or withdrawals by customers are entered on the keyboard console in the branch bank. The branch bank is connected by leased telephone line with the computer in the home bank, where each customer's account information is stored in the memory unit of the computer. In seconds the transaction performed at the branch bank is recorded in the main bank, and its results reported back to the branch bank.

Insurance Companies. The major insurance companies find the electronic computer ideal for keeping policyholder information up-to-date. Information regarding premium payments, loans against policies, cash reserves, and dividend payments can be made available at a moment's notice.

The loan departments of insurance companies have also found magnetic tape and the automatic typewriter helpful in the study of financial reports. When a business applies to an insurance company for a loan, it is asked to submit a copy of its financial report. If the loan application involves a large amount of money, the report is investigated thoroughly; and the report on the application may be updated many times. As new data are reported, the financial report is revised and reprinted.

Under the traditional method of preparing new typewritten reports, the entire report had to be checked for accuracy in copying. Through the use of magnetic tape that reproduces verbatim all of the old data in the report, only the changes made in the report need to be verified. Since the automatic typewriter prints copy from the tape, this saves time in two ways: the work is done at speeds much faster than that of the highest-skilled human typist, and the old data in the report need not be proofread for accuracy.

An example of a successful management information system exists at the Radio Corporation of America's parts and accessories operation in Deptford, New Jersey. This parts and accessories operation is responsible for providing replacement parts for all of the commercial equipment built and distributed by the other RCA divisions and for merchandising accessories for use with this equipment. These parts and accessories are distributed through the same channels as the parent equipment.

Orders for parts and accessories are received from over 8,000 customers at the rate of over 300 orders per day. These orders average about 10 items each and are filled from an inventory of over 70,000 stock parts. This inventory represents an investment of approximately $10 million.

It was determined early in the planning stage that the MIS system would be a decision-making system and not a reporting system. The system was not designed to generate reports which would go to clerks or analysts for manual review in order for decisions to be made. This is based upon the belief that there were very few decisions made by these clerks and analysts that couldn't be programed, no matter how complex, no matter how unique, and no matter how varied these decisions were.

The necessary logic for decision making is incorporated in the system so that, instead of giving a report to an inventory control analyst enabling him to determine which items and what quantities are to be ordered, this type of work is now performed in the computer system. Decisions are reviewed by analysts on an exception basis and, from time to time, the computer's decisions are revised by a human being who is "on-line."

But basically, the routine decisions are being successsfully made by the computer system. Reports were designed to include only those items which required specific action by someone. Comprehensive status listings and other reports of a detailed nature are also produced; however, these are intended for reference and audit trial purposes only and are not distributed to operating personnel for routine day-to-day decision-making purposes. For example, there is a complete listing of all items on open order distributed to the purchasing group. This listing is issued both in part number sequence and in purchase order number sequence and also grouped by specific buyer and vendor.

The accompanying flow chart shows how information is fed into and through the system.

DATA-PROCESSING SERVICE CENTERS

Although the recent trend in computers has been toward small units as well as huge systems, the development of the small unit has not led to the installation of data processing equipment in the offices of as many small businesses as one might imagine. This is largely because literally hundreds of

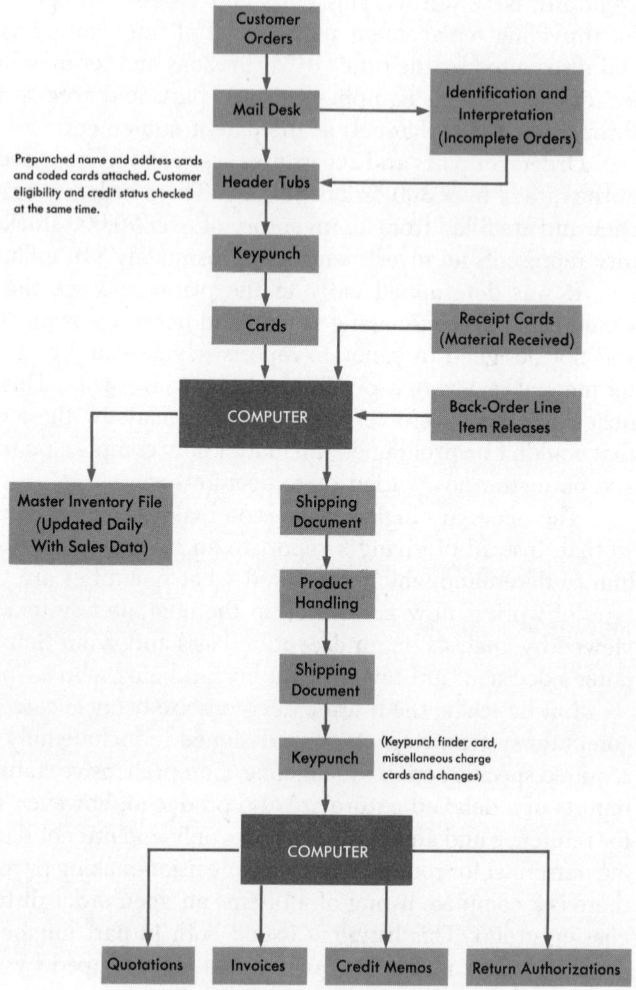

Source: Reprinted from *Business Automation,* Nov. 1967. © Business Press International, Inc.

thousands of businesses cannot afford to buy or lease even the cheaper computer equipment—it would actually be used very little, and thus might not even "pay its own way," as every worthwhile piece of equipment should. Out of the need for the part-time use of computers has developed *time shar-*

ing, which, as practiced in *computer service centers,* enables several businesses to use the same computer. These service operations (or bureaus) have complete equipment installations and a full staff of specially prepared personnel. In addition they maintain a depository of hundreds of different types of "programs"—even complete data-processing accounting systems. Through these centers the advantages of electronic data-processing are available to businesses, educational institutions, and hospitals that cannot afford even limited computer installations. This aspect of data processing is expanding rapidly.

THE ACCOUNTANT AND DATA PROCESSING

In the preceding chapter you learned about the work of accountants. Here let us consider the accountant's relationship to data processing. It is the accountant who determines the choice of data to be fed into the computer, who establishes an organizational pattern for that data, and who takes over where automation ends. Machines process basic data accurately and rapidly according to the program given them, but their tabulations must be interpreted by and for management. Machines calculate, but they do not think; and therefore they cannot replace the accountant-management relationship. A machine may show the amount a business has lost during a given period, but it cannot tell the causes of the loss. The machine's report may show that overhead is too high, but it will not tell how it should be reduced. Machines can calculate tax liabilities, but they cannot advise on legal ways to minimize them. The accountant is the interpreter of the machine's findings.

You will recall that one type of work accountants perform is setting up accounting systems. Systems analysis and design is an integral part of installing a computer program. An accounting system must be developed in terms of the firm's specific objectives and of the requirements that records management poses. The systems analyst must have a knowledge of accounting applications, of programming, and of the types of reports the equipment is capable of producing.

The transfer from a traditional basic accounting system to one based on the use of electronic computers is a gradual process requiring a period of several months. Time is needed to plan the program and prepare key personnel to use it. But even then, as certain operations are put on tape for use on the computers, some types of records are continued for a period on traditional equipment. There are several reasons for this. Not all new equipment is added in a single stroke, and of course personnel cannot be properly trained to operate new pieces until they are installed. Also, exactly how many and which kinds of additional machines are needed depends to some degree on how equipment already purchased works out. It is sort of a time of "developing transition."

THE CENTRALIZED COMPUTER SYSTEM AIDS IN MANAGEMENT DECISIONS

Up to this point our emphasis has been on the services that a data processing system renders a business enterprise in a specific location. Now we shall see how and why large corporations utilize centralized computer systems to coordinate a wide (and widespread) variety of activities.

Prior to the introduction of electronic data processing to their business equipment, most large corporations were obliged to use the relatively unsophisticated telephone or telegraph leased-wire services to provide a complete communications network between and among their far-flung industrial plants and offices. Now, by hooking them up with an electronic data-processing system, such traditional intracompany communications networks can be rung in as an integral part of a modern centralized computing center's operations. When production, sales, and financial data are all communicated into a company's home office, management has available up-to-the-minute information on which to base its decisions.

In addition to the vast assortment of general intracompany communications, the central tele-computer center often handles conventional inventory and payroll records (which were discussed earlier in this chapter). Then, too, there are customers' orders. The central computer's storage component always has the latest information on exactly how many units of every type of product are on hand in every warehouse. This means that all orders, together with shipping instructions, can be sent immediately to the warehouse nearest the customer which stocks the wanted items.

The cash analysis is an item of real interest and significance to management. Extremely large corporations have funds deposited in hundreds of different bank throughout the country. A centralized tele-computer system can in a matter of minutes make available to management a complete status report on the corporation's cash balance.

Sales records and customer billing may also be kept current. Under conventional records systems there exists a five- to 10-day delay in entering company records of sales, and in customer billing. The computing center provides instant information and makes possible simultaneous recording and customer billing. In addition, company management may have a daily report on total company sales. Furthermore, the computer can break the sales report down by products, by regions, or in any other way that management would want such data.

Such data handling improves decision-making at all levels. It frees divisional accounting managers from mountains of paperwork and enables them to function as true financial planners.

CAREER OPPORTUNITIES IN DATA PROCESSING AND RECORDS MANAGEMENT

Job opportunities are currently no more promising in any area of business than in data processing and records management. The employment opportunities section of the classified ads of any metropolitan newspaper includes notices of such employment needs. There are positions for persons to operate various types of equipment, for programmers, and for systems analysts. In addition, there are opportunities for promotion to supervisory and management positions.

Actually, in data processing one's title does not delineate clearly just what his work is. One person with the title of programmer may spend most of his time writing out specific directions for the computer. Another person who is called a programmer may spend his time in developing problems and even doing systems design. The systems analyst is concerned with designing programs to achieve particular objectives. To design an information system, a systems analyst must know not only what the computer equipment can do—he must have some understanding of the business operation that is to employ the system. Usually, representatives of the equipment manufacturer, and accountants or records managers in the employ of the business that will use the equipment, work together in designing an information system.

There are job opportunities in management positions for college educated persons with an understanding of data processing. Business executives need to know what types of informational reports to expect from computers, and something of the special applications that may be made in their particular businesses.

Accounting firms are now installing computer equipment and offering programs and information systems services to their clients. All of the types of positions discussed above would exist here, as well as with businesses that have their own installations.

Educational Requirements

Persons who wish to enter data-processing positions should prepare themselves broadly in the area of business administration, including as part of their study courses in business management. They would do well to pursue accounting and statistics to some depth. These persons should possess competency in being able to rationalize, and to see and understand mathematical relationships. The field of information management is one of the more promising areas for young educated persons who plan to make a career in business management. In preparation, courses in records management and computer systems are essential.

The personal qualities needed by the office manager are the same as those needed by other business executives. You must be a leader of men. You must be capable of thinking and planning constructively, and of seeing that your plans and decisions are carried through to completion. You must be able to look at the entire scope of the organization rather than at isolated phases. In addition to having administrative ability, you must be a good salesman, because you will have to sell your ideas to top management and influence your co-workers so they will see the importance of the services rendered by the office. You should be able to express yourself simply and clearly, and you should possess the following attributes: tactfulness, imagination, patience, willingness to cooperate, initiative, openmindedness, loyalty, sincerity—and a sense of humor.

A survey of company presidents in the Detroit area showed that honesty and integrity are the characteristics they most appreciate in an office manager. Other qualities these presidents regarded as necessary to success as an office manager are intelligence, loyalty, willingness to work, the ability to get along with people, and the ability to produce helpful suggestions.

SUMMARY

The ever increasing load of paperwork makes machine processing of records information a most welcome accomplishment. Data processing has not decreased the number of persons required to handle records information, but it has raised the level of the tasks they perform. Its net effect has been to provide management with up-to-the-minute information and with reports not previously available.

The basic elements of information handling, or data processing, are coding, computing, communicating, recording, sorting, storing, and summarizing. In addition to speeding information handling, electronic data-processing is more accurate than the work done by human beings, and it eliminates considerable duplication of effort in records management.

A computer consists of three basic units—input, processor, and output. It performs its work at fantastic speeds and with a high degree of accuracy. It operates automatically—that is, independent of human effort—but it receives its directions from a "program" that some person prepares.

Almost every aspect of modern business operation—finance, manufacturing, and selling, as well as the government—utilizes electronic computer services. Businesses that are too small to have their own installations may contract with data-processing centers for selected computer services. A variety of programs and systems is available at these centers.

Career positions are available for college educated men and women who have the right preparation, interest, and competencies. The top position would be that of the office manager. To qualify for this position, one would of course need practical experience in addition to his college preparation.

VOCABULARY REVIEW QUIZ

Match the following terms with the statements below.

a. binary system
b. coding
c. computation
d. console
e. data processing
f. input
g. output
h. processor
i. program
j. storage

1. The process of making different types of number calculations
2. The operation of filing data in the memory unit of a computer
3. Assigning identification or classification numbers to merchandise or expense items
4. The feeding of data into a computer
5. That part of a computer installation that performs arithmetical computations
6. The instrument panel or control device for a computer
7. A set of coded instructions that tells a computer what to do
8. An arithmetic system that employs only two digits, 0 and 1
9. That part of the computer which takes information from the processor unit and prints it in the form of a report
10. The process of working with or handling data

QUESTIONS FOR REVIEW STUDY

1. How would you define the term "electronic data processing"?
2. What are the various basic elements that are involved in data processing?
3. What are the advantages of processing data by computers as compared with doing the work on traditional equipment?
4. What are the three essential units in a computer installation, and what is the function of each unit?
5. What "bits" would be needed to express the number 75 in the binary system?
6. Explain how some business with which you are familiar utilizes the services of a computer in handling its records.
7. How does a knowledge of accounting relate to data processing?

8. What kinds of jobs are available to persons who are interested in finding employment in the field of data processing?
9. Explain how the use of punched paper tape or magnetic tape might be used to reduce duplication in records handling.

PROBLEMS AND PROJECTS

1. Assume that you have been asked to devise a system of keeping a perpetual inventory of goods on hand by using electronic data-processing equipment. What are the types of information you would need? Where would you find this information?
2. Suppose that the home office of the electric utility that serves your community wished to calculate and print its bimonthly statements to its customers by using a computer. What data would the computer need to use, and what would be the sources of that data?
3. Indicate the bits needed under a binary arithmetic system to make up the numbers 28, 40, 55, and 60.
4. In the example of the REA Express which was explained in this chapter, what information would the transmitting station need in order to communicate all the essential information to the destination office?
5. Examine the numbers encoded in magnetic ink in the lower left-hand corner of a bank check form. What are the numbers written there and what do they represent? Why is it important that these numbers appear in the same place on all checks?

A BUSINESS CASE

Case 10-1 A College Computer Problem

A small college is contemplating installing a small computer. You are a member of the committee appointed to recommend whether or not to make the installation. The big problem stems from the fact that no one aspect of the college program has sufficient need to utilize the equipment full-time. The matter of time apportionment is somewhat of a problem too in that all departments that are interested in using the equipment, want it sometime between 8 a.m. and 5 p.m.

1. Which aspects of the administrative office functions might be interested in using the computer?
2. Which academic departments might need the computer equipment for instructional purposes?
3. How would you schedule all potential users so as to make the maximum use of the equipment and also satisfy everyone's needs?

PART 4
OPERATIONS OF THE ENTERPRISE

The Management and Motivation of Personnel

11

You will recall that the single proprietor usually goes into business on a small scale, doing all the work himself or having at best only a few employees to help him with it. The small businessman is usually closely associated with his help; he is familiar with their work and perhaps knows something of their home relationships and personal problems. And, likewise, employees in a small company usually "know the boss" and may even be acquainted with members of his family.

But as the business prospers and grows, the proprietor discovers that he can no longer be personally acquainted with each employee. As a matter of fact, in large organizations with several thousand employees, top management seldom knows more than a small fraction of them. Of course this does not mean that top management or the owners have no interest in their employees' welfare. It simply means that employer-employee relationships change as a business becomes larger.

Since owners or top managers in large organizations cannot maintain personal contact with each employee, there is a need to organize the large company into smaller units or departments with some person designated to direct each. The smaller units make it easier for persons in management positions to be personally acquainted with their employees, and thus ensure that each worker contributes to the efficient functioning of the organization.

WHAT IS PERSONNEL MANAGEMENT?

If a worker is to contribute effectively to the operation of his company, a few basic conditions must be met. First, management must study thoroughly the job that is to be done, and define the personal requirements for doing it. Then, management must scientifically select the person whose qualifications satisfy those job requirements. And if, as sometimes happens, the person hired possesses only the minimum qualifications for doing the job, then management must train him to ensure proficiency.

It should go without saying that every conscientious employee ought to know how to perform knowledgeably and skillfully the tasks for which he is responsible. But proficiency takes more than knowledge and skill alone; it takes the desire to do a good job. Indeed, even the most informed and able worker may perform at a low level if he is not interested in what he is doing. The really effective employee is the interested one who has a genuine desire to do the best possible job, and strives constantly to improve his performance. And—hardly less important—he can work well with others as well as alone. We shall see, later in this chapter, that one of the major concerns of the personnel function is to help provide an environment in which people can function well as members of a group.

Effective, highly-motivated employees are essential to the efficient operation of every business. Owners or managers working alone cannot get the job done; they must have active cooperation from those working with them. So it is that in every business the personnel function attempts to build a team of effective employees who have high morale, a spirit of teamwork and cooperation, and a desire to see the business thrive.

Personnel management is not the sole concern either of the personnel department or of top management. It is part of the job of every manager, for the personnel function is necessary in every operation where people are employed. Although it is true that where companies have personnel departments, some line managers can be relieved of various of the personnel functions, not all of them can.

Personnel management has the responsibility of planning, organizing, directing, coordinating, and controlling all activities that concern employees: selecting, developing, compensating, and meeting their needs in a number of respects. It is a goal of personnel management to utilize effectively

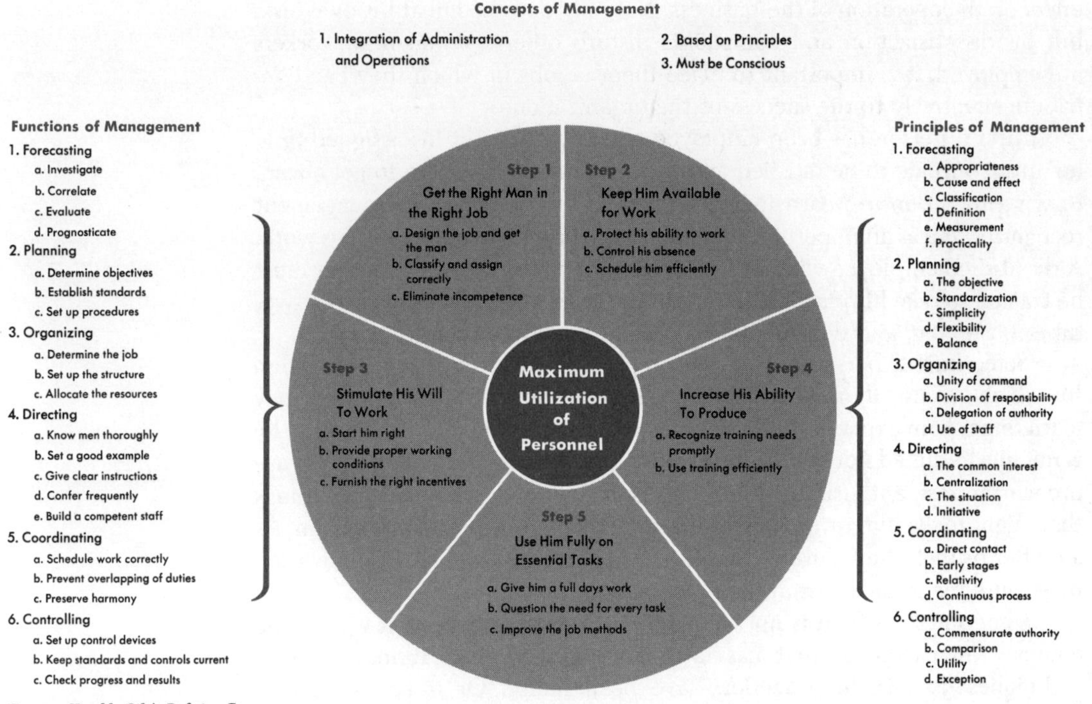

Courtesy Humble Oil & Refining Co.

A Philosophy of Management.

each employee's talents so that company objectives are attained efficiently and economically.[1] This implies that each employee is enabled to use his competencies, interests, and opportunities to his and the company's best advantage. Although mainly the personnel department promotes this point of view and coordinates the personnel function, goals of personnel management are, we repeat, the responsibility of all managers in every area of operation.

THE SIGNIFICANCE OF PERSONNEL MANAGEMENT

If a worker is to be motivated and productive, he must be placed in a job in which he is interested and for which he possesses the needed qualifications. Even a "right" person in the wrong job position can have a disturbing

[1] One company's efforts to secure maximum utilization of personnel is shown in their philosophy of management—see illustration at the top of this page.

effect on the operation of the business. Not only does he fail at his own task, but his dissatisfaction and complaints disturb others. When new workers are employed, it is important to place them in jobs in which they can contribute effectively to the success of the organization.

After a person has been employed and is working at his assigned task, he must continue to be satisfied and feel that he has a chance to get ahead, to win promotions, to earn increased pay. He must feel that management recognizes him as an important member of the firm and appreciates his work. A dissatisfied employee will not remain with the business, and another must be trained to take his place. A too-rapid turnover of employees is expensive, time-consuming, and detrimental to general employee morale.

Sometimes a person chooses to prepare for an occupation or position for which he (usually unknowingly) really is not suited. Such a person may learn to perform expertly the basic skills required on the job, but because he is not ideally suited nor much interested in the work he is doing, does not approach the task enthusiastically. As a result, he never masters those things that might make him invaluable to the firm and earn promotions for him. As a matter of fact, the failure to function well as a result of lack of motivation may cause his dismissal from the organization.

Sometimes the fault is not so much with the employee as it is with the company management that has improperly placed him. It may be that techniques used in his selection have been faulty. Or it could be that he lacked proper training for the position to which he was assigned. At any rate, he is living proof that when errors are made in selection or placement, a company invariably will have dissatisfied, nonproductive employees on its hands.

Because manpower is the most important asset of business and industry, the full and effective utilization of this wellspring of employee talent is a major responsibility of management. Improving working conditions, rising wages, and increasing benefits make employees better satisfied, more loyal, and more productive. Management and ownership enjoy the resulting benefits of increased production, reduced labor turnover, and decreased labor-management conflict.

Most small businesses have no need for a separate personnel department. A small group of likely employees—and sometimes only one—is asked to do the interviewing, testing, employing, and placing of new people. Someone (often the same person or persons) must also be responsible for training, disciplining, promoting, and discharging employees. In small businesses, either the top management or the owner must have a working knowledge of the personnel function if proper personnel policies and rules are to be established. The widespread lack of this knowledge is evidenced by the fact that many small businesses never do establish an adequate and consistent personnel program. This is an unfortunate fact of business life, because an adequate personnel program is as necessary for the small business as it is for the large.

THE PERSONNEL DEPARTMENT

Although the management of personnel is, as we have seen, the job of every supervisor and manager in a business, many of the duties it involves are assigned to the personnel department. This is done because that department is staffed by experts specially qualified not only to select new help but to train both new and continuing employees.

The authority and function of the personnel department vary tremendously from company to company. You will recall from an earlier discussion of the internal organization of businesses that the personnel department usually operates as a *staff function.* In other words, its task is to serve and advise other staff personnel as well as all line personnel, which includes both line and staff functional areas. In a staff capacity the personnel department assists other departments in the hiring and training of employees and in serving their needs. But final decisions concerning personnel matters are made by the department heads.

Sometimes the personnel department is given *functional* authority. In this capacity it does not just assist or serve other departments but actually makes the final decision in hiring, conducts specialized training, decides who is to be promoted, and so on. The important thing to remember is that the function of the personnel department is determined by the authority granted to it by top management. If this authority is staff, it serves and advises other departments. If it is functional, the personnel department has the power to command and to carry out programs it has designed for other departments.

It can be said that activities of the personnel department involve the following:

1. The selection of the best workers available to fill specific positions
2. The development of selected workers to ensure that they are well prepared for their assignments
3. The creation and maintenance of working conditions that are conducive to high morale and high production
4. The development and operation of a fair and adequate wage-and-salary program
5. An honest concern with the wants, motivations, attitudes, morale, and safety and health needs of employees

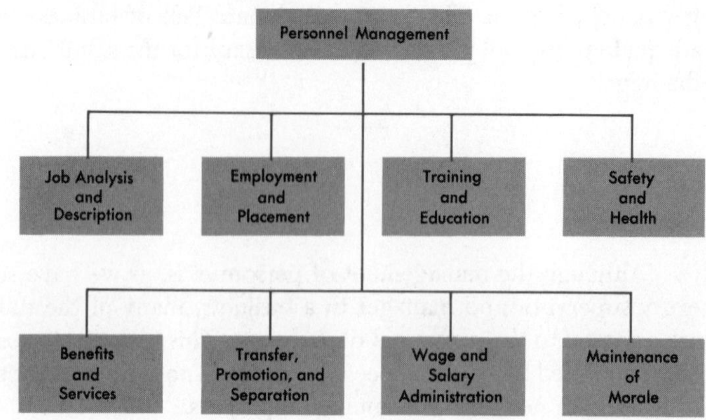

Areas of personnel management.

FUNCTIONS OF THE PERSONNEL DEPARTMENT

Long before the personnel department seeks out, interviews, tests, and evaluates prospective employees in its efforts to fill every available position with the most qualified person it can secure, it must be thoroughly acquainted with those positions. Experience has proven that familiarity of this sort comes only through *job analysis*, which involves the preparation of job descriptions and job classifications.

Job Analysis

The six briefest questions that can be asked about any occurrence are (in their usual order): What? When? Where? How? Why? Who? The six basic questions to be answered by job analysis are the same. They are: (1) What is to be done? (2) When is it to be done? (3) Where is it to be done? (4) How is it to be done? (5) Why is it important? (6) Who is to do it? The answers obtained during job analysis should reveal the degree of skill and the personal qualifications needed for the efficient performance of the task under consideration.

Job Description. The *job description* is a written report based on the analysis of a particular job. It should include or describe: (1) the job title; (2) a statement of where the work is to be performed; (3) the job's relation to other jobs, as well as its importance to the operation of the business; (4) the tools, machines, and equipment to be used, as well as the ways in which they are to be used; (5) the materials and supplies to be used, and the ways in which they are to be used; (6) the physical and/or mental skills required; (7) the working conditions; and (8) the duties and responsibilities assigned to the job. The importance of the job description becomes clear when we realize that management uses it as the basis for selecting and training workers and for promoting and transferring employees.

Job Classification. In a large organization there are usually hundreds of different jobs. Rather than assign a different wage-scale to each job, the problem of wage administration is simplified by assigning specified rates to a group of jobs that fall within a certain range of values. A job classification, therefore, is the grouping together of several positions into a single bracket or class. The "GS" ratings employed by the Federal Civil Service Commission are examples of job classification. The technique of classifying is useful for determining wages and in the transferring and promoting of employees. Job classification, therefore, serves as a guide to the selection of the right person for each position.

Selection and Placement

We have seen that job analysis is the first step to the wise selection of workers. Making use of information obtained during the analysis, the personnel department can then carry out the important task of selecting new workers and placing them in the jobs for which they are best qualified. So, the next step in the selection process might be called *applicant analysis*.

Application Forms. Almost every business uses some type of application form to obtain information that will be needed for the applicant's personal file. Such personal information as name, education, age, address, and telephone number is always included.

The would-be employee's history of work experience is probably the most important information provided by the application form. This record indicates more than the type and extent of his experience; it indicates whether or not he sticks with an assignment or whether he changes jobs frequently. In the application form, emphasis is given to the applicant's work history.

Space for listing the names and addresses of people for whom the applicant has worked is provided on the application form, too. Letters and telephone calls to former employers are frequently useful in securing information about an applicant's attitudes and personal qualities.

The accuracy, care, and precision with which an applicant completes this form may give the company a valuable clue concerning his work habits. One who is careless in the preparation of an employment application may well prove to be careless in his work habits, too.

The Employment Interview. Very often the next step in the selection process is an interview of the applicant by a member of the personnel de-

Gates

APPLICATION FOR EMPLOYMENT

THE GATES RUBBER COMPANY 999 So. Broadway, Denver 17, Colorado

INSTRUCTIONS: Fill out carefully in INK all the blanks. DO NOT WRITE ON THE BACK.

Please Print Name — LAST — FIRST — MIDDLE — Date / / MO. DAY YEAR

STREET ADDRESS — CITY — STATE — Telephone Number — Own ☐ Neighbor ☐

Social Security Number | Date of Birth: Mo. Day Year | Married ☐ Single ☐ | Widowed ☐ Separated ☐ Divorced ☐ | Women—if married, give maiden name | No. of Children Under 21 Ages

Male ☐ Female ☐ | Right ☐ Left ☐ Handed | Height: ft. in. | Weight: lbs. | Do you have any physical disabilities? Yes ☐ No ☐ Describe:

Type of work for which you are applying? Factory ☐ Office ☐ Trade ☐ | Have you ever before worked for Gates or an associate company? Yes ☐ No ☐ What Dept.? Date Left? | Are you willing to work any Shift? Yes ☐ No ☐

How long have you lived in Denver or Colo.? | Do you own your home? Yes ☐ No ☐ | Have you ever been arrested or convicted of any law violation (except minor traffic violations)? Yes ☐ No ☐ | Citizen of U.S.? Yes ☐ No ☐

Have you ever received funds under the Workman's Compensation Act for occupational injury____If yes, how many times?____

While employed by what companies?____Were you ever seriously injured or ill?____

If yes, give details____Do you have any chronic or recurring illness or ailment?____

Does your wife (or husband) or any of your dependent children have any chronic or recurring illness or ailment? Yes ☐ No ☐. If YES, give details

EDUCATION

CIRCLE the highest grade completed High School 1 2 3 4 5 6 7 8 9 10 11 12 College 1 2 3 4 5 6 | Did you graduate? Yes ☐ No ☐ | Age at which you left school

Name of last school attended — Address

College Major | Business or Trade School attended | No. of Years

PREVIOUS RECORD

Starting from today's date and working back for a period of 10 years **account for all of the time by recording all of your activities, such as** employment, military service, schooling, periods of unemployment, etc. Your application cannot be accepted as complete unless this has been done, and unless all information requested below is recorded as indicated.

Name of present or last employer | Exactly what did you do?
STREET ADDRESS — CITY — STATE | Why did you leave the job?
MO. & YEAR STARTED | MO. & YEAR LEFT | STARTING PAY | FINAL PAY | If still there, may we contact your present employer?

Name of employer | Exactly what did you do?
STREET ADDRESS — CITY — STATE | Why did you leave the job?
MO. & YEAR STARTED | MO. & YEAR LEFT | STARTING PAY | FINAL PAY

Name of employer | Exactly what did you do?
STREET ADDRESS — CITY — STATE | Why did you leave the job?
MO. & YEAR STARTED | MO. & YEAR LEFT | STARTING PAY | FINAL PAY

Name of employer | Exactly what did you do?
STREET ADDRESS — CITY — STATE | Why did you leave the job?
MO. & YEAR STARTED | MO. & YEAR LEFT | STARTING PAY | FINAL PAY

Relatives Now Working for Gates — Relationship — Dept.: — No. of Years
Relationship — Dept.: — No. of Years

FORM 161 (1-58)

Job application form

partment. The chief purpose of the interview is to gather additional information about the applicant. It also gives the interviewer a chance to have the applicant validate his answers to any or all questions on the application form. Through carefully phrased questions, the interviewer attempts to discover how the applicant might fit into the organization and what his attitude probably would be toward his associates on the job. The interviewer also explores the applicant's attitude toward his work in former jobs, his ability to express himself clearly, and his personal traits and characteristics. Many business firms have had great success with interviews because they have seen to it that interviewers were trained and unbiased, and that interviews were carefully planned to bring forth specific information.

But interviews are not always completely reliable as a means of selecting employees. Indeed, they are sometimes very unreliable. One reason is that the interviewer is seldom entirely free from prejudice, and it is prejudices that make it hard to conduct an interview with scientific objectivity. Another reason is that the (in some way) "weak" applicant may just happen to be having one of his rare and lucky "strong" days, and may fairly mesmerize the interviewer (who may be having a "weak" day).

Approximately three-fourths of the employees who lose their jobs do so because of personal reasons. But not all these people are misfits with undesirable or unacceptable personalities; some are doomed from the start merely because they are placed in jobs for which they are not suited. In trying to prevent matching the right man with the wrong job, the interviewer who knows his business tries to determine what sort of job will suit the personality and talents of each applicant. And he can do this only by taking all relevant facts and factors into consideration. The knowledgeable interviewer realizes as do few others that when the qualified employee is properly placed, when he is given the necessary training, and when he associates with individuals with whom he enjoys working, chances are that he will succeed—on behalf of his employer.

The interview is intended to achieve yet another important function—that of supplying the applicant with information about the firm, including its policy on salaries and promotions, working hours and conditions, and skills required.

The usual practice is to hold a preliminary interview and later a follow-up interview. The purpose of the preliminary interview is to size up the applicants in a general way and to eliminate those who obviously would not fit into the company organization. This interview may be held even before the application form is completed. The follow-up interview may be held at the time the worker is finally accepted or rejected. For this interview, a prescribed form may be followed to assure that critical questions are not overlooked.

The Use of Tests. In addition to interviewing the applicant and investigating his record, many companies make use of tests. Among the various types of tests that have found wide acceptance and use in recent years are interest tests, knowledge tests, tests for special aptitudes and abilities, and skill or performance tests.

The most widely used are the *aptitude tests*. If a person is being considered for a clerical position, let us say, he will be tested for potential talents (aptitude) in that area of work. A wide variety of aptitude tests is available, and some industries have developed specialized tests of this sort to serve their particular needs. Most people will respond to training if they have ability (or at least potential ability) in the area for which they are being trained. But if a person is weak in the special aptitudes needed to perform successfully in a particular type of work, no amount of training or experience will make a master workman of him. Aptitude is what separates the gifted artist from the well-meaning, hard-working, but at best merely "adequate" artisan.

Performance tests are designed to indicate the degree of skill an applicant has for a specific type of work. Such tests show whether the worker is qualified to perform the tasks required, or needs further training.

It is important to note that aptitude and performance tests require a skilled person to administer them. A poorly administered and poorly evaluated test is worse than no test at all.

The Physical Examination. Almost every modern firm now requires an applicant to submit evidence of physical health. He may have to produce a certificate from his family physician, or undergo a check-up by the company doctor. More and more firms are following the latter procedure.

The purposes of the physical examination are threefold. In the first place, the company must know whether the applicant is physically able to perform the work that his job assignment calls for. It might require constant standing, manipulative skill, extremely good eyesight. The physical test, then, is designed to discover any impairments that might prevent satisfactory performance on the job.

The second purpose of the physical examination is to ascertain whether or not the would-be employee has any basic trouble that might serve as the basis for a future claim against the company for physical disability.

Thirdly, the company wishes to protect its employees against the possibility that a new employee may have a communicable disease that would endanger their health or well-being. The company also has an obligation to make sure its customers will not be exposed to company employees who have a communicable disease. (Obvious examples of this would be the restaurant and food-processing industries.)

EMPLOYEE DEVELOPMENT

After an applicant has been selected for employment, he is assigned the task for which he was chosen (unless that job is not yet open, in which case

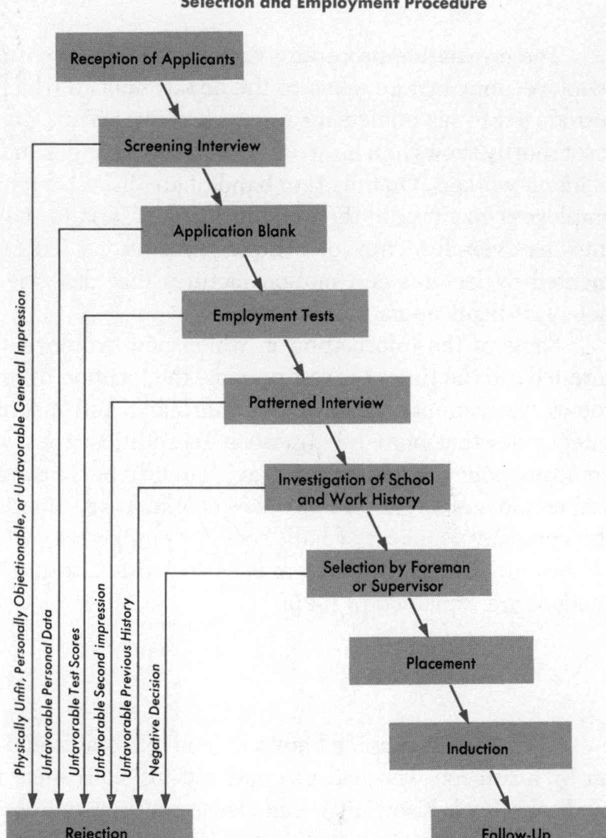

Selection and employment procedure

he will do something else temporarily). If necessary, he will undergo training to whatever extent his job-needs demand. Sometimes the applicant is given specialized training before, and sometimes after being assigned to a job. In either case, the new employee embarks on a training program, planned or not, that never really ends.

A college gives incoming freshmen some instruction about the college, its history, its goals and ideals, and its rules and regulations. A business firm must also provide information about the company, its purposes, and its organization. Such instruction is known as company *orientation* and *indoctrination.* A member of the personnel department usually provides this orientation for newly hired employees. For obvious reasons, the new worker must become familiar with basic company policies as soon as possible, particularly those of the department in which he is to work.

Orientation and Indoctrination

The orientation procedure varies from company to company. The new employee may first be taken to the department to which he is assigned, and introduced to his immediate foreman or supervisor. In this case the supervisor shortly shows him his work station and arranges an introduction to some of his co-workers. On the other hand, many firms prefer first to conduct new employees on a tour of the building or plant, and to show them how they fit into the over-all picture of company operations. This tour may be supplemented by lectures and motion pictures that describe phases of company policy or plant operations.

Some of the information in which new employees are particularly interested are the times for rest periods, the location of lunch facilities, locker rooms, recreational facilities, the infirmary, and first-aid stations, and the safety rules that must be observed. In addition, they want information on company policy regarding sick leave, medical benefits, vacation, pay periods, and employees' organizations. New workers are sometimes given a copy of the company's manual or handbook for employees. After they have had an opportunity to read it, they are encouraged to ask questions, and important sections are explained to them.

Training Techniques

The need for training knows no end. No one would wish to be operated on by a surgeon who had not updated his skills since his graduation from medical school. Knowledge and skills soon become obsolete unless there is a conscious, concerted, and continuous effort to supplement and improve upon them.

We have seen that a new employee must be trained to perform his job successfully. But we have also seen that a well-developed training program will also embrace employees who have been with the firm for years. Workers who are transferred or promoted to new jobs need training for those new jobs; foremen, supervisors, technicians, and executives often need special training.

A firm pays for training although there may be no formal training program. An inefficient worker has to learn by experience—trial-and-error—if there is no one to help him learn the way to do his best work. This type of training is more prolonged, and often is much more expensive, than training in an organized program. On-the-job training, formal and informal, will probably continue to be the most commonly employed means of qualifying people for work.

There are six approaches to the development of a company's personnel:

1. *On-the-job training* provides the worker with specific training for one job while under supervision. This is at present the most commonly used type of training, for it is simple, easy to administer, and interesting to the trainee. The primary burden for training is on the trainee's immediate supervisor.

2. *Vestibule training* is conducted away from the job, but in a simulated job situation. In this program, skilled instructors from the training department strive to develop techniques and working processes that are identical to those needed on the job. The advantage of the vestibule school is the high degree of specialization provided through the instructors. They are skilled both in technical knowledge and in the teaching process. The vestibule school also frees the trainee from the pressure of the production line and permits him to concentrate on the learning process.

3. *Technical training* is a relatively new development in business and industry. The rapid increase in the use and application of computing equipment and other automated devices has increased the demand for persons trained to utilize, operate, and maintain such equipment. Many persons currently employed in business do not have at their command skills required, though they often have the potential ability to perform the tasks with proper training. Companies, therefore, frequently call upon nearby colleges and equipment manufacturers to train company personnel in the use of automated devices. Such training may be conducted within company premises, on the college campus, or at special schools maintained by manufacturers of automated equipment. (Also included in technical training are programs designed to make all specialists aware of current developments in their fields.)

4. *Apprenticeship training* is similar to job training, except that here the worker is learning a craft that involves many related tasks, rather than just one job. Apprenticeship programs give more emphasis to education than do job training programs. They combine on-the-job training and experience with formal classroom instruction.

5. *Supervisory training* is basically leadership training in orientation, administration, human relations, technical knowledge, and instruction. Employees who rank high in desirable personal qualities, get along well with others, and exert leadership in group situations are those most often promoted to supervisory positions. Frequently they enroll in formal classes for instruction provided or arranged by company executives.

6. *Executive training,* the highest level of training, is designed to build the highest quality of administrative leadership. This preparation is usually provided through experience in junior executive positions, supplemented by formal courses of study. The latter may be given by the company or supplied by staff members of a nearby college or university.

Training Patterns

Modern firms usually provide training in one of three ways: (1) The training department organizes courses taught on the premises by employees of the firm or by outside specialists. (2) Schools and colleges teach certain academic courses to specific company employees. (3) Employees are encouraged to attend courses regularly offered at night on the campus of the educational institution; in many instances the company pays all or part of the tuition.

Many universities, particularly urban universities, maintain special departments to serve the training needs of business and industry. These departments are frequently called Management Centers, or Management Institutes. Management Centers serve business in two major ways. (1) They offer short-term, college-level courses of instruction designed to upgrade the job performance of supervisory and nonsupervisory personnel. A wide range of courses too numerous to list are offered, though some examples are: Supervisory Training, Decision-Making, Labor Relations Seminars, Managerial Economics, Managerial Accounting. (2) Management Centers also work with company training departments to develop and conduct courses and seminars especially designed to meet the special training needs of the company or one of its departments. These types of courses are usually coordinated with training sessions conducted by members of the company's own training department.

Trade associations, as well as business and professional organizations, also provide training and educational opportunities for employees, managers, and top executives of business firms. Many businesses send their executives to special workshops in executive training conducted by universities or business and professional societies.

Follow-up Evaluations

A practice that has become popular among large companies is the periodic follow-up of new workers. The purpose of such evaluations is to determine if the workers are happy and successful in their positions. The first evaluation is usually scheduled several days after a new employee has joined the company's work force, and subsequent checks are made at regular intervals thereafter, at least once or twice a year.

Should the first follow-up reveal that a worker does not seem to fit into the job to which he has been assigned, he may be given special training, or transferred to another type of work. Later follow-ups serve as the basis for retraining, transfer, promotion, or dismissal.

EMPLOYEE COMPENSATION PLANS

The development and operation of a fair and equitable wage-and-salary system is perhaps the most difficult function of personnel management. Since the amount of money a person earns determines the quantity and quality of goods and services he can purchase, the compensation function is very important to each employee. Of course, the function is important to the company, too. When employees are overpaid, a company's products may be overpriced in a competitive market. When employees are underpaid, turnover is high, morale is low, and production is inefficient. In an effort to determine the amount of compensation a worker should receive, scores of plans have been advanced. Most workers in the United States today are paid either time wages or piece wages. *Time wages* are based on the amount of time spent on the job. *Piece wages* are based on the number of units produced.

Time Wages

In many types of work it is more practicable to base wages on the employee's responsibilities rather than on his productivity; in fact, in many instances it is impossible to objectively measure output. When quality rather than quantity is important, or where the employee is continually interrupted in his work, time wages are usually more appropriate.

Secretarial work, training, supervision, and machine-tooling are functions for which time wages are desirable. The employee is paid a certain amount per hour, week, or month. Accurate records of how much time each employee puts in can be maintained through the use of time cards and time clocks, which record when each worker arrives and departs.

Time wages do have one serious disadvantage, though. They fail to encourage some employees to make their maximum effort. Because there is no immediate recognition of a worker's superior performance, he may become discouraged and put less than his best into the work.

Piece Wages

Under the piece-rate payment plan, a certain sum is paid for each unit a worker produces. (Of course this plan can be used only when the output can be counted or objectively measured in some way.) The unit payment may be based on the output of an individual worker, or it may apply to the work of a group or even an entire department. The system is particularly valuable when applied to work wherein loitering is difficult to detect. By encouraging the workers to "supervise" themselves, it decreases supervisory costs.

When great emphasis is put on quantity, there is always a tendency among workers to sacrifice quality—so, management must keep under careful control the quality of the units produced. It is also good practice, management finds, to reward workers for maintaining a low level of material waste and spoilage. Sociologists have proven what management has long suspected of piece-rate workers: that they often hesitate to increase their production too greatly for fear that the employer will decrease the price paid per unit produced. The fear is not without grounds, because all too often employers *have* cut unit wages following an increase in production. You can see that such a move on the employer's part might well destroy any incentive that had been gained through using the piece-rate system.

Wage-incentive Plans

Some manufacturing firms have set up wage-payment plans designed to reward the worker with added compensation for exceptional performance. Known as *wage-incentive plans,* they are based on the piece-rate method of making wage payments.

In 1895, Frederick W. Taylor developed the first wage-incentive plan, the *Taylor Differential Piece-Rate Plan.* Here is how it works. First a careful scientific study is made of each worker's operations. Then a standard rate of output is established that is within the reach of the average worker. Two rates prevail—one for the worker who fails to reach the standard, and a higher rate for the worker who exceeds it. For example, if the standard output is 100 units per day, a worker who produces fewer than 100 pieces might receive 19 cents per piece. On the other hand, a worker who exceeds 100 units might receive 20 cents per piece. The worker who produced 95 units would receive $18.05 for his day's work, whereas the worker who produced 105 units would earn $21.00.

A second wage-incentive plan is the *Gantt Task and Bonus System.* Under this plan, if an employee exceeds the set standards by completing the work in less time, he receives as a bonus a percentage of the base rate. The bonus is usually figured on a sliding scale, varying from 15 to 35 percent of the base rate. A worker who fails to complete the task in the time allotted for it receives the regular hourly rate but no bonus. There are two special features of this plan: (1) The bonus rate usually begins when the worker does three-fourths as much as the standard. This serves to encourage those who are striving to reach the standard as well as those who have already bettered it. (2) The foreman is usually given a bonus also, depending upon the amount or number of bonuses paid to the workmen he supervises.

There are many other wage-incentive plans, such as the Rowan, Emerson, Bedaux, and Halsey plans, and the 100 Percent Time-Saving Plan. The ones we have discussed have been given to illustrate the manner in which such plans operate. Detailed study of the other plans is reserved for courses in personnel management and industrial relations.

A well-conceived wage-incentive plan will include the following objectives:

For management

1. Lowered costs resulting from increased productivity
2. Improved cost control leading to production which is more consistent, more uniform, and less variable in actual cost
3. Improved facility utilization
4. Improved worker morale as earnings become proportionate to individual effort

For employees

1. An opportunity to earn money in excess of base rate and in proportion to individual effort
2. An opportunity for individual recognition
3. An opportunity for a healthful competitive spirit among employees
4. An opportunity for employees to control (at least partially) the levels of their standards of living by their own initiative

Any wage incentive must recognize this dual direction of benefits.

Employee Profit-Sharing

The term *profit sharing* is used to refer to wage-payment plans that provide remuneration beyond basic pay schedules. These extra payments go to all employees; their amounts are tied directly to the profits earned. The Council of Profit Sharing Industries has defined profit sharing as "any procedure under which an employer pays or makes available to all regular employees, in addition to regular rates of pay, special current or deferred sums based on the profits of the business."

The basic philosophy of profit sharing is that it creates a "partnership relationship" on the part of employees. It draws labor and management closer together, and develops a working relationship and "atmosphere" favorable to efficient workmanship. Those who advocate profit sharing claim that it makes for high employee morale, reduces the number and extent of employee grievances, reduces labor turnover, provides greater security for workers, and improves public relations.

There is, of course, a wide variety of practices in profit-sharing programs. Some plans provide for cash payments while others provide for deferred payments which are frequently tied to the issuance of stock. Some of the factors entering into the framework of profit-sharing plans are: whether the percentage to be paid is to be a fixed or sliding rate; whether the percentage is to be applied to profits before or after taxes; and the amount of the profits to be shared.

Eastman Kodak's profit-sharing plan is determined by the amount of the cash dividend paid on the common stock. Employee bonuses are paid on the basis of individual total yearly earnings.

One of the best-known plans is that of the Lincoln Electric Co. of Cleveland, Ohio, which the company inaugurated in 1934. Under their system "each job is evaluated to establish its importance to the company's operations, and a pay rate is established for it . . . . The workers are rated twice a year and they are graded on the quality and quantity of their work, their skill, and their attitudes." These ratings determine the amount of bonus each worker is to receive in relation to his base salary.[2] According to the company president, productivity has increased on the average about 15 percent each year, as compared to the national average of slightly over 3 percent. Employees leave the company at a rate of less than 1 percent per year, as compared to a rate in 1959 for other manufacturing plants of 3.3 percent.

Organized labor looks with disfavor on wage-payment plans that sponsor competition among the workers, setting one against another. It prefers plans that are universal throughout the plant and that apply to all the workers. Labor leaders also oppose plans that reward only increased productivity which results directly from increased personal effort. They feel that wage-incentive plans should reward workers for increased output that results from other factors as well as from workers' personal skill and effort.

Production-sharing Plans

Production sharing is similar to profit sharing in that such programs utilize the cooperative efforts of both management and labor. Rather than shared profits, they represent a sharing of savings that result from reducing production costs. Since savings from production are much more narrow in scope than are company profits, it is easier to relate an individual's efforts to the results of a small group.

One of the best-known production-sharing plans is the Scanlon Plan. This plan was first used in the Lapointe Machine Tool Co. in Hudson, Mass., by Joseph Scanlon, an official of the United Steel Workers. Scanlon claimed that individual incentive plans lead to cutthroat competition among workers, at the expense of the best welfare of the group as a whole.

The Scanlon Plan emphasizes the sharing of savings in production with all workers. Under the operation of this technique, a normal labor cost is computed per unit of production. Then, if through the cooperative efforts of

[2] *The Plain Dealer*, December 10, 1961.

the group as a whole the improved efficiency results in lower unit labor costs, the amount of such savings is passed along to all workers as a bonus. In some cases the efficiency is measured in terms of productivity: if there is a 5 percent increase in productivity, wages are increased by the same percentage.

Under the Rucker Share-of-Production Plan, both company and workers share the increased value of goods produced, which results from the joint efforts of management and workers. This plan includes all hourly employees, not just those whose work can be measured. The standards employed are not based on the number of physical units produced, but on the ratio of sales income to the cost of labor input. It also shows a worker the relationship between the dollars he earns and the economic value of the goods he helps produce.

The Kaiser Long-Range Sharing Plan has received much attention in recent years because it has several unique characteristics. In order to discourage worker resistance to the use of modern equipment, the plan provides protection against layoffs resulting from increased mechanization. It also encourages waste reduction in materials and supplies as a factor in reducing the cost of production.

Actually, production sharing is more than a way of paying monetary compensation to workers. It represents labor-management cooperation. In some cases, such as under the Scanlon Plan, the awards for suggestions that improve production efficiency are paid to the group rather than to the individuals who submit the suggestions. The whole emphasis is on teamwork for the benefit of all. With teamwork, production increases of as much as 50 percent have been achieved.

EMPLOYEE BENEFITS AND SERVICES

We have seen that compensating employees for their services is an important function of the personnel department. Today most managers agree that compensation programs should include certain benefits beyond direct wage or salary payments. Since World War II, organized labor and management have been increasingly concerned with employee benefits and services. Indeed, such benefits and services are frequently given greater consideration than wages during the negotiation of a collective-bargaining agreement. Although benefits and services may not involve direct monetary payment to employees, they are costs to business; they frequently exceed the costs incurred by granting wage increases.

One of the earliest benefits to be provided was payment for holidays and vacation periods. Today it is common practice for businesses to pay their employees for one or more weeks of vacation time and for six to eight holidays each year. Some companies, in the metals industry for example, provide vacations of up to 13 weeks duration every five years or so for employees who have been on the payroll for a specified number of years. Other benefits that were among the first to be included in collective-bargaining agreements are hospitalization, and life insurance. It is now common practice for companies to pay a goodly portion of such insurance premiums, if not the full amount.

The benefits and services that we have been discussing are called *fringe benefits*. Other benefits or services that may be found include employee discounts on purchases of company products, and credit unions, retirement income provisions, and loans during layoff periods. An increasing number of companies also offer legal-aid counseling, income-tax counseling, low-cost cafeteria facilities, libraries, and educational opportunities.

Fringe benefits are important to the health and well-being of employees during their working years, and also provide security in retirement. You will also see that they are important in the development and maintenance of high morale among the work-force; a discussion of morale and its importance is included later in this chapter.

TRANSFER, PROMOTION, AND SEPARATION

Since transfer and promotion are such important phases of the personnel function, a definite and clearly understood policy regarding them must be established. A company that does not establish such a policy risks poor employee morale and high labor turnover.

Transfer

The term *transfer* refers to the shifting of an employee from one position to another without increasing his duties, responsibilities, or pay. Every business finds it necessary to transfer workers to different positions. There may come a time when older workers must be given assignments that require lighter work. Or, if a worker has been assigned to a job on which he is not doing satisfactory work, he may be shifted to another. There are times, too, when the work load is heavier in some departments than in others, or when it is desirable to rotate workers into and out of dangerous positions. Occasionally a transfer is necessary because of personal differences among employees, or because of personality conflicts between workers and supervisors. Also, employees are often rotated from position to position as a training device.

When a transfer has to be made, management must double-check to make sure that there are valid reasons for it, and that the employee will not suffer hardship as a result of it. And it is important for management to tell employees their reasons for moving them—to make them feel that they are being treated fairly, and are not being shifted merely for the convenience of someone else. Management should also tell people it shifts around whether the transfer is permanent or temporary, and, if it is only temporary, how long they will be working in the new job.

Rules and policies relative to transfers should be clearly stated, and understood by all members of the firm. This is essential to ensure that the workers being transferred will feel that they are being treated with justice.

Promotion

The term *promotion* refers to the shifting of an employee to a new position in which both his status and responsibilities are increased. (Higher pay does not always accompany a promotion, although it usually does—or at least follows soon after.) Promotions are advantageous to the firm as well as to the employee. Management knows that deserving employees have been taken care of, that workers are situated where they can produce the most, and that the cost of orienting and training new people has been reduced. When a promotion is made, however, it should be deserved. An employee should not be given a promotion when he has not earned it or when others are better qualified or more deserving. Length of service must also be considered. When two employees are equally deserving of being promoted, so far as ability and performance are concerned, the promotion usually goes to the person who has been either with the company or on the job the longest. This person is said to have seniority.

An advancement in pay that does not involve a move into a new job classification is called a *horizontal promotion.* An advancement that moves an employee into a job with a higher rank or classification is called a *vertical promotion.*

If management is to avoid increased labor unrest and labor turnover, it must develop a systematic plan for promotions. The best-qualified employees of a company become dissatisfied and leave if few opportunities for advancement exist or if promotions are made only infrequently. Employees should know all the factors included in the company's promotion policy and the relative importance of each.

Separation

Separations from the employ of a company may either be temporary or permanent, voluntary or involuntary. A layoff is temporary and involuntary, usually traceable to a lull in business. It is customarily assumed that those who are laid off will be re-employed as soon as business returns to normal. The usual procedure is first to lay off those workers with the least seniority.

A *discharge* is a permanent separation of an employee, at the will of the employer. A person may be discharged if he is not competent in his job even after (as often happens, though not always) an honest effort has been made, through transfers, to find a suitable job for him. A worker who is guilty of breaking company rules may also be subject to discharge if the seriousness of the infraction merits such action, or if the worker has a history of ignoring and breaking certain rules. Insubordination is also just cause for discharge. (Where the workers of a company are members of a union, the conditions that govern discharge are included in the labor agreement reached by the company and the union. This situation is discussed more fully in the following chapter on labor-management relations.)

When employees leave the company of their own free will, management should make a sincere attempt to find out the reason for their departure, for it can use this information to improve conditions and thus decrease labor turnover.

The basic reasons why employees leave businesses to take positions elsewhere are: inadequate pay (wages below the going rate in the area, at any rate), lack of security, lack of opportunity for advancement, lack of consideration or appreciation by the employer, internal politics, too much overtime, and favoritism shown to certain employees.

EMPLOYEE MORALE

Employee *morale* is the attitude or feeling of individuals or groups toward their jobs, their associates, and the company. It is affected by all the varied factors that make up the employee's environment, including the extent to which his needs and wants are satisfied by working in a particular job or for a certain company. (Employee needs and wants are discussed in more detail later in this chapter.)

If the employee feels that he is treated fairly by management, that his salary is adequate, and that working conditions are good, he is likely to have high morale. When employees have high morale they are enthusiastic and are inclined to cooperate with management. Employees with low morale are easily discouraged, tend to be uncooperative, and generally reveal negative feelings. Morale affects efficiency of operation and is therefore of great importance to management, especially to those involved in the personnel function. Many authorities believe that rates of production are more sharply influenced by a work force's morale than by any other environmental factor.

Morale Factors

Many factors combine to determine the level of employee morale. Unhealthful working conditions, including the prevalence of communicable diseases, the lax enforcement of rules, poor communications, and a feeling among employees that no one is interested in listening to sincere complaints or in improving the conditions that give rise to them, are all contributors to low morale.

Let us take a look at some of the specific facets of business life which (1) affect morale, or (2) are affected by the level of morale that exists in an organization.

Employee Needs and Wants. Management must remember that an employee's needs and wants are extremely important to him and that he will not continue working in a company where they are not satisified. *Basic human needs* such as food, clothing, and shelter; *social needs* such as friendly contact with people and acceptance by others; *egoistic needs* such as independence, recognition, and achievement, all are "translated" into specific employee *wants* on the job. Examples of such translated wants include, among others: adequate pay, friendly co-workers and supervisors, a job with opportunities for promotion, and sincere compliments for a job well done. In the early days of business operation, little attention was given to employee needs and wants. Today the effective manager is aware that employee needs and wants must be determined and that steps must be taken to ensure their satisfaction. He knows that employee satisfaction is absolutely essential if morale is to be maintained at high levels, and if thereby the worker is to be motivated to do a good job.

Health Programs. Because an employee who does not feel well physically is an unproductive worker, larger companies today maintain extensive on-the-premises health services. Besides working physically, this works psychologically to keep a healthy work-force on the job. Employees come to feel that management is interested in their physical well-being and is making a genuine attempt to provide needed health services—and thus are happier and more productive.

We have already noticed that the physical examination is an important consideration at the time of employment. But the "physical" is only the beginning of the ideal continuing health program. A complete health program (usually found only in the larger companies) provides for first aid, dental services, optical needs, mass X-rays and innoculations, periodic physical examinations, and even psychological and psychiatric counseling. Attention is also given to proper sanitation and lighting, adequate heat and ventilation, safety, and industrial hygiene. Since approximately 2 percent of a worker's productive time is lost because of illness, and illness is responsible for approximately 8 percent of all permanent separations from the labor force, the need for an adequate health program can be easily seen.

Safety. A poor safety record in any organization is extremely bad for employee morale. It results in increased costs of operation and in substantially reduced efficiency. Accidents can result in damage to machines and

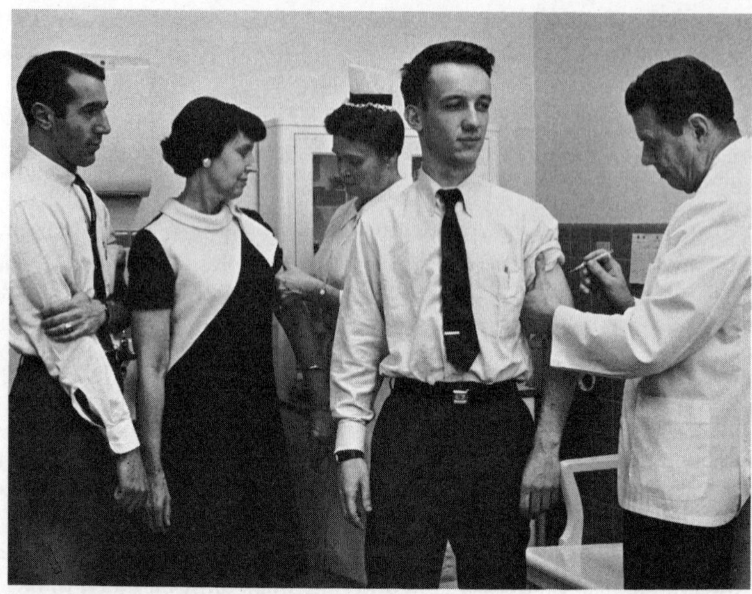

Company employees receiving free influenza shots

Courtesy Prentice-Hall, Inc.

supplies, to the physical plant, or to raw materials and products of the plant. Accidents may also result in physical injury to employees. Injury-accidents on the job cause lost time by not only the injured but also by other employees, who invariably stand around and discuss the details. And an on-the-job accident that results in the death of an associate lowers employee morale considerably.

Accurate figures on the frequency of industrial accidents are difficult to obtain due to the lack of uniformity in reporting accidents to state authorities. Usually, the only accidents that are reported are those that result in a loss of time greater than the shift during which they occur, and in some states only accidents for which compensation is paid are reported. Figures on costs of accidents are sometimes meaningless due to the lack of uniformity in computing such costs. It has been said that the true costs of an accident are like an iceberg; most of them are hidden "below the surface" and are discovered and measured only through extensive study. Examples of such "hidden" costs are time spent by management in compiling information and reporting the accident, loss of productive efficiency, work that spoils due to loss of production time, costs of training new workers, and several others. In spite of the difficulty in obtaining accurate figures concerning industrial accidents, we do know that approximately 2 million work injuries occur every year, of which one in 20 results in permanent total disability, and one in 23 in permanent partial disability. We also know that the cost of industrial accidents is probably in excess of 5 billion dollars annually. Accidents represent a tremendous loss of time and money that must be either absorbed by the company or passed on to the consumer as part of the cost of the article manufactured. In either event, it can be seen that it is to the advantage of both the business and the public to prevent industrial accidents.

In an attempt to work out preventive techniques and procedures, many investigators have undertaken research studies to determine the causes of industrial accidents. They have classified into two distinct types the many factors that contribute to industrial accidents: first, accidents due to the personal characteristics and attitudes of workers; and second, accidents due to impersonal factors—technical deficiencies in the work environment. Personal deficiencies include lack of knowledge on the part of the worker, improper attitudes, physical defects, reckless indifference to danger, and so forth. Technical deficiencies include inadequate lighting and ventilation, poor design of equipment, improper materials-handling techniques, ineffective safeguards on machinery, and others. However, it is significant to personnel management that four out of every five accidents are caused by personal rather than technical deficiencies.

An effective safety program involves establishing safety standards and policies, conducting safety inspections, utilizing up-to-date engineering techniques to assure that equipment and working conditions are satisfactory, educating the workers to become safety-conscious, and enforcing safety rules and regulations. Some of the techniques used by modern firms in educating for safety and in safety enforcement are: records of injuries, posters, the plant magazine, individual and group conferences, films, training in the use of fire equipment, and safety manuals that include safety rules and penalties for infractions. Some companies conduct safety contests and reward workers whose records indicate that they are observing safety rules and regulations.

Workmen-compensation laws give a company a financial incentive to maintain safe working conditions. A company with a high accident rate or a poorly-run safety program must pay higher premiums for its workmen's compensation insurance coverage than one with a good safety program or a good record.

Absenteeism. The term *absenteeism* refers to the failure (whether voluntary or involuntary) of a worker to be present at his assigned place of work as scheduled. It should be remembered that according to this widely accepted definition, tardiness is also a form of absenteeism. Studies show that there is a close relationship between absenteeism and unrest; excessive absenteeism is an indication of low morale, whereas high morale results in a lower rate of absenteeism.

Management sometimes uses the rate of absenteeism as an indication of the level of morale. If an employee who is eligible to work 25 days during a month fails to work on three of these days, his absentee rate would be 3 ÷ 25, or a rate of 12 percent. By utilizing this same method, the rate of absenteeism for a department or entire firm could be computed. Rates are sometimes computed for various groups of employees according to age, sex, level of job, and so on. Such analyses make it much easier to determine causes for absenteeism.

The rate of absenteeism varies considerably from one industry to another and from peacetime to wartime. It also varies with age, length of service, status of health, and sex. There are several significant factors that contribute to absenteeism. Illness and personal injury account for approximately 50 percent of all justifiable absenteeism. The search for other employment, home-related duties, poor job attitudes, poor working conditions, poor housing, the lack of adequate transportation and child-care facilities, and other factors contribute significantly to a high absenteeism rate.

We all know the importance of having every worker in a job he can perform well. Excessive absenteeism frequently indicates that an employee has been improperly selected or placed. Due to the high frequency of illness and personal injury as causes for absenteeism, it can be seen that effective measures to improve the health and safety of workers tend to reduce absenteeism. Management has only recently discovered that attempts to get at the causes of absenteeism are far more effective in reducing the rate than are penalties imposed on "absence prone" employees.

Labor Turnover. The phrase *labor turnover* refers to employees moving into and out of employment in an organization. The most commonly used measure is *net labor turnover rate,* which represents the number of replacements per hundred workers—that is, the number of employees who are hired to fill positions left vacant by separations. A firm that has an average workforce of 100 and has to replace five men who have quit and five who have been discharged would have a net labor turnover of (5 + 5/100), or 10 percent.

Naturally, an excessive labor turnover is to be avoided. It is undesirable for a variety of reasons; the fact that it is very expensive is but one. It must be analyzed carefully and its causes corrected. Several of the more important causes of turnover are marriage, transfer of spouse to another community, "raiding" by a competitor, retirement, poor working conditions, inadequate supervision, poor pay and promotional opportunities, and poor selection and placement procedures. Turnover rates vary with the workers' degree of skill —unskilled workers show higher turnover rates than semiskilled and skilled workers.

Grievances. *Grievances* are the complaints, discontents, or dissatisfactions existing when workers feel that they have been done injustices by the company or by their superiors. Regardless of whether or not the company is at fault, management must give adequate consideration to all grievances. It must be remembered that although not all grievances may be valid, many will present valuable opportunities to improve the over-all organization.

Grievances may involve (1) an individual, (2) a small group of workers, or even (3) all the employees in a plant or company. A grievance might arise, for instance, if (1) an employee feels that he is being asked to perform tasks not included in his job classification; (2) a group of employees have tried unsuccessfully to have a ventilating fan placed in their section of the plant; or (3) the employees in general or *en masse* feel that management is violating the terms of the seniority clause in the labor agreement. Whatever the complaint, and whether or not a union exists, a formal procedure should be developed that will ensure employees an opportunity to voice their complaints. When such opportunities do not exist, minor complaints may grow and become sufficiently serious to cause real trouble.

Grievance procedures vary from company to company. If the aggrieved employee cannot get a satisfactory settlement after consulting with his supervisor, the grievance is usually submitted to a committee composed of the supervisor and the union steward. If there is no organized union, the union steward's function is carried out by an elected or appointed employee representative. In any event, the aggrieved employee is present at the meeting of this committee, which constitutes the first step in the grievance procedure. In case grievances are not settled at the first step, procedures normally include several steps, each one involving progressively higher-ranking employee and management representatives. At each step, attempts are made to reach an acceptable solution. If an agreement is not reached after each of these steps is utilized, the grievance is sometimes submitted to an impartial arbitrator, who renders a binding decision. It must be remembered that grievances can be settled at any one of these steps, in which case progressively higher steps are made unnecessary for that particular case.

In any event, a definite grievance procedure should be established so that the employee can air his case for himself or have a union or employee representative speak for him. The grievance procedure gives management a chance to study the cause of such problems, and if necessary to make adjustments in keeping with established policy. It is to the advantage of both the employee and management that a formal procedure exist, and that its provisions be well publicized throughout the plant. A prompt disposition of grievances is important because in the long run it saves money and increases the level of morale.

Employee Participation. Many up-to-date organizations have found employee participiation in policy formulation and decision-making an effective means for developing and holding workers' interest in their jobs. When used discreetly, it has been found to be a tremendous boost to employee morale levels. Of course, the extent to which employees become involved in so-called "participative management" techniques varies from company to company and within companies. Likewise, the ability of a particular supervisor to create an atmosphere conducive to participation also varies among managers.

Employee participation may be of the formal or the informal type. Examples of the *formal* type include suggestion systems, junior boards that include workers and lower-level managers, and employee membership on important committees. *Informal participation* exists when employees are consulted by their superiors as to certain decisions, or when they are asked to assist in the development of specific plans or programs. In some companies, managers request the assistance of their subordinates in establishing job goals. For example, a salesman might be consulted by his superior and asked to help in the development of sales quotas for his territory for the coming year. In this way the employee feels that his ideas are important to the company and that his established objectives are more realistic than when arbitrarily imposed on him by management. There is a strong possibility that the quality of the management function is enhanced by employee participation.

The degree to which employees participate in decision making or policy formulation is usually a reflection of their superiors' skill and philosophy. For example, a superior may simply command his subordinates to do something, and they proceed—in effect, no employee participation exists. A degree of participation exists when the superior asks for employees' advice on a decision, then utilizes their comments in making the decision himself. The highest degree of employee participation exists when the manager permits the group to make a decision or formulate a policy through the democratic process, while he simply leads the group in discussion.

It should be remembered that employee participation has several limitations. It has not worked well with immature employees, nor with employees in jobs having extremely low educational requirements. An environment that creates too much freedom may encourage rule violations and poor performance, and even result in lowered morale. It is essential that all employees realize that although they have been invited to participate in the management function, their superior is still the manager and must arbitrarily make some decisions. A proper balance between the autocratic and democratic approaches seems to be gaining favor in modern management.

SUMMARY

Personnel Management is concerned with planning, organizing, directing, coordinating, and controlling the activities of employees. The personnel department has the primary responsibility for personnel activities, but all managers perform personnel functions. The extent to which the personnel department exercises control over the total personnel function is determined by the authority it receives from top management.

The personnel department works closely with all other departments. It is concerned with selecting new employees, with assigning them to jobs, and with their continuing development. Special tests, interviews, and physical examinations are used to insure that the best workers available are hired.

The safety and general welfare of the workers are the responsibility of personnel management. Health programs are established to keep employees well and on the job. Pleasant working conditions and effective supervision are provided to maintain employee morale and to reduce absenteeism and labor turnover.

Employee attitudes and their needs and wants, including adequate and equitable compensation programs, are vital concerns of personnel management. Effective and well-understood grievance procedures are essential for maintaining high levels of morale. Newsletters and company magazines are utilized to keep workers informed. Participative management techniques, including suggestion plans, are used to show the employee that his ideas are important to the company and its management.

VOCABULARY REVIEW QUIZ

Match the following vocabulary terms with the statements below.

a. Absenteeism
b. Apprenticeship training
c. Aptitude test
d. Discharge
e. Grievance
f. Job analysis
g. Job classification
h. Job description
i. Labor turnover
j. Layoff
k. Morale
l. Performance test
m. Piece wages
n. Production sharing
o. Profit sharing
p. Promotion
q. Separation
r. Supervisory training
s. Time wages
t. Transfer
u. Vestibule training

1. A test for potential talents
2. The shifting of an employee to a new position in which his status and responsibilities are greater
3. An employee's leaving the company for any reason—voluntary or involuntary, permanent or temporary
4. A measure of the degree of skill that a person has for a specific type of work

5. Complaints, discontents, or dissatisfactions existing when workers feel they have been done injustices
6. The grouping together of several positions into a single bracket or class
7. A temporary employee separation from an organization
8. A sharing of savings that result from reduced production costs
9. Basically, leadership training—but not of the highest level
10. Wages based on responsibilities rather than productivity
11. The attitude or feeling of groups or individuals toward their job, their associates, and the company
12. The failure of a worker to be present at his assigned place of work as scheduled
13. Wages paid for each unit produced
14. A payment to employees based on profits of the business
15. A permanent separation of an employee, at the will of the employer
16. Training in a craft involving many related tasks
17. The study of a job in an effort to answer what, when, where, how, why, and who
18. A written report based on the analysis of a job
19. Training conducted away from the job, but in a simulated job situation
20. The movement of employees into and out of employment in an organization
21. The shifting of an employee from one position to another without an increase in his duties, responsibilities, or pay

QUESTIONS FOR REVIEW STUDY

1. What is personnel management? Whose job is it?
2. Why is a separate personnel department needed in a large business?
3. How do the powers of a personnel department differ when it is granted *staff* rather than *functional* authority?
4. What is the purpose of the job description?
5. What are the three purposes of the physical examination as it is used in the selection process?
6. Why is technical training so significant today? Do you believe its importance will increase in the future? Why?
7. As an industrial worker would you prefer a production-sharing or a profit-sharing plan? Why?
8. What are several indicators of high employee morale?
9. What are the three types of human needs? Which of these is most difficult for management to satisfy? Why?
10. Distinguish between technical and personal deficiencies as contributors to industrial accidents.
11. How can management reduce labor turnover?
12. Of what value to management is the grievance procedure?

PROBLEMS AND PROJECTS

1. Assume that you have been given the authority to establish a training program for newly hired clerks and stenos (stenographers) in your office. Outline a plan for this program, including ways to determine training needs, the training approach (on-the-job, vestibule, etc.) to be used, where the training will take place, and qualifications of the teacher-trainer.
2. Assume that there has been an increase in employee turnover among the office workers in your company and that you have been asked to determine the causes. How would you proceed with this assignment?
3. Of the 25 employees in the department which you head, three are what you consider "absence prone." Outline a plan for bringing the three workers "back in line."
4. Management in your company tends to look upon each grievance as just another chore to take up time. State several arguments for taking a more positive approach toward grievances.

A BUSINESS CASE

Case 11-1 The Case of Arny

Schumacher & Smith, Inc., is a firm specializing in men's clothing and furnishings. It has 37 outlets in a certain eastern state. With few exceptions, its policy has been to fill vacancies in its managerial staff from within. Last year, Bob C. was given responsibility for a store in a community of some 400,000 people. Although the sales force increases at peak periods, Bob, as manager, is normally responsible for the supervision of 11 employees. All work, including merchandising and window-decoration, is performed by the manager and his staff.

Scheduling the work-force is a problem, since the store is open from 9 a.m. through 9:30 p.m., six days a week. If there is to be an adequate number of sales personnel on the selling floor at all times, and all necessary stock work is to be done, it is essential that all the people take an active interest in the work and show considerable initiative and inventiveness.

One sales clerk, Arny, a 20-year-old employee of six months, has shown little individual initiative. When assigned a task, he does it quite well. As soon as he has finished, however, he stops to await further directions. He is extremely defensive about anything he does, and has frequently pointed out that he is working as fast as he can, even when there has been no doubt that the job he has been doing has required a good bit of time.

Bob has come to realize that Arny is friendly with no one on the sales force, and indeed appears to regard his co-workers with a reserve that borders on belligerence. Bob has also found that Arny trusts no one. But perhaps, thinks Bob, Arny is not alone in his mistrust, contempt, and whatever. One employee, Bill D., has offered the information that Arny is frequently in desperate need of a bath!

Uncertain of what action he should take, Bob plans to go to the home office of S & S and to seek the advice of the personnel manager. He doesn't want to fire Arny because, bathless though he may be, Arny does a pretty good job. At the same time, though, Bob can't afford to have dissension in the ranks of his staff. Neither can he afford to have Arny offending the delicate nasal sensibilities of the customers.

1. If you were the personnel manager, what advice would you give that might aid Bob in resolving the problem of Arny?
2. Suppose you were Bob: what action would you take to remedy the situation?

Labor and American Business

12

The term *labor* has come to be widely used largely because it can be interpreted to mean different things under a variety of circumstances and in combination with myriad other business terms. For example, you often read and hear statistics pertaining to the number of persons in the "labor force." You also come to know from time to time that "labor" has taken a position in favor of, or in opposition to, certain business or governmental policies. In the first instance, "labor" is used inclusively because the labor force includes not only everyone who is actively employed, but also the unemployed. In the second instance, "labor" is used exclusively in that when labor endorses or opposes a stated policy, it is undoubtedly only *organized labor*—those workers who are members of labor unions—doing so.

The employed labor force includes professional people—attorneys, teachers, physicians. It is also made up of office workers such as accountants, clerks, and secretaries. These latter are sometimes referred to as white-collar workers, though the "white-collar" category properly includes most persons in management and supervisory positions. The term "blue-collar" is sometimes used to refer to workers engaged in manual tasks—skilled, semiskilled, and unskilled laborers. Although organized labor is strongest among blue-collar workers, a number of office employees and a limited number of public school teachers belong to unions.

In this chapter we shall be chiefly concerned with organized labor—with its types of organizations, with its objectives and accomplishments, and with its power and influence. First, however, we shall take a look at the total labor force.

THE LABOR FORCE

In the fall of 1966, civilian nonagricultural employment totaled approximately 72 million persons. This was 2.6 million more than a year earlier. During that same 12-month period the armed forces expanded by 482,000 men and women to a total of 3,178,000. When agricultural employment of 4½ million is included, the total labor-force in 1966 was rapidly approaching 80 million people. About 4 percent of this number were unemployed. The expected increase in the labor force for the immediate future is approximately 1.5 million persons per year.

Approximately one-third of the total labor-force is women, and it is anticipated that by 1980, women will constitute 36 percent of the total work-force. Women, together with young workers under 20 years of age, make up the main group being added to the labor force today. The distribution of the labor force by sex and by age is shown in the graph on the facing page.

Changes by Ages and Regions

The makeup of the labor force by age groups varies with the birth rate. During the 1960 to 1970 decade the greatest growth occurred in the 20-to-24 age-group. The projections for the decade between 1970 and 1980 indicate that the 25-to-34 age-group will expand much more than any other. The growth rates for the different age-groupings are shown by the graph at the top of page 332.

The labor force in the Pacific region—Alaska, California, Hawaii, Oregon, and Washington—is increasing at almost twice the growth-rate for the nation as a whole. The Mountain states have the next highest growth-rate with the South Atlantic region in third place. The East South Central region has the lowest growth-rate.

Projections of the labor force for the period from 1970 to 1980 are shown in Table 12.1, page 332.

Distribution of Total Labor—Force
Millions of Persons

By Sex

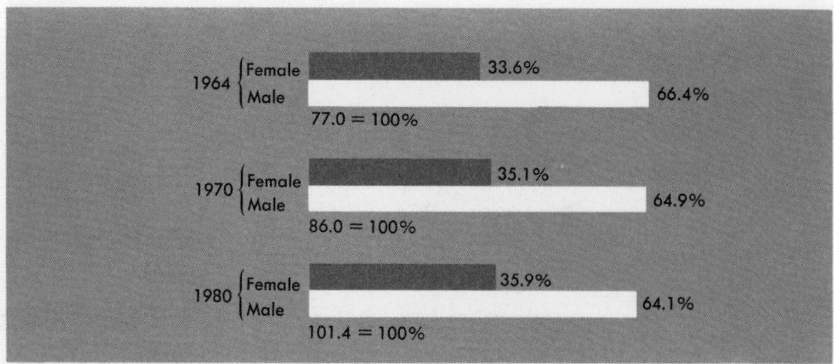

By Age

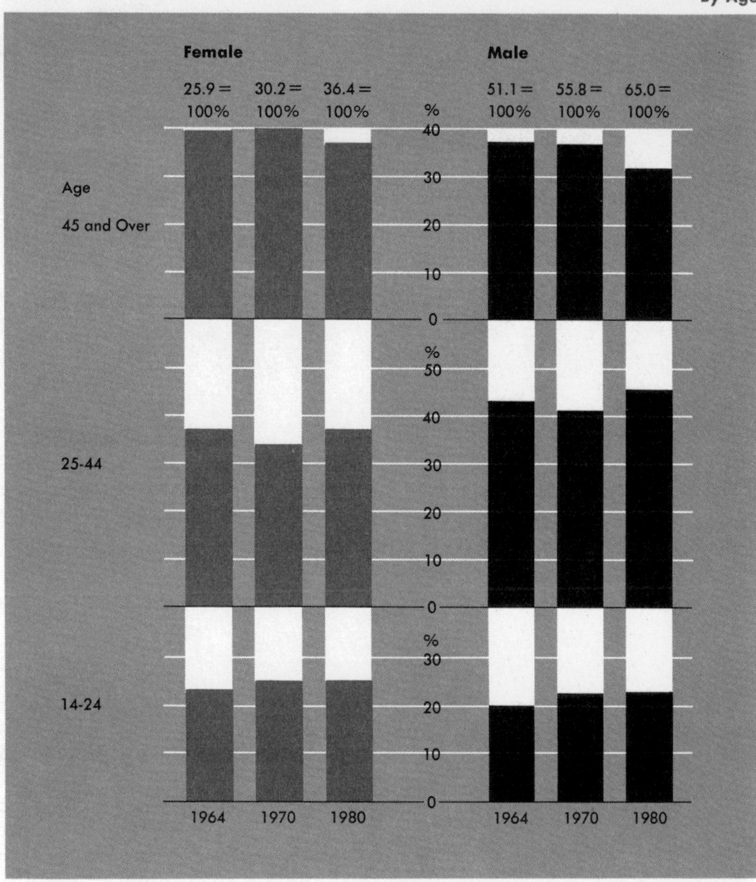

The female portion of the labor force is expected to continue increasing and to approximate 36 percent of the total by 1980. Females 45 years or older will constitute the biggest segment of the female labor force in 1970, but will be slightly outranked by the next younger group in 1980. The male labor force will show a relative decline in the oldest age category by 1980, and a slight rise in the youngest.

Sources: Bureau of Labor Statistics; Bureau of the Census; National Industrial Conference Board, Inc.

Changes in Total Labor—Force
By Age and Sex

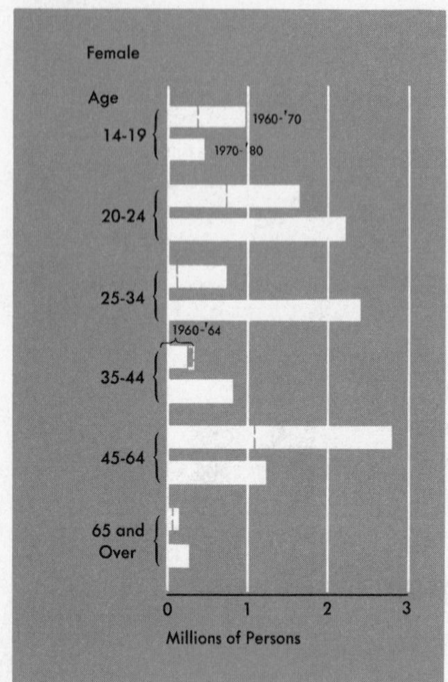

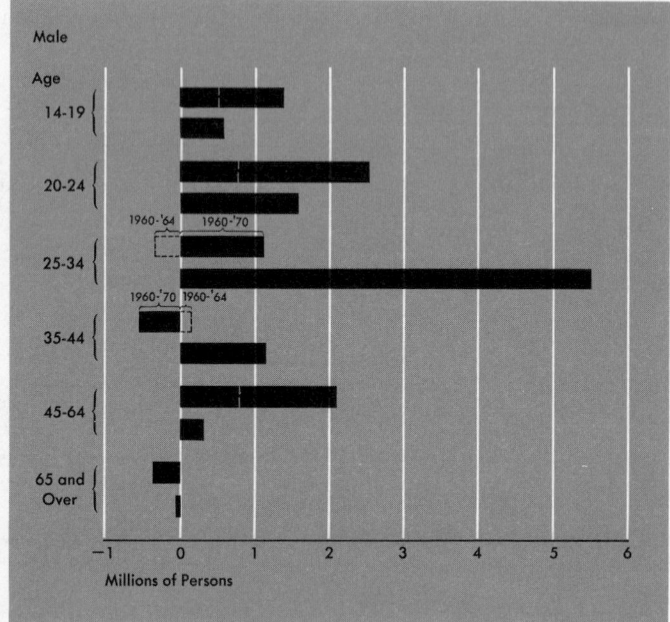

For females, the greatest additions in the present decade will be in the 45–64 age-category; for males, in the 20–24 age-group. The largest part of the addition for both sexes accurred between 1964 and 1970.
Source: National Industrial Conference Board, Inc.

TABLE 12.1

LABOR FORCE—1960 AND 1965 AND PROJECTIONS, 1970 TO 1980

	Total Labor Force (in thousands)				
	1960	1965	1970	1975	1980
Male	49,563	51,705	55,844	60,281	64,981
Female	23,518	26,653	30,155	33,365	36,427
Total	73,081	78,357	85,999	93,646	101,408

Sources: Department of Labor, Bureau of Labor Statistics; *Projections of the Labor Force, 1970–1980, Statistical Abstract of the United States.* 1966, p. 219.

The Job Outlook for the Next Decade

White-collar workers outnumbered blue-collar workers for the first time in 1956. Over the next decade, expectations are for the continuation of more rapid growth in white-collar occupations, the slower growth in blue-collar occupations, the faster-than-average growth among service workers, and a further decline among farm workers.

The greater growth expectation for white-collar jobs reflects the continued expansion anticipated for the service-producing industries that employ a high proportion of white-collar workers; the growing demand for personnel capable of performing research and applying scientific findings in industry; the increasing needs for educational and health services; and a continuing growth in the amount of paperwork necessary in all types of enterprises. Although the number of blue-collar workers as a group will increase at a much slower rate than that of white-collar workers, the number of craftsmen will grow at about the same rate as total employment.

While Total Employment Will Go Up by One-Fourth by 1975...
Industry Growth Rates Will Vary Widely

Decline	Industry	Projected Employment Growth: No Change	Less than Average	Average	More than Average
	Government	———	———	———	→
	Services	———	———	———	→
	Contract Construction	———	———	———	→
	Wholesale and Retail Trade	———	———	→	
	Finance, Insurance, and Real-Estate	———	———	→	
	Manufacturing	———	→		
	Transportation and Public Utilities	———	→		
←	Mining				
←	Agriculture				

Job Opportunities Generally Will Increase Fastest in Occupations Requiring the Most Education and Training

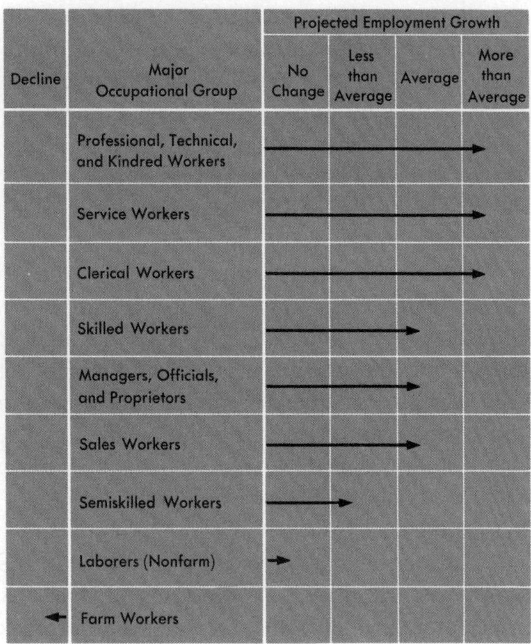

Decline	Major Occupational Group	Projected Employment Growth: No Change	Less than Average	Average	More than Average
	Professional, Technical, and Kindred Workers	———	———	———	→
	Service Workers	———	———	———	→
	Clerical Workers	———	———	———	→
	Skilled Workers	———	———	→	
	Managers, Officials, and Proprietors	———	———	→	
	Sales Workers	———	———	→	
	Semiskilled Workers	———	→		
	Laborers (Nonfarm)	→			
←	Farm Workers				

Source: National Consumer Finance Association.

Growth expectations in several employment areas are shown in the graphs on the preceding page.

THE HISTORY AND GROWTH OF LABOR UNIONS

The history of the labor movement dates from the beginning of this country. Even before the Declaration of Independence, skilled artisans in handicraft industries joined together in benevolent societies. Their primary purpose was to provide members and their families with financial assistance in the event of serious illness, debt, or the death of the wage earner. Although these early associations had little resemblance to present-day labor unions, they did bring workers together to consider problems of mutual concern, and their solutions.

Crafts such as those of carpenters, shoemakers, and printers formed separate organizations in Philadelphia, New York, and Boston as early as 1791, largely to resist wage reductions. These unions were confined to local areas and were usually weak because they seldom included all the workers of the craft. The first recorded meeting of workers and employer representatives for the discussion of labor demands occurred between the Philadelphia shoemakers and their employers in 1799.

Between 1827 and 1832, workers' organizations gradually turned to independent political activity. This idea of improving their status by political action soon spread to many leading industrial communities. Organization of union groups beyond a single local area was first tried in 1834, when the central bodies from seven cities met in New York to form the National Trades' Union. These experiments in federation, however, did not withstand the financial panic of 1837 and the period of depression and unemployment which followed.

Actually, the first national union was the Noble Order of the Knights of Labor, which was founded as a local union of garment workers in Philadelphia in 1869, and which by 1886 claimed more than 700,000 members throughout the country. Internal conflict between those who favored processes of collective bargaining and those committed to political means and basic social change, together with a conflict of interests between the skilled and unskilled workers, led to the weakening and dissipation of the Knights of Labor. This gave rise to the American Federation of Labor, which was founded in 1886 with Samuel Gompers as its first president.

During the first three decades following 1890 the AFL consolidated its position as the principal federation of American trade unions. It had approximately 2 million members by the outbreak of World War I, and surpassed the 4 million mark by 1920. In all there were more than 5 million union members by 1920. The economic prosperity which followed World

War I, together with protecting legislation during the 1920's and 1930's, brought about rapid growth in union membership. The greatest impetus to union growth was the passage of the Wagner Act in 1935. During the 10-year period from 1935 to 1945, union membership increased fourfold, from fewer than 4 million to almost 15 million. By 1958, union membership in this country had exceeded 18 million, but had decreased slightly by 1961. Growth in union membership is shown in Table 12.2.

TABLE 12.2

NATIONAL AND INTERNATIONAL UNIONS—MEMBERSHIP: 1940 TO 1964

Item	1940	1950	1955	1960	1961	1962	1963	1964
Unions Affiliated With AFL-CIO	147	137	139	134	131	130	129	129
Membership* (in thousands)	8,944	15,000	17,749	18,117	17,328	17,630	17,586	17,976
Percentage of Total Labor Force	15.5	22.0	24.4	23.3	22.0	22.2	21.8	21.9
Percentage of Employment in Nonagricultural Establishments	26.9	31.5	33.2	31.4	30.1	29.7	29.2	28.9
AFL-CIO (in thousands)	7,872	12,143	16,062	15,072	14,572	14,835	14,818	15,150
Independent or Unaffiliated Unions (in thousands)	1,072	2,600	1,688	3,045	2,756	2,794	2,768	2,825

* Includes Canadian members of labor unions with headquarters in U.S. (1,068,000 in 1960; 1,025,000 in 1961; 1,044,000 in 1962; 1,062,000 in 1963; and 1,135,000 in 1964).

Source: Dept. of Labor, Bureau of Labor Statistics; *Handbook of Labor Statistics, Statistical Abstract of the United States,* 1967, p. 246.

The degree of union organization varies considerably throughout the different regions and industrial groups in the United States. The most highly organized unions are in the long-established industries. The transportation industry, which includes the Teamsters, the railway unions, and the public transit unions, is almost fully organized. Contract construction, wherein the workers are organized on a craft basis, is also highly organized. Union membership as a percentage of the total employment in selected industries is shown in the chart on page 336.

The largest single union is that of the Teamsters, which has more than 1.5 million members; the second largest group, the United Auto Workers, has more than a million. The relative strengths of the 10 largest unions in this country is shown in the bar graph on page 337.

The largest unorganized occupational groups are farm hands, domestic help, and white-collar workers. The latter group includes about 18 million workers in clerical, professional, technical, and sales occupations, of whom only about 2 million are now in labor unions.

In discussing union membership, we should remember that the hours,

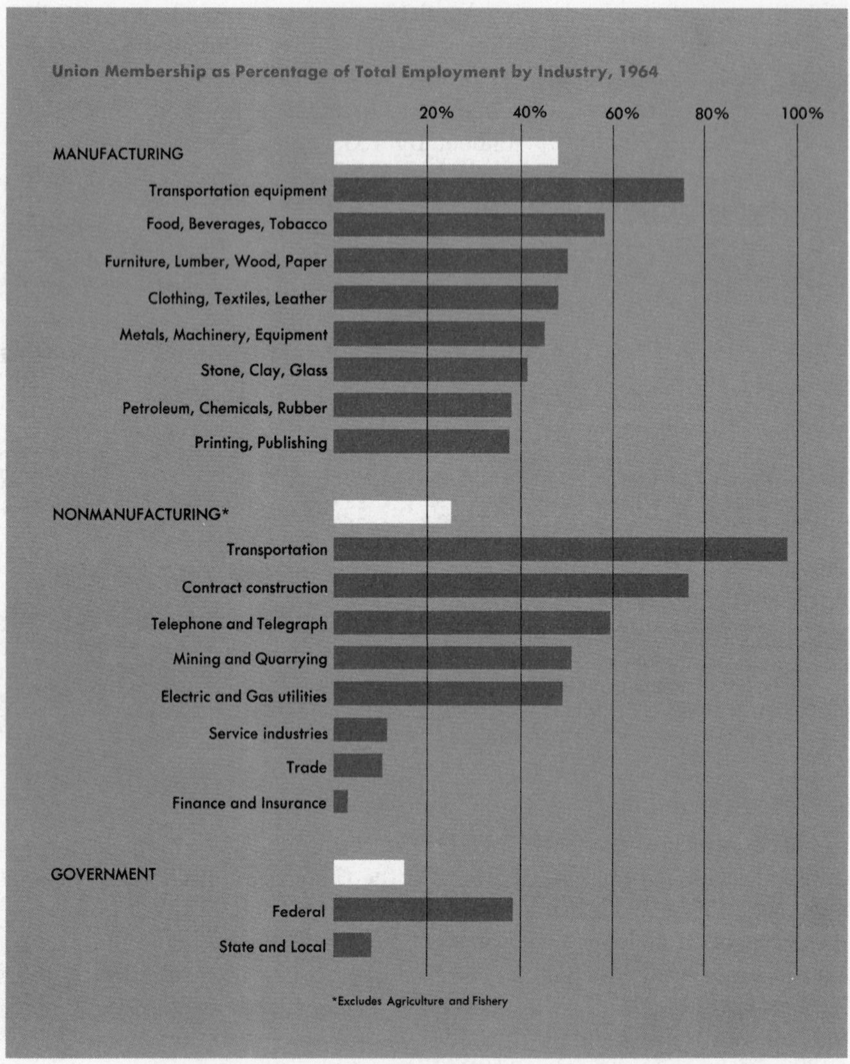

Most of the above percentages have been slightly inflated by the unavoidable inclusion of 1.2 million foreign workers belonging to U.S.-based unions, while the industry employment totals, used in the computation, relate to the U.S. only. Despite this distortion, it is clear where unionization has made the sharpest impact.

The transportation industry, where the Teamsters, the various railway unions, and the public transit unions have firm positions, is almost fully organized. Contract construction, with its many craft unions, and the transportation equipment industry, where the Automobile Workers are strong, are also highly unionized.

Sources: Bureau of Labor Statistics; National Industrial Conference Board, Inc.

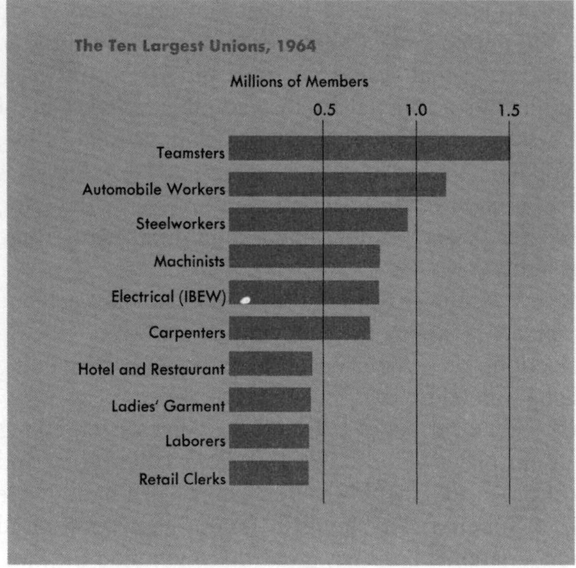

Source: National Industrial Conference Board, Inc.

wages, and working conditions of many workers who are not union members are often shaped by the bargaining successes of the unions themselves. Whereas only slightly more than one-third of all "organizable" workers are actually union members, about half of all such workers are now covered by *collective* agreements.[1]

THE POWER AND INFLUENCE OF LABOR

The labor movement in this nation has gained strength and momentum with the over-all economic development of the country. In the early days of our business history, the labor force was entirely unorganized. The individual worker had little authority and was without any effective way to promote his own interest. During most of the century from 1785 to 1885 there was no real labor movement in the United States, and in fact no logical reason for the existence of one. Large-scale organization of production was still in the future.

The trade-union boom of the early 1920's continued through the brief post-war prosperity period that followed. Contrary to what might be ex-

[1] A *collective* agreement is a written contract between the management of a firm and its workers as a group. Such agreements are discussed in the next chapter.

pected, however, the power and influence of labor as an organized group steadily declined during the period from 1930 to 1936. It was not until the second Roosevelt Administration that American trade unions began to respond to the series of stimulants advanced by that administration. One of these stimulants was the passage of the National Labor Relations Act of 1935, better known as the Wagner Act.[2] The principal aim of this law was to strengthen organized labor's power to deal with employers. In 1938, the Fair Labor Standards Act was passed, establishing a minimum hourly wage for employees in certain industries.

Today the unions have vast power. And the right to strike has been one of organized labor's strongest weapons in achieving that power. Once a union wins a bona fide election, the recognition of that union as a bargaining agent for the workers is guaranteed by law.

A look at the charts shown on pages 336 and 337 reveals something of the relative strength of our major unions. The Teamsters Union is far and away the largest and most powerful. Should the Teamsters call a nationwide strike, they would bring commerce to a standstill. The organization of all forms of transportation on a national basis has given this one union the awesome power to cripple the mightiest nation in history.

Now that big unions have grown into economic giants, with monetary powers equal to those of many large corporations, many people are asking this question: Have labor unions become monopolies and should they be regulated in the same manner as business monopolies are?

The United States Department of Commerce, concerned with the impact of labor on business, has asked Congress to amend Section 6 of the Clayton Act to describe the legitimate functions of labor unions. Many serious observers think there is a need for firm governmental control over unions. They argue that making labor unions subject to the authority of federal antitrust and antimonopoly laws would be neither discriminatory nor punitive.

Legislative correction is not a simple matter of applying the antitrust laws to unions. Rather, it should involve the application of American principles of power dispersion to unions in a way that would safeguard the full benefits of collective bargaining and prevent any new form of bargaining inequality. The ultimate objective of any legislation of this kind is to prevent either combinations of employers or combinations of unions from destroying our competitive system.

Since union negotiators bargain for whole groups of workers, thousands of individuals and their families have a vital interest in the results of labor-management negotiations. Everyone has a stake in these bargaining sessions: the workers, management, and, indirectly, you as a consumer, because the

[2] This act is discussed in Chapter 13 in the section dealing with labor legislation.

price you pay for the finished product is affected by the cost of producing it. Our government is responsible for representing the American public, and in achieving a peaceful and fair settlement of labor-management differences.

Idleness due to strikes in industry and business is costly to labor, management, and the public. Thus, it is to the advantage of everyone to settle labor-management controversies in order to avoid a work stoppage.

TYPES OF LABOR ORGANIZATIONS

There are two basic types of unions in the United States: craft unions and industrial unions. *Craft unions* are organizations of skilled workers engaged in various crafts or trades. All the members of a given craft union do the same kind of work. For example, there are craft unions for machinists, carpenters, painters, and plumbers.

Industrial unions are not restricted to skilled workers; they also include semiskilled and unskilled workers. The nature of the industry, rather than the special skill of the individual worker, forms the basis of membership. For example, workers in the automobile industry are represented by the United Automobile Workers, in the clothing industry by the Amalgamated Clothing Workers Union, and in the mining industry by the United Mine Workers of America.

The American Federation of Labor

The Federation of Organized Trades and Labor Unions was organized in 1881 through the coming together of a number of craft unions. In 1886 another group of unions, which previously had been affiliated with the Knights of Labor, broke away from that group and joined in with those unions in the Federation. At that time the union adopted the name of the American Federation of Labor (AFL). It was in truth a federation of affiliated autonomous groups. As an organization it had little power over its sovereign units, but it did have the power to expel a union or a group of unions from membership. Historically, the AFL was predominantly a craft union, although some industrial unions were affiliated with it. Perhaps the most notable and powerful industrial union affiliated with the AFL was the International Ladies Garment Workers Union. The affiliated unions found that by joining together into one organization they commanded greater strength in securing favorable congressional legislation than they could by working separately.

Under the able leadership of its president, Samuel Gompers, the AFL grew and prospered. Much of its appeal lay in its radical departure from the traditional philosophy of unionism. Previously, unions had been chiefly concerned with social objectives. Samuel Gompers led the AFL to emphasize the economic aspects of unions—what is known as *business unionism* or "bread and butter unionism." The AFL can truly be said to have constituted the cornerstone of the organized labor movement in America.

For many years the AFL followed a policy of neutrality in political activity. In addition to business unionism and nonparticipation in politics, Gompers strongly advocated the principle of the autonomy of each craft. He felt that this principle was inherent in forming a strong foundation for successful union growth and influence.

The Congress of Industrial Organizations

The AFL adherence to a policy of a single union for each craft led to the formation of a new labor organization, the Congress of Industrial Organizations (CIO). As American industry became more mechanized, there were increasingly larger numbers of workers operating machines rather than following a trade or craft. Understandably, these men could not qualify for membership in the "trade" unions. So in 1935 the presidents of eight of the AFL unions formed what was called the Committee for Industrial Organization. Opposing the AFL's emphasis on craft unionism, this new group wanted to organize large industries (such as rubber, steel, and automobiles) along the lines of industrial unionism. The feeling became so intense that in 1936 the unions that had associated themselves with the Committee for Industrial Organization were suspended from membership in the AFL. This move resulted in the group's formation as a rival labor organization, which in 1938 adopted a name very much like their own: Congress of Industrial Organizations. During the following decade, by pushing the organization of workers in many fields that had not previously been organized, the burgeoning CIO grew in power to the extent that it came to seriously compete with the AFL.

Merger of AFL and CIO

In the early 1950's, the leaders of these two rival organizations realized that the cause of organized labor would be greatly strengthened if they could join forces again. So in 1955 the leadership of the AFL and the CIO took initial steps to unify the two federations. Since that time, separate labor groups in particular areas—such as individual states—have come together into one group with one set of officers. Now four out of five labor unions are affiliated with the AFL-CIO.

The Independent Unions

Unions not affiliated with a labor federation are known as *independent unions.* Among the large and well-established unions that have not affiliated with the AFL-CIO is the United Federation of Electrical, Radio, and Machinists Workers of America. And the United Mine Workers of America, which is an industrial union, is not now affiliated with the AFL-CIO, although at one time or another it was associated with both the AFL and the CIO.

One of the large, powerful, and well-known independent unions (which we have already discussed) is the International Brotherhood of Teamsters, commonly referred to as the Teamsters Union, which was formerly affiliated with the CIO. It was expelled from membership in the AFL-CIO in 1957, and is currently an independent union. The United Automobile Workers Union was expelled from the AFL-CIO in the spring of 1968 for failure to pay dues to the federation.

The railroad brotherhoods—the Locomotive Engineers, the Locomotive Firemen and Enginemen, the Railroad Trainmen, and the Order of Railway Conductors—were organized shortly after the Civil War. They are recognized as among the most efficiently functioning unions in the country, and their conservative practices and strong discipline over their members have gained for them great importance and prestige.

FACTORS THAT ENCOURAGE LABOR TO ORGANIZE

There are many factors that lead members of the labor force to band together. Perhaps the most important ones, in our country at least, are the added strength that comes from effective organization, and the advantages that go with representation by qualified negotiators.

Strength of Numbers

As an individual worker, you are at a decided disadvantage when you are dealing with the management of a large corporation. If your requests for better working conditions, shorter working hours, or higher pay are refused or only partially granted, there is little you can do. Once you unite with other workers, however, your own bargaining position, and that of every other member of the group, is strengthened.

Representation by Qualified Negotiators

Organization makes it possible for workers to select their own representatives. As an individual worker, you may not feel qualified to argue your own

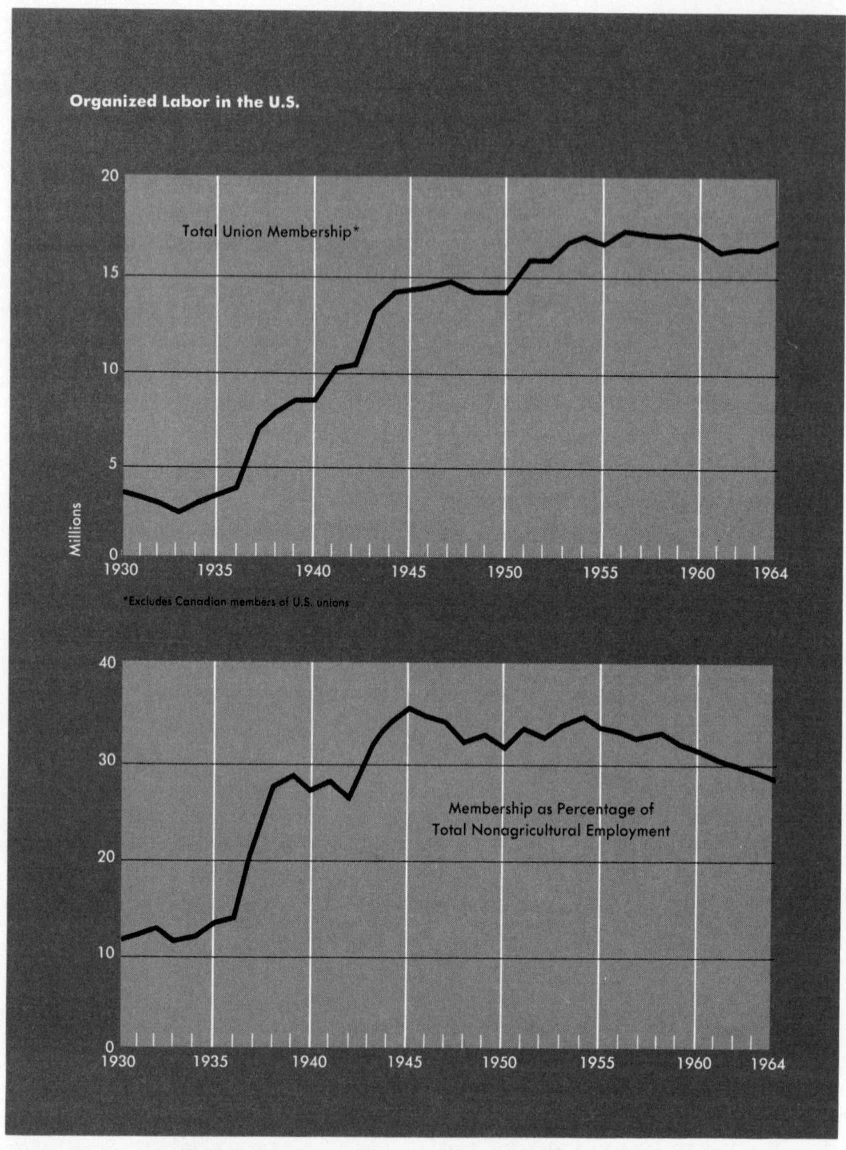

Total union membership has remained roughly unchanged in recent years, after a period of rapid growth between 1936 and the end of World War II, and a more modest expansion through 1956. This recent stagnation in the face of ever-increasing employment rolls has led to continuing decreases in the ratio of membership to total nonagricultural employment.
Source: National Industrial Conference Board, Inc.

case, but once you have joined with your fellow workers you have the advantage of being represented by the most able persons in the group. In fact, local labor groups often make use of the services of experienced negotiators who are members or employees of the parent union but who are not members of the local group.

OBJECTIVES OF LABOR ORGANIZATIONS

The over-all purpose of labor organizations is to gain greater benefits and advantages for their members. These include higher wages, shorter hours, better working conditions, and greater security.

One of the early demands that organized labor made on management was for higher wages; closely associated with it was the demand for a shorter working day. As the result of continued union pressure over the years, both demands have been met. The 40-hour week has become standard, and hourly wage rates have been greatly increased.

The further shortening of the work-week (without a corresponding decrease in pay) appears to be one of organized labor's chief long-term objectives. Recently there has been considerable talk by labor leaders suggesting that a shorter work-week would rank high in future contract negotiations. Walter Reuther, president of the United Automobile Workers, I. W. Abel, president of the United Steelworkers, and A. F. Hartung, president of the International Woodworkers of America, have taken the lead in this development. Also, the International Association of Machinists and the International Typographical Union have called for the eventual establishment of a shorter work-week. Most of these groups are asking for a 32-hour week.

A second major objective of organized labor that has become increasingly important in recent years has been the strengthening of the unions themselves. Unions have fought to gain recognition as the official representatives of all workers, and they have taken an active role in politics in order to win a more favorable position in the eyes of the government, the public, and business management. They are dedicated to unity and equality regardless of one's race, religion, color, creed, or political party.

A third major consideration lies in the area of the continued improvement of working conditions within the plant. It is quite common to have local unions in individual plants continue on strike after a national settlement is reached in a major industry such as the automotive or electrical equipment manufacturers. The industry-wide bargaining brings about agreement on the major issues of wage rates, seniority recognition, pensions, paid holidays, and other fringe benefits. But specific provisions regarding sanitary conditions, rest periods, and other similar grievances vary considerably from plant to plant within a given industry. These are usually hammered out at the local level.

A fourth major objective is a general membership concern with legislative, political, social, and civic matters. Union members are urged to active participation, both directly and indirectly, in all such activities that concern their best interests as union members and as citizens.

The Guaranteed Annual Wage

Organized labor has in recent years fought for the so-called guaranteed annual wage. We say "so-called" because actually it is not so much a matter of guaranteeing a certain number of dollars as it is a minimum number of weeks of work. The "guaranteed annual income" provision has received considerable publicity in recent years because organized labor has made it a chief objective.

Contracts that have been negotiated assure employees of a minimum number of hours or weeks of work during the year. This is especially important to workers in seasonal industries. Employees are as interested in the regularity of their compensation as they are in the amount of it. They want a steady income regardless of whether or not the work is steady.

There are several companies that have guaranteed their workers a minimum amount in wages during the year. (Actually, most plans guarantee a minimum amount of *work*.) Some plans supplement the payments employees receive, as unemployment compensation. Procter & Gamble guarantees its workers who have two or more years of service 48 weeks of work per year. Hormel guarantees 52 paychecks a year, with a minimum weekly wage based on 38 hours of work. The basis for determining annual wages is the annual sales forecast. Annual wages are paid in 52 equal weekly checks. Although the number of hours worked varies from week to week, the number of hours over 38 that one works in a given week is used to make up for those weeks when he works fewer than 38 hours.

Other companies that have several years of experience with guaranteed-annual-wage programs are Eastman Kodak, Sears, Roebuck and Co., and the Nunn-Bush Shoe Co. All these companies produce and sell consumer goods. The primary requisite for a satisfactory guaranteed-payment plan is a high degree of stability of operations, and this stability is easier to achieve in consumer-goods industries than in those that manufacture goods for producers. Consumer-goods industries are better able to diversify their production, produce during slack seasons and store the product until peak seasons, and transfer personnel to different departments within their organizations.

Organized labor wants a guaranteed annual income because it provides workers with better financial security than they enjoy otherwise. Some families face hardship when layoffs become prolonged, especially after unemployment benefits stop. Unions also argue that the steady employment provided by the annual-wage scheme benefits the over-all economy, tending to give it stability. This of course helps to increase the standard of living for all workers.

Management, on the other hand, objects to paying employees when they are not working. This practice tends to raise unit production costs, and thus the cost of goods to consumers. However, it must be taken into account that because of the seasonal nature of some products, it is difficult to spread production evenly over the entire year. Even diversification of company products cannot solve the problem entirely because differing products require different types of production processes. And it is not feasible to transfer workers from one type of production operation to another.

The guaranteed annual wage is one of the problems that labor and management must try to solve cooperatively. Although it has not made rapid progress, it certainly seems worthy of serious study and honest attempts to make it work.

Early Retirement and Sabbatical Leave

Among the newest benefits being received by labor are early retirement and extended vacation leave. Employees in many companies may now retire at 60 or 62 and qualify at that time for their company pensions. Earlier retirement under Social Security has helped bring this about. Another benefit of a similar nature is the sabbatical leave. After a worker has been with a company a stated number of years, he is granted an extended vacation with pay for a period of from three to six months.

TYPES OF UNION SECURITY

Among the chief objectives of organized labor are the maintenance of unions' existence, their protection, and their security. Of course, laws have been passed to guarantee their right to exist, but they had to work hard to secure this protective legislation. Unions utilize various types of recognition in the form of different shop agreements to provide their security.

The Open Shop

An open-shop situation exists when there is no union and no effort on the part of management either to promote or prevent the organization of one. Employees enjoy the freedom of choice as to whether or not they wish to organize. In many such situations there are some employees who are members of unions, and this makes the open shop an attractive target for union organizers.

The Simple-Recognition Shop

Under this type of agreement, some designated union has been recognized by the management as the rightful and exclusive bargaining agent of its employees. If more than 50 percent of the workers vote favoring a specific union as their official bargaining agent, a simple-recognition shop exists. This union is recognized as the workers' bargaining agent for all employees for a period of at least 12 months, since the National Labor Relations Board will not hold recognition elections more often than once a year. Under this type of shop, all employees enjoy the benefits that result from the union-management negotiations.

The Agency Shop

A modification of the simple-recognition shop is the agency shop. Under this agreement the nonunion employees as well as the union members pay the union dues. The nonunion workers, however, do not participate in determining union policies, are not subject to disciplinary action by the union, and do not attend union meetings. Their payment of dues to the union is in return for the benefits they receive because of union negotiation with management.

The Preferential Shop

In the preferential shop not only is the union recognized as the bargaining agent for all employees, but union members are given some preferences over nonmembers in certain areas of employment, and when new workers are employed, union members are given preference over nonmembers. In fact, when new workers are needed, the employer asks the union to supply them before he seeks to fill the positions in other ways. In some preferential shops, union members enjoy preferences over nonmembers in transfers and promotions, and are the last to be laid off. Because excessive preference for union members could, in reality, constitute a closed shop, which is forbidden by the Taft-Hartley Act, this type of shop setup is subject to close governmental scrutiny.

The Union Shop

The union shop is the most commonly found type of union security. It recognizes compulsory union membership on the part of all employees. The management of a business may employ anyone it desires, but he will be required to join the union within a stated period of time after he is employed. The Taft-Hartley Act provides a minimum of 30 days as the grace period prior to compulsory membership, but the Landrum-Griffin Act permits a minimum period of only seven days for workers engaged in the construction industry. The Bureau of Labor Statistics reports that of the contracts it has surveyed in recent years, almost three-fourths provide for the union shop.

The Closed Shop

Under this agreement any new employee would have to be a member of the union before being hired. In this way, the union would be the only source of employment available to the employer. But the closed shop was declared illegal by the Labor Management Relations Act, passed in 1947.

THE FUTURE OF ORGANIZED LABOR

The early 1960's brought a decline in union election victories. During the past decade, in the elections to determine whether unions would represent workers, the unions have been selected as the bargaining agent less frequently than was true before 1950. Also, the size of the new worker groups which unions have been able to organize has been smaller.[3]

The major cause of attrition in union membership has been the shrinkage of blue-collar employment in the organized industries. The changing occupational and industrial pattern is unfavorable to employment in the older industries, in which unions have their most substantial foothold. As technology, competition of products and services, changing consumer demands, and rising labor productivity take their toll of employment, unions in older economic areas necessarily decline in size. Many unions have sought to offset the shrinkage by broadening their industrial coverage, but few have been successful in extending their membership.

Unionization by Industries

Among the organized industries that have suffered losses in employment is the coal mining industry, where 65 percent of the production jobs have been eliminated since World War II (at the same time that the number of nonproduction jobs in the industry has remained stable). The attrition in railroad and bus employment, both union strongholds, has been only slightly lower—40 percent—with further cutbacks impending. The tele-

[3] Joseph Krislov, "New Organizing by Unions During the 1950's," *Monthly Labor Review*, (September, 1960), pp. 922–924.

graph industry has cut its jobs by one-third. The unionized service industries, such as hotels, and most particularly laundries and motion pictures, also have suffered major losses. In the manufacturing industries, the severest cuts in production jobs in the period from 1947 to 1959 took place in textile mill products, lumber and wood products, food and kindred products, and petroleum and coal products. In all groups employment of nonproduction workers actually increased, but employees of this kind are not usually candidates for union organization.[4]

A study of union membership trends from 1951 to 1958, conducted by the United States Bureau of Labor Statistics, highlights the effect of both employment shrinkage and geographical movement. This study of 131 national unions shows that 49 suffered a net reduction in membership; 16 had cuts of 10,000 or more members. The most serious cutbacks occurred among the textile unions, with losses of 164,770 by the Textile Workers Union of America, and 44,000 by the United Textile Workers. The Amalgamated Association of Street, Electric Railway and Motor Coach Employees of America reported a decline of 75,363 members because of the curtailment of urban transportation and the invasion of its jurisdiction by other unions.

As for the future of union membership in the currently established jurisdictions, there is little likelihood of any considerable growth as employment among production workers and unionized occupations continues to shrink or hold steady. The proportion of nonproduction employees in manufacturing industries rose from 16 to 24 percent between 1947 and 1959, as employment of production workers declined. Employment in the East and Midwest has not increased as rapidly as in the remainder of the country. The established union centers are not growing in strength.[5]

Only one of the five industrial sectors of the economy that showed a rise in employment of more than 25 percent between 1947 and 1959 also had a substantial percentage of union membership. While the proportion of eligible employees in the construction industry, according to official union estimates, is about 80 percent, the ratio for the four other sectors is very low. Five percent union membership prevails in finance, insurance, and real-estate industries; 10 percent in the government and wholesale and retail industries, and 20 percent in the service and miscellaneous industries. The absence of substantial organization in the service and retail industries is most significant, since they include many low-income earners.

The percentage of union membership is slightly higher in the three moderately growing sectors where the rise in production-worker employ-

[4] Solomon Barkin, *The Decline of the Labor Movement* (The Fund for the Republic, Inc., 1961), p. 11.

[5] *Ibid.*, pp. 12–15.

ment was between 11 and 15 percent over the same period. The ratios of union membership were 35 percent for crude-petroleum and natural-gas production, 55 percent for communications, and 65 percent in gas and electric utilities. The highest ratios of organization were in the declining employment sectors: manufacturing (55 percent), transportation (70 percent), and mining (75 percent).

The Effects of Geographical Industrial Movement

Another disturbing trend has been the shift in industrial location from the East and Midwest, where unions have been strong, to the South and to smaller communities where unions still have only limited influence. Bargaining rights do not move with the plant. Unions have to start organizing drives at the sites of the new plants, and frequently find their task most difficult because of unfriendly local attitudes. Even where the national employment figure is maintained in a union's jurisdiction, the shift to unorganized areas represents a serious setback in immediate membership potential, and in cases where a decline in the size of the industry is combined with a change in its location, the impact can be severe.

Future expansion of union membership must come from organizing efforts outside existing frontiers. And the area that seems to offer the most substantial potential growth is the southern geographic region. If each of the industries that exist in the southern region were to be unionized to the same degree that they are in other regions, union membership would increase by more than one and one-half million persons. And this potential membership will be even greater as the South becomes more industrialized.

But the South is a region where there is a surplus of labor. Also, in some communities where significant efforts have been made to attract industry, the public attitude is not especially warm toward strong unionization of workers. Many of the industries in the South are relatively small in size, and the scope of their operations gives them a strong local flavor. In addition, many of the southern industrial operations are highly competitive. And the people of the South are traditionally resistant to change. All of these factors combine to make the southern region one that is difficult to organize easily and rapidly.

It may be that a breakthrough of some type may be made in the white-collar area, especially in the government, finance, and clerical sectors. In many government offices, and in other large offices, workers are grouped together under working conditions that are very much like those of factory workers. Clerical jobs pay little more than unskilled labor, and less than skilled and some semiskilled occupations. Possible displacement by automated equipment is just as threatening for low-level office employees as for other machine operators. Discriminatory practices in salary schedules and in fringe benefits offered, and inconsistencies in supervisory practices, may cause unionization to become attractive to these workers in the near future.

State "Right-to-Work" Laws

You will recall that one of the major objectives of organized labor is the strengthening of the labor unions themselves. But labor has been unsuccessful in getting the national Congress to repeal Section 14-B of the Taft-Hartley Law. This provision permits the various states to enact laws prohibiting the union shop; it has been a strong influence in preventing continued union growth, and its repeal is currently one of the primary goals of organized labor.

Under the Taft-Hartley Act, Section 14-B, the union shop was declared legal except in states prohibiting it. As a result of this provision, 19 states now have laws to prohibit union-shop contracts which compel a worker to belong to a union before he can hold a job. These laws are commonly known as *"right-to-work" laws.* Under a union-shop agreement, an employer agrees that all his workers will have to join a union within a certain time after being hired. But the state right-to-work laws make it unlawful for an employer to enter into such an agreement.

Florida enacted the first right-to-work law by constitutional amendment in 1944. In 1956, Louisiana repealed a general right-to-work law but substituted a new law banning union-shop agreements involving workers in agriculture and in certain agricultural processing operations. Right-to-work laws have been passed by other states, mostly in agricultural areas, including Alabama, Arizona, Arkansas, Georgia, Indiana, Iowa, Kansas, Mississippi, Nebraska, Nevada, North Carolina, North Dakota, South Carolina, South Dakota, Tennessee, Texas, Utah, and Virginia.

There are two sides to the argument over right-to-work laws. One, shared by many employers, is that it is morally improper to require workers to join a union in order to obtain or hold a job, and that union-shop agreements are actually intended to perpetuate the bargaining power of unions. On the other side, the unions argue that right-to-work laws actually are designed to wreck labor organizations, and that any worker who benefits from union activities should be obliged to share in the cost by paying union dues.

Unquestionably, right-to-work laws hinder union growth in those states where such laws exist. Therefore, the repeal of Section 14-B of the Taft-Hartley law is high on organized labor's list of priorities. In fact, following the 1964 general elections, a highly organized campaign was launched to influence members of Congress to repeal Section 14-B. The drive had the endorsement and support of President Johnson. The House of Representatives passed the needed legislation, but the bill was defeated in the Senate in the spring of 1966. But organized labor has not given up on this objective, and will be heard from again.

SUMMARY

The labor force is made up of all working persons and all those seeking work. It includes persons employed on farms, and members of the armed forces. The total labor force is currently increasing at the rate of 1.5 million persons per year.

The most rapid growth-rates among various employed groups occur in the professions, technicians, service occupations, and clerical workers.

Early attempts at organizing the labor force were largely ineffective, with social objectives as their motivational impetus. However, with the formation of the American Federation of Labor in 1886, a definite shift occurred, both in purpose and growth. Under the able leadership of AFL president Samuel Gompers, business unionism was the order of the day, with economic benefits for union members the chief objective.

The era of most rapid union growth occurred during the 10-year period following the passage of the Wagner Act in 1935. Union membership increased fourfold during this decade. Then, in the early 1950's, the AFL and the CIO merged. This considerably strengthened organized labor, and union membership jumped to 18 million by 1958.

The chief objectives of organized labor are increased pay, including additional economic fringe-benefits, improved working conditions, and strengthening of the unions themselves. The so-called "guaranteed annual wage" is one of labor's strong talking-points, but it is far from becoming a reality.

The union shop is one of organized labor's chief means of strengthening itself. However, the passage of "right-to-work" laws in a number of states is hindering union growth in those states. Organized labor made an all-out campaign during 1966 in an attempt to influence Congress to repeal Section 14-B of the Taft-Hartley Act, but failed to marshall sufficient votes in the Senate to achieve this goal. This repeal still remains high on labor's priority list of current objectives.

VOCABULARY REVIEW QUIZ

Match the following terms with the statements below.

a. Agency shop
b. Business unionism
c. Craft union
d. Guaranteed annual wage
e. Independent union
f. Industrial union
g. Labor force
h. Open shop
i. Organized labor
j. Preferential shop
k. Right-to-work laws
l. Union shop

1. All workers who hold membership in a labor union of some kind, considered as one group
2. The total of all persons employed and looking for work, including members of the armed forces
3. A union whose members follow a particular trade
4. A union the membership of which is open to all workers in a particular industry
5. Unionism that is concerned about the economic aspects of its members
6. A union that is not affiliated with a labor federation
7. The assurance to employees that they will be paid for at least a stated minimum number of weeks each year
8. A working situation in which there is no union but also no attempt being made to promote or prohibit the formation of a union
9. An arrangement whereby both the union and nonunion members of a given company's work-force pay dues to the union
10. Where union members are given preferences over nonmembers when new workers are employed
11. A shop where all employees are union members—nonunion workers may be employed but they must join the union within 30 days
12. State laws that prohibit the union shop

QUESTIONS FOR REVIEW STUDY

1. What are the various groups of workers who together constitute "the labor force"?
2. In what age-groups is the labor force growing most rapidly? How do you explain this?
3. What factors combine to give the Pacific coast region the most rapid growth rate in the labor force?
4. What do you think are the chief reasons that farm laborers and domestic workers have not been organized into strong labor unions?
5. How do you account for the very rapid growth in union membership between 1935 and 1945, and the leveling off since 1958?
6. What arguments do you see in favor and opposed to regulating labor unions as business monopolies?
7. What are the chief objectives of organized labor?
8. Which of the goals of organized labor do you see as being of greatest importance today? Why?
9. What is your position regarding the guaranteed annual wage? Justify your position.
10. In what way is automation bringing about changes in the labor force?
11. The matter of the union shop and the so-called state "right-to-work" laws is currently an important and lively issue facing Congress. List the arguments for and against legal barriers to the union shop.
12. What do you think is the immediate future of the organized labor movement in the United States?

PROBLEMS AND PROJECTS

1. Consult several business magazines that were published during the past 18 months, and write a short essay explaining the current status of and trends in employment and unemployment. Include data on the number employed, the unemployment rate, and the changes currently taking place.
2. Study the graphs shown on page 333 and explain why you think the expected employment growth-rates are so much greater in some fields than in others.
3. Study the union membership chart shown on page 336, then write a paragraph, based on your outside reading, explaining why there are such great variations (as those shown in the graph) in percentages of unionization in these major industries.
4. Examine the graph on union membership shown on page 337. Gather some statistics on the number of persons working in those fields represented by the five largest labor unions. To what degree is the rank in union size at variance with the size of the employed labor force in each of these fields? Explain this difference.
5. There are varying positions regarding the effects of automation on labor employment. Read several periodical articles on this subject and state two opposing points of view. Then choose one position on this issue, and give your arguments supporting it. (A helpful reference is Chapter 13 of the *Sourcebook on Labor* by Neil W. Chamberlain, revised edition, published in 1964 by the McGraw-Hill Book Co.)

A BUSINESS CASE

Case 12-1 Union Growth and Expansion

Assume that you have been employed as a consultant by the AFL-CIO to suggest ways and means of achieving increased union membership. Union officials have asked your opinions regarding: (a) which industries among those that are already well organized offer the greatest promise for increased membership; (b) what fields of employment among those where unionization has previously made little progress seem to be most promising; and (c) in which geographic regions enlistment efforts should be concentrated.

1. Explain the procedure you would follow in attacking the problem.
2. What are your opinions regarding the three questions to be answered? Give reasons for your answers.

Labor-Management Relations

13

In every business enterprise the owners of the business and the employees are, ideally at least, bound together by strong common interests. Both are interested in sharing in the material gain that results from their joint efforts. Both have pride in the products they create and the services they render. Both are dependent upon and subject to the needs and wants of the buying public. And both are greatly affected by the attitudes and policies of government.

Employer and employee must work together to achieve their common goals and satisfy their mutual interests. Their efficiency and output, and consequently their standard of living and other rewards, are significantly determined by the degree to which they labor in an atmosphere of mutual cooperation, confidence, and respect.

Although both labor and management recognize (though sometimes grudgingly) their mutual dependence on each other, they admit that there are basic differences of opinion between them. Issues arise from different points of view regarding common problems. For example, management sometimes feels that labor fails to work for the highest production possible—workers waste time, "soldier" on the job, even fix restrictions on the amount each man can produce in a day. Workers, in turn, feel that management regards labor as a "cost of production" rather than as a "partner" in the business enterprise. Management usually considers policy-making as its own prerogative, while organized labor feels that it should share in policy formulation. There is nearly always a conflict over each group's evaluation of the other's contribution toward achieving increased production. (For example, to what degree was increased production the result of increased capital investments and efficient management, and to what degree was it the result of labor's efforts?)

When these issues involving differences are cooperatively and fairly resolved, both the ownership of the business and the employees benefit economically, and the service to society is made more effective. This means that honest efforts must be made to arrive at reasonable conclusions regarding matters of mutual concern—such matters as working conditions, hours of work, hiring and firing practices, and financial sharing in the fruits of production.

In this chapter we shall look at some of the ways in which labor and management both work together and combat each other. We shall examine the techniques used by labor to gain concessions, and the counter-measures used by management. We shall consider the bargaining process and the important elements of formal agreements between labor and management. We shall also look at the role of the government in helping to settle disputes between labor and management, and at some of the key legislative acts that have been enacted by Congress.

DIFFERENCES IN VIEWPOINTS

The basic point of conflict between management and labor is an economic one. To begin with, the central purpose of most business enterprises is to earn a profit: the income from sales must more than pay for the costs of producing the goods. The basic material costs are raw materials, land and buildings, and utility services. Beyond these, both the managers and the workers must be paid, and of course the owners are entitled to a return on their investment.

Cost, or Partner in Production

What about labor: is it one of the costs of production, or are the workers partners in production? Here is a real basis of conflict between management and labor. After the material costs have been purchased, the workers must be paid. Obviously the more labor costs, the less there is left as profit for the owners. So it is only natural that the owner-manager is interested in hiring workers at the lowest possible figure. There is a strong tendency for management to consider labor as a "cost" to be kept as low as possible, just as attempts are made to keep other costs low. On the other hand, labor is inclined to see its role as that of a "partner" in the production process rather than as a "cost." So here we have a clash in the basic point of view of management and labor.

Risk and the Return on Investment

There is little argument in the matter of risk. Labor seldom has capital funds invested in the business enterprise. If the business fails, the owners stand the loss. So owners are entitled to a payment representing an interest return on their investment. In addition, ownership is entitled to payment for the risk taken—the original investment might be lost. But no one seems to know what represents a fair return for risk and investment.

Labor holds the point of view that after fees for management have been paid and the owners have received a "reasonable return" on their investment, the workers should share in any excess profits. Management, however, sees these profits as rewards for risk and for initiative and ideas in administration. In general, management does not see any percentage figure as constituting a "fair return" for risk and investment. Rather, the accepted view is that one is entitled to as much profit as the traffic will bear—as much profit as the competition will allow.

One of the basic problems here is that it is difficult to determine the degree to which profits are the direct result of labor, and the extent to which they result from the contributions of management.

Participation in Decision-Making

The prevalent view among owner-managers is that decision-making regarding the running of a business is an inherent right of ownership. They agree that workers should be paid reasonable wages and provided with good working conditions. However, they hold that the right to hire and supervise workers and otherwise manage business operations is the right of management.

In contrast, organized labor feels that the workers should be represented in at least certain types of decision-making. One point on which labor maintains a strong position has to do with modernization techniques, especially those that automatize mechanical operations. These usually reduce the number of workers needed to perform routine tasks and operate the machines. Labor also feels it has a legitimate stake in decisions pertaining to employment, transfer, promotion, seniority rights, and the discharge of workers.

These basic differences in attitudes on the part of management and organized labor sometimes lead to serious conflicts. When negotiation breaks down, labor may go out on strike in order to reinforce its bargaining position.

LABOR VERSUS MANAGEMENT

One of the most important functions of labor organizations is *collective bargaining*, a process by which labor representatives bargain with management over the terms and conditions of labor contracts or labor agreements. It is called collective bargaining because labor acts collectively—that is, as a group (employers also may act collectively). The individual workers authorize their union to act as their agent. The employer bargains with the union representatives and recognizes the union as the authorized agent of the workers. Employers in the United States have preferred not to share power in employer-employee relations with organizations of their employees, because collective bargaining places restrictions on the employer's actions.

There has emerged in this country a public policy toward the unionization of workers that protects them against many forms of coercion by either employers or union officials as they choose the unions that are to serve as their representatives. This policy has been established through laws passed by the federal government. The Labor Study Group appointed by the Committee for Economic Development gave its support to this principle of self-determination because it extends into employer-employee relationships a procedure that is basic to democratic values. It helps avoid an undesirable alternative: a decision for or against collective bargaining based solely on an employer's or union's power to coerce.

Bargaining Pressures Used by Labor

In collective bargaining, union negotiators try to secure the highest possible price in terms of wages, fringe benefits, and working conditions, in return for the services of their union members. Unions have developed several devices to help win their objectives. The principal weapons used by them are *picketing*, the *boycott*, and the *strike*. In the following paragraphs we shall look at these techniques.

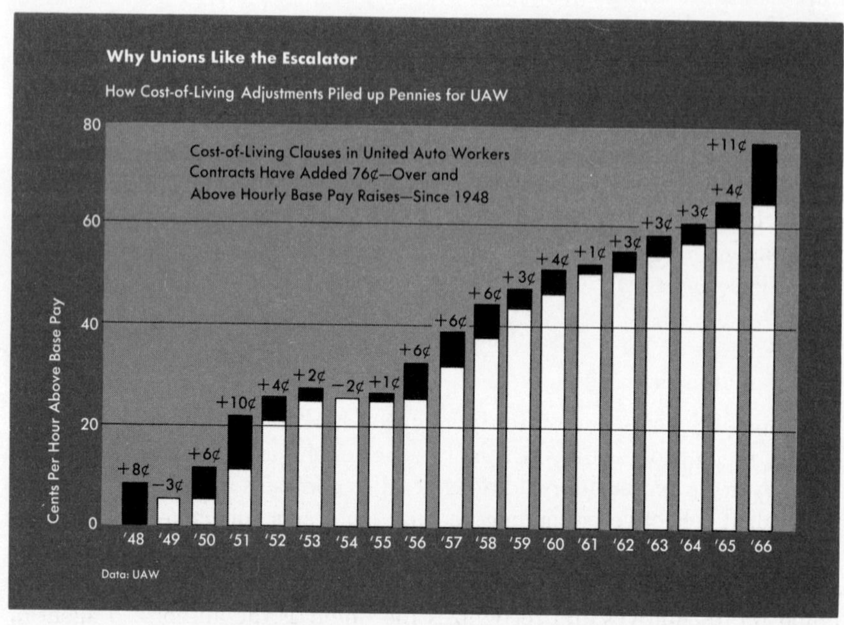

Source: Reprinted from the February 11, 1967 issue of *Business Week* by special permission. Copyrighted © 1967 by McGraw-Hill, Inc.

Picketing. Picketing has proved to be one of labor's most effective techniques in winning concessions from management. Union members carrying banners and placards that announce their complaints against the management are stationed at each entrance to a business or industrial establishment. The purpose is to inform the public of their case and to enlist sympathy and support. Picketing's greatest effectiveness is in cutting down the available labor supply by preventing union men from reporting for work. In addition to members of the union directly concerned, members of closely allied unions may respect the picket line and also refuse to report for work. If the employer hires nonunion workers to do the work of the striking union men, associated unions will sometimes refuse to work even though they did not respect the picket line originally.

Boycott. The boycott is a attempt on the part of a union to restrict the patronage of a business firm by influencing people not to do business with the firm. In the *primary boycott,* employees of the firm refuse to buy from their employer. Obviously, this is effective only when the amount of their patronage is significant.

A *secondary boycott* occurs when a union that is seeking concessions from its employer (Company A) places pressure on another firm (Company B) in an effort to get the second firm to influence the union's employer. The idea here is to influence customers of Company A to refuse to do business with the company unless the union's demands are met. The purpose is to threaten Company A with the possible loss of business from one or more of its best customers. In some instances the pressure by the union takes the form of a strike, or the threat of a strike, against Company B. This tactic is usually used where the union is already recognized by Company B and it is attempting to organize the workers of Company A.

The secondary boycott is defined as an unfair labor practice by one of the provisions of the Taft-Hartley Act. However, it is often difficult to determine whether or not a threatened strike is truly a secondary boycott. Therefore, it continues to be one of the weapons used by labor.

The Strike. When all other devices fail, a union may decide to go out on strike. Although there are many different kinds of strikes, the net effect is always the same: the workers refuse to work until their demands are met or a compromise is reached. Either a partial or a complete work stoppage results. Most strikes are called by unions to back up their demands for increases in wages, shorter hours, recognition of the union as the bargaining agent, improved working conditions, and job security. Whatever the ultimate outcome of a strike, the workers lose their weekly pay, and business costs are increased. Both business and the public suffer. But without the possibility of a strike there can be no true collective bargaining.

The chief purpose of the strike is to injure the business by halting production at a time when it is most damaging to the business. Thus, the ideal time to call a strike is when production is high and inventory accumulations are low. Another effective time is when the employer is in a strong competitive battle with a rival business.

There are various kinds of strikes. The *recognition strike* is an attempt to force the employer to recognize the union as the legal bargaining agent of the workers. This type of strike has been largely replaced by elections conducted by the National Labor Relations Board. The *jurisdictional strike* develops when two unions disagree as to which one should perform certain types of work. For example, the labor contract may specify that certain types of operations are to be performed by iron workers and that other types are to be done by sheet-metal workers. Sometimes it is difficult to determine just which group is responsible for a given task, and the jurisdictional dispute arises. When the dispute develops to the degree where it leads to a walkout by one of the unions, a strike is in progress. The *sympathetic strike* results when a union that is not a party to the original walkout refuses to cross the picket line and agrees to strike in sympathy with the original union that is on strike.

Strikes make news, and sometimes they get out of control. However, to repeat, they are a necessary complement to the collective-bargaining process. The general impression given the public by the news stories about strikes seems to be out of proportion to the strike record in recent years. There are more than 150,000 collective-bargaining contracts in force in this country, covering more than one-third of all the workers employed in non-farm labor. The man-days lost through strikes during a recent year, for example, amounted to only four hours per worker (for all persons working), or 0.17 percent of the total man-days worked during the year.

Techniques Used by Management

Management counters the pressure of labor by group action through *employers' associations*, the *court injunction*, the *lockout*, and *direct appeals to the public.*

Employers' Associations. Employers' associations have been in existence for many years, rendering such services as advertising, research, and lobbying. In addition, they sometimes function in labor-management negotiations. These associations may be formed on a city, regional, or national basis. Some of the best-known employers' associations are the National Association of Manufacturers, the Chamber of Commerce of the United States, and the Appalachian Coal Association. The formation of an association for labor negotiation purposes usually takes place when there are many small employers and a single large union that represents all the employees of the many small businesses. Representatives from the association and the union come together to negotiate the terms of the labor contract.

The Court Injunction. Court injunctions make it possible for employers to prevent certain specified undesirable acts on the part of labor groups—acts such as coercive practices, and destruction of a firm's property. Violating an injunction places the union in contempt of court and makes it subject to punishment by fine or imprisonment, or both. Perhaps the most notable examples of the use of this weapon, although it was not employed in this case by an employer but by the federal government, were the rulings of Judge Goldsborough against John L. Lewis and the United Mine Workers of America in 1946 and 1948.

The Lockout. A lockout exists when management closes its factory and refuses to permit the workers to enter the plant. The lockout is seldom used today because it is the employer who establishes the working environment in the first place. Most employers prefer to have the workers strike rather than employ the lockout because in the eyes of the public the strike makes him appear to be the injured party.

Appeal to Public Opinion. You sometimes see full-page newspaper or magazine advertisements used by a company or industry when it is being struck by labor. This is an attempt on the part of management to explain its side of the issue directly to the general public. The purpose of this direct appeal is to counteract the pressure of the union by giving the public information in the hope of winning support to the cause of management rather than of labor.

Perhaps it should be stated here that not all business enterprises are opposed to collective bargaining with labor organizations. Many businessmen feel that collective bargaining is advantageous to management as well as to labor. They realize that a collective labor agreement makes it unnecessary for management to deal with individuals on matters of wages, overtime, and working conditions. Then, too, since collective bargaining tends to promote uniform labor policies and practices within a given industry, management knows that competitors are not gaining an advantage by hiring cheaper labor or by maintaining inferior working conditions.

THE COLLECTIVE-BARGAINING PROCEDURE

The purpose of collective bargaining is to reach an agreement between management and labor regarding their mutual rights and responsibilities. All collective agreements run for a specific period of time, usually from one to three years. Months before an agreement is to terminate, representatives of both management and labor sit down together to negotiate terms for a new contract.

Generally, collective agreements cover the workers in a single plant or the workers of a single company that has several plants. The idea of collective bargaining is an accepted procedure in American industry today. In fact, many employers prefer to bargain with labor collectively rather than as individuals.

The first meeting between labor and management negotiation teams usually establishes rules, policies, and schedules for future meetings. Sometimes at this first meeting the representatives of labor formally present their specific proposals for changes in the existing labor agreement. At succeeding meetings management submits counter-proposals. Both groups seek opportunities to suggest compromise solutions in their favor until an agreement is reached. If labor and management find it impossible to come to an agreement, a third party may be brought in from the outside. This might be a governmental or a private mediator, or a mediation team.

Industrywide Bargaining

Oftentimes, similar industrial operations in a geographic region will bargain as a group. And there is some trend toward nationwide bargaining for a particular industry.

In the automobile industry, labor bargains with a particular employer—Chrysler, Ford, or General Motors, for example. The agreement covers all the workers who are members of the United Automobile Workers employed by that company. When an agreement is reached with that company, it then becomes the pattern for settlements with the other companies.

Coalition Bargaining

Organized labor favors coalition bargaining because this tends to strengthen bargaining lines where they are weakest—among small and weak unions. In *coalition bargaining*, several different unions within a given industry will collaborate in bargaining with an employer.

An outstanding recent example of union success in coalition bargaining occurred in the fall of 1966. The General Electric Co. had historically insisted on bargaining separately with each individual union. However, in the summer of 1966, 11 different electrical unions—all affiliated with the AFL-CIO—formed an alliance cutting across union jurisdictions to bargain as a group with General Electric. The largest and strongest of the 11 unions, the International Union of Electric Workers, took the lead in the negotiations. The AFL-CIO backed the negotiation team by pledging a sum of $8 million to carry out the negotiation effort. It employed a nationwide network of teletype stations in strategic cities to keep union members informed and in line. Although the General Electric management at first resisted the idea of coalition bargaining, in the end it settled with the coalition group.

THE LABOR AGREEMENT

The labor agreement is the result of negotiations that may extend over a considerable length of time. It may cover a single shop with only a few workers, or an entire industry with thousands of workers. The usual agreement specifies those workers for whom the employer recognizes a particular union as their representative or spokesman. Different groups of workers within one business organization may be members of different unions. The labor agreement provides for wage rates and policies, working hours, working conditions, employment and dismissal policies, seniority clauses, vacations, grievance procedures, and the life of the agreement.

Labor agreements are the result of give-and-take negotiation, reflecting union pressure and employer resistance. They may be only a few pages in length, or more than a hundred. Although management and labor are chiefly concerned with immediate issues when they are negotiating a labor agreement, a carefully prepared document should also provide for everyday relations between union and management. Only in this way can administrative difficulties be avoided. For example, an agreement should:

1. Indicate clearly which workers are included and which are excluded under the terms
2. Provide machinery for settling alleged violations of the agreement
3. Establish a procedure for settling future disputes
4. Define some orderly procedure for renewing the agreement

Wage Rates and Policy

One of the most important and extensive provisions in a labor agreement is the one in which the basic wage policy is outlined and detailed. If piece rates are to be paid, for example, the clause carefully describes the scheme to be followed and stipulates whether or not time-clocks are to be used, and what the rates for overtime will be. Sometimes the agreement provides that wage scales may be reviewed during the life of the agreement without affecting its other clauses.

Hours of work

The labor agreement also specifies the normal workday or work-week. If more than one shift is in operation, it stipulates the time of each shift and the times and methods of transferring workers from one shift to another. Other provisions cover how overtime is to be calculated (by the day or week), how much time is to be taken for meals, regulations for making up lost time, what is to be done about working on Sundays and holidays, and what happens when holidays fall on Sundays.

Working conditions

One part of the agreement covers the degree of sanitation to be maintained, what restroom facilities are to be provided and how they are to be used, provisions for safety rules and devices, and the amount of medical care to be furnished.

Employment and dismissal policies

A carefully prepared labor agreement must record the agreement that labor and management have reached on methods of selecting, promoting, and laying off workers. It must state clearly the degree to which seniority is to be recognized and how it is to be determined. This clause also lists the rules governing the transfer of workers, the hiring of temporary workers, and the apprenticeship program.

Vacations

One clause in the labor agreement specifies all the details governing vacation policy, including the length of vacations, when they may be taken, whether an employee may work instead of taking his vacation, how the length of vacation varies with length of service, what rules will determine the individual worker's vacation privileges, and whether vacations may be divided or must be taken all at one time.

Grievance procedure

This clause defines what is to be regarded as a grievance and outlines how the grievance policy is to be administered. It also specifies what use is to be made of shop stewards and grievance committees in handling problems.

Life of agreement

In this country, labor agreements usually run for one year, although the agreement itself must specify its own length of life. A clause is usually included that describes how the agreement must be renewed.[1]

SETTLEMENT OF LABOR DISPUTES

As we have seen, a labor agreement outlines a grievance procedure that will guarantee employees a hearing when they feel they are being treated unfairly. It also indicates the procedure to be followed when differences arise that are not covered by the agreement or when a difference of opinion develops on the interpretation of certain agreement provisions. The methods most commonly used in settling labor-management differences are *conciliation, mediation,* and *arbitration.*

Most grievances are settled at the first level in the grievance procedure (company supervisor, union steward, and worker). Only a relatively small percentage of the grievance cases ever pass unsuccessfully through all management-labor procedural levels, finally requiring the use of a third party to settle the dispute.

[1] This treatment of the labor agreement has of necessity been greatly abbreviated. Some of the other clauses frequently included pertain to recognition, representation, health and welfare funds, absenteeism, leaves of absence, holiday pay, production standards, strikes and lockouts, and disciplinary layoffs and discharges.

Conciliation and Mediation

In *conciliation*, a go-between makes every effort to bring the two groups in a dispute together. The conciliator encourages them to continue negotiations, trying to get each group to see the other's point of view, and helping them settle their differences themselves. In one sense, conciliation is an effort to correct unforeseen weaknesses in the labor agreement.

Mediation goes further than conciliation by offering specific suggestions in addition to those proposed by management and labor. The mediator does not act as a judge who holds hearings and renders decisions. Rather, his task is to influence each group to make concessions, helping them to narrow the gap between their demands, and aiding in bringing about a compromise that is acceptable to both groups.

There is nothing compulsory about conciliation or mediation. They simply represent the efforts of unbiased outsiders to help the disputants to reach an agreement. They are both constructive processes, since they offer the disputants no escape from the responsibility of making their own decisions and attempting to understand and evaluate each other's position.

Arbitration is similar to mediation, but there is one important difference. The mediator can only recommend a solution to a dispute between management and labor, but the arbitrator is authorized to determine the solution. This means that the arbitrator serves in the role of a judge who hears both sides of the case as an impartial authority. When arbitration is used, both sides agree in advance to abide by the arbitrator's decision. Sometimes a panel of several persons, usually three, serve rather than one person. In this case, one member of the panel is nominated by the company, one by the union, and the third is an impartial outsider who is experienced as an arbitrator. When both parties to the dispute agree to arbitration, the process is known as *voluntary arbitration*. If the union and the company are required by law to submit their dispute to a third party for a decision, the process is known as *compulsory arbitration*. Arbitration is commonly used in labor and industrial disputes when it is provided for in the contract.

Most collective-bargaining agreements provide that specific disputes that cannot be resolved by any of the other procedures established by the agreement must be submitted to voluntary arbitration for a final decision. The prevailing procedure in collective bargaining is to designate the type of arbitration procedure to be used when grievances cannot be settled by management and labor themselves without third-party assistance.

According to a study made by the Bureau of Labor Statistics of 1,254 labor agreements in 14 industries, three out of four union agreements, covering about 83 percent of the workers under the agreements analyzed, provide for arbitration as the terminal point in the grievance machinery. Of the 1,254 agreements, that is, 915 provided for arbitration. Of the total number of workers covered by agreements containing the arbitration provision, 28 percent were subject to permanently established arbitration machinery. The remaining 72 percent were subject to procedures calling for the selection of arbitrators whenever the need arose.

Of all the arbitration agreements, 93 percent (covering 91 percent of the workers) provided for *automatic* arbitration, or arbitration at the request of either party. Under this procedure, arbitration must be carried out if either party requests it, and both parties agree in advance to accept the decision as final and binding.

Several private organizations have been established to serve management and labor in settling industrial disputes. The Council on Industrial Relations for the Electrical Contracting Industry, for example, was established in 1920 for the purpose of serving the entire industry. Any segment of the electrical industry where contractual relations exist between employers and the International Brotherhood of Electrical Workers may make use of the Council's arbitration machinery. The American Arbitration Assn. serves management and labor by helping to select permanent arbitrators, by appointing fact-finders, and by conducting polls to determine whether the members of a union approve a collective-bargaining agreement, and which union they prefer to have represent them in negotiations with management.

The Government's Role in Settling Disputes

Industrial disputes have long been the concern of the federal government. Whenever a strike jeopardizes the public welfare, the government usually steps in and either takes over the industry or forces an immediate settlement of the controversy. Two of the most important government agents in labor-management negotiations are the National Mediation Board and the National Labor Relations Board.

The Federal Mediation Service. The National Mediation Board was formed in 1934 to aid in the settlement of disputes arising out of new agreements involving railroads and airlines; the National Railroad Adjustment Board has jurisdiction over disputes that arise out of agreements already in existence. The Federal Mediation and Conciliation Service helps to formulate new labor agreements and interpret existing ones. It helps to settle labor-management disputes by furnishing a panel of arbitrators. The Service also makes available to industry a roster of arbitrators, and otherwise aids employers and unions in handling labor-relations problems. Requests for such assistance are usually made by one or both parties to a labor dispute, although the Service can enter cases on its own initiative where the public interest requires. Cases handled by the Service fall into these categories:

Work stoppage. A strike or lockout.

Threatened stoppage. A situation where a definite strike date has been announced or a 30-day strike notice has been filed.

Controversy. A dispute that has not reached the stage of a work stoppage or a threatened stoppage.

Arbitration. Upon the request of both parties to a dispute, arbitrators nominated by the Conciliation Service render final and binding awards that the parties agree in advance to accept.

Technical activities. Upon the joint request of both parties to a dispute, the Service will offer advice on such technical matters as wage-incentive plans, time studies, and job evaluations.

Special services. Upon request, the Service will furnish labor-relations information, consult with labor and management on specific problems, and provide speakers for groups who are interested in the Conciliation Service, labor problems, and related subjects.

TABLE 13.1

WORK STOPPAGES RESULTING FROM LABOR-MANAGEMENT DISPUTES, 1940–1965

			Man-days idle		
Year	Number of Stoppages	Number of Workers Involved (thousands)[1]	Number (thousands)	Per Worker Involved	Percentage of Estimated Working Time[2]
1940	2,508	577	6,700	11.6	0.10
1945	4,750	3,470	38,000	11.0	0.47
1950	4,843	2,410	38,800	16.1	0.44
1955	4,320	2,650	28,200	10.7	0.26
1958	3,694	2,060	23,900	11.6	0.22
1959	3,708	1,880	69,000	36.7	0.61
1960	3,333	1,320	19,100	14.5	0.17
1961	3,367	1,450	16,300	11.2	0.14
1962	3,614	1,230	18,600	15.0	0.16
1963	3,362	941	16,100	17.1	0.13
1964	3,655	1,640	22,900	14.0	0.18
1965	3,963	1,550	23,300	15.1	0.18

[1] Workers counted more than once if involved in more than one stoppage during year.

[2] Estimated working time computed by multiplying average number of employed workers by number of days worked by most employees.

Source: Dept. of Labor, Bureau of Labor Statistics; and annual bulletin, *Analysis of Work Stoppages.*

The National Labor Relations Board. Another government organization that aids in the settlement of labor disputes is the National Labor Relations Board, which was created by Congress in 1935 to guarantee labor the right to organize and bargain collectively. The board consists of five members appointed by the President; each member serves for five years.

There are two types of labor hearings. The first type pertains to the investigation of employers who are accused of unfair labor practices. The Labor Management Act of 1947 assigned responsibility for this type of case to a general counsel. If the employer is found guilty, he is ordered to stop interfering with the workers' right to organize; if necessary, the federal courts may be called on to enforce the counsel's rulings.

The second type of case pertains to representation. This type comes under the direct jurisdiction of the Labor Board. The board provides election machinery to determine the workers' preferences on how they want to be represented in collective bargaining. According to the policy of the board, the workers have the exclusive right, without any interference from the employer, to decide whether they want to be represented by any union, and if so, which union they want. The union that receives a majority of the votes cast is selected as the workers' official representative. The board also initiates procedures for orderly collective bargaining between the union that is chosen, and the employer.

Many cities have mediation boards (New York, Newark, and Toledo are noted for their leadership in this service). Several states have conciliation boards to serve in disputes that do not fall under the jurisdiction of the National Labor Relations Board.

LABOR LEGISLATION

The subject of labor legislation has long been a sensitive topic among politicians. Over the years, both labor and management have struggled for power, security, and status.

Two distinct types of legislation affecting labor and employers have been enacted. The first pertains to working hours, wages, safety regulations, and health; the second concerns the rights and responsibilities of labor unions and employers.

The earliest control over working hours applied specifically to women and children. In 1924, Congress proposed a constitutional amendment granting itself power to limit, regulate, and prohibit the labor of persons under 18 years of age, but an insufficient number of states approved it. All the individual states, however, have laws of one kind or another governing the length of the working day and the use of child labor. Many states have legislation restricting the hours women can work in specified employment, but only a few states have attempted to regulate the minimum wages paid to male workers. The federal government is, of course, concerned only with the regulation of businesses engaged in interstate commerce. Those firms whose activities and operations are within a single state are regulated by state labor laws.

The Norris–La Guardia Act of 1932 contained the first statement of general policy toward unionization of labor ever adopted by the United States government. This policy said that workers should have the right to organize into unions if they choose to do so. This act outlawed the "yellow dog" contract, whereby workers, as a condition of employment, would agree not to join a union, and it restricted somewhat employers' utilization of the labor injunction to halt work stoppages. The following year the right to organize was incorporated into the National Industrial Recovery Act, but that act was declared unconstitutional in 1935.

The National Labor Relations (Wagner) Act of 1935

The labor provisions of the NIRA were incorporated into a separate law passed in 1935—the National Labor Relations Act, otherwise known as the Wagner Act. This statute is clearly a workers' law, for its regulations are designed to control the actions of employers. In fact it has sometimes been referred to as labor's "Magna Carta." In general, it guaranteed workers the right to organize. This was accomplished by making it unlawful for employers to:

1. Refuse to bargain collectively with representatives chosen by employees
2. Interfere with the employees' right to bargain collectively
3. Dictate in any way to labor officials about their administrative procedures
4. Discriminate against members in either hiring or firing
5. Discriminate against employees who take advantage of their rights under the law

The law established the National Labor Relations Board to administer the provisions of this act in settling disputes, and also to serve as a quasi-court in protecting workers against unfair practices. Its chief functions were to prevent or correct any violations of the five practices enumerated above, and to establish proper bargaining units and organizations to represent the workers. In substance, what the Wagner Act did was to set up an orderly process of democratic elections by the workers to replace the former tactic of striking in order to force the employer to recognize the union as the employee's rightful bargaining agent.

Fair Labor Standards Act of 1938

In 1938 Congress passed the Fair Labor Standards Act which contained provisions related to both wages and hours in industries that engaged in interstate commerce. This act stated that beginning on October 24, 1940 and thereafter, workers should be compensated at a rate of one- and one-half times their standard rate of pay for any hours they worked over 40 hours during any given week.

This act also set a floor under minimum wages that could be paid. The first minimum wage was set at 25 cents an hour, and it was to increase to 40 cents on October 24, 1945. This "floor" or minimum was and has repeatedly been raised—to 75 cents an hour in 1949, then to one dollar in 1955, and to $1.25 in 1961.

This act was amended in 1966 raising the minimum wage to $1.60 effective on February 1, 1968. The law specifies that any time an employee is "suffered or permitted to work" is to be counted as working time. All time spent by an employee in physical or mental exertion, whether burdensome or not, that is "controlled or required" by the employer, and pursued necessarily and primarily for the benefit of the employer is to be counted as working time. Thus, work not requested, but suffered or permitted, is working time. If work is permitted away from the premises or even at the employee's home it is counted as working time.

The law stipulates that an employer may not discriminate on the basis of sex by paying employees of one sex at rates lower than he pays employees of the opposite sex for doing equal work on jobs requiring equal skill, effort, and responsibility and which are performed under similar working conditions.

The Labor-Management Relations (Taft-Hartley) Act of 1947

There were many causes of industrial unrest and work stoppages in 1945 and 1946. Collective bargaining was still comparatively new in many situations; a considerable measure of employer opposition to unions existed. Some of the newly formed or rapidly growing unions could not maintain union discipline under the accumulation of wartime grievances, or accustom themselves to the less militant methods of collective bargaining after winning recognition. Neither group adjustment nor individual self-discipline was aided by the wholesale shifting of workers to war industries and new industrial centers and then to other jobs and locations during reconversion. The quick withdrawal of wartime public controls over labor-management relations and also over production, prices, and wages placed additional responsibilities on both unions and employers at a time when the cost of living was rising rapidly.

The series of post-war work stoppages symbolized serious industrial unrest in the public mind. Strike idleness as a percentage of total working time (perhaps the best measure for comparison over a period of years) began to rise soon after the war from the unusally low wartime levels. Even in 1937, a pre-war year of above-average strike activity, strike idleness had been less than 0.05 percent of total working time; in 1946, it was 1.43 percent—the highest ever recorded.

The unsettled labor-management situation after the war revived and greatly strengthened opposition to the Wagner Act. Senator Robert A. Taft, one of the leaders in the demand for change, argued that although the act had been passed to aid unions in maintaining an appropriate balance of rights and responsibilities between workers and employers, it had gone far beyond such a balance in its actual administration. He and Congressman Fred A. Hartley sponsored a rewriting of the act. The resulting measure, the Labor-Management Relations (Taft-Hartley) Act, gained such widespread support that despite strong objections by organized labor and a Presidential veto, it became law on June 23, 1947.

Some provisions of collective agreements which many unions had obtained or sought were banned or limited under the revised law. Provision for the so-called "closed shop" can no longer be included in agreements. Other widely adopted provisions of agreements, such as the union shop, check-off of union dues, welfare funds, and contract termination arrangements, are regulated.

The concept of striking a balance between unions and employers led to the inclusion of a list of unfair labor practices applying to unions, along with the list applying to employers. Among various other practices, refusal to bargain in good faith, engaging in secondary boycotts, stopping work over a jurisdictional or inter-union dispute, and charging excessive initiation fees to keep new members out of the union are considered by the law to be unfair. Employers, as well as workers, are permitted to appeal to the National Labor Relations Board against unions in connection with such practices. Certain practices may be penalized by court action and law suits for damages. Restrictions on the use of injunctions are eased.

Special rules were written into the Taft-Hartley Act for handling controversies or strikes which, in the judgment of the President, create or threaten emergencies by imperiling the national health or safety. In any such dispute or strike, the President is authorized to appoint a board of inquiry to investigate the facts. Thereafter, a court injunction can be obtained forbidding the occurrence or continuance of a stoppage for a period of 80 days. During this "cooling off" or waiting period, further efforts are to be made to settle the dispute. If no voluntary agreement can be arranged within 60 days, the employees are to be polled by secret ballot as to whether they will accept the final offer of the employer. After all these steps are taken, however, the injunction must be dissolved whether or not the dispute is settled. This procedure—government attempts to force the settlement of labor-management disputes—has been used sparingly in recent years.

Union opposition to the Taft-Hartley Act was intense in the first few years after its passage. The act was denounced as a slave-labor law and its repeal became a major goal of the labor movement. Many proposals were made for changes in the new law by its critics and also by its sponsors—changes which, for the most part, would ease the restrictions on unions. Revision proved to be difficult, partly because of the problem of reconciling the views of those who were fearful of going too far in modifying the law with the views of those who felt that any obtainable amendments would not satisfy their objections. By 1951, practical circumstances had brought about general agreement to repeal the requirement that elections be held to validate union-shop agreements. Experience had shown that in nearly all cases, large majorities of workers voted for the union shop. Accordingly, the law was amended to eliminate this requirement.

The Labor-Management Reporting and Disclosure (Landrum-Griffin) Act of 1959

Working under some of the most intense public pressure in years, Congress passed on September 4, 1959, the first major labor reform amendments to the Taft-Hartley Act. This act was the Labor-Management Reporting and Disclosure Act, commonly called the Landrum-Griffin Act. It is quite correctly titled, because the major portion of the law requires a series of reports to be made to the Secretary of Labor by both labor unions and business management. Among the reports required are:

1. Reports of the constitution and bylaws of union organizations
2. Reports of union administrative policies pertaining to initiation fees, union dues, and other financial assessments; calling of union meetings; qualifications for membership in the union; and the ratification of contracts
3. Annual financial reports by the unions, showing the amounts of assets, liabilities, and cash receipts; salaries of officers; and loans to members, union officials, or businesses
4. Reports of personal financial transactions on the part of union officials that might in any way conflict with the best interests of the union
5. Reports by employers of any expenditures made in order to prevent their employees from organizing

This law gives to employers new protection from union racketeers and unscrupulous labor leaders. Members have more voice in their local union affairs. Elections must be by secret ballot. Local officers must be elected at least once every three years and every five years at the national level. Union members can sue in federal courts if justice is not provided. The law prohibits Communists or anyone convicted of a felony within the previous five years from holding union office. A union official permitting a felon to hold office is subject to a year in jail and a $10,000 fine.

SUMMARY

Labor and management are bound together by a strong common interest and a common goal. They are in the business of meeting people's economic needs and wants as a joint venture. But in spite of their mutual dependence on each other, basic differences often arise between them.

Most of the issues between management and labor are basically economic or jurisdictional. Historically, management has looked upon labor as a cost of production, whereas persons who make up the labor force see themselves more as partners in production. Other issues revolve around the questions of who should share in the excess profits, and the degree to which representatives of labor might share in policy formation and decision-making at the operational level.

The principal techniques used by labor in attempting to secure benefits for workers are standardization, jurisdictional limitations, limitation of output, the union shop, picketing, the boycott, and the strike. Employers may use appeals to the public, the court injunction, or the lockout. Both management and labor attempt to reach an agreement on the main factors that concern their relations with each other.

The process of bargaining between representatives of management and labor is called *collective bargaining* because labor is acting collectively as a group. The agreement drawn up by representatives of management and labor covers a variety of factors, such as wage rates, hours, working conditions, paid holidays, dismissal policies, and a procedure for hearing workers' grievances.

When labor and management are not able to reach an agreement, they may call in outside help. This help may take the form of conciliation, mediation, or arbitration. There are private organizations whose sole function is to help management and labor reach agreement. The federal government is also very active in this field. The National Mediation Board and the National Labor Relations Board are the chief agencies of the federal government for assisting labor and management in settling their disputes. When it is possible for disputes to be settled without a strike, not only do both management and labor gain, but the general public benefits as well.

The public, acting through the federal government, has established the policy of self-determination by workers in deciding who their representatives should be in negotiations with their employers. The right to organize has been guaranteed through the enactment of the Wagner Act. The Taft-Hartley Act prohibits certain unfair practices of labor unions, and the Landrum-Griffin Act provides protection to workers from certain types of abuse by both their employers and their union officials.

VOCABULARY REVIEW QUIZ

Match the following vocabulary terms with the statements below.

a. Arbitration
b. Boycott
c. Coalition bargaining
d. Collective bargaining
e. Conciliation
f. Controversy
g. Grievance procedure
h. Injunction
i. Jurisdictional dispute
j. Labor agreement
k. Lockout
l. Mediation
m. Picketing
n. Secondary boycott
o. Strike
p. Wagner Act

1. The bargaining process, between labor and management, wherein workers act as a group through their representatives
2. A dispute between two groups of workers over the right to perform certain types of tasks
3. The stationing of banner- and placard-carrying workers at the entrance of a business
4. A refusal on the part of employees to patronize their employer's business
5. When the employees of a business attempt to influence the public not to transact business with the firm
6. When workers walk off the job and refuse to work until their demands are met (or a compromise is reached)
7. A court order preventing labor or management from carrying out an announced course of action
8. When an employer does not permit his employees to work until they agree to his stipulation
9. The collaboration of several different unions within an industry, in bargaining as a group with an employer
10. A contract, between management and labor, outlining in specific terms their working relationships
11. A provision in a labor contract that explains how employees who feel they are not receiving just treatment may be heard

12. A go-between in a labor dispute who attempts to bring the two parties to the controversy together to continue negotiations
13. Where the outside party who is attempting to get labor and management to agree offers suggestions as to a possible compromise
14. Where the outside party in labor-management negotiations serves as a judge in the dispute, and renders a decision
15. A labor dispute that has not yet reached the stage of a threatened work-stoppage
16. The common name for the National Labor Relations Act—sometimes referred to as labor's "Magna Carta"

QUESTIONS FOR REVIEW STUDY

1. What are some of the common interests of employers and employees?
2. What are some of the basic matters over which labor and management often are in conflict?
3. What procedures does organized labor employ in an attempt to enforce their demands upon management?
4. What is the most effective restraining action used by management?
5. Next to the strike, what is labor's most effective weapon?
6. What are the advantages to labor of coalition bargaining?
7. What are the most important items usually included in labor agreements?
8. What are the differences in meaning and function of conciliation, mediation, and arbitration?
9. What is the difference in purpose and function of the National Mediation Board and the National Labor Relations Board?
10. Why is the Wagner Act often called labor's "Magna Carta"?
11. Why did Congress enact the Labor-Management Relations Act of 1947?
12. What are the chief provisions of the Landrum-Griffin Act of 1959?
13. Why does the federal government take such an active role in settling labor disputes?
14. How does labor influence governmental policy through its political activities?

PROBLEMS AND PROJECTS

1. Write a short essay on the influence of organized labor and of employers' associations in national elections.
2. The strike is usually considered to be labor's most effective weapon in forcing its demands.

    (a) What are some factors that help determine whether a strike is successful?

(b) What factors might cause a strike to be considered as being against the public interest?

3. The Teamsters Union is in a position to tie up business by calling a nationwide strike of transportation facilities. Give arguments to support the breaking-up of the Teamsters into several smaller unions.

4. Assume a wage scale of $2.50 per hour and a work week of 38 hours. The employees strike for 12 weeks in an attempt to secure a new wage-rate of $3.00 per hour, but in a compromise settlement they agree to accept $2.80 an hour.

   (a) How much in wages did an individual worker lose during the 12-week period?
   (b) Assume that he received one-third of his regular wages as strike benefits from the union. How long would he have to work at the new wage of $2.80 in order to make up for the wage loss he suffered while on strike?

5. Read several articles from recent periodicals pertaining to labor-management negotiations in major industries.

   (a) What are the chief things labor is seeking?
   (b) Are the new contract agreements considered to be pro-labor?
   (c) What are the current guidelines for wage negotiations as suggested by the federal government?

BUSINESS CASES

Case 13-1 A Grievance Procedure

The Winchester Corp. manufactures an assortment of parts for auto bodies, and is a supplier to a half-dozen assembly plants in its area. Its recent growth has been quite rapid, with the number of employees having doubled in the past three years. However, the expansion at the middle and operational management levels has not kept pace with worker and production growth.

There are obvious inefficiencies in operational techniques, and the supervisory relationships are very ineffective. Worker grievances are numerous, and there is no uniform practice for hearing grievances, and no written procedures for handling them.

You have been promoted from a supervisory position to a staff position in the labor relations department, with your special assignment that of handling employee grievances. Outline a four- or five-step procedure for handling employee grievances.

Case 13-2 Should the Workers Organize?

The Uniform Products Corp. makes typewriter parts that it sells to various typewriter manufacturers. There are no union members among its employees. In the past the company has always paid the going wage-rate in the community—the same rates paid by its competitors whose workers are organized. Its fringe benefits include paying the operation costs of a credit union secretary-treasurer, low-cost hospitalization and life-insurance, paid holidays, paid vacation-time, and sick-leave. Its fringe-benefits package is reported to be slightly better than that of other similar manufacturers in the community.

Three key persons among the work force have been urging other employees to work with them in the formation of a union. Their idea is to form an industrial union with all plant employees eligible for membership in it.

1. What advantages would there be to the employees in organizing such a union?
2. What advantages and disadvantages might there be for the management should a union be formed?

Manufacturing Facilities and Materials Purchases

14

One of the most important early decisions which must be made when a new industry is to be established is the choice of its location. There may be many desirable locations from which to make a selection, but in all probability there will be a few sites which are more suitable than the others. In most instances the three major factors that enter directly into location selection—raw materials, transportation facilities, and qualified labor—must be present in the right combination. In other instances, nearness to other plants that supply parts may also be a significant influence; and in yet others it may be the availability of sufficient land area to meet the total needs of the plant. In this chapter we shall take a look at the different location factors and the ways in which they influence the location decision.

The type of manufacturing operation to be carried on greatly affects the space needs. If a single-story building is to be constructed, this naturally increases the acreage needed. The number of persons to be employed determines the size of the area needed for parking. And anticipated growth is not only an important space factor; it also influences building layout and design —so these, too, will be discussed.

No manufacturing enterprise can operate effectively and economically without quality materials. And these materials must be on hand in sufficient quantity to keep the manufacturing processes in continued operation. So the third area of study with which we shall be concerned is that of materials. Some of the aspects discussed are materials purchasing policies and procedures, maintenance of quality standards, storage, and inventory control.

CHOICE OF PLANT LOCATION

During recent years, with the rapid expansion of the economy, industries have been faced with countless decisions relative to decentralization and expansion. Should the present plant be enlarged? Should new plants be built at new locations in the same community? In new communities? In some instances, what was established originally as a branch factory is later expanded to become the main plant. And, occasionally, the original base is deserted and the firm moves its entire operation to one of the locations selected earlier for a branch plant.

The early history of the location of manufacturing plants was one of *concentration.* Factories were concentrated in or near urban centers like New York, Chicago, Los Angeles. The concentration of population living in these cities provided a nearby market and a readily available labor supply. New England was naturally the nation's first important industrial region. But as the population of the Middle Atlantic states increased, they first equalled, then surpassed New England as a manufacturing region. In later years, the rapid population growth of Los Angeles enabled it to become one of our leading manufacturing centers.

Currently, *dispersion* in manufacturing is the order of the day. By building branch factories in different geographical areas, a company can be near several separate market centers, lessen the threat of destruction from atomic warfare, avoid paying the high cost of land for industrial sites in older cities, and facilitate the diversification of product manufacture.

Some of the factors that a forward-looking management must take into consideration when it is evaluating possible plant sites are: nearness to markets; proximity to sources of raw materials; availability of labor; adequacy of transportation facilities; supply of cheap fuel, power, and water; and attitude of local government and residents toward industry. These are referred to as *location factors.* It is impossible to rank them in order of importance, since for one type of industry nearness to raw materials may be the most important consideration, and for another type availability of transportation facilities may take precedence. The best location is the one that provides a good balance among all these factors.

Nearness to Markets

In the beginning of our nation's industrial development, nearness to markets was one of the most important factors when selecting a plant location. Locating near the market was important because of transportation costs. However, the development of economical air transportation has brought most communities within range of the "market." A good example is the growing of flowers at Aalsmeer in the Netherlands. In this community alone there are 10,000 acres under glass, a tremendous development devoted to the production of flowers. The flowers are cut by six o'clock in the morning, and trucked immediately to the auction house. They are then loaded on airplanes at the Amsterdam airport by noon, and reach New York that same day. From New York they are shipped again by air to cities throughout the United States.

Transportation cost is not a critical factor for products that have a high value per small bulk—such as fountain pens, cutlery, and jewelry. However, it is important for products of large bulk. Automobile assembly plants are widely distributed because it is cheaper to transport parts than to move the completed cars.

The *service* factor is important in some instances, making it very desirable to locate production facilities near the market. Being near the principal market area increases efficiency and decreases installation and maintenance costs because company-trained personnel are close at hand.

Nearness to Raw Materials

In our modern economy there are three distinct types of raw materials: (1) perishable produce, such as fresh fruits and vegetables; (2) unprocessed materials from mines and wells; and (3) semifinished goods, such as leather, chemicals, and metals.

Plants that process perishable fruits and vegetables—such as food-canning and food-freezing establishments—clearly have no choice other than to locate in the agricultural communities in which these products are grown.

It is advantageous for plants that process bulky raw materials, which have a low dollar value and that lose considerable weight during the processing operation, to locate near the source of raw materials. Gold and silver smelteries and saw mills are excellent examples, because in each case the raw materials bulk they handle is greatly reduced.

The oil refineries in Texas and Illinois and the ore smelteries in the West are examples of factories that process raw materials from mines and wells. Because of the great bulk and weight of these raw materials, it is more economical to process them before shipping the finished product to distant markets.

Brick, tile, cement, and potteries always locate in communities where the raw materials are present in abundance. Furniture is manufactured in Indiana, Michigan, and North Carolina because of the abundant supply of hardwood in these areas.

Sometimes a wide variety of raw materials is used in a single manufacturing process. If these materials must be assembled from many different places scattered throughout the country, other location factors are of greater importance in selecting a plant site than is the availability of raw materials.

Adequacy of Transportation Facilities

In the two factors discussed thus far, the cost of transportation has been the paramount issue. When transportation costs are the deciding factors in being able to meet competition, an industrialist has no choice but to locate near the market or near the raw materials—or, if possible, near both.

The adequacy of effective transportation service may be as vital as its cost. One reason why such cities as Chicago, New York, New Orleans, and St. Louis became important trade and industrial centers was the adequacy of their transportation facilities. At first these cities had an advantage over many others because of their strategic location in relation to water transportation. Because they were important industrial cities the railroads, the major highways, and in turn the airport facilities were developed there. And these excellent transportation facilities have enhanced their attractiveness as industrial centers because manufacturing and transportation are *interdependent.* Industrial areas both depend on transportation facilities, and attract them.

When several methods of transportation are available—such as air, rail, highway, and water—you must strike a balance between urgency and economy in choosing the particular methods to use in procuring raw materials and in getting your finished products to market.

Availability of Labor

The degree to which labor costs determine the cost of production, the availability of the type of labor needed, and the wage differentials in various communities, must all be considered by management in selecting new locations. There is usually an adequate supply of unskilled labor in any large city. Skilled labor, however, has a tendency to concentrate in areas where specialized skills are most needed and best rewarded. Likewise, industries that require a particular type of skilled labor usually locate in regions where such labor is already concentrated. (Some examples of skilled workers are die-makers, pattern-makers, and machinists.)

The picture is quite different in industries that rely primarily on unskilled labor, for here the manufacturers are more interested in areas where the lowest rates of pay prevail. Lower labor costs is one of the primary reasons for the development of the South as a manufacturing region since World War II.

In the past, industrialists who were looking for new plant sites preferred regions in which labor unions were not highly organized. Now, however, three factors operate to make this consideration far less important than it used to be. One is the fact that formerly unorganized areas are becoming increasingly unionized. A second is industrial management's increasing recognition that collective bargaining is a desirable procedure that offers advantages to management as well as to labor. A third factor is the tendency for the wage rates of unorganized labor to approach those for organized labor.

Today, the stability of the labor force and the capacity of the people to respond to company training programs are probably as important as are prevailing wage-rates. Skilled labor can be moved to new plant locations, and persons can be trained for semiskilled and unskilled positions. The location of the cigarette industry in the South and the development of the textile industry there are two examples of how the availability of labor and the source of raw materials combine to establish the location of important industries.

Supply of Cheap Fuel, Power, and Water

Fuel. Areas that are rich in natural gas, oil, and coal are able to attract industries that need large amounts of fuel in their factory processes. Pittsburgh, Pa., became the center of the steel industry because of its nearness to a plentiful supply of coal and coke. The fact that iron ore could be shipped into this area by water also played a part in determining its popularity. The pottery industry has been concentrated in Ohio not only because of the rich deposits of clay in that state, but also because of a plentiful supply of the cheap natural gas that is used in firing the clays.

Power. Industries that use heavy machinery are obliged to choose locations that offer a large supply of cheap power. It was for this reason that our early industries located along the swift streams of New England, with their tremendous waterpower potential. The Niagara district attracted the industry not only of the northeastern part of the United States, but of southeastern Canada as well. More recently, the giant Tennessee Valley Authority has drawn heavy industry to Tennessee, Alabama, and Kentucky, and the chemical industry has also established many new plants in this region. And atomic energy plants have been located here because of the availability of ample sources of cheap power.

Water. An abundant supply of water—either in large quantities or of great purity—is important to certain industries, such as the manufacture of rayon, the making of paper, and the production of chemicals. The strong trend toward air-conditioning in modern plants and offices has also increased the importance of an abundant water supply. Communities which have not practiced water conservation, and/or planned for an increase in their water-supplying sources, are having a rough time, and will find things rapidly worsening if they do not take immediate action.

Community and Government Attitude

The migration of families from rural areas to urban communities has increased the need for industry in those communities to provide employment. Since these people can no longer look to the land for their support, it becomes increasingly important that suitable employment be found for them. And the establishment of even a relatively small industry may help a community immeasurably by providing new employment opportunities, both directly and indirectly. The realization of this fact has caused urban residents and governments not only to welcome industry, but to seek it actively and make land and tax concessions to induce new industrial enterprises.

Some companies have indicated that community attitude toward industry is the highest-ranking factor they consider when seeking a favorable location. In addition, these firms seek land at reasonable prices, and favorable building and zoning ordinances.

Some communities have actually set up foundations for the express purpose of attracting new industry. The Lexington Industrial Foundation in Lexington, Ky., for example, was organized in 1955 by the Chamber of Commerce for the purpose of attracting new industry to the city. The Foundation purchased 140 acres of land located on the edge of the city. Railroad sidings were already available to this area, and the city government was induced to service it with city sewers. Land tracts were made available to new industries, and within a period of two years all the sites had been taken.

City governments sometimes offer to bestow immunity from local property taxes on new industry for a period of from one to five years. The reasoning is that the entry of new enterprises into the area will increase the amount of taxable property by bringing the factory property itself to the tax rolls, and by encouraging the building of new homes and the establishment of new retail stores.

The educational level and the cultural facilities of a community also are important in selecting plant locations. People who live well make good employees. The adequacy of churches, schools, hospitals, and recreational facilities makes a community a desirable place to live and enhances a company's ability to attract a high type of person to live and work in that community.

Climate and Other Factors

In choosing the location of certain industries, climate is an extremely important consideration. The airplane industry has become concentrated in the Far West and the Southwest because the climate there provides good flying conditions over long periods of time.

The availability of land is in itself becoming a significant location factor, for good industrial sites are not as plentiful as they once were. In fact, in some of our well-established industrial cities it is becoming extremely difficult to find available land areas large enough for the construction of factories. Approximately one-third of all new factories are being built in cities under 100,000 in population.

Industries that manufacture automobiles and machines must consider nearness to small plants that supply component parts in making a choice of their plant sites.

The ease of securing financial backing from banks and other lending agencies, and construction costs, zoning regulations, availability of housing for employees, and nearness to competitors are all factors that modern industrialists must weigh very carefully in choosing industrial locations.

A recent survey of 100 new plants in the South, sponsored by the National Planning Assn., showed that the rising importance of the South as a consumer market has been the leading factor in attracting new industries. Sources of raw materials (including electric power and fuel) ranked second, and availability of labor ranked third.

The periodical *Modern Industry* has published a checklist which has proved helpful to many companies in selecting their plant locations. The major questions that the checklist aids management in answering are:

1. How good is the community setup?
2. Are transportation facilities what you need?
3. Are plant services (power, water, etc.) adequate?
4. Is the labor picture promising?
5. How will the site characteristics affect construction and operating costs?
6. Is the site suitable in terms of your building requirements?

THE GEOGRAPHICAL DISTRIBUTION OF MANUFACTURING

All the factors that we have been discussing combine to make certain areas highly desirable as factory locations. Table 14.1 gives the distribution of wage-earners, and the value added by manufacturing, for nine geographical areas, and shows how various sections of the country compare. Notice that 59 percent of the manufacturing labor-force is employed in the three sections comprising the northeastern part of the United States—a group of 14 states north of the Ohio River and east of the Mississippi, extending from Illinois north to Wisconsin, and east to Rhode Island. This same group of states also accounted for 59 percent of the value added by manufacture.

This table also shows that there has been a slow but continuous decline in the percentage of the total manufacturing done in this area. The three divisions making up this 14-state area employed 68.4 percent of all factory personnel in 1939, which decreased to 64.1 percent in 1954 and to 58.8 percent in 1963. This is a decrease of almost 10 percent during that 24-year period.

There was a corresponding decrease for this region in the value added to goods through manufacturing—a drop from 71.1 percent in 1939 to 59.3 percent in 1963. Most other geographical divisions showed increases during the corresponding period. The geographic regions that have increased most rapidly are the Pacific, Mountain, and the West South Central regions. The states that make up each census region are shown on the map on the next page.

TABLE 14.1

GEOGRAPHICAL DISTRIBUTION OF MANUFACTURING: 1939, 1947, 1954, 1959, AND 1964

	Percentage distribution of wage-earners					Percentage distribution of value added by manufacturing				
Division	1939	1947	1954	1959	1964	1939	1947	1954	1959	1964
New England	12.1	10.5	8.9	8.8	8.2	9.8	9.3	7.8	7.5	7.4
Middle Atlantic	28.5	27.3	26.6	25.2	23.8	29.8	27.9	26.0	23.8	22.2
East North Central	27.8	29.9	28.6	26.8	26.8	31.5	31.5	31.2	29.9	29.4
South Atlantic	12.5	11.3	11.0	11.8	12.6	9.1	9.3	9.1	10.3	11.1
East South Central	4.5	4.7	4.5	4.9	5.4	3.4	3.9	4.2	4.4	4.8
West South Central	3.3	3.8	4.6	4.9	5.3	3.3	4.1	4.9	5.4	5.9
West North Central	4.9	5.3	6.0	5.9	6.0	5.5	5.5	6.0	6.2	6.2
Mountain	0.9	1.0	1.3	1.5	1.6	1.1	1.1	1.2	1.5	1.7
Pacific	5.5	6.2	8.5	10.2	10.3	6.5	7.4	9.6	11.0	11.3
Total	100.0	100.0	100.0	100.0	100.0	100.0	100.0	100.0	100.0	100.0

Percentages calculated from data obtained from the U.S. Dept. of Commerce, Bureau of the Census.

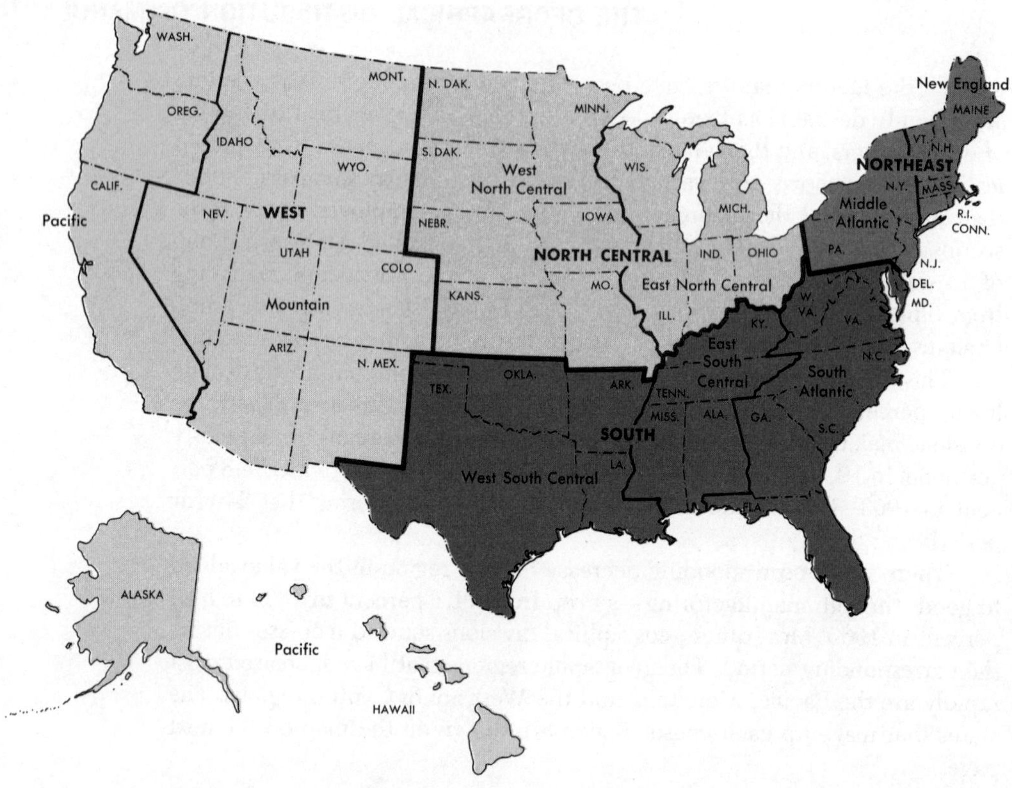

Map of The United States, Showing Census Regions and Divisions [Alaska and Hawaii are drawn at different scales from conterminous United States and are not shown in their correct relative geographic positions].
Source: Dept. of Commerce, Bureau of the Census.

PLANT LAYOUT

Let us assume that you have carefully weighed all these location factors and have decided on the site for your new plant. The next big step is to decide on plant layout. *Plant layout* refers to the arrangement of the work processes to be performed. Machines and work stations should be arranged so that production operations are carried through to completion with efficiency. A good layout eliminates, as far as possible, waste motion of both men and materials. As was pointed out earlier in this chapter, the amount of space needed for an efficient layout helps determine site selection.

Since management is concerned with producing quality merchandise at a low unit-cost, it must make careful, detailed plans for plant layout and the placing of equipment. To keep unit costs low, the layout must permit a free flow of work, a minimum investment of capital, and desirable working conditions for employees. Here are some of the factors that must be considered in planning plant layout: (1) the nature of the manufacturing process, (2) the type of product, (3) the extent and nature of mechanization, (4) provisions for heat, light, and power, and (5) allowances for flexibility and future expansion.

The type of building you erect will be closely related to the plant layout you need—in fact, the two are usually planned simultaneously, each influencing the other. If you purchase or lease a building, the layout must of course be adapted to the building—either as it stands or within the limits of possible alterations. The ideal situation, naturally, is to plan and construct a new building that will give precisely the plant layout you desire.

The Manufacturing Process

If you are going to manufacture only one or two stock products, you can plan a continuous-production process in which the machines are arranged in an orderly sequence. On the other hand, if you are going to manufacture many different products, or if you will have to make adaptations for special orders, you will usually find it better to group similar machines together.

The steel industry is an excellent example of the *continuous-production* process. The hearth furnaces are kept hot 24 hours a day, and are operated by three work-shifts. The continuous-production process is also well suited to the glass and rayon industries.

The production of automobiles, appliances, and machines illustrates factory processes that do not require continuous operation. Here, factory processes may be halted at intervals without damaging the finished product. This is known as *intermittent production.*

Of course, the differences between continuous and intermittent manufacturing processes necessitate different types of layouts for plants and equipment.

Type of Product

The plant layout best suited to a particular factory is also influenced by the type of product turned out. A plant that simply assembles component parts requires one sort of layout; a plant that produces parts and also assembles them requires another. Similarly, whether the article being produced is standard or made-to-order also makes a difference. Made-to-order work rules out the uniform procedures that may be followed when standard products are made. Moreover, specially produced articles are usually shipped out shortly after being completed, whereas standard articles are often kept on hand for a time and must be accommodated in storage facilities.

Extent of Mechanization

In a plant where most of the work is performed by machines, the layout must promote the free flow of work from one stage of production to another with a minimum of handling. If various workers, such as machinists or carpenters, play an important role in the production process, the layout must provide for freedom of body movement and for the frequent handling of materials.

Provisions for Heat, Light, and Power

In Chapter 11, you will remember, we mentioned the effect that working conditions have on worker morale and efficiency. Earlier in this chapter we discussed how the question of fuel and power influences management in determining plant location. Fuel and power are equally important in planning plant layout; a sudden interruption of the power supply throws both men and machines into idleness. If production is to proceed smoothly and efficiently, proper wiring and fuse installations must be provided that will handle peak loads. Special power engineers should be consulted to insure that the layout will be adequate.

Flexibility and Future Expansion

Unless production procedures have become thoroughly standardized so that there is little likelihood of your having to make changes in the future, the layout should be kept flexible and adaptable. The installation of new and larger machines at a future date may mean that you will need more floor space. Or, if your business prospers and expands, you may want to shift the departments around and add to plant facilities. How well you anticipate these changes and plan for them in the early stages will in large measure determine how efficient your layout will prove to be with new and enlarged production facilities. Buildings should be designed so that additions can be made with a minimum of disruption and expense. If plant layout has been properly planned, alterations and enlargements can be carried out without interfering with existing facilities.

Other Factors

Whether the building is all on one floor or occupies several floors makes a difference in placing heavy machinery and planning for storage space. The amount and type of elevator service available is another important consideration. The existence of loading docks and railroad spurs, or the possibility of building them, must also be taken into account.

PLANT BUILDINGS

Years ago, most factory buildings were of the multi-story type. When factories were being built in cities, where land costs were high, the multi-story buildings were almost mandatory. Now, however, new plants are locating in suburbs and in small communities where large tracts of land are available for plant sites at relatively low cost, making it possible to erect single-story plants. Of course, in factory processes that rely on the use of gravity in the processing or flow of materials, the multi-story building is still in demand.

Types of Buildings

Most industrial buildings may be classified into one of four basic types: single-story buildings, high-bay and monitor types, multi-story, and special structures. The manufacturing process to be used, the layout needed, and the cost of the land all influence the choice of type of building.

Single-Story. The current trend in factory construction is toward the *single-story*, rectangular building. This type of building can be constructed quickly and economically, affords great flexibility, and is easily heated and air-conditioned. The single-story building is not concerned with load capacities on the floors, and gives greater protection to employees in case of fire.

High-Roof and Monitor. Either the *high-roof* or the *monitor* type of building is used when overhead crane operations are required. (The *monitor* type of building has a two-level roof; the upper level runs down the center of the building.) This type of building is usually used for steel mills and foundry operations. It is frequently designed to provide maximum light and natural ventilation by constructing the walls largely of windows.

Multi-Story. The *multi-story* building is found in districts of high land prices because it gives the largest operational area per square foot of land. A multi-story building is well adapted to the manufacture of light goods which do not place great stress on the floors. Its greatest weaknesses are the high cost of transferring materials from one floor to another, and its inflexibility. Because of the large number of interior rooms, air-conditioning is essential to provide constant temperature and proper ventilation. Flour mills, sugar refineries, and drug and chemical producers find the multi-story building suitable for their use.

Building Design

Two factors which must be considered in building design are *flexibility* and *expansion.*

Flexibility. Flexibility is very important in building design because it gives versatility and makes buildings less likely to become obsolete. A building that uses large steel trusses to support the roof provides large working areas free of column obstructions. Placement of the heating and plumbing lines and equipment overhead also frees large floor areas of obstructions. These unobstructed areas enable a company to rearrange layout procedures to keep abreast of technological improvements. They also make it easy and inexpensive to change production processes or inaugurate the manufacture of new products.

The single-story building is the most flexible design because of the ease and economy of knocking out walls and of constructing additions.

Expansion. Long-run factory planning provides for future growth and increasing productive capacity.

The first step in providing for expansion is the acquisition of a large enough land area to provide for larger buildings without reducing parking and other outdoor facilities. Multi-story buildings designed to have new floors added must be structured to bear the added weight. Utility services

Courtesy General Motors Photographic, by Ezra Stoller.

This foundry, operated by the Metallurgical Engineering Department at the General Motors Technical Center, is equipped for virtually all types of experimental melts. Like the other special-purpose areas at the Center, it features maximum flexibility.

must be installed which will efficiently and economically connect with those serving the new floors.

In order to place the building properly for maximum use of loading and docking facilities, railroad sidings, parking areas, and the power plant, the location of building additions must be a part of the original building design.

MACHINERY AND EQUIPMENT

Many different types of equipment are needed for the great variety of factory processes that characterize modern industry. First, there is what is commonly called *general-purpose equipment*—such as lathes, drill presses, milling machines, and shapers. This type of equipment is specially suited to job-shop conditions where the customer specifies the characteristics and design of the product he wants. General-purpose equipment has great flexibility and can be used to make almost any type of product desired.

A second type of equipment is *special-purpose equipment,* such as a die designed for a specific purpose. When the manufacturer wants to produce a new model of his product, he must have new dies prepared. Special-purpose equipment is widely used in high-speed, mass-production operations.

What is known as "materials handling" has received special attention from the designers of modern plants. Efficient conveyor-belt systems have been devised to transport materials to the processing area of the plant and to carry small finished products away from the assembly lines. Conveyor belts also find many applications along assembly lines in the manufacturing process itself. The gravity conveyor is popular for transporting materials from high levels to lower ones, and pneumatic tubes are finding wide applications for carrying coal dust to furnaces and sand to foundry operations, and for loading and unloading grains.

In many industries, materials-handling equipment plays a very important role in the whole operation. Motorized tractors are used to deliver heavy material or large quantities of material to the operations center, and to carry cartons of the finished products to the storage areas. This type of equipment is also used to lift heavy objects from the floor to a machine or a workbench, and then to return the objects to the floor again. Mechanical aids of this sort are important where operations along the processing line are performed by women.

MATERIALS PURCHASES AND INVENTORY CONTROL

Before any type of production can get under way, the necessary raw materials must be purchased and delivered to the factory. Since the expenditure for raw materials is one of the largest cost-items in modern production, it is essential that high-quality materials be purchased at a favorable price. And, once delivered, they must be carefully controlled to prevent their being lost, wasted, or stolen.

Organization for Purchasing

In a small operation all purchases may be handled by the purchasing agent and his clerical assistants. Most large organizations have the purchasing function centralized in one department under the jurisdiction of a director of purchases who has several *purchasing agents* serving as his assistants. All purchases of raw materials, supplies, equipment, and machinery are made through this department. This leaves other departments free to concentrate on their chief functions. It also makes for specialization and efficiency in buying. Each purchasing agent can become an authority on one or more types or groups of products.

The advantages of centralized purchasing include:

1. Specialized knowledge of material markets
2. Assignment of responsibility and corresponding control procedures
3. Standardization of materials and purchasing procedures
4. Coordination of purchasing and receiving
5. Concentration of purchasing in one place, and uniform purchasing routines

Purchasing Policies and Procedures

In purchasing for production, the purchasing agent is concerned almost exclusively with buying to meet the specifications supplied by the engineering staff. The agent places the orders and follows through to see that the materials are delivered. The specifications for such items as lumber, bars of iron, and raw wool are standard throughout industry. In order to buy intelligently, the purchasing agent must be familiar with the manufacturing processes employed by his company, and with the purposes for which materials are to be used. He must know the different qualities available, and what qualities are needed. He must also be watchful for new products, improvements, and acceptable substitutes.

Purchasing Policies. When prices tend to remain stable or when they are increasing, a company is likely to buy in relatively large quantities. When prices are fluctuating considerably or are declining, however, a company is likely to place smaller orders at more frequent intervals. If you are acting as a purchasing agent, you must know how to strike a proper balance between volume buying and "hand-to-mouth" purchases. You will want to keep a constant check on both the availability of needed goods and the amount of capital to be invested in materials inventories. You will also want to know what discounts you can get by buying in quantity lots, and what storage facilities you will need to house your purchases.

Whether to purchase the company's total needs for a particular item from one firm, or to split it up among several suppliers, is a matter of company policy. Doing all your business with one supplier means that he will give your orders special attention, but in times of shortage it is valuable to have contacts with several different suppliers. Are your own customers to be given preference when you purchase supplies—that is, are materials to be purchased from customers whenever possible? Is it advisable to make a contract with a particular firm, insuring that you will purchase from it for a relatively long period of time? Should speculation enter into your purchasing plans, or should all risks connected with price fluctuations be covered by hedging?

All these factors enter into the determination of company policies, and the director of purchases carries out the policies after they have been established. He must be careful to maintain a supply of materials slightly above the amount required to meet current needs. He must place his orders, and time their delivery, in such a manner as to correlate delivery with production schedules.

Purchasing Routines. In firms that use a centralized purchasing system, the preparation of a *purchase requisition* is the first step in procuring materials. This requisition simply sets forth the specifications for the materials needed. Requisitions are sent to "purchasing" from all the departments of the business. If these materials are those regularly used by the firm, the purchasing department knows immediately which suppliers to contact. But if the purchase requisition is for new types of materials, the purchasing agent may have to write letters of inquiry to both old and new suppliers for quotations on the materials needed. Usually these quotations are based on the specifications furnished by the purchasing agent.

The purchasing department must maintain an up-to-date file of detailed information on all available suppliers. Before placing large orders, many businesses ask for competing bids from several different suppliers. Some firms follow the practice of requiring sealed bids when ordering extremely large quantities of materials; the order is usually granted to the lowest bidder if he is in a position to render prompt delivery and give satisfactory service. The use of sealed bids is common among government agencies.

The second step in the purchasing routine is to prepare the *purchase order*. Whereas the purchase requisition is an intracompany form—that is, it never leaves the firm—the purchase order is mailed to the supplier. The purchase order contains information picked up from the purchase requisition about quantity, description, and specifications. In addition, it clearly indicates the price of the material, shipping instructions, and the date on which it must be delivered. The purchase order may either be a letter written by the purchasing agent, or a form that has been designed for the specific purpose of ordering goods. It is normally signed by the purchasing agent, and one or more carbon copies are prepared for use by the company ordering the materials.

The next step is to *follow up on the purchase order,* to make sure that the materials ordered are delivered on schedule. This follow-up is usually the responsibility of some person in the purchasing department. Since goods are ordered and delivery dates specified to assure that there will always be adequate materials on hand, it is important that the director of purchases be kept up-to-date on all outstanding orders. If materials are overdue and the supply is beginning to run low, he should be alerted at once. When materials are ordered on a very tight time-schedule, it is sometimes desirable to contact the supplier a few days before delivery is expected, to make sure that the shipment will arrive as planned.

The *receiving report* indicates that the goods have arrived, and whether or not they have met the specifications described on the purchase order. The receiving clerk checks the goods and the vendor's invoice against the information shown on the purchase order. (A copy of the purchase order is usually sent to the receiving department when the order is placed.) The receiving clerk is responsible for seeing that the quantity and quality are correct, and for reporting any discrepancies to the purchasing department.

Storage

Since enough materials must be kept on hand to keep production moving smoothly, the problem of storage is of critical importance. Storage facilities must be provided for the raw materials that enter directly into production, such as minerals, lumber, and cotton. Then there are supplies such as oils, chemicals, and abrasives that are consumed in the production process; these are usually stored in areas separate from the raw materials.

Storage must also be provided for service materials such as tools, cleaning fluids, and replacement parts for machinery. Goods that are partially manufactured but awaiting completion, finished goods, and shipping cartons complicate the storage problem even further.

Remember that storage is an important production cost, because capital is invested in all the items for which storage is provided. Also, the labor costs for handling materials often are considerable. Management is faced with the problem of striking a proper balance among several factors, such as keeping adequate stores on hand to assure a continuous flow of work, purchasing in quantities that afford attractive prices and discounts, and keeping the capital investment in storage facilities and materials to a minimum.

Inventory Control

If shortages are to be avoided, if production is to be kept moving, and if investment in inventories is to be kept at a minimum, there must be wise management and a sound accounting for all raw materials and goods in process. This management of goods on hand is known as *inventory control.*

If the supply of raw materials falls too low, production delays result. If inventories are maintained at too high a figure, company funds are tied up that might be used more advantageously elsewhere. Also, too large an inventory enhances the chance of loss due to a price decrease.

When materials are received, accurate records must be prepared and systematic procedures followed so that management will know the amount of material in the factory, and its progress through the production operation. The information kept on raw materials must include descriptions of the materials, the amounts in stock, when new orders should be placed, the period of time needed for their delivery, and the amount of goods already in transit.

The simplest way to take an inventory is by actual count of all materials on hand. But it is impossible to make such a count often enough, so day-by-day records are kept of receipts of new materials and their issuance to be placed in production. Such a day-by-day record is called a *perpetual inventory.* But even when perpetual inventories are maintained, they should be verified at regular intervals by an actual physical inventory count.

One common practice in inventory control is to issue both raw materials and supplies only upon written requisition. Each requisition should be dated and signed, and should show exactly what was issued, to whom, and for what purpose. Standardizing materials when practicable, and establishing the limits within which the inventory is to be maintained, also are helpful control procedures.

THE NEW EMPHASIS IN PURCHASING

The new emphasis in materials management considers purchasing from the management rather than the marketing point of view. In a recent year a survey of the 100 largest U.S. manufacturing companies revealed that purchasing of materials and services accounted for 52 percent of the sales dollar. At the same time, labor costs consumed only 10 to 20 percent. Thus, for manufacturing concerns there is more opportunity for a reduction in the cost of materials to reflect a significant increase in profit than is true in the labor sector. The average company can effect a 10 percent increase in profit by reducing supply cost by 2 percent. Materials management encompasses to some degree the functions of purchasing, traffic, inventory control, receiving, shipping, and production planning.

The most common method of updating purchasing is broadening the purchasing function to include certain aspects of economic forecasting, commodity projection, contract analysis, information processing, and purchasing research. This means that today's purchasing function is no longer restricted to materials supply and the buying, repair, and maintenance of equipment. It has moved from a realm of "things" to a realm of *people*, with the purchasing department being staffed with specialists in production, statistics, and finance. This means also that the burden of paperwork which is generated through purchasing must be shifted from the purchasing department to electronic data-processing equipment.

Today's purchasing agent is not so much concerned with materials *per se*, but with their function in the manufacturing operation. He may find it advantageous to buy from new suppliers. He gives more attention to quality and value than to the lowest price. He is concerned with reducing inventories in items that represent the largest dollar investment. (Inventories make up, on the average, 15 to 20 percent of a company's assets.) Modern distribution systems have reduced the need for large stock accumulations, thus increasing stock turnover. The purchasing agent encourages standardization practices. This permits contracting for goods in large quantities at lower prices, and makes possible savings through competitive bidding according to specifications.

SUMMARY

One of the most important decisions related to production is the proper choice of a plant location. There are several factors that help to determine the best possible location, such as proximity to raw materials, nearness to markets, adequacy of transportation facilities, and availability of labor, fuel, power, and water. For a given industry, one of these factors may outweigh all others, whereas for another industry it may be much less important.

Good plant layout is essential to efficient, economical production. The nature of the manufacturing process, the type of product being made, and the extent of mechanization employed all play important roles in planning plant layout.

The type of building needed varies for different types of manufacturing. In some cases multi-story buildings are better, but single-story plants are more common, especially among new buildings. The cost and availability of land are sometimes significant in the choice of the type of building to be constructed.

The number and variety of types of machines are important in planning plant layout and in building construction.

Maintenance of an adequate supply of materials is another important factor related to production. The purchasing department attempts to buy in quantities large enough to meet production demands and to effect economy in purchases. At the same time, it tries to avoid large storage costs. Probably as important as securing materials is providing for proper control over them. This is a problem that requires well-organized procedures, and faithfulness in their administration.

VOCABULARY REVIEW QUIZ

Match the following vocabulary terms with the statements below.

a. Concentration
b. Director of purchases
c. Dispersion
d. Intermittent production
e. Inventory control
f. Layout
g. Location factors
h. Monitor-type building
i. Perpetual inventory
j. Purchase order
k. Purchase requisition
l. Purchasing agent
m. Receiving report
n. Semifinished goods

1. The tendency to group factories in or near a central location
2. Those items that combine to determine the selection of a plant site
3. The scattering of a company's factories, placing them in a variety of locations
4. A good that is the end-product of one manufacturing operation but is considered as raw material for another factory
5. The over-all arrangement of plant space, and the placing of machines and equipment
6. A production process where manufacturing operations may be stopped and restarted without doing harm to the finished product
7. A building with a two-level roof whose upper level runs down the center of the building to accommodate an overhead crane operation
8. The person with over-all supervision of and responsibility for all purchasing operations
9. A written request that certain specified materials or equipment be ordered
10. A letter giving specifications and ordering the goods described
11. The person who buys materials and/or equipment
12. A statement showing that materials ordered earlier have arrived and have been unloaded
13. A scheme for assuring that sufficient materials will always be on hand and that they are not wasted, lost, or stolen
14. An inventory that is kept up to date on a day-by-day basis

QUESTIONS FOR REVIEW STUDY

1. Explain the ways that transportation enters into the selection of plant sites.
2. Give some examples of production operations where nearness to raw materials is especially important.
3. Why is a good water-supply becoming increasingly important as a plant location factor?
4. What type of labor is most likely to be a plant location factor?
5. What types of concessions are sometimes granted to new industrial enterprises in order to attract them to a given community?
6. Which geographic regions are decreasing and which are increasing their percentages of the total manufacturing done in this country? Why?
7. Name several factors that must be considered in factory layout.
8. What are the steps in a good purchasing routine?
9. How does the problem of storage enter the purchasing picture?
10. What factors determine the purchasing schedule for raw materials?
11. What types of control are necessary for raw materials?
12. What types of records must be kept in order to have up-to-date inventory accounting?

PROBLEMS AND PROJECTS

1. There are seven "location factors" discussed in the first part of this chapter. Using these factors as your criteria, evaluate your home community as a possible location for a factory that makes men's suits, sport coats, and topcoats.

2. Refer to the map showing the nine census and manufacturing regions of the United States. Using this map, the *Statistical Abstract of the United States,* data given in Table 14-1, and your personal knowledge of the region in which you live, answer the following questions about that region:

   (a) How does it rank with the other regions in value added by manufacturing?
   (b) Is it currently producing a smaller or larger percentage of the total manufacturing of the country than it did a decade ago?
   (c) What are the principal types of raw materials produced in your region?
   (d) What are the chief types of manufacturing that are carried on in your region?

3. Answer the following questions about the manufacturing region in which you live (refer to the map shown earlier in the chapter to identify your region):

   (a) Which is the leading industrial city in the region?
   (b) What is the leading type of production in that city?

(c) Which city in your region is reputed to have the best rail, trucking, and airline terminal facilities?
(d) Which city is the leading port city of the region—the one that ships the largest tonnage by water?
(e) Which principal city is most nearly located in the geographical center of the region?

4. For each of the following types of industry, indicate which factors (proximity to markets, nearness to raw materials, labor supply, fuel and power, water, climate) are most important: petroleum, meat-packing, watch-making, plastics, furniture, and textiles.

5. Is your state more industrial or agricultural? Is the climate mild or rigid? Is the growing-season short, average, or long as compared to those of other states? Is it made up principally of large, small, or average—size cities when compared with other states? What is its chief attraction as a potential location for industry? What type of a factory would be most suitable as an industry in your home community?

BUSINESS CASES

Case 14-1 Fraud in the Purchasing Department

The Harper Co. manufactures hi-fi record-players, radios, and television sets for "private brand" retailers. An audit of the company books revealed that payment had been made for several dozen expensive cabinets that apparently had never been received.

There were four men who worked for Harper in purchasing and receiving, and their functions overlapped and duplicated one another. Each man initiated purchasing requisitions and checked receiving reports, okaying them for payment. It was discovered that one of these men had been working with an outside accomplice, ordering cabinets and okaying payment for them, when they had never been received by the company.

1. How could you determine which of the men was the guilty party?
2. How could the purchasing and receiving procedures be reorganized to eliminate and make impossible the described practice?

Case 14-2 Inventory Control

The Zonker Corporation's present practice is to allow all workmen who need raw materials or supplies to enter the storerooms, take whatever they need for the work they are doing, and simply write out a list of the supplies and/or materials taken. The cost of materials are considerably out of proportion to other costs when compared to the published norms for similar types of businesses. The company management has concluded that several of the men are using materials for their own personal projects.

You have been asked to set up a procedure that would stop the use of company material for personal projects, reduce the unit materials cost, provide a record that would show the amount and types of materials used on each project turned out, and maintain a perpetual inventory record for all types of raw materials on hand. What steps and procedures would you propose be put into operation?

Manufacturing Processes and Control

15

Almost everything consumers buy today—the chief exceptions being fresh fruits and vegetables—has been manufactured. Most manufactured products are a blend of raw materials gathered from the earth or the oceans. The process of removing these raw materials from the mines, oceans, forests, and farms is part of the broader process termed *production*. Production includes, in addition to the raising of crops and the removal of lumber and minerals, *manufacturing—the process of making finished goods*. Although all phases of production are important, we shall restrict our discussion in this chapter to manufacturing. We shall be concerned chiefly with the means of production as they relate to manufacturing; the characteristics of manufacturing—mechanization, standardization, specialization, and automation; and the role of computers in product design and control. Also included will be a study of organization for manufacturing; research; development; the various types of factory processes; operational procedures; and control techniques and methods.

Courtesy of the Standard Oil Company of New Jersey

This $7 million offshore drilling rig is called the "Ocean Traveler" for it can be towed across the ocean to search for oil. It is about the size of a football field and the platform includes living quarters for 51 men. When the rig arrives at the drilling site, its tall columns and horizontal pontoons are partially flooded with sea water to give it stability.

MANUFACTURING: THE CORNERSTONE OF AMERICAN BUSINESS

In light of what we have said, manufacturing may be defined succinctly as "the process of converting raw materials into useful products." A fuller, more formal definition might say that manufacturing is *the process of coordinating materials, men, machines, and money to create material goods that will satisfy human needs and wants.* Materials, men, machines, and money together are sometimes called the *means of production.*

The lesson of how to produce goods on a mass scale came to us from England, where, in the middle of the eighteenth century, the Industrial Revolution was booming along, making our parent country pretty much unmindful of the comparatively primitive state of her American colonies' basically agricultural economy. Only as thousands of practiced and potential laborers and sufficient numbers of enterprising businessmen migrated to America from England and Western Europe did manufacturing follow.

Then, already-large cities quickly grew larger as capital resources flooded the country, spurring industrial production, factory proliferation, and population growth alike.

Following the Civil War, America's factories converted from producing war materials to satisfying the needs and wants of a burgeoning nation headed for affluence. The rapid population growth, the development of the western states, and the recovery of the South supplied an increasing market for manufactured goods. The era of industrialization in America was upon us. And with industrialization came a principle and a practice with which we are familiar and about which we shall have more to say shortly: the specialization of labor.

At first, manufacturing was largely concentrated in New England and the Middle Atlantic states. Then it expanded into the East North Central region north of the Ohio River. Since World War II, all sections of the country have become industry-conscious, and many small communities have sought and found industries suited to their localities. Even the once almost wholly agricultural southern region is becoming important in manufacturing.

Modern factories give employment to millions of workers. In fact, more people are employed in manufacturing than in any other major industry. Manufacturing offers jobs to many different kinds of workers—the unskilled laborer, the semiskilled machine-operator, the machinist, the engineer, the stenographer, the production manager. It directly supports approximately one-fourth of all workers who are gainfully employed in the United States.

Not only does manufacturing employ millions of workers directly, but it also supports additional workers in other fields of employment. The Industrial Bureau of the Atlanta Chamber of Commerce reports that the payroll of one factory employing 150 men supports on the average 383 occupied homes, 24 professional men, 6,000 acres of farm products, 18 teachers, and 33 retail stores. All this accounts for $500,000 in retail sales annually, 320 automobiles and the services needed for them, and $2.5 million in tax valuation.

The importance of manufacturing is shown by Table 15.1, which gives the employment, annual payroll, and value added by manufacturing for each major industry group.

CHARACTERISTICS OF MANUFACTURING

As production progressed from the handicraft to the machine stage, industries became large and complex business structures. Today, businesses apply scientific principles to work-processes, and present-day manufacturing industries require well-trained and experienced executives in industrial management.

TABLE 15.1
PRODUCTION EMPLOYMENT AND PAYROLL BY INDUSTRY GROUPS, 1964

Code	Major Industry Group	All employees: Number (thousands)	All employees: Payroll (million dollars)	Production workers: Number (thousands)	Production workers: Wages (million dollars)	Value Added By Manufacture, Adjusted* (million dollars)
	All manufacturing establishments, including administrative and auxiliary units (total)	17,281	106,032	12,430	65,761	205,962
20	Food and Kindred Products	1,648	9,039	1,095	5,375	23,055
21	Tobacco Products	79	353	70	291	1,772
22	Textile Mill Products	877	3,651	782	2,966	6,736
23	Apparel and Related Products	1,305	4,696	1,149	3,643	8,150
24	Lumber and Wood Products	562	2,535	493	2,047	4,361
25	Furniture and Fixtures	386	1,838	323	1,369	3,225
26	Paper and Allied Products	593	3,683	470	2,676	7,805
27	Printing and Publishing	935	5,849	570	3,319	11,065
28	Chemicals and Allied Products	749	5,240	481	2,926	19,133
29	Petroleum and Coal Products	149	1,127	105	743	3,774
30	Rubber and Plastics Products	429	2,544	339	1,796	4,984
31	Leather and Leather Products	327	1,287	292	1,024	2,270
32	Stone, Clay, and Glass Products	581	3,369	460	2,449	7,520
33	Primary Metal Industries	1,179	8,477	991	6,570	16,732
34	Fabricated Metal Products	1,116	6,857	870	4,807	12,636
35	Machinery, Except Electrical	1,537	10,587	1,108	6,877	19,763
36	Electrical Machinery	1,484	9,417	1,029	5,573	18,040
37	Transportation Equipment	1,624	12,265	1,171	8,128	23,961
38	Instruments and Related Products	309	2,021	209	1,151	4,333
39	Miscellaneous Manufacturing	629	3,836	423	2,031	6,647
	Administrative and Auxiliary	783	7,361	—	—	—

Source: Bureau of the Census, *1964 Annual Survey of Manufacturers.*

*Represents the value of products shipped less cost of materials, supplies, fuel, electric energy, and subcontract work.

We can get a good idea of manufacturing in America today by looking in detail at several of its characteristics: *mechanization, large-scale operations, standardization, specialization,* and *automation.*

Mechanization

Manufacturing in America today is based firmly on the use of machines. The machine was once secondary to the worker, but now the worker supplements the machine. For instance, whereas all shoes were once made by hand, the shoe industry is now almost completely mechanized. Furniture manufacturing is another example of an industry that has become largely mechanized; usually it is only the more expensive custom-built furniture that is still handmade. And the automobile, office-appliance, and clothing industries, to name but a few others, depend almost completely on mechanized manufacturing processes. Laborers are used in large numbers along with machines, but only to operate them or to supplement their work. More and more, manufacturing processes are being built around the machine rather than around the man.

This mechanization of industry not only yields greater over-all production but also increases the productivity of each worker. Productivity has increased on the average approximately 3 percent per year. During the past 100 years, the employed labor force has increased tenfold, and the gross national product thirtyfold. Mechanization leads to a higher quality and an increased uniformity of the product, and with a greater degree of accuracy in the manufacturing of it.

Large-Scale Operations

The use of machines makes it possible to manufacture goods by mass production. Because overhead charges do not increase greatly as production volume is enlarged, the trend has been toward larger business units; mass production has thus brought about lower unit-costs. Lower prices for raw materials, resulting from the purchase of larger quantities, and lower unit-costs for labor have further helped to bring about lower selling-prices for manufactured articles. Lower prices, in turn, have helped to increase demand. Mass production has also made it profitable to manufacture useful byproducts from substances that were formerly waste materials.

Standardization

Standardization in industry simply means setting up uniform methods for the performance of each task, and then seeing to it that these methods are always followed. Standardization may include more than method, however; equipment, machine parts, products, procedures, and processes are all made to conform to uniform patterns. Standardization makes it possible to specialize the handling of each step in a process, and to reduce costs through quantity purchases of raw materials.

One of our earliest records of standardization in manufacturing is from the area of the production of firearms. Eli Whitney established a gun factory in 1789 and began to produce firearms by a new principle. He standardized all parts so that replacements could be used in different models. Formerly, guns for which no spare parts were available had simply been thrown away. The idea of standardization was greatly extended during World War I; the War Industries Board, for example, encouraged standardization of materials and supplies. After World War I, the American Standards Assn. encouraged cooperative efforts toward increased standardization of products. During World War II, several Allied nations used the same standards for war supplies and materials.

Frederick W. Taylor, whose contributions to scientific management are discussed in Chapter 11, suggested that raw materials, tools, machinery, and supplies must be standardized before work methods can be.

Standardization brings about cost reductions because once a machine is set up it can run for an extended period of time, producing the same item repeatedly. It reduces tooling costs because fewer dies, casts, and molds are required. Labor cost is also reduced because workers do not have to alter their routines or adjust their machines to accommodate different types of operations. Also, raw materials can be ordered to specification in large quantities, thus qualifying for lower price-rates.

Specialization of Labor

When this country was first settled, the family was an almost self-sufficient unit. Each family grew (and raised) its own food, made its own clothing, built its own home. Today, the family calls in a contractor to build a new home. The contractor then hires plumbers, carpenters, painters, and unskilled laborers, each to do a specific type of work. This same principle of specialization is very apparent in modern industry. Not only does a worker restrict his activities to operating a lathe, for example, but he machines only specified parts on it. One factory worker inserts bolts in a machine casing and starts the nuts on the bolts; another worker takes over and tightens them.

Not only does the individual worker specialize by narrowing the scope of his work, but businesses also specialize. A particular plant restricts its manufacturing activities to a narrow line of products. Even large corporations that are diversifying their manufacturing operations will build a new plant for a complete new line of products. For example, the International Business Machines Corp. will produce its typewriters in one plant but build its computers in a different location. And Procter and Gamble manufactures soaps and detergents in one factory, but its perfumes and related products in another.

In the preceding chapter we discussed the location of certain types of manufacturing enterprises near the sources of raw materials. This creates to some degree a geographical specialization: the production of automobiles in the Detroit area, furniture in Michigan and North Carolina, petroleum refining in Oklahoma and Texas, and so on.

Although specialization goes hand-in-hand with mass production, and makes for efficiency in manufacturing, it has some shortcomings as well. Many a worker's activities are narrowed to such an extent that his work lacks motivation. Specialization also makes the operations of any given plant dependent upon many others. A strike in a company that produces parts may shut down assembly lines in several other factories. Likewise, a strike in an assembly plant may close down several factories where parts are made by its suppliers.

Automation

The newest development in manufacturing is automation. This means that both the handling of materials and the control of production processes is done automatically—without the utilization of human labor. It includes not only the moving of parts and materials from one work station to another, but also automatic positioning and machining throughout the production cycle.

Automation in factory processes requires expensive, highly specialized equipment. In a sense, automation is an extension of the principle of mechanization in industry. In mechanization, mechanical effort is substituted for human effort, but men still operate and control the machines. In automation, however, manual control of the machines is eliminated—only electronic control is employed (except of course for "setting them up" and servicing them).

Automation has been in operation for some time in such industries as bottling plants and canneries, and it is currently being extended to many other types of production processes. The automotive industry, for example, has developed electronically-operated equipment for the production of engine blocks. Each block is moved from station to station, positioned, and drilled, and comes from the production line ready for assembly. It is estimated that this automatic process saves from two-thirds to three-fourths of the time and labor cost formerly required.

Several factors combine to increase the utilization of automation in industry. Automated machines handle many jobs too complicated to be done efficiently by hand, and performs numerous mechanical operations so rapid that the human eye and hand cannot stay with them. Also, automated machines are more accurate than human beings, and are invaluable in their ability to execute hazardous operations in such industries as munitions factories, chemical plants, and atomic-energy installations.

Some people have expressed the fear that automation will replace so many workers that mass unemployment may result. The history of mechanization processes in industry does not support this argument. Although machines may replace workers temporarily, they nearly always increase production sufficiently to create many new jobs for which workers are required. Furthermore, these new positions are more technical in nature than the routine processes that were eliminated, thus increasing the demand for more highly skilled and higher-paid workers.

THE USE OF COMPUTERS IN INDUSTRY

Computers are used in many different ways, but in manufacturing operations their chief uses are in the areas of design and control.

Product Design

The computer is in reality the heart of the scientific research laboratory. Here the computer is used to simulate in detail hypothetical operations. The design engineer furnishes the creative ideas, and the computer expedites the handling of repetitive routine details. We might say that the designer and the computer work as a team. The designer who is strong on creativity can hold a "conference" of sorts with the computer, which is strong on detail.

For example, the General Motors Research Laboratory uses a computer system, built to their specifications, called the DAC-1 (Design Augmented by Computer). The DAC-1 can display a video picture of an image which has been stored electronically in its memory component. It can change this picture, both on the screen and in the storage component, as the designer makes alterations in the sketch by using a light-pen. It can also develop, for remote viewing, a 35 mm. transparency of any image in storage. And it will even "read" original drawings of key lines, and convert them to machine language. As a matter of fact, using a blank screen and his light-pen, the designer can have the DAC-1 recall a sketch from storage, and have it prepare an enlargement of a particular segment of the drawing. And he can rotate the image like a three-dimensional model and, again through the use of his light-pen, make changes in the original design!

Under traditional procedures, many new detailed drawings had to be made, and then numerous tedious mathematical analyses had to be calculated, in order to make any change in design. The computer eliminates both the manual drawings and the calculations. The versatility and speed of the computer makes possible its acceptance of a variety of design factors, such as wind resistance and road conditions, and quickly evaluate their effects on the problem at hand. Auto makers feel that as they gain more experience, and as computers become more sophisticated, as much as a year may be cut from the time formerly required to make the necessary dies to stamp out a body shell for a new car.

At the Lawrence Radiation Laboratory in Livermore, Calif., is one of the largest computer facilities in use in laboratory research. The computers simulate the behavior of nuclear devices as part of their work in evaluating how these devices will pan out in practice. This laboratory made the breakthrough that made possible the development of the Polaris missile warhead. The Atomic Energy Commission states that this accomplishment would not have been possible without the use of computers.

Planning in Agriculture

Computers are used in design and planning in agriculture as well as in manufacturing. For example, The Department of Agriculture is concerned with flood control. This problem involves the building of an entire system of dams, catch-basins, and spillways in the uplands. Since a single watershed covers hundreds of square miles, it used to require weeks of tedious work to determine the most desirable locations, sizes, and types of dams to be built. Land contour, rainfall, storm history, and soil composition all are factors that enter the picture. Computers have reduced this watershed planning time to a few hours.

In 1951, the Dairy Herd Improvement Assn. experimented with computer-programmed feeding formulas on dairy farms in Illinois and Utah. In 1956, the New York Dairy Records Processing Laboratory was established. This laboratory handles the records on 400,000 cows in 10,000 herds (which constitute about 18 percent of the dairy cows) in New England, New Jersey, New York, Delaware, Maryland, and West Virginia. The yields of these cows were analyzed by computer, and improved feed formulas were prescribed. As a result, the milk output of these herds increased from 25 percent to 60 percent. In 1962, the cows in these herds that were managed and fed according to computer-determined data produced 50 percent more milk than the national average.

In 15 seconds a computer can analyze a herd's records, relating 38 factors affecting feeding and milk-production. The computer then prints out specific feed recommendations for each cow in the herd. *Farm Quarterly* forecasts that within a decade most of agriculture's major farm management decisions will be based on data analyzed by electronic computers.

Production Control

Virtually all major petroleum and chemical plants built within the last 15 years are fully automatically controlled by computers. And automatic packaging machines are the practice rather than the exception, in the major industries that produce consumer goods. For example, the manufacture of a typewriter part made by one of America's leading manufacturers contains 92 setscrews. This company has installed an automatic assembling machine that eliminates all manual labor and has reduced the assembly time by 70 percent. And a major U.S. clock manufacturer has automated its whole assembly line for one of its leading models. A single machine, 180 feet long and utilizing more than 50 assembling steps, assembles 6,000 clocks per day. The only workers used are involved with loading the work-stations, and machine maintenance.

The use of computers in quality control is commonplace today. By using a computer card for each machine being put together, inspectors can check on each step in the assembly process. Defects are recorded on these cards, and an engineer can track down the source of the trouble and take immediate steps to correct it.

CAPITAL INVESTMENT FOR PRODUCTION

Large-scale manufacturing using expensive machinery controlled by electronic computers calls for large sums of money capital. The capital investment for all manufacturing enterprises in 1964 amounted to approximately $23,000 per production worker. The highest capital investment is found in the petroleum industry, where the capital investment is $153,000 for each production worker. The capital investment per worker for the major industrial groups is shown in the bar graph on the following page. (The ways in which business raises these huge sums of capital are discussed in the following chapter.)

Output per Worker

The use of automated equipment enables each worker in manufacturing to increase each year the value of the goods he produces. (Increases in production go up faster than costs, because of increases in both speed and efficiency.) This makes for a higher standard of living for all. One way to show each worker's production is to divide the gross national product by the number of persons employed. In order to account for price changes, this must be calculated in constant dollars. Using 1958 as the base year, the output per worker is shown by the line graph on page 412.

ORGANIZATION FOR PRODUCTION

In a manufacturing plant the final responsibility for producing the goods that the business sells is that of top management, usually one of the vice-presidents. His task is to work closely with those in charge of other depart-

---

Capital invested comprises total assets less investments in government obligations and securities of other corporations. Since it is stated at book value, capital invested reflects the prices underlying the original cost of the assets and not the cost of these assets in current prices. It is stated after deducting all reserves, such as for depreciation, etc. The figures for workers are annual averages of those actually employed in the industries, as reported by the Bureau of Labor Statistics. Capital invested per worker is the total capital invested, divided by the number of workers. The data are for 1964; they are directly comparable to those reported in *Road Map* No. 1550.

Source: National Industrial Conference Board, Inc., *Road Maps of Industry*, No. 1579, Oct. 1, 1967

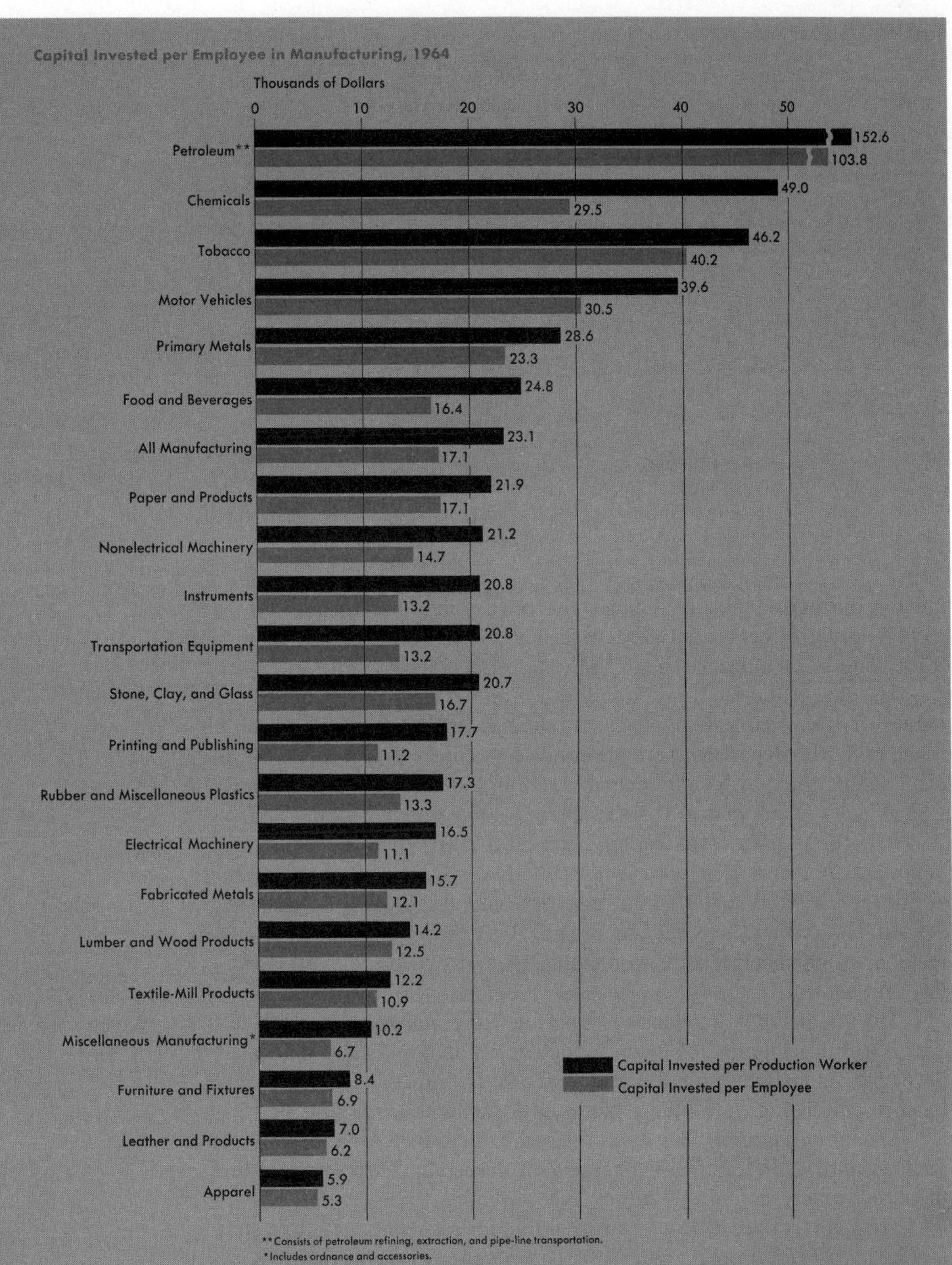
Capital Invested per Employee in Manufacturing, 1964
Thousands of Dollars
0
10
20
30
40
50
Petroleum**
152.6
103.8
Chemicals
49.0
29.5
Tobacco
46.2
40.2
Motor Vehicles
39.6
30.5
Primary Metals
28.6
23.3
Food and Beverages
24.8
16.4
All Manufacturing
23.1
17.1
Paper and Products
21.9
17.1
Nonelectrical Machinery
21.2
14.7
Instruments
20.8
13.2
Transportation Equipment
20.8
13.2
Stone, Clay, and Glass
20.7
16.7
Printing and Publishing
17.7
11.2
Rubber and Miscellaneous Plastics
17.3
13.3
Electrical Machinery
16.5
11.1
Fabricated Metals
15.7
12.1
Lumber and Wood Products
14.2
12.5
Textile-Mill Products
12.2
10.9
Miscellaneous Manufacturing*
10.2
6.7
Furniture and Fixtures
8.4
6.9
Leather and Products
7.0
6.2
Apparel
5.9
5.3
Capital Invested per Production Worker
Capital Invested per Employee
**Consists of petroleum refining, extraction, and pipe-line transportation.
*Includes ordnance and accessories.

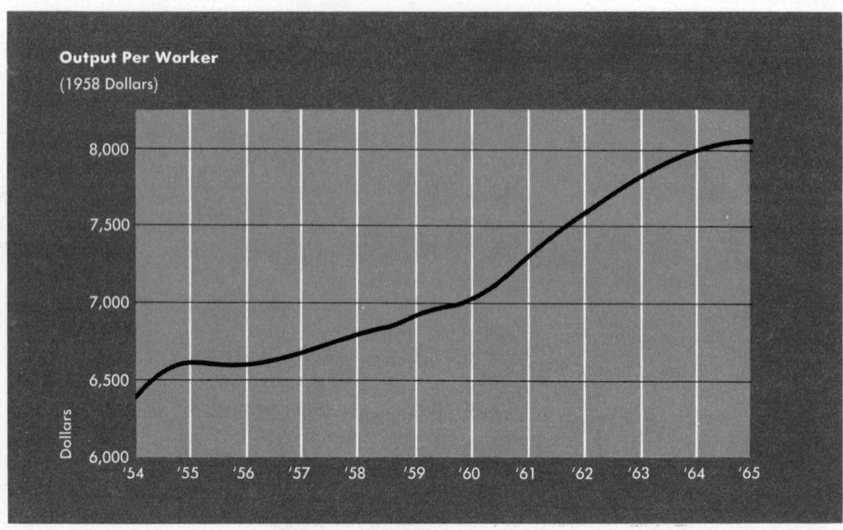

ments—the personnel, the finance, the purchasing, and the sales departments—and to direct the activities of the specialists who work under him. He is the plant's "organization man" and master trouble-shooter.

The size of the factory determines to some degree the complexity and nature of the organization of the production department. However, the functions of this department are primarily the same in all factories. In a small plant one person may handle several functions in the production, whereas in a large factory each person is responsible for only one major function.

In setting up an organization chart for a production department, it is important to ensure that each major function is the definite responsibility of one person, and that relationships between responsibilities are clearly defined. Notice that the preceding organization chart has four divisions: two major ones, engineering and manufacturing, and two lesser ones, plant service and control.

The *engineering division* is responsible for conducting research in the design and development of new products. This division is also delegated to develop plant layout, standards, and methods. Its third function is the maintenance of buildings, machinery, and power facilities.

The *manufacturing division* is the heart of the factory, with four major sections, and with a foreman in charge of each section. This division is under the direct supervision of the factory superintendent.

The *plant service division* is responsible for receiving materials, storing raw materials and supplies, and maintaining tools in usable condition.

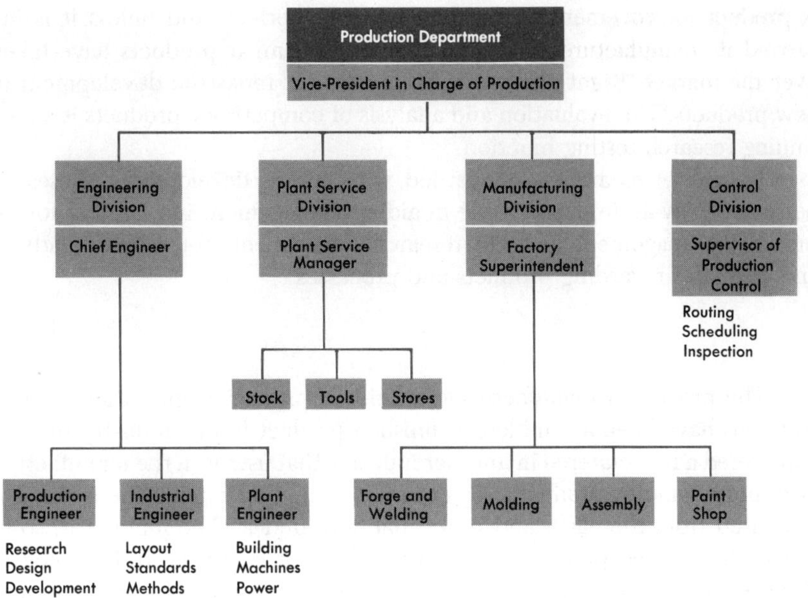

Production department organization chart.

The *control division* is concerned with scheduling, routing, and inspection.

Industrial Research

Industrial research is as old as production, but it was not given the same emphasis as sales and finance until relatively recently. Research in industry started in a small way at the turn of the twentieth century, and a few small research laboratories were established. At first researchers were concerned with attempts to solve special problems; they later turned toward the development of new processes aimed at product improvement. During the past two decades there has been a rapid growth and expansion of research development.

As was pointed out in Chapter 9, the total amount spent for research and development in 1965 totaled more than $21 billion, which was 3½ times as much as was spent a decade earlier. All manufacturing industries combined spend almost 4 percent of their total income from sales for research and development. The aircraft industry leads the way, spending almost 9 percent of every sales dollar; the electrical equipment industry spends 6 percent.

The Functions of Research. Perhaps the leading function of research is product improvement. A product is never perfect, and unless it is improved its manufacturer may find that other, similar products have taken over the market. Right along with improvement ranks the development of new products. The evaluation and analysis of competitors' products is a continuing research testing function.

Basically, research is concerned with future development. Research personnel play an important role in aiding management in planning for tomorrow. Management looks to research departments for scientific advice and estimates regarding products and processes.

MANUFACTURING PROCESSES

The process of manufacturing a finished product begins after the raw materials have been assembled. A finished product in one industry may be considered a raw material in another industry that uses it in the manufacture of a more complex product. For example, in a copper mine the mineral is separated from the earth and rocks that surround it. The mineral is, so to speak, the finished product of the mine. When it is sent on to the smelter, however, it is regarded as raw material, and is processed to produce pure copper, which is the smelter's finished product. Then other industries take the copper as a raw material and use it in manufacturing such finished products as wire and cooking utensils.

In order to manufacture the wide variety of goods that we use in this country, modern industry has developed several different types of production processes. The term *manufacturing process* refers to the method used to change the form of materials. Most processes fall into one of the following classes or types: *extractive, analytical, synthetic,* and *fabricating.*

The Extractive Process

The raw materials used in manufacturing are found in the land, the air, and the oceans. The term *extractive process* refers to the method (such as mining or quarrying) of removing these materials.

Examples of extracting industries are salt, coal, copper, lead, zinc, silver, and gold mines, and refineries that extract petroleum products. Some minerals, such as magnesium, chlorine, and sodium, are taken from the ocean. Nitrogen and oxygen are extracted from the air.

The Analytic Process

An *analytic process* is one in which a raw material is broken up into its components. After petroleum is extracted from the earth, it is refined. Refining is an analytic process by which petroleum is broken up into gasoline, lubricating oils, fuel oil, and bases for the making of petrolatum, paraffin, vaseline, tar, coke, asphalt, etc. The chemical industry is another example of the analytic process whereby raw materials taken from the air, water, or minerals are refined into a wide assortment of useful products. The meat-packing industry is still another well-known example of the analytic process. The main product is dressed meat; the hides, from which finished leather is made, are considered a byproduct, and from the wastes are manufactured many products, such as fertilizers, soaps, chicken feed, and dog food.

One of the problems faced by management in industries that use analytical processes is getting all the products to "come out even," not in the sense of equal volumes, but from the standpoint of production time and marketing schedules. The processing of the main product often is a big enough job to continuously support a full complement of workers. In contrast, some of the minor products may be produced only irregularly, and this can cause the people employed to work on them to be kept busy only part of the time—and of course during the off-periods some other work must be provided for them. (A related problem is that in some cases the production of a main item may result in larger quantities of byproducts than the company is able to market.)

The Synthetic Process

The synthetic process is exactly the opposite of the analytic—to synthesize is to put together. The *synthetic process* combines raw materials to form new products. Plastics, paints, drugs, fertilizers, and concrete are examples of products made by the synthetic process.

The fact that such processes require several different types of raw materials in varying quantities sometimes gives rise to serious storage problems. Manufacturers must exercise care to ensure that adequate supplies of all needed materials are on hand.

The Fabricating Process

To fabricate is to put together to form a whole. The *fabricating process* includes the shaping of materials into new forms (stamping an auto fender from sheet metal, for instance) as well as the assembling of many parts into an integrated product. The automobile industry is one of the best-known examples of an industry that utilizes the fabricating process: tools and dies are employed to stamp out new designs, and manufactured parts are assembled from many sources and combined into the finished product. Other industries utilizing the fabricating process include the manufacturers of aircraft, makers of glass products, shoemakers, fabricators of steel files, and furniture makers who construct metal tables and chairs. In all fabrication processes the work proceeds in a preplanned, orderly sequence toward the completed product.

CONTROL IN MANUFACTURING

The purpose of production control is to maintain a smooth, constant flow of work from raw material to finished product so that the product will be completed in the shortest possible time and at the lowest possible unit cost. This requires careful coordination of all the factors that enter into the production process—materials, machines, men, and methods.

Types of Factory Processes

There are two basic types of factory processes—continuous and intermittent. *Continuous* manufacturing refers to those types of production in which the factory operates around the clock. The maintenance of blast furnaces in the steel industry in a good example of this type. Continuous manufacturing also refers to assembly-line production in which different types of machines are used to perform the same operations for long periods of time. The production of appliances is a good example of this type of operation.

In *intermittent* manufacturing, the factory processes may be stopped at regular or irregular intervals. In some types of production the worker may leave his work at almost any point, and pick it up again when he returns, without in any way damaging the work process. Most types of job-order and custom manufacturing fall into the category of intermittent manufacture.

From the control standpoint, the continuous type of manufacturing is the simpler of the two, for the raw materials usually proceed through the production cycle at a regular rate of flow and along a definite path of movement. Consequently, both the rate of flow and the path of movement may be easily kept under control.

Intermittent manufacture, however, creates many control problems. The path of movement through the factory may vary from one job order to another. Since this type of work is usually laid out on a departmental basis, the materials used are drawn by personnel in the different departments rather than by a single group of individuals. Different combinations of specific parts are employed on different models of similar products. Moreover, there is always a problem in scheduling the work, since various orders from different departments may all require the services of a particular machine. Several job orders may all reach this stage at the same time unless the work is scheduled carefully. The control group needed for intermittent manufacture is always larger than for continuous manufacture.

Procedural Control

There are four steps in production control: (1) *planning,* (2) *routing,* (3) *scheduling,* and (4) *dispatching.*

Planning. Efficient production is rooted in proper *planning.* Everything that comes afterward in routing, scheduling, and dispatching reflects the quality of the planning that has taken place in the early stages. In order to plan effectively, management must have a realistic knowledge of the plant's limitations and must be constantly informed on the total amount of work in process.

Planning is more than setting up over-all procedures and objectives. It calls for close attention to specific details. For example, the type and quantity of materials that will be needed must be determined in advance by the production foreman and his assistants. Where a large quantity of material is involved, it is necessary to check the inventory records to see if sufficient quantities are on hand. Secondly, if finished parts manufactured by other firms are to be used in the assembly process, the number of each kind needed must be determined by the executive in charge of production, and ordered in time to have them when they are needed. Purchase requisitions for these parts, and for any materials needed that are not on hand, must be issued by the production department to the purchasing department.

In addition to planning for materials and parts, the work must be distributed to the different departments, the number of men needed must be determined, the number and types of machines required must be decided upon, and the time for the completion of each stage must be assigned. All this is the responsibility of those in charge of the production department.

In a small industrial plant that employs only a few workers, the foreman often handles this detailed planning in an informal manner, particularly where the production processes are standardized. On the other hand, in a large industry such as the automobile industry, where dozens of different materials and scores of finished parts from other factories are assembled, management usually sets up a planning department. The complexity of the operation makes such a department a "must." Each model manufactured is a separate planning problem, and many different operations are performed simultaneously. Although some pass through only one process, others go through several operations before they are completed.

Routing. Control over the sequence of operations that are performed in the manufacture of a particular article is called *routing.* When you realize that some articles involve the use of several machines, and that some machines must be used for several different processes, you can see how important routing is in a modern plant. To complicate matters even more, several different jobs are "in process" at the same time.

The person responsible for routing determines the order in which different operations are to be performed, which personnel are to do the work, and which machines, tools, and supplies are to be used. He must indicate the route for each individual part produced, and its relation to the other parts in process. He then issues route cards to each department, showing the sequence of operations for each part that passes through that department. Detailed drawings are sometimes prepared to chart all necessary production processes and assemblies.

Scheduling. The purposes of *scheduling* production work are to ensure a smooth flow of work through the production process, to avoid conflicts and delays in the use of men and machines, and to set time-tables for the arrival of needed materials and the shipping of finished goods in such a way as to keep costs to a minimum. Scheduling is necessary in order to finish stock items at a rate that will avoid the depletion of items on hand, and in order to meet time limits on job-order work.

The person responsible for scheduling must prepare a master schedule that shows the number of items he expects to complete during each week or month. For job-order work, the schedule can be worked backwards from the desired delivery date; he determines a definite time as the date on or before which each operation or part must be completed. Since he makes known to the supervisors the schedules for the different jobs, rush orders can be accommodated, and jobs that permit an extra allowance of time can be used to avoid idle periods, and thus keep costs down.

The person responsible for schedules must keep in mind the amount of plant capacity already committed to jobs in process, and he must maintain a balance of work assignments to different departments, thus avoiding overloading. He is responsible for coordinating the delivery of parts from other plants with the completion of parts within the factory, and for avoiding overloaded periods for the most frequently used transportation facilities (to avoid delay in delivery of raw materials and finished goods).

Dispatching. The issuance of work orders for each job is necessary for the planning to be carried through, for proper routing to be arranged, and for the schedule to be maintained. The preparation and issuance of these work orders, which entails considerable clerical work, is known as *dispatching*. The dispatcher must prepare requisitions for needed materials and supplies and see that the required tools are assembled.

The dispatch clerk must use follow-up routines to keep abreast of the progress of each task. He must record the times of starting and completing each task. He must deliver work orders and submit reports of completed work. The dispatch clerk uses messengers, pneumatic-tube conveyors, and dispatch boards for delivering and receiving records. He must have a systematic filing plan for each type of record. The dispatcher is also responsible for seeing that work progresses in accordance with the routing cards and time schedules. He must avoid idle time for machines and men by issuing new work orders as soon as they have completed their tasks. The dispatcher has a responsible job, for he determines how effectively planning is translated into actual output.

Performance Control

Performance control utilizes many techniques. Among the most commonly used are the *planning board, progress charts, time-and-motion studies, standards,* and *inspection.*

The Planning Board, and Progress Charts. When several types of work are in progress, involving dozens of different types of machines, management must use some system for exercising over-all control. Many modern industrialists set up a visual display called the planning board. This shows in detail the plans for three classes of work: jobs in progress, jobs to be started when the work in process is completed, and job orders not yet scheduled. The planning board also provides a separate record for each machine. The shop foreman can see at the beginning of each day or week exactly what management has planned for his department.

Boston firm nearly doubles production—through Wassell scheduling. Without adding either equipment or men, Barnstead, Still & Sterilizer, a large Boston manufacturing firm, has increased production through better scheduling of manpower and order control. Manpower is scheduled on the two VU-9074 Wassell VU-boards and order control is tracked on three 100-200 85P Produc-Tol Boards, one of which is visible at the far right of the picture.

A progress chart serves much the same purpose as a bar graph. Posted on the bulletin board or on a wall, it shows at a glance the dates on which each job is to begin, the number of units to be produced, and the date by which each job is to be finished. Lines on the chart indicate whether each job is on, ahead of, or behind schedule.

Motion Study. The purpose of motion study is to discover and eliminate waste motions and to develop the most effective method of performing each job. The motion-study analyst, who is a trained specialist, breaks each job down into all the elementary motions that the worker uses, such as reaching, selecting, picking up, putting together, and replacing on the conveyor belt. Then the analyst studies both the separate motions and the operation as a whole in order to discover the rhythm of movement, distances covered, coordination, and sequence. After he has completed his study, he recommends that certain distances be shortened and that certain movements be eliminated. He tries to advise the worker on the most desirable rhythm and timing, and helps him to work out the proper sequence of steps.

Time Study. Time study is usually associated with motion study. When the observer breaks down the whole operation into the elementary motions that the worker goes through, he also determines the time required for each motion by using a stopwatch. He selects a location that permits him to see every action of the worker. Each time the worker makes a motion, the observer times it and records the time on an observation sheet. He also records all work stoppages and delays, and anything else that seems to be significant. Every elementary motion that the worker makes during the completion of one unit of work (that is, during what is referred to as the "job cycle") must be timed many times. Then the average of all these timings for a single movement becomes the base time for that motion, and the total of the averages for all the separate motions involved on one operation becomes the standard time for the complete job-cycle.

Sometimes the worker's motions are so rapid that the observer cannot do an accurate job with a stopwatch. Then he uses cameras to make what are called "micromotion studies." A large clock having a face divided into hundredths of seconds is placed behind the worker, and a motion-picture camera records both the movement and the position of the clock's sweep-hand. By studying the series of pictures, the analyst can calculate with great accuracy just how long the movement took.

As you can see, success in time-and-motion studies requires the full cooperation of the worker being studied. If he is not in sympathy with the idea, the results are very likely to be invalid. Then, too, he should be a typical worker and not one who is exceptionally slow or fast, efficient or inefficient.

It is a good practice to invite labor representatives to participate in time studies. Workers must be given assurance that a study will not be used to force more work from them in less time just to save production costs. If they feel that the result will be higher standards for them to meet for the same pay, they are not likely to be very cooperative.

Standards. No production-control system can function effectively without standards. This part of the control system does not have to be an elaborate one, but it must provide standards for operation, standards for quality, and standards for working conditions. Operating standards, which are expressed in terms of time and procedure, indicate the amount of time needed to perform a particular job and thus to provide the data needed for scheduling. The quality-control department establishes apparatus for use in comparing parts or products with established quality standards. Good standards for working conditions include good ventilation, adequate light, noise control, clean working areas, and freedom from hazards. Periodic lubrication of machines and equipment, and a constant supply of materials to all work stations, are essential to the proper functioning of this part of the control program.

Inspection. The most important function of inspection is to enforce standards. Carefully prepared plans and carefully observed schedules are of no value if the finished product proves unacceptable, and establishing standards is useless unless you take steps to ensure that they are met.

In addition to maintaining quality standards, inspection serves three other functions:

1. If you can catch defective material or workmanship early in the production process, you can prevent the waste of additional labor later on.
2. Careful inspection at various stages during the completion of a product helps you to discover points of weakness in the manufacturing process.
3. Thorough inspection of the finished product helps prevent the shipping and delivery of defective or substandard products, and helps you to maintain goodwill and a good reputation among your customers.

Inspection enters the picture even before the production process begins. For example, the receiving department inspects raw materials before accepting them, and the supervisor inspects tools and gauges at regular intervals to make sure they are still up to standard. Since one of the chief purposes of inspection is to see that set standards are being upheld, the worker must be held responsible for poor-quality workmanship. In fairness, though, he must be supplied with sound materials and effective machinery; otherwise he cannot be held accountable.

How thorough the inspection is to be, at what stages it is to take place, and who is to conduct it, are matters of company policy that depend on the nature of the articles being manufactured and the production processes involved. For example, if you are manufacturing parts for precision machinery that have to be accurate to within .005 of an inch, your inspection will be far more elaborate and meticulous than if you were turning out toys, pencils, or paperweights. For most products, a sampling inspection is all that is necessary, but in some cases every item must be inspected (this is called 100 percent inspection).

Through experience, most manufacturers have found that it is better to make the inspection crew responsible to the production manager rather than to the shop foreman. Since the foreman is intent on keeping schedules and pushing production ahead, he sometimes shows a tendency to treat quality standards rather loosely. After all, a high rejection rate would slow up his production and reflect upon him and his department.

There are two types of inspection: *centralized inspection*, in which the inspectors are grouped together in one area, and *floor inspection*, in which the inspectors are scattered along the assembly line.

Testing is one phase of inspection; it is especially useful for inspecting completed products. For example, cans are tested under pressure at high temperatures, and automatic washing machines are put through test runs before being crated for shipment.

CAREER OPPORTUNITIES IN PRODUCTION MANAGEMENT

One of the chief characteristics of production management is that there are many different types of positions within this field. Probably no other area of business offers the variety or number of supervisory jobs found in production—both line and staff positions. Line positions range from that of department foreman to plant superintendent. Staff positions include positions dealing with all types of job analyses, supervisory functions, time study, and inspection. Large companies require highly specialized personnel to fill certain staff positions.

In addition to the large number of different positions, there is also a variety of types of industries. This means that those persons interested in production management have a wide choice in selecting a career well suited to their interests and abilities.

Opportunities for advancement in production are quite good. In addition to strictly industrial engineering functions, production requires the same types of specialized services available in nonmanufacturing enterprises: cost accounting, statistical analysis, personnel management, merchandising, and advertising.

In short, production industries offer most of the career opportunities available in retail merchandising and service businesses, and in addition offer opportunities in production management, planning, development, and plant management.

Most large corporations send their personnel recruiters to college and university campuses to select graduates who have the potential for succeeding in middle and top management positions. College courses in industrial management, personnel administration, and marketing management provide the type of background suited to modern industrial management. This college preparation speeds the trainee along the advancement trail.

SUMMARY

Manufacturing pertains to the coordinated employment of men and machines to produce economic goods from raw materials. It is the cornerstone of American business because it employs directly approximately one-fourth of all gainfully employed persons, and in addition supports many other closely related business activities. Without manufacturing there would be little need for transportation and communication, and few goods to merchandise.

Manufacturing is characterized by the practices of specialization, mechanization, and mass operations. The machine is the key to modern industrial processes; manpower is utilized to supervise, maintain, operate, and coordinate mechanized operations. An ever-increasing number of production processes and machines are becoming automated in today's factories. Continuous engineering and developmental research is required to perfect the current methods, machinery, and products, and develop the new.

Production processes refers to the way that materials are changed in form. There are four principal types of industrial processes: extractive, analytic, synthetic, and fabricating. Although these processes differ from one another, the problems of management are very much alike in all of them. In many types of industry, several of the processes are used in producing a single finished product.

Procedural production-control is secured through planning, routing, scheduling, and dispatching. Performance control is obtained by time-and-motion studies, and comparisons of outputs with expected standards. Inspection is used to maintain standards, catch defective material and workmanship, and discover places where improvement in the manufacturing processes are needed. Most operations utilize both centralized and floor inspection.

Testing is one phase of inspection. Samples of raw materials are tested to assure quality products; the completed products also are examined carefully. Mechanically operated products are usually put through test runs as the final production phase prior to being packaged for shipment.

VOCABULARY REVIEW QUIZ

Match the following vocabulary terms with the statements below.

a. Analytical process
b. Automation
c. Continuous manufacture
d. Dispatching
e. Extractive process
f. Fabricating process
g. Intermittent manufacture
h. Motion study
i. Performance control
j. Routing
k. Scheduling
l. Specialization
m. Standardization
n. Synthetic process
o. Time study

1. The setting of uniform methods for the performance of production tasks
2. The performance of machine operations automatically, without the use of human labor
3. The narrowing of a person's effort to one type of operation which he performs repeatedly
4. The method of removing raw materials from the earth or sea
5. The division of one substance into several products
6. Changing the form or shape of a product, or the bringing together of many parts to make the whole
7. The manufacturing process that is carried on around the clock without cessation of operations
8. Factory processes that are interrupted or stopped at intervals
9. The process of combining two or more elements to form a single product
10. The ordering of the steps in a manufacturing process, organizing them in a logical sequence of activities
11. The setting of time-tables for the performance of specific manufacturing operations
12. The issuing of work-orders for the different production operations
13. Breaking a job down into its individual motion components
14. Control gained through improving workers' conduct and procedures on the job
15. Using a watch to determine the length of time needed to perform specific operations

QUESTIONS FOR REVIEW STUDY

1. How would you distinguish between the terms *production* and *manufacture?*
2. Justify the statement that manufacturing is the "cornerstone" of American business.
3. How would you describe American manufacturing operations to a person who was unfamiliar with it?

4. What are the chief advantages of automation in manufacturing?
5. How and why did standardization come into being in manufacturing operations?
6. Give some examples of specialization in production.
7. What are the chief contributions of research in industry?
8. Name four types of manufacturing processes and give an example of each.
9. What are the steps in production control?
10. How do time-and-motion studies improve manufacturing efficiency?
11. What are the chief functions of product inspection?
12. What is the role of standards in production control?

PROBLEMS AND PROJECTS

1. Classify the following as extractive, analytical, synthetic, or fabrication processes: petroleum, detergents, appliances, sugar refining, automobile tires, glider aircraft, plastics, shoes, silver, meatpacking.

2. We often hear and read statements about the effect of automation on labor. Usually the arguments given say either that automation eliminates jobs, or that it creates more jobs than it destroys. Read several articles in business periodicals that discuss this topic, then prepare a paper supporting one of these two positions.

3. Study the data contained in Table 15-1 and then answer these questions:
   (a) Which of the industry groups constitute the "big five" in terms of the number of production workers employed?
   (b) Which industry groups make up the "big five" as far as value added by manufacture is concerned?
   (c) How do you account for the fact that these are not the same five industries?
   (d) Which of the industry groups has the largest dollar figure for value added by manufacture per production worker?

A BUSINESS CASE

Case 15-1 Stabilizing Output

Smith & Co., Inc., manufactures refrigerators and air-conditioners, which it markets largely through small chains of department stores that handle furniture and appliances. Their products are sold under several different brand-names.

Smith buys its electrical motors from Company X and its cabinets from Company Y. During the past two years, Smith has had difficulty in meeting its delivery dates because of labor and material problems at both X's and Y's plants, which have caused delays in their delivery of parts to Smith.

Smith has made good profits over the years, and has accumulated a significant surplus in relation to its capital investment. However, its profits the past two years have been low due to the inability to secure motors and cabinets on time from its suppliers.

The questions before management are:

(a) Shall we try to purchase these two companies that serve as our principal suppliers?
(b) Shall we switch to new suppliers?
(c) Shall we build a new plant and produce our own motors, or cabinets, or both?

1. What do you see as the important factors that enter into the problem of restabilizing production and providing protection against spotty future delivery of parts?
2. Are there alternatives other than the three we have mentioned?

PART 5
FINANCIAL MANAGEMENT

Capital Financing

16

All business organizations, regardless of their size, face the same difficult problem: finding the capital with which to finance their operations. (*Capital,* as used here, includes money and credit needed to operate an enterprise; but besides cash and credit, it covers assets such as land, buildings, equipment, inventories, and permanent fixtures.) Basically, the financial needs of a business, its sources of funds, and the methods it uses in raising capital, all depend largely on whether the firm is a sole proprietorship, a partnership, a corporation, or some other form of ownership, and on its size.

"Capital" can be divided into *long-term* and *short-term.* Short-term capital, which is discussed in the next chapter, is needed to pay current operating expenses. In general, obligations or debts that have a maturity of less than one year are used for short-term financing. In this chapter we are largely concerned with long-term financing, although a portion of the discussion is devoted to intermediate-term financing.

In addition to studying the basic types of securities used in each type of financing, we will devote considerable attention to the capital markets where stocks and bonds (generally referred to as securities because of their investment nature rather than debt obligation) are traded. Because of the importance of the subject of securities and the security exchanges, particularly the New York Stock Exchange, a substantial part of this chapter is devoted to these financial markets—to observing how they operate and what they contribute to our total economic climate.

CAPITAL REQUIREMENTS

The logical course of action for any business either just beginning or about to expand is (1) to determine the amount and kind of capital it needs, and (2) to plan its financial structure and operations to fit these needs.

Types of Capital Requirements

The financial needs of a business, regardless of its size, normally require two types of capital: *fixed* and *working*. There is a definite distinction between these that is evident mainly in the way they are used.

Fixed capital is money used to buy fixed assets, which consist of such items as real-estate, machinery, and fixtures. Ordinarily, during the course of business, fixed assets are not intended to be converted into capital, as are current assets.

Working capital is funds invested in the current assets of the business (inventories, accounts receivable—amounts due from customers, for example), and in cash. Working capital becomes a part of the funds used up and replaced in the normal operating cycle of a business. Indeed, there is a continuous flow of current assets in the direction of cash as merchandise inventories are sold and receivables are collected. (You will recall that we observed this in our earlier study of accounting in Chapter 8.) In general, working capital should be sufficient to meet both current debts and peak requirements of seasonal variations, and it should be able to take care of special purchasing opportunities, too.

The distinction between the two types of capital is essential because long-term financing is appropriate for acquiring fixed capital, whereas short-term financing is better suited to satisfy most of the needs of working capital. In this chapter the major emphasis is on the various sources of long-term capital.

Long-Term Capital Sources

Few businesses desire to remain the same size over an extended period of time; the goal of most owners and managers is to achieve financial growth.

But this usually requires additional financing. And even those firms that originally had sufficient working capital, provided from long-term sources, often fall into the error of neglecting to provide additional long-term working capital to maintain growth.

Means of Capital Financing. A large part of the working capital of a business should come from long-term sources. Such financing, called *long-term financing*, represents a financial obligation that ranges from five to 15 years or more. The basic types of securities available to corporations in raising long-term funds are bonds and stocks.

There are times when a business needs capital for a period of at least one, but not more than five years. This is commonly known as *intermediate-term financing*, because it represents a period of time less than a long-term loan but longer than a short-term loan. *Short-term financing*, which is discussed in the next chapter, is credit for one year or less. Several of the more important short-term obligations are promissory notes, commercial drafts, and trade acceptances.

While there may be some degree of uniformity in raising long-term and intermediate-term credit, there is no pattern common to all firms. However, regardless of the legal form of ownership, among the sources frequently used are the following:

1. Owner's capital (sole proprietorships and partnerships)
2. Profits reinvested (retained earnings)
3. Sale of securities (stocks and bonds)

The matter of obtaining long-term funds for a sole proprietorship or partnership presents quite a different picture than does that for a corporation. The major source of long-term financing for both the proprietorship and partnership is *equity capital*, the personal-savings funds invested by the owners. In part, this accounts for the small size of most unincorporated businesses, and is responsible for the conversion of many of them into corporations.

Although corporations depend most heavily on funds obtained from selling bonds and stocks, they may also use the same sources of debt capital which noncorporate businesses use. Indeed, the ability to borrow funds, as well as to market stocks and bonds to the public, has made possible the burgeoning of many a corporation. (In actual practice, many corporations sell stocks and bonds for reasons we have not even mentioned yet, but which we shall explore shortly in this chapter.)

The diagram (top of page 432) illustrates the various sources of capital financing and the purposes for which these funds may be used.

Pros and Cons of Equity Financing. Maximum use of equity financing offers several advantages:

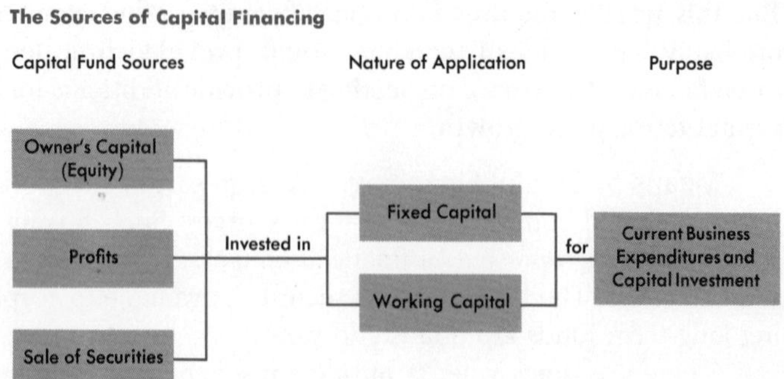

1. There is the avoidance of interest charges normally paid on borrowed capital.
2. The business is financially stronger to withstand a business recession because there are no fixed interest charges.
3. Assuming that the business is well financed in the beginning, the ability to borrow funds at a later date is enhanced by a strong underpinning of equity investment.

The chief disadvantage of equity financing, except during periods of high business activity, is the difficulty the owner may have in being able to provide funds in sufficient quantities to meet the needs of the business. He may also have difficulty in keeping his capital working; if part of it remains idle in cash balances, it will not be earning income for the firm.

Reinvestment of Profits. This is also a satisfactory means of obtaining new capital, though there are times when funds from this source are not adequate. Some large and successful corporations prefer to borrow heavily to finance their growth, rather than retain substantial amounts of profits. This makes it possible to pay larger dividends to stockholders. But financing with debts obviously can be a risky business. In the final analysis, consideration must always be given first to the nature of the firm's financial management policy and objectives.

Depreciation of Assets. In addition to the sources of investment funds previously discussed, depreciation provides a means of retaining funds in a business. In every business there are certain costs of operation which are not readily apparent, but which must be taken into account in the long run. One of these costs is *depreciation,* which is the amount of economic loss of a fixed asset, such as a building or machine, as a result of its use. The theory of this concept is that fixed assets begin to lose their value from the day they are put into use, and therefore some provision must be made for the allocation of these depreciation costs to the business operations during the life of the asset.

The amount of annual depreciation taken is recorded on the firm's books in a special account as a depreciation allowance, which is deducted from the value of the asset. Thus, depreciation becomes a charge against current income of the business, and this in turn reduces the amount of profits from which dividends may be paid.

The whole subject of depreciation is one which has been discussed at great length among accounting practitioners and financial managers because of the different methods and formulas used and the net effect on the financial condition of the business. Whether the depreciation rates are a fair appraisal of the actual wearing-away of assets or not, the amounts written off each year affect profits. A company can distort its profits by taking a high or low depreciation. When used for income-tax purposes, depreciation rates are regulated by the Internal Revenue Service. In a sweeping revision of depreciation standards, after a year-long study, the United States Treasury on July 12, 1962, announced new policy guidelines for depreciation of assets in computing federal income taxes. New guidelines were added in 1965. These newer guidelines allow for more rapid depreciation than formerly. It is believed that this action by the federal government gives business owners added encouragement to increase their capital expenditures because of the more rapid rate of depreciation allowed, thereby encouraging investment spending on the part of business firms.

LONG-TERM CAPITAL SECURITIES

We have seen that capital for a proprietorship is normally obtained from the owner. If at a later date he wishes to increase his capital because he thinks he can make more money, one way he may do this is by taking in a partner who has funds to invest in the business. Further expansion requiring more capital usually suggests forming a corporation. In this case, the corporation has the option of selling either stock or bonds.

The managements of public utilities, natural-gas pipelines, and (often) railroads need large sums for expansion. These funds are commonly obtained from the sale of bonds, which many investors prefer over common or preferred stock. Many times, the financial position of such companies is such that whereas they would experience difficulty selling common or preferred stocks, they can borrow through the sale of bonds.

If the corporation can earn 10 percent on new capital which it can borrow from bondholders at 5 percent, the difference of 5 percent becomes available for the stockholders. The bond interest of 5 percent is fixed, and it has no relationship to company profits earned on borrowed money. The principle of borrowing funds at a lower rate than the rate of expected earnings on these funds, with the difference becoming available to stockholders, is called *trading on the equity.*

Trading on the equity is considered a sound business principle at the start. However, it becomes increasingly risky as the percentage of borrowed capital increases in proportion to the total assets.

When the situation arises wherein a corporation has securities outstanding which are entitled to only a fixed rate of return, this is what is known as a leverage factor. The *leverage factor* is, properly, the effect on the per-share earnings of common stock when large sums must be paid for bond interest or preferred-stock dividends before common stockholders are entitled to receive a share in the earnings. From an investor's standpoint, he will want to examine the corporation's income statement carefully to determine the amount of leverage existing. Common stock of companies with a high leverage factor is more speculative than that of companies with little or no other outstanding securities requiring a priority over common stockholders.

Types of Securities

You might well ask: "What is the source of the money used in long-term financing?" The answer is that there are many sources. A substantial amount comes from individuals who buy stocks and bonds as an investment through organized security markets. Another source is the group of institutional investors including pension funds, insurance companies, trust funds and philanthropic foundations, universities, and charitable organizations. All of these have financial resources which must be invested so that earnings sufficient to carry on the institution's operations may be provided. Still another source is the assortment of banks, savings institutions (such as savings-and-loan), and investment trust companies (mutual funds) which invest in securities the financial resources belonging to other people.

One of the major recurring problems of the financial manager is the selection of the type of long-term security which is the most satisfactory source of capital, at the lowest cost, and in adequate quantities of money. The three types of securities most frequently used in long-term financing are common stocks, preferred stocks, and bonds. Each of these offers the financial manager certain advantages as capital sources; each serves a particular need. (A corporation may not necessarily issue both types of capital stock: when preferred stock is issued, its purpose is to raise funds by appealing to a different type of investor. The term *capital stock* refers to the total aggregate ownership interest in the corporation. This total, less unissued capital stock, represents the capital stock outstanding.) Let us see the significance of each type of security and examine some of the more important implications to the security holder.

Financing by Common Stock. The *common stock* of a corporation, divided into transferable shares, is the original investment by the corporation's owners. Every common share is equal in value and privileges to all other common shares. Financing a corporation by selling common shares involves several factors that affect both the stockholder and the corporation. From the viewpoint of the corporation, the management may use at its discretion money obtained from common stock. There is no legal requirement on the part of the company to pay back to the investor the value of the stock, nor is the company required to guarantee a dividend.

Common stock carries no fixed maturity date and, therefore, does not require a refinancing program at a later date. It is generally easier to sell than either preferred stock or debt financing. From the investor's viewpoint, common stock is often sold at a price less than the book value. This is appealing to investors. In a majority of cases, management must price its stock when first issued so that it will yield a higher return than that paid to preferred stockholders. Finally, an additional issue of common stock has a tendency to dilute the control of existing shareholders.

It is common for corporations to issue either par value or no-par value stock. The term *par value* stock denotes an arbitrary value placed on the certificate. This printed value may range from one cent to $100 or more. "Par value" suggests the original price, although more often than not the stock is originally sold for less than par. (When stock is sold at a price above par, the difference is called *paid in surplus.*)

From the standpoint of liability, the "par value" stipulation is important. By law, an investor who bought original common stock at a price below its stated par may later be assessed enough to make up the difference. On the other hand, par value stock sold at the stated par is generally marked "fully paid and nonassessable," to show that the investor has no additional liability at some later date.

If no stated value appears on the certificate, the stock is known as *no-par value* stock. Its major advantage is that it may be sold for any price without subjecting the buyer to a later assessment. Generally speaking, today there seems to be less emphasis upon the importance of par value than formerly.

Of course, stock has other values in addition to par. The price that it brings on the market is called *market value,* which changes from time to time, usually depending on the firm's financial condition. *Book value* is the actual value of the stock as shown on the corporation's balance sheet. For example, if your corporation has assets of $85,000 and liabilities (debts) of $35,000, its net worth—the difference between assets and liabilities—is $50,000. If the company has 25,000 shares outstanding of common stock at no-par, the book value of each share is $2. Its market value, however, may be several times more than $2, or it may be worth less than $2.

Common stock is usually "voting stock." It bestows on the holder the right to vote for the directors of the corporation, and on matters that may be presented at the stockholders' meeting. Since 1926, the New York Stock Exchange has refused to list any common stock that does not carry with it the right of stockholders to vote on corporation affairs.

The outstanding characteristic of common stock is its complete and final claim to profits of a corporation after all other classes of debt have been satisfied. Both preferred stockholders and bondholders have a prior claim on company earnings, over common stockholders. This same priority applies in the distribution of assets when the corporation is liquidated.

When earnings are high, the investment yield on common stock may be substantially above the fixed return on bonds or preferred stocks. But when earnings are down, the company may omit dividends to common stockholders. Thus the common stockholders may experience "feast or famine" in dividend returns. This is a fact every stockholder should know.

Despite the disadvantages of common stock as an investment, it is the least complicated of all long-term securities. This factor probably accounts to some extent for its popularity as a means of raising long-term capital.

Stock Rights. As a corporation's business expands and more funds are needed, the directors may recommend increasing the number of capital stock shares. The corporation, therefore, may give its stockholders the privilege of subscribing to additional stock at a price below the current market price. This privilege is called a *stock right.* This stock right, when exercised, is evidenced by a *subscription warrant* filled out by the stockholder to indicate that he desires to exercise this right, and to state the number of additional shares he will take within the terms of the formula. Stock rights usually must be exercised within a comparatively short period, during which they have a market value and are traded in the market. Normally, the prices of these rights are quoted daily.

An illustration of the use of rights is that of a company that offered its shareholders the right to subscribe to shares of common stock, the subscriptions to be based on a formula of one share for each 10 shares of common stock held by the shareholder and at a price of $20 per share. Actually, these shares were selling on the market at $23.75. Thus, the stockholder owning 100 shares could buy an additional 10 shares at a savings of $3.75 each. If the investor decided not to buy more shares, he could then sell his rights on the market.

For a rights offering to be successful, stockholders must believe that the company is efficiently managed and that the new capital resulting from the sale of the rights will produce a profitable expansion of the business. Moreover, the stockholders must believe that net earnings will increase at least as much as the proportional increase in capital. As a rule, rights offerings state why the funds are sought and how they are to be spent.

The general condition of the business cycle has much to do with the success of rights offerings. If there is a recession and corporations tend to have idle cash or unused production, then stockholders are skeptical that an issue of stock rights will greatly enhance earnings. But if business is good and conditions appear to be favorable ahead, then the prospects for profit seem better, and shareholders are more interested in stock rights.

Stock Purchase Warrants. Earlier in this discussion the term "subscription warrant" was used in relation to stock rights. Sometimes the word *warrant* is confusing to investors because of its several meanings. In the present discussion it is used to mean *the physical certificate which a stockholder receives as evidence of his stock rights subscription.* Warrants are also used to apply to long-term options to buy shares of stock at a stipulated price. These are usually called *stock purchase warrants.*

Some warrants expire on a given date; others are issued for the lifetime of the company or until exercised. These warrants have value on the market, and they fluctuate in price. For example, a warrant entitling its holder to buy a share of XYZ stock at $25 has a basic value of $5 if the stock is selling currently at $30 on the market. Depending upon the price of the stock, the $5 basic-value warrant may sell at a premium (above $5) or at a discount (below $5).

The Stock Split. Sometimes companies will vote stockholders a *stock split,* which may be defined as *the division, into additional units, of common stock outstanding.* In other words, the total ownership "pie" is simply cut into smaller pieces without changing the value of the original portions. If you owned 30 shares of stock and received a two-for-one split, your 30 shares would become 60, each new share now worth half of one original share. The usual reason for a stock split is to bring the unit market price of a share into a trading range or price range which more investors can afford to pay. If a stock were selling for $200 a share and a four-to-one split occurred, the new price "when issued" would be set at $50 a share. Each holder would now have four shares for each one he held previously. Stock splits help to widen the market for a stock. (Naturally, the shareholders hope the price of the stock after the split will again rise.)

In the history of most successful companies will be found numerous splits, and frequent stock dividends (which will be covered next). For example, 100 shares of General Electric bought during the mid-1920's has now become 4,800 shares due to accumulated stock splits. Had there been no splits, General Electric would be quoted today at nearly $5,000 a share. This illustrates the prime reasons for splitting: to reduce the shares to a popular price-level, broaden public interest, and increase the number of shareholders.

The Stock Dividend. A *dividend* is a distribution of earnings among stockholders. A *stock dividend* is a distribution of shares among stockholders from surplus earnings. The declaration of a stock dividend does not increase the net worth of a corporation. Instead, each share of outstanding stock henceforth represents a smaller proportion of the total net worth, which has not changed. The directors may vote a stock dividend, if the surplus is available, without putting it to a vote of the shareholders. Stock dividends are more frequently paid on a percentage basis. For example, a 10 percent stock dividend means that one new share will be issued for each 10 shares outstanding. If a shareholder holds 12 shares at the time a 10 percent stock dividend is declared, he is entitled to receive 1⅕ (or, 1.2) new shares. Since fractional share certificates are normally not issued, the shareholder can buy on the market enough additional fractional shares to equal a full share, or he can sell his ⅕ share at the current market price.

Distribution of stock, rather than cash, permits the retention of cash for use in the company. But then, sometimes a corporation will pay both a cash *and* a stock dividend. The company's dividend policy depends on the corporation's choice of whether to plow back all the earnings to avoid borrowing, or to issue part in new stock or part in cash.

Financing by Preferred Stock. In addition to issuing common stock, many corporations raise additional capital by selling *preferred stock.* This may be defined as stock that carries certain preferences over common stock, preferences stated on the preferred-stock certificate and in the corporation charter. Here are some of the special features of preferred stock (although these are not necessarily found in all preferred stock):

1. Preference as to assets
2. Preference as to dividends
3. Guaranteed dividends ahead of common stockholders
4. Convertibility
5. Redeemability
6. Cumulative and noncumulative

As a holder of preferred stock, one is entitled to receive a stated dividend ahead of all common shareholders. The amount of the dividend generally appears on the stock certificate. If the corporation assets are liquidated, holders of preferred stock have a preference over common shareholders when funds received from the sale of assets are distributed. As a rule, however, preferred stock does not give the holder voting privileges, whereas common stock does.

Preferred stock may be cumulative or noncumulative. Should a company's directors decide not to pay a dividend one year, the dividend on cumulative stock carries over to the next year or until it is paid in full. Noncumulative stock, however, provides that if the dividends are not paid during the year in which they are earned, the company is not obligated to carry the dividend forward. In other words, in no event are dividends, once skipped, payable out of future earnings of the corporation.

Sometimes a corporation may find it desirable to have one issue of preferred stock take precedence over the next, just as ordinary preferred stock takes precedence over common. These classes of stock are identified as 1st preferred and 2nd preferred, or preferred A and preferred B. Preferred stocks are also issued as participating-preferred and nonparticipating-preferred. Holders of participating-preferred stock receive their stipulated share of dividends ahead of common stockholders, and also share with the common stockholders in the division of any remaining dividends. Owners of nonparticipating-preferred stock receive only their stated dividend. Any remaining dividends are divided among the other classes of shareholders.

In recent years the use of convertible preferred stocks in planning corporate mergers has become more popular. The renewal of this interest in convertible preferreds has been dictated by tax motives. For example, an exchange from common to preferred is not a taxable transaction on the exchange. It is often a common practice in a merger for the acquiring company to offer shareholders of the other corporation convertible preferred stock for their common. This can result in a higher dividend rate on the preferred than may be paid on the common. Then there is the factor of a capital appreciation potential. When the preferred reaches a point where it is selling near or at the level at which conversion into common becomes profitable, a capital appreciation is possible. Thus, if the preferred is exchangeable share-for-share into common, the market price of the preferred and common tend to move together.

Preferred stocks, both convertible and straight, are often desired by investors because of the higher yield they ordinarily pay than do common shares, because of their appreciation possibilities, and finally because of the defensive characteristics inherent in this fixed-income type of security.

Financing by Bonds. When a corporation wants to borrow funds for a period longer than six months or a year, a common practice is to sell bonds rather than to issue more stock. You have seen that a stockholder is a part owner in a corporation; a bondholder is one who lends money to it. A *bond* is a certificate of indebtedness issued under the seal of the corporation. It is a kind of promissory note, for it is a written promise by the borrower to pay the lender a specific sum, called the *principal,* at a stated time with a stipulated rate of interest. Bondholders actually have a claim on the assets of the corporation which is prior to that of holders of common and preferred stock.

Bonds are classified in different ways. Among the different classes are: *mortgage bonds, collateral trust bonds, income bonds, equipment trust bonds,* and *debenture bonds.*

Bonds may be either secured or unsecured. A *mortgage bond* is one that is secured by a mortgage on the real property of the corporation. If the principal cannot be paid when due, the bondholders have a legal right to foreclose on the mortgage and sell the property to recover the loan. An example of a mortgage bond is Consolidated Edison's 5 percent Series N mortgage bonds that mature in 1987. These bonds were issued in the amount of $60 million, secured by a mortgage on the corporation properties.

When one series of mortgage bonds ranks ahead of others, they are known as first-mortgage bonds. Later issues are referred to as second-mortgage bonds, third-mortgage bonds, and so forth. Public utilities frequently issue bonds in this manner.

Bonds may be secured by collateral rather than by real property. Such bonds are called *collateral trust bonds,* because securities in the form of stocks or other bonds are pledged with a trustee as backing for the bonds.

Bonds are sometimes issued with the provision that interest at a certain rate will be paid, provided it is earned in excess of other fixed charges. Bonds issued under this provision are called *income bonds.* During the reorganization of a corporation, income bonds may be issued to replace fixed-interest obligations that have proved too burdensome for the company to pay. Income bonds have maturity dates, as do other bonds, but the interest payments are contingent on company earnings.

Equipment trust bonds are used mainly by railroads to raise funds to buy new equipment. For example, a railroad may want to buy 25 new locomotives but cannot assemble enough cash to make the purchase without impairing its cash position. So it makes a down payment of 15 or 20 percent of the total cost, and finances the balance by selling equipment trust bonds to insurance companies and trust companies, under an equipment trust agreement with a trustee named in the agreement. Interest is paid at fixed periods to the trustee, who in turn pays the bondholders. When the bonds are fully paid, title to the equipment reverts from the trustee to the railroad company.

Debenture bonds are the type backed solely by the general credit of the company, and not by a mortgage or any pledged assets. They have been popular in business as a means of refinancing old debts. Since 1946, the American Telephone and Telegraph Co. has sold nearly $5 billion worth of debenture bonds for its equipment expansion program. Of this total, $3.2 billion was raised by selling debenture bonds that could be converted into common stock under certain conditions. The Standard Oil Co. of New Jersey, Consolidated Edison of New York, and the Coca-Cola Co. are among the large companies that have sold huge sums of debenture bonds at low interest rates. (It was easy to find buyers for these bonds because of the sound financial condition of these corporations.) As a rule, these debenture bonds carry a slightly higher interest rate than other bonds because they are not secured by a mortgage; therefore, the risk to the investor is greater.

When a single issue of bonds is divided into several groups with differ-

Courtesy Merrill Lynch, Pierce, Fenner and Smith

A coupon bond differs from other types of bonds. The principal is payable to the bearer of the bond, and the interest is payable to any one who detaches the coupon, as shown in the photograph, and presents it to a banking institution for payment.

ent dates of maturity, they are called *serial bonds*. Each group within the series matures at a different time and is paid off by the corporation at maturity. The holder buying a serial bond knows when he will be paid.

A *registered bond* is issued in the owner's name, which appears on the face of the certificate and on the books of the corporation. *Coupon bonds*, on the other hand, are payable to the bearer, and do not show the owner's name on the certificate. When coupon bond interest is due, the holder simply clips a coupon from the bond and presents it to the bank that the corporation has authorized to make interest payments.

Considerations in Raising Long-term Capital

A factor which financial management must consider in raising long-term capital is the cost of borrowing as compared with the cost of ownership capital (stocks). If the firm can earn 8 percent net after taxes and expenses, and bonds can be sold at 5 percent net interest charge, then the financial managers will likely elect to issue bonds rather than sell stock in order to raise more capital. The major disadvantage in issuing bonds as opposed to selling stock is that interest payments become a charge against income. In a business recession it may become difficult to pay the interest cost. Borrowed money offers a tax advantage, because interest is a deductible expense under federal income tax laws, while dividends are not.

There are times when the prevailing market prices of common stocks are too high to yield the investor a reasonable return. The more conservative-minded investor then would prefer not to risk his money in common stocks. Hence, to raise sufficient long-term capital, it may be necessary to issue bonds or sell preferred stocks, because to the investor the yield is higher and the investment more attractive. It is difficult for the typical financial manager to forecast trends in the capital market. The impact of economic conditions, coupled with changing investor interests in various kinds of securities, makes it more complicated to engage in long-term financing.

Another consideration in determining the size and form of long-term capital financing is the matter of the tax policy of the federal government. Since corporations normally pay a higher federal income tax rate than most single proprietorships or partnerships, there is logic in the use of debt. The use of common stocks involving the payment of dividends does not involve a debt expense and therefore cannot be deducted from earnings, as can interest on bonds.

These are only a few of the issues which financial managers must face in making the decision whether to use common stocks, preferred stocks, or bonds, to raise long-term funds.

Choosing the Type of Securities To Be Issued

There are certain principles that may serve as guides for financial managers in helping them to make the decision as to the kinds of securities a corporation should use to obtain additional capital. The three most basic principles are:

1. Bonds should be issued only when earnings are expected to be maintained well above the interest and amortization requirements.
2. Preferred stock may be issued when, over a period of several years, the average earnings are anticipated to remain well above the prevailing dividend requirements for preferred stock.
3. Common stock should be used when earnings cannot be accurately predicted with reasonable certainty to cover interest and sinking-fund requirements.

STOCK EXCHANGES AND SECURITY MARKETS

Thus far in this chapter we have dealt primarily with the types of securities—preferred and common stocks, and bonds—that are used as sources of long-term funds for business. Because there is such a widespread use of stocks and bonds by individual investors as well as by business firms seeking money sources, more than a dozen large and small security markets, commonly referred to as *stock exchanges,* have been organized in the United States to provide centers for *trading* (buying and selling securities by auction). These markets are an essential part of our economic system. They are the meeting-places where the agents of those seeking capital can negotiate with the agents of those who wish to invest.

The Scope of the Securities Exchanges

The New York Stock Exchange is the nation's largest; the American Stock Exchange, also in New York, is the next largest. These two exchanges alone account for over 90 percent of the total dollar volume of all transactions on registered exchanges. The Midwest Stock Exchange ranks third in dollar volume, with the Pacific Coast Exchange in fourth place. The other exchanges (in no particular order) are the National Stock Exchange in New York City, and those located in the Philadelphia-Baltimore-Washington area and in Detroit, Boston, Cincinnati, Pittsburgh, Spokane, Salt Lake City, Wheeling, Colorado Springs, Richmond, and Honolulu. Table 16.1 shows how regional exchange volume has soared since 1962.

The Over-the-Counter Market. Many stocks and bonds are not listed on an organized exchange. Called *unlisted securities,* these are bought and sold in the "over-the-counter" market, which is a collection of brokers and dealers connected by nationwide communication services. Stocks in banks, insurance companies, and mutual funds are generally sold "over-the-

TABLE 16.1

GROWTH IN REGIONAL STOCK EXCHANGE VOLUME AS COMPARED WITH THE NEW YORK STOCK EXCHANGE (VOLUME OF SALES AT MARKET VALUE IN MILLIONS OF DOLLARS)

	1963	1964	1965	1966	1967
New York Stock Exchange	$54,887	$60,424	$73,200	$102,785	$130,790
Midwest Exchange	1,756	2,286	3,086	3,887	4,995
Pacific Coast Exchange	1,540	1,790	2,173	3,524	4,538
Philadelphia, Baltimore, and Washington Exchange	686	828	1,009	1,365	1,832
Detroit Exchange	335	481	630	706	715
Boston Exchange	271	310	382	700	1,086
Cincinnati Exchange	41	46	72	97	62

Source: Securities and Exchange Commission.

counter" rather than on one of the organized exchanges. Generally, over-the-counter securities involve stocks that are mainly locally or regionally owned. This is commonly true of banks and many insurance companies, but not of mutual funds.

Most security dealers operating in this market buy stocks on their own account for resale to their customers—or over the counter, the same as goods are sold in a retail store. When this happens, the security dealer quotes the stock at an "asked" price. Customers offer a "bid" price which is usually lower than the asking price. By negotiation, the parties agree on a price. The difference between bid and asked prices in any quotation is called the *spread,* which cannot be less than ⅛ point. When the security dealer buys or sells for his own account, hoping to make a market for it, he is said to "take a position" in that stock, which means he is willing to buy or sell the stock. The profit that he derives from the transaction is the difference between the price he paid and the price he received, which is the spread.

Security dealers who do not wish to make a market for over-the-counter stocks but who accept orders for these unlisted securities will endeavor to obtain them for clients at the lowest price. In these cases, the dealer or broker is paid a regular commission for rendering this service. The commission rate is in line with the rates established by the New York Stock Exchange.

As you can see, there are two sets of prices for stocks traded in the over-the-counter market: the wholesale price (the price at which one securities firm will sell to another securities firm), and the retail price (the price which the public pays).

The New York Stock Exchange. Most major corporations list their securities on the New York Stock Exchange, commonly known as "the Exchange." Common and preferred stocks of 1,274 companies were listed at year-end, 1967, on the Exchange.[1] An estimated 20 million Americans owned shares in publicly-held companies during 1965, as compared with 17 million in 1962, and 6½ million at the time of the first New York Stock Exchange census in 1952.[2] As the accompanying graph shows, the value of the shares listed on the New York Stock Exchange at the end of 1965 was nearly $550 billion as compared with slightly more than $100 billion in 1953. For more than a decade the price of shares listed on the New York Stock Exchange has advanced. This has served as a hedge against inflation.

The Function of the Securities Exchanges

In the framework of our economic system, these various exchanges function, as we have said, as market places where buyers meet sellers through

[1] *New York Stock Exchange Annual Report,* 1967, p. 23.
[2] *New York Stock Exchange Annual Report,* 1965, pp. 18–19.

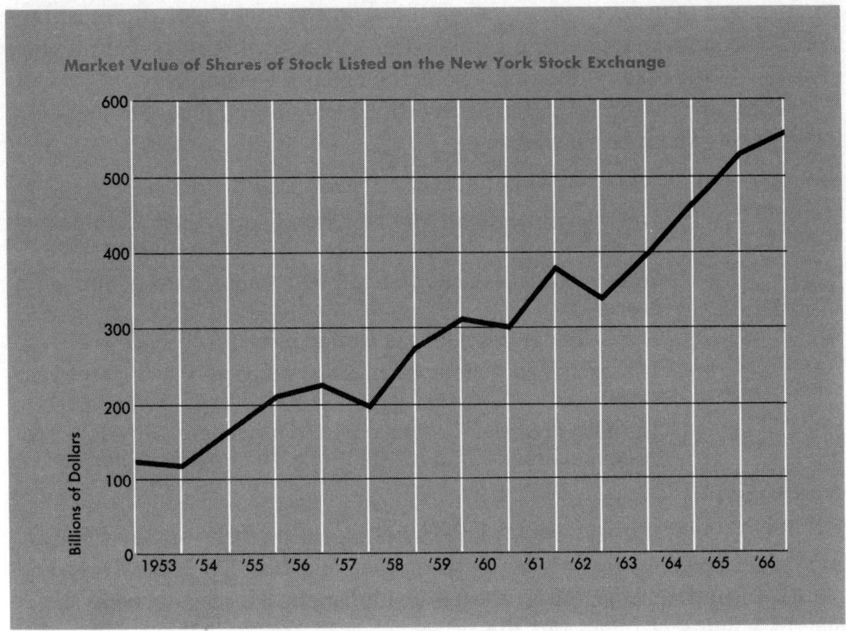

Source: Securities and Exchange Commission.

agents who are authorized to do business on the exchange. It is possible for two persons in widely separated parts of the United States, through their brokers, to trade with each other without any personal contact. You may wonder why you cannot buy a stock directly from an exchange or from a corporation, just as you buy an automobile from your dealer. This is because a corporation has only so many shares outstanding. Whether you want to buy

TABLE 16.2

THE 10 MOST WIDELY HELD CORPORATE STOCKS, AND THE NUMBER OF THEIR SHAREHOLDERS

American Telephone and Telegraph	3,089,600
General Motors	1,418,000
Standard Oil (New Jersey)	710,000
General Electric	515,290
General Telephone & Electronics	487,750
Ford Motor	393,000
United States Steel	372,513
International Business Machines	275,650
E. I. du Pont de Nemours	257,100
Bethlehem Steel	245,000

Source: *Financial World Stock Factograph*, 1967.

25, 100, or 1,000 shares of any stock listed on the exchange, you must buy from someone who owns (or a combination of those who own) that number of shares. The broker is the one who is the agent for each party.

There are certain facts that are worth keeping in mind concerning buying or selling stock on an exchange:

1. When you buy stock, you buy from another person through a broker.
2. When you sell stock, you sell to another person through a broker.
3. The exchange provides the market place for the sale.
4. The exchange neither buys, sells, nor sets the price of your stock.
5. Through their daily operations, the exchanges provide a continuous market with a constant release of market information.

Stock Quotations. Most daily newspapers publish, on the financial page, prices paid in stock transactions on the New York Stock Exchange and the American Exchange. This report is an alphabetical listing of stocks showing the volume of sales, and the prices, of each stock. The accompanying illustration (see facing page) is a partial list of stock quotations reported daily by *The Wall Street Journal.*

You will observe from this list that sales are recorded in lots of 100 shares, or in "round lots" on stock exchanges. "Odd lot" sales (less than 100 shares) are usually listed in a separate section of the newspaper. Price quotations are in dollars and fractions of dollars ranging from ⅛ to ⅞. Hence, a quotation of 25⅝ indicates the price is $25.625 per share. Following the name of each stock is the amount of the dividend paid to date, or other information, such as a footnote reference to a key shown below the list of stocks.

The diagram on page 448 explains in detail how to read a stock market quotation. (Your newspaper may not carry the various columns as shown in the illustration from *The Wall Street Journal.*)

Bond Quotations. In addition to stock prices (common and preferred), many newspapers list daily bond prices and their averages. Like stock quotations bond prices vary from day to day. The movement of these prices reflects the opinions of investors toward the value of bonds in relation to other types of investments. A bond selling below par or at a price less than face value is called a *discount.* A bond selling at higher than its face value or the amounts of its denomination is sold at a *premium.* By observing these daily fluctuations and the yields, businessmen can evaluate how the cost of financing by bonds compares with other forms of borrowing. If bond interest-rates are consistently low and at the same time there is a reasonable

Wednesday's Volume, 14,090,000 Shares

Volume since Jan. 1:	1968	1967	1966
Total sales	800,144,256	730,590,671	670,410,255

MOST ACTIVE STOCKS

	Open	High	Low	Close	Chg.	Volume
Occiden Pet	39¾	39¾	38¾	38¾	− ⅞	247,600
McDonnD	46⅜	46⅜	44⅞	45⅝	− ⅝	201,700
Libb Mc Nl	18¼	18¾	18¼	18¾	....	171,800
Benguet	11½	12¼	11⅜	12¼	+ ¾	165,700
Sunasco	9⅛	10½	9⅛	10⅛	+1⅞	143,700
Gulf Wn In	46½	46½	45	45⅛	−1⅞	130,000
Pan Am Sul	35	37⅜	35	36⅞	+2⅜	114,100
Glen Ald	12⅝	13⅜	12½	13¼	+ ⅞	113,000
Chrysler	65⅜	67½	65¼	66⅞	+1¾	104,000
Am Tel Tel	50⅝	50¾	50¼	50⅜	− ¼	99,400

Average closing price of most active stocks: 33.80.

A-B-C

−1968− High	Low	Stocks Div.	Sales in 100s	Open	High	Low	Close	Net Chg.
17⅛	15½	Abacus .62t	2	16	16	16	16	+ ⅛
53	41⅞	Abbott Lab 1	111	51⅝	52⅜	51	52⅜	+1¾
31¼	28	Abex Cp 1.60	117	29¼	29⅜	29¼	29⅜	+ ⅛
46½	39½	ACF Ind 2.20	42	45½	46¼	45½	46¼	+ ¼
40	36	Acme Mkt 2b	37	38¾	39	38¼	38½	..
17	16	Adams Exp	27	16⅞	17	16⅞	16⅞	− ⅛
63¾	38¼	AdMillis .40a	30	49	49	48¼	48⅝	− ⅜
25¼	22⅞	Ad Millis wi	18	24⅝	24⅝	24⅛	24⅛	− ⅝
80½	52	Address 1.40	45	63⅞	64	63⅜	63⅜	− ¼
25⅛	16½	Admiral	120	23⅛	23⅜	22½	22¾	− ¾
64	47¼	Aeroquip 1b	14	53⅞	53⅞	53⅛	53⅛	− ⅜
41⅝	32⅝	Air Prod .20b	27	35⅜	35½	35⅛	35¼	+ ¼
123½	106	Air Pd pf4.75	1	112	112	112	112	− ¼
36⅞	28½	AirRedtn 1.50	109	30⅞	30⅞	30½	30⅞	+ ⅜
12⅝	8⅛	AJ Industries	122	8⅝	8¾	8½	8¾	+ ⅛
19½	17⅜	Ala Gas .96	10	17⅞	18⅛	17⅞	18⅛	+ ⅛
43⅞	32	Alberto C .20	44	39¼	39¼	38½	39	− ⅛
27⅜	22	AlcanAlum 1	222	23	23¼	22¾	23¼	+ ¼
17⅞	12¼	Alleg Cp .20g	77	15⅝	15¾	15¼	15½	− ⅛
65	45	Alleg 6pf .60	8	54¾	54⅞	54	54	− ½
72¾	61¼	AllegLud 2.40	30	68	68	67⅜	67⅜	− ¾
24¼	20⅞	Alleg Pw 1.20	38	22	22¼	22	22⅛	+ ⅛
31⅞	24¾	AllenInd 1.40	30	30¼	30½	30	30½	..
43	34	AlliedCh 1.90	269	37	37⅜	36¾	37¼	+ ½

Courtesy The Wall Street Journal, Dow Jones & Co., Inc.

demand for bonds, a corporation may abandon plans to sell a new stock issue in favor of floating a bond issue.

Most bond quotations are in denominations of $100, although the usual face value is actually $1,000. For example, a bond quoted at 95 means that the actual trading price is $950 as of that quotation date. Actually, the quotation of 95 means the price is 95 percent of par or the price of its denomination.

There are several important differences between stock and bond quotations. For one thing, separate listings are shown for different types of bonds, such as U.S. Government bonds, foreign bonds, and domestic bonds. Another difference is that bond prices are quoted in denominations of $100 regardless of their face value. For example, a bond selling for 81½ would cost $815. The quotation of 81½ means 81½ percent of par, or of a denomination of $1,000. One selling for 124¼ would cost $1,242.50.

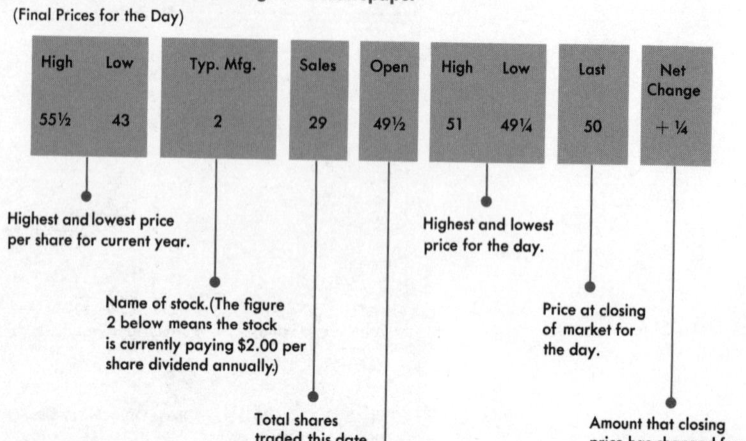
How to Read the Financial Page of a Newspaper
(Final Prices for the Day)
High
Low
55½
43
Typ. Mfg.
2
Sales
29
Open
49½
High
Low
51
49¼
Last
50
Net Change
+ ¼
Highest and lowest price per share for current year.
Name of stock.(The figure 2 below means the stock is currently paying $2.00 per share dividend annually.)
Total shares traded this date in round lots.
Price for first sale this date
Highest and lowest price for the day.
Price at closing of market for the day.
Amount that closing price has changed from previous day's close.

Courtesy The Wall Street Journal, Dow Jones & Co., Inc.

The trading-unit price variations for corporation bonds and foreign government bonds are quoted in ⅛ points and are expressed as a percent of par value. U.S. government and state bonds listed on the New York Stock Exchange or in the over-the-counter market are quoted in 1/32 points. Thus, a federal treasury obligation quoted at 102.12 is the same as 102 12/32, or 102⅜. On a $1,000 par bond, the price, therefore, would be $1,023.75. Stocks are traded and quoted in dollars a share in fractions of ⅛, ¼, ⅜, ½, ⅝, ¾, and ⅞.

Bond interest rate is also quoted as a percentage of par; thus "4½s" means that interest payments are 4.5 percent of par value of the bond per year. The list of bond quotations shown on page 449 from *The Wall Street Journal* shows a variety of quotations. The majority of bonds sell "with interest" or, as it is more often stated, "plus accrued interest." This means that if you sold the bond through your broker you would receive not only the sales price but the accrued interest from the date of the last payment, excluding the day of delivery.

Note the following illustration. Assume that you invested on December 29, 1968, in a $1,000 American Car 5 percent bond due in 1978 at 125. Interest is paid on February 1 and August 1. Because interest is computed on the basis of a 360-day year, every calendar month should be considered to be 1/12 of 360 days. In this case, a purchase on December 29, 1968, would not be delivered until January 5, 1969, which is the end of four full business

Corporation Bonds

Volume $16,050,000

A-B-C

—1968— High	Low	Bonds	Sales in $1,000	High	Low	Close	Net Chg.
118¼	97¼	Air Red cv3⅞s87	89	105	103¼	105	+1½
136	116¾	Allegh L cv4s81	1	128½	128½	128½	+1½
81½	77½	Allied Ch 3½s78	22	79⅝	79½	79½	−1¼
165	127¼	Allied St cv4½s81	33	165	158¼	164	+2½
111⅞	94½	Allied Str cv4½s92	238	110¾	109	110¾	+ ¾
114¼	103	AlliedSup cv5¾s87	69	110	108½	109	
113½	101½	Alcoa cv5¼s91	48	108	107¾	108	+1½
83¼	78½	Alcoa 4¼s82	5	79¾	79¾	79¾	.....
.....	.....	Alcoa 3s79 reg	10	73⅞	73⅞	73⅞	.....
97	94	Alum Can 3⅞s70	4	95¾	95¾	95¾	....
111⅛	95	Amerace cv5s92	15	108½	108	108	−1
113½	101¼	AAirFilt cv4⅞s87	1	110	110	110	..
119½	104⅜	AmAirlin cv5½s91	56	109½	109½	109½	− ½
89¾	76⅝	AmAirlin cv4¼s92	110	81½	80½	81½	+ ¾
114⅞	93	Am Airlin cv4s90	88	99¼	99	99¼	+1
100	96⅞	Am Can 6s97	4	96⅞	96⅞	96⅞	..
91⅛	84	Am Dist cv4⅜s86	50	88	88	88	+1
73	64¾	Am FP 5s2030	66	67	66¼	67	+ ¾
76½	65⅝	Am FP 4.80s87	63	70	70	70	
149	115⅝	Am Hoist cv4¾s92	27	122½	120	120½	− ½
79½	73¼	AmMFdy cv4¼s81	30	76½	75	76¼	+ ¼
85	79⅝	Am Sug 5.30s93	1	80⅛	80⅛	80⅛	+ ⅛
.....	.....	AmSug 5.30s93reg	2	80	80	80	...
83	79	Am T&T 4⅜s85	65	81	80¼	80⅞	+ ⅜
76⅛	71	Am T&T 3⅞s90	5	73½	73⅛	73⅛	+ ⅛
87½	84	Am T&T 3⅜s73	28	86⅛	86	86	− ¾
74½	68	Am T&T 3¼s84	16	69¼	69	69	−1
91⅝	89½	Am T&T 2¾s71	20	91⅛	90⅞	91⅛	...
82	77	Am T&T 2¾s75	61	78¾	78¼	78¾	+1
72⅞	67	Am T&T 2¾s80	17	70	69½	70	+ ½
70⅞	66½	Am T&T 2¾s82	1	68½	68½	68½	+ ½
67½	62½	Am T&T 2⅝s86	9	64	63	64	+1
99⅞	88	Am Tob 5⅞s92	5	93⅞	93⅞	93⅞	
97⅛	95	Am Tob 3s69	7	96¾	96¾	96¾	− ⅜
138	110	Ampex cv 5¼s91	52	122	121	121½	+1½
116	102⅛	Apco Oil cv5s87	16	108⅛	108	108	+1½
82½	78¼	Armco 4½s 86	2	79¾	79¾	79¾	− ¼
84	76	Armour&Co 5s84	9	79	78	78	− ½
103	85	Armour cv 4½s83	77	91	88½	88½	−2½
107	99	ArmsRub cv4½s87	16	105⅜	105⅜	105⅜	− ½
101	99½	Assoc Inv 6¼s70	46	100⅛	100	100	− ⅛
76¾	72	Atchison 4s95	18	72½	71½	72½	+ ½
73½	69	Atchison 4s95st	2	69	69	69	− ⅛
88¾	79	AuroraPl cv4⅝s80	20	88	85	85	−3
100	91½	AutoCan cv4¾s81	21	94½	94	94½	+1
126	74½	AutoSpkr cv4⅜s87	82	79½	78⅝	78¾	− ¾
109	90	B&O cv 4½s2010f	10	104½	104	104	− ½
62	58	B&O cv4½s2010 A	1	58¼	58¼	58¼	− ⅛
66½	60½	B&O 4¼s 95	1	61⅛	61⅛	61⅛	+ ⅝
72⅛	68	B&O 4s 80	2	70	70	70	+ ⅜
93¾	91⅛	B&O 3⅞s 70	4	93½	93½	93½	
78	70¼	BangorPun 5¾s92	7	71¼	71¼	71¼	+ ¼
201	120	BangPun cv5½s87	65	146	145	145½	+2¾
....	..	Baxt Lab cv4½s88	37	116	115½	115½	
142⅜	112	Baxter Lab cv4s87	16	135½	135½	135½	+ ½
80¾	72	Beaunit cv4¼s90	30	76	75	76	..
103¼	98¼	BendixCorp 6⅝s92	9	101¼	101¼	101¼	− ½
102	98	Benef Fin 6¼s70	20	101	100½	101	+ ½
101½	96	Benef Fin 5.60s71	115	97⅞	96¾	97⅞	+ ⅝

Courtesy The Wall Street Journal, Dow Jones & Co., Inc.

days (Saturday, Sunday, and holidays are not counted). The computation would be:

$1,000	American Car 5% bond 1978 at 125	$1,250.00
plus	Accrued interest (154 days as shown below)	21.39
plus	Commission	2.50
	Total cost	$1,273.89

Interest on American Car bonds is paid semiannually—let us say on February 1 and August 1. Each payment amounts to $25. Therefore, in this example, accrued interest from the date of last payment to January 5 would be for the following days:

August	30 days
September	30
October	30
November	30
December	30
January	4
Total	154 days

As the seller, you are entitled to interest on the $1,000 bond for 154⁄360 of a year at 5 percent. Based on the 154 days, the interest amounts to $21.39. In addition to the interest, you would receive $1,250, because the bond sold at a premium, less the $2.50 commission, less the Securities and Exchange registration fee of 3¢ and a transfer tax of 50¢, or a net of $1,268.36, assuming that this transaction occurred on the New York Stock Exchange market.

The Role of the Stockbroker

Whether you live in Cheyene or Chicago, if you want to buy or sell stocks or bonds, you place your order with the local stockbroker. It is the role of the stockbroker to deal with the public interested in buying securities, and actually, as we have seen, it is stockbrokers who make organized exchanges possible. The modern brokerage house is the source of a vast amount of information on market conditions, on the financial condition of individual companies and various industries, and on the general economic conditions prevailing. Much of these data are gathered by the research departments of brokerage firms. Each brokerage firm consists of several brokers skilled in investment counseling and in helping customers to reach a decision as to which securities to buy or sell.

The Member Firm. On January 1, 1967, there were 649 member firms with over 3,701 offices in approximately 865 cities in the United States and

24 foreign countries. These member firms own seats on the exchanges as private partnerships or corporations. Stockbrokers working for these member firms receive orders from customers and transmit them to the New York or American Stock Exchange or to the smaller regional exchanges. In some brokerage firms, the stockbroker is called an "account executive," a "customer's man," or a "stock salesman." The Securities and Exchange Commission often refers to him as a "registered representative." Regardless of the title you may use to identify him, as a member of the firm, he must have passed the examinations given by the New York Stock Exchange or American Stock Exchange and by the National Association of Security Dealers. Adequate training by the firm is a prerequisite to successful completion of the required examinations. Even security salesmen of member firms that limit their activities to local trading in over-the-counter securities must take the examination.

Many brokerage offices are equipped with a large Teleregister board, which automatically records price changes of several hundred popular stocks. The board may show the symbol for the stock, plus the previous day's closing price and the open, high, low, and last prices—or perhaps simply the symbol and the last price. Through the courtesy of Merrill Lynch, Pierce, Fenner & Smith, Inc., a national brokerage firm, a sample ticker-tape is illustrated below.[3] Only the price is shown when the sale is for 100 shares (a "round lot"). For sales from 100 to 1,000 shares, the number of 100's is printed. For sales above 1,000, the exact number is printed.

J	SOM	T	BSP_r	F
$50\frac{7}{8}$	3s49	$108\frac{1}{2}$	$146\frac{1}{4}$	1000s$82\frac{1}{2}$

If the stock you are interested in is not on the "Board," your account executive in his office can dial a special number, and the last sale- and bid-and-asked prices of that stock will appear on a vacant panel in the board via Telequote service. Board-watching has in recent years become a favorite activity for many Americans.

Brokerage firms also provide customers with such market services as financial facts about corporations whose stock is listed, and all kinds of announcements about business conditions. This information is useful to buyers in helping them to select securities.

[3] A small portion of the tickertape is shown in this illustration which shows the following sales of common stocks: J—Standard Oil Company (New Jersey), 100 shares at \$50.87½ per share; SOM—Socony Mobile, Inc., 300 shares at \$49 per share; T—American Telephone and Telegraph Company, 100 shares at \$108.50; BSP_r—Bethlehem Steel Corporation, 100 shares preferred at \$146.25; and F—Ford Motor Company, 1,000 shares at \$82.50 per share.

Investing vs. Speculation

Should you decide to invest in securities (stocks or bonds), be certain that you are really investing to achieve a clearly defined objective, and not just speculating in an effort to make a big profit quickly. The stock market offers many speculative opportunities, but one should not attempt to take advantage of such opportunities unless he can afford to lose what he invests, for the risks are ever-present. (However, it is a fact that the professional market speculator plays a valuable role in the market. Prices of stocks might drop drastically if it were not for the willingness of such speculators to assume more risk than conservative investors do.)

Before buying any stock, one should have a savings account, which may be used if necessary for an emergency, and a reasonable amount of life and health insurance. The emergency fund should be adequate to carry dependents (if only oneself) through a temporary loss of employment, or a period of illness. The important point is to have sufficient savings so that the investor will not be required to sell his securities to meet an emergency.

Three Major Investment Objectives. If you have a sum of money that you want to keep intact for a specific purpose, *safety of principal* becomes your first important objective. Since safety of principal has historically been associated with bonds, some people assume that any purchase of bonds is safe investing, and that all investing in stocks is speculative. This is a false assumption because some bonds are highly speculative and some stocks offer a high degree of safety.

Let's assume that you are primarily interested in supplementing your regular income and that *dividend income* (or just plain income) is your second investment objective. According to the brokerage firm of Merrill Lynch, Pierce, Fenner & Smith, Inc., more than 85 percent of common stocks listed on the New York Stock Exchange during the past decade have paid cash dividends averaging from 3.3 to 6.1 percent. Some companies have yielded more, and others less.

Income that you receive from your securities may be called the "return on your investment" or "the yield." How do you calculate yield? A stock that cost you $50 a share and pays $2 annual dividend is yielding a return of 4 percent ($2 ÷ $50). Should the stock advance to $60 with the annual dividend remaining the same, the yield will change to slightly over 3 percent ($2 ÷ $60). If the stock goes down to $40 and the dividend remains the same, the yield will change to 5 percent ($2 ÷ $40). In all three of these illustrations, the yield changes when either the price or the dividend changes.

A popular third objective is to achieve *growth of capital*. This is accomplished by investing in growth stocks. A *growth stock* is one whose earnings

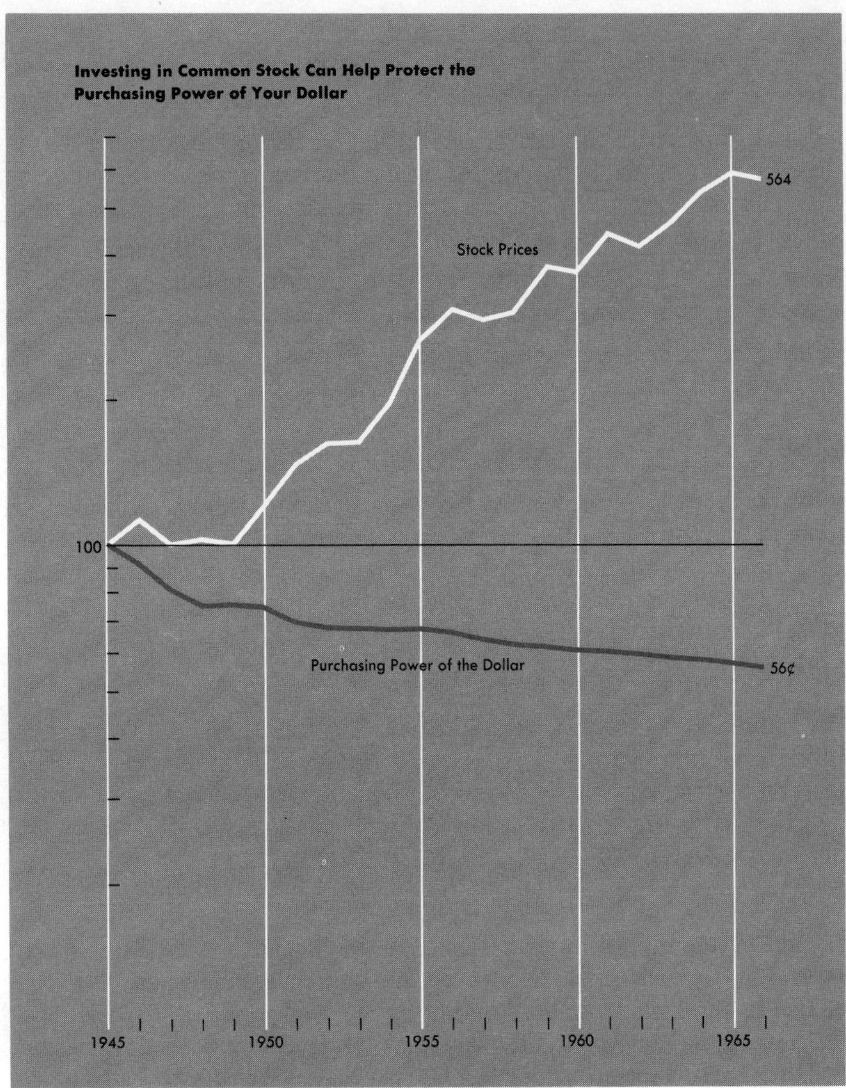

Courtesy Merrill Lynch, Pierce, Fenner & Smith, Inc.

have increased, and are anticipated to continue increasing, at a faster-than-average rate over a period of time (such as several years). Growth companies usually plow back into the business the bulk of their earnings, and consequently pay smaller dividends as compared with income stocks. When you buy a growth stock, it is generally assumed that you are willing to forego present income for the possibility that your stock will increase substantially

International Business Machines

Courtesy: M. C. Horsey & Company, Salisbury, Maryland

in value in future years. International Business Machines is an example of a well-known growth stock. Notice on the accompanying chart how the market price of the stock rose during the 10-year period 1957–1966; also that during the same period the company engaged in five stock splits and that dividends jumped from 55¢ to $4.30 per share. (There is a tax advantage in owning growth stocks when you sell your shares, assuming that you owned them six months or longer and that they have appreciated substantially.) Choosing growth industries is not as difficult as selecting promising growth-stocks in individual corporations.

Some companies enjoy a high level of prosperity when general business conditions are good, but their earnings decline, sometimes rather sharply, when the economic cycle turns down. To investors such companies are known as *cyclical companies* and their securities as nongrowth securities. The prices of nongrowth securities rise and fall in varying degrees depending

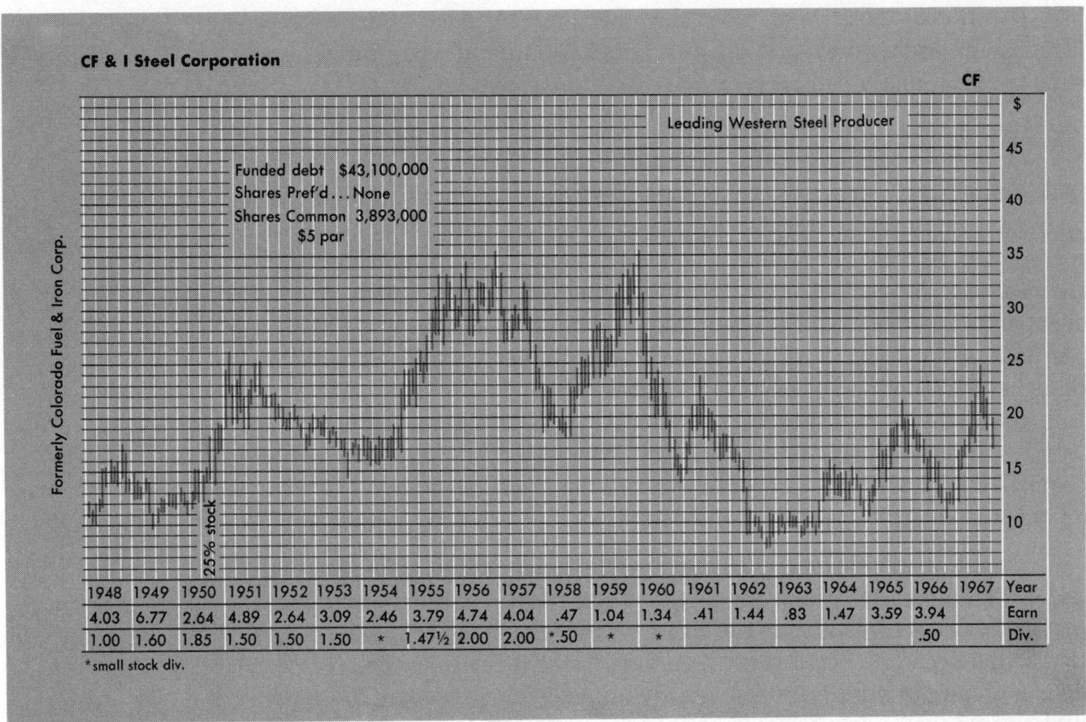

Courtesy: M. C. Horsey & Company, Salisbury, Maryland

upon the annual earnings. The accompanying chart of the CF&I Steel Corporation is an example of a cyclical company. Notice from the chart how the market prices and earnings of the company over a 15-year period fluctuated with changing business conditions. During periods of business prosperity both earnings and stock prices increased sharply. Conversely, a downturn in business conditions produced a drop in earnings followed by a decline in security prices. So-called growth stocks are popular with investors who seek a substantial return over a long-range period. Cyclical stocks more often appeal to investors looking for short-run returns.

Dividends

As we previously noted, a dividend is a distribution of corporate earnings paid to stockholders in the form of cash or in property, or it may be in additional shares of stock. At the time the corporation directors declare a dividend, there are four important dates to be established. They are (1) the declaration date, (2) the record date, (3) the ex-dividend date, and (4) the payment date.

The Declaration Date. The day the directors meet and declare a "regular" or "extra" dividend is known as the *declaration date.* (Under most state laws, dividends can be paid only if there is a surplus.)

The Record Date. The date on which a list is made, by the corporation, of all the stockholders who will receive the declared dividend, is the *record date.* To be eligible to receive the declared dividend, you must have your name on the list of stockholders, as an owner of shares, on or before the record date. As soon as you buy a share of stock, your name is recorded on the company books, usually by a bank acting as the corporation transfer agent. Often a corporation appoints another bank to act as the registrar. It is the duty of the registrar to check the transfer agent to make certain that there has been no fraudulent issue of shares.

Were you to buy stock up to four days prior to the record date, you would still have time to obtain delivery of this stock through the regular channels and have your name placed on the books in time to become a holder of record to receive the dividend.

The Ex-Dividend Date. The term *ex-dividend date* is used to establish the date on and after which the buyer of stock is *not* entitled to receive a previously declared dividend. The rule for determining the ex-dividend date is that the securities (common or preferred stock) shall be declared "ex-dividend" *on the third full business day* immediately preceding the record date, provided this date falls on a full business day. Should the record date fall on a holiday or any day other than a full business day, the ex-dividend date is the *fourth* full business day preceding the date of record.

For example, if you buy a share of stock traded ex-dividend on a Tuesday which is the third business day before the date of record (and Friday is the date of record), then you acquire the stock without the right to receive the dividend. But if you buy the stock on the preceding Monday, you receive the dividend.

The Payment Date. On the *payment date* you are eligible to receive the dividend.

Investment Procedures

Having determined an investment objective, the investor must then select one or more of the individual corporations in which he desires to invest. Even with the advice of a competent security broker who may have numerous financial services at hand, making the choice is difficult.

Selecting a Stock. The first step in selecting a particular stock is to pick out an industry which produces goods or services that are widely used and needed. For example, picking out a growth industry (if growth is your investment objective) is not too difficult, but choosing the most promising stock in the industry requires more study and analysis. Even in an industry wherein companies are expanding and increasing their profits, there may be other companies that are not showing signs of growth. You should note whether the industry is cyclical (subject to major ups and downs) or relatively stable. Does the industry as a whole depend to a great extent on war for its business? Or is it a non-war-dependent and growing industry, with new products and discoveries?

The second step is to select two or three better-grade stocks in the industry. Ask these questions about each of the stocks:

1. How good is the company's management record?
2. Has the company's past performance been good? A good performance record is one when the company has been doubling its per-share earnings every five to eight years.
3. What is the growth record of the company's dividend performance over the past several years? Have dividends increased or decreased?
4. What is the relationship of the price of the stock to the company's earnings per share? (The ratio of price to earnings for a given fiscal period is called the *price-earnings ratio.* For example, if a company is earning $2 a share annually and selling for $30 a share, its price-earnings ratio is 15 to 1.) For growth stocks, the price-earnings ratio is well above a 20-to-1 ratio as a general rule; whereas, for income stocks the price-earnings ratio is more likely to be lower.
5. Have annual sales as well as earnings been increasing?
6. What rating does the company have in published investment manuals?
7. Is the stock listed on one of the major exchanges? (There are two advantages to being listed. One is that more facts about the stock, such as daily quotations and financial information, are available. The other is that the stock can generally be sold without delay or difficulty.) One must recognize that there are good stocks whose companies are not on major exchanges, but available over-the-counter.

Opening an Account. Your next step may be to open an account with a broker. The procedure is much like opening a charge-account with a merchant. You need to furnish such information as your occupation and address, the name of your employer, and your Social Security number. When your account is open, you can buy or sell over the telephone. You are expected to pay for your purchases within the four business days shown on your invoice from the broker. (You will of course want to discuss fully with your broker the two or three stocks you have selected, before making a final choice.)

HOW COMMON STOCKS GROW IN VALUE

Company	$1,000 Invested in These Companies in 1917 Was Worth in 1967	Company	$1,000 Invested in These Companies in 1945 Was Worth in 1967
General Motors	$84,977.80	International Business Machines	$98,529.26
Eastman Kodak	84,244.85	Eastman Kodak	21,703.10
National Lead	66,828.18	Lockheed Aircraft	14,527.83
E. I. du Pont	63,829.02	Radio Corp. of America	12,114.83
Sears, Roebuck	54,102.29	Texas Corp. (Texaco)	11,563.02
Corn Products	49,725.38	United Aircraft	11,439.58
Gulf Oil Corp.	41,111.29	Goodyear Tire & Rubber	11,411.12
National Distillers & Chemical	36,667.47	Sears, Roebuck	11,053.68
General Electric	35,329.24	Shell Union Oil (Shell Oil)	10,624.65
American Can	33,972.12	Union Oil of California	10,467.65
International Nickel	31,159.95	Gulf Oil Corp.	10,095.20
Deere & Co.	26,793.22	Firestone Tire & Rubber	9,883.67
Procter & Gamble	25,654.17		

Source: Adapted from *Forbes* magazine Vol. 100, No. 6 (September 15, 1967) pp. 92–98.

Security Analysis Sources

Whether one merely dabbles in the stock market or invests many thousands of dollars, he invariably demands up-to-the-minute financial and business information beyond that which is published in the daily newspaper. There are numerous sources of information available, and we shall discuss these under two general headings: *financial services and annual reports* from corporations, and *professional investment counseling.*

Financial Services and Annual Reports. Two of the best-known stock market services that contain stock prices, corporate earnings, dividends, and summaries of financial data are *Moody's Investors' Service* and Standard & Poor's *Industry Surveys.* Both of these services may be purchased by subscription in the form of a loose-leaf type of publication. Annual reports of corporations have a large amount of current information on sales trends, the products of the companies, earnings, and the growth of company income and assets. Most of these reports contain pictures of company products.

There are also several well-known investment services, such as *United Business Service,* 210 Newbury St., Boston; *Babson's Investment and Barometer Letter,* Wellesley Hills, Mass., and *The Value Line Investment Survey,* 5 E. 44th St., New York, N.Y. All three of these investment services are sources of financial information about stocks and bonds reflecting professional opinions as to security ratings, market trends, and investment recommendations.

Among the better-known financial magazines published either weekly or twice monthly are *Forbes* magazine, 60 Fifth Ave., New York, N.Y.; *Financial World,* 17 Battery Place, New York, N.Y.; and *Barron's,* 30 Broad St., New York, N.Y. Several of these publications make stock recommendations. They are primarily useful for keeping abreast of company and industrial developments. Several magazines also list periodic reports on corporation earnings.

Professional Investment Counseling. Some investors rely mainly on their stockbrokers in making decisions as to what to buy and sell. Others use the services of a professional investment counselor, even assigning him full responsibility for making portfolio investments and paying little or no attention to his routine investment decisions. The usual charge by the counselor is an annual fee of ½ percent of the average value of the portfolio, with a minimum fee of $500. Counselors with 10 or more clients are required to register with the SEC. Pages of financial journals and business newspapers abound with advertisements of investment counselors, who often maintain a stock-market publication service. (The drawback for the small or modest investor is that the fees charged may cost more than the gains received from such service.) Another type of investment counselor is the *investment trust manager,* the kind employed by mutual funds and trust estates that hold large blocks of stocks and bonds.

Stock Averages and Price Indexes

To keep up-to-date and at the same time understand the daily market behavior as reflected by advances or declines of stocks and bonds is difficult and time-consuming. Accordingly, several different indexes are compiled daily to show price trends in security investments. In the field of stock prices there are two types of indexes: *averages,* and *index numbers.* Both of these terms were discussed in Chapter 9.

Two of the better-known stock-price averages are the *Dow-Jones* and *New York Times* averages. Both of these are averages of daily stock prices quoted in dollars. Whenever you want to know how the market is doing, you can find out by checking one of the quotations which tells the average price decline or advance for a given number of companies for that day. These averages are published in newspapers and reported over radio and television. The Dow-Jones averages consist of four different groups of stocks and five bond price-indexes. The four stock-indexes are based on the average of (1) 30 selected industrial stocks, (2) 20 representative railroad stocks, (3) 15 public-utility stocks, and (4) a composite of all 65 representative stocks. The bond indexes consist of the average prices of a certain number of high-grade railroad bonds, selected second-grade railroad bonds, selected public-utility bonds, representative industrial bonds, and a general composite of selected bonds.

A *stock price-index* such as published by *Standard & Poor's* or the *New York Stock Exchange Common Stock Index* is an average of the relative changes in prices of all the common stocks used in the index stated with reference to a base—usually 100. In the case of Standard & Poor's daily stock price index, the market value is expressed as an index number with the period 1941 to 1943 serving as the base equal to 10. The New York Stock Exchange Common Stock Index uses 50 as its base. The following illustration showing the New York Stock Exchange index compares the common-stock index with the average daily volume for approximately 1,250 common stocks traded on the New York Stock Exchange.

The Mechanics of Placing an Order

Let's assume that you have talked with you local stock broker and now you have decided to buy some shares of stock in General Electric as an investment. First, your broker tells you that General Electric common is being quoted on the New York Stock Exchange "65 to a quarter." This means that, at the moment, the highest bid to buy General Electric common is $65 a share, and the lowest offer to sell is $65.25. You decide to order 100 shares, which will cost you about $6,500, plus commission of $45.50, and state tax, if any.

Your order for 100 shares is teletyped to the New York office of your brokerage firm and relayed to your broker's booth on the floor of the Exchange. There, one of the firm's floor brokers goes to the trading post where G.E. is being bought and sold. There are 18 of these posts on the floor, and all transactions in a given stock must take place at its assigned post station. About 80 different stocks are traded at each of these posts.

At just about the same time you decide to buy G.E., a certain Mr. Snow in St. Louis decides to sell 100 shares of G.E. He calls his broker, obtains a "quote," and then instructs him to sell the shares at the market price.

Mr. Snow's "sell" order is teletyped to New York. His broker also goes to the G.E. post. Your broker calls out, "How's G.E.?" Someone answers, "65 to a quarter." Your broker could, without further thought, buy 100 shares at 65¼, or Snow's broker could sell his 100 shares at 65. Now, had the former occurred, both customers might have said to their brokers, "Why didn't you try to get a better price for me? After all, this is what a broker is supposed to do for his client."

Actually, your broker knows that someone has already bid 65 for 100 shares and has found no one willing to sell at that price. So he raises the offer to 65⅛. And, since Snow's broker has had no luck trying to sell at 65¼, he decides he had better try to get 65⅛. So when he hears your broker bid 65⅛, he instantly shouts, "Sold 100 at 65⅛." This means that both parties to the transaction have agreed on a price and that the transaction is now completed. This is the sort of transaction that is constantly taking place on the Exchange floor.[4]

Suppose you had wanted to invest on a more modest scale and had asked your broker to buy only one share of stock. Such an order is known as an odd-lot share. An additional fee is charged for this service by the odd-lot dealer, who must buy 100 shares in order to furnish anyone with any number less than 100. After delivering your share to your broker, he must be able to sell the remaining 99 shares to other buyers without taking a loss. For this added risk he is allowed an *odd-lot differential.*

The entire transaction is made with remarkable speed and accuracy. Within a day or two you are notified of the cost of your stock, including commission and tax. Your shares are delivered to you by mail at the address you gave your local broker. Or you may have the shares sent to your broker, who keeps them for you as your agent.

The stock exchanges require that all stocks bought and sold must clear through a duly appointed transfer agent and a registrar who are responsible for all transfers and recordings of the stock. In larger companies they are usually trust companies. In quite small corporations, a company officer is used as the transfer agent. The transfer agent is required to maintain a stockholders' ledger which shows the names and addresses of all shareholders, the date of acquisition, number of shares, and serial numbers of each stock certificate, and the amount paid for each share.

The corporation registrar keeps records of the total number of authorized shares of all kinds, the number outstanding, the number unissued, and the total shares in the treasury. He is responsible for seeing that no fraudulent issues or errors occur. He must sign every stock certificate that is issued.

The commission paid the broker is based on the number of shares and the amount of money involved in each transaction. On the average, the commission amounts to about 1 percent, with a $6 minimum. For odd-lot transactions the commission is slightly higher than for round-lot orders.

For example, if you bought or sold one share priced at $24.38, the commission would be $1.46. On 10 shares priced at $50 a share, the rate is $10.

[4] Since 1954, the New York Stock Exchange has operated an installment stock purchase plan known as the "Monthly Investment Plan," which is operated by the members of the Exchange for the public. This plan makes it possible to buy listed common stocks through regular monthly payments, which may be as low as $40 quarterly. It works this way: you go to a broker who is a member of the New York Stock Exchange, and select your stock. Then you decide how much you can afford to invest each month or quarter. You sign a cancellable agreement whereby you undertake to make payments regularly. There is no penalty if you miss a couple of payments. Your broker, however, reserves the right to terminate the plan if you miss four consecutive payments. Each payment, less the commission, will be invested in full and fractional shares of your stock. (The Los Angeles Stock Exchange operates a similar plan.)

New York Stock Exchange Common Stock Index and Daily Average Volume

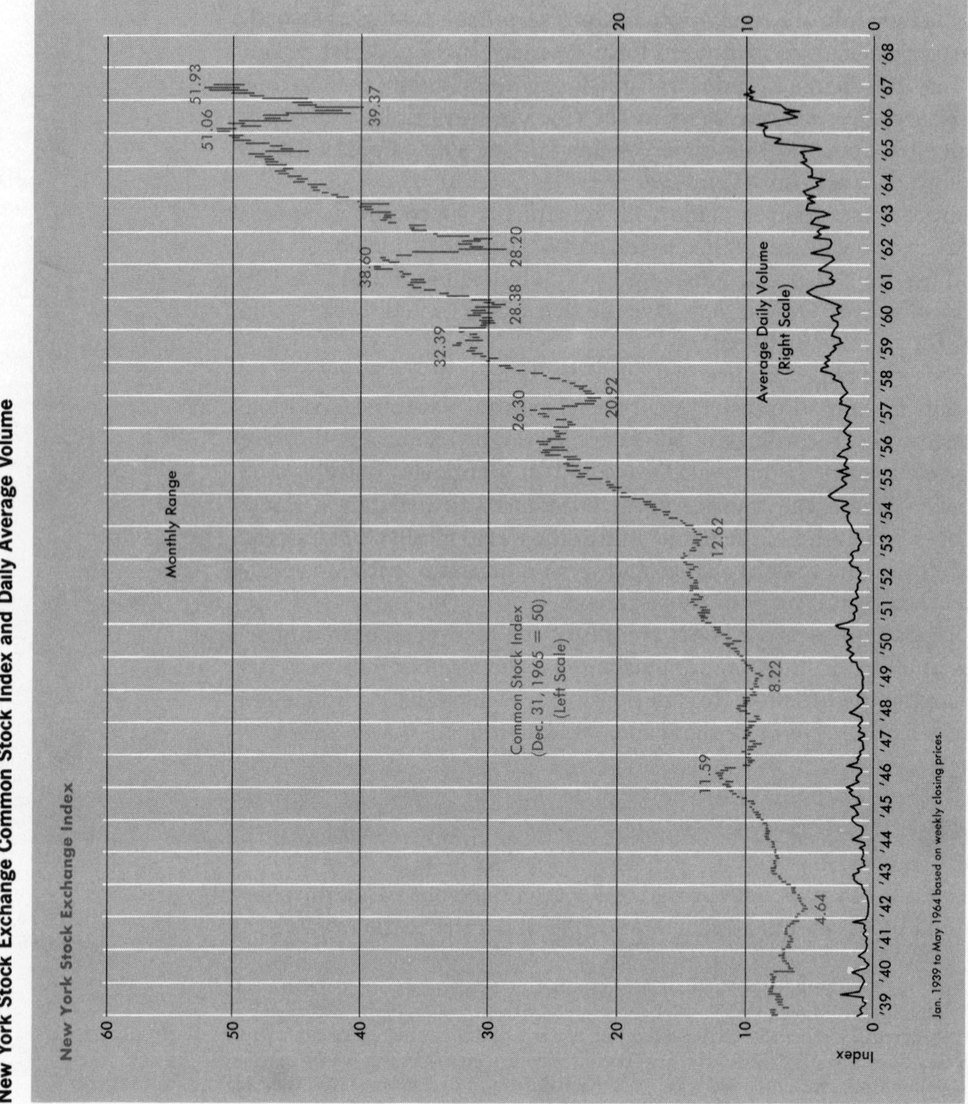

Courtesy New York Stock Exchange.

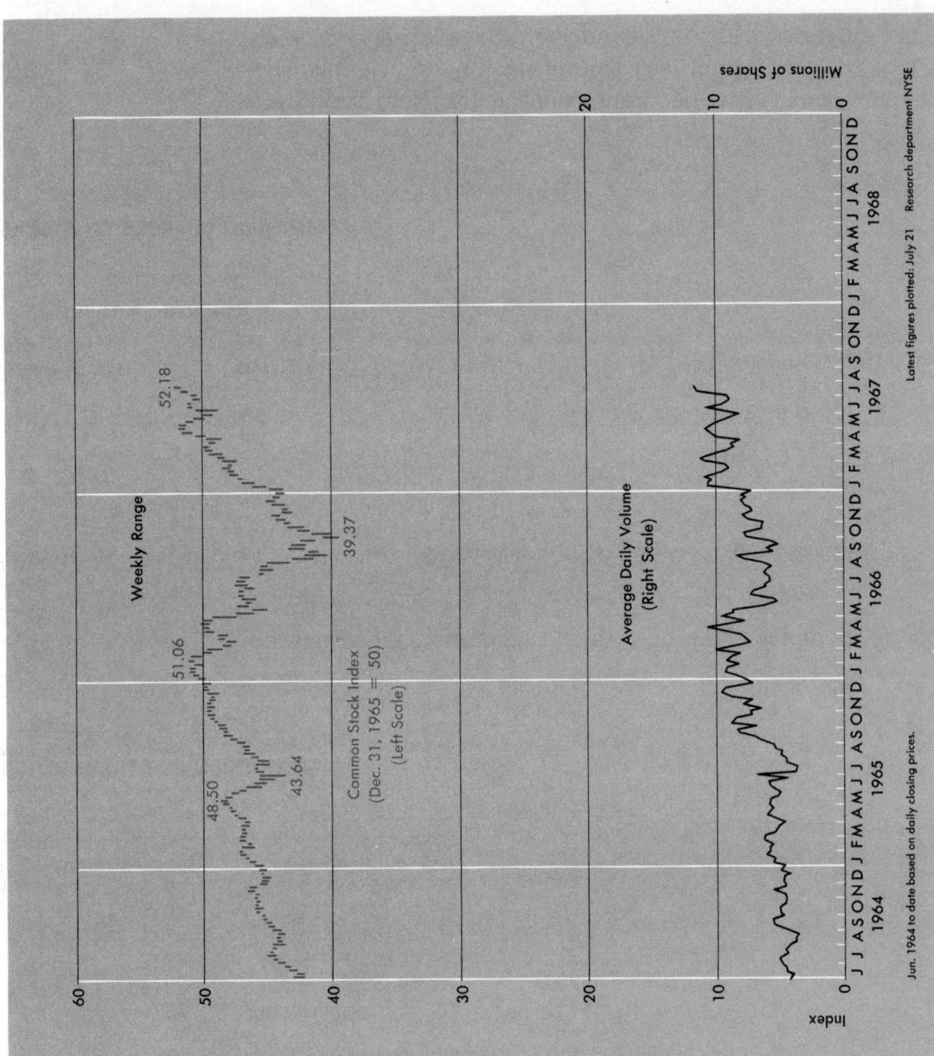

Courtesy New York Stock Exchange.

For 100 shares at $1.50 per share, the commission is $6. If the total value of a single transaction is $100 or more, the minimum commission is $6 per transaction. On a transaction involving $5,000 or more, the rate is ⅒ of 1 percent of the amount of the sale, plus $39. The minimum commission on a 100-share transaction is $75.

The commission varies with the size of the order—a proportionately smaller amount is paid on large orders than on small ones. The following shows the minimum commission per transaction on the New York Stock Exchange.

COMMISSION CHARGES ON STOCKS

	Minimum commission per transaction		
		Plus stated amounts	
Total Amount Involved	Percent of Money Involved	For 100 Shares	For Less Than 100 Shares
$ 100 to $ 399	2	$ 3*	$ 1*
400 to 2,399	1	7	5
2,400 to 4,999	½	19	17
5,000 and above	⅒	39	37

* Minimum $6. If money involved is under $100, minimum commission is mutually agreed upon.

The following examples show how these commission rates may be applied.

COMMISSION PER TRANSACTION

Money involved	100 Shares	Less Than 100 Shares*
$ 100	$ 6 (minimum)	$ 6 (minimum)
400	11 ($3 + 2%)	9 ($1 + 2%)
2,000	27 ($7 + 1%)	25 ($5 + 1%)
4,000	39 ($19 + ½%)	37 ($17 + ½%)
10,000	49 ($39 + ⅒%)	47 ($37 + ⅒%)
25,000	64 ($39 + ⅒%)	62 ($37 + ⅒%)
50,000	75 (top minimum)	75 (top minimum)

* Subject to the top minimum of $1.50 per share.

The following is a comparison of commission charges on a small order and on a large one based on round-lot-orders prices for 100 shares.

Name of Company	Price Per Share	Price Per 100 Shares	Broker's Commission	Percent of Commission to the Total Purchase Price
Alpha	$ 6	$ 600	$13.00	2.16
Beta	30	3,000	34.00	1.13
Gamma	100	10,000	49.00	.049

In addition to commission charges, both the federal government and the state of New York levy a tax on the transfer of shares which is paid by the seller. The federal transfer tax—4¢ per $100 of actual value of the shares transferred—is paid by the seller. The minimum tax per transaction is 4¢; the maximum is 8¢ (on stocks selling at $200 or more). Odd-lot (less than 100 shares) purchases on a national exchange are exempt from the federal transfer stock tax. The New York state tax ranges from 1¢ to 4¢ per share.

Selling Short. Another type of stock exchange transaction is known as *selling short,* which may be defined as *the sale of stock which the seller does not own but which he expects to acquire in the future.* In practice, it works like this: you predict a drop in the price of a certain stock, so you decide to sell some of that stock "short" (in one respect, short of owning it), hoping at a later date to make a profit because you plan to buy it back at a lower price than you will shortly have sold it for. Of course, in order to deliver the shares you are selling short, you must borrow them from someone. The broker to whom you give the order will arrange for you to borrow the stock, either from one of his clients who has authorized his stock to be used for this purpose, or from another broker. Actually, there is no time limit within which you must return the shares to the lender. So, when you feel that the price of the stock has dropped to the point where you can make a sufficient profit, you place a "buy" order with your broker, to buy back the same number of shares you previously sold short. This enables you to return the shares you borrowed, and complete the transaction. If the price per share for the stock you just bought is lower than the price at which you sold short, you have made a profit. If the stock failed to drop, and actually advanced, then you have incurred a loss.

Here is an illustration. Assume that you sell short 100 shares of X stock at $50 a share. Two weeks later this stock drops to $35 a share, so you buy it back. You have made a gross profit of $15 a share. If, however, during this period the stock jumps to $60, then you have lost $10 a share (assuming you executed your order to buy it back). There are regulations in effect under the Security Exchange Act of 1934 both to permit the justified use of short selling and to curtail its abuses.

REGULATION OF SECURITY TRANSACTIONS

Control over the securities market is a responsibility of both the states and the federal government. It was not, however, until federal legislation was passed in the early 1930's that any degree of success was achieved in detecting and prosecuting market manipulators and stock swindlers.

State Regulation of Securities

"Blue-sky" Laws. To create more confidence among investors, nearly all states have in recent years enacted legislation in some form aimed at regulating the sale of new securities and activities of security dealers and brokers. Kansas, in 1911, passed the first of these laws, which came to be known as "blue-sky" laws because they were intended to stop the sale of fraudulent securities with nothing of substance—"nothing but the blue sky"—to back them. There is wide variation among state laws, and generalizations are difficult. Suffice it to say that today all states except Nevada have blue-sky laws designed to: (1) provide more supervision over registration of securities, (2) require registration of dealers, and (3) protect the public against fraud in the securities market. Although these laws are somewhat effective within each state, they offer no control over interstate sales. Thus, by residing in one state and doing business in another, a promoter can escape the regulations of *both* states. It is evident why federal laws have had to be enacted.

Federal Regulations of Securities

Early in 1928, when stock prices were skyrocketing, almost everyone on Wall Street who followed the market knew about (but was not concerned over) certain manipulative practices that were taking place. Rather than condemn such deception, the general public seemed to welcome it—tips of all kinds with the aid of which they could buy and sell stocks and bonds and thus share in illegitimate profits. The collapse of the market in October of 1929, which resulted in financial ruin for thousands of persons and subsequently in economic chaos for the nation, produced a popular clamor for federal legislation.

In March, 1932, the Senate passed a resolution calling for investigation, mainly of short selling. By the time Ferdinand Pecora was appointed as counsel to the committee, the scope of the committee's activities had been broadened to include a study of the entire securities market, involving organized exchanges in New York.

The Securities Act of 1933. The first Congressional effort to eliminate abuses involved in the interstate sale of securities was the Securities Act of 1933. The primary purpose of this act was to require that the public be furnished with financial and related information concerning securities. A second purpose involved prohibition of misrepresentation and other fraudulent acts in the sale of securities, regardless of whether registration of the securities is required. This law made anyone who signed a registration certificate of new-stock issue liable to the purchaser for any investment losses sustained if the certificate omitted material facts or included any misleading statements. Also, every investment bank was required to furnish a *prospectus*—a detailed description of the business, its properties, its proposed capitalization, and its financial condition—when new stock was offered for sale.

The Securities and Exchange Act of 1934. The "Act of 1934" was designed to accomplish three major goals:

1. To prevent a disproportionate amount of the reserves of a financial institution from being spent on stock-market securities. The SEC is authorized to restrict *margin* borrowing by members of exchanges, brokers, and dealers.[5]
2. To give the public current information about the financial condition of corporations whose securities are traded on the security market.
3. To prevent corporations from manipulating stock-market transactions in order to give misleading information about the popularity of a stock.

The requirement that all corporations having their securities listed on a national exchange must file a registration statement with the SEC was further strengthened by requiring from these corporations periodic reports, thus helping investors to keep better informed of company conditions.

The over-the-counter markets in addition to the national exchanges, were included under the jurisdiction of the SEC as defined in the 1934 Act. Restrictions have also been placed on the trading activities of corporation officers, to prohibit them from taking advantage of secret information to

[5] When stock is bought "on margin," the buyer puts up the "margin" and borrows the remainder of the price from his broker. The buyer pays interest and pledges the stock as collateral. If the price of the stock drops, the borrower's equity, which is the value of the stock minus the loan, drops, too. When the value of the stock falls below the minimum required, the broker will call for more margin. If the borrower cannot do this, the broker will sell the stock and collect the loan. Buying on margin is a means to magnify gains. Prior to 1929, the margin requirement was 10 percent. It has been as high as 100 percent. On July 9, 1962, the margin was lowered by the Federal Reserve Board to 50 percent. This means that the buyer then had to put up 50¢ on every dollar invested in stock, with the broker lending 50¢. More recently the margin was raised to 80 percent.

make a profit. Corporate officers owning 10 percent or more of the stock of a company that is listed on a national exchange are required to list their holdings with the SEC. Furthermore, if a company officer buys and sells securities of his own company for a profit within six months, this profit must be awarded to the company.

Corporate officers cannot sell short securities of their own company. The Commission has the power to issue a "stop order" when it is not satisfied with published facts about a firm's stock. This is a very drastic step, even if the defect is corrected, because it can adversely affect the marketing of the stock in the future.

The Securities Act Amendment of 1964. Under this amendment large publicly-owned companies, regardless of whether their stocks are listed on an exchange or not, must make more information available to the public about the financial condition of the corporation. This legislation extended the registration, periodic reporting, proxy solicitation, and insider reporting and trading provisions of the Securities Exchange Act of 1933 to include the over-the-counter issuers. Heretofore, this group of stocks had not been included in this type of regulation. Insurance companies are exempt from these requirements, provided they are appropriately regulated by the state in which they are incorporated.

The Act also empowered the Commission to conduct administrative proceedings to determine if an issuer has been guilty of violating the law and, if so, to release to the public its findings and to require the violator to comply with the Act. Written examination requirements are now imposed on new salesmen selling over-the-counter securities.

The Maloney Act of 1938. The Maloney amendment to the Securities Exchange Act of 1934 was the result of negotiations between security dealers and the SEC. This amendment authorized investment bankers to form associations for the purpose of self-regulation. The National Association of Securities Dealers, Inc. (NASD) was the first (and thus far has been the only) such organization formed. The Association has the power to limit price concessions, discounts, allowances to members, and withdrawal privileges concerning those members who fail to abide by the rules. Today the NASD includes most over-the-counter security dealers in the United States. It has become the only self-regulating body concerned with unlisted securities.

Investment Trust Regulations. In the early history of this nation the trust form of ownership, which we discussed in Chapter 3, was fairly popular. Over the years, however, many of these trusts became corporations. More recently, several investment companies have been organized using the trust device.

The New York Stock Exchange defines an *investment trust* as a company "engaged primarily in the business of investing and reinvesting in securities of other corporations for the purpose of revenue and for profit and not in general for the purpose of exercising control." Investment trusts are also called "investment companies" or, even more popularly, "mutual funds." These companies issue their own shares to anyone who desires to invest. In return, the funds collected are invested in the stocks and bonds of qualified companies considered to be good investments. The list of stocks and bonds selected for the trust to buy is known as its *portfolio.*

In view of the increasing popularity of investment companies, Congress in 1940 enacted two measures. One was the Investment Company Act (Wagner-Lea Act) requiring all investment trusts to register with the SEC, and that managers of trusts which send securities by mail across state lines be registered. No trust can issue nonvoting shares. A minimum capital of $100,000 is necessary to start an investment company, and its directors are prevented from paying dividends out of capital.

The second measure was the Investment Advisers Act, a companion law. This legislation requires all investment counselors and advisory services to be registered with the SEC. Prohibitions are placed on any scheme to defraud or mislead a client by any device or practice.

Mutual funds, an outgrowth of the aforementioned legislation, are a popular form of investment. Of the two types, the *open-end* fund is the more popular. It issues as many additional shares as it can sell, and expands its portfolio as sales are made. The *closed-end* fund limits the number of shares issued at one time. After the initial offering, shares can be bought and sold on the open market in the same way as any corporation's securities are distributed.

There are different types of mutual funds. For example, *balanced funds* divide their investment among common stock, preferred stock, and bonds. The *stock funds* restrict their investment to common stocks. Then there are *specialty funds,* which purchase securities in special fields such as electronics, banking, chemicals, and aviation. Investment companies are large buyers of stocks and bonds on the regular exchange markets. Therefore, they are an important segment of the investing public, supplying large sums of new capital.

INTERMEDIATE-TERM FINANCING

Thus far no mention has been made concerning the nature of the source and the use of intermediate-term credit, which is generally considered to be from one year up to 10. Credit of this type is commonly known as *term loans.*

A more precise definition of a term loan is that it is an intermediate-term credit to be repaid in installments over a period of more than one year. Some may run as long as 15 years. Loans made to business of this type are often made to buy machinery and other fixed assets, or to supplement working capital. These loans are an important source of credit to metal-products manufacturers, transportation companies, small petroleum refineries, and public utilities. Rates of interest often are negotiated. Insurance companies, particularly life-insurance companies, make term loans for large sums to manufacturers, very often at lower interest rates than those available from other sources. Advantages of the investment company lie in its diversification of its investment, which tends to spread the risk of each individual investor.

Small-term loans ($25,000 or less) usually can be handled by individual commercial banks. Larger sums, amounting perhaps to several million dollars, are financed through groups of large commercial banks. A loan agreement, which may or may not provide for collateral (security), depending on the firm's general credit rating, is of course signed by the borrower.

Term loans, as compared with other forms of debt, may create operational problems. Often a bank will require the borrower to maintain a compensating balance, and this tends to increase the effective cost of funds. Also, because term loans are repayable in installments, the amount of each installment is considered during the current year as a current liability, and serves to reduce net working capital by the amount of the installment. A third disadvantage of term loans may arise when payment of principal and interest is scheduled regularly: an interruption in the cash flow can produce a financial crisis.[6]

Savings-and-Loan Associations

Savings-and-Loan Associations, sometimes known as "building-and-loan associations," are privately-managed associations owned by stockholders who buy varying numbers of shares. The association serves two purposes: it helps investors who want to save and invest small amounts; and it pools these funds and lends them to borrowers for five to 20 years, taking a mortgage on the real-estate that is bought with the loan. The total number of these organizations is now in excess of 6,000, with assets nearly $14½ billion. These

[6] The concept of "cash flow" is actually an estimate of the total receipts expected to be available to meet expected expenditures for a specific period of time. Generally, six months is used. *Cash flow* is defined as *what is left of income after every expense except depreciation, and every cash distribution except common-stock dividends, have been deducted.* It may be computed by adding depreciation expenses to earnings available for common stock expressed on a per-share basis. Another way to express cash flow is to add net profits after taxes to the amount set aside for depreciation and depletion. By dividing this by the number of shares of common stock outstanding, you can get cash flow per share. Cash flow can be a main source of company expansion. In industries such as oils, and in extractive industries, where the law permits large deductions for depreciation and depletion, cash flow is particularly important, because of the large amount the accountant charges against gross income for depreciation, for which there is no cash outgo. This income becomes available for expansion or other use.

organizations are under state supervision, and their deposits are insured with the Federal Savings and Loan Insurance Corporation.

SUMMARY

Every business, regardless of its size, needs some kind of financial planning as part of its regular policy. A business requires funds not only for initial establishment but for the financing of normal growth and modernization of its equipment. In addition to funds invested by the owner (equity funds), a business uses capital for many other purposes. The source of the capital and the length of time it is to be used are generally determined by the use to which the funds are put. Funds for fixed capital expenditures (buildings, machinery, land, etc.) generally come from sources that will not require immediate repayment, such as long-term and intermediate-term loans. A long-term loan is one ranging from five to 15 years, while an intermediate-term loan is credit for at least one year, but often not more than five. Short-term financing involves credit for one year or less.

Sources of long-term working-capital financing include capital invested by owners (sale of stock), sale of bonds, accumulated profits, and depreciation allowances on fixed assets. A term loan is an intermediate-term credit source. Among the sources of short-term working capital are bank loans and trade credit.

A corporation has the advantage of being able to raise funds by selling common and preferred stock. Common-stock holders may receive dividends which represent a share of the firm's profits. Holders of preferred stock likewise participate in the distribution of profits, but have a higher priority than holders of common stock. Unlike shares of stock, bonds must be paid when due, and interest is payable periodically. The holder may foreclose if the borrower is unable to pay the interest or principal.

Among the different kinds of bonds are mortgage bonds (secured by mortgage on real property), collateral trust bonds (secured by stocks or other bonds), income bonds (on which interest at a certain rate will be paid only if earned), and equipment trust bonds (secured by certain operating equipment). Bonds may be either registered in the name of the owner (registered bonds) or issued payable to the bearer as coupon bonds. When interest on a coupon bond is due, the holder simply clips the coupon and presents it to a designated bank for payment.

Corporation securities are marketed in different ways. Stocks and bonds may be sold in a local market over the counter by local brokerage firms. These are unlisted securities. Or they may be sold through an organized exchange using brokerage firms that hold membership on the exchange. The largest exchange is the New York Stock Exchange, located in the heart of the financial district on Wall Street. Security prices are quoted daily in most newspapers when listed on an organized exchange. Businessmen and the general public watch these daily prices in order to keep informed of changing financial conditions.

The New York Stock Exchange is the leading exchange engaged in trading in listed securities. The American Stock Exchange and the National Stock Exchange, both smaller in volume of daily trading, are also in New York. Regional exchanges are in many of the larger cities.

To qualify for listing its securities on the national exchanges, a corporation must meet certain requirements of the SEC, plus specific requirements that the Exchange itself imposes. The most difficult membership requirements are imposed by the New York Stock Exchange.

Both the Securities Act of 1933 and the Securities and Exchange Act of 1934 provide for strict regulation of securities exchanges and brokers doing business in interstate commerce. In addition, all companies listing stocks and bonds on these security markets are required to register and file periodic statements. Other restrictions include regulation of "margin" buying and control of security brokers by requiring a license.

VOCABULARY REVIEW QUIZ

Match the following vocabulary terms with the statements below:

a. Bond
b. Book value
c. Capital stock
d. Debenture bond
e. Fixed capital
f. Investment trust
g. Par value
h. Preferred stock
i. Portfolio
j. Prospectus
k. Price-earnings ratio
l. Short-term financing
m. Stock dividend
n. Stock right
o. Term loan

1. Money invested in fixed assets of a business such as land and buildings
2. Total aggregate ownership interest in a corporation
3. An arbitrary value placed on the face of the stock certificate
4. Actual value of stock shares as shown on the corporation's financial statement
5. A distribution of shares of stock from surplus obtained from profits to shareholders
6. Stock that carries certain preferences over other stock
7. A type of bond backed solely by the general credit of the company without pledging any assets
8. The ratio of the market price per share to its earnings per share during a financial period

9. A detailed description of the business, including its financial condition, capitalization, record of earnings and profits, and dividends, prepared to accompany a new issue of stock for use of the public
10. A company engaged primarily in the business of investing its funds in the securities of other corporations for the purpose of receiving dividends and gain rather than for acquiring managerial control
11. The list of securities bought for the trust for investment purposes
12. Credit in the form of a loan ranging from one to 10 years
13. Loans having a maturity of less than one year
14. The right of a stockholder to buy additional shares of stock within a stipulated time at an agreed price
15. A certificate of indebtedness, issued under the seal of the corporation, providing for the payment of a stated rate of interest

QUESTIONS FOR REVIEW STUDY

1. Explain the difference between a corporation bond and common and preferred stock from the standpoint of the corporation.
2. What are the main sources of capital financing for corporations?
3. How does equity capital differ from borrowed capital?
4. If a business desired to construct its own building, using debt capital as much as possible, what possible sources might be used?
5. Explain the meaning of the term *leverage factor* as it might apply to the investor.
6. A board of directors is debating whether to issue bonds or preferred stock to secure additional long-term capital. What factors might influence this decision?
7. Does the term *par value* establish the stockholder's liability?
8. What purpose does a stock right serve, and who benefits from its use?
9. What are some of the features found in preferred stock that are not present in common stock from the viewpoint of the investor?
10. Explain why a company can issue and sell a debenture bond.
11. What is the difference between a listed security and an over-the-counter security?
12. Explain what is meant by having an investment objective.
13. Describe how to distinguish a growth stock from an income stock.
14. What are the major factors to be considered in raising long-term capital?
15. Assume that you wanted to sell short. Explain exactly what you would have to do to make arrangements with your broker.

PROBLEMS AND PROJECTS

1. The A. B. Dawn Co. has assets of $3 million and liabilities of $2 million. A total of 100,000 shares of $50 par-value common stock is outstanding. The

market value of the common stock as quoted last is $20 per share. Calculate the book value of this stock. How do you explain the fact that the market value is different from the par value?

2. Two years ago Jim Dix bought 100 shares of ABX Co. common ($50 par) for $30 per share. This past year the company paid total dividends of $2, and the current market price is $100 a share. What is the current rate of return at the present market price? If the company earned $4 a share on common stock, what would be the price-earnings ratio? From the investor's point of view, how would you regard ABX as an investment stock?

3. The Jewels Co. has decided to raise $300,000 additional working capital by making a term loan. Explain what a term loan is and why the company might prefer to raise the funds this way rather than sell bonds.

A BUSINESS CASE

Case 16-1 Securing Capital for Business Expansion

The Marlton Corp., a family-owned company, has for many years manufactured a line of kitchen appliances sold to three chain department stores, each having its own private-label brand. For the past five years the three chains have increased their orders each new contract period. Word was received recently that two of the chains want to increase their order again for next year. The facilities cannot be increased without instituting a program of modernization, including the installation of new equipment. Recently the executive committee recommended a plant expansion involving approximately $5 million in new financing.

Presently the company has a capitalization of $5 million, with 100,000 shares of common stock, par value $50, outstanding. No preferred stock or bonds have ever been issued. The company has on several occasions borrowed up to $100,000 from a Chicago bank for one year. According to Dun & Bradstreet, the Marlton Corp. has the highest credit-rating available.

Last year the annual sales reached an all-time high of $45 million, with profits after taxes amounting to $3 million. Dividends on the common shares have been $25 a share. Five members of the family own all the common stock.

The stock is sold over-the-counter. About six months ago there was a rumor that the company was to merge with the Apex Co., the largest manufacturer of electric vacuum sweepers and automatic dishwashers. As a result, the price of the Marlton common jumped 15 points, from $55 to $70 per share. The plans for the merger were dropped when it was determined that Marlton was unwilling to meet the terms of Apex.

The corporation's executive committee are in agreement that the company needs to expand, or it will lose its contracts with the chain stores. But they are not in agreement as to the best way to raise the necessary capital.

The company's latest financial statement showed the book value of the

100,000 shares of common stock to be $90 per share, which was equal to nearly four times the par value proposed in the reorganization plan. Anticipated earnings for this year are expected to reach $4 million after taxes.

One suggested plan of financing is to fund the total expenditure out of earnings, with a term-loan for the balance of the required capital.

A second plan is to amend the charter and increase the number of common shares from 100,000 to 400,000, using a new par value of $25 per share. This would require calling in the outstanding stock and exchanging it for new shares at the new par-value ratio. The company would then sell 100,000 shares of common stock to the public at about $50 per share, less brokerage costs. This would produce slightly less than $5 million.

A third plan calls for no changes in the organization's financial structure but to sell 6,000 corporate bonds in $1,000 denominations bearing 6 percent interest, callable in 10 years at $101 but with the special provision that half the total bonds may be called for repayment after six years, at the regular par value of $1,000.

1. Assuming that you were a stockholder, which method of financing would you prefer?
2. Which method of financing would you recommend if you were not a stockholder but an employee?
3. How would you as a stockholder feel about the stability of a company that has only three customers?

Short-Term Financing

17

In the preceding chapter we observed how long-term capital financing is achieved when relatively permanent investments in new equipment, additional manufacturing plants, land, warehouses, and so forth, must be made. Little has been said, however, to indicate how an established business obtains credit for *short* durations, and what sources are available to businessmen for short-term loans. Funds of this nature are needed to finance short-term business activities, to buy goods for resale, to "carry" customers until they pay for the goods, to meet payrolls, and to be available for emergencies of various kinds.

The purpose of this chapter is to establish a meaningful frame of reference within which each of the various sources of short-term credit may be examined. In addition, we will concentrate on the following topics: credit; credit instruments; banks; the national banking system and its relation to the Federal Reserve System; finance and loan companies; commercial-paper houses; factoring companies; and the regulation of financial institutions.

CREDIT

Credit is so much an integral part of our business system that its real significance is often taken for granted. Yet it is doubtful that many businesses could operate very long without it.

What Is Credit?

The word "credit" is derived from the Latin *credere,* "to trust." (*Creditum* means "a loan.") When associated with business transactions, *credit* is defined as *the power or ability to secure goods or services* (or money) *in exchange for a promise to pay later.*[1] Popular usage of this term, however, has turned its meaning around, until it denotes something that the seller and not the buyer gives. In the strict sense, it is incorrect for the seller to state "we give credit," for it is the prospective buyer who actually extends the credit in exchange for the goods purchased or services obtained.

From certain points of view the term "credit" may be better understood if it is explained rather than defined. Credit necessarily involves two characteristics. First, there is the element of *faith* on the part of the creditor in the willingness and ability of the debtor to fulfill his promise to pay. When such faith is present, the creditor is willing to give goods, services, or money in consideration of the debtor's ability to pay. The second element of credit is *futurity:* in every credit transaction the seller or lender accepts some risk over a period of time. Credit instruments always involve a *time* during which the creditor's confidence is placed in the debtor's promise to pay, and until payment is made there is always a *risk* that it will not be made. It is by these characteristics that credit instruments are distinguished from other commercial documents that resemble them.

Functions of Credit

Credit serves business in several ways. It makes capital available that would otherwise be idle. Induced by payment for the use of their funds, thrifty persons are willing to entrust their personal savings to banks and other financial institutions which, in turn, lend these savings to business. A direct result of the use of credit has been the development of enterprises of all sizes.

Credit also serves as a medium of exchange. Through its use, transactions can be quickly accomplished with a minimum of work and without the exchange of money. Without credit, the high level of economic activity enjoyed by business would disappear. The development of large-scale enterprise is the result of credit.

[1] For a more complete discussion, see Ernest W. Walker, *Essentials of Financial Management* (Englewood Cliffs, N.J.: Prentice-Hall, Inc., 1965), pp. 105–119.

Thirdly, credit is a tool of business promotion which enables the entrepreneur to adjust his volume of capital to the varying needs of his business. By borrowing additional capital, he may be able to increase production during peak periods of business activity. By extending credit, he can induce a desired class of customers to buy, thus gaining a competitive advantage over the entrepreneur who does not give credit.

Trade Credit

Trade credit differs radically from other forms of short-term credit primarily because it is not obtained from a financial institution. This type of credit is an obligation typified by the common "open-book account" extended by credit managers. It has become the most common source of working capital. In accounting language, it comes under the heading of accounts receivable for the seller, and accounts payable for the buyer. It starts when goods are sold to the buyer on a 30-, 60-, or 90-day credit. Other than the invoice, no formal instrument is involved.

Reasons for Trade Credit. From a creditor's point of view, a firm is willing to grant credit in order to increase sales. If a firm's sales volume can be raised without spending large amounts of funds on production equipment, it is possible to spread the fixed costs over a larger number of units and reduce the unit cost of production.

From the debtor's viewpoint, firms make use of trade credit largely because they are unable to obtain adequate financing from other credit sources, such as banks and finance companies. Commercial banks are either unable or unwilling to assume the costs or the risk inherent in many trade credit sales. On the other hand, the seller can assume both because trade credit is about the only avenue open to him to stimulate sales without resorting to long-term credit of some kind. Many firms would find it most difficult to maintain suitable inventories in the absence of trade credit.

Credit managers estimate that *open-book accounts*, a form of short-term credit, constitute approximately 85 percent of the total volume of retail and wholesale sales in the United States. The seller enters into no formal written agreement acknowledging the debt, but relies instead on the buyer, whose integrity he respects, to pay for the goods at the appropriate time. However, since the seller's record alone does not constitute the best type of legal evidence of debt in the event of dispute, it is common practice to support these credit transactions with sales slips or delivery receipts.

Trade-credit debt accounts traditionally are payable in 30 days. Wholesalers, jobbers, and manufacturers may sell goods on such terms as "2/10, net 30," which means that a discount of 2 percent on the amount of the invoice will be allowed the buyer if he pays his bill within 10 days, and that the entire amount is due in 30 days. The buyer's ability to take his discount promptly is evidence of his satisfactory financial condition.

Needless to say, trade credit is an important and advantageous source of credit for any business. It should be carefully used. We may conclude that there is a definite cost of trade credit when the buyer fails to take his discount.

Credit Instruments

Each of the several types of credit instruments common to short-term finance possesses certain attributes. These instruments may be divided into two broad categories: those based on *promises to pay,* and those based on *orders to pay*. The former group (promises to pay) includes promissory notes and bonds. The latter classification comprises drafts of all kinds, and the general category of trade acceptances. These instruments have two things in common: they involve the element of time during which the creditor's confidence is placed in the debtor's promise, and the degree of risk until payment is made.

Promissory Notes. Ranking second in order of importance as an unsecured obligation in the promise-to-pay category is the *negotiable promissory note.*

Section 3-104 (1) of the UCC defines a negotiable promissory note as *an unconditional promise in writing made by one person to another, signed by the maker, engaging to pay on demand, or at a particular time, a sum certain in money to order or to bearer.*

In the illustration of a negotiable promissory note on page 480, Joseph Doe, Jr. (the maker) agrees to pay to the East End State Bank (payee) $100, with interest at 6 percent, 60 days from the date of the note. A promissory note is preferred to an open-book account because it represents prima-facie evidence of the debt. (The term *prima facie evidence* denotes that the evidence is sufficient to establish the fact in question unless rebutted.) An advantage in using the promissory note over the open-book account is that when signed by the debtor it acknowledges the accuracy of the debt at the time he agreed to it. The note may be written so that it bears interest either at maturity or at specified intervals during the life of the debt, or it may be a discounted note, in which case the interest is deducted from the principal at the time the note is made.

For example, Tom Jensen wishes to borrow $1,000 from his bank at 6 percent interest for 60 days. The money is to be used for a short-term business debt. When he signs the note, the bank accepts it and pays him the money. If he used a discounted note, the bank would subtract $10 interest immediately from the face of the note and pay him $990. He will pay $1,000 to the bank at the end of 60 days.

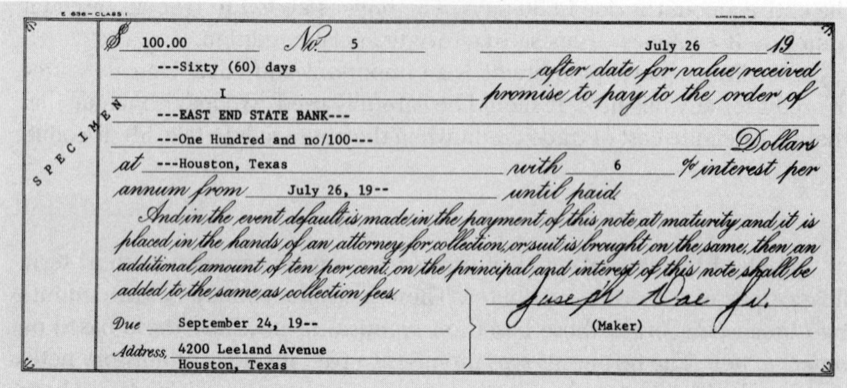

$ 100.00 No. 5 July 26 19
---Sixty (60) days after date for value received
I promise to pay to the order of
---EAST END STATE BANK---
---One Hundred and no/100--- Dollars
at ---Houston, Texas with 6 % interest per
annum from July 26, 19-- until paid.
And in the event default is made in the payment of this note at maturity and it is placed in the hands of an attorney for collection, or suit is brought on the same, then an additional amount of ten per cent. on the principal and interest of this note shall be added to the same as collection fees.
Due September 24, 19--
Address, 4200 Leeland Avenue
Houston, Texas
(Maker)

SPECIMEN

Courtesy East End State Bank, Houston, Tex.

A negotiable promissory note.

When a firm accepts a promissory note from a customer, the note is carried on the firm's books under "notes receivable." But if the firm needs cash before the note is due, it may be indorsed and sold to a commercial bank at a discount. Discounting promissory notes is one of the services of commercial banks.

Bonds. Although the subject of bonds was discussed in the preceding chapter, we mention it again simply to remind you that a bond is a written credit instrument in the promise-to-pay category.

Drafts or Bills of Exchange. Thus far we have discussed only the promise-to-pay type of credit instrument. One of the common orders-to-pay negotiable instruments is the *draft* or *bill of exchange*. This instrument is an order to pay money. A draft may be defined as a written instrument created by the *drawer* (the one who draws up the instrument), addressed to a second party, the *drawee*, who is ordered to pay "a sum of money certain in amount" to a third party, the *payee*, on a fixed or determinable future date. A draft or bill of exchange can be drawn so that a payee is not named, merely by drawing it to the *bearer*, who would be the person holding the instrument and presenting it for payment.

Certificates of Deposit. Commonly known as a CD, the *certificate of deposit* is an interest-bearing negotiable instrument representing a time certificate. Issued by a bank, it acknowledges receipt of a specific sum of money with an obligation to repay it only when the certificate is surrendered. Since it is in part an acknowledgment of receipt of money, it is distinguished from a promissory note, which is solely a promise-to-pay instrument. It is negotiable if it meets the requirements for negotiability contained in Section 3-104 of the Uniform Commercial Code. From the banks' standpoint, CD's are desirable because they are a means of attracting time deposits from profit-making corporations, which according to the laws of some states are not permitted to open a savings account in the name of the corporation as a means of obtaining short-term interest on funds that are idle for only a brief period.

Certificates of over $100,000 value may bear as much as 5½ percent interest. For certificates of less than $100,000 value the rates vary from 3½ to 5 percent. A bank is allowed to negotiate the rate, which is determined both by the amount of competition among banks for CD's, and by the size of the customer's bank balance. Each certificate is issued for six months and may be renewed at the expiration of that time. Interest is forfeited if the certificate is cashed prior to the maturity date. Payment prior to the maturity date may be made by the bank but requires an affidavit of hardship from the holder. If the CD is lost, the bank requires an indemnity bond equal to double its value. An illustration of a CD is shown below. This certificate may be so drawn to make it negotiable. Interest rates for CD's were established under amended Federal Reserve Regulations "Q" and the Federal Deposit Insurance Corporation ruling effective September 26, 1966.

A draft differs from a promissory note in that it is an order rather than a promise to pay. If the draft is payable on demand, it is called a *demand* or *sight draft.* If it orders payment at a designated future date, it is a *time draft.* In the illustration on page 482, Richard B. Brown is the drawer of a sight draft payable to Joseph Doe, Jr., from funds in the drawer's account, First City National Bank. This draft is issued to the drawer through the courtesy of the East End State Bank as an accommodation to Richard B. Brown.

NON-NEGOTIABLE

CERTIFICATE OF DEPOSIT

FORT LEE TRUST COMPANY
FORT LEE, NEW JERSEY

$____ Fort Lee, N. J.____ 19__ No. 464

This certifies that ____
has deposited with Fort Lee Trust Company, Fort Lee, New Jersey
the sum of ____ Dollars.

The said Company will allow interest at the rate of ____ per cent per annum from this date, and on ____ will repay the like amount with the interest. Neither the deposit evidenced hereby nor the interest hereon may be withdrawn except on or after the maturity date hereof and upon presentation and surrender of this Certificate to the Company. The rate of interest payable hereunder is subject to change by the Company to such extent as may be necessary to comply with the requirements of the constituted authorities.

AUTHORIZED SIGNATURE AUTHORIZED SIGNATURE

A certificate of deposit is issued by banks to attract time deposits from corporations as well as from individuals.

CUSTOMER'S DRAFT

SPECIMEN

At sight HOUSTON, TEXAS July 26 196-

PAY TO THE ORDER OF Joseph Doe, Jr. $ 100.00

---One Hundred and no/100--- DOLLARS

VALUE RECEIVED AND CHARGE TO ACCOUNT OF WITH EXCHANGE

TO First City National Bank
Houston, Texas
(Drawee)

Richard B. Brown
(Drawer)

ACCOUNT NUMBER 956-391

IF YOUR BANK HAS ASSIGNED YOUR ACCOUNT AN IDENTIFICATION NUMBER, PLEASE FILL IN ABOVE BOX.

COURTESY OF East End STATE BANK HOUSTON, TEXAS

Courtesy East End State Bank, Houston, Tex.

A sight draft payable when presented for payment.

A sight draft may also be used in collecting an overdue account. The debtor may find his credit rating impaired if he refuses to accept the draft. A sight draft has another use: it may be used when goods are delivered by freight on a cash sale. As the shipper, you secure from the transportation company an order bill of lading. This document is an enforceable agreement, usually prepared in several copies by the transportation company when the goods are delivered to the transportation company for shipment to the consignee (buyer). One copy of the bill of lading is used as the shipping order by the transporter; another is retained by the shipper (seller). The transportation agent at the destination point cannot release the goods to the buyer until the bill of lading is presented to him. As seller, you can attach a sight draft to the bill of lading and mail both to the bank of the buyer. In order to obtain possession of the goods, the buyer must then pay the sight draft. At this time he receives the bill of lading, and the transportation agent is authorized to release the goods to him. All this has happened because the buyer has honored the sight draft.

The main distinction between a time draft and a sight draft is that the former is payable at a stipulated time as shown on the draft, whereas the sight draft is payable on presentation, which may be any time. The time draft, after it has been accepted by the drawee, may be sold at a discount. To this extent, it represents a debt on the part of the buyer (drawee) which he agrees to pay at the time the draft is due.

Checks. Another kind of bill of exchange is a *cashier's check.* It is a check drawn by a bank against its own funds, and signed by the cashier or some responsible person representing the bank, instead of by the depositor. A cashier's check may be used by a bank to pay its own debts, or it may be purchased by any person who wishes to send a remittance through the mail

Courtesy East End State Bank, Houston, Tex.

A cashier's check. This type of check may be purchased from a bank.

to individuals who are not willing to accept a personal check. A cashier's check is illustrated above. It has all the characteristics of a negotiable instrument that you studied in Chapter 3.

You may make your check payable to "Cash" or to "Bearer," or to a named person. Any check made payable either to cash or to bearer may be cashed by any person who gains possession of it. For this reason, it is not a safe business practice to write such a check until you are ready to cash it at the place where you write it.

You will observe from the following illustration of a check that there are several parties to this instrument: (1) the *drawee* (the bank on which it is drawn); (2) the *payee* (the person to whom the check is made payable); and

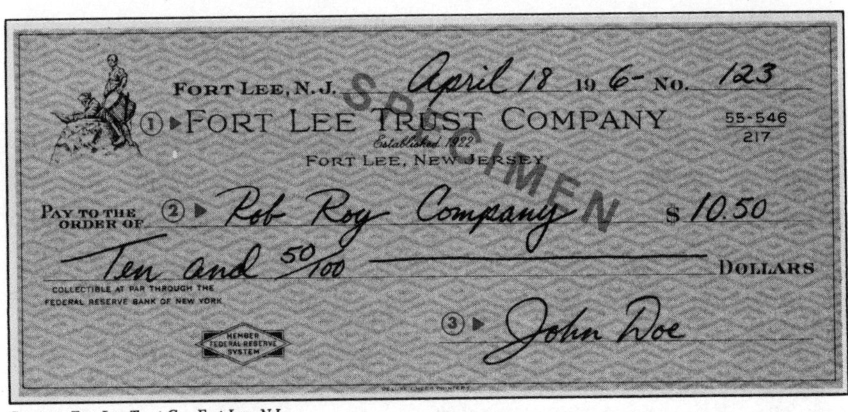

Courtesy Fort Lee Trust Co., Fort Lee, N.J.

Parties to a bank check: (1) Drawee bank, (2) payee, (3) drawer of the check. Notice that the amount of the check is entered in two places. In case of dispute, the amount spelled out in words takes precedence.

(3) the drawer (the one directing the bank to withdraw funds from his account).

Checks differ from money in at least two ways. First, a check is an individual credit instrument and therefore does not have the accepted qualifications of money. Second, there is a legal liability involved in passing a check which is absent when transferring money. As a negotiable instrument, a check involves both the faith and the futurity mentioned earlier as characteristics of credit.

Still another special form of check is a *certified check*, illustrated below. Certification is accomplished when a bank officer where the account is kept authorizes the amount of the check to be deducted from the customer's account, and stamps "Certified" on the face of the check. As a result of certification, the check becomes an obligation of the bank rather than of the drawer.

Trade Acceptance. When a time draft is sent by the seller (drawer of the draft) to the buyer (the drawee) for his acceptance of the debt, this instrument is called a *trade acceptance*. Thus, a trade acceptance is in reality a draft drawn by the seller, accompanying the shipment and directing the buyer to pay the debt at a fixed future time. Because it is a negotiable instrument, a trade acceptance must follow the requirements of negotiable instruments. The additional security of goods involved causes trade acceptances to be regarded as rediscount paper by Federal Reserve banks. The Federal Reserve Board has adopted several requirements as to the form of trade acceptances:

1. The face of the instrument must be labeled "Trade Acceptance."
2. The instrument must be accepted in writing on its face.

Courtesy Hackensack Trust Co., Hackensack, N.J.

A certified check is a safe and convenient instrument for paying accounts.

3. The instrument must indicate on the face that it arises out of the sale and purchase of goods.

Despite the indorsement by the National Association of Credit Men and the influence on the part of the Federal Reserve to encourage the use of trade acceptances by favoring them for discount and rediscount purposes, they are not as widely used as other credit instruments in this country. The primary reason is that most buyers prefer to buy on an open account.[2] Moreover, some buyers think a trade acceptance is used only for customers with poor credit ratings.

From the standpoint of the seller, there are at least three advantages to the trade acceptance:

1. It is a negotiable instrument that the creditor can discount at his bank more readily than a promissory note.
2. It is easier to bring suit on a trade acceptance than on an open account.
3. It puts pressure on the buyer to pay on the due date.

As to disadvantages of the trade acceptance, there is danger that the seller will discount too many of them and run into financial difficulty if the acceptors do not pay them when due. The seller (drawer) who discounts the trade acceptance is liable as an endorser, and the bank looks to him for payment if the acceptor defaults.

OUR BANKING SYSTEM

Thus far in our coverage of short-term financing we have studied mainly the various credit instruments used by business. The use of these credit instruments is possible only because this nation has developed an efficient and strong monetary system, which is a prime requisite for a progressive capitalistic economy. In some countries wealth is highly concentrated but dormant. This is usually the case among nations that lack the facilities for putting wealth to work. In the United States our wealth, not being highly concentrated, has "velocity"; with the aid of the commercial banks, which are a major source of credit for commercial establishments, it moves freely from one venture to another.

Our banking system is composed of several types of banks (among which are commercial, savings, and investment banks), and also of trust companies. Much of the stability of our system is due to the Federal Reserve Bank

[2] The terms "open account" and "open book account" are used interchangeably.

TABLE 17.1
ALL BANKS IN THE UNITED STATES

Kind of bank	Number
Federal Reserve Member Banks	6,194
Nonmember Commercial Banks	7,608
Total	13,802
Classes of Member Banks:	
National Banks	4,811
State Banks	1,383
Total	6,194
Classes of Nonmember Banks:	
Commercial Banks	7,608
Mutual-Savings Banks	505
Total All Banks	14,307

Source: *Federal Reserve Bulletin,* August, 1966, p. 1192.

System, which we shall study in considerable detail later in this chapter. Federal Reserve Banks are called "bankers' banks" because they provide financial services to the total monetary operations of this country.

Each state maintains its own system of banks through *state banks* chartered by a state authority and subject to rules and laws of the state as well as of the Federal Reserve System.

Banks that receive their charters from the Comptroller of the Currency, United States Treasury Department, are known as *national* banks. These banks are corporations whose stock, like that of the state banks, is owned by stockholders. Their operations are supervised by national bank examiners who periodically go over their books to make certain they comply with the laws and regulations laid down by the Congress and implemented by the Federal Reserve Board. All national banks operate under the National Banking Act of 1863, the Federal Reserve Act of 1913, and the Gold Reserve Act of 1934.

Table 17.1 gives you some idea of the total number of national, state, and mutual savings banks in the United States. By far the largest number of banks are commercial banks, of which there are slightly more than 13,800; and there are 505 mutual savings banks. Approximately 4,800 are national banks, and about 9,000 are state banks.

Commercial Banks

Commercial banks differ from other banks in two important respects: they accept *demand deposits*—that is, deposits that the depositor may withdraw at any time without giving prior notice to the bank—and they specialize in making loans to businessmen and individuals for short periods of time. These loans are called *short-term loans* because they are in effect for a period of one year or less. If you needed a personal or business loan, perhaps for a short duration, chances are you would go to a commercial bank in your community.

The list of services provided by commercial banks is a long one. Obviously, not all of these services can be listed here, but you should be aware of the following:

1. As a depository for money
2. As a collection agency of negotiable instruments
3. As a source of loans
4. As a source of credit information and advice
5. As a trustee of funds
6. As an administrator of estates and trusts
7. As a source of letters of credit
8. As a dispenser of travelers' checks
9. As an agency to handle foreign-trade transactions

Commercial Bank Loans. Of the many banking functions performed, perhaps the most important to business is that of supplying short-term capital in the form of loans. Borrowing from a bank requires both a good credit rating and some acceptable form of collateral. *Collateral* is marketable assets —goods, land, equipment, or negotiable instruments. Among the common collateral instruments used are: (1) stocks or bonds, (2) warehouse receipts, (3) trust receipts, (4) mortgages, and (5) order bills of lading.

1. Since *stocks* are ownership in a corporation, they are considered acceptable security provided they are marketable and may continue to be so for the duration of the loan. *Bonds,* such as corporate or municipal, are acceptable if they, too, are sound and marketable. Stocks are not used as extensively for commercial loans as they are for personal loans.
2. A document that serves as a receipt for goods stored in a warehouse is called a *warehouse receipt.* This receipt may be either negotiable or non-negotiable. Negotiable warehouse receipts are used as collateral for loans against goods held in storage. When properly indorsed, the receipt entitles the holder to take possession of goods listed on the document in the quantity and condition specified. In the event of default by the borrower, the goods can be seized and sold at auction to benefit the lender. This type of financing has been encouraged by the provisions set forth in the Uniform Commercial Code.

3. Loans made on *trust receipts* are similar to those secured by warehouse receipts. When a bank is in possession of a warehouse receipt or a bill of lading, it is impossible for the merchant concerned to obtain possession of his goods before paying the loan. But under a trust receipt agreement with his bank, the merchant may obtain the goods so that he may be able to sell them to pay off the loan. Under this arrangement, the bank pays for the goods and the borrower agrees to hold in trust for the bank both the goods and proceeds until the loan is repaid. When this type of financing is used, a letter of credit is first sent to the vendor, stating that the bank will honor drafts up to a certain amount for the borrower. Such a draft is called a *banker's acceptance.* Titles to automobiles may be transferred to a bank on a trust receipt while remaining in the dealer's showroom. Then, as the cars are sold, the dealer pays off portions of the loan. This practice is commonly called *floor-plan financing,* and is one that is used by most automobile dealers.
4. A *real-estate mortgage* is the most widely used security for a debt. In case of default, the trustee acting for the lender can foreclose on the mortgage and seize the property for the unpaid claim. In addition to the real-estate mortgage, a *chattel mortgage* may be used as security for a bond. It represents a mortgage on personal property (movable) in contrast with real property. Automobiles, agricultural equipment, and household appliances are commonly used for chattel mortgages. There are some states that do not recognize a chattel mortgage on personal property. Instead, a *conditional bill of sale* is used. Even under this arrangement, however, title remains with the seller until the debt is paid.
5. When goods are shipped by rail or truck, the shipper receives either a "straight" or an "order" *bill of lading.* The *straight* bill of lading is non-negotiable; it conveys title to the goods and must be surrendered to the transportation company before the goods can be delivered to the buyer. For this reason, it is regarded as satisfactory security for a loan, provided the goods are nonperishable.

With respect to *intrastate* shipments, bills of lading in most states are governed by the Uniform Commercial Code; in those states that have not adopted the UCC, they are governed by Article 7 or the Uniform Bills of Lading Act. Bills of lading used in *interstate* transportation are regulated by the Federal Bills of Lading Act.

Savings Banks

A second type of bank, not nearly so common as the commercial bank, is the *savings bank.* These banks accept deposits on savings accounts, which funds the banks use primarily for making loans. The surplus deposits in excess of total cash reserves and loans may be invested in such investments as real-estate, mortgages, government bonds, and corporation stocks and bonds if approved by law.

Savings banks are of two types: *stock companies* and *mutual companies.* The former companies are owned by stockholders who receive dividends from net profits. Mutual-savings banks are owned by depositors. The net profits are prorated to the depositors on the basis of the size of each deposit. At present, mutual savings banks operate in only 18 states and the Virgin Islands. Since they are chartered by state governments, the amount of interest they may pay and the ways in which they may invest their funds are regulated by the state.

Savings bank deposits may be insured under the Federal Deposit Insurance Corporation up to $15,000 for each depositor. Many state laws limit the amount a person may deposit in savings to $10,000. This limitation is intended to prevent large amounts from being withdrawn at any one time. For persons of small or moderate wealth, the savings banks perform a most useful service in protecting their savings and earning for them a fairly dependable income. (Business firms rarely use savings banks for this purpose.) Most savings banks are located in New England and other northeastern states.

Investment Banks

The *investment bank* is a highly specialized financial institution. It does not accept deposits from the public. It serves business by helping corporations sell long-term securities. Many firms that otherwise might find it difficult to market stocks and bonds make use of these banks, which are often called "security houses" because they underwrite the securities issued by corporations. In a broad sense, the total structure of the investment banking industry includes commercial banks, broker-dealer firms, and investment banking firms that engage primarily in underwriting and distributing public corporate securities. Commercial banks are mentioned because they are important underwriters of local, state, and federal agency bonds. However, for our purposes our interest in this discussion is concerned mainly with investment banking firms engaged primarily in underwriting securities.

In underwriting securities, the investment bank takes a stock or bond issue at an agreed price and pays the corporation the total cash value before the securities are sold. The bank then assumes the risk involved in selling these securities to the public. If the issue represents a large sum of money, several investment banks may join together and form a syndicate. Each bank in the syndicate agrees to take a portion of the total securities offered for sale, and distribute them through the regular channels. In 1954, when Ford Motor Co. stock was offered to the public, over 700 firms participated in underwriting the sale of it. These firms included broker-dealers as well as investment banks.

The investment bank makes its profit by charging a commission for selling securities or by bidding for stocks or bonds at a discount and later selling them at a slightly higher price. If the market price drops before the entire issue is sold, the bank must take a loss on some of the securities. Of the New York security brokers, such as J. P. Morgan & Co., and Kuhn, Loeb & Co., few are willing to handle a security issue of less than $1 million, since the expense of selling a small issue is almost as great as the cost of marketing a large one.

Trust Companies

Originally, *trust companies* were authorized by state laws to serve as trustees of funds and estates. In this capacity they acted to safeguard the property entrusted to them. In recent years, however, their services have been extended to include the role of registrar and transfer agent for corporations. As transfer agents, they record changes in stock ownership, and many even issue dividend checks to stockholders. As registrars, they accept the responsibility of certifying to the public that stock issues are correctly stated and in accordance with the provisions of the corporation charter. Some states allow commercial banks to perform certain functions that are ordinarily performed by trust companies. Thus you may see a commercial bank with the title "_______ Bank and Trust Company."

THE FEDERAL RESERVE SYSTEM

The early banking history of this nation is one of which there is little to be proud. The United States had a central bank from 1791 (First Bank of the United States) until 1811, and from 1816 to 1836 (Second Bank of the United States). From 1836 to 1863 there were no national banks, no federal regulations, and virtually no controls by the states. It was during this time that "wildcat" banking was at its height. Banks were started without proper financial backing, and quite naturally many failed, resulting in heavy losses to stockholders and depositors. Finally, following the nationwide money panic of 1907, Congress decided that federal action was needed to bring order out of chaos: in 1908 it authorized a National Monetary Commission to study banking needs. The outcome was a proposal for a Federal Reserve System, which resulted in passage of the Federal Reserve Act in 1913.

In the United States the Federal Reserve System serves as the nation's central bank. In Europe, the well-known central banks include the Bank of France, the Bank of England, and the Reichsbank in Germany. Central banks in most foreign countries are owned and operated by the various national governments. In the United States this is not the case. The Federal Reserve System is owned by member banks, and the employees of the Federal Reserve are not government employees. They are paid out of earnings of the Federal Reserve instead of from federal funds. The law was purposely written to provide this kind of separation. As a result, the Federal Reserve has not been subjected to the kind of political pressure that other federal agencies frequently experience.

Organization

The law that created the Federal Reserve System was entitled, "An Act to provide for the establishment of Federal Reserve Banks, to furnish an elastic currency, to afford means of rediscounting commercial paper, to establish a more effective supervision of banking in the United States, and for other purposes."

At the time of publication of this book, the Federal Reserve System was composed of 6,194 member banks, 12 Federal Reserve Banks, and 24 branch banks. There is in conjunction with it three important groups: a Board of Governors, the Federal Open Market Committee, and the Federal Advisory Council, all of which are shown in the illustration on page 492.

The Board of Governors is appointed by the President of the United States with approval of the Senate. Each of the seven members on the board is appointed for a 14-year term unless the appointee is replacing a member whose term has not expired. Every second year, the term of one member expires and he is replaced. Anyone serving a 14-year term is not eligible for reappointment. This board is regarded as autonomous and nonpolitical in the sense that it is free from control by any executive branch of the federal government.

Functions

The Federal Reserve System performs two major functions. One is to supply certain basic banking services, such as acting as a clearing-house for checks, serving as a fiscal agent for the government by distributing currency and coins, and supervising the operations of the member banks. The second function is a dual one: to maintain a sound credit policy for all member banks (by controlling the volume of credit in circulation so as to avoid sharp fluctuations in the business cycle), and at the same time to promote a high level of consumer buying. This is a very significant function because it serves the entire economy. (The methods by which credit and the circulation of money are regulated are described later in this chapter.)

Federal Reserve Banks

The United States is divided into 12 Federal Reserve Districts, as shown on the map on page 493, each with its own Federal Reserve Bank located in the following cities:

THE FEDERAL RESERVE BANKS OF THE UNITED STATES

District	*Bank location*	*District*	*Bank location*
1	Boston	7	Chicago
2	New York	8	St. Louis
3	Philadelphia	9	Minneapolis
4	Cleveland	10	Kansas City
5	Richmond	11	Dallas
6	Atlanta	12*	San Francisco

* Includes Alaska and Hawaii

Each of the 12 Federal Reserve Banks (one in each district) is a corporation organized and operated for public service. These banks differ from privately managed banks in that profits are not the object of their operations; furthermore, their stockholders, which are the member banks of the system, do not have the powers and privileges usually belonging to stockholders of privately managed corporations. (See Chapter 4.) Each Federal Reserve Bank has nine directors who conduct the business of that bank.

Branch Banks. Within the 12 districts, there are 24 branch banks. For example, in District No. 12, the Federal Reserve Bank is located in San

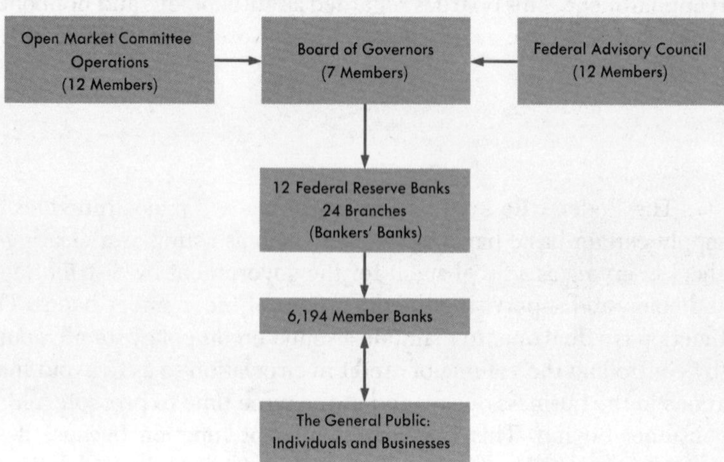

Adapted from *The Federal Reserve System*, 1963, p. 22.

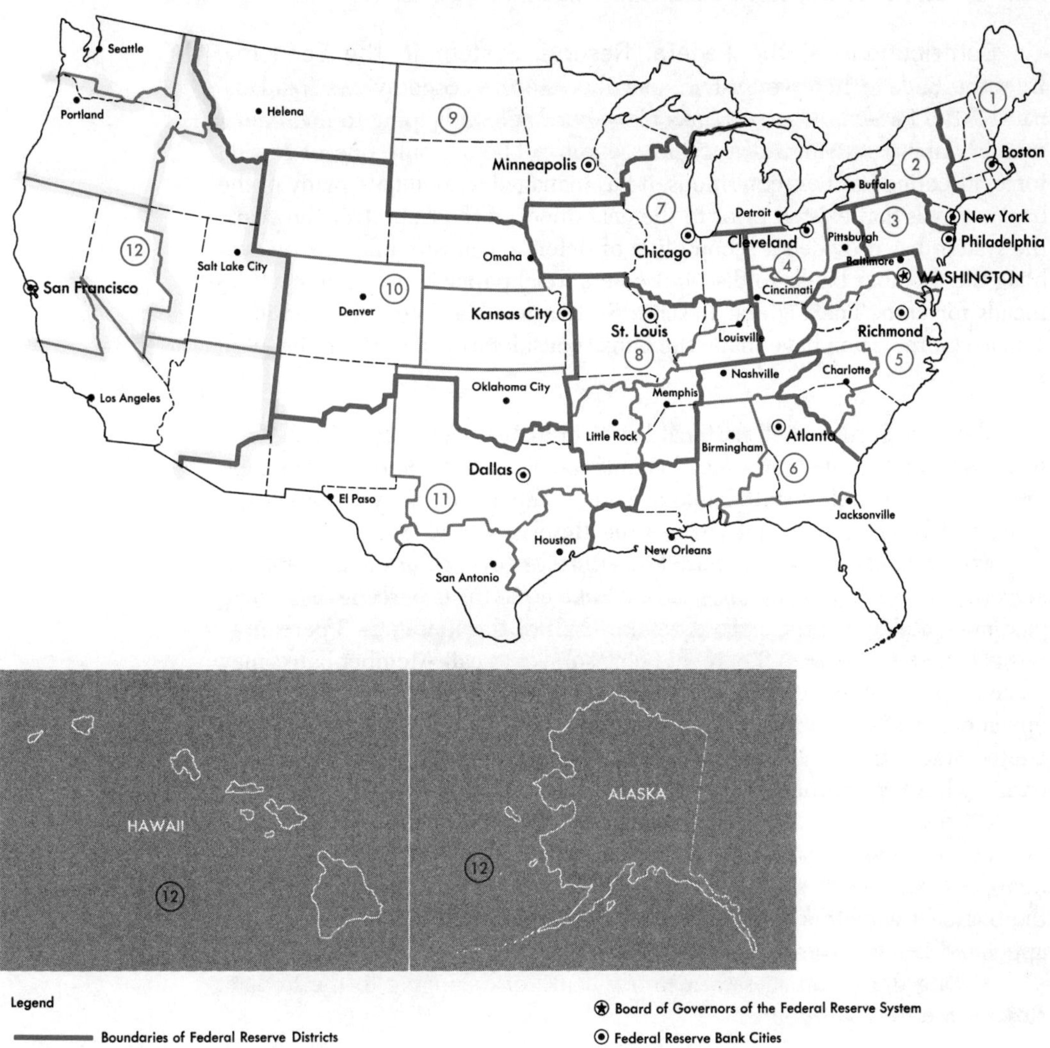

Courtesy Board of Governors, Federal Reserve System.

A map of the Federal Reserve System composed of 12 district banks and 24 branch banks.

Francisco, and the branch banks are in Los Angeles, Portland, Salt Lake City, and Seattle. These four branch banks, together with the Federal Reserve Bank of San Francisco, serve the member banks of their district.

Contributions of the Federal Reserve System to the Economy. Does the Federal Reserve System contribute to the economy? As "bankers' banks," the Federal Reserve Banks play a vital role in helping to maintain a sound banking system and a stable economy. Though only one of several forces affecting business conditions, it has managed to eliminate many of the banking evils that existed prior to the enactment of the Act. Over the years, the system has provided a second line of defense against bank runs by enabling the member banks to discount commercial paper in order to meet demands for cash. The Federal Reserve System and the Federal Deposit Insurance Corporation have made the banks considerably safer than they used to be.

Member Banks. All national banks must be members of the Federal Reserve System. State banks may become members provided they can meet the requirements. Most state banks are nonmembers, probably because their volume of business does not require the Reserve's services.

Each member bank is required to subscribe to stock in the Federal Reserve Bank to which it belongs, an amount equal to 6 percent of its own paid-in capital and surplus. To date, only half of this amount—3 percent—must be paid in, the other 3 percent being subject to call. Member banks may receive up to 6 percent cumulative dividends on their stock. Income above operational requirements of any Federal Reserve Bank is turned over to the United States Treasury. In recent years over half a billion dollars in surplus earnings has been turned over to the Treasury annually.

On the basis of a classification established by the Board of Governors, member banks are divided into three sizes: small, medium, and large. Member banks in each size elect one Class A member and one Class B member of the Board of Directors of their Federal Reserve Bank. Class C directors are appointed by the Board of Governors.

Among the advantages to member banks of belonging to the Federal Reserve are the following:

1. Currency can be obtained immediately from a Federal Reserve District Bank.
2. Drafts may be drawn on the Federal Reserve Bank.
3. Deposits may be transferred by telegraph between one bank and another through a Federal Reserve Bank.
4. Eligible commercial paper may be discounted and advances obtained from the Federal Reserve Bank.

5. Deposits are insured in each member bank up to $15,000 for each depositor by the Federal Deposit Insurance Corporation.
6. Federal Reserve Banks may be used to collect checks and clear other negotiable instruments.

Operational and Credit Functions of the Federal Reserve System

From the viewpoint of the national economy, the most important function of the Federal Reserve System is the regulation of the volume of bank credit—that is, the amount of demand deposits, or checkbook money, that banks create by making loans. The system uses several different methods to accomplish this function. These may be identified as follows: (1) open market operations, (2) legal reserve requirements, (3) the rediscount rate, and (4) margin requirements for the sale of securities.

Open Market Operations. The Open Market Committee increases or decreases the amount of bank reserves by directing the Federal Reserve System to buy or sell United States government securities in the open market. Buying or selling in the open market involves buying from or selling to the general public. Briefly, it works like this. Suppose business gives evidence of slowing down. The Open Market Committee may direct the Reserve to buy $1 billion worth of government bonds. The persons who sell these bonds deposit the money in their banks. By buying these bonds the Federal Reserve puts that much more money into the banking system and thereby increases bank reserves. This enables the banks to increase their loans.

Conversely, if business seems to be expanding too rapidly because there is too much "easy" money in circulation, which could have the adverse effect of reducing the purchasing power of the dollar, the committee can direct the Federal Reserve System to sell government bonds. If, for example, banks are directed to sell $1 billion in bonds, the persons who buy the bonds pay for them by drawing checks on their banks. This reduces the amounts on reserve in the member banks. Thus, the cash reserves of the banking system are reduced by $1 billion and its lending capacity is likewise reduced. As a result, credit becomes "tighter," banks make fewer loans, business firms find it more difficult to obtain credit for expansion, and the dangers of overexpansion of business activity are prevented.

Legal-Reserve Requirements as Against Demand Deposits. In addition to the requirement that every member bank must subscribe to a certain amount of stock in the Federal Reserve Bank in its district, each member bank must maintain a minimum legal reserve. The amount of this legal reserve can be increased or decreased by the Board of Governors, when in their judgment there is a need to increase or decrease the amount of money member banks have available for credit financing.

The effectiveness of changes in reserve requirements depends on much the same conditions as open-market operations. Increasing excess reserves when the supply is already excessive encourages banks to put idle money to work by making more loans. If the increase in reserve requirements tends to reduce excess reserves to a dangerously low point, then the reserves will be decreased in order to curtail bank lending. This is a blunt and general means of credit control compared with the open-market operations, and when used it has proved to be most effective in discouraging or encouraging bank credit. It is used only infrequently.[3]

The Rediscount Rate. There are times when a member bank needs money for a short period. These banks may borrow from Federal Reserve Banks in two ways: they may rediscount, or sell, the promissory notes or other commercial paper they hold, or they may borrow on their own secured notes in a way similar to the way a customer borrows from a commercial bank. The former transactions are called *rediscounting*, and the latter, *advances*. When a bank obtains an advance, eligible commercial paper (negotiable promissory notes, for example) or government securities must be offered as collateral. Reserve authorities are inclined to raise the rediscount rate to discourage member-bank borrowing from a Reserve bank, and lower the rate to encourage it.

If the Federal Reserve decides that easy credit is contributing to inflation, it can raise the rediscount rate so that borrowers will have to pay a higher interest-rate. Raising the rediscount rate tends to raise interest rates so that borrowers find it too expensive to borrow money either to expand their businesses or to make additional purchases.

Regulation of Margin Requirements. As has already been mentioned in our discussion of the New York Stock Exchange in Chapter 16, the Board of Governors by law has the power to set minimum margin requirements. Regulating the margin requirements is a means of encouraging or discouraging lending. The smaller the margin required of the buyer, the more he can borrow against the purchase price; the higher the margin that

[3] In the United States, commercial banks are required to maintain legal reserves equal to a certain proportion of total deposits. This requirement is intended to place a legal limit upon increasing or decreasing demand deposits. For example, if a bank's reserve requirement were 25 percent, total deposits could not exceed four times the amount of reserves. But if deposits already were four times the reserves, for the bank to increase its demand deposits it would have to increase further the reserves.

By controlling reserve accounts, it is possible to regulate demand deposits. Originally, the Federal Reserve Act called for a reserve requirement of 3 percent on time deposits, and demand deposits required a reserve of 13, 10, and 7 percent, applicable to central reserve city, reserve city, and "country" banks, respectively. Recently, Congress consolidated the reserve classes of cities. The Board is empowered to vary reserve requirements on demand deposits between 10 and 22 percent at reserve city banks, and between 7 and 14 percent at country banks, but still only between 3 and 6 percent on time deposits at any class of bank.

is required of him, the less he can buy against the price of the stock. Consequently, buying on margin makes it possible for a person to buy more stocks with less money. The current margin rate is 80 percent.

Besides the direct controls over margin borrowing, the Federal Reserve for many years had the power to set limits on installment sales contracts. During the years of the Korean conflict, the Federal Reserve established a regulation requiring buyers of cars, household goods, and other items under "Regulation W" to pay up on charge accounts before buying more goods on credit. This regulation was very effective in controlling credit, but it became unpopular, and when the Korean crisis ended, this power of the Federal Reserve was permitted by Congress to expire.

Clearing Bank-Checks. Another function of the Federal Reserve System is to establish procedures for clearing bank-checks. About 90 percent of the total dollar volume of business involves payments by check. Most checks are drawn on one bank and deposited in another. When the banks involved are located in the same community, the clearance is conducted by the local clearinghouse association of local member banks. This procedure involves tabulating, accounting, and exchanging local checks, with account differences being paid to the appropriate bank each day. When banks are not local but are in the same Federal Reserve District, handling the checks is called the *clearing process*. When there is an exchange of checks between banks located in two or more Federal Reserve Districts, the check-clearing process is known as the *transit process*. Any bank that acts as a representative of another bank is a *correspondent bank*. In the accompanying illustration, the transit process is indicated step-by-step, involving check-clearance concerning banks located in two Federal Reserve Districts.

The illustration below shows the transit process for handling checks between two Federal Reserve District Banks. In this example, Mr. Jones in Richmond, Va., writes a check on his bank in Richmond and mails it to C Co. in Atlanta, Ga. That company then deposits the check to its account in an

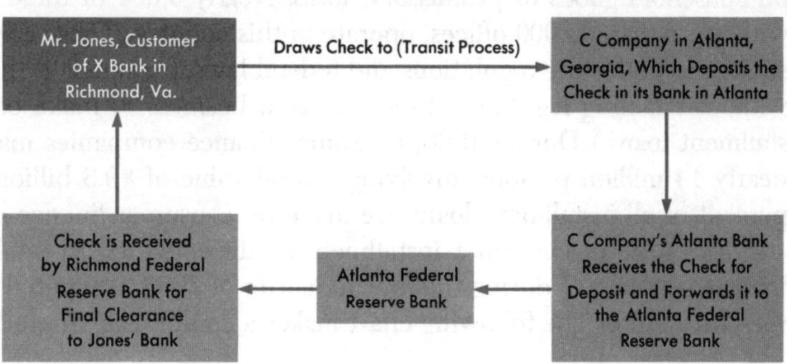

Atlanta bank. This bank sends the check, together with other out-of-town checks, to the Atlanta Federal Reserve Bank, which sorts the checks by districts and sends Mr. Jones' check back to the Richmond Federal Reserve Bank. All checks are again sorted by cities, and the various checks are returned to each drawer's bank. In this case Mr. Jones' check is received, and the amount is deducted from his account.

OTHER SOURCES OF COMMERCIAL CREDIT

In addition to short-term loans supplied by commercial banks, there are other sources of funds which business firms and individuals may use. Among these are *sales finance companies, consumer finance companies, factoring companies, credit unions,* and *industrial banks.*

Sales Finance Companies

These specialize in financing the sale of consumer goods bought on installment sales contracts from retail merchants. The loans are made directly to the customer, repayable on an installment plan. Examples of sales finance companies are the General Motors Acceptance Corp. (GMAC), which does financing for General Motors cars sold through dealers. Ford dealers are served by the Commercial Investment Trust (CIT). In addition, there are many smaller privately-owned sales finance companies. These firms acquire their funds mainly by borrowing from commercial banks at a low rate of interest because of their excellent credit-ratings and their ability to collect on installment loans. In the automobile business less than 10 percent of the dealers "carry the paper" on their retail sales.

Consumer Finance Companies

These are in the business of making consumer installment loans mainly on household goods or promissory notes. Nearly 9,000 of these companies, with more than 21,000 offices, operate in this country. These companies are subject to both state regulations and federal laws. (Arkansas is the only state without enabling legislation to authorize a business to make consumer installment loans.) During 1966, consumer finance companies made loans to nearly 14 million persons, involving a total value of $9.3 billion. About 40 percent of all installment loans are made by consumer finance companies.[4]

The ratio of consumer installment credit extended to total disposable income was 15 to 1 during the fourth quarter of 1966, compared to 15.9 to 1 the year before. The following chart makes a comparison of credit extended

[4] National Consumer Finance Assn., *Finance Facts Yearbook,* 1966, p. 2.

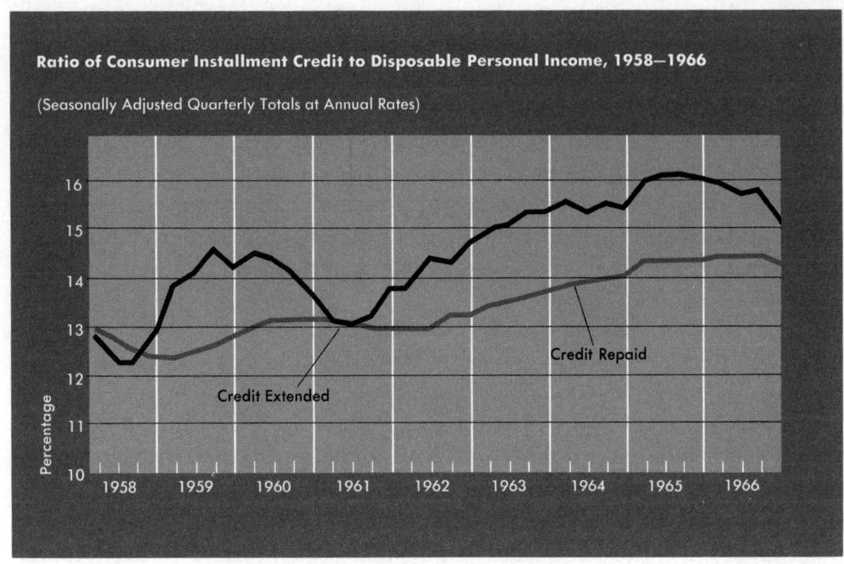

Source: Federal Reserve Board and Dept. of Commerce

to credit repaid, representing ratio of consumer installment credit to disposable personal income, 1958–1966.

Factoring Companies

These specialize in loans on accounts receivable which they actually take over from business firms; they perform the work of collecting each account. For this service, they receive a fee as well as interest on the loan. Factoring is practiced largely in the manufacture of furniture, glassware, textiles, and shoes. Although the primary financing functions performed by factors is to purchase accounts receivable without recourse for credit losses, factors also make secured and unsecured loans to their clients. In these instances, the factor is acting in the capacity of the commercial finance company. There are about two dozen well-known factoring companies, located mostly in New York and Chicago.

Credit Unions

These are cooperative associations composed of groups of people having a common bond (employees of the same company or members of the same union) who agree not only to save their money together but at the same time to make loans to one another at low interest-rates. Most loans are small—from $10 to $300.

Credit unions may be chartered under state or federal laws. Almost all of the states have passed legislation to charter credit unions as nonprofit associations. Federal credit unions are chartered and supervised by the Bureau of Federal Credit Unions, an agency affiliated with the Department of Health, Education, and Welfare. Members in the credit unions buy shares in the association which may be bought back from the member by the association at any time, without loss of principal. Compared with commercial and mutual-savings banks, the dividend rate of credit unions tends to be from 1 to 2 percent higher. The legal maximum dividend rate that a federal credit union can pay is 6 percent.

Industrial Banks

These are institutions chartered and supervised by the states. Their main purpose is to make nonbusiness loans to be repaid by borrowers out of income. These banks obtain their capital from individual savers, either through deposits or from the sale of investment certificates.

One of the better-known industrial banks is the Morris Plan Bank found in many metropolitan areas. Arthur J. Morris was the originator of this plan of banking, and out of his idea has grown the concept of industrial banks. The Morris Plan Bank plan avoids the usury laws by the simple device of selling installment "investment certificates" to borrowers. Technically, the advance of money is not a loan. Regular payments are made on this certificate over a period of time agreed upon, and when the loan is fully paid, it is cancelled against the loan contract. The Morris Plan introduced the idea of using the "co-maker" on a note. This means that borrowers are required to furnish one or more co-signers who guarantee that the contract will be performed. Actually, industrial banks, including those using the Morris Plan, provide other banking services, including personal and savings accounts, checking-account privileges, and financial advice.

REGULATING FINANCIAL INSTITUTIONS

During the course of our discussion of various fields of business, we have noted several illustrations of governmental control. Both the states and the federal government have in a similar manner enacted legislative measures to control financial and credit-type institutions.

Regulatory Measures

Congressional authority to regulate money and credit is chiefly based on Section 8 of the Constitution of the United States. Under this provision,

Congress has certain rights, among which are those of borrowing money on the credit of the United States, of coining money, of paying debts, and of performing certain other responsibilities vital to the common defense and general welfare of this nation.

For many years, financial institutions such as banks, savings-and-loan companies, investment trusts, finance companies, and stock exchanges were subject to very little federal control, and often to even less state control. As early as 1900, however, it became evident that government supervision of our national banking system was needed. During the boom period of the late 1920's, the public was victimized by dishonest schemes and abuses involving the purchase of overvalued corporation stocks. Even more significant was the number of bank failures that occurred. These could have been avoided had there been proper legislation to provide for greater controls. Fortunately, corrective legislation, such as the following, eventually was enacted.

The Federal Reserve Act. One of the four purposes of the Federal Reserve Act of 1913 was to provide supervision of banking in the United States. The Board of Governors of the Federal Reserve System makes general monetary credit policies as a whole, and formulates rules and regulations necessary to carry out the purposes of the Federal Reserve Act. Their controlling of credit conditions, and supervising of Federal Reserve Banks and member banks, is indeed important to the general welfare of this nation.

The Federal Reserve Board has the power to examine Federal Reserve Banks, and to control the admission of state banks or trust companies to membership in the Federal Reserve System. It may also terminate membership, approve or disapprove bank mergers or consolidations, and pass upon applications of national banks for authority to act in a fiduciary capacity (a special duty of care and confidence between the parties). In addition to its credit operations, the Federal Reserve can establish or discontinue branch reserve banks, and exercise supervision of those banks in their relations with foreign banks or bankers. In this chapter we have already noted many of these areas of control, particularly over practices that affect banking operations, and over credit policies toward business. The value of this legislation is self-evident.

The Federal Deposit Insurance Corporation. Few people today worry about the safety of their money on deposit in national and state banks that are insured by the Federal Deposit Insurance Corporation (FDIC). As we said earlier in this chapter, one reason for this public confidence is that the FDIC Acts of 1933 and 1950 require all national banks to insure their deposits with the FDIC. State banks are also eligible to participate, provided

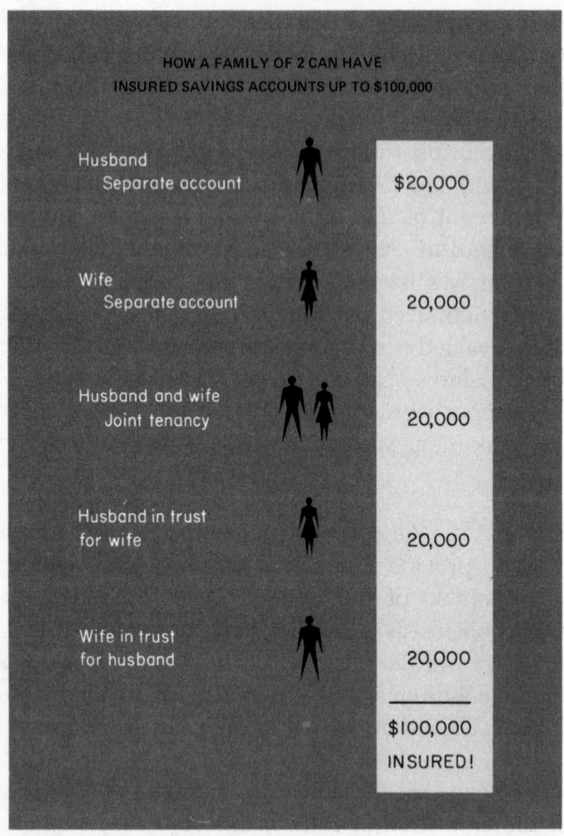

these institutions can pass a careful examination conducted by the FDIC. The amount to which each account is insured was recently increased from $15,000 to $20,000. Funds for this program are obtained by assessing each member bank an annual fee equal to one-twelfth of 1 percent of all deposits in that bank. The illustration above shows how a family of two can have insured savings up to $100,000.

The Truth-in-Lending Law. The Consumer Credit Protection Act (otherwise known as the "truth-in-lending" bill) was passed by Congress in May, 1968 with an effective date of July 1, 1969. This law requires loan companies, banks, retailers, and other businesses engaged in installment consumer selling to publish—in terms of an annual rate—the cost of consumer credit charged the buyer. Whereas stores formerly listed the cost of a revolving charge account as 1½ percent per month, they must now state the cost as 18 percent (the cost per year). The law covers loans and credit purchases up to $25,000 and home mortgages of any amount.

Certain exemptions are provided in the Act. No disclosure of lending costs is required on installment purchases of $25 or less; items which cost between $25 and $75 if finance charges are less than $5; and purchases over $75 if the total finance charges do not exceed $7.50. The Federal Reserve Board has responsibility for preparing the regulations to implement this law. Massachusetts enacted the first truth-in-lending law in 1967. Seven other states adopted such legislation prior to May, 1968, the date the federal legislation was passed.

YOUR CAREER IN FINANCE AND BANKING

Over the years there has been developed in this country a variety of financial institutions to serve short-term, intermediate-term, and long-term financial needs. Through the medium of these financial institutions personal and business savings are put to work to provide large amounts of capital. The fact that banking services are in great demand to help maintain a growing economy has made career opportunities in finance and banking unusually good for those who are qualified.

Qualifications for Banking Positions

Since banks are constantly handling money belonging to other people, honesty and integrity are two important personal requirements for bank personnel. Among other requirements are the ability to meet and work with others, politeness, neatness, and initiative. Of course, all bank employees must be able to keep confidential any information about their customers. And last, but not at all least, collegiate training in business administration will enhance a job applicant's qualifications.

Under the sponsorship of the American Institute of Banking, a series of special courses to help employees advance is offered in many of the larger cities. These courses cover every phase of banking and are regarded as a prerequisite for advancement.

Employment Opportunities in Banking

Banks are constantly complaining that there is a shortage of college-trained men and women interested in careers in banking. In the past, the relatively low starting salaries offered by banks tended to discourage young people from entering this business, and banks made little effort to carry on an aggressive campaign to inform college students of the expanding opportunities. More recently, however, starting salaries have been increasing, and banks are doing a better job of informing young people of the advantages of a career in banking.

Courtesy Provident Tradesmens Bank and Trust Co. Philadelphia, and International Telephone & Telegraph Corp.

Bank teller compares check signature with TV signature sent from a central file by means of VIDEX installation of International Telephone & Telegraph Corp. The system enables a television picture of the depositor's signature to be transmitted for verification over ordinary, inexpensive telephone lines, between the central signature file and branch offices.

Kinds of Employment. Several kinds of employment are open to beginners in banking. The bank operations department is a good place to learn mechanical operations and accounting procedures. Other good opportunities for advancement are to be found in the loan department and in the department responsible for new-business development and public relations.

Larger commercial banks have trust departments to handle estates and administer trusts; legal training is essential in these activities. Some banks maintain a foreign or international trade department to handle trade documents used in foreign commerce (described in Chapter 24). And in every bank, no matter what its size, there are numerous clerical positions that may serve as steppingstones to higher positions. These positions involve machine operators, messengers, typists, clerks, and secretaries. In Chapter 10 you learned that a new field, that of the electronic computer, requires specialists in computer programming.

There are also positions as tellers, personnel managers, auditors, economists, tax specialists, and loan officers. The American Institute of Banking reports that out of every 100 jobs in banking, 17 are filled by administrative officers and 10 by senior supervisors.

The highest position in most banks is the chairman of the board of directors, who is promoted from the office of president. The regular officers are: president, vice-president (usually several), secretary, and cashier. Large banks assign each of the vice-presidents the responsibility for directing the functions of certain departments. Some banks have several assistant cashiers. One of the most interesting and responsible positions is that of loan officer, who is in charge of all loans. In very large banks, all loans are ultimately approved by a loan committee after the loan application has been analyzed and prepared by the loan officer.

The Investment Banker and the Stockbroker

The *investment banker* is a specialist who advises corporations on the most profitable methods of marketing their securities. He provides information about the proper timing of a sale, about what type of securities can be distributed at a minimum cost, and about legal and technical matters, and he also provides general economic information. He is actually the intermediary between two parties—the issuer and the investor.

When the corporation officials have decided to sell the firm's securities through the investment banker, he assumes the responsibility for marketing these securities. Planning the sale of corporate securities requires months of careful preparation and entails a knowledge of legal procedures, government regulations, stock-market operations, and current economic conditions. All of this necessitates a broad background in finance and banking.

Closely identified with the investment banker is the *stockbroker,* who as agent executes orders for his clients. To qualify for this position you must pass an examination conducted by the Securities and Exchange Commission. Virtually all of the larger brokerage firms conduct special training programs for beginners in this field. Training in business finance, economics, law, accounting, mathematics, and investments will provide you with a good background for one of these positions.

Career Opportunities in Other Finance Fields

There are career opportunities open in many other fields of finance. These include employment in the Federal Reserve System and the Small Business Administration, and in insurance companies, savings and loan associations, commercial-paper houses, and mortgage companies. Positions with any of these organizations should be well-paying and offer good future expectations. Here again, broad training in business administration is a valuable asset. Other requirements are similar to those discussed previously. A background in liberal-arts subjects, including English, is highly important.

SUMMARY

In addition to permanent financing, every business uses various forms of credit as sources of funds for short-term financing. Our business system is such that credit is the basis for all loans. Credit furnishes a convenient means of making debt payments, and enables the proprietor to adjust his volume of capital to meet the changing financial needs of the business that result from seasonal variations in production and sales.

Credit instruments used in financing working-capital are based on either the principle of promise-to-pay or order-to-pay. Credit instruments that are promises to pay are the open-book account, the promissory note, and bonds. Included among the orders-to-pay instruments are checks, drafts (bills of exchange), and trade acceptances. Each is designed to serve a particular purpose.

Short-term credit is available through such credit arrangements as pledging of accounts receivable, bank loans, installment credit, and loans from finance companies and government agencies. Security for short-term loans consists of corporation stocks, bonds, order bills of lading, warehouse receipts, trust receipts, and chattel mortgages.

Commercial banks are the principal sources of short-term business loans. These banks also supply business with a variety of other financial services, such as accepting deposits which can be withdrawn without notice (demand deposits), discounting negotiable instruments, renting safe-deposit boxes, issuing letters of credit, servicing foreign-trade transactions, and serving as trustee or executor of estates.

Commercial banks are classified as either state or national banks. State banks are chartered by the state in which they are organized; national banks receive their charter from the federal government.

Under federal law, all national banks must be members of the Federal Reserve System and the Federal Deposit Insurance Corporation. State banks may also be members if they qualify.

The main function of the Federal Reserve System is to make more funds available when warranted by business activity, and to restrict funds when the economic condition justifies contraction of credit.

In addition to the regulation of credit exercised by the Federal Reserve, the Securities and Exchange Commission exercises various forms of control over stock-market operations and corporate financing procedures. The Secretary of Agriculture supervises transactions on commodity markets.

There are few fields of endeavor that offer greater career opportunities for college graduates than banking and finance. Levels of employment in banking are varied and interesting. For every 100 jobs in banking, there are 17 administrative and 10 supervisory positions. College-trained students are in demand, especially those with training in business administration. Salaries are higher than in many other fields of employment.

VOCABULARY REVIEW QUIZ

Match the following vocabulary terms with the statements below.

a. Cashier's check
b. Certificate of deposit
c. Collateral
d. Correspondent bank
e. Credit
f. Drawer
g. Investment banker
h. Negotiable promissory note
i. Payee
j. Sight draft
k. Stock companies
l. Time draft
m. Trade credit
n. Warehouse receipt

1. A financial obligation, typified by the "open-book account," which is extended by credit managers and proprietors.
2. The one who draws a negotiable draft
3. The name of a draft that is payable on demand
4. A bill of exchange drawn by a bank against its own funds
5. The person to whom a check is made payable
6. Marketable assets—goods, land, or negotiable instruments used as security for a loan
7. What businesses owned by stockholders are called
8. A bank that acts as a representative for another bank
9. One who advises corporations as to the most profitable method of marketing their securities to the public
10. The ability to secure goods or services in exchange for a promise to pay later
11. A written promise made by the borrower to the lender, agreeing to pay, either on demand or at a certain time, a specified sum of money to order or to bearer
12. A document that serves as a receipt for goods stored in a warehouse
13. An interest-bearing negotiable instrument, in the form of a time certificate, issued by a bank acknowledging receipt of a specific sum of money to be repaid by the bank
14. A draft payable at some designated future date

QUESTIONS FOR REVIEW STUDY

1. In what way do "promises to pay" instruments differ from "orders to pay" credit instruments?

2. Analyze the meaning of "credit" and explain how it serves the businessman.
3. What makes a promissory note a better credit instrument than an open-book account?
4. Identify the various parties to a check.
5. Explain the difference between a time draft and a sight draft.
6. Explain the meaning of the term "trade acceptance" and indicate how it is used.
7. A customer with a good credit-rating places an order with your firm, but says he is temporarily short of working capital. Suppose you are not willing to ship the goods on an open-book account. What form of credit instrument would be the most desirable for you to use in order to make this sale?
8. Illustrate the uses of the following types of collateral: a chattel mortgage, a negotiable warehouse receipt, an order bill of lading, and a trust receipt.
9. Identify at least five services rendered by commercial banks to business.
10. Analyze the two main functions of the Federal Reserve System.
11. Discuss some of the advantages banks find in belonging to the Federal Reserve System.
12. What is the purpose of open-market operations as performed by the Open Market Committee of the Federal Reserve System?

PROBLEMS AND PROJECTS

1. Patrick Hix has both a good credit-rating and a position that pays him $10,000 a year. He plans to buy a new automobile that will cost about $4,000. His dealer has offered him $1,000 for his present car. Describe which sources of credit are open to him, assuming he cannot pay cash for the car.
2. From the viewpoint of a financial manager, compare commercial banks, sales finance companies, and consumer finance companies as sources of short-term financing. Analyze the kinds of short-term loans each of these companies makes.
3. The San Jacinto Canning Co., producers of fruits and juices marketed through retail stores in Washington, Oregon, and California, needs a short-term loan of approximately $20,000. Most of the fruit is harvested during the summer season and canned in the company's three plants. To meet the heavy costs of operation during the canning season, the company temporarily needs additional working capital to carry them over. By January all the fruit has been sold to wholesalers, which means the company can pay this obligation. What sources of credit would you recommend to the company, in addition to their present bank-loans?

A BUSINESS CASE

Case 17-1 ASA Manufacturing's Need for Short-Term Credit

The ASA Manufacturing Co., weavers of cotton cloth (mostly sheets and pillow cases), needs about $60,000 to carry it until the end of the selling season. The firm has already exhausted its short-term credit with three local banks. One of the local bankers, however, has suggested the company use some other means of financing.

Analyze the following financial statement and recommend to the company president some other possible sources of credit.

ASA MANUFACTURING COMPANY

Statement of Financial Position December 31, 19—

Assets		Liabilities	
Cash	$ 20,000	Notes Payable	$ 35,000
Accounts Receivable	75,000	Accounts Payable	73,000
Merchandise Inventory	35,000	Total Liabilities	$108,000
Total Assets	$130,000	Owner's Equity	22,000
		Total Liabilities and Equities	$130,000

Risk Management and Insurance

18

Under our system of private enterprise, every business venture involves some amount of risk, and therefore a degree of uncertainty. But then, everyone, even in private life, is constantly exposed to a multitude of risks, and some of these bring with them a feeling of uncertainty that oftentimes is almost unbearable. Indeed, risk is so universal that it is unlikely that any firm or individual will escape, for very long at least, the company of one or another kind and degree of uncertainty. Because this is a book about business, however, we will limit our discussion mainly to business risks and uncertainties.

Some business risks can be overcome by good business practices. In certain cases, it is possible to adjust or absorb losses that otherwise cannot be removed or shifted. Other perils must be guarded against by the use of insurance in one form or another. But even the shifting of risks to an insurance company, while it may minimize the loss to the insured, does not relieve the individual or business as a whole from responsibility for all loss. Moreover, insurance cannot make up entirely for the loss of goods, the destruction of which makes society poorer through a reduction of its economic potential.

In this chapter we will analyze how insurance in its numerous forms, through the practice of risk management, is used as a safeguard against misfortune and loss. Although admittedly insurance cannot prevent such unfortunate occurrences as death, sickness, floods, and auto accidents, and, as we have said, cannot really make up for lost goods, it can reduce the burdens they produce. When a businessman insures his plant against loss by fire, it may burn, but he will have peace of mind that the loss will be borne by the insurance company more economically than by him.

In order for you to understand the kinds of risk which may be insured against, and the various types of policies available, it is also important that you become familiar with the essential principles of insurance, and the general provisions of insurance contracts. The final portion of this chapter is devoted to a discussion of career opportunities in insurance that are open to college graduates.

THE NATURE OF RISK

As has already been noted, one of the characteristics of our environment is the presence of risk. (Perhaps this is the reason why for many people life does not get monotonous—one cannot accurately forecast the uncertainties ahead.) Through an understanding of the various types of insurance contracts, you will be better prepared to deal with risk as it comes your way time and again under numerous guises.

Risk may be defined as *the chance or uncertainty of loss.* The loss may take many forms, such as loss of life, property, or health. Because people are unable to predict misfortune, risk causes a great deal of anxiety. Little wonder, then, that people constantly seek to shift the burden of risk or attempt to prevent it. Often, mere token efforts to reduce risk pay big dividends.

Types of Risk

There are two broad types of risk: *speculation* and *pure risk.* At this point a distinction needs to be made in order to determine which one is insurable.

A *speculative risk* is generally defined as *one in which there is both a chance of loss and an element of gain*—such as a business venture or a gambling transaction. Wagering, for example, is a speculative risk because those who wager may either gain or lose. Hedging, one of the topics discussed in Chapter 19, is a means of neutralizing a speculative risk. The kind of loss

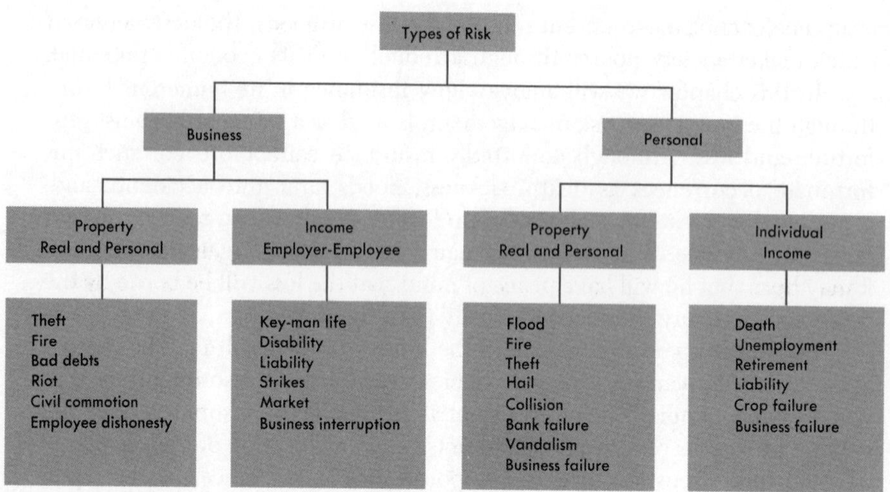

against which insurance offers protection may be called *pure risk.* In *pure risk* there is no chance of gain—only of loss. Examples of a pure risk include loss by fire or flood, and the death of a key executive. The distinction between these two is significant because allowance for compensation for speculative risk generally is handled by methods other than insurance coverage, while pure risks are usually insurable. The diagram above shows the kinds of pure risks, classified as "Business" and "Personal," for which it is possible to buy some form of insurance protection. It also brings us to the subject of the various ways of meeting risk, which we shall discuss next.

Methods of Meeting Risk

Obviously, one person alone cannot reduce his risk, unless he is able to control a large enough number of factors that have a direct bearing on that risk. After all, each of us has but one life; most of us own little property; and only a comparatively few persons own more than two automobiles. Even if three or four autos are owned, this is an insufficient number to permit adequate spreading of the risk.

What, then, are the methods of meeting risk that are open to individuals and business concerns? In addition to hedging, there are four other methods of meeting risk. They may be grouped under the following headings:

1. Remove the risk or its cause.
2. Establish a reserve fund in anticipation of loss.
3. Practice good management to prevent causes of risk.
4. Shift the risk by buying insurance.

Removing the Chance of Loss. Among the most effective ways of removing the chance of loss, or its cause, are installing safety devices on machinery, and replacing equipment that constant use has made defective and dangerous. Fireproof structures help to eliminate losses from both fire and the damage by water that frequently follows. Safety campaigns among workers help to decrease the number of accidents by curtailing carelessness. The same goal can at times be achieved by eliminating the causes of fatigue, including poor ventilation, unhealthy working conditions, and long hours.

Self-Insurance Plans. A second method is to set aside a reserve fund on which to draw when losses occur. This method assumes that it is more profitable for a businessman to assume his own risks than to insure against them. It is not a practical method for most small businesses. Assume, for example, that the owner of a $60,000 business building decides to set aside $1,000 per year as a reserve fund to protect his property against fire. It would obviously take almost a lifetime to accumulate sufficient reserve funds to cover a total loss. Furthermore, most business firms cannot afford to carry an excessive amount of risk during the early years of their operation under this plan.

This plan is often more successful when used by companies with widely scattered operations. Since the chance of a severe loss in property during any one year at several locations is remote, if each unit in the company contributes to a self-insurance fund, that fund will ordinarily be adequate to compensate for any loss the company might sustain. Such risks as those caused by cyclone, tornado, hurricane, and flood require excessively high insurance premium rates. Yet companies need some kind of protection. So electric, gas, and water utility companies as well as telephone companies set aside annually a self-insurance reserve fund to cover losses of these kinds. These funds remain in the business until needed. If losses occur requiring expenditures in excess of the fund, then the company makes up the difference. The method of determining the amount to be set aside is rather arbitrary, since past records are not an accurate guide to future perils caused by nature.

Good Management. The best way, and often the only way, to meet certain kinds of business risk is to exercise sound business judgment when making management decisions. For example, sharp changes in the economy which affect the demand for a product or service are a risk for which insurance is not available. About the only effective way to meet this kind of economic risk is for management to be alert enough to changing conditions, to prepare in advance an appropriate plan of action. To be properly informed and prepared, many companies maintain a research department which studies economic trends, analyzes customer demands, and tests new products and ideas.

Insurance. Businessmen have found that one of the most satisfactory ways to deal with risk is insurance. Insurance combines the risks of many people in a group, using the money collected from each person in the group to meet losses as they occur. The purpose of insurance is not to prevent losses, but to spread the risk burden resulting from such losses. Thus, insurance is a means to enable an individual to transfer his risk to a larger number of people who are liable to suffer similar losses.

Insurance involves a contract that specifies what each party agrees to do. It represents, in the highest degree, cooperation for the mutual benefit of the insurer and the insured.

Principles of Insurance

Both the function and the method of operating an insurance company are unique in modern business. It is not difficult to understand why the *modus operandi* of an insurance company should have to differ from that of other businesses when it is realized that the function is that of a professional risk-taker. Even the fundamental principles (so to speak) of the insurance company are unlike those of other business, for insurers alone rely heavily on the principle of the *law of large numbers* and the *principle of insurable risk.*

The Law of Large Numbers. Has it ever occurred to you how an insurance company can afford to assume a $50,000 risk for an annual premium of $1,000?

The explanation lies in the application of the law of large numbers, often referred to as the *law of averages.* According to this mathematical law, if you use a very large number of similar risks, only a certain number of losses will occur. For example, if you study the number of fire losses annually of, say, 25,000 similar types of buildings over a three-year period, it is possible to predict with surprising accuracy how many of these structures will be destroyed by fire during a given year. The important factor in predicting losses by this principle is the use of large numbers of cases.

The law of large numbers, therefore, may be stated as follows: *The larger the number of cases used, the more nearly will the actual experience approximate the probable outcome.* This law uses the application of probability to past experience. Consequently, when past experience reveals the total losses, the share to be assigned to each individual insured during the next period can be equitably calculated by actuarial methods. This is the basis of all mortality-table calculations used by life-insurance companies. In a similar manner, fire-insurance companies study fire losses, using large numbers of cases in order to predict losses.

The Principle of Insurable Risk. While it is a fact that insurers have demonstrated a remarkable ability to predict losses by the application of a large number of cases where pure risk is involved, certain other requirements must be met if a risk is to be insurable. A second basic principle of insurance, the principle of insurable risk, involves the conditions under which a risk can be economically insured. This principle simply states: *If the requisites of insurability are not met, the risk is not economically insurable.*

From the standpoint of the insurer, the following requisites of insurability must be satisfied for a risk to be insurable:

1. *Should the loss occur, it must be the kind that is purely accidental and unintentional.* There must be some uncertainty attached to the loss. Otherwise, if the risk has been eliminated, insurance serves no useful purpose. As a matter of fact, insurance is one item that *must* be bought *before* it is needed.
2. *The nature of the loss must be determinable and measurable.* Before an insurer can accept a risk burden requiring payment of a claim, he must set up procedures to determine if the loss has actually occurred, and if so, how much of a loss it is.
3. *The loss must not be subject to incalculable catastrophe hazard.* It is a theory of insurance that only a small percentage of the group exposed to a risk will suffer a loss at any one time. But if conditions are such that all or most of the objects in the group may suffer loss at the same time from the same peril, then this requisite for insurability is not present. This is the reason why an insurance company will limit itself to an amount it will commit for any one risk, and why fire companies limit their total commitments in any one geographical area.
4. *There must be a sufficient number of cases to measure, and the nature of the risk must be similar.* When only a few objects are covered, the insurer is unable to make an accurate calculation of the probable loss. In addition, the quality of the objects to be insured must be homogeneous in order to formulate reliable statistics of loss. This is the reason why, in computing fire losses for rate-making purposes, it would be improper to group commercial buildings with private residences; the hazards facing these classes of buildings are different.

TYPES OF PRIVATE INSURANCE COMPANIES

Insurance is a highly specialized business, and each company engages only in certain types of risk. Most insurance business, however, is handled by two common types of insurance companies: *stock companies,* and *mutual companies.*[1]

Stock Companies

The stock company is a corporation owned by stockholders, who need not necessarily be policyholders. The initial capital subscribed by the stockholders constitutes the company's working capital, and the company's income is earned from premiums paid by those who buy insurance policies. The *premium* is the amount paid by the insured for the protection purchased. Premiums may be paid weekly, monthly, quarterly, semiannually, or annually, depending on what the insurance contract calls for. Stock companies usually write their business through local agents, paying them a commission on the amount of business they obtain.

Profits earned by stock companies go to the stockholders, who are really the owners of the company. In some stock companies the policyholders also share in the earnings after the stockholders have received their investment dividends. Policies that provide the policyholder with a dividend (a share in the surplus earnings) are called *participating policies,* and the company issuing the policy is often referred to as a *participating company.* Insurance on which no dividends are paid is called *nonparticipating insurance.*

Stock companies do not assess policyholders when losses are greater than anticipated. The company must bear the loss through its stockholders.

Mutual Companies

Mutual insurance companies are associations of persons organized under the insurance code of each state as nonprofit corporations. Since each policyholder is legally an owner of the company, in this dual role he is in theory both an insurer and an insured. There are no profits as such, since any excess income goes to the policyholder as a dividend, or is used to reduce premiums. The policyholders elect a board of directors who are responsible for managing the company.

[1] Lloyd's of London, one of the oldest insurance associations in the world, is sometimes classified as a third type. It is operated as a corporation composed of members in much the same way as the New York Stock Exchange. Insurance contracts are written by individual member underwriters. If any single risk is too great for a member to carry alone, one or more of the other members share the contract. Lloyd's has approximately 1,400 members, many of whom have joined together in syndicates. Lloyd's transacts business in all parts of the world and insures extremely varied risks, such as the birth of triplets or changes in the weather. Lloyd's of America is organized like Lloyd's of London, but it has no connection with the English company.

Besides stock and mutual companies, life insurance is also sold by other organizations such as savings-bank life-insurance plans (Massachusetts, New York, and Connecticut), the National Service Life Insurance (a part of the Veterans Administration), and fraternal organizations. These organizations and companies are commonly referred to as *life-insurance carriers.*

The Institute of Life Insurance has reported that by the end of 1967, mutual life companies had 54 percent of the total life insurance in force, and stock companies carried 46 percent. Mutual companies also operate in other fields of insurance, but they are used to the greatest extent in the life-insurance field.

We shall now discuss only the more prominent of the several other types of mutual companies.

Fraternal Societies. These organizations, which are nonprofit ventures, are operated very much like lodges or societies. A fraternal society issues life insurance, and sometimes sickness and accident insurance. It may pay dividends to the policyholders, and in every way functions as do the other mutuals. Under state laws, fraternal societies are required to maintain reserves. In 1955, the National Association of Insurance Commissioners adopted a Uniform Fraternal Code to regulate fraternal insurance societies. The code requires virtually the same standards for life-insurance companies operating as fraternal societies as for other insurance companies.

Class Mutuals. These are mutual companies that insure only a specific class of property, such as factories, lumber mills, and farms. A mutual insuring farm property exclusively is called a *farm mutual.* In a few instances the name "farm mutual" is also applied to companies whose insured must be members of a grange—a type of farm organization.

The *factory mutual* specializes in writing coverage on factories. Eight completely independent mutual companies have organized an association known as Associated Factory Mutual Fire Insurance Companies. These companies accept only risks that meet high standards of building construction.

Stock- and Mutual Companies Compared. The question that often arises is: Which of these two types of companies charge the lowest premiums? A comparison is difficult to make. For one thing, most stock companies write only nonparticipating policies (a few write participating policies), which means that *the policyholders do not participate in dividends.* Thus, the premium rate for the nonparticipating policy becomes the cost of the policy. Mutual companies, however, issue participating policies in which the premium includes enough to cover all expenses, plus an added amount to safeguard the company. If the company management is highly efficient and part of the premium is not used, the company may return it in the form of a dividend. Hence, the net cost of the policy is determined by subtracting the dividend from the premium paid. It would seem that the net premium cost should be lower for mutuals than for stock companies, but competition tends to keep the net cost of insurance sold by mutual and stock companies about the same except where rates are set by a state insurance commission or equivalent agency.

GENERAL PROVISIONS OF INSURANCE CONTRACTS

The insurance contract is the policy that describes in detail provisions and coverages provided for, and also provisions which the company will not honor. Every policy covers a specified risk. The following information is usually contained in the policy contract:

1. The name of the insured or the identity and description of the property to be insured
2. A statement of risks covered and exempted, and a definition of terms
3. The amount of insurance to be paid in event of loss
4. The amount of the premium, and basis of payment
5. The method by which claims will be paid by the insurer
6. The period of coverage
7. The limitations of the insurer's liability

Common Policy Conditions

All insurance contracts stipulate that certain conditions must be met before any payment can be made. If the insured violates or fails to comply with any one of these conditions, there may be grounds for refusal to pay claims. It is important that each policyholder read his contract carefully, since most conditions have to do with loss settlements.

Insurable Interest. A fundamental principle underlying insurance contracts is the doctrine of insurable interest, which simply means that the policyholder must demonstrate a financial loss to himself in order to collect amounts due him when the insured peril takes place. Insurable interest is a legal requirement; otherwise, one could collect when he suffered no personal loss. This requirement is a necessity to prevent insurance from becoming a gambling contract. A man is considered to have an insurable interest in his own life, and in that of his wife and his children or even his business partners. But he is not considered to have an insurable interest in anyone else outside his family.

When does an insurable interest exist? In general, insurable interest in life insurance must be in existence at the inception of the policy, but not necessarily at the time of the loss. This adheres to the principle that life insurance is not a contract of indemnity, while property insurance is. It is established by the courts that in the case of property insurance, insurable interest need exist only at the time of the loss and not at the preparation of the policy. This principle should not be confused with the *principle of insurable risks* studied earlier in this chapter.

Fraud or Misrepresentation. Most contracts stipulate that misrepresentation of facts, or fraud, will void the contract. Failure to reveal facts about the risk which are material but known only to the insured will also invalidate the policy.

Notice of and Proof of Loss. Virtually all types of insurance contracts require the insured to give immediate written notice of loss, if practicable, or within a reasonable time (often 30 days). The insured then is generally allowed a certain number of days, say 30 or 60, to provide written formal proof of loss. Usually the company adjuster or agent provides copies of proof-of-loss forms and helps the insured to verify the losses.

Cancellation. All contracts of insurance specify the conditions under which the policy may be terminated. Property and liability contracts may be canceled by either party upon written notice. Life- and certain health-insurance contracts may be canceled by the insured, but not by the company except as may be provided in the "incontestable" clause. This clause governs payment of life-insurance claims in the event of suicide. It provides for reinstatement and a grace period, and in general stipulates a time limit within which the insurer must discover any fraud or misrepresentation in the application or be barred thereafter from asserting a legal right to cancel the contract. Some life policy contracts exclude death from war or from certain aviation accidents as an insurable risk. Refusal by the insurer to pay claims from these two excluded perils would not be in violation of the incontestable clause regardless of when the death occurred.

The Principle of Indemnity. The principle of indemnity is closely related to the doctrine of insurable interest, which states that a person may not collect more than his actual cash loss for damage caused by an insured peril. Thus, a person may insure property in excess of its actual value, but he cannot collect damages for more than the actual loss if the property is destroyed. As a general rule, only contracts for property and liability insurance are subject to the principle of indemnity. Contracts for life insurance and most health insurance are not contracts of indemnity.

TYPES OF INSURANCE COVERAGE

Insurance may be divided into the following broad classifications: (1) fire and allied lines, (2) marine, (3) casualty (including automobile, burglary, robbery, larceny, theft, workmen's compensation, public liability, accident, and health), (4) fidelity and surety bonds, (5) title, (6) credit, and (7) life insurance. In the discussion that follows, we shall stress points that are pertinent to business, but we shall also refer to personal insurance whenever such references are appropriate.

Fire and Allied Lines

Fire insurance indemnifies (pays for loss or damage) the insured (the policyholder) for the actual loss or damage to property due to destruction by fire or lightning up to the full amount of the property.[2] Fire insurance accounts for a large share of property insurance—fire losses each year are the highest. Since 1957, total property losses by fire have exceeded $1 billion annually.

Standard Fire Policy Form. Many states have adopted the New York standard fire contract, and those which have not, require a form similar to it. The advantage of the standard form is that the wording has been tested by the courts; as a result there is no doubt as to the meaning of the language.

If you want protection against such hazards as windstorm, riot, smudge, water, hail, aircraft damage, civil commotion, or explosion (which hazards are normally not contained in a standard form), you may obtain it by buying

[2] Except where there is a coinsurance clause. This clause is explained later in this chapter.

Every year fire destroys millions of dollars' worth of real and personal property. Fire damage is one of the common risks against which insurance is carried.

additional insurance under the extended-coverage endorsement to the standard fire-policy. This added coverage is usually referred to as *allied lines.*

The standard fire-policy contains the name of the insured, describes the property and its location and the perils covered, and gives the rate and premium.

The Coinsurance Clause. Business property in good condition and under the protection of a first-class fire department is seldom completely destroyed by fire. As a result, businesses have a tendency to underinsure. To prevent this, fire-insurance companies are permitted by state laws to insert one or more clauses that will limit the liability of the insurance company. When this type of limitation is in force, the amount of the premium may be lowered without sacrificing protection. The coinsurance clause requires that the insured carry insurance up to a stipulated percentage of the property's value. The most common coinsurance clause requires that insurance equal to 80 percent of the value be carried. A typical clause reads: "In the event of loss this company shall be liable for no greater proportion thereof than the sum hereby insured bears to ______% [usually 80 percent] of the cash value of the property described herein at the time when such loss shall happen."

In its simplest form this clause requires that if a building is insured for substantially less than its value, the owner must bear part of the loss of a firm. But in return, a reduced rate is given on such policies.

If a building is valued at $50,000, a policy with an 80 percent coinsurance clause would require the owner to carry at least $40,000 (80% × $50,000) of fire insurance.

How much could the owner collect if he carried only $30,000? On losses, he would collect only that proportion of the loss which the amount of the policy ($30,000) bears to the required amount ($40,000). If a $10,000 fire-loss occurred, the owner would collect $7,500 $\left(\frac{\$30{,}000}{\$40{,}000} \times \$10{,}000\right)$. The formula to determine the amount to be collected is as follows:

$$\frac{\text{Amount of Insurance Carried}}{\text{Amount of Insurance Required}} \times \text{Loss} = \text{Amount of Recovery}$$

In the following examples you can see the amount of fire-losses that would be paid on an 80 percent coinsurance contract:

Example I

Value of building = $30,000
Insurance required (80% × $30,000) = $24,000
Insurance carried = $24,000

The full amount of all losses up to $24,000 would be paid because the owner carried insurance equal to the percentage required in the coinsurance clause.

Example II

Value of building = $30,000
Insurance required (80% × $30,000) = $24,000
Insurance carried = $26,000

The amount of all losses up to $26,000 would be paid.

Example III

Value of building = $30,000
Insurance required (80% × $30,000) = $24,000
Insurance carried = $18,000 (less than the 80% required by clause)

Should a $20,000 loss occur, the amount to be recovered is $15,000.

$$\left(\frac{\$18{,}000}{\$24{,}000} \times \$20{,}000 = \$15{,}000.\ \text{See formula above.}\right)$$

In Example III, regardless of the loss, the owner could collect no more than $18,000, which is the amount of insurance carried. As a rule, coinsurance clauses do not apply to residences, household furnishings, or other personal property in a building.

Consequential Loss. Normally the standard fire contract reimburses the insured only for losses that can be traced directly to fire. Sometimes, however, all or part of a business is destroyed by fire; then the owner will suffer indirect losses resulting from his inability to carry on the business in a normal way. Losses of this nature are called *consequential losses.* Ordinarily, the standard fire-policy does not provide coverage on food that is damaged in a locker under conditions starting from fire, but a consequential-loss clause that specifically assumes this risk may be added to the policy for an additional premium at the time the policy is written.

Other kinds of consequential losses related to fire are loss of rental income if the building has previously been rented, extra expenses incurred in obtaining temporary quarters to carry on the business, and continuing expenses in the business after the fire loss is sustained, such as salaries and rent on equipment.

Figuring the Amount of Premium. Fire policies are usually written for one, three, or five years. A businessman may reduce the cost of his premiums by buying coverage for more than one year; however, he must pay the premiums in advance for the life of the contract.

The total premium for a fire-insurance policy is determined by multiplying the rate for each $100 of insurance by the amount for which the property is insured. This means that if you have a business building insured for $50,000 and the premium is 25 cents per $100 of insurance, your premium for one year is $125. But you can save money by paying the premium for three years, because the amount you pay is only two and one-half times the amount you would pay for one year. You can make even greater savings by buying a five-year policy, because the premium cost is only four times the annual rate.

Premiums vary according to the type of building construction (wood, brick, or concrete), its location in the community, and the record of fire losses over a certain number of years in that community. In many states, rates are set by a state commission.

Determining the Amount of Insurance. Astute businessmen will tell you it does not pay to overinsure property, since the maximum damage that can be collected from total loss is usually only the present value of the structure. In no case can the amount collected as damage exceed the face value of the policy, the amount stated in the policy contract. As a matter of fact, in most states the actual amount of the loss is paid rather than the face value of the policy. When policies are renewed, the amount should be revised to cover the real value of the article at time of renewal.

Assume that a building built five years ago cost $20,000 and is insured against fire under a standard contract. Since the building was built, building costs have advanced 50 percent. If the building were depreciated at an annual rate of 2 percent, the insured should carry $27,000 of fire insurance, computed as follows:

$20,000	original cost
10,000	increase in cost of materials ($20,000 × .50)
$30,000	replacement cost now
3,000	depreciation for 5 years at 2% ($30,000 × 2% × 5 = $3,000)
$27,000	amount of insurance to be fully insured

Marine Insurance

Marine insurance is the oldest type of insurance; its use dates back some 5,000 years. Originally it covered loss of vessel and cargo at sea. Coverage at sea is now called *ocean marine insurance,* while coverage on land is called by a somewhat contradictory term, *inland marine insurance.*

Ocean Marine. This type of protection covers all kinds of hazards to the vessel and cargo while in port or at sea. Some of the perils include sinking, capsizing, stranding, collision, and theft. Each contract is "custom made." It may be written for a specific period of time or for a single voyage.

Inland Marine. Inland marine insurance includes coverage of all forms of transportation over land and on rivers, lakes, canals and coastal waters, and in the air. The perils include such items as fire, lightning, wind, hail, theft, flood, and collision. Of special interest to businessmen is the form of inland marine insurance that covers the shipment of goods by parcel post. The shipper may either buy a blanket policy covering all parcel-post shipments, or else purchase a book of insurance coupons and insert one coupon in each parcel shipped by parcel post. Generally, risks such as theft, robbery, riot, and strikes are covered only if specifically indorsed.

The *personal property floater policy* is a variation of inland marine. This policy insures household goods and personal effects of the insured in the home or away from home, whether in transit or not.

Automobile Insurance

Automobile insurance is one of the several kinds of insurance coverages included in the term "casualty," which is a generic term applicable to various kinds of insurance other than life, marine, and the hazards of fire and windstorm. A *casualty* is an accident—a mishap that happens unintentionally.

If you own a car, you can buy insurance protection to cover any of the six basic automobile insurance coverages listed in the following diagram. As you can observe from the diagram, automobile owners face two major classes of risk: (1) the possibility that the car will be damaged, stolen, or destroyed by collision, theft, or fire (respectively); and (2) the possibility that the car may cause injury or damage to others.

SIX BASIC AUTOMOBILE INSURANCE COVERAGES

	Coverages on persons		Coverages on property		
Type of Automobile Insurance Protection	Insured and Members of Family	Others Than Insured	Insured's Car Only	Cars Other Than Insured's	Property Other Than Cars
Comprehensive damage losses			X		
Collison or upset			X		
Bodily injury liability		X			
Property damage liability				X	X
Medical payments for injury	X	X			
Uninsured motorist protection	X	X			

Comprehensive Damage Losses. This type of policy covers the cost of damage or loss of an automobile due to fire, theft, windstorm, hail, riot, lightning, flood, and damage to glass from flying objects. The policy also covers loss by theft of articles from a locked vehicle. The first automobile policies ever issued insured the car for the hazard of fire only. Now these various kinds of hazards are grouped together and are included in a single policy covering a comprehensive line of risks. Virtually all finance companies and banks require this kind of protection for automobiles sold on an installment plan.

In case of fire or theft, indemnity is based on the current or present value of the automobile and not on its original cost. Fire and theft rates are based on the age of the car, its use (for business or pleasure), and the rate of fire-losses in a given community or state for a prior period. About half of all claims paid under the comprehensive coverage is for the replacement of glass in the vehicle.

Automobile Collision or Upset. This insurance pays the damage to the insured car resulting from collision with either a moving vehicle or a stationary object. Collision insurance may be either full-coverage or deductible. Under full-coverage, the company compensates for all losses, regardless of the amount or who is at fault.

Under the deductible plan, no liability rests with the company until the loss from collision or upset exceeds a specified amount. To illustrate: Assume that your policy is written with a "$50 deductible" clause. If your car is damaged in the amount of $300, you bear the first $50 of the cost, and receive indemnity for the remaining $250 from the company. The higher the deductible clause, the lower are the premium rates because there are fewer claims filed. The two most popular deductible clauses are for $50 and $100. Many firms carry deductible policies on company cars, but more often for larger amounts than for $50 or $100.

Bodily-Injury Liability. The purpose of automobile bodily-injury liability insurance is to furnish protection to the insured against claims resulting from the injury or death of a person for whom the owner of the vehicle is liable. Most bodily-injury policies are written for a stated amount to cover one or more persons injured in the same accident. Thus, a policy with limits of $5,000/10,000 covers injuries to one person up to $5,000; if two or more are injured in the same accident, $10,000 could be paid, but no more than $5,000 to any one individual. For a slightly higher premium, the owner can buy a policy reading $25,000/50,000 (which pays up to $25,000 for death or injury to one person, and $50,000 for two or more persons). Some persons buy policies as high as $300,000/300,000. Since juries in recent years have tended to allow increasingly high awards, the need for added protection has increased correspondingly.

Some states have *financial-responsibility laws.* Drivers who fail to buy automobile liability protection, and cannot put up the required cash as proof of their liability to pay claims when an accident happens, generally lose their driving privileges.

Property-Damage Liability. In addition to being liable for bodily injury or death, an automobile owner is liable if his auto causes damage to the property of others. If your car damages another vehicle, a dwelling, or other property, the insurance company will settle the claim within the limits of the face value of your contract coverage.

Medical Payments. If the insured has an accident involving his automobile in which any passenger is injured, he may be liable for that person's medical expenses. Even if he is not liable, he will no doubt want to be certain that these expenses are paid. Therefore, *medical-payments insurance* is designed to pay for all reasonable medical, surgical, dental, hospital, nursing, and funeral expenses incurred within one year of the accident. This insurance covers the driver, his family, and his guests while they ride in the car, regardless of who is responsible for the accident. Coverage can be bought ranging from $250 to as high as $5,000 per person. However, medical-payments insurance does not apply when the insured's car is used as a public or livery vehicle. Also, if the insured is operating a nonowned car in his business, medical-payments coverage is denied for injuries to passengers if the nonowned car is a commercial vehicle, but not if it is of a passenger-vehicle type. The sale of medical-payments insurance is restricted to drivers who have purchased liability insurance.

Uninsured-Motorist Protection. The *uninsured-motorist indorsement* which may be added to your automobile policy is a fairly recent innovation. Under this indorsement the company agrees to pay damages which the insured is entitled to recover from the owner or operator of an uninsured automobile. If the insured and the insurance company cannot agree on the amount of bodily-injury damage you have sustained, provision is made to settle the dispute in accordance with the rules of the American Arbitration Assn. This type of protection is actually designed to protect automobile owners and occupants injured by hit-and-run drivers. There is no reimbursement under this indorsement for damage to property of the insured. Instead, damage is restricted to bodily injury, sickness, or disease sustained by the insured and the occupants of the insured's car.

Burglary, Robbery, Larceny, and Theft Insurance

Individuals and business firms are exposed to risks involving the taking of property by unlawful means. For purposes of this discussion, such losses are grouped under the headings of *burglary, robbery, larceny,* and *theft.* While there is a variety of meanings attached to these terms under the law, they are carefully defined by contracts for insurance purposes.

Burglary is breaking into a premises by force and violence for the purpose of stealing. Standardized burglary policy-forms require that there must be visible evidence of forced entry, such as marks made upon the premises. This requirement is designed to prevent the unscrupulous proprietor from claiming a fictitious loss. On the other hand, *robbery* is the felonious taking of property from another by violence, or threat of violence. Whereas burglary is a crime against property, robbery is a crime against a person.

Larceny is the legal term for theft. It means the stealing of property regardless of methods used. *Theft* is the act of stealing. Theft insurance is the most expensive of the crime coverages because its coverage is so broad.

There are approximately 14 different types of burglary, robbery, and theft insurance policies. The storekeeper's burglary and robbery policy is a combination policy which many insurance companies write. It is a "package" policy especially designed for small retail establishments. A single contract may include as many as seven different types of peril. Among these are safe-burglary and mercantile open-stock burglary; damage by burglary or robbery to money, securities, merchandise, or furniture and equipment; theft of money or securities from a night depository of a bank; robbery inside or outside the premises; and kidnaping of a messenger for the purpose of giving the thief access to the premises in order to take money, securities, goods, or equipment.

Workmen's Compensation Insurance

Industrial accidents seem to be inevitable despite constant reminders to employees to observe safety rules. To protect injured employees, legislatures of the various states have enacted workmen's compensation insurance legislation, thus providing them with the cost of medical care and weekly benefits as required by law. The employer pays the premium. If the employee loses a hand, an arm, or his life, a lump-sum payment is made. If due to an injury he is unable to work, he receives his weekly payment. And, all or most of his medical and hospital expenses are paid. Compensation insurance now ranks second in size among all casualty lines, with annual premiums of nearly $1.4 billion.

Public-Liability Insurance

So far, except when we mentioned bodily-injury liability insurance for automobiles, we have been talking only about loss or damage to the property or person insured. But businesses and individuals are also subject to a class of risks in which injury is caused to the person or property of a third party. The insurance covering risks of this sort is known as *public-liability insurance;* sometimes it is referred to as *third-party insurance.* Under our system of laws, you may be held liable for damage caused to a third party by an act of negligence on your part—that is, an act in which you failed to exercise due caution or prudence when involving others.

Here are some of the more common types of risk covered by public liability insurance:

1. A theater may be held liable if a patron is injured on the premises.
2. Druggists making errors in compounding prescriptions may be sued by a third party if physical harm results.
3. Contractors may become liable for injury caused by materials that fall on or otherwise strike a third party on the premises.
4. Restaurant owners may be held liable for sickness or death caused by contaminated foods served on their premises.
5. Storekeepers may become liable for accidents on the premises resulting in injury to customers.
6. Manufacturers and food-processers have liability for any injuries sustained from harmful ingredients contained in their products.
7. Attorneys, physicians, and Certified Public Accountants may be sued by clients or patients for malpractice.

Accident, Health, and Group Medical Insurance

Many business firms supplement the wages and salaries paid their employees by offering fringe benefits. Among these benefits are accident and health insurance and group medical insurance, including hospital and surgical coverage. In some states the workmen's compensation laws require employers to provide employees with medical and hospital care. The purpose of accident and health insurance is to shift part of the expense incurred as a result of injury or ill health. Casualty-insurance companies issue policies that make it possible for employers to guard against this risk. Although these policies vary with the kind and amount of protection provided, all of them offer the following basic benefits:

1. Weekly indemnity for loss of wages, but not the full amount that the employee might otherwise earn working full-time
2. Total disability payments for as long as 26 weeks, and partial disability for a limited number of additional weeks
3. Payments in lump sum for loss of an eye, hand, foot, thumb, or finger
4. Death-benefits when death is caused by an accident

Group medical insurance differs from both accident and health plans in that it provides either all or part of the cost of hospital expenses. One of the most popular plans is Blue Cross and Blue Shield.

Fidelity, Surety, Title, and Credit Insurance

Businessmen use fidelity and surety bonds as a means of protecting themselves against losses caused by dishonest acts of a third party, or losses resulting from a third person's failure to perform an obligation or contract. Because of the complex nature of these losses, our discussion will be limited to the chief differences between fidelity- and surety bonds and their uses.

Fidelity- and Surety Bonds. There are two types of coverage: the *fidelity bond,* which protects the employer against the acts of a dishonest employee, and the *surety bond,* which guarantees performance of an obligation or contract. The purpose of the fidelity bond is to reimburse the employer should his employee misappropriate money entrusted to him. This bond may be purchased to cover one employee or to cover all workers. A fidelity bond that covers a group is known as a *schedule bond* and requires that the names of all employees be listed. Fidelity- and schedule bonds are usually carried by banks, trust companies, and other commercial establishments to cover cashiers, bank tellers, salesmen, and others who handle large sums of money.

The purpose of the surety bond is to guarantee that the terms of a contract will be fulfilled. For example, contractors for buildings are generally required to post a surety bond (sometimes called a "performance bond"); if the contractor fails to complete the construction as agreed, the insurance company assumes the responsibility of completing the job.

A *payment bond* is a supplementary agreement to a performance bond, usually in connection with a building contract, and guarantees to the assured that the finished structure or product will be turned over to him free of labor and material costs incurred by mechanics and subcontractors. This protection is especially important to a firm that is planning to expand its facilities by constructing new buildings or by remodeling existing plants.

Bonds covering faithful performance of duties by public officials are called *public-official bonds.* Special bonding companies and insurance firms issue fidelity- and surety bonds in various forms.

Credit Insurance. Credit insurance covers losses arising out of the inability of credit customers to pay their debts. When goods or services are sold on credit, the seller is bound to suffer some loss through the failure of certain customers to meet their obligations. Insurance companies sell policies to manufacturers, wholesalers, and jobbers, and occasionally to retailers, to cover these anticipated credit–losses. *Credit insurance,* however, covers only the loss in excess of normal losses for the year. Prohibitively high premiums would have to be charged for policies covering all losses from bad debts. Credit insurance is generally written for a 12-month period, at the end of which it is subject to renewal.

OTHER USES OF INSURANCE PROTECTION BY BUSINESS

1. *Boiler and machinery policy*—insures against damage from steam-boiler explosion and loss of machinery due to accident.
2. *Plate-glass insurance*—protects against losses caused by breakage of glass in the plant.
3. *Power-interruption insurance*—covers loss from interruption of operations, and loss from damage to property of the insured through spoilage.
4. *Furnace explosion*—covers losses resulting from the explosion of furnaces (as opposed to explosion of the steam boilers which they may serve).
5. *Rain insurance*—intended to cover loss of profits or fixed charges due either to abandonment or postponement of public events in the event of rain, hail, snow, or sleet.
6. *Accounts-receivable insurance*—covers losses brought about because of the inability of the business to collect from open-account (unsecured) debtors because a fire destroyed accounts-receivable records.
7. *Rent insurance*—covers insurable interest in rents which must be continued even though the premises were partially or wholly destroyed by fire.
8. *Comprehensive general liability insurance*—insures the businessman against such classes of liability as elevator accidents, product liability, liability arising out of use of premises, and contingent liability (imposed on the insured by law for actions of his independent contractors).
9. *Water-leakage insurance*—covers damage from a broken water-pipe or water accidentally discharged from a sprinkler system.

Title Insurance. The risks attending ownership of land, such as losses resulting from defects in the title of the property, are not uncommon. Title defects may be caused by forgery of records by prior property owners or others, by defective probate procedures involving titles, by invalid or undiscovered wills, by debts against the property, or by errors in court proceedings. These defects usually are discovered when property is being transmitted to the new owner.

A property owner may protect himself against such losses by purchasing a *title insurance.* The insurer agrees to indemnify the owner against any loss he may suffer resulting from defects in the title to the real property. This kind of protection is written by a corporation known as a "title company." It is most often a local corporation operating within a limited geographical area because of the high cost of building up abstracts of title files on local real estate. An *abstract of title* is a summary of all the conveyances, mortgages, and liens affecting a parcel of land on which the new owner's title to the real property depends.

A title company will not issue a policy to the new property owner without first making a thorough search of the records in the court house of the county or parish in which the property lies. If irregularities or defects in prior titles are discovered by the search, they must be corrected by the owner selling the property, or by the title company if it is at fault. The title company will not issue a new policy until the defect on the title has been corrected.

A lump-sum premium is charged each time the real property is sold and a new policy is issued. Title insurance is effective either indefinitely or until the property changes hands. Title policies are not cancelable by either party. The premium is paid in advance, and there is no refund under any conditions.

Life Insurance

Unlike other forms of insurance you have been studying in this chapter, life insurance is the only form designed to cover the loss of future income as a result of death. People buy life insurance for various reasons, but the main one is to obtain financial protection for their families in case they themselves should die. A man creates an estate immediately when he buys a life-insurance policy, and he protects the future of that estate as he continues to pay his premiums. It should not be concluded that one must die in all cases in order to get his insurer to pay a death claim. Many policies contain features which provide either retirement income, paid-up insurance, or cash savings.

Before noting some of the other purposes of life insurance besides the family-protection objective, let us review briefly a few pertinent facts about the size and importance of the life-insurance industry.

Life insurance in force in the United States with *legal-reserve companies* (i.e., companies operating under state laws requiring specific minimum reserves which a company must provide for its policies) exceeds $980 billion. With coverage provided by other private insurers, such as savings banks, private banks, burial companies, and by insurance written by the federal government, the total life insurance of all kinds at the end of 1966 amounted to about $1,045 billion. The head of the family was insured in nine out of 10 families in the United States. Among all income groups, 89 percent of the husbands under 65 owned life insurance. For this group the average amount owned was $11,400. About two out of three wives were insured. Excluding wives covered by life insurance under the family-plan policies, the average-size policy owned by a wife was about $5,500. Excluding the families that owned no life insurance, the average ownership for insured families was $19,800.

Of the 23.7 million new life insurance contracts bought by individuals and group-life plans during 1966, 10.2 million were ordinary life, 9.6 million were industrial policies, and 3.9 million were group certificates. The average-size policy issued was $8,810.

Money at work through the assets of U.S. life insurance companies reached $167.0 billion at the end of 1966. The most important of these assets were mortgages amounting to $64.6 billion, and industrial and miscellaneous bonds valued at $41.2 billion. Other assets included common stocks, corporate bonds, and government securities.

Purposes of Life Insurance. As has already been stated, the primary purpose of life insurance is to afford financial protection to dependents when the head of the family or the breadwinner dies. In addition to this purpose, however, life insurance may be used to serve other purposes, including the following:

1. To promote individual and group savings
2. To supply funds for education
3. To serve as a source of credit for business and personal loans
4. To provide an estate for old-age security
5. To pay off long-term business and personal debts
6. To indemnify a business against loss of key executives or other valuable employees
7. To provide employee-group insurance

The Mortality Table. Like some of the other forms of insurance we have studied, life insurance is based on the "law of large numbers." For life-insurance companies to be able to charge a proper and adequate premium, they must have some means of gauging the risks they assume. The only way in which they can estimate the death claims of the future is by the experience of the past, and this is embodied in a so-called "mortality table." The table which all companies use is the Commissioners' 1958 Standard Mortality Table (CSO), portions of which are illustrated in Table 18.1.

The full table shows for each age, starting with zero (those born but who are not yet one year old) and up to and including age 99, the number of persons alive at the beginning of the year, and the number dying during the year. From these statistics it is possible to compute the deaths per 1,000 persons. For example, in Table 18.1, we see that the number of deaths per thousand at age 15 is 1.46. The life expectancy at this age is calculated to be 54.95 years. At this age only 146 persons in every 100,000 are expected to die before they become 16. At age 90 the death rate is slightly over 22 percent, since 228.14 per 1,000 persons are expected to die during that year. At age 100 it is assumed that death is a certainty. It should be noted that the

TABLE 18.1

COMMISSIONERS' 1958 STANDARD ORDINARY MORTALITY TABLE (CSO) (SELECTED AGES)

Age	Number Living	Deaths Each Year	Deaths Per 1,000	Expectation of Life
0	10,000,000	70,800	7.08	68.30
1	9,929,200	17,475	1.76	67.78
10	9,805,870	11,865	1.21	59.58
15	9,743,175	14,225	1.46	54.95
20	9,664,994	17,300	1.79	50.37
25	9,575,636	18,481	1.93	45.82
30	9,480,358	20,193	2.13	41.25
35	9,373,807	23,528	2.51	36.69
40	9,241,359	32,622	3.53	32.18
45	9,048,999	48,412	5.35	27.81
50	8,762,306	72,902	8.32	23.63
60	7,698,698	156,592	20.34	16.12
90	468,174	106,809	228.14	3.06
99	6,415	6,415	1,000.00	.50

probability of death expressed in a mortality table is based on insured lives and not on the entire population; consequently, the death rate is overstated.

Table 18.2 shows how life expectancy at birth has increased since 1900. Longer life expectancy will mean lower premium rates at each age.

For years the mortality table has been compiled by life insurance actuaries who are highly trained persons qualified to make these computations. More about the role of the actuary appears at the end of this chapter.

TABLE 18.2

EXPECTATION OF LIFE AT BIRTH IN THE UNITED STATES

	White			Nonwhite			All Races		
Year	Male	Female	Both Sexes	Male	Female	Both Sexes	Male	Female	Both Sexes
1900	46.6	48.7	47.6	32.5	33.5	33.0	46.3	48.3	47.3
1920	54.4	55.6	59.9	45.5	45.2	45.3	53.6	54.6	54.1
1930	59.7	63.5	61.4	47.3	49.2	48.1	58.1	61.6	59.7
1940	62.1	66.6	64.2	51.5	54.9	53.1	60.8	65.2	62.9
1950	66.5	72.2	69.1	59.1	62.9	60.8	65.6	71.1	68.2
1960	67.4	74.1	70.6	61.1	66.3	63.6	66.6	73.1	69.7
1961	67.8	74.5	71.0	61.9	67.0	64.4	67.0	73.4	70.0
1962	67.6	74.4	70.9	61.5	66.8	64.1	66.8	73.4	70.0
1963	67.5	74.4	70.8	60.9	66.5	63.6	66.6	73.4	69.9
1964	67.7	74.6	71.0	61.1	67.2	64.1	66.9	73.7	70.2

Source: U.S. Dept. of Health, Education, and Welfare, National Center for Health Statistics.

For years, several different mortality tables have been used. The CSO table, which was computed by the National Association of (State) Insurance Commissioners, using data obtained from American life-insurance companies between 1950 and 1954, has been adopted by all U.S. insurance companies.

Life-Insurance Premium Computation. The primary use of the mortality table is to provide data on which to base life-insurance premium rates. A simple illustration shows the general procedure for calculating the cost of a one-year term policy at age 35, disregarding interest, expenses, and profits. Referring to the 1958 CSO listing (Table 18.1), we see that 23,528 persons of the group living at age 35 will die during the year. If the insurance company agrees to pay the beneficiaries of those at age 35 who die that year, how much money must the company collect from each member of the age-35 group? In order to pay claims, the company will need $23,528,000 (23,528 × 1,000). Assuming that there are 9,373,807 persons in the group, as shown in the table, the following computation is necessary to arrive at a premium cost:

$$\frac{\$23,528,000}{9,373,807} = \$2.51$$

The company will, however, have other expenses—salaries, clerical costs, sales commissions, office expenses, etc., which the above cost does not reflect. These costs are called the "loading." This amount must be added to the amount required to pay claims for that year. It should be observed that a person buying life insurance at age 35 would pay a progressively higher premium to renew it each year because the chance of death increases with age. Since people like to know, when they buy insurance, exactly how much they must pay each year, the constantly increasing rate would be very unpopular. To obviate this criticism, practically all policies are now sold on a *level-premium plan,* which means that the insured pays exactly the same amount annually for the life of the policy. (The level premium is computed by averaging the premiums for all ages which the insured is expected to reach.) Actually, the insured pays more than his *pro rata* share during his early years, and less when he is older. Part of the excess paid during the early life of the insured, together with the earned interest, becomes a reserve that belongs to the insured. This becomes the *cash-surrender value* of the policy.

Types of Life-Insurance Contracts

There are only three basic types of life-insurance policies: *term,* which is temporary protection; *straight life,* which is lifetime protection with limited savings values; and *endowment,* which is mainly savings with protection until the policy matures. Straight life may be bought as a limited-payment contract. All other policies are a variation or a combination of the three basic types. As you can see from the following diagrams, the element of protection is common to all three basic policies. Savings is offered in limited amounts in the straight life and the endowment types.

Term Insurance. This type of policy gives protection only during a definite period of time. It is somewhat like fire insurance, since it provides only temporary protection. Actually, it offers none of the savings or investment features found in other types of policies. In term insurance, the face amount of the policy is payable only if the insured dies within the period stated in the contract. Some term policies may be renewed at the end of the contract period without another physical examination, but at a higher premium rate. Most companies will permit the holder to convert a term policy to a permanent contract by adjusting the premium. Any conversion is of course subject to the insurance company rules.

Term policies are often bought to furnish temporary protection against a business risk, such as the risk a construction firm faces through the death of a key individual in charge of an important contract. Term insurance is popular among young professional men who want maximum coverage at a minimum cost during the early part of their professional careers when their incomes are low. Term policies are usually for 5, 10, or 15 years, although some companies issue policies for longer than 15 years.

Straight Life-Insurance. Next to term insurance, *ordinary* or *straight* life-insurance has the lowest premium. This is sometimes called *whole* life-insurance because the premium continues to be paid throughout the life of

Comparison of the Three Basic Life-Insurance Policies
(Issued at Age 25)

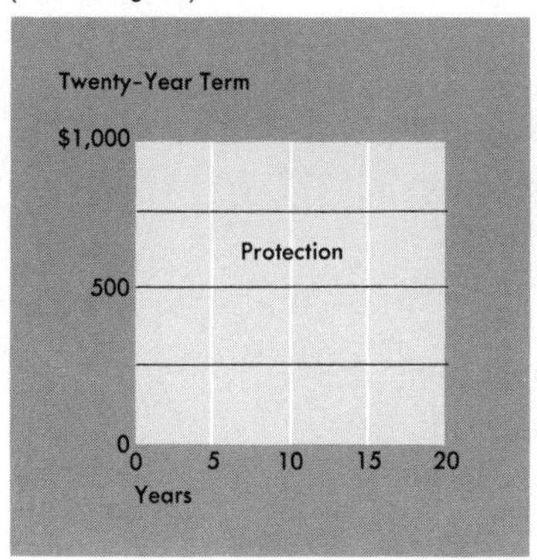

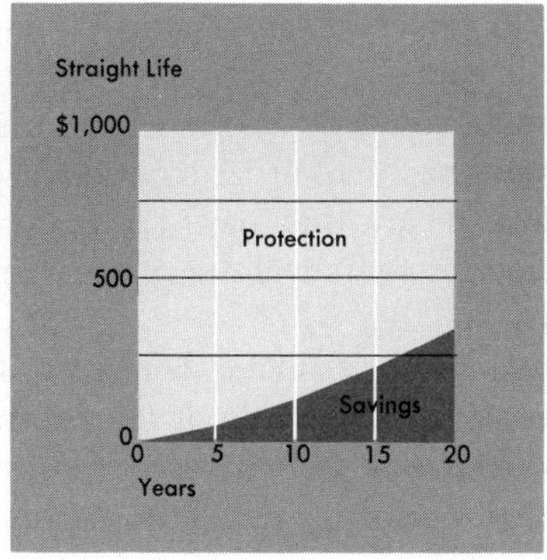

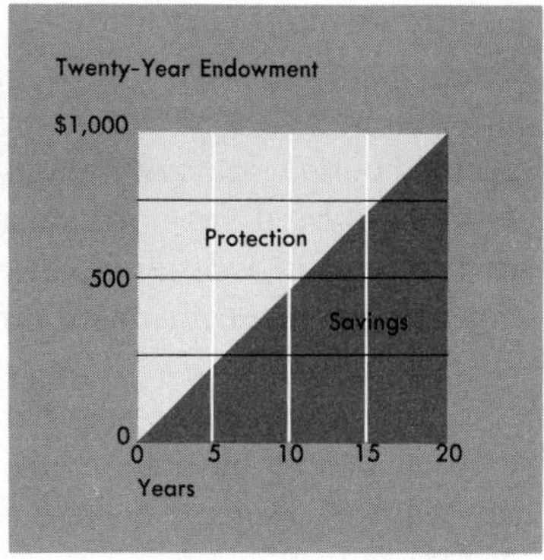

Figures in this example courtesy of *The Prudential Insurance Co. of America.*

the insured. When death occurs, the face value of the policy, which is the value stated on the contract, is paid to the beneficiary. This policy has a cash-surrender or loan value, and it may be converted to one of the other types of insurance. It has long been the most popular type of life insurance.

The flexibility of the straight life policy is one of the reasons for its popularity. For example, after several years (usually the second or third) the policy has a cash or loan value. The cash value may either be withdrawn in whole or in part should the policy be surrendered, or the insured may borrow the amount of the loan value. This loan privilege is often very valuable in that it provides a source of funds to meet emergencies. It may happen that the policyholder is financially unable to continue making premium payments. Under such circumstances, the insured may elect to take the option of "extended-term insurance," which means that he can, without further premium payments, enjoy the full benefits of his policy for a designated number of years and days. Finally, the insured may choose the option of stopping premium payments and take a paid-up policy, for a reduced amount, payable upon death to his beneficiary or estate. The amount of paid-up insurance increases the longer the policy is in force and as long as premiums are being paid.

One variation of the straight life policy is the *limited-payment contract.* It is similar to straight life in all respects but one: premiums are paid not for an entire lifetime, but for a definite number of years, usually 20 or 30. After that time, protection continues for life without further payments. Like a straight life policy, this contract carries both a cash and a loan value. For a given amount of insurance at a specific age, annual premium payments are larger than for the straight life policy. The face value is paid only upon the death of the insured. Another variation is the *single-premium payment life,* which requires the insured to make only one premium payment. After that payment the policy is paid up in full.

Endowment Insurance. *Endowment insurance* is a combination savings plan coupled with a small element of insurance protection. The endowment policy promises payment upon death if such occurs within a specified period. It also agrees to make payment in case of survival at the end of the stipulated time. Obviously a policy that pays for either death or survival beyond a designated number of years will cost more than one that stipulates payment for death only.

A *pure endowment policy* provides no insurance benefits to those who die during a specified time, but pays the face value of the contract to the survivor. People buy endowment insurance for various purposes. A father may want to ensure a college education for his daughter. At her birth, he can take out a 20-year endowment policy on himself for $10,000. It will take him 20 years to pay it off. If he dies in less than 20 years, the policy is considered paid up as of the time of his death, and when his daughter turns 20 the full face value is made available to her for her college education. A man wishing to provide for his retirement at age 60 may take a 30-year endowment policy for $30,000 at age 30. If he dies before reaching 60, the named beneficiary receives the $30,000. But if he lives to 60, he receives the face value paid to him according to the contract. If the insured elects to take monthly payments at 60 but dies after reaching that age, the payments are made to the insured's beneficiary or to his estate.

Package Life-Insurance Contracts. There are several types of special contracts which are combinations of the more standardized policies. We shall discuss the *family income policy* and the *modified life-insurance contract.*

The *family income policy* is a combination of ordinary life- and term insurance. It is designed to provide a larger amount of protection when the children are young, and still allow for some permanent insurance. This is a popular contract because it furnishes a solution to the dual needs of both permanent and temporary life insurance.

A *modified life-insurance contract,* another example of a package contract, is one in which the premiums are arranged so that they are small during the first five or 10 years, and higher thereafter. This is accomplished by combining term insurance with some other form of permanent type.

Annuities. *Annuities* are contracts in which the life insurance company agrees to pay you, the *annuitant,* an income in return for a certain sum. An annuity is one way of assuring retirement income. It is a calculated method for taking a certain sum of money and using it up month by month, but in such a manner of payment that the annuitant will receive payments as long as he lives. Of course, annuities are not the only way to build a retirement program.

Although annuities are sold mainly by life insurance companies, they are different from life insurance contracts. As we have seen, the purchase of insurance requires a series of payments, in return for which the company agrees to eventually pay either you or your beneficiary a certain sum of money. When you buy an annuity, you promise to pay the company a specific sum of money according to certain terms, and the company promises to eventually pay you a specific amount for as long as you live after the payments begin. The primary purpose of the annuity, unlike that of most life insurance, is to protect the annuitant, not his dependents.

Annuities fall into two general classes. One type, known as an *immediate life annuity,* starts paying an income immediately after it is bought for a lump sum. However, all payments cease when the annuitant dies. Thus, although the annuitant may live a lot longer than expected, and therefore collect much more than he has invested, he may not even live long enough to collect more than a small part of his total investment.

The second type of annuity, called the *deferred annuity,* guarantees an income to begin at some future time. The deferred annuity is typically bought on the installment plan, although some companies will accept a lump-sum payment. Usually the income begins at retirement. If the annuitant dies before collecting any payments, his beneficiary receives either a death benefit equal to the cash value of the annuity at the time of the annuitant's death, or the sum of premiums paid, whichever is larger.

Annuity contracts include various combinations of features, and some are even contingent upon the survival of more than one life. Suppose we examine several types of annuities.

The Straight Life Annuity. This type of annuity, sometimes known as a "pure annuity," is one in which the payment to the annuitant is made only during his lifetime. If he should die after the annuity begins, there is no obligation for the insurer to return any of the purchase price. On the other hand, he may live to collect more than his original investment.

When it is desired to obtain an annuity that guarantees a minimum number of payments, the *life annuity with installments certain* guarantees payments for a certain number of years. For example, if payments are guaranteed for 20 years and the annuitant dies at the end of five, payments will be made for 15 more years to a designated beneficiary. If the annuitant outlives the guaranteed years, then payments will be made to him during his lifetime, but nothing goes to the beneficiary upon the annuitant's death.

The *group annuity* uses the same principle as the individual annuity, except that the employer pays the premiums on a contractual plan covering all employeees. Generally, the employee has no withdrawal rights before his retirement unless he leaves the group. Business often uses this plan to fund a private pension program.

The chief criticism of the annuity discussed thus far is the fact that the annuity contract yields an income of a fixed number of dollars, which rising prices may devaluate. To offset this danger, the Teachers' Insurance and Annuity Assn. in 1952 introduced a new type of annuity called the *variable annuity.* The idea of the variable annuity is to invest each annuity payment in common stocks, which will hopefully rise in price with the cost of living. Each periodic investment buys "so many units" in the investment fund, which are expected to rise and fall according to the performance of the investment portfolio and the general level of the securities market. When it comes time for you to collect, the insurance company may simply buy you a regular annuity with the money that's been amassed for you. Or it may hold onto the stocks and provide you a monthly income, based on your life expectancy, that varies with the value of the stock.

Since it was introduced, the variable annuity has been the subject of nationwide controversy. In 1959, the Supreme Court ruled that insurance companies selling variable annuities were subject to Securities and Exchange Commission regulations. Also in 1959, the New Jersey legislature was the first state body to approve the sale of variable annuities to individuals. Only a few states thus far have approved the sale of variable annuities to individuals by life insurance companies. Most states allow the sale of variable annuities only to company groups as part of a company pension plan.

America has been a leader in pioneering the variable annuity as a group annuity for employees of business firms, and the sale of individual annuity plans in states that have legalized the variable annuity. Some insurance companies have declined to sell variable annuities mainly because they do not regard them as life insurance. There is an inconsistency in trying to sell fixed incomes on the one hand and speculative variable annuities on the other hand. Also, there is too much risk involved for the average annuitant. Among the several arguments in favor of variable annuities is the one claiming that any rise in the cost of living will be accompanied by increased earnings and higher market-values of stocks. Where these increases work out, the variable annuity is a hedge against inflation.

Group Life Insurance. This is one of the popular forms of coverage sold to business as part of a fringe-benefit program for employees. The policy is written under a single master policy, with or without medical examinations. The plan may be either term, straight life, or some combination. For this reason it is not included in the discussion of the three major types of life insurance policies.

Industrial Insurance. Under this type of life insurance, which is written usually without medical examination, the face value averages about $300 per individual. Premiums are paid weekly to company agents who contact the insured. Straight life and endowment policies are the two most popular types of industrial insurance. This policy is issued to both children and adults. Unlike group life-insurance, which in 1961 represented about 30 percent of the total of life insurance in force, industrial insurance in force amounted to about 7 percent.

Comparison of Life-Insurance Premiums. One of the perplexing questions about life insurance is, "Which kind of insurance is best for me?" For most persons, one important consideration is cost. Table 18.3 compares premiums for $1,000 worth of insurance for persons of standard risk (that are in satisfactory health).

Other Business Uses of Life Insurance

Every proprietor or manager has certain objectives for his firm. One is profit. Another is to render a service. A third is growth. A fourth is survival.

TABLE 18.3

TYPICAL ANNUAL PREMIUMS PER $1,000 LIFE INSURANCE FOR VARIOUS TYPES OF POLICIES ISSUED BY A PARTICIPATING COMPANY (AT SELECTED AGES) AND BASED ON STANDARD RISK

Age	Straight Life	20-pay Life	20-year Endowment	Endowment at age 65	5-year Renewable Term
19	$17.25	$27.94	$49.48	$20.29	$ 9.92
21	18.01	28.90	49.63	21.46	10.14
22	18.41	29.40	49.71	22.10	10.27
25	19.74	30.99	49.98	24.20	10.44
30	22.49	34.11	50.62	28.62	11.15
35	26.01	37.80	51.69	34.67	13.04

In their desire to achieve these objectives, managers often overlook the tremendous risks which the firm faces if a key executive or partner dies.

Key-Man Insurance. Since the prosperity and growth of the business generally depends to a great extent upon the continued existence of the owner or manager, it has become a custom for the firm to buy life insurance on the owner or manager—the top executive. This is called *key-man insurance.* The company pays the premium and is the beneficiary. The firm cannot deduct the premium costs from gross income for federal income tax purposes, but when a key man dies, the proceeds received by the firm from the policy are not subject to taxation for federal income tax purposes.

Partnership Insurance. As has been pointed out in Chapter 4, when a partner dies, the partnership is dissolved. This may result in a loss to both the deceased's family and the other party. The solution is the purchase of partnership insurance supported by a buy-and-sell agreement. Such agreement assures that funds will become available upon the death of one partner to buy the share of the deceased partner. What the buy-and-sell agreement does is to spell out in detail the authority to use life insurance funds to purchase the partnership interest from the estate of the deceased partner. The agreement establishes the value of the partnership shares for tax purposes, assures funds to pay the heirs, eliminates the need for forced liquidation of the business, and preserves the business for surviving partners. The purchase of partnership life-insurance has no direct tax effect because the partnership income is the income of the partners for federal income tax purposes. And premiums on partnership life-insurance are also not deductible as a business expense.

In a close corporation with only a few stockholders, a buy-and-sell agreement may be executed to provide life insurance on important stockholders. This protection gives the remaining stockholders a source of funds with which to buy stock from the estate of the deceased.

Credit Life-Insurance. A substantial amount of consumer sales are on credit. If the credit purchaser dies, the heirs are subjected to the debt. This kind of risk has led to the development of credit life-insurance. It is customary for commercial banks, finance companies, and credit unions, in making loans, to require the borrower to buy a credit life policy. The premium cost is included in the person's monthly payment. The creditor is named as the beneficiary in the insurance policy.

The Cost of a Key-Man Life-Insurance Policy

When a firm decides to buy a straight life-insurance policy on an executive from a typical mutual life-insurance company, this is what happens:

1. An annual premium is paid to the insurance company. This premium is calculated to provide some margin for adverse developments in mortality and expenses, and for decreases in the rate of interest.
2. Each year, except possibly in the very early years, the company determines whether the accumulated funds and future premiums are sufficient to provide, again with some margin, for the future benefits guaranteed by the policy. If so, there is credited to the policyholder an annual dividend, which will be seen to be essentially a return of the unneeded portion of past premiums.
3. Each year, the insurance company deducts from the premium the following costs:
   a. Taxes imposed by state and national governments.
   b. Commissions and operating expenses. These are usually high in the early policy years and very low thereafter.
   c. Mortality costs, which are an individual policyholder's contributions to cover the death claims of all other policyholders in the same classification.
4. The difference between premiums paid (net of annual dividends) and the costs of doing business is invested at interest. The resulting accumulated funds provide the means for the company to pay annual dividends, as already mentioned, guaranteed cash surrender values and, in the later policy years, possibly further amounts in the event of termination.

Here is how these various items will work out in a typical whole life policy of $50,000 purchased on an executive age 35 if he lives to a retirement age of 65:

The premiums paid at about $25 per $1,000 per year would in 30 years		= $37,500
Assuming current experience continues unchanged over this period, annual dividends would about		= 15,300
Thus, the firm's expenditure, net of annual dividends, would		= $22,200
If the policy is surrendered when the executive reaches age 65, the guaranteed cash value would	= $27,350	
If current conditions continue, so that present termination dividend scales are still in effect, there would further be payable a termination dividend	= $ 1,200	
So that the total proceeds of the cash surrender would be		$28,550
Thus, the net gain under the contract for the business firm would		= $ 6,350

Figures in this table courtesy of *The Prudential Insurance Co. of America.*

This gain is possible because over the 30-year period, under the stated assumptions, interest earnings would have more than covered taxes, operating expenses, and mortality costs.

GOVERNMENT REGULATION OF INSURANCE COMPANIES

Traditionally, all forms of the insurance industry have been regulated mainly by the separate states. One reason for this is the fact that insurance companies are chartered to operate under individual state laws. Each state has its own insurance department, and an insurance superintendent or commissioner who has the responsibility of supervising insurance companies. Regulation of insurance companies is necessary because experience has demonstrated over the years that some government supervision is needed to protect both the interests of the public, and the insurance companies. Because insurance is a social device that occupies a position of public trust, federal government supervision will become a practical necessity if the industry continues to exercise such a far-reaching influence on the public.

For many years insurance company officials have been confronted with the argument over whether federal regulation would be superior to state control. No serious objection to state regulation was made until the 1860's, when a Virginia agent for several New York insurance companies maintained that the state of Virginia had no jurisdiction over the companies he represented because they were transacting interstate commerce, which could only be regulated by the federal government. The United States Supreme Court in 1868 (*Paul v. Virginia*) held that insurance is not interstate commerce and, therefore, that the federal government should have no regulatory powers over insurance companies. This decision was upheld repeatedly until reversed in 1944 by the Supreme Court in the *South-Eastern Underwriters Assn.* case. But despite this reversal, Congress has left the regulation of insurance companies pretty much to the various states.

In any discussion of insurance regulation the question arises: Can competition exist in an industry subject to extensive regulation? The answer is that there are other industries, more highly regulated than insurance companies, in which there exists tremendous competition. In fact, a great deal of evidence can be marshalled to prove that much competition does exist in spite of insurance rating bureaus and state regulatory bodies.

CAREERS IN INSURANCE

Not only is the insurance business one of the fastest growing in the United States, but it is in control of more wealth than any other single industry. It employs a vast army of workers in a great variety of occupations. In the casualty field alone, there are about half a million workers, including approximately 200,000 agents located in practically every community. Over 700,000 persons are employed in life insurance.

Careers in insurance fall into two broad areas: *selling* (or *production*) and *administration*. Under each of these two classifications there are many different kinds of employment and occupational specialization. The two principal areas of employment in the insurance business are *home offices* and *field offices*.

Employment in the insurance industry continues to increase. As you can see from Table 18.4, the number of persons thus employed has more

TABLE 18.4

NUMBER OF PERSONS EMPLOYED IN ALL FORMS OF INSURANCE IN THE UNITED STATES

Year	Annual Average
1945	600,000
1950	800,000
1955	900,000
1960	1,105,000
1962	1,145,000
1964	1,195,000
1966	1,260,000

Source: Institute of Life Insurance.

than doubled since 1945. The rate of growth since the 1960's has been slower than between 1945 and 1955, probably due in part to the increasing use of automation.

The insurance companies employed about 660,000 men and 600,000 women in 1966. Sales personnel numbered about 415,000, of whom about half derived 50 percent or more of their income from the sale of life insurance. Slightly over half of all non-sales personnel work in home offices. The remainder are employed in field and agency offices, or in service organizations such as rate bureaus and industry organizations. Table 18.5 gives a more detailed analysis of insurance employment data by sex and type of work in life and non-life insurance.

TABLE 18.5

TOTAL EMPLOYMENT IN INSURANCE IN THE UNITED STATES, 1966

Sex	
Male	660,000
Female	600,000
Total	1,260,000
Work Related to	
Life or Life and Non-life Insurance	720,000
Non-life Insurance Only	540,000
Total	1,260,000
Type of Work	
Sales: More than 50% of Income from Life Insurance	205,000
Less than 50% of Income from Life Insurance	210,000
Total Sales	415,000
Non-sales: in Home Office of Insurance Company	435,000
in Agency, Field, Brokerage, or Other Offices	410,000
Total non-sales	845,000
Total	1,260,000

Source: Institute of Life Insurance.

Home-Office Occupations and Operations

Every insurance company has as its administrative nerve-center a home office. The home-office operational structure generally is organized along departmental or sectional lines in order to furnish general administrative direction to the company as well as to facilitate the specific supervision or direction of the operations of those working in the field. "General administrative direction" may include direction of the agency section (which deals with the supervision of field agents), the underwriting section, and the claims section, as well as of actuaries, insurance statisticians, and investment specialists. (These sections and groups are rather more peculiar to the insurance business than to other kinds of enterprises, and thus will be discussed in detail here. The workings of sections and groups assigned to handle problems common to all businesses—personnel administration, advertising, general accounting, employee training, marketing, and transportation—should by now be familiar enough to require no further delineation.)

The home office uses the services of a highly-skilled staff of accountants, statisticians, lawyers, mathematicians, investment analysts, economists, training directors, and computer programers, and the assistance of numerous competent machine operators, clerks, typists, and secretaries. Although a college education is not a prerequisite for the clerical-type positions, it is for the higher ones. Let us look briefly at certain home-office sections and positions.

The Agency Section. Persons employed in this section generally supervise field agents (salesmen), determine commission rates, supervise the issuing of state licenses to field agents, and make certain that the company is qualified to operate in the various states. The individual in charge of the agency section is usually an experienced salesman.

The Underwriting Section. This home-office section obtained its name during the early days of marine insurance, when a person who was willing to insure ships and cargo signed his name on the documents that described the risk. This ceremony, often occurring in the English coffeehouses, resulted in coining the term "underwriter." Whenever you make application for a policy for life- or property insurance, someone must determine your insurability. It is the duty of the underwriting section to analyze the risk. In life insurance, the underwriter reviews the applicant's medical record and credit reports, and it is upon his recommendation that you are approved or rejected.

Underwriters specialize in different types of risk. They work in companies that write life, fire, casualty, liability, automobile, and marine insurance. They collect many kinds of facts having to do with physical and moral hazards, and they compile summaries of the company's experience within each territory as to premiums received, accidents reported, and losses paid. A beginner in this work usually starts as a clerk, progressing through the successive steps of assistant underwriter, underwriter, supervising underwriter, chief underwriter, and head of the section. A college education is very helpful as part of the training, and a broad business background plus special training in insurance is essential.

The Claims Section. This section handles claims that arise from losses by policyholders. It approves payments of claims where the investigation shows the company is responsible. The claims adjustor, who determines whether the company is liable for a loss under the terms of its contract, needs a knowledge of law, and a broad business background. Some companies employ lawyers in the claims section.

The Actuaries. In the life insurance field, one of the most complex and indispensable occupations in the home office is that of the actuary. He is the person who collects, compiles, and analyzes mortality statistics. The actuary uses the mortality tables, together with various mathematical formulae, to determine premium rates on new policies, and helps to plan new types of life insurance policies. In preparing for a career as an actuary, mathematics and English are extremely important tools. And so are finance, economics, law, and accounting. Another important requirement is the ability to pass a series of written examinations to qualify for membership in the Society of Actuaries.[3] The Society conducts these periodically.

The Insurance Statisticians. The insurance statistician compiles and analyzes all kinds of mathematical data on the company and its policyholders. For instance, the statistician compiles special reports pertaining to claims payments, policy renewals, premium rates, insurance losses, and investment earnings. Because the statistician works principally with mathematics, he should have a special aptitude for this subject, and thorough training in statistics and higher mathematics. Furthermore, he must know a great deal about the operations of the insurance company that employs him. The job takes infinite patience and an aptitude for details. A college education, including a knowledge of business administration, statistics, and insurance, is essential. Every type of insurance company uses the services of a statistician. This position is well-paid, mainly because the high degree of specialization discourages many persons from entering it.

The Investment Specialists. Since part of an insurance company's income is derived from dividends and interest, each company requires the services of an investment specialist. His work involves the analysis of all kinds of investment suitable for insurance-company reserve funds. Surplus funds may be invested in real-estate, corporation bonds, government bonds, municipal bonds, and mortgages. The investment specialist must be qualified to analyze these securities to determine whether they are safe and adequate investments. He must also be able to write comprehensive reports for review by company executives. For this work, you would find it helpful to have training in law, business finance, economics, accounting, statistics, investments,

[3] Organized in January, 1949, as an international body, the Society of Actuaries is the result of a merger between the Actuary Society of America and the American Institute of Actuaries.

and insurance. But before reaching one of these top-level positions, you will need to acquire a wide background of practical experience, perhaps in a brokerage firm.

Field-Office Occupations

The field office of an insurance company is similar to the branch office of a manufacturing concern. The personnel of this office make direct contacts with prospective purchasers of insurance coverage and with policyholders. In other words, the field office performs a service function.

Field Agent. By far the largest number of persons employed in field offices are the insurance agents (salesmen) who contact all prospective policyholders. They are the insurance company's direct representatives.

Most life-insurance field agents specialize in selling either ordinary insurance, industrial insurance, or group insurance, although in some companies field agents sell all three types. As a rule, an agent represents only one life-insurance company. This is known as the "American Agency System" in life insurance. Some life-insurance agents, however, share or *broker* their business with other companies, particularly when the risk is not entirely acceptable to their own company. The brokerage practice is more common in fire and casualty insurance than in life companies because the latter companies prefer to build up their own agency system rather than use brokers.

A qualified agent must hold a contract with an insurance company, and in all states a license is required. Some states require the agent to pass a written examination before he is granted a license. Other states grant a license upon direct certification by the company.

Selling life insurance is a highly personalized business. As an agent, you must be able to explain various policies, and advise your clients on the most desirable forms of coverage. Agents are paid either on a straight commission basis or on a combination salary and commission. Commissions range from 25 to 75 percent of the first year's premium, with a small percentage on subsequent premiums. This so-called "renewal" commission is paid for a limited number of years. In the general insurance field, the agent is paid a percentage of each year's premium (it ranges from 10 to 25 percent) when the policy is renewed.

During the past few years, increasing emphasis has been placed on training for field agents in both the life and casualty fields. In 1927, the American College of Life Underwriters was created for the purpose of establishing higher educational standards in life-insurance training. The College does not offer courses itself, but it cooperates with universities and colleges by encouraging educational programs and by providing study outlines and textbook recommendations to schools. The College offers annually a series of nationwide examinations.[4] Candidates who successfully pass these examinations and meet certain other requirements are awarded the coveted Chartered Life Underwriter (CLU) designation.

The success of the American College of Life Underwriters prompted the organization in 1942 of the American Institute of Property and Liability Underwriters, Inc., sponsored by the industry and by the American Association of University Teachers of Insurance. The designation CPCU (Chartered Property Casualty Underwriter) is awarded to those who meet the general requirements and pass a series of examinations prepared by the institute in insurance other than life. These examinations cover several areas of education in addition to insurance. This organization also cooperates with colleges by encouraging courses in insurance and by publishing study materials. The earning of either of these two designations is regarded as a mark of distinction and professional accomplishment.

SUMMARY

Risk, in business parlance, is the uncertainty of the occurrence of an economic loss. Since risk imposes an economic burden on both society and the individual, it becomes important to find a way of handling it. Various kinds of risk faced by both individuals and business can be covered by insurance. It is the function of insurance to provide certainty; it does this by spreading the consequences of loss among a large number of persons subject to a similar risk. But insurance is not the only way of handling risk; it is possible to remove it, or its cause. A reserve fund in anticipation of the loss can be established. Hedging is another means of shifting the risk. And one of the best ways to meet certain kinds of business risk is by the practice of good management.

The two types of insurance companies are stock companies and mutual companies. The former are owned by stockholders, who need not be policyholders. Mutual companies are owned by policyholders, who may receive a dividend if collected premiums are in excess of the amount required to operate the company, including the payment of claims.

Insurance requires that a person must have an insurable interest in property in order to recover any loss or damage on it. This doctrine is what prevents insurance from becoming a gambling contract. The principle of indemnity states that a person may not collect for damages more than his actual cash loss caused by an insured peril.

[4] The American College schedules the examinations in the spring, usually on the campus of a university or college under the auspices of the institution. All examination papers are graded by the American College of Life Underwriters.

Life insurance policies are sold in various forms, such as term, straight life, endowment, group life, and industrial and family income policies. "Key-man" insurance is used in business to cover the lives of important company officers, providing funds to defray expenses incurred upon their death and until they can be replaced.

Casualty insurance covers such risks as damage to an automobile, burglary, robbery, public liability, and workmen's compensation. Fire insurance accounts for the largest amount of property insurance in force; annual fire losses are among the highest in all fields of insurance.

VOCABULARY REVIEW QUIZ

Match the following vocabulary terms with the statements below.

a. Burglary
b. Credit insurance
c. Consequential losses
d. Endowment policy
e. Family income policy
f. Fidelity bond
g. Insurable interest
h. Key-man insurance
i. Larceny
j. Mutual insurance company
k. Nonparticipating insurance
l. Principle of insurable risk
m. Premium
n. Pure risk
o. Public-liability insurance
p. Personal property floater policy
q. Risk
r. Schedule bond
s. Speculative risk
t. Straight life insurance
u. Surety bond
v. Theft
w. Title insurance
x. Term insurance
y. Variable annuity

1. An insurance company owned by its policyholders
2. Life insurance offering protection for only a specified number of years, usually without cash surrender or loan value
3. The amount of money one pays periodically for the cost of an insurance policy
4. A situation in which there is both a chance of loss and a possibility for gain
5. A term used to define the uncertainty as to the occurrence of a loss of life, property, or health
6. A type of risk that can result only in a loss
7. An insurance principle that states that if the requisites of insurability are not met, then the risk is not economically insurable
8. An insurance contract on which no dividends are paid the policyholders
9. An insurance principle that requires the policyholder to demonstrate that he has suffered a financial loss before he can collect on an insured peril
10. A type of loss suffered by the insured that results in his inability to carry on a business in a normal way due to destruction by fire

11. Insurance protection covering losses caused by a breaking into the premises, using force or violence in the taking of property
12. A legal term that describes the act of stealing property regardless of methods used
13. A bond that protects an employer against acts of dishonest employees
14. A legal term that represents the act of stealing
15. A bond that guarantees performance of a contract or legal obligation
16. An insurance policy providing protection against any defects in the title to real property
17. A life insurance contract requiring payment of the premium during the life of the insured
18. A life insurance policy that combines the element of life insurance with the investment feature
19. Insurance on the life of an important executive that is bought by his company with the company named as beneficiary
20. A bond, listing a group of employees by name, written for the purpose of protecting the employer against possible dishonest acts on the part of any of these employees
21. Insurance covering risks, to which businesses and individuals are exposed, that may result in injury to another person, or in damage to his property
22. An insurance contract combining the features of ordinary or whole life with those of term insurance
23. A future income of uncertain amount, bought by periodic payments in advance, which payments are invested in securities (stocks and bonds), and represented by units measuring the share in the investment fund
24. A policy insuring household goods and other personal effects of the insured while in the home or away from the home, whether in transit or not
25. Insurance that reimburses a seller for any losses arising out of his inability to collect a debt arising from a sale

QUESTIONS FOR REVIEW STUDY

1. How does pure risk differ from speculative risk?
2. In addition to insurance, what are other means by which a businessman may reduce or eliminate his risks?
3. Some companies find it desirable to self-insure. Why don't all firms do this?
4. What does the term "insurable interest" mean, and how does it differ from the "principle of insurable risk"?
5. How does the mutual-insurançe company differ from a stock-insurance company?
6. What actually is standard in a standard fire-policy?
7. What is the reason for coinsurance?
8. Why is it often impractical for even large businesses to use self-insurance?
9. How does the "law of large numbers" apply to insurance?
10. What are the major differences between term and ordinary life insurance?

11. What are the different kinds of insurance coverage available to automobile owners?
12. What is a buy-and-sell agreement, and how is it used in insurance?
13. What are the two types of liability insurance that can be carried by a business firm?
14. How is it possible for an insurance company to pay for a $50,000 loss even though the policyholder has paid only $2,000 in premiums?

PROBLEMS AND PROJECTS

1. Larson, who owns and operates a successful cafeteria, wishes to borrow $15,000 for a year from his bank, but the bank has informed him that it cannot lend him the money unless he will buy a policy on his life, naming the bank as beneficiary. Larson already has $20,000 in life insurance, of which $10,000 is ordinary or straight life, and $10,000 is an endowment policy. Both were taken out 15 years ago, when he was 29. Since Larson does not wish to assign to the bank any of the life insurance he now has, it is doubtful he will get his loan. What can you suggest as a solution to his problem that will help Larson obtain the loan?
2. A modern, fireproof building valued at $300,000 is insured at 75 percent of its actual value. Compute the premium cost for one year at an annual rate of 40¢ per $100. How much would the owner save in premiums if he bought a three-year policy?
3. A retailer insured his store building, valued at $80,000, for $40,000 under an 80 percent coinsurance clause. He has suffered a fire loss of $32,000. How much is he entitled to receive by way of insurance compensation?

A BUSINESS CASE

Case 18-1 Life Insurance as an Investment

Not long ago, Robert Dexter retired at the age of 65 after working for 37 years in a local department store, first as a clerk and then as a buyer. Throughout his employment he invested virtually all his savings in a self-styled life-insurance program aimed at giving him a comfortable, worry-free retirement, and providing for his survivors (who are now his wife and their two married children). He obviously liked the 20-year endowment plan, for when he retired he had $75,000 paid-up insurance in the form of 20-year endowment policies, and an additional $25,000 endowment policy due to mature in two years. From time to time he spends some of the proceeds of this life insurance to supplement his income, which comes mainly from social security benefits.

Mr. Dexter has always contended that life insurance is safer than other investments and that it gives one a return on his investment that is comparable to that from other low-risk investments. In his case, he says, insurance combined both investment and protection during his years of employment. He always believed that he was storing away a sum of money that would guarantee his family a good living when he retired, with some left over for his family when he died—or, conversely, which would leave his heirs well-off if he died before he reached retirement age. Since his firm was a family-owned business, no stock was sold to employees, and he never invested in the stock of any large corporations listed with any of the exchanges because he felt they were too much of a gamble for him.

Recently, Mr. and Mrs. Dexter each had a physical examination, and both were found to be in good health. In fact, the attending physician half-jokingly told both of them, "You may live another 20 years." Over the past few weeks, the newly invigorated Mr. Dexter has been advising his 27-year-old son, a chemical engineer with two children, to start a similar insurance plan for his retirement. The son, who earns $15,000 before taxes, is buying a home requiring monthly payments of $178.00. His company allows its employees to buy stock. But Mr. Dexter has advised his son to buy life insurance, such as his favorite 20-year endowment contracts, rather than stock in the corporations listed on the New York Stock Exchange. The son contends that, with so much inflation, life insurance as an investment is not good. Mr. Dexter points out that should a severe depression or recession occur, one could borrow against his endowment policy and not have to pay it back as long as he continued to pay the interest and the annual premiums. Although Mr. Dexter admits that inflation is a problem, he feels that the risk is not enough to offset the advantages of insurance as a form of saving for the future and creating an estate.

Since the son and his wife are undecided as to what is the best course of action, they have sought your advice as to what procedure to follow. Presently, the son has a $20,000 term life-insurance policy on himself, but no insurance on his wife.

1. Is Mr. Dexter giving his son sound advice?
2. What arguments could you give to the son and his wife to support the idea of investing heavily in endowment insurance?
3. What specific arguments would you make to the son regarding the advantages of buying stock in his company, or some other listed security?
4. What are some of the weaknesses of depending too heavily on the purchase of stock in the company where the son works?

A BUSINESS CASE

Case 18-2 The Tweedy Brothers Produce Company

The Tweedy Brothers Produce Co., owned by John and Ralph Tweedy, was a well-established wholesale fruit and vegetable business in Lincoln,

Neb., until it was ruined by a fire six days ago. The company last year had gross sales of $350,000, earning a profit, after taxes, amounting to $32,000. The firm occupied a combination frame and brick structure located in the downtown district, and rented for storage an adjacent wooden building, which was also completely damaged by the fire. Total loss to real property owned and rented by the firm has been estimated at $200,000. Four delivery trucks were also lost. Cost of destruction of fruit and vegetables amounted to about $2,500. (Luckily, all records were saved.) The firm will remain closed for at least 30 days until a suitable building can be located to serve as a temporary office and market place.

A fire-related tragedy has caused additional complications. An employee, attempting to drive one of the trucks out of the building during the fire, was blinded by smoke and collided with a fire truck on the premises. A city fireman died from the collision and the employee was hospitalized for a few days.

At the time of the fire, Tweedy Brothers carried fire insurance amounting to about half the replacement cost of the building, which was considered to be $90,000. Their automobile insurance included fire, theft, and comprehensive policy on 12 trucks, and an automobile bodily injury liability policy in the amount of $25,000/50,000.

Appraise this situation for Tweedy Brothers and recommend an insurance program adequate to serve the future needs of this business.

PART 6
MARKETING MANAGEMENT

Marketing in Our Economy

19

In our earlier study we learned that the American business system is characterized by specialization. Each geographic region has some advantage in production over other regions because of the abundance of certain raw materials in that region. This causes certain areas of the country to specialize to some degree in the types of goods manufactured in it.

But the people who live in all parts of the country are prospective buyers of all types of goods regardless of the area in which they are made. So our business system must be concerned with getting goods, regardless of where they are manufactured, to the customers who wish to buy them, regardless of where they are located. This distribution of goods is called *marketing*.

The term *market* as commonly used refers to different things—sometimes its scope is quite narrow, while at other times it includes a wide range of activities. For example, some cities have what is generally referred to as "the farmers' market," a trading place where all types of fresh fruits and

Courtesy, Board of Trade, City of Chicago

Trading on the floor of the Chicago Board of Trade.

vegetables are sold. The Chicago livestock "market," the nation's largest marketplace of its kind, includes both the stockyards and the sales that take place there daily. Sometimes the term "market" is used to refer to sales trends or fluctuations in consumer demand. We say that the automobile market is picking up or that the cattle market is down, meaning that customer demand is strong or weak. Persons frequently refer to the "stock market." This refers to the sale of corporation stock on the stock exchanges (which was discussed in Chapter 16). *To the economist, the market for a specific economic good (or service) is the sum of all exchange transactions between buyers and sellers of that good at any designated time.* To constitute a market there must be a buyer and a seller, a commodity or service, an exchange, and an agreed-upon price.

In this chapter we shall study the nature and scope of marketing, its economic significance, management's role in marketing, the basic types of goods distributed, the cost of marketing, and the functions of marketing. In succeeding chapters, we shall take a closer look at some specific aspects of marketing.

THE NATURE AND SCOPE OF MARKETING

The committee on marketing of the American Marketing Assn. has defined *marketing* as *the performance of business activities that direct the flow of goods and services from producer to consumer or user.* This includes all the activities concerned with the processing, sale, and physical distribution of goods that take place after they are manufactured until they are delivered to their ultimate users. It includes marketing research, transportation, product packaging, and also, the use of advertising and credit as means of influencing consumer patronage.

Actually, today the marketing function is thought of as beginning before goods ever enter the manufacturing process. The emphasis in marketing is no longer centered on *things;* rather, it is largely concerned with *people* and their wants. A business that is truly marketing-minded concentrates on creating goods of value that satisfy potential patrons' needs. So *we* shall define "marketing" for the purpose of our discussion as *the system of interrelated business activities that pertain to designing, promoting, pricing, and distributing goods and services to potential users.*

This definition of marketing presents it as a comprehensive term, more or less synonymous with distribution. It encompasses merchandising promotion, selling, and transportation, which are more narrow in scope. It emphasizes the management function of marketing, and the concept that the whole scheme of business activities should be customer-oriented. It presents marketing as a coordinated and integrated function rather than one of fragmentation.

THE ECONOMIC IMPORTANCE OF MARKETING

When you envision the mountains of goods and the huge quantity of services that together make up today's gross national product, you catch a glimpse of the magnitude of today's marketing function. Only a small percentage of any product is consumed in the local community where it is produced. To distribute these mountains of products to the consumers who want them requires the service of between one-fourth and one-third of the employed civilian labor-force. (This is including all employees in the wholesaling, retailing, warehousing, and transportation industries, and those engaged in marketing activities for the manufacturing, agricultural, and mining industries.)

Looking at it from another point of view, marketing considerations are central in corporate business management and decision making. The National Association of Manufacturers has put it this way:[1]

> Marketing is the beating heart of many operations. It must be considered a principal reason for corporate existence. The modern concept of marketing recognizes its role as a direct contributor to profits, as well as sales volume.
>
> No longer can a company just figure out how many widgets it can produce and then go ahead and turn them out. To endure in this highly competitive change-infested market, a company must first determine what it can sell, how much it can sell, and what approaches must be used to entice the wary customer. The president cannot plan; the production manager cannot manage; the purchasing agent cannot pur-

[1] *Sales Management,* March 20, 1959, p. 7.

chase; the chief financial officer cannot budget; and the engineer and designer cannot design until the basic market determinations have been made.

MANAGEMENT'S ROLE IN MARKETING

The thing that makes a marketing program successful is what has been termed the proper "marketing mix." By *marketing mix* we mean a combination of four basic elements: the product, the channels of distribution, the pricing policies and practices, and the methods used in promotion. A company may manufacture a single line of products, or several lines. Its products may be packaged singly or in groups; by brand or unbranded. It may be distributed through wholesalers only, through jobbers, directly to retailers, or by a combination of methods. It is management's responsibility to see that all these variables are combined in the right "marketing mix."

It was pointed out in earlier chapters that management is involved with setting objectives, organizing, planning, coordinating, staffing, directing, analyzing, decision-making, and evaluating. The term *marketing management* refers to the carrying out of these management functions through marketing processes. The ways that they are performed vary from company to company.

As an example of how one company administers its marketing management program, let us consider the brand-management practices of Procter & Gamble. This firm manufactures a wide range of consumer products, many of which are familiar to you—Ivory soap, Tide detergent, Crest toothpaste, Folger coffee, and the Duncan Hines mixes, to name only a few. Each marketing manager at Procter & Gamble is responsible for his own brand (company product). In many ways, "P & G's" brand managers enjoy much the same freedom in decision-making and in administration as they would if they were in business for themselves. They set marketing goals and formulate marketing budgets. They develop the strategies to be used in achieving these goals. They stimulate and coordinate the total marketing package that supports their respective products. Of course, they are free to draw upon the competencies of company personnel in the areas of copy editing, television programming, and other specialities. However, it is again they alone who have the task of synthesizing all the marketing efforts (pertaining to their respective brands) that are focused on satisfying the consumers' wants.

PRODUCT PLANNING AS MARKETING

Whether a company is developing a new product or redesigning an old one, the development process must be preplanned. Some companies have special departments for this work, while others carry it through as a part of the marketing function. The chief purpose of continuous product planning is to make sure that a company will not be left behind either by its competitors or by changes in consumers' fancies.

There are eight stages in product planning. Although they normally follow one another, some steps may be performed simultaneously.

1. The first step is a market forecast to estimate the size and type of product to introduce.
2. The basic market study attempts to make an assessment of consumers' needs. This tends to establish the over-all market potential for the product, not the product of a particular company.
3. The product concept is concerned with the specific qualities of the product. This is vital to the over-all product development and must be kept in constant review during all remaining stages.
4. The product objective sets out the product's dimensions as to sizes, colors, prices, and quantities.
5. This is followed by an evaluation or feasibility study which is done by the engineering staff. It answers the question of whether or not the product will perform the functions planned for it.
6. Consumer reaction is needed at this point in order to prevent the waste that would result from proceeding too far in the wrong direction. This is a preliminary sounding of consumer acceptance.
7. Models or prototypes are then tested in a limited market.
8. Tooling up for production is the final stage. At the time this is done, consumer testing is continued on a broadened scale. Attempts are made at this time also to perfect the product, eliminating all possible defects before full-scale marketing begins.

BASIC TYPES OF MARKETED GOODS

All the goods that flow through our marketing system may be classified into two main groups: consumer goods and industrial goods. Since it is the goods themselves that give meaning and purpose to our marketing system, let us look closely at these two basic types of commodity.

Consumer Goods

Goods that consumers buy from retail outlets for their own personal satisfaction are called *consumer goods.* On the basis of the way in which these goods are purchased, we can break consumer goods down into three different types: *convenience goods*, *shopping goods*, and *specialty goods*.

Convenience Goods. Convenience goods are those products that consumers buy at retail outlets near their homes. They are usually staple items of low unit value, purchased frequently and in small quantities. Soft drinks, drugs, tobacco, gasoline, newspapers, and ice cream are typical of this class. Consumers are not especially interested in comparing prices or checking quality when they purchase such goods, many of which are bought on impulse and are so well adapted to self-service methods. Good display is necessary in order to secure maximum sales.

Manufacturers attempt to secure distribution of convenience goods in as many stores as possible. To secure even wider distribution, these items are frequently offered for sale through vending machines in offices, factories, schools, and public buildings.

Shopping Goods. Shopping goods are that group of consumer goods whose price, fashion, quality, and service are of considerable importance to the buyer. They are relatively high in value, and are bought infrequently and only after deliberation. Instead of simply buying where it is most convenient, the consumer shops around in the hope of finding precisely what he wants. Items typical of this class are furniture, jewelry, rugs, shoes, and china.

Stores that specialize in the selling of shopping goods are customarily located within a block or two of one another, in busy shopping areas. Shopping goods are heavily advertised by the merchants in local newspapers and other local advertising media, and the manufacturer often cooperates with the merchant in the advertising program. The number of outlets that sell shopping goods is small compared with the number that distribute convenience goods.

Specialty Goods. Goods that possess some distinctive quality for which the consumer has a strong preference are classed as specialty goods. They are usually (but not necessarily) items of high unit value, such as television sets, appliances, and automobiles; you might be willing to walk several blocks to obtain a relatively low-cost specialty item, such as your favorite box of candy, simply because it possesses some distinctive quality that you happen to value. This class of goods differs from shopping goods in that price is not the principal consideration in one's choice of stores. Some marketing authorities contend that the line between shopping and specialty goods is scarcely discernible, however, and suggest that the latter term be discarded.

Notice that these three kinds of goods are classified on the basis of consumers' shopping habits. There is considerable variation in the shopping habits of consumers. This means that a given article may represent convenience goods to one person, shopping goods to another, and specialty goods to a third. To the man who is unwilling to spend time shopping around, for example, the purchase of a pair of shoes might be a convenience item. Most women, however, are accustomed to buying their shoes only after deliberation and comparison; to them, shoes constitute shopping goods. But then, too, many purchasers have a favorite brand of shoe that they habitually purchase at a particular store, and to these people, shoes represent specialty goods.

Industrial Goods

Industrial goods include all the various kinds of goods used or consumed by a business, and those that are used in the production of other goods. Approximately 45 percent of all manufactured goods are sold for industrial use, and 80 percent of all farm products are sold on the industrial market. The following classifications will suggest to you the different kinds of industrial goods that find their way through our marketing system:

Raw Materials. Raw materials are, as we saw in Chapter 15, basic items that come from farms, mines, and forests. They include such commodities as grain, wool, ore, tobacco, petroleum, and wood.

Semi Manufactured Goods. These are goods that have been processed but will be sold to another manufacturer for further processing. Examples are pig iron, leather, industrial chemicals, and sheet aluminum.

Parts. This class includes manufactured items that will serve as components of larger articles—such as tubes for radios, bearings for machinery, and wheels for automobiles.

Supplies. Although supplies are not physically incorporated into the manufacturer's finished product, still they are essential to the operation of his business. Examples of supplies are wrapping paper, machine oil, cleaning compounds, and fuel. Such goods may be purchased for use in factories, offices, or mercantile businesses.

Machinery and Equipment. This category includes all machines—large and small—used in production and office work.

The use that a purchaser intends to make of the goods he buys determines whether they should be regarded as industrial or consumer goods. Goods that are all finished and ready to be consumed, and are purchased to be resold to an ultimate consumer, are regarded as consumer goods. But if they are purchased by a business for its own use, they are classified as industrial goods. Certain articles, such as coal and automobiles, will at times fall into both categories, depending on the use that is to be made of the product. Coal burned by a utility or business concern would be classified as industrial goods, but coal purchased for home use would be classified as consumer goods. The automobiles that a wholesaler purchases for the use of his sales force would constitute industrial goods.

Contrasts in Marketing Industrial and Consumer Goods

A look at the markets and marketing techniques commonly associated with industrial and consumer goods reveals a number of clearly identifiable contrasts.

1. There is a very narrow market for many kinds of industrial goods. For example, the market for certain industrial chemicals and automobile body hardware is limited for the most part to a small group of manufacturers. The consumer goods market, on the other hand, often has millions of potential customers for a product. A narrow market at times simplifies the task of marketing because it facilitates the making of sales directly from the producer to the industrial user. On the other hand, such a restricted market makes it impractical for the producer to employ a sales organization large enough to contact all potential customers. When these conditions exist, it is not uncommon for industrial consumers to seek out the seller of the goods. For this purpose, the purchasing department usually has an assortment of catalogues and an index of sup; liers, such as Thomas' Register. This four-volume set has 500,000 listings of manufacturers under thousands of product classifications.

2. It is more difficult to discover in the industrial market the party who actually makes buying decisions than it is in the consumer goods market. Retailers can usually assume that any person who visits their stores and shows an interest in their goods is the potential purchaser. On the other hand, it is often difficult for the salesman of industrial goods to determine which persons in the customer firm really make buying decisions. In the purchase of an item used in manufacturing, for example, the decision may be made by the purchasing agent, the plant superintendent, the foreman, the product engineer, or the plant manager. Sometimes the salesman feels that no one will give him a candid answer when he asks who has the final authority over purchases.

3. Reciprocity of orders between buyer and seller is a common practice in the industrial market, but relatively unimportant in the consumer goods market. Many companies buy goods or services produced by their customers. For example, a steel producer may buy its chemicals from the chemical manufacturer that buys its steel. The steel producer may adopt this practice because it makes the chemical firm a more loyal customer. A salesman of industrial goods may therefore attempt to influence the purchasing department of his firm to patronize his potential customers.

4. A single sale of industrial goods often represents a large sum of money. The sale of a single machine, for example, may amount to thousands of dollars, and a contract for materials and parts may run into millions.

5. Buyers of industrial goods are usually well-informed and make their purchasing decisions on the basis of the product's proven performance. The industrial purchasing agent is not emotionally motivated, as the buyer of consumer goods often is, and is under no pressure to "keep up with the Joneses."

6. The demand for certain types of industrial goods is extremely sensitive to changing business conditions. The demand for machines, for instance, drops precipitously when business slows down. In fact, the entire industrial market suffers more than the consumer market during periods of declining business activity. But in normal and boom periods the demand for machinery, equipment, and parts is greatly accelerated.

7. Industrial goods are commonly sold directly by the producer to the user without the intervention of the middleman characteristic of the consumer market. Engineers representing both the buyer and the producer may work together in setting up specifications for the product. And the producer often furnishes expert advice, machine installation, and repair service after the goods have been sold. A relationship of this sort increases the likelihood that future dealings will be kept on a direct, face-to-face basis. Approximately 80 percent of the industrial goods manufactured in this country are sold directly to the industrial user.

THE COST OF MARKETING

The all-around cost of distributing to their ultimate users all the goods manufactured in the United States runs into fantastic amounts of time, energy, and money. And little wonder, for this function furnishes employment to a major portion of the working populace. All types of commercial transportation—railroads, trucks, airplanes, and ships—are involved. In addition, much equipment (such as tractors and forklifts) is needed to move the finished product from the assembly line to storage areas, from storage to commercial transportation lines, and so on. And of course the cost of all the advertising done in newspapers and magazines, and by direct mail, radio, and television, is included in the cost of marketing. We must also keep in mind that part of the cost of marketing is for research to determine in advance exactly what sizes, designs, and colors the consumer wants.

On the average, all things considered, the cost of marketing accounts for approximately 50 percent the total cost of a typical good. At first this might seem excessive. But when you stop to consider the low cost of the raw materials in a rubber ball, a writing pen, or a lamp, for example, and the relatively short time required to make any of them, in comparison with all that is involved in the total marketing function, the figure seems rather reasonable.

And there are many secondary benefits that come to consumers more or less as byproducts of the marketing function. For example, a daily newspaper costs only a dime, and a monthly periodical only a quarter. But were it not for the financing of these publications by advertising, they would cost many times that much. And television programs are free to their viewers only because their cost is underwritten by advertising.

Perhaps we should not use the term "cost of marketing." For some time now we have talked and written about the "value added" by manufacturing. It is just as logical to talk about the *value-added concept in marketing.* Just as manufacturing gives a product form-utility, marketing gives it *time-and-place utility.*

THE FUNCTIONS OF MARKETING

One of the best ways to develop an understanding of how goods are marketed in our modern economy is to examine the various functions that are performed as goods move from producer to consumer. These functions may be listed as follows: *buying, selling, transporting, storing, risk-bearing, standardizing, grading, pricing, financing and market information.*

Each of these functions is essential to the success of the over-all marketing activity. To illustrate: the marketing of the shoes you are wearing began the moment they were completed at the factory. First they had to be stored at the factory and then in the retail store where you bought them. Sales efforts were expended by the manufacturer, the wholesaler, and the retailer through whose hands they passed. The retailer spent time and money selecting his stock of shoes; they had to be shipped to him; someone had to assure that they conformed to certain standards of size and color. The wholesaler extended credit to the retailer, thus assisting him to finance his business. And at every step along the way, efforts were made to keep abreast of information on the leather market and on fashion trends.

Buying

For the consumer who walks into a retail store, the buying function is usually a simple enough matter, but in a business concern it involves several distinct activities. First the buyer must determine his needs, based on his knowledge of the preferences of customers. Customer "taste" in one locality may differ greatly from that in other communities, and he must be able to predict whether the goods he chooses to sell in any particular area will appeal to the tastes of his customers there. This is a fine art that demands extensive experience and is one of the key functions in successful buying at the retail level.

After the buyer determines what his customers' wants are likely to be, he must select his sources of supply. A buyer normally deals with the representatives of dozens of different companies, and must decide which one or ones will give him the best terms—quality merchandise at reasonable prices. This is true whether he represents a wholesale or a retail business enterprise.

The third phase of the buyer's task is negotiating with the suppliers for the delivery of the merchandise. Generally, these negotiations are most successful when detailed specifications can be given. This helps assure that exacting quality standards will be met. Purchase-order and delivery schedules must be arranged and clearly understood by both parties engaged in the negotiation procedures. Through all this, the buyer is constantly concerned with maintaining the correct inventory balance within the minimum and maximum limits necessary to keep production going.

Selling

Selling is the very heart of the marketing function. It includes the location of buyers whose wants can be satisfied by the kinds and quantities of goods that have been purchased. A significant aspect of selling is promotion. Advertising, window displays, sales demonstrations, special prices for limited periods of time, trade movies, trade exhibits, and samples all are important aspects of promotion. The selling of industrial goods differs somewhat from that of consumer products, just as the selling efforts at the wholesale level differ from those of retailers. (The discussion in Chapter 20 discusses in considerable detail the various channels of marketing.)

Transporting

Transportation of goods is essential in any marketing activity. Of primary concern to both buyer and seller are the speed and cost of this service. Although cost is usually the determining consideration in choosing the method of transportation, speed and special services (such as refrigeration) determine the method of shipment of certain goods—perishable commodities, for example.

A highly developed system of transportation enables us to benefit from large-scale operations and regional specialization. Thus we are able to produce goods here and there, according to where the most favorable conditions are, and yet make them available in all parts of the nation. Improvements in transportation service also broaden the market for goods. For example, the inauguration of air freight extended the market for California strawberries to many distant parts of the United States.

Storing

Adequate storage is essential to marketing because of the lag between the production and ultimate consumption of a product. In certain marketing situations it is necessary to store reserve supplies of goods that are produced seasonally but consumed regularly throughout the year. In other situations it is necessary to store goods that are produced regularly but are consumed irregularly from one season to another.

Clearly, the physical location of storage facilities is of paramount importance in the successful performance of this function. Reservoirs of consumer goods must be maintained and made readily accessible in the vicinity of retail outlets, since the retailer can profitably store only enough goods to supply the needs of his customers for a relatively short period of time. Instead of using his valuable display space as a storage area, the retailer insists that goods be kept on hand in the wholesale house, the chain-store warehouse, the manufacturer's branch warehouse, or a public warehouse.

The storage of agricultural products requires an especially complex set of facilities, organized in an elaborate geographical pattern. In the producing areas, for example, middlemen must operate extensive storage facilities to care for the commodities they purchase from farmers. Then the commodities must be transported and stored in tremendous elevators and warehouses located in or near the large centers where the commodity is widely traded. For example, in Chicago, one of the greatest grain-trading centers of the world, huge grain-storage facilities are maintained. Other storage facilities must be available in areas where commodities are processed, and at seaports and railroad terminals where they await shipment to their destinations.

Risk-Bearing

The ownership of valuable stocks of industrial or consumer goods carries with it a heavy burden of risk, for the major portion of the capital at the command of most marketing firms is tied up in their physical inventories. Fire, storms, and theft are common types of risk that may be covered by insurance, but other risks cannot be guarded against by this means. Sudden shifts in styles of dress, for example, may result in severe losses to dealers in fashion goods. The only way this risk can be reduced is through careful market analysis. Every marketer is faced with the possibility that price levels may decline sharply, leaving him with a warehouse full of goods on which he must take a loss. Careful control of inventory is the usual way of minimizing this risk, but even that will not eliminate the danger entirely.

Controlling the costs of bearing these risks is a test of the skill of the marketer. The cost of risk-bearing varies widely with the type of goods handled, but some loss is inescapable in almost every business that distributes goods.

Standardizing

Standards must be firmly established before merchandise can be accurately catalogued and described in a fashion that is meaningful to the buyers and sellers of goods. A *standard* is a constant physical characteristic that gives uniformity to a group of products. For example, when a plumber orders a length of ¾-inch pipe and the fittings necessary to use it in an installation, he has no doubt that all the critical measurements will be uniform. Because electric light bulbs are standardized, we have no hesitancy in ordering by telephone a quantity of 60-watt bulbs. Manufacturers observe an industry-wide standard in designing the bases of bulbs, making it possible for us to screw any ordinary bulb into virtually any light socket. Moreover, when you see a bulb labeled "60-watt," you know without experiment just how much light you can expect to get from it.

During the early days of trading, when the "let the buyer beware" attitude was accepted by buyer and seller alike, there was little need for standardization. Buyers inspected the merchandise and made their own selections, and descriptions were unimportant. But now, when the buyer and seller are often far apart, sales transactions must be made in faith and confidence based on mutually accepted standards. Life would be primitive indeed if goods were not standardized.

Even so, the observance of standards for certain products could still be improved, with a consequent increase in marketing efficiency and consumer satisfaction. Not all size-six shoes or size-12 dresses, for example, are cut to precisely the same dimensions—a lack of uniformity that leads to a waste of time when customers try them on in stores, and that also serves to increase the number of returns.

Grading

Grading is another process that improves marketing efficiency. This is the process of sorting goods into a number of classes, or grades, according to quality. The term is most commonly applied to agricultural products, such as grain, fruits, eggs, and meat. For each grade of a commodity certain specifications have been established, usually by federal agencies. The Agricultural Marketing Service of the Department of Agriculture has developed standards of quality for approximately 100 commodities.

In most cases, grading eliminates the necessity of inspecting the product at the time of sale. Thousands of bushels of grain are sold daily, completely on the basis of grade. Trading in the futures market would be impossible were it not for a universally accepted system of graded products. Furthermore, grading improves marketing efficiency by channeling different qualities of goods to the markets best suited to them. Only grade-A eggs can be sold successfully in certain stores, while lower grades may be quite satisfactory for processing as powdered eggs. The cost of grading is negligible compared with the economies and improvements it makes possible.

Pricing

The degree of freedom that a seller has in setting prices varies according to several factors. To begin with, the cost of the product sets the absolute floor for pricing. But one tries to sell for more, of course, because a sale at cost price results in a loss of sorts, since that sale does not bear its proportionate share of the overhead expenses. There was a time when one could charge whatever the traffic would bear, but this is hardly possible any more. Actually, the price ceiling varies according to the keenness of the competition. In some industries a few giant businesses may try to set pricing patterns and force the smaller companies to "follow the leader" in raising or lowering their prices. But government pressure is often exerted in these cases to prevent pricing practices that will lead to monopoly or increase inflation. In the absence of competition and where government pressure is not required, consumer demand limits the price.

Financing

Regardless of the sales policy (cash or credit) followed by the retailer, someone must finance the marketing function. Because large sums of capital are required to provide marketing services and maintain an adequate inventory of goods in stock, credit frequently has to be extended all along the marketing line: by the retailer, by his wholesaler, and even by the manufacturer. If credit suddenly were discontinued, the economic system would suffer dire effects.

Retailers are usually engaged in keen competition with one another in their attempts to offer credit terms attractive to customers. Now, a liberal credit policy, though a powerful force in attracting customers, also increases materially the capital requirements of the business. Nevertheless, a variety of credit plans are offered by retailers today. Many offer credit either on a 30-day payment basis, or by means of a "revolving" plan of payment. Under the latter plan, the customer makes regular monthly payments of a previously agreed amount, and may make additional purchases so long as the account does not exceed an agreed maximum balance. Retailers also offer the installment plan of credit, which is evidenced by a conditional sales contract with payments extending over a period of several months.

Providing Market Information

A constant flow of information about both sources of supply and market conditions is essential to firms that market goods. They must know, for example, about price fluctuations in commodities at the wholesale level, and must keep posted on subtle shifts in fashions. The job of collecting, interpreting, and disseminating all this information falls under the function of providing market information, which is performed by government agencies, trade associations, news services, commission firms, and the sellers themselves.

Alfred Politz Research, Inc., conducted a detailed *Study of Consumer Expenditures* for *Life* magazine which was published by *Life* in 1959. The purpose of the study was to describe the consumer markets for all categories of products and services. These markets were described in terms of the kinds of people and households that make the purchases. The households were classified on the basis of market size, income, geographic location, socio-economic status, and other related items. The study was designed to serve as a background for making marketing decisions. It is probably one of the most complete analyses of the buying public completed in recent years. Because of the extensive nature of this study, the findings are reproduced here as a simple "pie graph" (page 572). And because the average family income has increased tremendously since this study was made, the way in which today's U.S. family spends its income is shown in the accompanying table. You can see how the percentages have changed since the *Life* study was made.

EXPENDITURES FOR CONSUMER GOODS AND SERVICES IN 1966

		Percent
All commodities		65.03
All services		34.97
		100.00
Food		22.94
Housing		32.89
Shelter	(20.32)	
Fuel and Utilities	(4.96)	
Furnishings and Operation	(7.61)	
Apparel and Upkeep		10.54
Transportation		13.70
Medical and Personal Care		8.66
Recreation		5.80
Other Goods and Services		5.09
		100.00

Source: *Statistical Abstract of the United States,* 1967, p. 357.

How the Average U.S. Family Divided Its Dollars for Consumer Goods and Services in 1956

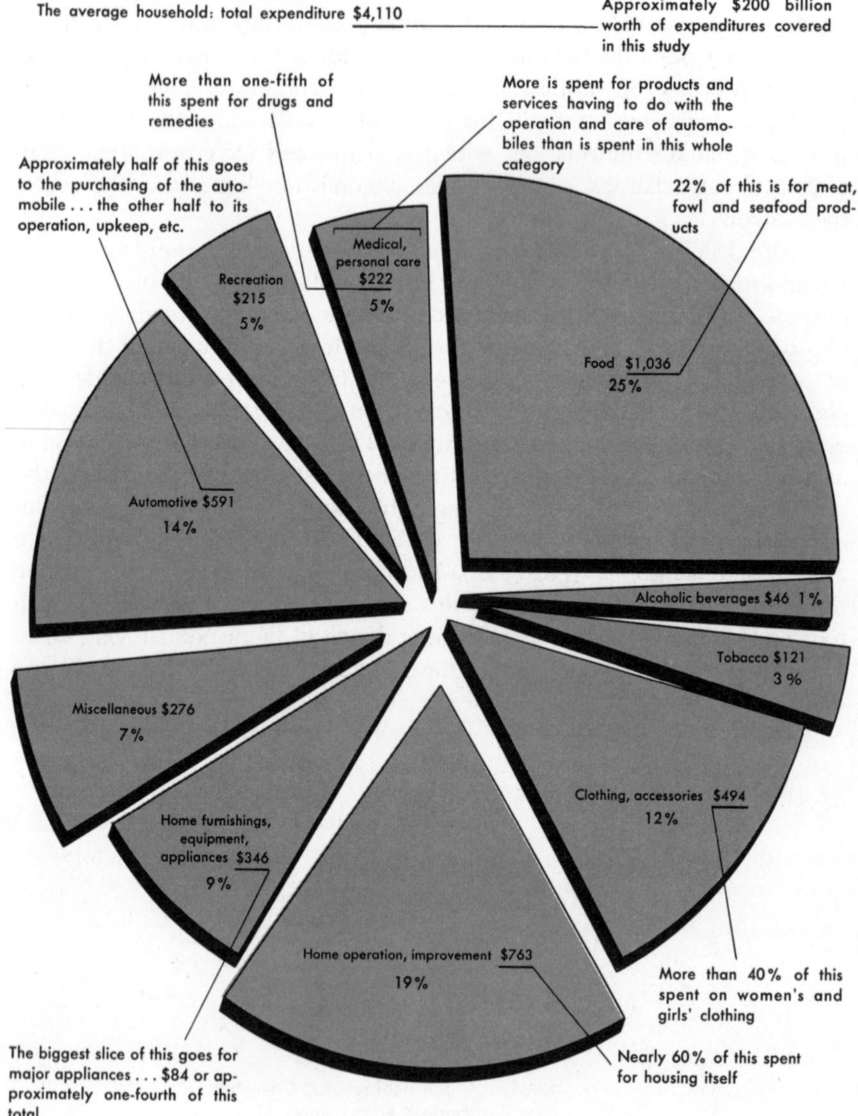
The average household: total expenditure $4,110
Approximately $200 billion worth of expenditures covered in this study
More than one-fifth of this spent for drugs and remedies
More is spent for products and services having to do with the operation and care of automobiles than is spent in this whole category
Approximately half of this goes to the purchasing of the automobile . . . the other half to its operation, upkeep, etc.
22% of this is for meat, fowl and seafood products
Medical, personal care $222 5%
Recreation $215 5%
Food $1,036 25%
Automotive $591 14%
Alcoholic beverages $46 1%
Tobacco $121 3%
Miscellaneous $276 7%
Clothing, accessories $494 12%
Home furnishings, equipment, appliances $346 9%
Home operation, improvement $763 19%
More than 40% of this spent on women's and girls' clothing
The biggest slice of this goes for major appliances . . . $84 or approximately one-fourth of this total
Nearly 60% of this spent for housing itself

Source: LIFE *Study of Consumer Expenditures,* © *Time, Inc.,* 1959

COMMODITY EXCHANGE MARKETS

One of the important marketing agencies within our total economic system is the *commodity exchange.* This may be defined as an organization or association of individuals which provides a place for its members to buy and sell commodities both for themselves and for nonmembers. Commodity exchanges do not actually exchange commodities *per se;* instead, all transactions are made "on the floor" by persons who have a membership in the association similar to membership in a stock-market exchange. The list of commodities traded in these markets is numerous. It includes raw materials like rubber, hides, silver, tin, and copper; such grains as wheat, soybeans, oats, cotton, barley, sugar, and potatoes; and certain frozen foods.

There are over 40 such exchanges in the United States. On 15 of these, "futures trading" is conducted in about 30 commodities under regulations made by the Grain Futures Act of 1922 and the Commodity Exchange Act of 1936. The Chicago Board of Trade has the largest volume of trade in grains. The New York Cotton Exchange and the New Orleans Cotton Exchange specialize in cotton.

TYPES OF TRADING

The dealing in grain which occurs on the larger exchanges is of two types: cash (or spot) and futures. *Spot transactions* are purchases or sales of commodities in specific amounts, requiring immediate delivery of the commodity and payment in cash. The seller either owns, or has the assurance of being able to deliver, the commodity. *Futures transactions* are purchases or sales that call for future delivery contingent upon the payment of presently agreed-upon prices. The main purpose of the futures market is to provide price insurance against loss due to price fluctuations in the future.

A Future Transaction

A typical futures transaction may be as follows. In March, a commodity speculator named Hensen decides that May wheat is low, so has his broker buy 5,000 bushels (a unit of trading) of May futures at $2.06 a bushel. Hensen is taking a "long" position in making this purchase. He does not expect delivery, however. If he had ordered his broker to sell 5,000 bushels of May wheat, this would have been a "short" sale. (You will recall the explanation of selling short in Chapter 16's discussion of the stock market.) In April the price of May wheat reaches $2.12 a bushel. So Hensen decides to take his profit by selling his 5,000 bushels of futures contract wheat. The first transaction offsets the second, and the $300 difference becomes his gross profit, from which he must pay his broker his commission.

Commodity Specification and Prices

The commodity exchange specifies the unit of trading for purchases and sales. Most grain transactions are in multiples of 5,000 bushels, known as a "round lot" similar to the stock-exchange round lot of 100 shares. A "job lot" consists of 1,000 bushels, or multiples thereof, for all grains except oats, the lot for which is 2,000 bushels.

The exchange also designates certain months to identify futures prices contracts. For wheat, corn, oats, and rye, these months are September, December, March, May, and July. It is interesting to know why these months were selected. December represents the end of the harvest period, and the beginning of winter storage (navigation is closed on the Great Lakes). March is the time when many Southern Hemisphere crops come on the market in volume. May is the "clean-up" month prior to the harvesting of small grains, and the month when the Great Lakes are again fully navigable. July is the time when there is the heavy movement of winter wheat and some oats, barley, and rye to the markets. September is the month when new spring wheat begins to come to the market.

The spot price of wheat is affected both by consumption demand and by supply from marketing channels or from storage. If the current demand increases, the spot price generally rises. This has a tendency to induce storers of wheat to sell more to consumption channels.

The difference between spot and futures prices for grains is called the "basis," a term widely used by the trade in quoting prices. Much of the trading by grain speculators is done in the belief that the "basis" will either widen or become narrower in the future, and a transaction is made to take advantage of the direction the basis seems to be taking. The difference between the spot price and the futures commodity trading price is the "spread," which often is less than the average of storage costs. It is important to note that futures and spot prices, over a short period, tend to move up and down together by more or less the same amount. It is because there is this relative stability of spreads between spot and futures prices that it is possible to hedge.

Under normal conditions the futures price tends to exceed the spot price at any given time by the average of storage costs for the commodity from that time to the delivery date of "futures." It is through this process of pricing that it becomes possible to shift the risk of loss (on commodity manufacturing or processing) to the professional speculator who deals in futures contracts involving hedging.

Hedging

Hedging is a procedure used by grain dealers, flour millers, elevator operators, processors of food commodities, and others engaged in commodity marketing to protect their legitimate profit by minimizing inventory price-risks. *Hedging* consists of buying a quantity of a given commodity in the ordinary trade (spot) market and, at about the same time, selling the same quantity in the "futures" market. The hope is that any loss sustained from a drop in price on the first transaction will be offset by an increase in price on the second transaction. Such increases enable the businessman who is the hedger to make his regular trade profit by giving him advance protection against unpredicatable price fluctuations.

Hedging against price changes is possible under two circumstances: (1) where a business is involved with maintaining an inventory of a commodity *for which there is a futures trading on a commodity exchange;* and (2) where a company is in the business of making commitments *which require future purchases of a commodity,* and at the same time desires to protect itself against a *rise* in price.

A Hedging Transaction. At this point let us examine, by way of a rather simple illustration, the mathematics of hedging. Let us assume that on May 15 a flour miller realizes that he needs more wheat to keep his mill grinding. So, he buys 10,000 bushels of wheat at $2.15. But he knows full well that prices fluctuate in both spot wheat and flour, and thus that he must take steps to protect himself. Therefore, when he buys his 10,000 bushels at $2.15, he immediately sells a September "futures" contract of 10,000 bushels at a price of $2.22. You will recognize that this is a short sale. These two transactions constitute the first half of the hedging price and may be summarized as follows:

I. May 15, a flour miller	
Bought 10,000 bushels wheat for cash @	$2.15
Sold 10,000 bushels September futures @	2.22
Net gain per bushel on transaction	.07

On June 10 the miller accepted an order for flour from a Chicago baking company (the flour for this order having been ground from the wheat purchased for cash on May 15 at $2.15 a bushel) at a price adequate to give him his normal milling profit. Although the miller had actually paid $2.15 for his wheat which he purchased for cash, in the intervening time December futures prices declined along with the drop in the price of spot wheat, falling from $2.22 as of May 15 to $2.16 as of June 10 (the date he received his order for flour). In summary, his June 10 transactions were as follows:

II. June 10, a flour miller

Sold 10,000 bushels of wheat as flour @	$2.09
Bought 10,000 bushels September wheat @	2.16
Net loss on transaction	.07

As a result of the entire transaction, the miller earned his regular milling profit on the flour he sold, but this was because he priced his flour so that he could make a profit even if the wheat for the flour had cost but $2.09 a bushel. Although he paid $2.15 for his spot wheat, he had a 6¢ profit on his futures purchase ($2.22 – $2.16).

This illustration is perhaps oversimplified. In actual practice, the hedge is not always expected to jibe to the penny, since prices in the spot and futures markets seldom move in perfect parallel with each other. It is common, however, for the hedger to produce either a small profit or a small loss. At any rate, the lesson is clear: hedging reduces the risk of price fluctuations so that a businessman, like the grain-elevator operator or flour miller, is able to quote prices to his customers with the assurance that he will not suffer a loss while he holds the commodity in storage or in processing.

REGULATION OF MARKETING PRACTICES

Control over pricing and labeling practices in marketing has been of concern to the federal and also to state governments for many years. Legislation at both levels of government is aimed at preserving competition in marketing, and providing protection for consumers.

The Robinson-Patman Act

The Robinson-Patman Act was passed in 1936 to prohibit certain types of price discrimination. It was intended to curb the practices of large retailers but was written in so general a manner that it has been applied to manufacturers as well. It prohibits price discrimination between different purchasers of goods of like quality if such discrimination would lessen competition with either the person (or company) who grants or receives the benefits of such discrimination.

The Robinson-Patman Act includes an interesting provision in that the buyer, as well as the seller, is guilty if he *knowingly* accepts an unlawful discrimination.

The Miller-Tydings Resale Price Maintenance Act

On occasion, the courts have held that contracts between manufacturers and retailers fixing the resale price of an article have been in violation of the

Sherman Antitrust Law; on other occasions, the courts have declared agreements of this kind lawful. To clear up this confusion, the Miller-Tydings Act of 1937 amended the basic antitrust law by making agreements of this nature lawful. Although the Miller-Tydings Act, and various state "fair-trade" acts passed later, apply only to trade-marked or branded goods, they still cover a wide variety of merchandise. The Miller-Tydings Act actually changed public policy on resale price agreements from an attitude of opposition to the government view, to one of complete support of it. Since this federal law was passed, some 45 states have also passed price-maintenance statutes. California was the first to adopt this kind of statute, in 1931.

One of the significant features of the Miller-Tydings Act was a provision permitting a manufacturer of brand-name products to enter into contracts with retailers in a given state; the retailers would agree not to sell the products below the list price set by the manufacturer. Furthermore, such a contract would be binding on all sellers in that state, whether they signed a contract or not. In 1951, however, the Supreme Court declared that part of the law affecting nonsigners to be unconstitutional. Other parts of the Miller-Tydings Act still remain in force.

The McGuire Act

No sooner had this Supreme Court decision been announced than manufacturers and retail associations again put pressure on legislators to pass a new price-maintenance law that would cover nonsigners of these agreements. So Congress enacted the McGuire Fair-Trade Act of 1952, which specifically declared that fair-trading under the nonsigner agreement was not illegal provided it was approved by the state legislatures concerned.

But the controversy was not over. Many state legislatures made nonsigner arrangements legal, and immediately several state courts declared these clauses unconstitutional. Fair-trade laws incorporating nonsigner clauses are now in effect in about three-fourths of the states.

Many large retail outlets like Macy's and Gimbels in New York have challenged fair-trade legislation on the grounds that such laws, both state and federal, restrain competition. They contend that these laws open the door to monopolistic activity. Trade associations can use these laws as legal authority for collective action by going through the motions of making a "cost survey," and then establishing a minimum retail price below which competitors are forbidden to sell.

Effects of Fair-Trade Laws

The items most commonly subject to *fair-trade price agreements* are food, drugs, tobacco products, soaps, photographic supplies, and electrical appliances. From the consumer's viewpoint, fair-trade laws prohibit retailers from cutting prices on popular brand-name goods. Some merchants, in an effort to free themselves from price controls, have resorted to promoting private-label brands (brands sold by only one firm) as substitutes for the much better known, nationally advertised articles on which there is some kind of price control.

Manufacturers complain that they cannot police all retailers to make sure that set prices are being maintained. General Electric for several years tried desperately to do just this, but finally gave up. Furthermore, neither the Department of Justice nor the Federal Trade Commission has the necessary personnel or the funds to detect and prosecute violators. And state agencies are reluctant to take action against large companies about which complaints have been received.

Faced with the futility of trying to maintain price agreements on a national scale, a growing list of manufacturers have abandoned price agreements on many lines of merchandise. However, fair trade is by no means dead. The privately operated Bureau of Education on Fair Trade contends that the death of fair trade would bring the end of small business. Some observers are of the opinion that the decision of companies like General Electric, Eastman Kodak, Sunbeam Corp., and Westinghouse Electric, to end fair-trade practices has made more imperative the passage of a bill that would extend resale price maintenance on a national scale to all forms of distribution.

Regulation To Control Quality of Goods

In the interest of public welfare, the federal government and several state governments have passed laws to protect you from unscrupulous vendors who would sell you inferior goods improperly branded or marked. As early as 1900, the public was spending as much as $90 million annually for misbranded and adulterated foods and drugs. Although not all these articles were actually harmful, they were definitely inferior. Because there were few state laws, and no federal statutes to protect the public, little could be done until the federal government passed appropriate legislation.

The Pure Food and Drug Act of 1906. A typical example of how the federal government has sought to protect you against impure and misbranded articles is the Pure Food and Drug Act. Under this law, an article is considered "misbranded" if its "labeling" is false or misleading. The term "labeling" includes both written and printed matter that appears on the article or the container. In 1938, the Copeland Act amended the Pure Food and Drug Act of 1906 by requiring that the Commissioner of Food and Drugs approve all new drugs before they are marketed. The Copeland Act also prohibits the interstate shipment of misbranded or adulterated foods, drugs, cosmetics, and therapeutic devices. The penalty for violating this law is a fine of up to $1,000, or imprisonment for one year, or both. More serious violations involve a fine of $10,000 and imprisonment for three years.

The Wool Products Labeling Act. Food, drugs, and cosmetics are not the only items whose quality is subject to federal regulations. You are also protected against the misbranding of woolen fabrics, by the Wool Products Labeling Act of 1950. If you purchase a nationally advertised woolen blanket, you can be sure of its condition and wool content, because this law requires the manufacturer to show how much new and used wool has been used in the blanket. Other kinds of materials used with the wool must also be indicated on the label, along with the manufacturer's name. (Carpets and upholstery materials are exempt from this law.)

Other examples of federal legislation to control the quality of goods are the Federal Tea Act, the Federal Import Milk Act, and various meat inspection acts. The Tea Act prohibits importation of tea that does not meet government standards of quality. The Import Milk Act requires that foreign milk and cream received into this country must meet certain standards of quality and purity. The Department of Agriculture has meat inspectors at all packing plants where meat is prepared for interstate shipment. You have no doubt seen beef that carried the Department of Agriculture stamp of approval, which means that the meat has been inspected for quality.

CAREERS IN MARKETING

Persons who have a strong interest in the field of marketing should have little trouble establishing a career suited to their aptitudes and abilities. Among the fruitful areas of specialization are selling, statistical work, research, copywriting, and art. Some areas of opportunity in marketing require technical training—product design, product development, and testing. The position of purchasing agent also requires technical training.

Marketing research is a good possibility for those who have a solid preparation in statistics, for it involves market analysis as well as sales procedures. It supplies information for the marketing manager and serves as a guide for judging sales performance. Sales promotion and advertising occupations are highly rewarding to persons with imagination, initiative, and resourcefulness.

Selling is the most common marketing vocation and offers opportunities on almost every educational level. The sales force is the group charged with the responsibility for producing the revenues of the firm and is usually rewarded liberally if successful. Accordingly, compensation is higher in the sales field than most areas of business. The amount sold is the usual measure of success in selling, but the satisfaction that comes from successful selling is also very rewarding.

Young people with college preparation are often given initial employment in selling not only because they are promising salesmen but because of their potential ability to handle management responsibilities. Sales experience provides valuable preparation for attacking many types of problems common to all business, and good experience for managerial responsibility.

Many young people look forward to owning their own business; some day *you* may be the owner of one of the 5 million small businesses operating in the United States. With a steadily expanding population and a continuing rise in per capita income, there will be excellent opportunities for industrious young men and women who set out on their own in marketing.

SUMMARY

Marketing and manufacturing are the two major areas of American business, each sharing approximately equally the consumer dollar. The term *market* has several meanings, depending upon the intent of the one using it. As defined here, it refers to the system of interrelated business activities that pertain to the designing, promoting, pricing, and distributing of goods and services to customers. Marketing furnishes employment to between one-fourth and one-third of the labor force.

The combining of the various aspects of marketing into an integrated function is the task of marketing management. Goods are distributed in two different markets: the industrial market and the consumer market.

The marketing of goods is accomplished by the performance of a number of activities or functions. Buying and selling are the key functions, because they effect changes in ownership until the goods are in the hands of the consumer. Other essential functions are transporting, storing, standardizing, risk-bearing, pricing, financing, and providing market information. All these functions must be performed even when the goods are sold directly by the producer to the consumer.

Control over marketing practices has been a concern of state governments and the federal government for many years. The purpose of most government legislation is to preserve competition in business and to protect consumers.

Marketing affords a variety of job opportunities for young people with a college preparation. Salaries are commensurate with the individual's ability to produce for the business.

VOCABULARY REVIEW QUIZ

Match the following vocabulary terms with the statements below.

a. Consumer goods
b. Convenience goods
c. Fair-trade agreement
d. Grading
e. Industrial goods
f. Management
g. Market
h. Marketing
i. Marketing mix
j. Miller-Tydings Act
k. Risk-bearing
l. Shopping goods
m. Speciality goods
n. Standard

1. A buyer and a seller who exchange a good at a negotiated price
2. The system of business activities concerned with the flow of goods and services from producer to consumer
3. The combination of the four basic elements in marketing
4. Goods that are sold to the consuming public
5. Where responsibility for the marketing-mix lies
6. Goods that are easily accessible to consumers in their neighborhood stores
7. Goods with whose fashion and quality the user or purchaser is concerned
8. Goods that have some distinctive features for which the consumer has a strong preference
9. Goods that are sold to businesses to be used by them rather than resold to consumers
10. Taking the chance that merchandise may be stolen or destroyed
11. A uniform characteristic or quality applied to a group of products
12. The process of sorting products into classes according to their quality
13. An act passed by Congress to clarify the legality of marketing contracts and related price agreements between manufacturers and retailers
14. Contracts whereby retailers agree not to sell a product at a price below that suggested by the manufacturer of the article

QUESTIONS FOR REVIEW STUDY

1. What is your favorite definition of the term *marketing*?
2. Illustrate several ways that the term *market* may be used correctly but with different meanings.
3. What is meant by the term *marketing mix*?
4. Name, define, and give examples of three types of consumer goods.
5. How does the marketing procedure for industrial goods normally differ from the marketing of consumer goods?
6. What is the significance of the term "value added by marketing"?

7. What are some of the benefits that come to the public as a result of the marketing function?
8. Explain how marketing gives a product time-and-place utility.
9. Describe five important marketing functions.
10. What establishes the floor and ceiling in pricing practices?
11. Why is the government concerned with the marketing practices of business?
12. Is standardization more important when marketing industrial or consumer goods? Why?

PROBLEMS AND PROJECTS

1. Prepare a brief case either supporting or opposing the use of credit as a marketing incentive.
2. Briefly describe the various types of marketing activities performed between the time that a pair of shoes is manufactured and the time that it is delivered to your home.
3. Classify each of the following as convenience, shopping, or speciality goods: a lady's coat, a typewriter, an outboard motor, a color TV set, an electric range, automobile tires, a house trailer, groceries, drugs, carpeting, shoes, a shirt, a book, Christmas cards.
4. An independent grocer was making a profit of 3.8 percent of his gross sales, which were $360,000 annually. He adopted a trading-stamp plan to try to stimulate sales. The cost of the stamps to him was $1.95 per $100. After a trial period of six months, he analyzed the results of his experience, which were as follows: his sales increased by 25 percent, his profit (before trading stamps) increased to 4.4 percent. He found that since some customers did not take stamps, stamps were issued on only 80 percent of his sales.

   (a) What were his gross sales for the six months?
   (b) What was his profit before paying for his trading stamps for the six months?
   (c) What was his net profit for the six months (after paying for his stamps)?
   (d) What would his sales and profit have been had he not issued the stamps? (Use his former experience record for sales and profit margin.)
   (e) Would you recommend he continue the issuing of trading stamps? Give reasons to support your decision.

A BUSINESS CASE

Case 19-1 Consumer Market Change

Harvey Bills is an automobile dealer in a city of 150,000 people in one of the southeastern states. He has been selling the low-price models for one of the "Big Three" automobile manufacturers for the past 10 years. Recently the dealer franchise for the range of medium-price automobiles made by this same manufacturer became available, and has been offered to Bills.

Bills thinks that this might be a good time to move to a higher-price product, and feels that his repairmen can make the necessary adjustment if given the appropriate special training. He has been reading in his business journals about the shifting of increasing numbers of wage earners into the middle and upper income brackets. He thinks that many families might be ready to shift to the next price-range when buying automobiles. His reputation as an automobile dealer is well-known in the city and the surrounding community.

1. What factors enter into this decision, in addition to the upward shift in family income?
2. If he should shift to the new dealership, what changes is he likely to make in the various aspects of marketing automobiles?

Distribution Channels and Marketing Practices

20

In the preceding chapter we learned about the functions of marketing and the contribution of marketing to the nation's economy. In this chapter we shall see who it is that performs these marketing functions. We shall also study the interrelationships between and among the different groups that constitute the marketing channels.

We shall look first at several distinct patterns used in marketing. Then we shall study more specificially the chief middlemen groups—wholesalers, retailers, and agents. We shall also look at the part that co-operatives play in our marketing system.

CHANNELS OF DISTRIBUTION FOR CONSUMER GOODS

The *channel of distribution* for a product is the route it follows as it moves from the producer to the consumer. If middlemen are used, they are also included in the channel of distribution. *Middlemen* are business concerns or individuals whose principal functions are buying and selling. A common channel of distribution for aspirin tables, for example, includes a number of middlemen. This product is often sold by the drug manufacturer to the drug wholesaler, who sells to the retailer, who then sells to the consumer. The channel for college textbooks is usually shorter, running from publisher to bookstore to student.

Because of intrinsic differences among products and even among various producers of the same product, there are countless variations in the manner in which goods are distributed in our economy.

From Manufacturer Directly to Consumer

At first glance, this channel promises to be very simple and extremely economical. But actual experience has shown it to be relatively costly. Only a few types of manufactured goods, such as Fuller brushes, have been successfully marketed in this manner. The milkman still makes his rounds, but what with improved refrigeration, a great portion of our fresh milk is sold by food stores. Farmers still make limited use of the direct channel to sell small quantities of fruits, vegetables, honey, poultry, and eggs; but here again we find that most farm produce reaches the market through a more circuitous route. Manufacturers using this direct-selling channel ordinarily employ one or more of the three methods we shall now discuss: *manufacturer-owned retail stores, house-to-house selling,* and *direct mail.*

Manufacturer-Owned Stores. The most widely used method of selling "direct" from manufacturer to consumer is through the manufacturer-owned store. A limited number of manufacturers operate their own stores both in order to take full advantage of the profits from the retail sale of their products, and to promote the greatest possible volume of sales. We find manufacturer-owned stores in the shoe, paint, and men's clothing industries, for example. The basic items in these stores are produced in the plants of the owner, although, in order to carry a complete stock many items are pur-

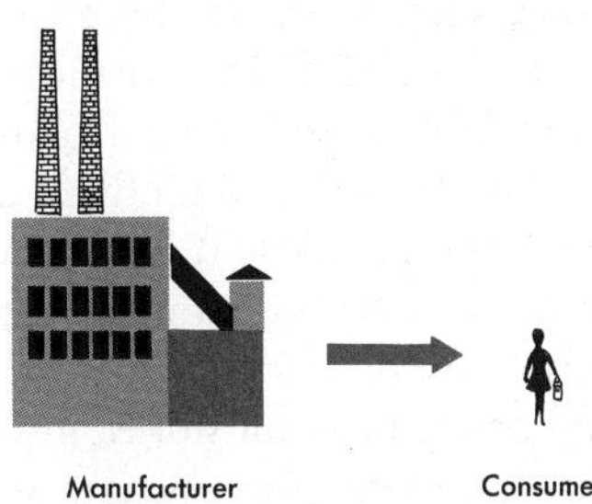

chased from outside sources. You may have observed manufacturer-owned shoe stores that carry hosiery, handbags, and gloves purchased in this manner. Few manufacturers enter into this sort of marketing activity, however, since it requires considerable amounts of capital and demands experience in the operation of retail stores.

House-to-House Selling. House-to-house selling has proved successful for only a few products—mainly brushes, mops, brooms, vacuum cleaners, silverware, cookware, and cosmetics. The success of this sales method depends largely on the company's ability to develop highly effective salespeople carefully trained to present a well-planned demonstration. The principal drawback of this approach is that it is extremely costly, for a salesman must spend a great deal of time with a single customer—or, at best, with a few customers gathered in a private home. Moreover, most housewives lack confidence in the door-to-door salesman and refuse to give him the time he needs to make an effective presentation. The system will, however, undoubtedly continue to be used for products that lend themselves to convincing home demonstrations. After all, at least *some* consumers will always be attracted by the opportunity of buying direct from the manufacturer. And most certainly there will always be people willing to try their hand at this type of selling because of the attractive commissions it pays.

Direct Mail. Another means of selling direct to the consumer is through the use of magazine ads and direct-mail brochures. This method has sometimes proven quite successful in marketing neckties, food specialties, and similar commodities. It has been especially effective in selling books and recordings to customers who contract to buy a specified number of items over an extended period of time. But this channel of distribution is generally regarded as costly and relatively inefficient, since only a small percentage of returns can be expected from even an expensive mailing-piece. Moreover, it is difficult for the small-scale seller, who typically uses these techniques, to generate public confidence.

From Manufacturer to Retailer to Consumer

Many kinds of goods, such as automobiles, furniture, appliances, and shoes, are sold through this channel. Certain manufacturers prefer it because they are anxious to retain a high degree of control over the manner in which their product is retailed. And by selling directly to the retailer they are able to influence the training of salespeople and see that the retailer's service staff provides consumer satisfaction. Some manufacturers even follow a policy known as *exclusive distribution*, under which each manufacturer deals directly with a restricted group of retail stores, instead of seeking wide distribution of his goods through as many stores as possible.

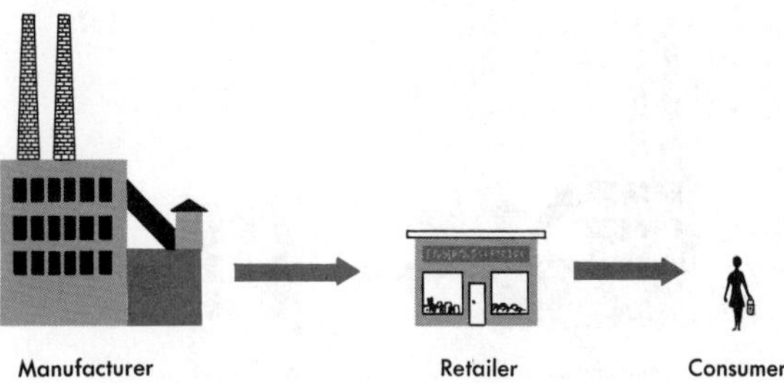

Since speed is important in the marketing of fashion goods (for instance), buyers from retail stores often prefer to go directly to the sales offices of the manufacturer to place their orders, instead of working through middlemen. And to expedite their dealings with retail buyers, frequently several manufacturers will join together to show their samples and take orders at a show or fair, such as the semiannual furniture show at the Chicago Furniture Mart.

Manufacturers who distribute their goods over a wide area sometimes establish branch warehouses in which they maintain a stock of goods adequate to meet regional demands. By shipping orders directly to retail stores, they render much the same service as does an ordinary wholesaler. Although these manufacturers incur many of the expenses inherent in wholesaling, they have more freedom to conduct an aggressive selling program than they would if they depended exclusively on wholesalers to distribute their goods to retail outlets.

Notice that although this channel of distribution bypasses the wholesaler, it does not eliminate any of the marketing functions discussed in Chapter 19. Every one of these functions must be performed, either by the manufacturer or the retailer. What this means is that the wholesaler must justify his position in the marketing system by competing successfully with this more direct method of distributing commodities.

From Manufacturer to Wholesaler to Retailer to Consumer

This is probably the most widely used channel to market the goods we buy most frequently. In Chapter 19 you studied about *convenience goods*—goods that consumers want to buy with a minimum of effort. Most convenience goods such as drugs, hardware, groceries, and bakery goods move along the route from the manufacturer to the wholesaler, to the retailer, and then to the ultimate consumer.

Wholesalers purchase goods in large quantities from numerous manufacturers. From their collection of a wide variety of types of goods, they supply the needs of retailers. Thus the wholesaler reduces the number of

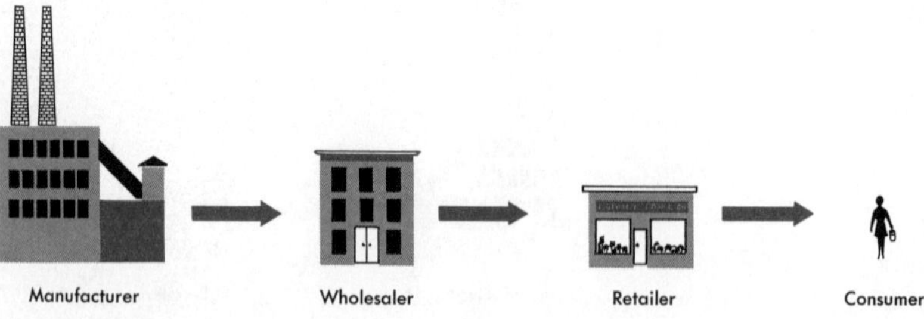

accounts with whom the manufacturer deals, and the manufacturer saves the expense of having to service thousands of individual retail businesses.

The wholesaler likewise saves the retailer money and time. An independent grocer normally stocks his shelves with thousands of different items. Instead of contacting hundreds of manufacturers, he would prefer to do business with just a few wholesalers.

From Manufacturer to Chain Store to Consumer

The chain organization performs most of the functions that wholesalers render. The chains have buyers who specialize in particular lines of goods. Chains buy in large quantities, have their own storage facilities, and in some instances own their own trucks for delivering goods to their outlets. (The delivery problem alone can be enormous, for a single warehouse might serve as many as 50 different company-operated retail sales outlets.) Safeway, Kroger, and A & P are well-known grocery chains that maintain warehouses.

Independent retailers sometimes group together to form a *voluntary chain* organization. These merchants pool their buying and certain other distribution functions in much the same manner as the large chains. In many instances the voluntary chain group is organized by a wholesaler who serves them by supplying their most important items, and then some. The Rexall drug stores, IGA grocers, and Ben Franklin variety stores are well-known voluntary chains.

CHANNELS OF DISTRIBUTION FOR INDUSTRIAL GOODS

The distribution channels through which industrial goods travel are markedly different from those followed by consumer goods. No retailers are needed, and fewer middlemen are used. Consequently, the marketing of industrial goods is usually a simpler process. The most commonly used channels are these:

1. Direct from factory to industrial user, sometimes by way of a factory sales branch
2. From factory, to agents (or brokers), to industrial user
3. From factory, to industrial distributor (wholesaler), to industrial user

Approximately two-thirds of the total volume of industrial goods marketed is sold direct from the factory by the manufacturers to the users. An additional 12 to 15 percent is sold to industrial users through the sales branches of manufacturers. One reason for this short distribution channel is the technical nature of products that require expert installation and maintenance service. The best way for the purchaser to insure getting this service is often through face-to-face dealings with the manufacturer. Another reason is that when most of a manufacturer's important customers are concentrated in a small geographic area, there is simply no reason to work through a middleman. Finally, many orders for industrial goods are so huge that the cost of direct negotiations between manufacturer and buyer is negligible.

THE WHOLESALERS' FUNCTION IN MARKETING

There are approximately 290,000 wholesale establishments doing business in the United States. Most of them limit their activities to areas of about 150 miles in radius, although some are large-scale businesses that serve the entire nation.

The Nature and Importance of Wholesale Trade

Before discussing the work of these wholesale establishments, let us look at a few facts about wholesaling that are frequently misunderstood. Almost all manufacturers, as well as wholesale establishments, sell their goods on a wholesale basis. In other words, manufacturers also engage in wholesale trade, but are not regarded as wholesalers because their primary function is manufacturing.

It is also important to recognize clearly the distinction between a retail sale and a wholesale sale. The former type consists of any sale of goods to an ultimate consumer for his own personal satisfaction. A wholesale sale, on the other hand, is any transaction in which the purchaser desires the goods for either resale purposes or for use in his business. Notice that neither the price of the goods nor the quantity purchased is a criterion that necessarily distinguishes the retail sale from the wholesale sale. Often the sale of a single item is a wholesale transaction. Wholesale sales are commonly made to manufacturers, wholesalers, retailers, public utilities, railroads, hotels, schools, colleges, and governmental units.

Surprisingly enough, wholesale establishments do a larger dollar volume of business than retailers. In fact, in recent years the wholesale sales volume in the United States has been 50 percent greater than the total sales of all retailers. Clearly, the activities of wholesale establishments include far more than simply supplying goods to retailers. True, retailers are their biggest customers, but they absorb only 38 percent of total wholesale sales. Industrial users account for 35 percent of the sales of all wholesale establishments, while other wholesale establishments, and also exporters, are responsible for the remaining 27 percent.

The wholesaler is the most important source of supply to many retailers. The small retailer especially could scarcely operate without his services. And for some kinds of goods—especially convenience goods—the wholesaler is the principal supplier to both small and large retailers. The importance of this middleman in our marketing system can best be understood by investigating the ways in which he serves the manufacturer and the retailer.

Merchant Wholesalers. The most important type of wholesale middleman is the merchant wholesaler, who distributes about 45 percent of all consumer goods. Most merchant wholesalers render a full range of wholesale services and are appropriately called *service wholesalers.* In serving their customers, they make regular visits to solicit business, grant credit, make deliveries, store goods until needed, check on the customers' stock, and provide them with current trade information. This type of merchant wholesaler secures about 95 percent of the sales volume of all merchant wholesalers.

Limited-Function Wholesalers. The remaining 5 percent represents the sale of *limited-function wholesalers,* who render fewer services. In some cases this method of operation makes it possible to sell at a slightly lower price, but it often lacks appeal to customers who desire the services that were eliminated. For example, the cash-and-carry wholesaler, who extends neither credit nor delivery service, may be unable to obtain orders from retailers who are accustomed to buying on credit or who do not wish to make the trip to pick up merchandise at a wholesale house. Because of the small share of trade obtained by this type of wholesaler, we shall confine our subsequent discussion to the service wholesaler.

How the Wholesaler Serves the Manufacturer

Why is it that so many manufacturers depend on wholesalers to distribute their products? There are several good reasons:

1. Most manufacturers are small firms with limited resources. They must direct their main efforts toward production and cannot afford to spend

time and money coping with the difficult problems of marketing. Because of their lack of "know-how" and capital, these firms are perfectly willing to rely on wholesalers to sell their output.

2. Since the wholesaler is in intimate contact with retailers, he is able to keep the manufacturer informed about such matters as desirable package styling, advertising appeals, and product features. Without assistance from the wholesaler, every manufacturer would be forced to make his own market surveys to keep abreast of changing market conditions.

3. The wholesaler provides manufacturers with thorough coverage of virtually every retailer who might be interested in stocking his product. The wholesaler counts among his regular customers all kinds of stores, large and small, in the city and in out-of-the-way country towns. This is an especially valuable service for manufacturers whose products, such as tobacco and groceries, need wide distribution.

4. The services provided by the wholesaler enable the manufacturer to keep at a minimum his selling cost per unit. The manufacturer of food products, for example, would have to maintain enough salespeople to call on thousands of retail stores and restaurants in order to serve the grocery trade himself. But by selling only to wholesalers he can get along with a relatively few salesmen taking orders for large quantities of goods.

5. A manufacturer can also minimize his clerical costs by selling only to wholesalers, because he needs to carry only a few accounts on his books and needs to make only large bulk shipments.

6. The manufacturer of a product with a strictly seasonal demand cannot afford to keep a sales force on the payroll throughout the year. But the wholesaler can carry the product along with others and provide the necessary sales coverage at the appropriate season.

How the Wholesaler Serves the Retailer

In order to appreciate the importance of the services rendered by wholesalers to retailers, let us compare what happens when a retailer purchases from wholesalers, with what happens when he purchases direct from producers.

1. Purchasing from wholesalers saves the retailer much time in the buying process. Imagine what would happen if every grocer had to buy direct from the 50,000 manufacturers of the goods he stocks. If only half of these manufacturers called on the grocer once every three months, he would be visited by approximately 400 salesmen daily! Obviously the retailer in most lines of trade could not deal with all the manufacturers who produce the goods he might be interested in stocking.

2. The wholesaler carries a complete line of goods from which the retailer can replenish his stock easily and swiftly. This means that the retailer

need not keep a huge supply of goods on hand, and it saves him from tying up large amounts of capital in inventory.

3. Freight costs are reduced when the retailer buys goods from nearby wholesalers. Few retailers enjoy a large enough volume of business to order carload lots from the factory, but goods are often shipped in carload lots to wholesalers.

4. The nearby wholesaler is in a better position to grant credit to the retailer than is a distant manufacturer. Even the small merchant, who would order only small quantities from an individual manufacturer, may provide a valuable source of business for the wholesaler. The high costs of making credit investigations and carrying on clerical work make it costly for a manufacturer to carry a host of small credit accounts on his books.

5. The retailer regards the sales representatives of wholesalers as a valuable source of information and advice. For example, they may give suggestions on display and sales promotion of the goods they sell. They suggest new items that might be added to his stock, and keep the retailer informed about trends in merchandising. The wholesale representative is, in fact, the principal business adviser to many small retailers.

THE ROLE OF AGENTS AND BROKERS IN MARKETING

Agents and brokers are often referred to as *functional middlemen.* They usually serve as the connecting link between the manufacturer and the wholesaler. The producer or manufacturer may choose to work through agents rather than hire his own sales force. Agents and brokers normally do not take title to or possession of the merchandise they sell. They may represent several different manufacturers, and are paid a commission by each manufacturer, based on the volume of goods they sell for him. Included in this group of functional middlemen are brokers, manufacturers' agents, selling agents, commission houses, and auction companies. The illustration on page 593 serves as a typical example of the way these middlemen function in the distribution channel.

Merchandise Brokers

The chief function of the *broker* is to negotiate transactions for goods that belong to his client, or "principal." He also keeps him informed on market conditions. In serving his principal he often brings about agreements to transactions on price, terms of sale, freight charges, and storage arrangements. In most cases he is a selling broker—that is, he represents the seller. But in some instances he serves as a buying broker, representing the buyer.

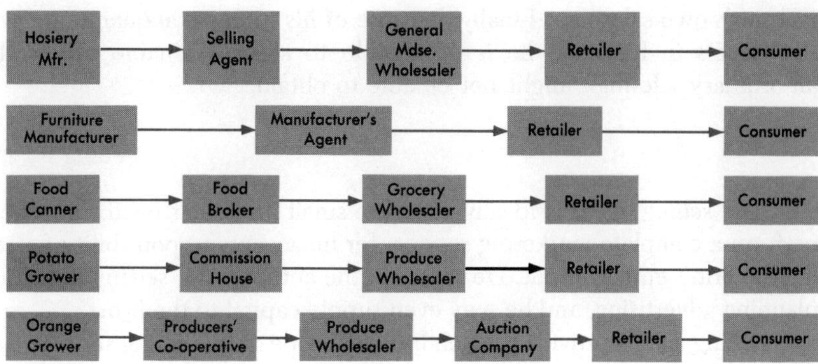

The principal either establishes the price on the commodities, or approves prices suggested by the broker. By concentrating in one specialized area of commodities, such as coffee, sugar, lumber, or cotton, the broker develops an intimate acquaintance with market conditions. Consequently, the broker is highly regarded by the people with whom he does business. He may represent a principal continuously, or for only one transaction.

The marketing service provided by brokers is very economical, for their commission rates are relatively low. For example, on canned goods the rates range from 2 to 6 percent. The broker is able to provide the small producer with marketing experience and skill, and the seasonal producer with a maximum sales effort during the seasons when it is needed, at low cost.

In the food-processing industry, the term "broker" is often applied to a middleman who actually operates as a manufacturers' agent rather than as a broker. Food brokers commonly serve as sales representatives in territories assigned to them by the manufacturer. They are able to sell more economically than the firm's own sales force, because by representing a number of firms their expenses are spread over a number of lines.

Manufacturers' Agents

Manufacturers' agents operate very much as though they were salesmen employed directly by the manufacturer. The only difference is that they represent several manufacturers simultaneously. They are independent operators who sell in an assigned territory on a commission basis. Although their services are best suited to the needs of the small manufacturer, these middlemen are used by large firms as well.

Selling through manufacturers' agents provides the manufacturer with several advantages. For one thing, no expense is incurred except on sales that are actually made. Moreover, since the agent carries several lines, he is able to cultivate and exploit his territory more thoroughly than could the manufacturer's own salesmen. Finally, because of his intimate acquaintance with the buyers in his area, he is often able to secure valuable orders that an ordinary salesman might not be able to obtain.

Selling Agents

The *selling agent* is ideally suited to small firms that need someone to perform a complete marketing service, for he accepts responsibility for selling the firm's entire output. He shares in the authority for setting prices and planning advertising, and he may even supply capital to the firm.

Selling agents provide a much broader scope of marketing services than do manufacturers' agents. Their service covers all phases of marketing in an unlimited territory, whereas the function of the manufacturers' agents is to sell in a limited territory. The typical selling agent represents a number of manufacturers and is particularly active in the coal and textile industries.

Commission Merchants

Unlike the agents we have discussed so far, the *commission merchant* actually takes possession of the physical goods he markets. He usually arranges for the shipment of goods, stores them temporarily, sells them, and delivers them to the buyer. At times he also grants credit to the buyer. For all these services he charges the owner a commission, and sometimes adds the expenses he incurs in handling and storing the goods.

The majority of commission merchants deal in agricultural products, such as melons, fruits, vegetables, and livestock. Since these products must be sold quickly once they reach the market, it is customary for the owner to instruct the commission merchant to sell at the best price obtainable. Under these conditions, the commission merchant assumes no risk from a change in market prices, nor does he have any capital invested in the goods. Some growers, however, will not turn their goods over to the commission merchant until a definite price has been agreed upon. In these cases the commission merchant may purchase the goods outright, and handle them in the same manner as a wholesaler. Thus, the so-called commission merchant may actually operate his business in mixed fashion, both as a wholesaler and a commission merchant.

Auction Companies

The auction method of selling is rarely used in the wholesale marketing of manufactured goods. Its most common use is in the wholesaling of certain fruits, vegetables, tobacco, live poultry, and livestock. Fruit auctions, located in large cities such as Chicago, St. Louis, and Detroit, handle a large share of the citrus fruits on their way to wholesale middlemen. The *auction company* receives the goods on their arrival and places them in storage until sold. It also supplies a salesroom and an auctioneer, who sells either from samples or a catalogue furnished to the prospective buyers.

Most tobacco is sold at auctions held in large warehouses in the tobacco-growing states. After each grower's lot has been sorted into different qualities and weighed, it is auctioned to buyers. Auction companies have also become an important agency in the marketing of livestock, especially in areas that are remote from the large terminal markets.

THE ROLE OF RETAILING IN MARKETING

Retailers are businessmen who purchase goods from manufacturers and wholesalers and sell them to final customers. Retailing is a heterogeneous business carried on in stores that differ as to the lines and quality of goods sold, services provided, price ranges, and types of locations. Each store has its own personality, layout, and customer-service policy. In the field of retailing are to be found small-, medium-, and large-scale enterprises, some individually owned and others operated as corporations, co-operatives, or manufacturers' retail sales branches.

In recent years, Americans have spent approximately two-thirds of their *disposable income* (income left after paying taxes) for goods and services purchased in retail stores. Of the approximately 8 million nonagricultural businesses in the United States in 1968, approximately 2 million were retail establishments.

Retailing Is Easy To Enter

You can start a retail store with a relatively small amount of initial capital—far less, for example, than is normally required to establish a wholesale or manufacturing business. Moreover, you will be subject to relatively few legal requirements. Experience, although an important requirement, is not a mandatory prerequisite. Manufacturers seeking new outlets for sale of their products may even prove willing to provide you with some financial assistance and merchandising advice.

Retailing Is Typically Small-Business

There are many large-scale retail chain organizations in existence, such as the Great Atlantic & Pacific Tea Co. (the familiar "A & P"), Safeway, Montgomery Ward, Sears Roebuck, J. C. Penney, and W. T. Grant. But by far the greatest number of retail stores are small, owner-managed concerns. As a rule, the independent retailer serves as both owner and manager of the business, especially if the operation is on a small scale. In about one out of every three retail stores, there are no paid employees outside the owner's family, and considerably less than 1 percent of all retail firms employ over 100 persons. About one-third of all retail stores sell less than $25,000 worth of merchandise a year. The fact that those entering retailing as proprietors usually start as independents accounts for the large number of small enterprises in retailing. It also contributes to their high failure-rate.

Retailing Is Highly Competitive

Retailing is one of the most competitive segments of our business economy. Competition is especially keen among grocery stores, restaurants, liquor stores, service stations, and automobile dealers. You will often find gas stations located on opposite street-corners. Probably if more people were aware of the high degree of competition that exists in these lines, they would be more reluctant to risk their money and time in starting such enterprises.

Retailing Is Highly Specialized

Like so many other segments of our economy, retailing has become highly specialized. A sizable amount of retail sales are made directly from factories by mail and by producers who sell at the place of production, and some (relatively small) amount by house-to-house salesmen. The great majority of all retail business, however, is, as we have said, carried on in stores. Many of these stores specialize in a particular line of merchandise—men's clothing, ladies' ready-to-wear, shoes, luggage, hardware goods. Later in this chapter we shall note some of the characteristics of the various types of retail operations.

THE FUNCTIONS PERFORMED BY RETAILERS

The purpose of our marketing system is to help fill the needs and wants of every consumer. This is also the general function of the various middlemen, one of whom is the retailer. A study of the retailer's functions shows that he has responsibility for two broad categories of operation: first, he performs the economic functions of place- and time-utility; second, he is responsible for several merchandising functions. In the pages that follow we shall note what these are.

The Economic Functions of Retailers

Retailing, as the final stage of marketing, is naturally concerned with selling consumer goods. This involves performing two important economic functions.

The Retailer Makes a Contribution to the Creation of Place-Utility. The presence of goods at the place where they are wanted is called *place-utility*. By having goods ready for consumption on hand in the store, the retailer is a direct contributor to this type of utility.

Equally important to the consumer is knowing that goods are available not only at the right place but at the proper time. Having goods on hand at the proper time involves cooperation of transportation facilities, and also storage.

The Retailer Contributes to the Creation of Time-Utility. The presence of goods at the time they are wanted is called *time-utility*. Just as goods may be more useful in one place than in another, so they may be more valuable because of the time when they are available. It is important—often essential—that the consumer have his goods on hand at the right time and place.

The Merchandising Functions of Retailers

You can think of the merchandising functions as broken down into the following simple steps: (1) buying merchandise; (2) dividing, packaging, and pricing; (3) storing; (4) selling; and (5) delivering. Let us examine these in greater detail.

Buying Merchandise for Resale. This function involves selecting the goods that will be offered for resale, determining the prices at which they will be offered, marking the goods, and planning sales activities. Many observers regard these as the most critically important activities of all the retailer's functions.

To do an effective job the buyer, who may likely be the owner if the store is small, must have not only an intimate knowledge of the markets from which he will obtain these goods, but an awareness of his customers' needs and tastes. He must carefully determine the quantity and quality of stock to buy—the right sizes, colors, and styles. Otherwise, he may find himself disastrously overstocked at the end of the season or year. Good buying comes only through meticulous planning, and the buyer must draw on every available source of information—his own sales staff, manufacturers' catalogues, and general market conditions—before making his final choices.

Except in stores that cater exclusively to the "carriage trade," proprietors should stock merchandise that appeals to medium-income groups, with perhaps a limited number of items for low- and high-income buyers.

Dividing, Packaging, and Pricing. The second retailing function involves getting the goods into the store and preparing them for resale. For example, some goods cannot be displayed until they have been unpacked and processed. Moreover, since consumers usually buy in small quantities, stock clerks have to divide case lots, cartons, boxes, and other shipments of goods, into small quantities. With some items, the clerks simply open a pasteboard box, price the items, and place them on the shelves. Others have to be weighed, sacked, wrapped, and price-marked before shelving.

Receiving and processing goods in retail merchandising make several demands on management. For example, the retailer must work out an efficient method for checking incoming goods against invoices, and set up a quick, accurate system of marking the goods with prices. Moreover, he must ensure that the stockroom is run efficiently. Effective housekeeping in the stockroom requires providing a clean storage-place, ensuring readily accessible shelves or bins, maintaining systematic arrangements for locating stock quickly, and making economical use of all space.

In order to enjoy the profits that go with a large volume of sales and in order to keep fresh supplies of goods on hand, retailers try to maintain a rapid turnover of stock. Various dating codes are used on price-tags as a means of keeping a record of the age of goods. Perhaps the most common code is simply to indicate, by means of a letter or a numeral, the month in which the merchandise was received. For example, January might be indicated by the letter A or the numeral 1; February, by B or 2; and so on.

In pricing goods, the retailer works on the basis of a *markup*. The markup is the difference between the retailer's cost and his selling price. Hence, if a product cost the merchant $20 and is marked to sell for $30, his markup is $10. Markup is generally expressed in terms of percentage.[1] Here, for example, the markup would be 33⅓ percent. Many retailers use a markup table similar to that in Table 20.1. It is easier to figure markup on the basis of cost than on the basis of selling price.

In lines where competition is not severe, or where the rate of turnover is low, the retailer's markup may be as high as 100 percent. Many merchants begin a particular selling season with their standard markup, and then toward the end of the season reduce their prices in order to clear out any remaining stock.

Normally, markup covers both the cost of the goods and an amount for expenses and profit. It may also include an estimated amount to allow for

[1] To find the percentage of markup when both the cost and selling price are known, first find the profit (difference between cost and selling price), and then divide that by the selling price. Markup is usually computed on selling price.

TABLE 20.1
MERCHANDISE MARKUP TABLE

Percentage of Margin Based on Selling Price		Percentage of Margin Based on Cost Price
10		11.1
11		12.4
12		13.6
13		15.0
14	Is equivalent to	16.3
15		17.7
20		25.0
25		33.3
30		42.9
33		49.1
35		53.9
40		66.7
50		100.0

an anticipated markdown in the future. This is often the case with highly seasonal merchandise, for there is always a chance that at the end of the season, quantities may remain on hand that must be reduced in price in order to ensure a quick disposal. *Markdown* is simply a reduction in the original selling price. It is generally expressed as a percentage, just as markups are. As a rule, the chief reasons for having to make markdowns are overbuying, poor selection of quality, shopworn goods, selecting too many units of a given size, unpopular colors, or just plain weak sales-effort.

Storing Merchandise. Storage is often regarded as a problem peculiar to warehousing, but actually it is as important in retailing. Retail stores use a great many different systems for storing merchandise. If space permits, the retailer may set aside part of his building or shop exclusively for storage; otherwise, he may store goods under counters and on open shelves. A good storage system ensures ready accessibility to the stock, a means of filing and classifying goods according to the different departments in the store, and protection against fire, breakage, deterioration, and theft. Large department stores maintain separate warehouses; or if the main building is large enough, they reserve entire floors for storage purposes.

Selling. Since the core of the retail operation is the volume of merchandise that passes over the counter, the selling function is of paramount importance. It involves every aspect of sales promotion, including advertising, store displays, special sales, and service to customers, as well as actually selling the goods.

The services provided by a retail store vary widely with the size of the store and the attitude of the retailer. The following services, designed to increase sales, are commonly offered by retail establishments, particularly department stores and household-goods stores:

Personalized Customer Service	*Credit Service*
Personal shopper	Open account credit
Mail-order service	Layaway privileges
Prompt delivery	Installment credit
Pre-sale announcements mailed to customers	COD deliveries
Nurseries	Goods on approval
Style shows	Return privileges

Delivery Service. The customers of today's retail stores expect free delivery on many purchases, and they insist that the service be prompt and efficient. In many stores, delivery service is just as much a part of retailing as cash-and-carry transactions are. Prompt, efficient, and courteous delivery service is an effective bid for customer goodwill. What many consumers fail to realize, however, is that "free delivery service" is a deceptive term. Theoretically, each customer should pay more for goods in a store offering free delivery service than in one that does not, because the cost of delivery must be in the markup.

TRENDS IN RETAILING

Since the early days of the itinerant peddler, retailing has undergone many and constant changes. The general store finally gave way to specialized types of stores, mainly because these outlets could render better service, provide customers a wider choice, and attract more customers with increased advertising and other sales-promotion aids. Continued expansion of suburbs and the increased use of automobiles for shopping not only has promoted the development of more suburban shopping centers, but also has multiplied the number of different lines of merchandise carried by these stores. Suburban stores now provide a full third of department-store sales, as against only 5 percent a decade ago. The giant supermarket, with its multiple lines of goods, is cutting down the number of small neighborhood stores. Supermarkets have also helped to promote the trend toward more self-service-type stores.

Variety stores, notably those in the "five-and-dime" category, are carrying higher-priced goods. Many outlets have been remodeled to provide for more self-service and at the same time to reduce selling costs by eliminating some clerks. Several variety chains have announced the construction of discount stores—all of which is part of the revolution taking place in retail merchandising. Drug chains are expanding their hard goods and houseware lines. And former "cash only" chains, such as J. C. Penney and Co., have joined the credit-customer parade.

The introduction of electronic data-processing equipment promises to improve stock-control and record-keeping operations, as well as to reduce clerical costs. Many downtown department stores are constructing suburban stores in shopping centers located away from the central business district.

The number of discount outlets is expanding rapidly in all parts of the nation. The *discounter* is a retailer who sells brand merchandise at less than the customary or fair-trade price. Price-cutting in retailing is not new, but the discount house makes the most of it: it carries many kinds of durable-goods items, competing on a price-appeal basis. The discount field, once characterized as a renegade form of retailing, is now being entered into by even such old-line retailers as variety chains, department stores, and drug chains. Wherever possible, large chains are attempting to eliminate middlemen in the marketing process, performing such wholesaling functions as storing, dividing, and packaging.

CO-OPERATIVES IN THE MARKETING SYSTEM

A *co-operative* is a business enterprise organized and owned by a group of people in order to serve their marketing needs. Each member has an equal voice in the control of the firm, which is sometimes operated without profit. If profits do accrue, they are distributed to members in proportion to their patronage. There are co-operatives in many areas of business, such as retailing, telephone service, farm products, and money-lending. In marketing there are three kinds of co-operatives: the *consumer* co-operative, the *agricultural marketing* co-operative, and the *agricultural purchasing* co-operative.

The Consumer Co-operative

The consumer co-operative is a retail store established by a group of consumers to make it possible for them to purchase goods at the wholesale cost. In other words, the objective is to eliminate the profit made by the ordinary retailer. Such stores are rare in the United States, and it is unlikely that their number will increase here substantially in the future. In Great Britain, however, 12 percent of the retail trade carried on is normally handled by consumer co-operatives.

Few consumers in this country have shown genuine interest in consumer co-operatives. The movement started in European countries under the sponsorship of subsistence-income groups and socialistic idealists. In the United States, where higher living-standards have prevailed, there has been little agitation for displacing privately-owned stores. Some marketing authorities believe that chain stores, with their emphasis on price appeal, have convinced consumers that there is little to be gained from sponsoring co-operative stores.

The Agricultural Marketing Co-operative

Agricultural marketing co-operatives are associations operated by the growers or producers of a single product, or a group of closely related products. Sunkist Growers, Inc., to name a familiar example, markets oranges and lemons, and Land-O-Lakes Creameries, Inc., markets dairy and poultry products. These middlemen are important agencies in the marketing of several kinds of farm products. They market the grain, dairy products, fruits, vegetables, nuts, and livestock of over 4 million producers. In addition to actual selling, these associations have several other purposes: (1) to improve merchandising practices; (2) to create demand through the use of brand names and advertising; (3) to promote more orderly marketing; (4) to extend financial assistance to members; and (5) to encourage the growing of higher-quality products.

The Agricultural Purchasing Co-operative

A second type of co-operative association that serves farmers is the agricultural purchasing co-operative. These associations purchase and resell to members and nonmembers alike such commodities as fertilizer, seeds, gasoline, feeds, and farm machinery. Many of them also stock household appliances, but they do not attempt to handle most kinds of consumer goods. The principal objective of these associations has been to enable their members to obtain their farm needs at lower prices. Their business has increased with the trend toward farm practices that require many kinds of equipment, seeds, and supplies. Membership is open to any farmer willing to buy one or more shares of stock in the association. Dividends, in cash or stock, are distributed on the basis of the patronage of members. Each member has an equal voice in controlling the affairs of the association.

CAREER OPPORTUNITIES IN MIDDLEMAN MARKETING

The career opportunities in wholesaling and retailing are excellent. Nearly 10 million people work in the latter field alone. The college graduate is in demand, with excellent opportunities open to both men and women, especially in department stores. Although a majority of the higher executives are men, an increasing number of women are holding positions as manager, buyer, and personnel director.

If you are interested in wholesaling or retailing as a career, there are two types of opportunity you may consider: self-employment (that is, owning your own business), and working for a small-, medium-, or large-size establishment.

Regardless of your area of specialization in college, you will find an opportunity in wholesaling or retailing. Majors in business administration with training in such fields as marketing, advertising, accounting, personnel administration, and statistics are especially well equipped. Many of the larger stores, regardless of the employee's major, will train candidates for high-level positions in their own executive-training programs.

Opportunities in Self-Employment

The fact that a large percentage of the retail stores in the United States are small establishments suggests that there are many opportunities for owning your own business. But it also suggests that you will have to be prepared to cope with strong competition in this area. At one time, selling goods to consumers was a simple process. That simple process is gone now because giant organizations have entered the field with large-scale capital outlays and complex merchandising methods, thus creating a highly competitive situation.

Opportunities in Working for Others

Some people have the idea that the only jobs in retailing are those that involve direct selling. But the fact is that retail stores offer a great variety of career opportunities in nonselling activities. At the executive level, for example, the merchandising division of a large department store must be staffed by specialists such as these:

- Department buyers
- Department managers
- Comparison-shopping managers
- Fashion coordinators
- Divisional merchandise managers
- General merchandise coordinators
- General merchandise managers

And the field of general management offers additional opportunities to talented young people with managerial and selling experience:

- Store managers
- Store supervisors
- Employment manager
- Personnel directors
- Training directors
- Adjustment managers
- Delivery-department managers
- Receiving-department managers

Opportunities for Advancement

For the young man or woman who has what it takes and is willing to work hard, there are unlimited opportunities in retailing in chain-store organizations, department stores, mail-order chains, and self-employment. Competition is keen, but the qualified and ambitious person stands out, and can move rapidly up the ladder to better-paying positions. After you have worked as a salesman, the next assignment is likely to be assistant department manager, then department manager. Other responsible positions that may follow include buyer, merchandise manager, store manager, general superintendent, general manager, and president.

During the years immediately following World War II, retailing offered lower starting salaries to college graduates than most other industries. More recently this discrepancy has been corrected, so that now, beginning salaries are in line with those of other types of employment. In addition, many of the larger companies give substantial fringe-benefits, including a discount on store purchases, group insurance, profit sharing, social security, and bonuses.

SUMMARY

In this chapter we have examined several different channels or routes that goods take in the distribution process. Some goods move directly from the manufacturer to the consumer, but the distribution channel for most goods is more involved than this. The most commonly used channel for moving consumer goods is that from the manufacturer to the wholesaler, to the retailer, and then to the consumer. Some goods are distributed by chains of retail stores where the wholesaling services are performed by the purchasing function of the chain group. Industrial goods are marketed differently from consumer goods, for the retail function is not a part of the distribution channel for industrial goods.

We have also examined the service functions of wholesalers, agents, and brokers in the distribution process. We have noted the different kinds of wholesalers and agents, and the ways in which their modes of operation vary one from another.

We have examined the functions performed by retailers and some of the recent trends in retailing. And finally, we have studied about types of marketing co-operatives, and career opportunities in wholesaling and retailing.

VOCABULARY REVIEW QUIZ

Match the following vocabulary terms with the statements below.

a. Broker
b. Commission merchant
c. Co-operative
d. Disposable income
e. Distribution channel
f. Exclusive distribution
g. Functional middleman
h. Markdown
i. Markup
j. Middlemen
k. Place-utility
l. Retailer
m. Service wholesalers
n. Time-utility
o. Voluntary chain

1. The route a product takes as it moves from the producer to the consumer
2. Persons or business enterprises who buy and sell goods as a part of the distribution process
3. When a manufacturer markets his products through a few chosen retail outlets
4. A group of retail merchants who collaborate and pool their purchasing and advertising efforts
5. Merchant wholesalers who render a full range of marketing services
6. Agents who serve as the distribution link between manufacturer and wholesaler
7. A middleman who represents a manufacturer in negotiating sales contracts with a number of buyers
8. A middleman who temporarily takes possession of the goods he sells, and who works on a commission basis
9. A marketer in the distribution channel who buys from manufacturers or wholesalers and sells to consumers
10. The amount of income a worker has left after paying his taxes
11. The availability of goods at locations where there is a demand for them
12. The presence of goods at the time they are needed
13. Setting the sales price of goods at a percentage figure greater than their cost
14. A reduction made in the price originally asked for goods offered for sale
15. A business enterprise organized and owned by a group of persons for the purpose of serving their marketing needs

QUESTIONS FOR REVIEW STUDY

1. Describe four different common distribution channels, and for each channel name a product that is commonly distributed in that manner.
2. Which distribution channel is employed in most house-to-house selling?
3. When the wholesaler is by-passed, who renders the marketing services normally supplied by the wholesaler?

4. Which distribution channel is normally used for marketing convenience goods?
5. How does the distribution of industrial goods differ from the marketing of consumer goods?
6. What three groups purchase large fractions of the goods sold by wholesalers?
7. What are the chief ways that wholesalers serve manufacturers?
8. How does the wholesaler help the retailer?
9. Where do agents fit into the distribution channel?
10. Why is a retail business relatively easy to establish?
11. Which marketing functions are commonly served by both wholesalers and retailers?
12. What is a fair-trade agreement?
13. What are some of the current trends in retailing?
14. What are the principal types of co-operatives commonly found in this country?

PROBLEMS AND PROJECTS

1. A group of dairy farmers sells raw milk to the Rogers Dairy. Rogers' trucks pick up the milk at the farms in 20-gallon drums. The milk is then processed and delivered to residential homes and to retail stores. (a) Which type of distribution channel is utilized here? (b) Which marketing services are rendered by the Rogers Dairy?
2. Some middlemen do not take possession of the goods they sell. What are the advantages to them of not actually handling the merchandise?
3. Assume that you own a piece of land that is zoned for business purposes and you have decided to seek a buyer for it. What factors would be the most important in determining whether it was more suitable for a wholesale or a retail business? Be specific in your answers.
4. Some retailers give trading-stamps to their customers and some do not. What are the arguments for and against the use of trading-stamps?

BUSINESS CASES

Case 20-1 Should the Company Open a New Branch?

The Hawkins Corp. has a franchise to sell a famous-name motorcycle and motorbike in a city of 150,000 population. Hawkins is located on the northeastern edge of the city. Since the population of the metropolitan area is growing quite rapidly, the manufacturer is seriously considering a second franchise, to be located in the southwestern part of the city. Hawkins has been told that the second franchise is being planned.

Mr. Hawkins' son, James, is a junior partner in the business. He has proposed that the Hawkins Corp. apply for the second franchise. He would manage the business at its present location, and his father at the new location. His argument is that it would be better for them to "compete with themselves" rather than divide the potential business with an outside competitor. The elder Mr. Hawkins had been hoping to retire in a few years, and is reluctant to expand into this new operation.

What factors are important in making this decision?

Case 20-2 Wholesale or Retail?

C & O Jewelers have been operating as a wholesale company, supplying the retail jewelry stores in a mideastern metropolitan community with a wide variety of jewelry items. For a period of eight weeks now they have been issuing "membership cards" to individuals who may come in and buy articles on a cash-and-carry basis at wholesale prices.

The owners of a number of the retail jewelry stores serviced by C & O, having met to discuss the problem of what appears to them to be an act of unfair competition, have protested this new operation to the management of C & O. In fact, they have warned them: "You need to decide whether you are going to operate as a wholesale or retail business. Unless you discontinue this 'membership card' retail operation, we may be forced to cease patronizing your firm with our wholesale purchases."

The management team-members of C & O have told the retail jewelers: "How we operate is our business." They have done this although they recognize that by doing so they might well lose this group of customers who constitute the hard core of their regular sales volume.

1. Do you feel that this business can ethically run both wholesale and retail operations without making any differential in the prices charged these two groups of customers?
2. Has the time come to decide whether to operate at wholesale or retail?
3. Is there a third alternative open to C & O?

Advertising as Sales Promotion

21

Next to personal selling, advertising ranks as the most effective means of personal persuasion. As such, it performs a most important role in the marketing of goods and services. It is through advertising that individuals and business firms inform the public of the kinds of goods and services they have to offer. It is also through advertising that business communicates with the public on subjects of mutual interest. Business has found that advertising is an effective aid to salesmen because it informs consumers about products well before they have to buy, priming them to make the "right" choices when they do. It makes the final selling job considerably less difficult.

Advertising is everywhere that some form of industrialization exists and products are available for distribution to local and distant markets. All of us are familiar with its messages. We hear them as we drive along in our automobiles. We see them on billboards. We read them in the newspapers and watch them on TV. Because they are virtually omnipresent, and all too often objectionable, we have strong feelings about some of them. Yet not many of us fully appreciate the important role they play in bringing the buyer and the seller closer together.

In this chapter we shall examine the ways in which advertising is used as a marketing tool, and we shall explore such other aspects of our subject as the kinds of motives and psychological appeals used in writing copy, the relative advantages and disadvantages offered by various advertising media, the economic effects of advertising, and the nature of career opportunities that advertising offers.

THE NATURE AND OBJECTIVES OF ADVERTISING

Under our economic system, when goods are available they are moved into the channels of distribution, and through the selling process reach the industrial or other ultimate consumers. But before this is possible, those with goods to sell must seek to find buyers through the process of advertising. There are two elements in the selling process: *personal selling*, which you will be studying in the next chapter, and *advertising*, which is generally recognized as impersonal selling and is our present subject. Although manufacturers, wholesalers, and retailers send out their salesmen to contact their prospective customers, the effectiveness of these representatives often depends upon the amount and kind of advertising that precedes them.

Advertising Defined

According to the National Association of Teachers of Marketing and Advertising, *advertising* is defined as "any paid form of nonpersonal presentation of goods, services, or ideas to a group, such presentation being openly sponsored by the advertiser, involving the use of such media as: magazine and newspaper space, radio, motion pictures, outdoor media, car cards, catalogues, direct mail, directories, store signs, programs, novelties, circulars, and others." Obviously, among "others" we should include television.

Although publicity is not regarded as advertising, it is sometimes referred to as such. Actually, *publicity* is information concerning a firm and its product made available to the public by the use of various media of communication without charge because such information is regarded as newsworthy. Advertising, however, is paid for, and presented on a nonpersonal basis. Many concerns often supplement their advertising with publicity. For example, when an automobile company brings out a new model, it not only will plan a big advertising campaign, but it will also prepare news releases which will be sent to newspapers and television stations in the hope that these media will use them with each new model presented.

Types of Advertising

The two broad types of advertising are *product* and *institutional.*

Product Advertising. This type is used to sell a single product or a family of related products by extolling the good qualities or identifying the satisfaction-giving features which the product is said to possess. This type of advertising is used to sell both consumer- and industrial-goods. (You will recall that consumer goods are more-or-less finished items in such form as to be readily usable by the general public; industrial goods are items destined for further use by industry in the manufacture of other goods.) Because consumer- and industrial-goods possess different marketing characteristics, each type is sold in different trade channels, to different markets, under different pricing policies, and by dissimilar selling methods. Consequently, consumer goods are generally advertised by using different appeals than are normally used in industrial goods advertising.

Institutional Advertising. This type is intended either to promote a single firm's reputation or to enhance the prestige of the business in general. By means of institutional advertising, a firm announces (for instance) the appointment of new personnel, a change in location, or the acquirement of a new line of goods. Sometimes advertisers issue a joint advertisement for the benefit of several firms. For example, the Association of American Railroads may buy advertising space on behalf of all the railroads, announcing the position, on some current problem, of all railroads belonging to the Association. Large companies can afford to spend money on institutional advertising without mentioning a specific product. Small stores seldom find institutional advertising profitable, mainly because it is too costly for the benefits gained.

Advertising's Historical Background

Like most other institutions, advertising developed because there was a need for it. If you hope to understand advertising fully, it is important to know something of its origin and why it developed as part of our total environment.

Since speech preceded the written word by many eons, the earliest advertising was without a doubt vocal—the shout of a man with something to sell, perhaps. As such, it was limited in its scope—often to the range of the seller's voice. Formal writing permitted a wider dissemination of messages, but they had to be hand-copied to be reproduced, and this was slow and often expensive. Indeed, not until 1478 did the first printed advertisement in the English language appear—a poster announcing the publication of a book written by William Caxton. And this was 28 years after Gutenberg printed his first Holy Bible on the first printing press! When newspapers first appeared, the advertisements in them were usually in the form of terse, polite announcements. But as each significant improvement in printing was made, great floods of less and less inhibited advertising followed, presaging the modern day of ballyhoo and bluster, of subliminal appeals (subconscious projection) to the emotions, of gross exaggeration, and of outright pitches to snobbery and sex.

The first American advertising was similar to that of its conservative and even stodgy English big brother. The turning point in American advertising occurred after the Civil War, when America began its transition from an agricultural economy. Soon, young mechanized industries were turning out goods in such large quantities that they could no longer be absorbed in the region of the manufacturer. A method had to be found whereby distant consumers could be informed of new products—and advertising provided that means.

The Influence of Newspapers and Magazines in America. The growth of newspapers and magazines helped to stimulate the use of more advertising in the United States. *The Boston News Letter* in 1704 was the first newspaper to publish an advertisement. By 1830 there were about 1,200 newspapers printing advertisements. The total number of newspapers, all of which carried advertising, reached 2,400 by 1880. Today there are over 11,000 newspapers, serving the public and advertisers of America, which

TOP 15 ADVERTISERS RANKED ACCORDING TO ANNUAL EXPENDITURES IN MAGAZINES, NEWSPAPERS, AND NETWORK TELEVISION, 1966
(in millions of dollars)

Company	*Billings*
1. Procter & Gamble	$114.5
2. Bristol-Myers	89.1
3. General Motors	88.9
4. General Foods	57.0
5. Ford Motor	54.8
6. American Home Products	52.5
7. R. J. Reynolds Tobacco	52.1
8. American Tobacco	47.4
9. Colgate-Palmolive	42.8
10. Lever Brothers	40.4
11. Chrysler	39.7
12. Sterling Drug	39.6
13. Gillette	36.0
14. Philip Morris	30.1
15. Brown & Williamson Tobacco	26.1

rely heavily on advertising space for revenue. (Of course they also depend on subscriptions for income.)

Harper's Monthly carried its first magazine advertisement in May, 1864. *The Atlantic Monthly* followed suit in February, 1869. Whereas there were some 600 magazines in the United States in 1850, the number increased to 1,200 in 1870, and by 1880 doubled to 2,400, matching the number of newspapers. Today there are about 9,000 magazines in the United States, and virtually all accept advertising. Most large companies engaged in business on a regional or nationwide scale depend largely on newspapers and magazines as important advertising media. (Later in this chapter we shall discuss why these media are important in the marketing of goods and services.)

Advertising is a big business: advertisers spend in excess of $15 billion annually on all forms of advertising media. Most advertisers use more than

Courtesy The Bettmann Archive

Advertisements from around the turn of the century typically contained much more reading matter than do ads of today, in far less attractively designed layouts. Advertisers have found that the public respond best to simple, attractive, "punchy" ads, like the oil company ad at the right.

one medium to carry their messages to the public, but this is to be expected since advertising is a part of marketing.

The Functions of Advertising

As a tool of marketing, advertising generally performs three basic functions (sometimes called "the 3 R's of advertising"):

1. *Retain "loyal" customers:* persuade present customers to keep buying.
2. *Reduce "lost" customers:* slow down the flow of present customers away from the proffered brand.
3. *Recruit "new" customers:* increase the flow of customers toward the advertised product; replace those lost to competitors; widen the total market.

How Advertising Actually Serves Business. One of the most fruitful approaches to the study of advertising is to examine some of the more significant services that advertising provides a business firm's marketing program.

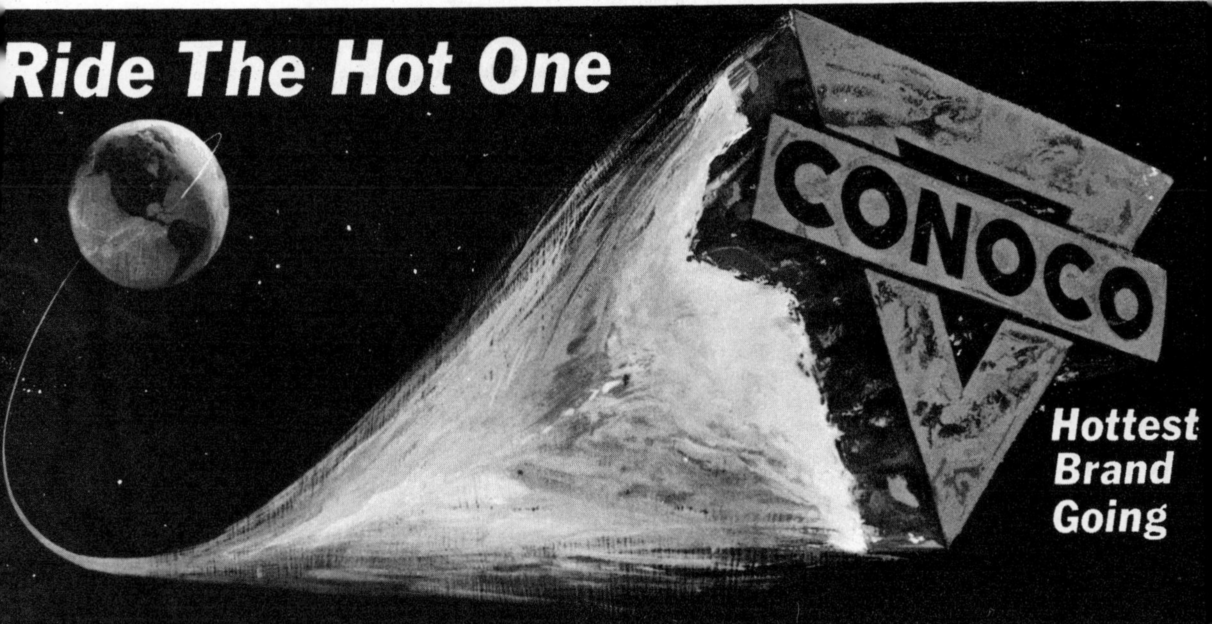

Conoco ad courtesy Continental Oil Co.

1. *Advertising has altered living habits.* So powerful is the influence of advertising that it is constantly changing our daily habits and attitudes. It has created public acceptance of new styles, new forms of entertainment, new modes of transportation. It has led to the greater use of color in the home, to the social acceptance of cigarette-smoking habits among adults, to the adoption of push-button devices which give families more leisure time. Family eating habits have actually been changed—housewives are buying more prepared and frozen foods, and are preparing fewer foods in the home. And by disseminating information about preventive medicine, infant care, diets, and personal hygiene, advertising has had a beneficial effect on the nation's health.
2. *Advertising helps to lower unit costs by increasing sales.* By increasing consumer desires, advertising enables a business to sell more units. This in turn allows the manufacturer to increase product output, which in turn reduces the cost of each unit. To the extent that advertising increases the cost of the product to the consumer, it is of course wasteful. In the long run, however, the main economic justification of all advertising is to reduce the price of goods by building up sales.
3. *Advertising helps support the total sales effort.* Since many of our wants are primarily psychological in character, the persuasive power of advertising is important in providing the public with facts about products so that they will continue to flock to the market place. Generally, products that are well-known to the consumer are easier to sell than unfamiliar products. Advertising is widely used by large corporations to develop a favorable "institutional image." For example, a large corporation may sponsor an hour-long televised symphony, during which the company's reputation and policies are emphasized, but no mention made of its products. In the accompanying illustration, *Newsweek* lists seven ways in which corporate advertising supports sales.
4. *Advertising can help to associate a whole family of products under one brand-name.* Manufacturers often find it more economical to produce a group of products, usually in a related field, rather than to specialize in one item.

How Corporate Advertising Supports Sales

1. Places corporate reputation behind new products
2. Paves the salesmen's way among new and unfamiliar prospects
3. Reaches those usually not contacted by salesmen — the top executives, scientists, engineers, technicians
4. Announces the company's scope and diversification by displaying all the product lines
5. Hastens the sale by beginning at the top
6. Seeks out minds which can see applications for the product lines which the company has not anticipated
7. Puts the full force of the corporate name behind the product in the public mind

Courtesy Newsweek, "The Case for Corporate Advertising."

A varied line enables a manufacturer to reduce the over-all distribution cost of each product. For example, soap companies often produce soap flakes, toilet soap, shaving soap, and toothpaste. Thus, it is possible to promote the sale of the entire line in single advertisements. Advertising costs may then be split among the various products. At the same time, the consumer becomes better acquainted with the company's entire line of products. When a new article is added, it automatically shares in the prestige that has already been established. In determining the difference between consumer acceptance and rejection, the image that a brand has acquired in the public mind is often as important as, if not more important than, the specific attributes of the product.

5. *Advertising can promote the development of an entire industry.* Sometimes various businesses within an industry voluntarily pool their funds and engage in a continuous advertising campaign to promote their industry. It may be that the industry itself is suffering from the competition of a new product or service. For example, during recent years the sale of synthetic fabrics has cut down the consumption of silk and wool. Several firms engaged in weaving woolen cloth have combined their efforts as an industry, and each contributes to an industry-wide fund which is used to promote the sale of woolen fabrics. Citrus growers' co-operatives spend substantial amounts each year on advertising to increase the consumption of citrus fruits. Other groups, such as the Association of American Railroads and the American Gas Assn., raise funds from the membership to carry on an aggressive industry advertising program.

The Effects of Advertising on the Economy and on the Public

We have seen that the primary purpose of advertising is to promote the sale of goods and services. There is little doubt that in doing this, advertising has made a substantial contribution to our standard of living. By the very same token, however, it has been accused of engaging in wasteful practices, creating monopolies, and disseminating false information. Advertising has also been criticized for making people want things they cannot afford, and thus promoting excessive personal indebtedness. On the other hand, there is consolation in the fact that, although the average American is exposed to a great deal of advertising, it is highly doubtful that his response to it is of such urgency as to cause unbearable unhappiness simply because he cannot afford to buy all the products advertised.

Economic Waste in Advertising. Advertising has long been the target for adverse criticism. Some of the sharpest condemnations come from observers who denounce advertising as an economic waste. For one thing, they claim that advertising does not create new demand, but merely results in brand-switching. Stuart Chase popularized this theory in his book, *The Tragedy of Waste,* when he wrote:

> Advertising creates no new dollars. In fact, by removing workers from productive employment, it tends to depress output, and thus lessen the number of real dollars. What it does is this. It transfers purchasing power from A to B. It makes people stop buying shaving soap in mugs and starts them to buying it in tinfoil sticks.[1]

While Mr. Chase's argument may have some merit in the case of industrial goods, it provides little if any validity when applied to consumer-goods advertising. Instead, evidence reveals that in the case of such consumer products as toothpaste, cosmetics, candy, and gasoline, whose advertising is highly competitive, the total per capita consumption has risen steadily over the years. To hold that all advertising is purely competitive and therefore wasteful suggests that competition itself is wasteful and should be abolished. As long as we favor maintaining competition as part of our economic order, to eliminate advertising probably would increase, rather than decrease, economic waste. As a competitive tool, advertising is perhaps less costly than other tools used to stimulate consumption would be if advertising were banned. Out total economic system, with its freedom of individual enterprise and its private-property rights, is a means of maintaining the competitive struggle. Any "fair" means of achieving a competitive advantage has long been accepted as such.

In his best-seller, *The Hidden Persuaders,* Vance Packard raised this question: Does advertising cause people to buy things they don't need? So the argument continues that advertisers are attempting to influence consumers to engage in purchases which offer little or nothing in the way of benefits. These critics imply that by eliminating this advertising, the producer or distributor would save the cost of advertising, and thus be able to lower the ultimate price to consumers. On this point we have to conclude, as did Neil H. Borden in his rather exhaustive study of advertising costs and pricing, that the evidence is inconclusive.[2] (It is common knowledge, however, that on many widely advertised products such as room air-conditioners, automatic refrigerators, power mowers, and electric dishwashers, prices have dropped as sales have increased. It is also no secret that in other heavily advertised areas such as cigarettes, soap, and cosmetics, quality has increased with no appreciable rise in prices—and this is tantamount to a drop in prices.)

Brand Monopoly. Critics claim that advertising tends to develop

[1] Stuart Chase, *The Tragedy of Waste* (New York: The Macmillan Co., 1928), p. 112.

[2] Neil H. Borden, *The Economic Effects of Advertising,* Chapters XVII–XXI (Chicago: Richard D. Irwin, 1942), pp. 424–28.

brand monopolies. The basis for this contention is that too much advertising is devoted to the promotion of branded goods. This, the critics say, builds up public preference for specific brands, and by having a monopoly, the advertiser is able to increase his prices. But any attempt by a producer to raise prices, even if the amount were small, will encourage other companies to enter the market with a lower-priced product. Furthermore, if any monopolistic position exists, it is in the area of increasing sales, not prices. And it is doubtful that advertising ever affords a producer a monopoly over an entire industry. Despite the large sums spent by Eastman Kodak to publicize the name Kodak, or by General Motors to promote the sale of Frigidaires, there is no evidence that either firm has obtained a monopoly because of huge advertising expenditures.

Truth in Advertising. Does advertising tell the truth? There is no simple answer to this question—yet this is probably one of the most important questions in this chapter.

In order to answer this question, we must first resolve what we mean by "tell the truth." Is advertising expected to tell the literal truth, or merely to give an accurate impression? Regarding fraudulent and misleading advertising, the Supreme Court has made these statements:

> Advertising, as a whole, must not create a misleading impression even though every statement separately considered is literally truthful.
>
> Advertising must not obscure or conceal material facts.
>
> Advertising must not be artfully contrived to distract and divert readers' attention from the true nature of the terms and conditions of an offer.

Although most advertising can be considered truthful, there are some unscrupulous advertisers who make misleading or untrue statements in their claims. Fortunately, much has been accomplished in recent years to stop these malpractices.

In 1938, Congress passed the Wheeler-Lea Act amending the Federal Trade Commission Act of 1914, which gave the FTC power over "unfair or deceptive acts or practices." The FTC constantly reviews magazine and newspaper advertisements, and monitors radio and television commercials, for violations of this law. Using the Supreme Court criteria for what constitutes fraudulent and misleading advertising, the FTC annually issues about 270 complaints against advertisers cited for alleged violations of the Wheeler-Lea Act.

There are a number of statutes aimed at specific industries wherein the FTC is granted authority to act over matters related to labeling and advertising. In this category fall:

The Wool Products Labeling Act of 1939
The Fur Products Labeling Act of 1951
The Flammable Fabrics Act of 1953
The Textile Fiber Products Identification Act of 1958

The Federal Communications Commission has regulatory power over television and radio broadcasters. The Commission grants to television and radio stations permission to broadcast, and assigns frequencies to them. Its effect on the advertiser is indirect, since it is concerned mainly with the broadcaster. However, by virtue of its authority it can maintain a watchful eye over the merits of particular advertising.

In 1965, Congress enacted the Highway Beautification Act prohibiting the placement of billboards and other signs within 660′ of the Interstate and Primary Road Systems. Unzoned areas, where other business is permitted, are exempted. Also in 1965, Congress passed special legislation (effective January 1, 1966) requiring that every pack and carton of cigarettes bear in a conspicuous place the following statement: "Caution: Cigarette smoking may be hazardous to your health."

Statutes enacted by the various states are intended to cover advertising that may not be subject to federal statutes. However, most of the hodgepodge of state laws are directed at specific practices or particular industries, and so at best enjoy results that are rather limited in scope.

The most meaningful of all forms of advertising watchdogging is self-regulation by the fraternity of advertisers and advertising agencies. The Association of National Advertisers, representing the largest advertisers, and the American Association of Advertising Agencies, which places about 75 percent of national advertising, work together through an organization known as the Committee for the Improvement of Advertising Content. This committee reviews complaints, and reports its findings to the advertiser or advertising agency. In many instances the advertiser and the agency have voluntarily changed the advertising to respect the criticism.

Printers' Ink, a leading marketing magazine, and the *Better Business Bureaus*, which are well known for their activities to protect consumers, have worked for many years to prevent unethical advertising and to raise standards of practice. Their weapons have been twofold: publicity unfavorable to offending firms and, if necessary, recourse to the federal courts when false advertising has been transmitted by mail. Many cases involving violations of statutes have been brought before the courts, and in most instances the law has been upheld and the violator punished. Despite all the progress that has been made to improve advertising standards, however, obviously there are still advertisers and a few advertising agencies far more interested in increasing sales by any means than in honestly advertising their products or services.

ADVERTISING MEDIA

The advertising *medium* (plural: *media*) is simply the means chosen by the advertiser to present his message—newspapers, magazines, or radio, for example. In a sense, the town crier served as an early advertising medium. Today, with our vast assortment of printed publications and communication devices, advertisers have many media at their disposal. Selecting the proper one is often an extremely difficult task.

Advertising media may be classified in the following manner:

Types of Media

Newspapers	Radio	Transportation
Magazines	Television	Specialties
Direct mail	Outdoor signs	Point-of-purchase displays

Some large companies use almost all these media, but small concerns are content, for financial reasons, to use only one or two of them. Many factors must be evaluated by the advertiser in selecting the proper media. Several factors are *cost, extent of coverage (circulation), amount of selectivity, degree of flexibility, timeliness,* and *effectiveness.*

Amount of selectivity refers to the ability of the medium to deliver the advertiser's message to a particular group of consumers he wants to reach. *Degree of flexibility* is the freedom the advertiser has to alter his message to meet changing conditions in a given medium. *Timeliness* has to do with the ability of the medium to keep abreast of local or national events or sudden changes in the advertiser's plans. *Effectiveness* relates to the degree of success enjoyed by his advertising in a given medium.

Other factors to be evaluated are size of audience, creative strategy,

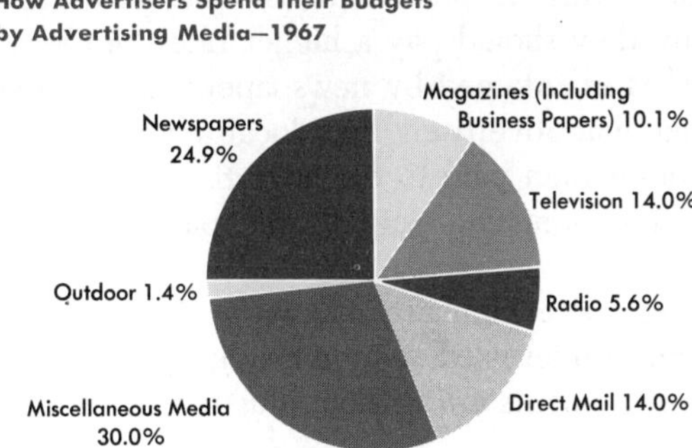

Source: *Printers' Ink.* June 19, 1967.

relationship of media to market, and editorial policy of media. There is no single medium "best" for all advertising; each choice must be based on the particular requirements of the advertiser's situation.

Now let us see how advertisers spend their dollars, and what each medium has to offer.

Newspapers

In terms of volume carried, the newspaper is the leading advertising medium in the United States, accounting for approximately 25 percent of total expenditures. Although newspapers carry both local and national advertising, about three-fourths of newspaper volume comes from local sources. The popularity of newspapers as an advertising medium is largely due to the fact that almost everybody reads at least one.

Types of Newspaper Advertising. The three principal types of newspaper advertising are: *local display, national display,* and *classified advertising.*

The backbone of newspaper income is advertising from stores, banks, insurance companies, and other establishments in the community. This is referred to as *local display advertising.* About 80 percent of all newspaper advertising is local display; only 20 percent is national.[3] Rates for local display are generally lower than for either national or classified advertising.

National display advertising is used for merchandise distributed in a national market under a trade-mark that identifies the manufacturer or distributor. Large national manufacturers often run the same advertisement in selected newspapers from coast to coast on a given day or during a given week. A substantial part of all national display advertising is created and placed by advertising agencies. The average national display rate for weekday insertions is approximately 50 percent higher than the average local rate for weekdays, and the Sunday rate is about 70 percent higher. National advertisers have fought against this rate differential for many years, for they see no justifiable reason why they should pay a higher rate than local buyers. But this rate differential is maintained by newspapers on the basis that it costs more to service national advertisers than local advertisers. Generally there is a 15 percent commission paid to the advertising agency involved, and a 10 to 25 percent commission paid to the paper's national sales representative.

Classified advertising, more familiarly known as "want-ads," appears in special classified columns under fixed column headings arranged in alphabetical order. These advertisements are without illustrations or artwork and

[3] *Printers' Ink,* February 2, 1965, p. 12.

are set in uniform type. You have undoubtedly seen such want-ad columns as Services Offered, Business Opportunities, Employment, Rentals, and For Sale. Want-ads are closely read, for the people who look at them already have an interest in what is being offered. Classified advertising is generally sold on an established rate per word or line, which varies with the paper's circulation.

Special Characteristics of Newspapers. From the standpoint of the advertiser, newspapers possess several characteristics not common to other media. One unique characteristic is that they serve a very large proportion of the population in a community, and enable advertisers to reach a broad local market. The time flexibility of newspapers is another desirable characteristic. Since advertisements may be prepared and submitted only a few hours before press time, it is possible for the advertiser to adapt his message to meet any emergency or sudden change in the community. Consequently, the advertising message can be as timely as the morning's news flashes.

Because of the numerous special-interest sections carried by newspapers, the reader's interest is sustained from day to day. Moreover, the low cost of the daily paper helps to increase subscription sales. On the other hand, it is considered to have a shorter life and is more hastily read than magazines. Studies show that the average length of time an individual spends in reading a newspaper is only about 20 minutes daily. Recognizing this fact, copywriters try to capture reader interest by preparing advertisements that contain a minimum amount of written copy and a maximum amount of white space.

Newspaper Rate Structure. The advertising rate structure for each newspaper varies depending upon the paper's circulation, labor costs, amount of advertising, and other factors. Almost all newspapers quote different rates to national and local advertisers. Rates are based on different units of space. For example, local advertising rates are frequently lower than national advertisers' rates. The local rate allows no commission to advertising agencies and is subject to appreciable discounts depending upon the amount of space used.

The basic unit of space for local advertising is the *column inch,* an area one column wide by 1″ deep. The standard rate for local advertising charged by *The Seattle Times* is $7.67 per column inch. However, a local advertiser can, by volume discounts based on increased purchase of space, reduce this cost by as much as 50 percent.

The national rate, which is quoted in terms of *agate lines* (or simply *lines*), provides for an advertising agency's commission, but seldom offers volume discounts. An agate line is a space one column wide and 1/14″ deep (there are 14 lines to the agate inch). In the case of *The Seattle Times,* the national rate is 78¢ per line, which is equal to $10.92 per inch (14 × 78¢), and the maximum discount for volume space bought reduces this by only about 10 percent. For 1,000 inches (14,000 lines), the national advertiser would pay $10,920 (14,000 × 78¢), instead of about half this amount, which the local advertiser pays for 1,000 inches a month. Of course, rates for color advertisements are higher than for black-and-white ads.

In making a comparison of the cost of newspaper space, two variables must be considered. One is the rate per line, and the other the circulation. To make a comparison of advertising costs among several different newspapers, regional and national advertisers use a theoretical figure called the *milline rate*. Specifically, the milline rate is what it would cost per line to reach a million circulation with one line of advertising. It is determined by multiplying the line rate by 1 million and dividing the result by the newspaper's actual circulation, in this way:

$$\frac{R \times 1{,}000{,}000}{C} = MR \qquad \begin{aligned} R &= \text{published rate per line} \\ C &= \text{actual circulation} \\ MR &= \text{milline rate} \end{aligned}$$

Let us compare the milline rate for the following two newspapers:

Newspaper A has a circulation of 2 million and a rate of $2 per line. What is its milline rate?

$$\frac{\$2 \times 1{,}000{,}000}{2{,}000{,}000} = \$1 \text{ milline rate}$$

Newspaper B has a circulation of 300,000 and a rate of 48¢ per line. What is its milline rate?

$$\frac{48¢ \times 1{,}000{,}000}{300{,}000} = \$1.60 \text{ milline rate}$$

In terms of the total circulation, or the total number of messages delivered, the advertiser pays 60 percent more for space in newspaper B than in A. In general, the milline rate goes up as circulation drops, and the greater the circulation, the lower the milline rate.

Magazines

Magazines are another important medium, ranking fourth in total dollars spent for advertising space. But while a tremendous amount of money has been spent for magazine advertising in recent years, the proportionate share of total dollars spent annually for it has declined. This decrease is due to a large extent to competition from television advertising.

Types of Magazines. According to Standard Rate and Data Service, a private organization that periodically publishes advertising rates, copy requirements, circulation data, and other facts, magazines are classified into three broad types, based on the audiences served:

1. Consumer magazines
2. Business publications
3. Farm publications (journals)

Consumer magazines are directed toward the household consumer. They are, for example, general-interest magazines, such as *Time, Look,* and *Life.* Some consumer magazines are especially designed to appeal to women; *McCall's* and *Good Housekeeping* are typical of this group. Magazines directed primarily to men include *Esquire* and *Playboy.* Some consumer magazines appeal to individuals with special interests, such as hobbies, health and diet, travel, and education. The special-interest publications must be distinguished from professional magazines, which are classified as business publications.

Included in the category of *business publications* are some 2,400 assorted magazines, written about many business subjects for business readers, including executives and employees of commercial and industrial concerns and members of the professions. Included in this category of magazines are various subclassifications, such as (1) industrial and manufacturing magazines, (2) trade magazines for retailers, wholesalers, and related groups, (3) professional magazines for the fields of medicine, law, education, and accountancy, and (4) general business magazines that appeal to a broad class of business readers. Many advertisers use these business publications to *supplement* their advertising in consumer magazines. Advertisers marketing products exclusively for business and industry depend largely on business publications as their *primary* medium.

Farm magazines are written primarily to appeal to farmers and others engaged in various aspects of agriculture. If you want to reach all types of farmers, you might use *Farm Journal, Successful Farming,* or *Progressive Farmer,* but if you are trying to reach a more specialized group, you might buy space in *Hoard's Dairyman* or *Turkey World.* Unlike consumer and business magazines, the majority of which enjoy nationwide circulation, most farm magazines, due to the nature of their contents, are distributed only in statewide or regional areas.

Characteristics of Magazines. Magazines are generally printed on top-quality paper stock that permits creative typography, excellent reproduction of illustrations, and full use of color. In spite of all this, however, and though they offer advertisers a wide range of audiences, magazines do not furnish advertisers with as much flexibility as do newspapers, television, or radio. And since most of them are widely distributed, it is not possible to adapt their advertising to meet local conditions. (Some publishers attempt to overcome this limitation by publishing regional editions.) Another difficulty with magazine advertising is that because ads must be submitted at least several weeks in advance of the publication date, it is difficult, if not impossible, to make last-minute changes of copy to meet an emergency.

The typical magazine reader spends much more time with a magazine than with a newspaper. Unlike the newspaper, which is often discarded the day it is bought, a magazine usually is kept for several weeks, or even months. This feature gives the advertiser a potentially larger reading audience than is normally reflected by actual circulation figures.

Since women both read more magazines and make more purchases than men, producers of consumer goods consider magazine advertising aimed at the female readership an extremely important sales promotion medium.

Magazine Rate Structure. Magazines, like newspapers, use the agate line as their basis for rates. However, in actual practice, most space is sold in terms of units of pages, and fractional pages. These rates include a commission to advertising agencies—usually 15 percent. At the time of publication of this book, rates (which change from time to time) ran as follows: a full-page, black-and-white ad in *Readers' Digest* (16,500,000 total circulation) cost $46,650; *Time* magazine, with a circulation of slightly more than 3 million, charged $28,860 for a full-page, four-color advertisement; *House Beautiful,* with a circulation of approximately 1 million, got $8,750 for a four-color, full-page advertisement. Space in color on one of the cover positions costs considerably more than space elsewhere. Discounts are given for frequency of insertions, cover ads included.

Since it is difficult for advertisers to make an accurate comparison between one magazine and another as to value received in terms of costs of space, professional media space-buyers have developed a yardstick known as the *cost-per-thousand of circulation.* On the basis of the cost of reaching 1,000 readers, the space buyer can compare magazine costs with those of other media, or the cost of one magazine with another. Thus, if the cost for a black-and-white full page is $24,000, and the average net paid circulation is exactly 4 million, the formula will look like this:

$$\frac{\text{Page rate} \times 1{,}000}{\text{Circulation}} = \text{Cost-per-thousand, or } \frac{\$24{,}000 \times 1{,}000}{4{,}000{,}000} = \$6$$

A magazine with a rate per page of $11,000 for a black-and-white ad and a circulation of 2 million would have a cost-per-thousand of $5.50.

Of course, this formula is more realistic when two or more magazines of the same type are being compared. And it should also be recognized that different types of magazines simply cannot be compared on a dollar-and-cents basis alone. Like the newspaper milline rate, the cost-per-thousand for magazines usually goes up as circulation goes down. However, often an advertiser is willing to pay a higher cost because of the qualitative selectivity of the circulation.

Rates are influenced by the publisher's guarantee (called the *circulation guarantee*) that he will print and distribute a certain number of copies of each issue. Naturally, even though the advertiser is guaranteed that a specific number of copies will be distributed, he cannot possibly be guaranteed that all subscribers will read every page.

Direct-Mail Advertising

This medium carries advertising messages directly to the prospective buyer—to either his home or office, or both. Direct-mail publications usually take the form of letters, postcards, catalogs, folders, or booklets.

Success in using direct mail depends largely on the quality of the mailing list. To elicit a satisfactory response, a mailing list must be accurate, up-to-date, and free of duplications. Moreover, it should contain only the names of persons who are really potential buyers of the product or service offered.

There are several reasons for the extensive use of direct-mail advertising in modern business. It can be adapted to firms of any size. It can be used for local, regional, or national coverage. It is a selective medium. It offers broad geographical flexibility.

There are at least two limitations to this medium, however. It is extremely difficult to prepare an effective mailing list and keep it up-to-date. Moreover, direct-mail advertising pieces often appear cold and impersonal, giving the impression that they were mechanically prepared in large quantities (even if they are, they shouldn't appear to be).

Because the expense of direct-mail campaigns varies with the size of the mailing and the nature of the piece itself, it is difficult to quote average cost figures. Authorities agree that if a mailing elicits a response of from 2 to 4 percent, it is worth the effort and expense. In fact, a 4 percent response is regarded as above average.

Broadcast Media

Radio and television are comparative newcomers to the ranks of advertising media. As channels of communication they differ greatly—TV combines the qualities of sight, sound, and motion; radio depends solely on sound—but as advertising media, they have much in common. For this reason, we shall examine them together, under the general title of *broadcast media.*

The Nature of Broadcasting. Broadcasting may be studied from three different points of view: production techniques, entertainment values, and advertising. Our interest is chiefly from the advertising standpoint.

It has been said, "Nothing has changed American family life since the advent of the automobile so much as television; nothing else has had such an impact on advertising."[4] (Of course radio, when it first became popular, had a similar impact on advertising.) As a communications field, broadcasting is dominated by four national companies, each of which has developed its own network system. These networks are the sources of programs other than those developed by local broadcast stations. On the other hand, local radio and television broadcast stations—with the exception of some metropolitan stations—invariably fall into the class of small businesses, no matter what criteria are used in judging them.

Radio. Commercial radio broadcasting started in the early 1920's. By the mid-1930's nearly 700 commercial radio stations were broadcasting; today there are well over 5,000. Most stations operate via amplitude modulation (AM), though about 23 percent choose to operate on frequency modulation (FM), which is practically static-free and therefore affords certain advantages over AM broadcasting. Today's radio stations specialize in program appeal. For example, one station specializes in news coverage. Another specializes in reporting on sports events. And a rather common goal is to become the leading station in broadcasting the latest "hit" records. Also, FM stations have become popular for their broadcasts of classical music. Advertisers usually take pains to select the kind of programs that they believe will give them the largest and most loyal (and necessarily the most patient) listenership. As a result, the use of radio as an advertising medium is more evident than many listeners wish it were.

Television. Well over 50 million American homes have at least one television set (the ratio of black-and-white to color sets is about 4 to 1). This means that the home penetration rate for television is almost 95 percent (the rate for radio is almost 100 percent). Home TV usage ranges from five to seven hours per day (radio listening averages about two).

One of the advantages of TV for the advertiser is that he can either use it on a nationwide or regional basis, or concentrate on only the local market. (This advantage is also true of radio, though to a lesser extent.) The advertiser who selects TV (or radio) faces a more complex situation than the one who buys printed space. The sole responsibility of the advertiser buying printed space is to make certain that his message is well written so that it will be read and understood; the printed medium is responsible for the reproduction problems. But the broadcaster, especially on TV, must make sure not only that his program is good—that it is worthy of listenership—but also that

[4] Otto Kleppner, *Advertising Procedures*, 5th ed. (Englewood Cliffs, N.J.: Prentice-Hall, Inc., 1966), p. 223.

his commercials are effective. And even though the broadcaster buys time on the air, he is not assured of a guaranteed audience. One reason is that the mortality rate of new TV shows, and even of some fairly old "standards," is awesomely high.

Broadcast Rates. Unlike magazines and newspapers, which sell advertising space by the agate line, broadcast media base their rates on units of time. Thus, radio and TV advertising time is sold in units of one minute or less, and five-, ten-, fifteen-minute, half-hour, and hour units. The cost per unit varies from station to station, depending on such factors as station strength, time of day, scope of station coverage, and cost of talent. For example, certain times of the day are considered by advertisers more popular than others, mainly because there are more viewers or listeners then than at other times. Usually, the most popular periods cost the most. Network broadcasting likewise costs more than local coverage. One hour of CBS-TV network time costs approximately $140,000, exclusive of talent.

Television and radio stations usually classify their broadcast period by time units in order to reflect differences in the size of audiences. For many stations, Class AA TV time, which is the most expensive, is from 7:30 p.m. to 10:30 p.m. daily. The cheaper Class A time covers from 10:30 p.m. to 11:00 p.m. daily, and from 6:30 to 7:30 p.m. on Saturday. Some stations have a Class D time, which extends daily from sign-on to 9:00 a.m., and from 12 midnight to sign-off. This is the lowest-priced time, because the audience is then smallest.

Prior to television, radio's evening time was substantially higher priced than other times. Today, however, radio time buyers find that some stations have a single-class price policy for all periods, day or evening.

Program Sources. A question facing many sponsors interested in buying broadcast time is, "Where can I get a good program?" Basically, there are three sources. The most common sources are the station and its network. If the sponsor desires a local program, it may be possible to obtain one that fits his particular needs, using local talent. Programs developed by the network often are more elaborate, and consequently more costly. In any event, the sponsor may elect to buy a regular show appearing daily or weekly, or only an occasional special event. The third source of programs is the free-lance operator who (often in conjunction with an advertising agency) develops "specials"—boxing matches, golf tournaments, track meets, political conventions, etc.

Due to the high cost of sponsoring a quality program at the more popular hours, many advertisers find it expedient to share both the billing and the bills. For example, two advertisers may elect to be *alternate sponsors*—that is, on one program the one will be given the lion's share of the

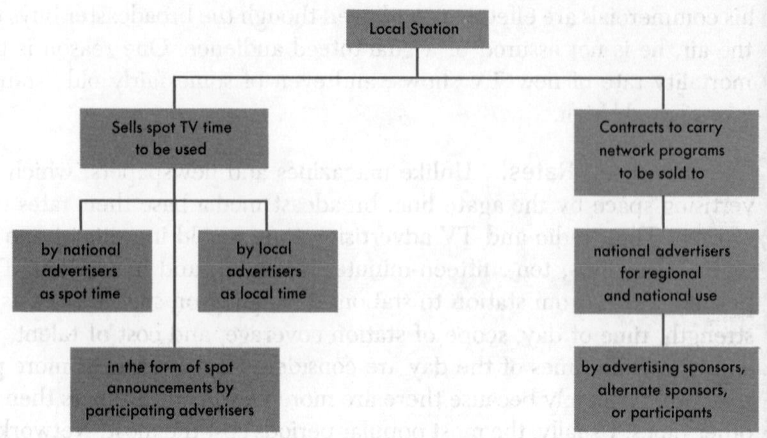

The Structure of Television Broadcasting

commercial time allotted, and on the following program the other will be in the main spotlight. (No doubt you have wondered from time to time why in the world "next week's sponsor" should be mentioned at all, no less given a portion of the time that might be used by "this week's sponsor.") When more than two sponsors use the same show, they are called *participating advertisers*. This arrangement allows the advertiser to buy time from the station for short announcements now and again, instead of presenting advertising messages as a regular show sponsor. On the national TV networks, the trend is strongly toward participating sponsorship because of the increasing cost of programs, and thus of both full and alternate sponsorships.

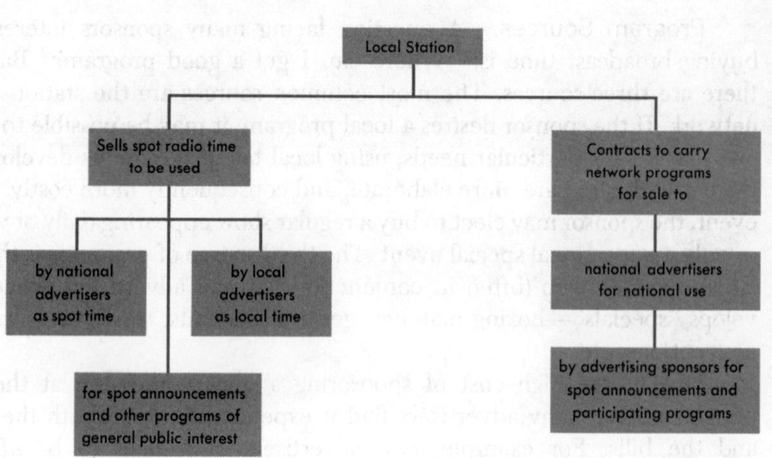

The Structure of Radio Broadcasting

The "structures" of TV and radio broadcasting are shown in the accompanying charts. These charts show how time is sold by the local radio and/or TV station in the form of network, local, and spot time to full sponsors, alternate sponsors, and participating advertisers.

Outdoor Advertising

The promotion of outdoor advertising as a local, regional, and national media has resulted largely from the efforts of an organization, founded in 1891, that is now known as the Outdoor Advertising Association of America. The association energetically promotes sound public-relations practices among its members, and conducts continuing research into the effectiveness of its medium.[5]

The three categories of outdoor advertising used mainly by national advertisers are *posters, painted bulletins,* and *spectaculars.*

The *poster,* often called a "billboard," is a standardized structure, 12′ high and 25′ long, made of weather-resistant materials. This is known as a "24-sheet poster." The message is printed or painted on sheets of heavy paper that are glued onto the poster. These poster signs are located along routes traveled by a large number of automobiles or pedestrians. Most posters are designed to be attractive both in daylight and when illuminated at night. A "six-sheet poster," more often known as the "junior panel," often is used in areas where space is limited.

The *painted bulletin,* usually more elaborate than the poster, is also used for outdoor advertising. Instead of being pasted on in the form of printed sheets, the advertisement is painted on the sign. The standard painted bulletin is 15′6″ high and 55′ long.

The third type of outdoor advertising is the *spectacular,* which is a sign, custom-made to fit a specific space, whose elaborate design, color, illumination, and perhaps even animation are designed to attract the attention of passers-by.

For outdoor advertising to be effective its message must be brief and its form attractive, and it must be in good taste. In recent years, outdoor advertising has had a number of critics who complain that these signs both distract the attention of drivers, and hide the natural beauty along the highways. Another complaint is that they are ugly. The amendment to the 1965 Federal-Aid Highway Act (that is, the aforementioned Highway Beautification Act) that requires that outdoor displays be located at least 660′ off high-

[5] Closely related to advertising is the much broader area known as *public relations.* One may define public relations as *the art and practice of creating a favorable image or personality in the mind of the public.* The modern firm is very much concerned with how the public feels toward it as an institution.

ways built with federal aid permits reductions in federal assistance to states failing to pass enabling legislation. (Interestingly enough, the bill also provides partial reimbursement to owners of displaced signs.) In many instances, the criticisms against outdoor advertising are aimed neither against the standardized poster and printed bulletin, nor toward the spectacular, but against the unsightly nonstandardized sign.

Since the enactment of this legislation, Congress has been subjected to pressures from outdoor-advertising sponsors to alter the existing guidelines by shifting to the various states the responsibility for determining the rules. This could result in altering highway advertising requirements in favor of the advertisers and against the wishes of the highway-subsidizing federal government.

Transportation Advertising

This medium consists of three types of displays:

1. *Car cards* placed in subway and elevated cars, streetcars, busses, taxis, and suburban railroad cars
2. *Traveling displays* painted or posted on the outside of streetcars and busses
3. *Station posters* located inside stations and terminals and on station platforms

Although these types of transportation advertising are well suited to promote sales on a local, regional, or national basis, they are used most often in large cities. In New York City the cost of an 11″-by-21″ subway card is $9,000 a month. Every year advertisers spend about $24 million for transportation advertising space throughout the United States, generally to supplement other media. This medium offers a low cost of coverage, a fairly high degree of flexibility, and good selectivity. It differs from outdoor advertising in that it is used primarily on or in various forms of transportation, and at transportation terminals.

Specialty Advertising

Advertisers have long recognized the value of such specialty items as blotters, pencils, calendars, matchbooks, paperweights, and memorandum pads, bearing the company name. The chief value of this type of advertising is that it provides a frequent reminder to patronize the business whose name appears on the article.

Advertising premiums are another commonly used specialty device. An advertising premium is simply any item given away free, or for a very nominal consideration in addition to the regular purchase price of a product. The hope, of course, is that it will serve as an additional inducement to steadily buy the advertiser's article. Premiums for children have proved particularly effective in selling breakfast foods and milk products. Games, coloring books, magic tricks, badges, hair brushes, flower seeds, paring knives, and silverware are only a few of the many premiums used by manufacturers to induce sales.

Point-of-Purchase Advertising

Point-of-purchase advertising consists of displays mounted inside the stores where consumers make their actual purchases. Unlike newspaper, radio, television, and magazine advertisements which carry the message into the home, point-of-purchase ads greet customers at the exact moment when they are deciding what to buy. These displays are designed to stimulate *impulse buying*—purchases made on sudden inclination and without specific prior intent to buy a particular item at a particular time or place.

Point-of-purchase advertising takes many different forms, including the following:

Counter displays	Floor racks
Wall displays	Door signs
Window displays	

Most national manufacturers prepare a wide variety of display material, furnished free to dealers, to help sell their products. Even so, it is often difficult to persuade a merchant to set up a display in some prominent location. To overcome this resistance, the manufacturer's salesman sometimes carries a set of display materials with him and installs the displays in the course of his regular calls. This practice is common in mounting elaborate window displays that call for specially prepared materials.

Certain store areas are preferred for point-of-purchase displays. Several of the favored positions are windows near the store entrance, a spot near the cash register or exit turnstile, and the area adjoining the bread counter. The next time you shop in a retail store, notice the number of different point-of-purchase displays and the positions in which they are located.

WRITING ADVERTISING COPY

In the final analysis, the success or failure of an advertisement is measured by how well it does its job. So far, we have discussed the importance of (1) various kinds of media, (2) the social and economic effects of advertising, (3) costs of media, (4) their advantages and disadvantages, and (5) the importance of selecting the proper medium. Now let us direct our attention to the preparation of the advertisement itself. In order to do this, we must first examine some of the psychological forces and social influences that motivate human behavior.

The Psychology of Advertising

What makes people think and act as they do is a complex subject. Psychologists generally believe that there are certain psychological forces and social influences that motivate human behavior. Individuals are said to be motivated when they show fairly definite directional trends. What then is the meaning of "motivation"? Essentially, *motivation* is a process of stimulus and response that activates or moves the individual's behavior toward an objective or goal. Thus, people are often motivated without realizing it.

Psychologists tend to agree that some motives stem from the physical or organic needs of the individual which are essential to his physical well-being. These are often referred to as "primary" motives because they are innate, biologically-based needs of universal existence. Motives not directly related to physical needs are known as "secondary" motives. Hunger, pain-avoidance, and social approval are examples of primary motives. Examples of secondary motives include beauty, economy and profit, cleanliness, and health. Advertisers make use of both primary and secondary motives.

By now you must realize that advertising, like economics and marketing, is closely involved with human behavior. But because in the market place behavior cannot be separated from behavior elsewhere, advertisers—especially copywriters—must have a good understanding of what actually motivates human behavior. They must avoid distinctions between physical and social needs, and study the problem on hand from the standpoint of buying motives, instead.

Buying Motives. The contributions of the behavioral sciences to business have been numerous and far too lengthy to recite here. Their language has stemmed from three separate disciplines: psychology, sociology, and anthropology. As a result of research, the behavioral scientist has identified certain motives known to activate human behavior. When these appear in an advertisement for the purpose of stimulating you to buy, they are referred to as *buying motives,* though psychologists sometimes refer to them as "consumer desires." Wales, Gentry, and Wales have identified the following as buying motives:[6]

[6] Hugh G. Wales, Dwight L. Gentry, and Max Wales, *Advertising Copy, Layout, and Typography* (New York: The Ronald Press Co., 1958), pp. 67–75.

1. Desire for recognition and superiority
2. Desire for good health and long life
3. Desire for appetizing food and drink
4. Desire to earn money
5. Desire for comfort
6. Desire for security
7. Desire to save money
8. Desire to save time
9. Desire to protect one's family
10. Desire to win approval of the opposite sex

At this point we are ready to explore copy objectives and the use of motives in the writing of advertising copy.

Advertising Appeals

We have already observed how necessary wants are in motivating consumer behavior. The advertiser, in presenting his message, must be interested in determining the type of stimulus that will obtain his desired response, which is to satisfy customers' wants and needs. The psychological stimulus used by the advertiser is usually referred to as the *advertising appeal.* Its function is to awaken the dormant desire in the mind of the individual which will set into motion the behavior mechanisms leading to the desired satisfaction. The appeal should always be directed in such a way that it takes advantage of a buying motive (which we have already noted is what causes people to act or react).

The first objective, then, is to get the prospect's interest and attention, which you will remember is the first step in selling. This should be followed by evidence to support any claim that might not stand by itself. The final step involves the necessary action that will result in the decision to buy.

Copy Appeals. Examine the advertisements in your favorite magazine or daily paper and you will find that in addition to the careful attention that has been paid to layout, photography, color, type faces and sizes, and literary style, stress has been placed on an underlying appeal based on a psychological motive. Copy appeals are used to state the benefits that the reader (or in the case of radio, if not TV, the listener) is supposed to receive from the use of the product described, or by accepting the proposition presented. In other words, *copy appeals are actually the selling points contained in the advertisement;* they should not be confused with the physical qualities of the product. The terms "copy appeal" and "advertising appeal," then, both relate to the same thing.

Among the most widely used copy appeals are these:

Better health	Greater prestige
Increased popularity	Added savings
Increased income	Relief from pain
More pleasure	Pride of ownership
Improved appearance	Sex appeal
Financial security	Greater beauty

The following copy illustrates some of these appeals:

HOW TO SAVE $100 OR MORE WHEN YOU BUY YOUR NEXT CAR
(Added Savings)

HOW WE RETIRED IN 10 YEARS WITH $400 A MONTH
(Financial Security)

IF YOUR NAILS BREAK OR SPLIT, CORRECT THEM
THIS MEDICALLY PROVEN WAY
(Improved Appearance)

DO YOU HAVE TO HIDE YOUR HAIR TO LOOK PRETTIER?
(Greater Beauty)

Headlines (or "headings") such as these are the most important of all copy elements. If they fail to attract attention and interest, the other parts of the advertisement are wasted. Copy designers who place great importance on illustrations might take exception to this statement because they consider that the reader's eye is more often attracted by a picture than by a series of words. The fact is, however, that words and pictures together, or either alone, may be used equally as well to attract attention. The important point is that the primary attention-getting device, the headline *idea,* be gotten across quickly and satisfactorily.

Learning how to write effective advertising copy calls for more than an understanding of psychological appeals and techniques. It requires practice in the use of these techniques, and the constructive criticism of that practice, just as learning to play a musical instrument requires both practice and acceptance of criticism. Copywriting is a difficult art—one that demands more skill than perhaps any other form of creative writing.

THE ADVERTISING AGENCY

According to the American Association of Advertising Agencies, Inc., an advertising agency is "a firm of specialists in creating advertising and in planning the entire marketing program of which advertising is a part."[7] The

[7] *Advertising: The Advertising Business and Its Career Opportunities* (New York: The American Assn. of Advertising Agencies, Inc., 1961), p. 4.

agency acts as an intermediary between the company that wants to advertise, and the various media that sell advertising space and time. Agencies work in the open, and always in the spotlight of competition. To meet their responsibilities, they have developed staffs of talented, experienced people—highly creative, and experts in all phases of art and layout work, typography, photoengraving, merchandising, public relations, print production, research, and writing.

Here are some of the business services an agency provides:

1. A study of the client's product or service
2. An analysis of the present and potential market
3. A knowledge of the distribution factors related to sales
4. A knowledge of all available media that can be used in selling the product to consumers, retailers, or wholesalers
5. The formulation of a plan and its presentation to the client
6. Development and execution of the plan
7. Close cooperation with the client's sales organization to ensure the greatest results from the advertising campaign
8. Preparation of the copy

Organization of an Agency

Agencies vary in size from the so-called "one-man" concern to those employing several thousand people. The large agencies tend toward a division of labor: specialists are assigned to departments charged with the performance of certain highly specialized agency functions. The following illustration shows a type of organization chart for a specialized-labor agency.

Agency Compensation. The advertising agency receives a commission for services it renders in preparing an advertisement, buying space, and following through to ensure that the advertisement is properly checked and edited before it appears. The usual commission rate is 15 percent; in outdoor advertising it is 16⅔ percent. (Other rates of commission are charged, but

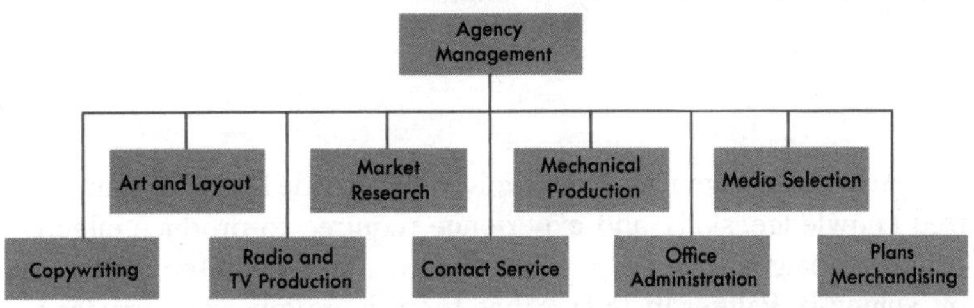

Organization chart for an advertising agency.

15 percent is virtually universal.) The advertiser pays the agency at the regular space rate, and the agency then deducts its commission and remits the balance to the medium. Technically, the agency receives its commission from the medium. For example, if the rate for a full page in a newspaper is $1,000, the commission paid the agency is $150. If the advertiser should place the order for this space directly, he still pays $1,000, assuming he has employed an agency. Hence, the advertiser enjoys no advantage when he bypasses the agency and deals directly with the medium in an attempt to save money.

The commission system has been under attack for many years by those who feel that the agency's clients, and not the media, should pay the agency for its services. There is no guarantee, of course, that a fixed percentage of the cost of the advertisement is an accurate reflection of the value of an agency's services. Moreover, on a fixed-percentage basis, the more the client spends, the higher the agency's fee; and this situation creates at least a suspicion that the agency has no real incentive to hold down the client's advertising costs.

Although most of the agency's income is derived from media commissions, it also charges the client for the cost of art work, engraving, research time in gathering facts about the market, and so forth. In the case of radio and television, the agency also charges the cost of talent. In addition to the actual cost of these services, the advertiser pays a service charge of 17⅔ percent. That is, the client is billed 17⅔ percent more for the work than the agency pays, and after the client takes the 2 percent discount from the gross bill, the service charge nets the agency 15 percent. This fee is not to be confused with the 15 percent commission paid by the media to the agency.

Advertising agencies have enjoyed a phenomenal growth in recent years. *Advertising Age* reports that there are about 4,200 agencies, including branches, doing business in the United States, and in 1966 their billings amounted to more than $5 billion. The term *advertising billings* refers to the amount of dollar business done by the agencies with the various media. Thus, if an agency placed $20 million with various media during the year, it "billed" $20 million. Its gross operating revenue, however, from this phase of its activities, totaled only $3 million.

ADVERTISING AS A CAREER

Advertising agencies have evolved to provide the chief source of specialized knowledge, skills, and experience required to produce effective advertising campaigns. The first agency of record in the United States was started by Volney B. Palmer in 1841. Since then the number of agencies has (as we have said) grown to over 4,200, employing about 65,000 people and serving nearly 16,000 clients. These agencies handle a volume of business (billings) estimated at slightly more than $5 billion. They have a gross income of approximately $800 million, but about two-thirds of this is paid out in salaries to employees who work in the agencies. The remaining third includes the cost of rent, taxes, traveling, supplies, and (hopefully) a reasonable profit.

Although some retailers employ the services of agencies, the bulk of retail advertising does not involve any advertising agency. Even large space-buyers such as department stores use advertising agencies on only a limited basis. And agencies seldom become involved in classified advertising.

Personal Qualifications Required

Since the services performed by advertising agencies vary from artistic skill to marketing research, it is somewhat difficult to be specific as to exactly which personal qualifications are generally required. These depend largely on the type of work to be performed. However, in addition to the qualifications ordinarily needed for a general career in business (as discussed in earlier chapters), there are at least four essential *personal* qualifications.

One personal qualification is the ability to create—to visualize and come forth with new ideas. It often helps to be an innovator. Another qualification is adaptability. The third is the ability to sell, and the fourth is patience. One who has studied college marketing, advertising, statistics, and other basic business-administration subjects has an advantage. And the study of written and oral communications is most essential if one has in mind an eventual position as an agency manager or accountant.

Positions in Advertising Agencies

All businesses strive to find ways to make work easier and more efficient. The most important fundamental procedure is of course the proper selection and assignment of personnel. Because large agencies tend toward a division of labor, qualified specialists are always in demand. Here is a brief description of positions commonly found in an advertising agency, and the qualifications needed for each.

Media Director. This person is responsible for selecting the best media for accomplishing the client's advertising purposes. He must be able to choose from among 1,600 daily newspapers, 800 weeklies, 900 consumer magazines and farm journals, 2,600 business and professional magazines, and 4,000 radio and 500 TV stations. These are in addition to outdoor signs, transportation advertising, and direct mail. All this requires that the director know a great deal about circulation, populations, audiences, rates charged, and classes of readers, viewers, or listeners presumed to use the medium involved.

Art-and-Layout Director. This individual, who must possess considerable art talent and skill, is mainly responsible for the quality of art work, which includes sketches, designs, drawings, and color selection. He confers with the client and with the account executive and others in the agency, to determine what is desired in the layout of the ad. There are some 3,000 art-and-layout directors in the United States. In many agencies, the positions of art director and layout director are separate, thus requiring two men to do the work.

Production Man. The production man is a specialist in all details of printing. His primary job is to keep the project—pamphlet, booklet, or ad—moving through the various processes. He is the equivalent of the radio or TV producer who supplies the story or format, performers, musicians, and others. All told, agencies employ about 1,000 production men. A smaller number work in publishing firms, for printers, and in various company advertising departments.

Copywriter. Often called the "idea man," the copywriter prepares the advertising copy—the message the advertiser wishes to present. In the final stages of copy preparation he works with various specialists, including the art-and-layout director and the account executive. Recent figures reveal that about 4,500 persons work in advertising agencies as copywriters. Another 2,000 are employed in the advertising departments of oil companies, department stores, manufacturing concerns, drug and food chains, and other retail outlets. You will find some of advertising's most imaginative minds in the field of copywriting.

Account Executive. This individual occupies one of the most important and "sensitive" positions in an agency: he is responsible for dealing with the client and keeping him satisfied with the agency's work. Besides being a creative person and a good salesman, the account executive must be familiar with business practices and have a working knowledge of marketing, merchandising, and advertising. Occasionally, an account executive will resign from an agency and start his own business, taking several clients with him. Little wonder that one of the qualities which an agency looks for when hiring an account executive is loyalty.

Researcher. Media decisions, creative problems, and advertising strategy often require a factual basis for executive action. The work of the researcher and his staff members is to ferret out facts about consumers, competitors, channels of distribution, and the public's buying habits. When an agency plans a campaign, either to promote a new product or to increase the sale of an old one, research experts are called on to make a comprehensive study of the market. About 1,000 researchers, trained in statistical methods, economics, report writing, and other business-administration programs, are currently working in agencies.

Merchandise Planner. The person who occupies this position is responsible for "developing" products for the client through the proper selection of middlemen to sell them. Many firms need a considerable amount of service from agencies when a new product is being offered to the public or to distributors.

Positions Outside of Advertising Agencies

Young men and women interested in careers in advertising need not work for an advertising agency. Many large companies employ their own advertising staffs. Among the positions they offer are director of advertising, market research analyst, media representative, and art-and-layout supervisor. And newspapers, magazines, outdoor advertising companies, radio and TV stations, and transportation companies employ salesmen to sell advertising space and time. For these latter positions, the ability to sell is often as important as a knowledge of advertising, marketing, and research.

Non-agency jobs in advertising are often obtained through college and university placement offices. Recruiters from business and industry visit colleges periodically, looking for men and women interested in an advertising career with companies other than advertising agencies.

Educational Requirements for an Advertising Career

The question is frequently asked: What is the best way to prepare for a career in advertising? As a general rule, for this purpose no single kind of educational background is superior to any other, neither will any particular one open the door to all positions in advertising. Those who want to do art work need a strong background in art. Educational requirements for other positions include preparation in English, history, psychology, economics, sociology, advertising, and statistics. And an applicant for a position is one jump ahead of the crowd if he has had good training in writing, speech, or research methods.

Today it is important for persons interested in advertising to get a good education beyond high-school. The American Association of Advertising Agencies ascertained from a recent survey that a large majority of the 56 agencies surveyed were inclined to favor candidates with a college degree. Many agencies and companies prefer *graduates* from colleges of business administration with sufficient general education to be assigned to any one of *several* positions.

Opportunities for Promotion

Advertising offers little room for mediocrity. It demands high-level hard work, and concrete results. And it rewards them: opportunities for advancement are excellent for persons with ability and "drive." In fact, there are few other businesses where talent (often a talent for getting things done) is so quickly recognized. Employers often transfer capable and conscientious employees from one job to another—sometimes to broaden their knowledge, sometimes as a promotion "up the ladder." Occasionally even a client will recognize an agency employee's ability and offer him a position as head of the client firm's own advertising department.

The highest level of employment you can reach in advertising is manager or owner of your own agency. Since advertising is essentially a service type of business, establishing an agency requires a relatively small capital investment, and subsequent growth is limited only by your own ability. Salaries in the higher-level positions are commensurate with those of persons of similar responsibility in business and industry.

SUMMARY

The general objective of advertising is to help a firm to achieve satisfactory levels of sales and profits by urging customers (1) to try a product for the first time, (2) to use it more frequently, (3) to buy it in larger quantities, and (4) to lengthen the buying season.

As a social force, advertising has altered living habits and has helped to raise living standards. Economically, it has promoted the growth of industry, helped to lower unit-costs, and served to identify in the minds of consumers families of products advertised under one name or brand.

The most popular advertising media are newspapers, radio and television, magazines, direct mail, and outdoor displays. Transportation advertising, specialties, and point-of-purchase displays are also effective, but are used less frequently. In choosing from among these media, the six basic factors that are commonly considered are: cost, extent of coverage, amount of selectivity, degree of flexibility, timeliness, and effectiveness.

On a cost-per-reader basis, newspaper advertising is expensive, but on a cost-per-prospect basis it is comparatively inexpensive. The total number of people that may be reached by a newspaper is greater than the number of copies circulated.

Newspaper advertising copy may be changed up to within a few hours of press time, thus assuring the advertiser a high degree of flexibility in presenting his message. Newspapers are widely read, but the average reading time is much less than that of magazines. Direct mail is the most selective medium, because it goes only to those persons considered good prospects.

Radio and television advertising reach large numbers of consumers at a comparatively low unit-cost, and are both highly flexible.

Outdoor advertising offers a great geographical selectivity, for it enables an advertiser to concentrate his message in any given locality. Transportation advertising is also suitable for appealing to local and regional markets, but it is selective only to the extent to which it is read by the riders. Transportation advertising is generally used to supplement local newspaper, radio, and television campaigns.

The chief value of specialty advertising is in reminding the user to patronize the firm whose name appears on the specialty article. Point-of-purchase advertising is designed to stimulate impulse buying.

Advertising copy is created to accomplish one of three objectives: the psychological objective, the institutional objective, or the marketing objective.

Every advertisement is based on a copy appeal. Among the most frequently used appeals are better health, increased income, improved appearance, financial security, relief from pain, and sex appeal. The copy appeal is meant to motivate the consumer to act.

The modern agency provides the advertiser (client) with all the important services needed to develop and place copy in the proper medium. The agency studies the client's product, analyzes his market, prepares the copy, helps select the media, and in general advises the client on his marketing problems. Agencies are staffed by copywriters, artists, layout men, production men, researchers, and media men.

As a career, advertising offers the young man or woman a variety of employment opportunities. The largest number of positions are in agencies and advertising departments of firms. Selling and writing experience, and a broad college education, provide excellent background for an advertising career.

VOCABULARY REVIEW QUIZ

Match the following vocabulary terms with the statements below.

a. Agate line
b. Alternate sponsor
c. Advertising medium
d. Poster
e. Point-of-purchase advertising
f. Classified advertising
g. Milline rate
h. Advertising billings
i. Impulse buying
j. Circulation guarantee
k. Product advertising
l. Consumer magazines
m. Advertising premiums
n. Advertising
o. Public relations

1. One type of advertising used to sell a product or family of related products by extolling their good qualities and uses
2. The communications channel used by advertisers to present their message
3. A form of local advertising more familiarly known as "want-ads"
4. A unit of space one column wide and 1/14" deep
5. A rate used by regional and national advertisers to make comparisons of advertising costs among several media, based on the cost-per-line method
6. A class of magazines published mainly for household consumers
7. A program sponsor who shares advertising time on TV with another sponsor
8. One form of outdoor advertising that uses a standardized structure 12′ high and 25′ long on which to place the message
9. A display mounted inside the store at the point where consumers make their purchases
10. A term that denotes purchasing based on sudden impulses
11. A term used to refer to the amount of total dollar business done by an advertising agency
12. A term, used by a publisher, implying that he will print and distribute a certain number of copies
13. A free item given in addition to one sold at the regular purchase price
14. A general term used to describe any paid form of nonpersonal presentation of goods, services, or ideas requiring the use of one or more media
15. A company policy designed to create a favorable image in the public's mind

QUESTIONS FOR REVIEW STUDY

1. Explain how advertising functions as a tool of marketing.
2. Contrast institutional advertising with industrial advertising.
3. What are the ways in which advertising serves business?
4. Do you concur with the critics who claim that there is too much waste in advertising?
5. Discuss what is being done by the advertising industry and by the federal government to keep advertising honest.
6. What are some of the advantages that a newspaper has over a magazine as an advertising medium?
7. What is the difference between milline rate, circulation guarantee, cost-per-thousand of circulation, and agate line?
8. Explain the advantages that TV advertising is considered to have over magazine advertising.
9. What are buying motives and how are they related to advertising copy?
10. What are the chief services rendered clients by advertising agencies?

PROBLEMS AND PROJECTS

1. Select from current magazines three advertisements for competing automobiles and underline the most important words used to describe them. Referring to these words, state in writing what you believe the copy appeal is in each advertisement, and describe the kind of mental picture each appeal created for you.
2. Prepare either a written or an oral report describing how the activities of one of the following organizations are related to advertising.

   The American Association of Advertising Agencies
   The Better Business Bureaus
   The Federal Trade Commission
   The National Association of Broadcasters
   The Standard Rate and Data Service

3. Which of the following newspapers is more reasonably priced for advertising?

Newspaper	*Line Rate*	*Circulation*
A	6¢	15,000
B	5¢	12,500

A BUSINESS CASE

Case 21-1 Tom Sawyer Peanut Butter

The Murdock Manufacturing Co., producer of a line of assorted jams, jellies, canned fruits, and (more recently) peanut butter, has enjoyed considerable success in the market. Their Tom Sawyer brand has been on the market only about 16 months. The other Murdock products have been popular for nearly two decades.

These products are sold in eight southern and southwestern states. The company's main plant is in Georgia. The complete line is sold through five large wholesale grocery companies and two large food brokers—one of the latter in Memphis, and the other in Denver. In five of its eight states the Murdock brand has had a distribution estimated to be 80 percent of all food stores. In the other three states the distribution has ranged from 55 to 70 percent of food stores. The Tom Sawyer brand, however, presently is sold in only about half of the retail outlets that carry the Murdock line of goods. This is both because the product is new and because the company has not previously engaged in any all-out advertising program for this brand. The officials feel it is time that something be done about either discontinuing the item or organizing an extensive advertising campaign.

Recently the five district sales supervisors met with the general sales manager and discussed the subject of how to improve sales of Tom Sawyer peanut butter. The group recommended that a special advertising budget be sought for the new product, and a few days later the general sales manager requested such a budget, in the amount of $300,000. The vice-president for finance shortly announced that $125,000 had been approved for the next year, subject to final approval by the advertising manager.

Although a majority of the Murdock executives supported the proposal to promote the peanut butter, feeling that the best way to increase sales of a specific item was to advertise so that customers would try the product, several objected to it. They were opposed to spending advertising funds on a single-line item, and also (somewhat on the other hand) argued that the appropriation was too small to make much of an impact on the peanut butter market, anyway.

If the company did decide to advertise Tom Sawyer peanut butter, decisions would have to be made as to how best to use the appropriation. For example, the company could run small ads in national magazines; it could buy short announcements on radio and television; it could develop point-of-sale posters; or it could buy space in trade papers. Another sales promotional plan might involve giving retail stores a special deal of one case free with every 10 cases purchased. This might encourage retailers to push the brand.

1. Should the Murdock company spend $125,000 advertising Tom Sawyer peanut butter?
2. If so, what kind of advertising campaign would you plan? With which medium or media would you spend the most money on advertising? Why?

Personal Selling and Sales Management

22

In the preceding chapters you learned that goods move through distinct marketing channels until they get to the ultimate consumer, and that each of the middlemen engaged in marketing distribution makes some kind of contribution to the flow of goods. The producer, for example, in his dealings with the consumer, may present his wares in a personal or in a nonpersonal manner. Personal presentations take the form of personal selling—salesmanship. Nonpersonal selling, as you know from your study of Chapter 21, may be presented by means such as advertising. In this chapter we shall deal with personal selling only, analyzing the salesman's role and the fundamental selling techniques he uses. We shall also survey the sales process and the work of the sales manager in the average large company.

In order to be successful, a firm must excel in all phases of marketing. And one of the most important phases of marketing is selling. It is generally agreed that effective selling affects our social standards and economic well-being in at least two ways: it stimulates the mass production of goods for wider distribution, and it is a desirable way to raise our standard of living.

But before we begin our discussion, we must first agree that it is the job of sales forces to see that the continuous stream of goods produced in our factories moves steadily through the various channels of distribution. In so doing, we will inevitably come to agree also that there is hardly any kind of venture that does not depend on salesmen. This may seem like a strong statement; but in a free economy such as ours, where people have the right to make a choice between one product and another, the salesman—as we shall see—can wield a direct and strong influence over consumers' choices.

WHAT IS PERSONAL SELLING?

Some people have the idea that salesmen perform a nonproductive role. This concept may have had some truth before the advent of mass production, when each consumer furnished most of his own needs. But with the rise in production rates that followed the application of nonhuman power to machines, producers soon discovered that they had a surplus of goods available to trade for other goods or services they lacked. In due time, this process of exchanging one product for another became so important that it provided not only a profitable, but a necessary component of business: selling.

The salesman has become an economic institution in our society. He conveys to the consumer information about his product or service. At the same time, he relays to his employer the demands of consumers. Although the salesman does not control the destiny of the market, he does play a vital marketing role by convincing the consumer to buy his goods. The personal salesman is indeed the link between the producer and the consumer.

Selling

When Emerson said "He is great who can alter my state of mind," he was in a sense speaking of the salesman. Definitions of selling and salesmanship vary widely: some call selling an art, others say it is a science. At any rate, most people agree that there are certain principles of salesmanship that can be taught the same as are those of any other activity taught as an academic discipline.

A simplified definition of *selling* calls it "The art of personal persuasion employed by the seller to induce others to buy what he wishes to sell."[1] *Salesmanship* is a broad term that includes the sales efforts of peddlers, retail clerks, telephone solicitors, and several other types of sales personnel. Sales-

[1] F. A. Russell, F. H. Beach, and R. H. Buskirk, *Textbook of Salesmanship*, 7th ed. (New York: McGraw-Hill Book Co., 1963), p. 13.

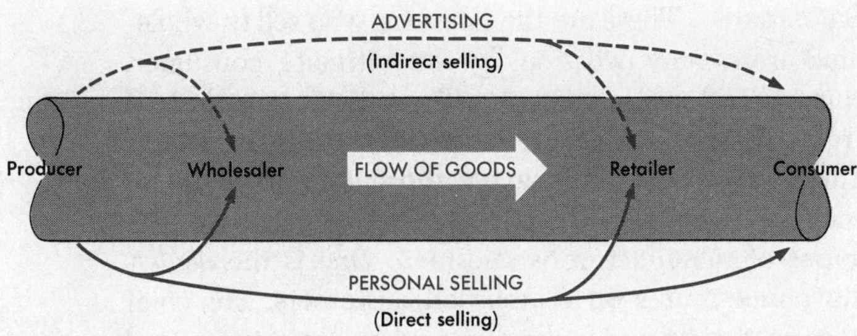

Personal selling and advertising expedite the flow of goods through the marketing channel, which involves—in most cases—the wholesaler and the retailer.

men in the "better" retail stores do not do clerks' work—that is, make change, wrap goods, etc.

Personal selling, the oldest and most important method of selling, is generally defined as *the activities of both the inside and outside salesmen involving direct contact of the seller with the buyer.* It is unique because it involves only a two-way communication of ideas between buyer and seller. It can take the form of house-to-house selling, as practiced by Fuller Brush Co. representatives; it may mean selling to manufacturers, jobbers, or purchasing agents; or it may involve across-the-counter selling, such as that practiced in retail stores. Regardless of its form, its immediate goal is the salesman's presentation of the product.

Advertising is very often used to introduce a new product to be sold through personal selling. The accompanying diagram illustrates the parallel relationship of advertising to personal selling in promoting the flow of merchandise through the channels of distribution. The combination of advertising and personal selling is often called the *merchandising mix.* The mix varies among firms: some companies emphasize advertising, while others use more personal selling.

Types of Personal Selling Jobs

According to the Census Bureau, about 4.5 million persons work directly in selling occupations. This is a ratio of one salesman to every 42 persons, considering the total population. Although the nature of these selling jobs varies widely, we can identify them for discussion purposes under five major headings: (1) manufacturers' salesmen, (2) wholesale salesmen, (3) retail salesmen, (4) specialty salesmen, and (5) door-to-door salesmen. In all of these selling jobs the object is to influence people's behavior through direct communication of facts about products and markets.

Manufacturers' Salesmen. These are the salesmen who sell to wholesalers, retailers, manufacturers, and occasionally the ultimate consumer. They usually sell machinery and semimanufactured products to industrial consumers, and as a rule the number of products each salesman sells is limited. The manufacturer's salesman must have a thorough knowledge of each item, including exactly how it may be used.

There are three types of manufacturer's salesmen. One is the *dealer-servicing salesman* who concentrates on established customers. His chief function is to call on these customers and make certain they are getting good service and that they understand how to use the product they are buying. Maintaining good customer relations helps to resell the product and assure more efficient use of it.

The second type is the *distribution-getting salesman.* His job is to convince wholesalers, dealers, and distributors that they should take on a new product his company has developed, and, perhaps, convince them that they should drop a competing line of goods.

The third type of manufacturer's salesman is the *merchandising man.* His job is to promote the use of his product among the jobbers who handle his goods. He meets frequently with jobber-salesmen and gives them ideas on ways to sell the merchandise his company produces. He also calls on local dealers to determine how much of his company's merchandise they are carrying in stock.

Wholesale Salesmen. The *wholesaler,* an important middleman who assembles merchandise in large quantities for redistribution in smaller amounts, must employ a highly effective sales staff. The alert wholesale salesman sees to it that retailers are well stocked with his brands of goods, that they are receiving satisfactory service, and that they are properly informed about the uses of these products.

Most wholesale selling is *low-pressure selling*—that is, selling based on the concept of service, with no attempt to use high-pressure techniques. Low-pressure salesmen obtain their business by being punctual, friendly, reliable, and ready at all times to extend special service.

Retail Salesmen. These are the persons from whom you buy merchandise over the counter in your favorite retail store. Retail selling differs from other types of selling in that the buyer seeks out the salesman instead of the salesman seeking out his prospect. The retail salesman must be familiar with a great many kinds of merchandise. In small stores, he is often required to demonstrate many kinds of articles and to explain their uses. In large retail establishments, salesmen usually specialize in selling the goods found only in one department. In either case, they must know how to handle people as well as how to present merchandise effectively.

Specialty Salesmen. Unlike the old-time "drummer" who carried his wares about the countryside in large trunks, the modern specialty salesman concentrates on selling one particular article—an adding machine, a typewriter, or a vacuum cleaner. This means that he must be thoroughly familiar with his merchandise and know precisely how it compares with competing products. And he must be able to explain to prospects how his product is manufactured and how it benefits its users.

In recent years many manufacturing companies have found that engineers trained in the mechanical, electrical, or chemical field make very successful specialty salesmen because of their highly specialized knowledge. The title "sales engineer" has actually come to replace the term "specialty salesman" in such industries as chemicals, machine tools, and electronics. Today's sales engineer is a highly trained specialty salesman qualified to serve as a counselor, trouble-shooter, and service representative.

Door-to-Door Salesmen. Some manufacturers who sell directly to consumers use door-to-door salesmen. As a rule, the items sold by these salesmen are the kind that require a more vigorous sales presentation than is normally made in regular retail outlets. The list of manufacturers that have used this form of personal selling is long, but the failure rate is high. Among the companies that have found this method of selling successful are the Wear-Ever Aluminum Co. and the Fuller Brush Co.

FUNDAMENTALS OF SALESMANSHIP

Although everyone in this country is a consumer of goods and services, not everyone is an active buyer. Some persons are confined to institutions, or to their homes with infirmities. Others are too young to make purchases. Someone else buys most, if not all of their goods. Most of the responsibility for today's family shopping falls on the housewife, although male members of the average household do buy some items. But regardless of who does the buying for whom, it is (as we shall shortly see) evident that the buyer is invariably motivated in one way or another to make certain purchasing decisions. Therefore, it is the responsibility of everyone who sells to understand as much as possible about buyers' motives.

What Motivates Buyers?

Psychologists have in recent years devoted a great deal of study to human behavior and its causes. Today, enlightened businessmen are also interested in the behavior of the individual—and not only for reasons of understanding what makes him buy. They want to know more about his behavior as a member of various groups that make up society. The shrewd salesman knows that "If you expect to sell John Doe what he wants, you must see things as John Doe does." So, in order to understand the consumer, we must endeavor to understand what motivates him to act.

Motivating Forces. Motivating forces may be innate (such as hunger, anger, fear, pleasure, and relief of pain), or they may originate within the environment and out of experience (for example, the desires for security and for achievement). The art of selling lies in the salesman's ability to sense the customer's motives (reasons) for wanting the product, and to present his product in such a manner that it appeals to one or more of these.

Some Common Buying Motives

We have seen that buying motives based on psychological drives are the underlying reasons why consumers purchase certain goods. Motives may be classified as either *emotional* or *rational*, and it is important to understand the distinctions between them.

Emotional motives are the result of impulsive, often illogical, subjective reactions. Included among these motives are pleasure, fear, and the desires for security, recognition, and superiority.

Rational motives are stimuli produced by a logical reasoning process. If a product is bought only after all the advantages and disadvantages have been considered, the buying may be said to be rationally motivated. Among the more common rational motives are the desires for economy, dependability, durability, quality, and a fair price.

In personal selling as well as in advertising, specific motives are used to persuade prospects. (Although a single buying motive may be important, it is not uncommon for both rational *and* emotional motives to be involved in a buying decision.) Motives are easier to understand if we have some orderly method of analyzing them. The following brief analysis of emotional and rational motives should explain how they are used in selling.

Pleasure. The rather common emotional buying motive of *pleasure* is what prompts many people to make certain purchases of goods and services. Sellers of such tangible products as musical instruments, sporting equipment, television sets, and radios use this motive to convince people of the joy they will receive from these products. Travel agencies in particular find that the desire for pleasure is a strong selling-point.

Fear. Much buying is motivated out of fear of one thing or another. This motive takes many forms. There is the form of fear of losing one's job. Another is fear of loss of life, health, or property. There is fear of social disapproval. Insurance salesmen show prospects how insurance can be used to eliminate financial fears associated with loss of health or life. Automobile tires are sold on the basis of relieving fear through the purchase of tires that will reduce accidents. Advertisers use fear of social disapproval as an appeal to sell mouthwash, toothpaste, and deodorants. As people grow older, the motive of fear naturally becomes stronger. There is a tendency of older people to build up greater security for their retirement by buying more stocks and bonds or putting more money in the bank.

Economy. Few consumers have all the income they need or would like. To buy the most possible with their incomes, most people are highly motivated by appeals to economy. Even wealthy people look for savings. The economy appeal is often used to induce the consumer to buy in larger quantities and save. Cut-rate drug stores and discount houses owe their existence to this buying motive. The economy appeal is indeed one of the most important rational buying motives.

Dependability. Another strong rational motive is the desire for dependability. The consumer wants to know what built-in qualities the product has that will give it longer life and greater dependability. This question is often asked about automobile tires and batteries. Many manufacturers, recognizing how important this motive is, will provide factory and dealer warranties on appliances, automobiles, furniture, carpets, and other durable goods to prove to the consumer that the product has guaranteed dependability backed up by repair- or replacement-service.

The Steps in Making a Sale

Despite the fact that there are different types of selling jobs, and numerous motives used in making a sale, selling may be broken down into specific steps on which the heart of the sales presentation is based. Although these steps cannot always be timed precisely, nor sharply distinguished from one another, they most often occur in the following order:

1. Locating the prospective customer
2. Obtaining the prospect's attention
3. Arousing the prospect's interest
4. Developing the prospect's desire for the product
5. Closing the sale

Locating the Prospective Customer. There are many products and services whose first sales step involves locating prospective customers. Usually, a considerable amount of initiative and originality is needed by the salesman in this initial step of the selling function. In selling life-insurance, for example, flushing out the prospect can be disappointingly difficult. But, as insurance sales figures show, "difficult" does not mean "impossible."

Obtaining Attention. The act of obtaining the prospect's attention is obviously the first thing the salesman must accomplish. Before a person can be aroused, it is necessary to get him to listen. Various devices are used to accomplish this step. Door-to-door salesmen use a sales "opener" to gain attention—a catchy phrase, a startling question, an offer of a free sample.

Arousing Interest. Arousing the prospect's interest is often even more difficult than gaining his attention. Moreover, the holding of his interest may depend on the effectiveness with which the salesman amplifies his original interest-arousing approach. Any of several methods may be used to arouse the buyer's interest; the following illustration is typical.

A salesman has experienced difficulty in getting an appointment with a buyer, but is finally admitted to the prospect's office. The prospect hardly looks up from his desk, however, and goes right on with his paperwork. "I'll be with you in a minute," he says. "Go ahead, I'm listening." Sensing that he does not have the buyer's undivided attention, the salesman replies "Well sir, I'd hate to interrupt you—if you're too busy to discuss this now, would you tell me when I might come back and see you again?" A remark of this sort, made in the proper tone, will in many cases produce the desired results. Better later than never.

Developing the Desire to Buy. The salesman's presentation gradually unfolds until it reaches the point where he brings the full force of his selling ability to bear on the buyer. If he is successful, the buyer becomes convinced that he needs the article or service, and that he should buy it. Here is the real core of selling, and the most difficult part to develop. If the sales presentation is convincing, the sale is practically made, and all that is left is to close it. But some salesmen lose sales because they block the prospect's desire to buy, by talking too long. They "oversell" the prospect and give him a chance to say, "I'll think it over and let you know when my mind is made up." Oversold prospects rarely call back.

Closing the Sale. The good salesman recognizes the precise moment at which the customer reaches a decision, and closes the sale promptly. This may be done by offering the customer a pencil or pen to sign the sales ticket or contract, or by actually wrapping the goods. If the sale is to be charged to the customer's account, the salesman prepares a sales slip and asks, "When shall we deliver your purchase?"

A good salesman studies his prospect carefully and discovers which technique will be most effective in closing the sale. For example, he finds out how the customer wishes to pay for the article, and then moves along smoothly to the right closing technique without offending his customer.

One sales manual of instructions says this about closing a sale:

1. When your prospect begins to pause in making the final decision, this is the time to step in and close.
2. Watch your prospect's facial expression. If the prospect indicates by a smile or a twinkle of the eye that she is pleased with the article, then get out your order book.
3. Listen to the prospect's voice; if there is a slight inflection or a raising or lowering of tone, this is your tip to make your closing remarks.

Some Selling Techniques

The ability to sell depends on the use of numerous techniques, and many pages would be required to explore all of them in detail. However, among those that are often mentioned as essential for successful salesmanship are these:

1. *A successful salesman knows his product and what it can do for his customer.* Without an understanding of his product, the salesman is unable to fit the right product to the prospect's needs. *With* that understanding, however, the salesman is never at a loss to emphasize the strong points that are needed to clinch the sale and bring it to a close. A knowledge of his product also enables the salesman to answer questions and meet objections raised by the customer.

2. *A good salesman is able to size up his customer.* Every customer is different from every other customer in some respect, and the salesman must discover early in his sales presentation the prospect's likes and dislikes as well as his needs. He is alert to his customer's reactions, as indicated by facial expressions and body movements. When he discovers that he is not communicating effectively with his prospect, the skillful salesman shifts his appeal tactfully and easily. For example, a salesman who is trying to sell a deluxe-model automobile observes that his prospect's interest is slipping away; immediately he shifts his customer's attention to a lower-priced car that he is better able to afford, enabling him to avoid any embarrassment about his ability to pay.

3. *A positive approach is more effective than a negative approach.* The salesman is more effective when he says, "May I show you our new line of electric clocks?" than when he says, "You wouldn't like to see our new line of electric clocks, would you?" The negative approach makes it easy for the buyer to say "No," while the positive approach carries with it a power of suggestion that creates interest. Another manifestation of the positive approach is to allow the buyer to talk freely in describing his wants. The alert salesman does not do all the talking.

4. *The wise salesman uses praise judiciously.* Some authorities state that praise is one of the salesman's least-developed resources. Praise costs little but often returns huge dividends. One type of approach of this kind is to compliment the prospective buyer for his desire to own the product the salesman is selling, and another approach is to point out how much the product will add to the prospect's pride, personality, or appearance. As a sales technique, praise should be used judiciously—otherwise, the customer will interpret it as false flattery.

By this time, you must be aware that the art of personal selling varies with each type of sale; there is a wide difference between the selling techniques used by a retail-clothing salesman and a manufacturer's representative selling a mechanical air-compressor. Nevertheless, in *all* forms of personal selling, there are at least two qualities that make a good salesman. First, the salesman must at all times display a genuine interest in his client's needs. This means he must render a distinct personal service to his customer by selling him the kind of product that best meets his requirements. Second, a good salesman does not high-pressure his customer into buying an article, knowing full well it is not the right product. Instead, the salesman should endeavor to learn what the prospect's needs are.

Nonselling Duties of Salesmen

Most salesmen are known to perform such duties other than those involved in personal selling, as traveling to the prospect's address, waiting for personal interviews, completing required records for home-office management, locating potential customers via the telephone, and responding to service calls or requests for information. Manufacturers' and wholesalers' salesmen are often required to perform a wider variety of nonselling duties than are door-to-door salesmen. Usually, this is because salesmen representing manufacturing concerns and wholesale houses must maintain detailed records of all customers these establishments serve, including names of buyers and purchasing agents, etc. Door-to-door salesmen operate on a different plan.

The following diagram shows approximate average percentages of time spent by salesmen in selling and nonselling duties.

In retailing, salesmen perform other duties in addition to selling. These include pricing and displaying stock, preparing sales tickets, making adjustments on unsatisfactory merchandise, and collecting credit information. In some retail establishments, salesmen help to stock the shelves, and assist in making inventories. It is obvious that salesmen must know far more than just how to sell effectively.

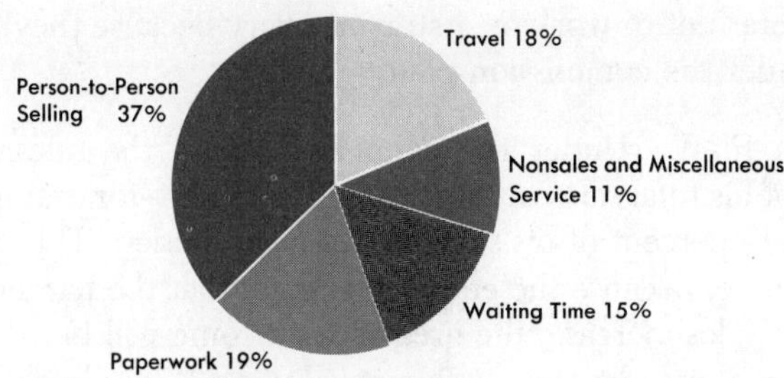

How the average wholesaler's and manufacturer's salesman spends his working time.

COMPENSATING SALESMEN

Business and industry use a variety of ways to compensate salesmen, but they all break down into three broad plans based on five basic factors. These factors are: straight-salary or time-wages; commission or piece-rate; profit sharing; bonus for above-average service; and reimbursement for expenses. The type of plan used depends largely upon the type, size, and financial condition of the business, and upon various factors relating to the ability of, and the owner's attitude toward, its sales staff.

Plans of Compensation

The three most commonly used plans for paying salesmen are *straight salary* with expenses, *straight commission* without expenses, and *salary and commission combined,* without expenses. In some companies you may find a variation in the application of expenses.

The Straight-Salary Plan. This plan, which compensates the salesman with a fixed amount of income regardless of his sales volume, is often preferred by the beginning salesman, for it gives him an assured income which may be more than he is actually worth as a beginner. In many cases it gives even the experienced salesman a sense of financial security. Moreover, it allows the business to exercise more control over what the salesman does during his working hours, especially where the work is largely routine and he can be assigned other duties when not engaged in selling. From the standpoint of the employer, the straight-salary plan is simple, and easy to administer.

Perhaps the main disadvantage of this plan is that it provides little incentive for a salesman to work harder: he knows in advance how much he will earn regardless of how hard he tries to increase his sales. (Generally, of course, his salary will increase in keeping with his effectiveness.) Many experienced salesmen prefer not to work on a straight salary because they feel they can earn more under the commission plan.

The Commission Plan. Under the commission plan the salesman receives a percentage of his total sales in return for his service—for example, his commission may be 5 percent of his sales over a given period. This plan provides a strong incentive, because the employee knows that the harder he works and the more his sales increase, the greater his income will be.

A man working on a straight commission usually is not so closely attached to his firm as the man on straight salary. His object may be to make quick sales that will bring him immediate returns, rather than to promote the company's reputation by rendering special services. Young salesmen just beginning their careers tend to dislike this plan, for they lack experience and are not entirely certain of their ability to sell.

The straight-salary and commission plans are compared in the following diagram. Notice that as sales volume increases, it becomes more profitable to work on commission than on straight salary.

Salary and Commission Combined. Often the most satisfactory arrangement—for both the company and the salesman—is a combination of the two plans discussed above. For instance, the salesman may receive, as salary, enough to cover his living expenses, and then receive a commission on all he sells beyond a specified amount. The commission serves as a stimulus to urge him to work harder. Some companies pay a *bonus*, in addition to the normal compensation, on the basis of the number of new accounts a salesman acquires, or on the basis of a certain number of sales above a fixed quota. A bonus is actually an added commission for achieving a special goal.

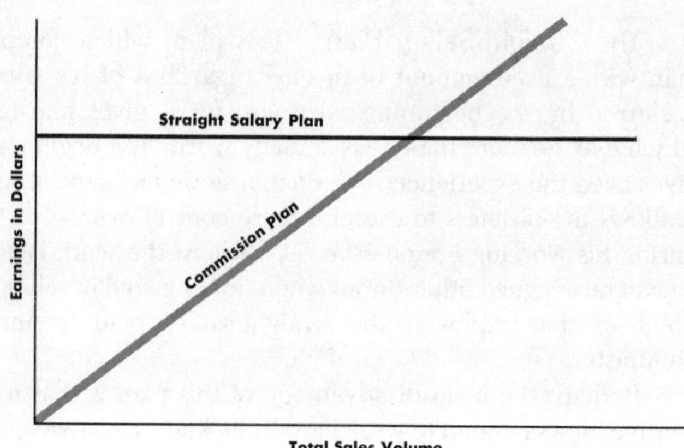

A comparison of two plans of compensation for salesmen.

SALES MANAGEMENT

Sales management is that part of a business organization responsible for management of two broad areas of selling and marketing: the personal selling function, and other marketing promotion activities. In some businesses, the term is synonymous with a newer term, *marketing management*.

In the area of personal selling, one of the important contributions of the sales manager is to provide sales leadership. This includes responsibility for the recruitment, selection, training, assignment, supervision, and general motivation of the sales staff. In some firms the personnel department performs part of this function, but in most larger companies other than retailing firms, it is a part of sales management's responsibility.

The trend in recent years has been in the direction of sales managers' exercising responsibility for the performance of virtually all marketing activities related to sales promotion. This includes sales budgeting, advertising, market research, product policies, and, occasionally, credit extension and product transportation.

Basic Functions of Sales Management

The basic functions of sales management fall into three general classifications: *administrative, operating,* and *staff functions.* Since each of these is intimately related to the over-all sales operation, only when all three are performed efficiently does the sales organization operate as an effective team. A discussion of these functions follows.

Administrative Functions. The administrative functions performed by sales executives encompass the following activities: formulating sales policies; organizing and planning the work of the salesmen; coordinating the activities of the sales department with other departments in the total operation; designating responsibilities; delegating authority; discovering new markets; planning products; analyzing competition; contracting salesmen; planning public-relations activities; and issuing communications.

Operating Functions. Operating functions differ from administrative sales management functions in that the former are related more to the actual work of selling the product, and the direct supervision of the sales force. Operating functions are performed by supervisors, the salesmen themselves, and branch executives at the operating level. These functions include such activities as recruiting, selecting, and training; conducting sales meetings; determining sales routes; reporting on sales operations; coordinating advertising and sales operations; and providing information about product service to salesmen for dissemination to customers.

Staff Functions. The various staff functions in a sales organization are generally directed toward providing the administrative staff with vital information useful for planning. These functions involve the following: planning sales campaigns, making sales analyses and cost studies, and developing specialized promotional plans for increasing sales.

In small companies, many of these three classes of functions are not actually performed by separate divisions of the sales management organization. Instead, they are the responsibility of the general sales manager, who may delegate some to subordinates. The functions of modern sales management are pretty much alike in all business. Usually, any differences are those of detail or special emphasis along certain lines.

Types of Sales Organizations

Fundamentally, the activities in which sales managers engage are similar in all types of businesses. Certain differences do appear, however, in the size of the actual sales organization and the manner in which it is set up. A manufacturer's sales staff, for example, must cope with different problems from those, say, of a retailer's sales staff, and sellers of industrial goods need a different organization from that used by sellers of services. Despite these variations, there are two basic types of sales-organization plans: *organization for direct selling,* and *organization for selling to middlemen.* Let us examine the differences as well as the similarities of these two types of organizations for selling to middlemen.

Organizations for Direct Selling. Sales organizations that sell directly to the consumer or user, eliminating the wholesaler and retailer, are known as *direct-sales organizations*. In this type of organization, all the selling functions and operations are concentrated in a single department, with a single head responsible to a higher level of management. Authority and responsibility are delegated on a line or functional plan of organization similar to that which you studied in Chapter 7.

In the following organization chart, observe how the various components are related in the direct-selling organization. The general sales manager is in charge of the organization, having authority to delegate to subordinate managers certain authority and responsibility appropriate to each position. For example, the advertising manager in charge of all advertising activities works directly under him. The sales manager also supervises the organization's retail salesmen.

Organizations Involving Middlemen. These organizations make their sales through independent jobbers and retailers. There may be many variations in their organizational setup, because of the different middlemen

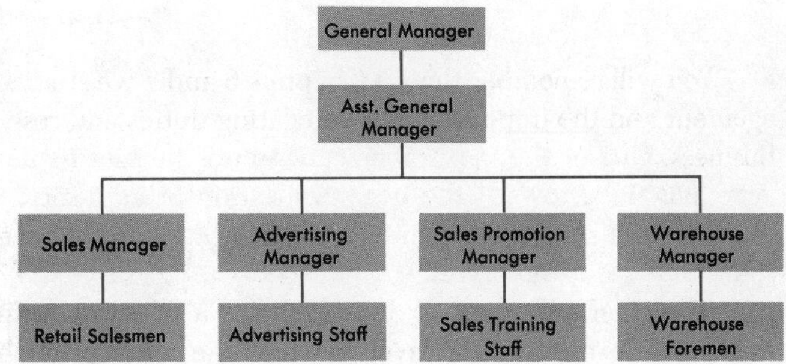

A line-plan sales organization for direct selling (producer to user).

involved and the different relationships between the manufacturer and the middlemen engaged in the distribution of goods and services.

The following chart shows that the line organization extends only to the jobbers and retailers. In other words, company salesmen have no contact with consumers. Instead, they deal solely with middlemen—the jobbers and retailers who make the final sale to the consumers. The success of this plan depends largely on how efficient a job is done in selling the goods, for the more the middleman sells, the more he buys from the producer. Notice the broken lines, which indicate that the salesmen exercise no direct control over the jobbers and retailers. This type of sales organization is generally believed to be the most common channel of distribution for manufactured consumer goods, mainly because of the services the middlemen perform for consumers.

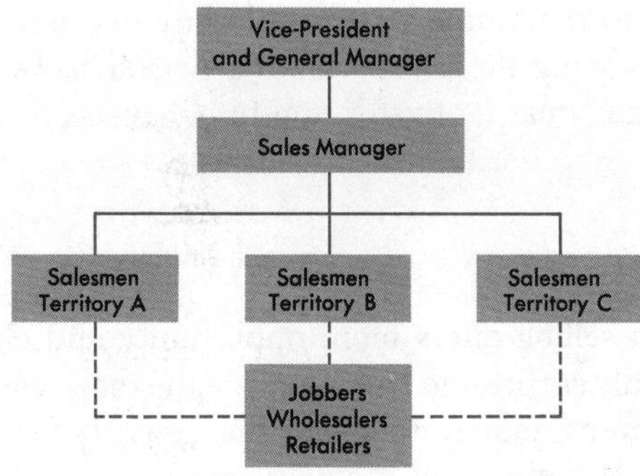

A line-plan sales organization involving middlemen—jobbers, wholesalers, and retailers.

Trends in Sales Management

You will remember that in Chapters 6 and 7 we studied the role of management and the importance of delegating duties and responsibilities in any business. One of the most significant trends in sales management in recent years has been toward the decentralization of authority. Many companies are decentralizing management by delegating greater authority and responsibility to lower levels.

The chief advantage of decentralizing a sales organization is that it permits more flexibility at the level on which the actual problems arise. This permits those in charge at this level to act immediately on local problems without first conferring with a higher authority. Among other things, it enhances the organization's ability to meet competition.

Decentralization also helps eliminate duplication of functions at several levels, and consequently helps conserve manpower. Moreover, it relieves top management of many burdensome details, and promotes the development of greater managerial ability.

In the area of recruiting and selecting salesmen, the trend is toward more extensive use of psychological tests to evaluate the applicant's ability. Most large companies have for a long time used psychological tests for employee selection. Now many medium and small companies have adopted this technique.

Another trend in sales management is in the direction of increased use of market research to get the facts about business environment and marketing problems. The concept is gaining acceptance that it is possible to plan marketing activities just as it is to plan production, provided marketing managers have accurate information with which to make these plans. A recent development in decision-making in marketing is the application of the psychological tool called *motivation* (or *motivational*) *research*, which is scientific inquiry to find the hidden or subconscious reasons for consumer behavior—in particular, to determine why people buy one brand or product instead of another. Knowing the social values a person seeks furnishes the means for understanding what motivates him to behave as he does.

SELLING AS A CAREER

Today a career in selling offers more opportunity and challenge than ever before. This is hardly surprising. If we analyze the facts, we will find that this country now has more money to spend than ever before because the personal income level is higher and includes more people. This nation is growing at the rate of more than 8,000 people per day, whose needs and wants must be satisfied by intelligent selling. We have long enjoyed a high living standard, and are accustomed to wanting the latest in technological advances, the most recent electronic miracles, more home comforts, and additional labor-saving devices. America demands the latest and the best, and, as a result, salesmen profit.

Vocational Considerations

A good salesman is rarely without employment. Also, for him every day is different; selling is not a monotonous occupation but one that offers stimulating, challenging, and interesting experiences.

Based on average compensation, personal selling is the best remunerated of all business professions and occupations. Moreover, the rise to high-level compensation is more rapid for successful salesmen than for persons in any other form of employment.

Selling is a stepping-stone to other careers in business; many of today's most successful executives began their careers as salesmen in retailing, manufacturing, or wholesaling. Famous Americans like Marshall Field, J. C. Penney, John Wanamaker, Charles Walgreen, H. J. Heinz, Harvey Firestone, and Walter P. Chrysler worked as salesmen, then launched their own businesses to achieve national recognition as outstanding executives.

Personal Qualifications

What is it that makes one salesman superior and another mediocre? Are there special personal traits which seem to make for success in selling? Research on this subject indicates that while certain so-called "success characteristics" do exist, there are some personal traits which seem to be universal as prerequisites for success in personal selling.

Universal Traits. Personal traits that seem to be universal among good salesmen are: (1) an interest in selling as a career; (2) the willingness to work hard on the job; (3) a strong personal desire to succeed; (4) a positive and enthusiastic attitude toward the job; (5) resourcefulness and imagination; (6) patience; and (7) tact. While it may be argued, and rightfully so, that these are useful traits that any person in business *should* have, there is substantial evidence that a salesman is not likely to be successful unless he *does* have them.

Selling is difficult work—much more so than many other types of endeavor. Because it often causes much mental strain and drains the energy, it requires a strong mind and a vigorous body. When a salesman demonstrates that he possesses a high degree of intelligence and a quick perception into problem situations, he is likely to be offered a more responsible job with a higher salary.

Opportunities for College Graduates. It is common for both large and small firms to seek college graduates for personal selling jobs. For example, a company selling chemical products very often employs a chemistry major for selling positions. Engineering or technological training provides a good background for sales engineers to work with manufacturers. The term "sales engineer" is used where the products are highly technical and require both engineering knowledge and sales ability. Many firms employ business-administration graduates for selling positions. Usually, however, they like their salesmen to have a background in marketing, management, finance, accounting, and advertising.

SUMMARY

There are two main methods by which goods are sold: advertising, and personal selling. Personal selling involves an oral presentation by the seller to his prospect. This type of selling includes manufacture-, wholesale-, retail-, specialty-, and door-to-door selling.

The five steps in selling are: (1) locating the prospect, (2) obtaining his attention, (3) arousing his interest, (4) developing his desire for the product, and (5) closing the sale. While each of these steps represents an activity in itself, they blend together to form the total sales effort.

The ability to sell depends on the use of numerous techniques. For example, a salesman should know his product and what it can do for his customer. This technique enables the salesman to fit the right product to the prospect's needs. A good salesman is able to size up his customer, including his likes and dislikes as they are related to his product needs.

It is more effective to use a positive than a negative approach in talking with a customer about his interests. Also, the wise salesman uses praise judiciously. One kind of praise is in complimenting the prospect on his desire to own the product the salesman is selling. Another kind is in associating the product with the prospect's personality or appearance.

Sales training is a prerequisite to successful selling. When properly trained, the salesman knows how to approach his customer, how to size him up, how to present his product or service, and how to apply certain techniques to appeal to the customer.

Although selling offers rich opportunities, and is a stepping-stone to other careers, it is a career that involves long hours and hard work. On the other hand, remuneration is generally based on the individual's ability and willingness to work. The three most common plans for paying salesmen are the straight-salary plan, the commission plan, and a combination of the two.

In recent years there has been a significant trend in sales management toward the decentralization of authority. Executives at lower levels of sales management are being assigned more authority to make managerial decisions. Another trend is the practice of making greater use of market research techniques in solving sales management problems.

VOCABULARY REVIEW QUIZ

Match the following vocabulary terms with the statements below.

a. Commission plan
b. Bonus
c. Distribution-getting salesman
d. Low-pressure selling
e. Merchandising man
f. Personal selling
g. Sales management
h. Salary and commission combined
i. Selling
j. Straight-salary plan

1. The activity of getting the buyer to accept the product being sold by the seller
2. The activities of both the inside salesman and outside salesman involving direct contact of the seller with the buyer
3. A salesman who has the job of convincing wholesalers, dealers, and merchandising men they should take on a new product for their company to sell
4. One who promotes the use of his product among jobbers
5. Selling based on the concept of service
6. A salary plan based on a fixed amount per month regardless of total sales volume
7. Compensation paid on the basis of a percentage of the total sales dollar
8. A term synonymous with marketing management
9. A plan for paying salesmen based on a fixed amount plus an added sum based on a percentage of sales
10. An added commission for achieving a special goal

QUESTIONS FOR REVIEW STUDY

1. Analyze the difference between personal selling and advertising.
2. In what ways does effective selling affect our social and economic well-being?
3. What is "low-pressure selling" as it relates to wholesale selling?
4. How does personal selling by manufacturers' salesmen differ from personal selling by wholesale or retail salesmen?
5. Explain the steps in making a sale, in the order in which they normally occur.
6. What is meant by the statement, "A positive approach is more effective than a negative approach"?
7. What are the factors that determine the method of compensating salesmen?
8. In what way or ways are the personal traits of a successful salesman different from the personal traits of persons successful in other occupations?

9. How do operating functions differ from administrative functions in a sales management position?
10. In your opinion, what are the most important personal traits a salesman must have? Rank them in their order of importance and explain the reasons for your ranking.

PROBLEMS AND PROJECTS

1. The Elsworth Air Conditioning Co., which has a factory in Atlanta and one in New Orleans, and its main office in Memphis, has just completed tests on a new home air-conditioner. This machine controls the humidity, cleans and purifies the air, and, since it also has a built-in heating unit, regulates the temperature. It will sell at retail in the neighborhood of $50 for the 1-hp unit and $90 for the 2½-hp unit. The latter unit is large enough to handle a room containing 1,500 square feet of space. A 5-hp unit will cost about $125 retail. For the present, the company plans to sell these units direct through door-to-door salesmen. Describe some of the buying motives the company salesmen can use in their sales presentations.
2. You have just been appointed sales manager of a new office to be opened in Chicago. Your company sells, through retailers, a fairly new product called "Clean-Rite," which is used on windows, porcelain, and enamel. It can be applied with a brush, cloth, or sponge. The company plans to introduce this product with a concentrated newspaper and television program. It will be your job to recruit and train 15 salesmen to call on retail outlets. Draw up a list of qualifications you think your men should have.
3. When he calls at homes, an encyclopedia salesman represents himself as a marketing analyst making an educational survey. After he is admitted to the home, he asks a few questions about the number of children in the family, their ages, and what schools they have attended. Then he starts his sales message on his product. If you were one of these salesmen, state how you would present your sales message, and what points you would emphasize.

A BUSINESS CASE

22-1 International Office Machines Company's Plan for Compensating their Salesmen

The International Office Machines Co. is a well-established manufacturer of electric adding machines. The company has one plant in the United States and two in Japan. In the United States the company employs 1,900 salesmen, all of whom work on a commission plan, assigned to 200 branch offices.

For the past year the company's present compensation plan for salesmen has been under study. During the past four years the general growth of the company, accompanied by increased advertising expenditures, has resulted in a substantial increase in the ratio of sales to calls made by salesmen. For this reason, the vice-president of sales decided that a study of compensation plans for all company salesmen in the United States should be made. A committee of four company officials, with the vice-president of sales as its chairman, was appointed by the president to make a recommendation.

Under the present plan, salesmen are paid a salary of $300 per month, plus a commission on sales. The commission is based on a point system computed on a basis of one point for each $30 in sales. For the first 50 points the salesmen receive $2 per point commission; for the next 50 points, $4 per point; and $6 for all points in excess of 100. The price list for all new machines for each of the four sales models is shown following in Schedule A:

SCHEDULE A

Models	*Prices*	*Points*
A	$1,000	30
B	800	25
C	600	20
D	450	15

For the last 24 months the salesmen have averaged sales of 10 machines per month, with the result that their salaries have averaged over $14,500 per year. A current study shows that this is about $3,500 above the salary level of salesmen from the two largest competing firms. Schedule A was originally based on a minimum sales of five machine-sales per month, averaging 20 points per machine. Later, a Model D machine was added to the line at 15 points per machine which reduced the minimum average points from 20 to 15 per machine.

The company also offers fringe benefits, including $10,000 convertible life insurance paid by the company, and a retirement fund to supplement social security enough to bring combined monthly retirement income up to $500 after 30 years of service.

The following schedule is proposed for study and analysis to replace Schedule A.

SCHEDULE B

Models	*Prices*	*Points*
A	$1,000	3
B	800	2
C	600	1.5
D	450	1

Under Schedule B, salesmen would receive $50 per point for total sales, and in addition would be paid a bonus of $600 if total quarterly sales exceeded 54 points. An analysis indicates that the average salesman would earn about 15 points per month. About one-fourth would receive a bonus each quarter.

Under this proposed plan, the $300 monthly salary would be eliminated. In its place would be a $350 monthly advance (draw) on commissions. And the company would continue to pay mileage of 8¢ per mile on individually-owned automobiles used by salesmen.

Two of the four officials on the committe have recommended this new plan, but no decision has been made as yet by the other two officials.

1. You are asked to study and evaluate this new plan, comparing it with the existing one. Compute the monthly commission on 12 machines, at an average selling price of $600 per model, under Schedules A and B. Make the same comparison under both plans, placing the average salesman's monthly sales at 15 machines, at an average selling price of $800 per machine.
2. Does Schedule B offer more or less incentive than Schedule A?
3. Explain your recommendations as to choice of plans that should be adopted.

Transportation and Physical Distribution

23

So far in our study of marketing we have examined its place in the national economy, and have traced the various distribution channels used to market industrial and consumer goods. We have also evaluated the role and contributions of advertising and sales management. Now we shall consider in detail a subject, basic to all aspects of marketing, which we have touched upon often, but only lightly, in the past: transportation and physical distribution. (For reasons which will shortly become evident, we shall consider the combination of these singular terms to be a single subject.)

We have seen the high degree to which both production and marketing have become specialized. This specialization could not be maintained without an efficient and orderly physical-distribution setup which provides for the *systematic* movement of goods from place to place. In this chapter we shall focus upon the *systems* concept of physical distribution, the significance of transportation services to the smooth operation of all businesses, and the different methods of transportation commonly employed. We shall also look at warehousing, leasing, and the federal regulation of transportation companies.

There are several different components which, functioning together, constitute physical distribution. Determination of the makeup of the shipment is the first element. This includes the minimum and maximum number of units to be shipped, and the size and nature of the package in which the goods are transported. The next element is the selection of a transport medium and a specific carrier. The other components are materials-handling, warehousing, inventory control, and order-processing. Although we can list these as separate components, it must be emphasized that all must be integrated into a well-coordinated system and must not be permitted to function as a fragmented series of operations. Decision-making in each area must be related to choices made in the other areas. For example, the location of the warehouse may in large measure determine the quality of transport facilities available. And the choice of a carrier may influence the most desirable unit-size of package to be shipped, and vice-versa.

The systems concept of physical distribution and transportation means that the movement of materials into the plant (warehouse or store), movement and handling within the plant, and the movement of finished goods from the plant, all are organized into systematic, coordinated flow. This concept makes it possible for the marketing manager to see his work from the viewpoint of the user of the goods as well as that of the seller. He can even study the handling and movement of goods by means of flow-charts. This concept focuses attention on the relationships between transportation expenses and warehousing expenses, and makes it less likely that savings effected in one area will cause increases in the other. The systems concept also means that one must strive for a balance between distribution costs and customer utility. It may be that a slightly higher freight-cost, because of using air transportation, would make money for the firm by generating greater customer satisfaction and repeat business.

An example which illustrates the systems concept is that of the Armour Pharmaceutical Co. This company discovered that the use of air freight was so much faster than other types of transport services that fewer distribution centers were needed to serve its customer territory. In fact, the number of warehouses was reduced to those in a single distribution center. The increased cost of air transportation was returned to the company through other savings that were effected. The stock inventory requirements were cut in half as well, and major reductions in packaging costs, in interest, and in insurance expenditures also followed.[1]

[1] George M. Shutes, "Airfreight from a Marketing Viewpoint," *Journal of Marketing*, October, 1960, p. 41.

THE ECONOMIC IMPORTANCE OF PHYSICAL DISTRIBUTION

In Chapter 19 we noted that the total marketing function accounts for approximately 50 percent of the price of goods. Similarly, the various components of physical distribution account for approximately half the total cost of marketing. (It should be understood that this is a rough estimate because the cost of physical distribution, like all other marketing costs, varies from industry to industry.) And, a recent survey made by *Distribution Age* indicates that physical-distribution costs for manufacturing enterprises account for approximately one-fourth of the sales price.[2] Specific figures reported are shown in the accompanying table.

TABLE 23.1

PHYSICAL DISTRIBUTION COSTS*

Industry	Percentage of Sales
Chemicals, Petroleum, and Rubber	26
Food Machinery	34
Machinery	11
Paper	20
Primary Metals	33
Textiles	16
Wood Products	17

* Includes warehousing, materials handling, transportation, and shipping costs.

It should be obvious from a reading of this table that in order to effect any real economies in marketing costs one must bring about increased efficiency in the various aspects of physical distribution.

The Transportation Labor Force

In 1945, approximately 3.2 million persons were employed in transportation in the United States. Today the figure is down to about 2.4 million —2 percent of our labor force. This shift in the employment pattern has resulted from technological improvements in industry, increased integration in the manufacturing industry, and the decentralization of distribution processes. It has raised the average level of jobs in the transportation in-

[2] Richard E. Snyder, "Physical Distribution Costs," *Distribution Age*, January, 1962, p. 47.

dustry. A larger percentage of all those employed utilize higher-level skills than formerly; the decrease has been in the semiskilled and unskilled groups.

Prior to 1920, the railroads employed 80 percent of those engaged in transportation, but today they employ less than 30 percent. Trucking and warehousing combined employ about the same number.

TRANSPORTATION SERVES IN MANY WAYS

We share in the benefits of transportation in so many ways that we tend to take it for granted. Our homes and businesses are equipped with merchandise and equipment that comes from every corner of the globe. Perhaps the severest tests of transportation's effectiveness come in times of emergency. For example, when a snowstorm buries the western plains, aircraft must be used to fly in emergency rations and medical supplies, and airlift hay to stranded cattle. And when a hurricane batters the Gulf Coast, railroads and trucks must be pressed into action to rush food and clothing to the area. But we are concerned with the variety of ways in which businesses use the various modes of transport in everyday commerce. In brief, transportation does the following basic things:

1. Moves raw materials from source to point of use
2. Conveys partially processed goods to other factories
3. Transports manufactured goods to warehouses for storage
4. Ships goods from a company's main factory to its various branch operations
5. Routes goods from storage to wholesalers, retailers, and consumers
6. Carries people from one place to another

Now let us consider in more detail four aspects of transportation that follow from the performance of these fundamental accomplishments.

Transportation Widens the Market

A bushel of corn sitting on an Iowa farm may be fed to farm animals or processed into meal for human consumption. But by utilizing transportation facilities it may be sold for use throughout the country. Steel made into sheets or bars at the mill may be shipped to any factory that wishes to use it anywhere in the world. Furniture manufactured in Michigan, Indiana, or North Carolina is available in short order to homes and offices wherever it is in demand because it may be swiftly transported to those places. By enlarging the market for raw materials and processed goods beyond the boundaries of the local communities where they originate, our transportation system contributes materially to the soundness and the successful functioning of our national economy.

Transportation Enhances the Value of Commodities

Transportation enhances the value of commodities in two ways. It enables us to move merchandise from a location of surplus where it is not needed to an area of scarcity where it is in demand. Also, because our transportation system works efficiently and rapidly, goods can be shipped from one location to another quickly and at a small unit-cost. You will recall that we call this *giving place- and time-utility to goods.*

Transportation Enhances Specialization

We studied about mass production techniques in an earlier chapter. Mass production is possible only because of modern transportation facilities for shipping raw materials to factories, and finished products to markets. Transportation also makes possible manufacturing specialization. To illustrate, automobile parts manufacturing can be concentrated in the Detroit area, but the parts shipped to assembly plants in other sections of the country. Steel production is concentrated in Pennsylvania and Ohio; textiles in New England and the Southeast.

Efficient transportation enables a geographical region to specialize in producing those crops best suited to its land and climate. For example, the western plains can devote its entire grassland area to sheep and cattle, and its cultivated lands to wheat. The South can best raise cotton, peanuts, and soybeans, while citrus fruits grow best in Arizona, California, and Florida.

Transportation also enables different countries to specialize by producing those things they can make best and most profitably. Because of the worldwide transportation system, petroleum is shipped from eastern Mediterranean countries to Europe and Asia. We buy coffee from Brazil, bananas from Guatemala, tin from Indonesia, and transistor radios from Japan.

Because of modern transportation facilities individuals, states, countries, and regions can specialize. By trading with one another, all benefit, and everyone can have more of the articles he needs and wants. Without an efficient transportation system, this high degree of specialization would be impossible.

Transportation Reduces the Need for Large Inventories

There was a time when many business firms were required to maintain large inventories because movement of goods from one point to another required relatively long periods of time. This situation no longer holds true, since it is now possible to ship goods posthaste. Today, many concerns that sell to a national market maintain decentralized warehouses, strategically located to supply wholesalers and retailers efficiently. This reduced delivery time eliminates the need for the small wholesaler and the retailer to maintain large inventories, as was formerly necessary.

The degree to which the centralized distribution center is replacing the former pattern of decentralized warehouses may be illustrated by the Corn Products Co., which has replaced its 221 consignment warehouses with 16 distribution centers. The General Foods Corp. has replaced more than 100 warehouses with 17 regional distribution centers. The Scott Paper Co. has so coordinated its distribution processes, through the use of strategically located shipping centers and by effectively coordinating traffic control with order processing and shipping, that whereas it once required eight days to process an order, it now takes only overnight.

TYPES OF CARRIERS

Transportation firms are legally classified as *common carriers, contract carriers*, or *private carriers*.

A *common carrier* offers its services to the general public to transport property for a stated rate and in accordance with standard rules. It is expected to give the same service and charge the same rate to all shippers. Examples of common carriers are railroads, bus lines, intercity freight motorlines, some air-freight lines, most airlines, most domestic water carriers, all freight-forwarding companies, and REA Express. Common carriers are subject to various kinds of state and federal regulations, which are discussed later in this chapter.

A *contract carrier* sells its transport services on the basis of individual agreements or contracts which specify the carrier's liability. Some contract carriers specialize, transporting only specific types of goods. Automobile trucking companies and chartered buses and planes are examples of contract carriers.

A *private carrier* is one who transports his own goods. Manufacturers, wholesalers, and retailers who make their own deliveries in their own trucks are classed as private carriers. Since they are usually small companies operating in small geographical areas, they are subject primarily to local and state regulations.

Until well into the 1950's, railroads were this country's most important type of transportation carrier (that is, they carried 50 percent or more of all freight loads). In 1930, three-fourths of all freight shipments were carried over the rails. By 1950, the fraction had dropped almost to one-half. Today, considerably less than half of the intercity freight shipments are carried by the railroads. Figures released by the Bureau of Railway Economics, Association of American Railroads, show that the percentage of domestic intercity freight for selected years was distributed as follows:

TABLE 23.2

INTERCITY DOMESTIC FREIGHT SHIPMENTS

	Percentage of total				
Type of Carrier	1930	1940	1950	1960	1965
Railroads	74.3	61.3	56.2	44.1	43.5
Motor Trucks	3.9	10.0	16.3	21.7	23.1
Oil and Gas Pipelines	5.3	9.6	12.1	17.4	17.3
Inland Waterways (Great Lakes, Rivers, Canals)	16.5	19.1	15.4	16.8	16.0
Air Carriers					.1
	100.0	100.0	100.0	100.0	100.0

THE RAILROADS AS CARRIERS

Some rail lines are great systems with thousands of miles of roadbeds—systems like the Penn-Central, the Santa Fe, and the Union Pacific. Because cars can be switched from one line to another, shipments often can be carried from coast to coast swiftly and without being disturbed. Approximately 215,000 miles of track link the principal cities and towns in this country, and over these the railroads shipped 745 billion ton-miles of goods in 1966 alone. (One ton moved one mile equals one ton-mile.)

Our railroads contribute materially to our economy in the amounts of money they spend for the maintenance of roadbeds and for equipment, salaries, and supplies. Class I railroads[3] spent $3 billion for the maintenance of plants and equipment in 1965, and $4 billion for transportation operations, and paid $916 million in federal, state, and local taxes. Their total operating revenue exceeded $10 billion, and they employed 640,000 persons.

Advantages and Disadvantages of Railroads

The chief advantage of railroads is that they can haul bulky goods over long distances at low cost in a relatively short time. One diesel engine can pull more than a hundred freight cars; a typical freight train carries as much

[3] Class I railways include those having annual operating revenues of $5 million or more. There were 76 Class I railroads at the close of 1965.

as 1,500 tons. A second advantage of railroads is that they are able to maintain regular, reliable schedules. Bad weather, except for unusually severe snow storms in the heart of winter, has little or no effect on their activities. Moreover, since railroads have established an impressive safety record, shippers can count on having goods arrive at their destination in good condition. Finally, railroads are highly flexible: extra cars can be dispatched to accommodate particular regions during peak periods of manufacturing or harvesting.

The chief disadvantage of rail transportation is that it does not always meet the needs of the small shipper. A freight train is made up of a great many cars, all traveling in the same direction. As a result, the shipper of a single carload, or less than a carload, often finds his goods held up for hours while other cars are loaded and made ready for departure. Other disadvantages are slowness and inflexibility in terms of shipping goods short distances, and inaccessibility. Freight terminals are frequently located in traffic-congested areas. Also, many small communities are not served by railroads at all, and many small factories not only are not located on rail lines, but are not even served by any of the systems of special "private" tracks (called "loading spurs") that branch off from the main line and lead to warehouses, loading docks, or whatever. (The railroads fully own the spurs; they do not lease them.) Off-the-main-line, no-spur companies often sustain considerable extra expense in moving their products from factory to freight terminal.

Special Service Features of Railroads

Railroads offer a number of "plus" features that make their services particularly useful to marketers. Some of these features have grown out of competition with other methods of transportation, such as motor lines and waterways. Most of them, however, have come about as a result of research conducted by railroads themselves in their attempts to provide shippers with specialized service.

Reconsignment and Diversion Service. Changing marketing conditions occasionally make it imperative for shippers to change the destination of their goods after they have been sent out. For example, a shipment of wheat might originate in Amarillo, Tex., and be consigned to Kansas City, Kans. But while the wheat is in transit, or even after it has reached Kansas City, the shipper might find it advantageous to reconsign and reroute it to Louisville, Ky. The railroad will do this for a nominal service-charge.

Or a fruitgrower in Lakeland, Fla., might ship a carload of oranges to a produce broker in Richmond, Va. While the oranges are en route, he might communicate with another broker along the way to promote the sale of oranges. If his broker in Birmingham, Ala., for example, wired him that the market price was up, he could notify the railroad to reroute the shipment. If the railroad received the notification before the oranges reached Jacksonville, Fla., the shipper would be entitled to a through rate plus nominal diversion charges to Birmingham. If the oranges had gone beyond Jacksonville, the shipper would have to pay additional freight charges. Changing the terminal point of a shipment before it reaches its original destination is known as *diversion.*

Pooling Service. Whether or not a merchant succeeds in making a profit often depends on his ability to get low transportation rates. One way that he can keep his transportation costs down is by pooling shipments that are going to several destinations along the route. A Minneapolis flour mill might sell flour to a buyer in Omaha, to another in Topeka, and to yet another in Tulsa. Assuming that the shipper was an efficient businessman, he would ship a car of flour nonstop to Omaha in order to take advantage of a carload rate. From Omaha, he would have the rest of the flour shipped to Topeka and Tulsa at less-than-carload rates. His total cost of shipping the flour this way would be less than if he had sent out a separate shipment to each of the three dealers.

Small retailers or wholesalers can also save money by pooling shipments. By consolidating their orders in one carload, they get the benefit of a carload rate. Grocery stores and feed dealers who order flour, stock feed, and poultry mash from a wholesaler or manufacturer often pool their orders.

In-transit Privileges. In their efforts to accommodate shippers, railroads provide them with countless in-transit privileges. For example, certain commodities that demand continuing attention while being moved by railroad car can be stopped in transit for manufacturing processes, storage, milling, feeding, creosoting, packing, cooling, grading, and concentrating. The railroad charges the shipper a through rate plus a fee for such in-transit service. Livestock producers make use of this service when shipping cattle over long distances. From time to time on the way to their destination, the cattle are taken off the train and fed, watered, and rested.

Terminal Services. To make it easier for shippers to unload their merchandise, railroads provide elaborate terminal services, including temporary storage and specialized trucking facilities. "Big" shippers are serviced from their own "spurs."

After a freight shipment has arrived in a railroad yard, it is officially *spotted* by railroad employees. *Spotting* means that its location in the yard is carefully noted and its track number recorded. Then the railroad notifies the person to whom the shipment is addressed (the *consignee*) and allows him a period of time in which to unload the freight. He is given 48 hours after 7 a.m. following the time that the car is *placed* (stationed in place). For example, if a car is placed at 10 o'clock Monday morning, he would have until 7 a.m. Thursday to unload the car. In order to encourage the consignee to move the shipment promptly, the railroad levies a *demurrage charge*—sort of an "overtime parking" charge—for each day thereafter. Although demurrage charges may seem high to some, other dealers find them so reasonable that they use the tracks for temporary storage while they are completing local sales contracts. Actually, demurrage costs are usually much less than the cost of moving heavy freight to a warehouse and then on to the point of consumption or sale.

Lumber dealers often buy a carload of lumber and sell it, directly from the track, to large contractors, rather than move it to their lumber bins and deliver it to the contractors from there. The same plan is often used in selling large quantities of other bulk commodities, such as cement, lime, sheetrock, and plywood.

Pickup, Loading, and Delivery Service. The railroad's service to shippers continues even after the freight has arrived in the railroad yard. Most railroads provide trucks that can be used for pickup, loading, and delivery in the city. However, this service is furnished only on less-than-carload lots.

Rail piggyback traffic rose 12 percent during 1966 over 1965, and by the end of 1966, containerized shipments had doubled the volume for 1961.

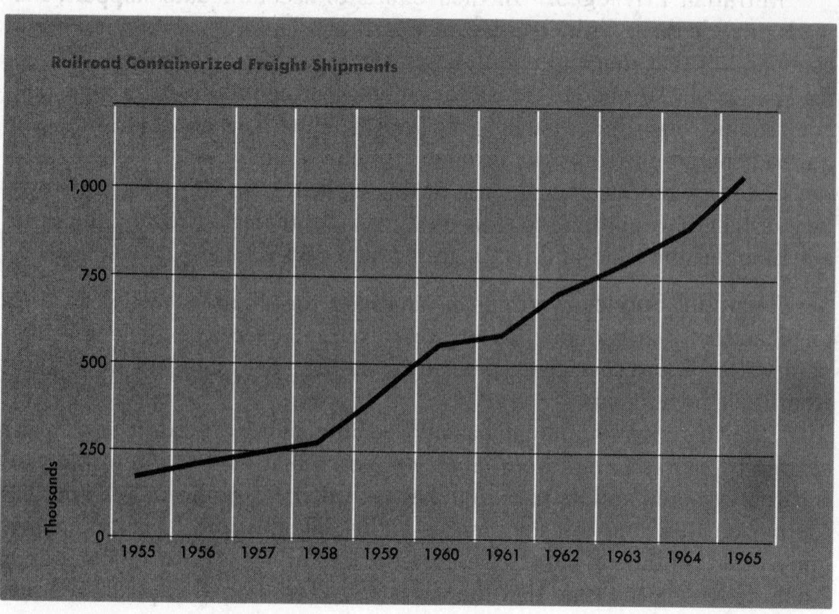

Courtesy The Boeing Company

The Boeing 727QC is specially designed for rapid conversion to all-passenger, all-cargo, or combination passenger-cargo use. Complete conversion to any of the configurations may be carried out in less than 30 minutes.

Railroads hauled 2.5 million truck trailers and containers on flatcars in 1966, and containerized shipping accounted for 4 percent of all freight carloadings.

But containerization is not restricted to railroad traffic. One of the country's large freight-forwarding companies, Wings and Wheels, announced in January, 1967, that it had designed a series of standard air-freight containers in varying sizes. The idea was to consolidate small air-freight shipments into bulk containers, thus moving air freight at a saving of approximately 15 percent over the cost of shipping "uncontainerized" packages. Wings and Wheels will pick up packages at the shipper's loading platform for delivery to the air terminal, and at the other end deliver the packages to the consignee. Their next step will be the construction of warehouses, where boxes may be loaded and unloaded, near air terminals in principal cities.

CONTAINERIZATION

The idea of *containerized shipping* is one of the most significant recent developments in physical distribution. It is the practice of placing goods in a sealed container which is carried by more than one type of carrier between the shipper and the consignee. It might travel first by truck, then by rail, then on a ship, and finally by truck again on the last leg to its destination city.

The original plan for containerization, introduced by the New Haven Railroad and approved by the Interstate Commerce Commission in 1954, involved nothing more than the transporting of the trailers of common carrier trucks on railroad flatcars. Then, in 1958, the railways began offering the shipper the choice of using his own trailer or one owned by the railroad. The use of standardized containers which are easily handled and are completely interchangeable between trucks, railroads, and barges, and which can be coupled together to make a single unit, holds great promise for future operations.

Shippers like "piggybacking" (trailer-on-flatcar hauling) for its convenience and economy. A long haul by piggyback requires 40 percent fewer man-hours than it does by highway, and offers great savings in wear and tear on the equipment as well. Containerized operations are not only cheaper than conventional truck shipment for long hauls, but require less effort on the part of the shipper, because he has to deal with only one organization instead of with connecting truck lines in different cities. Piggybacking also reduces damage and theft, because the cargo remains sealed in the container throughout its travels.

The airlines are now shipping containers in their large jets. The A-container fills the entire semicircular hold of a DC-8 or Boeing 707. This container accepts 10,000 pounds of weight and 457 cubic feet of bulk. B-size containers are half the size of A; C-size, half the size of B; and D-size, half the size of C. Combinations of B, C, and D containers build up to the size of an A container.

Containerized shipping-loading dock in New York City.

Courtesy, The Port of New York Authority

The European maritime industry is building port facilities for handling containerized cargo, and European shiplines are converting ships to specialize in carrying it. (The first containers manufactured for ocean shipping were made of steel or plastic, and generally measured 8′ x 8′ x 20′.) It has been estimated that containers can reduce port costs by as much as 50 percent. They also can reduce the time required for loading, transporting, and unloading cargo; the time required between England and Chicago, for example, can be reduced by several days.

It was announced by London shipping sources in the fall of 1966 that 33 "container ships" were already under construction or on order. An additional 20 ships were at that time being converted to handle containers. And it has been estimated that approximately half of all trans-Atlantic cargo will be carried in containers in the early 1970's.

Source: News Bureau, The Boeing Company

The United States supersonic airliner is shown in slow and high-speed flight in this drawing. One plane speeds toward a destination thousands of miles away with its wings swept back and integrated with the horizontal tail for 1,800-miles-an-hour flight. The other supersonic airliner gains altitude after takeoff with its wings extended for efficient subsonic cruising. The Boeing-designed variable-sweep wing was selected for the American SST as the most practical approach to efficient operations at both supersonic and subsonic speeds. The swift craft will be capable of transporting up to 350 passengers intercontinental distances at 2½ times the speed of sound, yet with wings extended and flaps lowered it will match the slow-speed performance of present-day jet airliners. The Federal Aviation Agency announced on December 31, 1966, that Boeing had won the federal design competition on the supersonic transport program.

MOTOR TRUCKS AS CARRIERS

Trucks have revolutionized cargo transportation in this country. From their first use, truck lines have capitalized on the flexibility of the motor truck in solving distribution problems. Speedy connections over state, county, and local highways have brought buyers and sellers into contract relationships in a way that would otherwise have been impossible. Door-to-door deliveries provided by motor trucks have eliminated the expensive handling of merchandise between terminal points and points of consumption.

Motor transportation has enhanced the development of the warehousing industry. Accessibility to local warehouses and wholesalers by truck has made it possible for retailers to buy in small quantities, to maintain limited inventories, and to minimize their capital investments. Then, too, highway transportation has minimized the handling of goods in transit. Since many deliveries are through-shipments (shipped directly from distributor to user), they do not have to be repacked with other freight in order to make up carload shipments in rail terminals.

Trucks continue to gain on railroads in carrying cargo. In 1940, motor vehicles transported only 10 percent of all intercity freight. By 1950 they were carrying 16 percent, and 23 percent by 1965.

Advantages of Truck Transportation

Trucks can reach all communities, many of which are inaccessible to trains or water transportation. They are very flexible and can be adapted to serve a variety of purposes: manufacturers will in fact build a truck to suit the needs of the purchaser. And the relatively low cost of a truck makes it possible for many individual businesses to own and operate their own fleets.

One of the greatest benefits of truck transportation is the quick and convenient delivery service it makes possible. Retailers rely heavily on free deliveries to stimulate buying; they have found the added expense more than compensated for by increased sales. Most retail stores that offer free delivery service maintain their own fleet of trucks, but some stores hire the services of local delivery companies that specialize in consolidating deliveries for several stores in the city.

More than 90 percent of all U.S. business firms use the services of trucking companies that operate as public carriers; the rest (whose vehicles in 1964 numbered 7½ million) operate their own trucks. The arguments given by companies owning and operating their own trucks are:

1. They save the company money.
2. There is better control over mechandise.

3. The driver is a company employee and better able to meet customer problems right "on the spot."
4. Trucks may be loaded at odd hours when this seems desirable.
5. During peak traffic periods the shipper, not the transportation company, sets the priorities.
6. The company reaps on advertising value, since the company name goes everywhere the truck goes.

WATERBORNE CRAFT AS CARRIERS

The oldest and cheapest means of transportation is by waterway. Centuries ago, men were using the oceans, lakes, and rivers as channels of transportation. In modern times, waterways have continued to have a significant bearing on domestic and foreign commerce because of their economy and accessibility.

Rates for water transportation are as little as one-third of those of the railroads. The reason for this wide difference is quite simple: more goods can be moved by barge at less cost and with less motive power and manpower. When it comes to cost, neither a train nor a fleet of trucks can compete with one towboat pulling a dozen barges, each loaded with a "trainload of boxcars."

In terms of cost, then, water transportation would seem ideal. However, the use of waterways imposes serious limitations on an efficient marketing and distribution program. For one thing, it is slow to ship by water. With our modern tempo of distribution, this time element alone is enough to rule out the possibility of water transportation for many commodities. Styles become quickly outdated, markets are seasonal, and losses are incurred through spoilage.

Export merchants and local dealers who use waterways sometimes find themselves handicapped by inflexible routes, little or no choice of ports, poor docking facilities, and high labor costs. Furthermore, distribution becomes bottlenecked if the ports are not strategically located near overland feeder lines. (*Feeder lines* are small lines that connect communities not located near main transportation lines.)

Most domestic shipping by waterways is carried on along the Atlantic, Pacific, and Gulf coasts; intercoastal shipping between the Atlantic and Gulf coasts on the one side and the Pacific coast on the other moves through the Panama Canal. The Great Lakes, various navigable rivers such as the Mississippi and its tributaries, and numerous local barge canals offer possibilities for inland transportation of goods by water.

The percentage of the total intercity freight traffic moved by inland waterways (rivers, canals, and the Great Lakes) has remained fairly constant

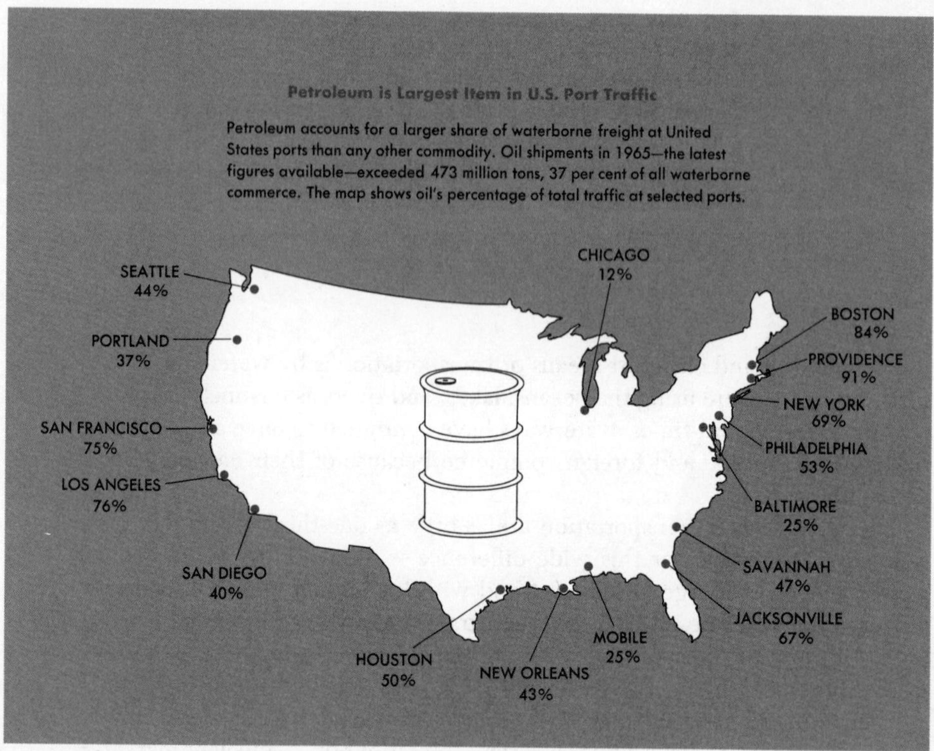
Petroleum is Largest Item in U.S. Port Traffic
Petroleum accounts for a larger share of waterborne freight at United States ports than any other commodity. Oil shipments in 1965—the latest figures available—exceeded 473 million tons, 37 per cent of all waterborne commerce. The map shows oil's percentage of total traffic at selected ports.
SEATTLE 44%
PORTLAND 37%
SAN FRANCISCO 75%
LOS ANGELES 76%
SAN DIEGO 40%
CHICAGO 12%
BOSTON 84%
PROVIDENCE 91%
NEW YORK 69%
PHILADELPHIA 53%
BALTIMORE 25%
SAVANNAH 47%
JACKSONVILLE 67%
MOBILE 25%
HOUSTON 50%
NEW ORLEANS 43%
Source: Oil Facts

during the past two decades, amounting to approximately one-sixth of all intercity freight shipments.

The successful use of hovercraft offers promise for transporting both passengers and freight over water. Hovercrafts suspend themselves on a cushion of air which enables them to skim over land and ice as well as water. They are already in use in Britain where they perform ferry service between coastal towns and across the English Channel. The largest of these craft to be placed into operation so far is the SR.N4. This craft, which was placed in commercial use late in 1968, is 130 feet long, 76 feet wide and is driven by four 19½ foot propellers at speeds up to 70 miles per hour. It can carry up to 600 passengers or 30 cars and 250 passengers.

PIPELINES AS CARRIERS

Although we hear less about pipelines than about other transportation media, they are one of the most important means of distributing certain commodities. Throughout the United States, large quantities of crude petroleum, petroleum products, and natural gas flow daily through thousands of miles of pipelines.

Limited quantities of powdered coal and wood pulp are now being transported by pipeline, too. In the pioneer years of transporting coal slurry (a mixture of crushed coal and water) by pipeline, it was necessary to remove almost all the water before the slurry could be burned. However, in 1961, furnaces were developed that can burn slurry with 30 percent water content. This has made pipeline-pumped coal almost as easy to handle as fuel oil.

Before World War II, pipelines, like railroads, were built and operated entirely with private capital. Following the war, however, government funds were made available to help in the expansion of pipeline transportation. The Big Inch and the Little Big Inch lines, which distribute natural gas from the great resource fields of the Southwest to the large metropolitan areas of the eastern and north-central United States, have been made possible because of government funds. Most pipelines run from the oil fields in the Southwest to the large industrial centers in the North and East.

Changing Patterns in U.S. Petroleum Transportation

(Crude Oil and Refined Products)

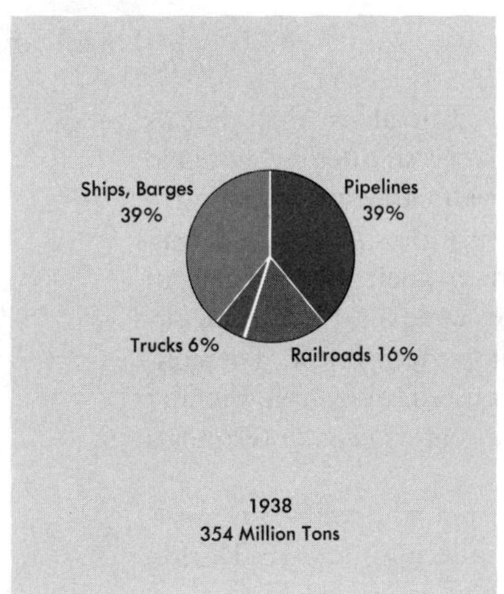

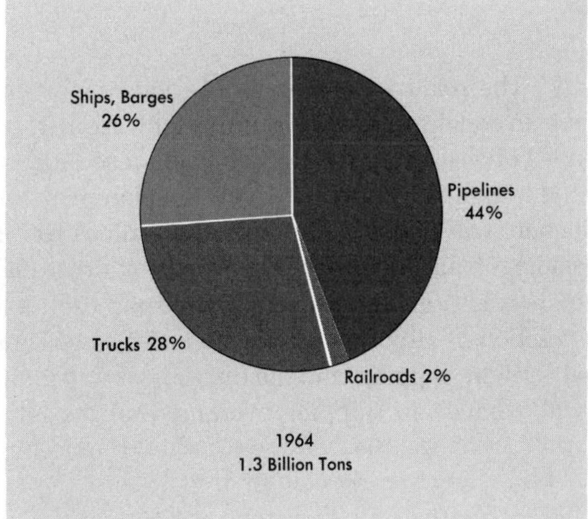

Pipelines and trucks increased their share of the U.S. petroleum industry's transportation business in the past quarter-century, while rail and water percentages decreased. Competition among transportation media helps keep petroleum prices reasonable.

Courtesy Ashland Oil and Refining Co.

Advantages of Pipeline Transportation

Transportation by pipeline is very economical and can be utilized day and night in all kinds of weather. Today's pumping stations are fully automated, thus keeping labor costs low and operations safe and efficient.

THE AIRLINES AS CARRIERS

The relative percentage of total freight shipped by air is small, but its role in freight shipments is important. At first, packages shipped by air could not be very large or heavy, but modern jetliners can carry almost any size and weight of container. The development and use of standardized containers will undoubtedly help the airlines to increase their share of freight shipments in the future. The economy of jet planes compared to engine aircraft is also giving air-freight transportation an important boost. The construction of airports near all the major towns and cities is also strengthening air-freight shipping, and the building of distribution centers near air terminals will enhance air shipping even more in the future.

Containerization, large jet aircraft, and improved equipment for material handling are causing air-freight shipping to come into its own. During 1967 more than 5 billion ton-miles of cargo—ranging from checks to computers to race horses—were flown between cities and between continents. This was up by a billion ton-miles over air shipments a year earlier.

When the jumbo jets become operative in the 1970's this will give air shipping another tremendous boost. Air-freight shipments are estimated to approximate 30 billion revenue ton-miles by 1975, with almost half of this being carried by United States airlines.

The quick-changeover technique is also playing an important role in air-freight shipments. The entire conversion from cargo to passenger accommodations (or vice-versa) requires only 20 minutes and the work of eight men. The passenger equipment is fastened to pallets which move on floor-mounted rollers. Pallet locks, folding hatracks, movable galley units and other hardware are designed for smooth, trouble-free operation. In this way a single aircraft may be used for passenger service during the day and cargo shipments at night. Plane utilization is thus raised to 2½ times normal operation.

Advantages of Air Transportation

Air shipments are fast and safe, and save on manpower. Air shipping cuts down time for delivery, and for perishables and goods that have great value but little bulk, offers rates that are highly competitive with those of other types of shipping. Air transportation also (as was pointed out earlier in this chapter) enables producers to maintain fewer distribution centers, and lower inventories. And it saves on packaging costs, since most goods can be shipped in inexpensive, lightweight containers.

TRANSPORT DIVERSIFICATION

Perhaps the next progressive move in the transportation industry will be in the field of *transport diversification*—common ownership of various modes of transportation. Under this plan a single transport company would own a railway system and a connecting barge line operation and/or motor carrier unit. Transport companies (whether railroad, motor carrier, barge, or airline) all sell the same commodity—the movement of goods from place to place. The variables in the different methods of transportation are: cost of service, flexibility, transit time, volume, pick-up and delivery, and frequency of trips.

Transport diversification appears to be a dynamic step forward that would strengthen the common carrier system. It would enable the transportation system better to meet the changing needs of industry and commerce, and has promise of reaping substantial benefits for the public. It represents a bold change in transportation policy and would necessitate a change in the structure and functioning of transportation in the United States. (Of course, safeguards would have to be provided through regulation and competition among the major transport companies.) This new concept of transport functioning could provide an efficiency and economy in the commercial movement of property that cannot be brought about in any other way. In the past the railroads have looked with favor on this idea, but most other types of transport have not.

Canadian Pacific has combined rail, truck, ship, and jet aircraft systems into one integrated freight system. The Canadian rail system extends all the way across Canada; Canadian Pacific steamship service extends from the Great Lakes to Europe, and their cargojets link the five continents.

Now that we have a Secretary of Transportation in the cabinet of the president of the United States, we shall undoubtedly see improved coordination of the various means of transportation. It will require time and diplomatic leadership to bring about substantial progress. However, there is the hope and promise that this will take place. Cooperation of all parties concerned is essential as is the support of the president.

WAREHOUSING

Warehousing is an important part of physical distribution. Storage is essential if production and consumption are to be coordinated in relation to time because, for one thing, not all goods can be consumed as they are produced. For instance, the growing of crops is seasonal, yet farm produce is in demand at all times. Therefore, produce such as orange juice must be canned or frozen in season, though it is sold throughout the year. The proper use of warehousing services thus enables the producer to store his surplus goods for the present and market them later. And the proper use of transportation in conjunction with warehousing helps the producer to adjust his operation to fit the time, place, and rate of consumer demand.

The reverse of this situation also exists. The demand for Christmas toys and outdoor sporting-goods is seasonal, yet manufacturers wish to maintain their operations the year around. Here, warehousing again helps the adjustment that must be made: to gear year-'round production to meet peak seasonal demands without the added cost of overtime or around-the-clock operations.

Types of Warehouses

There are essentially two types of warehouse operations: private and public. *Private warehouses* are owned or leased and operated by individual enterprises—manufacturers, wholesalers, and retailers—for their own use. They may maintain storage and distribution centers near their plants, or they may operate branch operations at other locations.

Public warehouses make their storage and handling facilities available to any businesses wishing to use them. Patrons of public warehousing facilities pay for the services they receive on the basis of space- and time-requirements. Some warehouses store all types of general merchandise while others store only special commodities such as farm produce or frozen foods. Public merchandise warehouses are in operation in all principal market areas in the United States. A recent U. S. census of business showed that there are more than 1,600 general warehousing and storage operations in the United States. In addition, there are many specialized storage facilities such as those for cold storage, frozen produce, and bulk liquids.

Warehousing Services

All too frequently, people are inclined to think only of storage in connection with warehousing. It includes storage, of course—in fact, this is its primary service—but warehousing is much more than storage. For instance, another of the services offered by public warehouses is the dividing of bulk shipments, and reshipping. They receive carload shipments, divide them into smaller units, and ship them to a number of customers in different geographical locations. Some of the large shipments may be stored for future demand, and the rest divided and shipped immediately. And in some instances the goods may be processed or packaged according to customers' specifications before being reshipped.

Warehouses may help the owner of goods being stored in financing his operation. A receipt is issued to the owner, showing the kinds and amounts of goods he has in storage. This warehouse receipt may be used as security for a loan at a bank. When the goods are sold, the loan at the bank is paid, and the goods are released and shipped to the new owner.

Because they are specialists, warehousemen can advise business management regarding specialized aspects of physical-distribution services. They can suggest ways in which available facilities may be used to the best advantage of both buyer and seller.

TRUCK LEASING

Full-service leasing companies provide annually approximately a quarter of a million trucks to business enterprises throughout the United States. Leasing eliminates the direct operating costs, frees working capital, saves record-keeping costs, and provides cash savings on procurement, maintenance, insurance, and licensing expenses. (Full-service leasing provides the trucks, their financing, maintenance, insurance coverage, and licensing.) It also takes the company out of the transportation business and frees administrative personnel from many problems that demand their attention when the company owns its equipment.

A study conducted in 1964 by the University of Chicago Research Center made a cost comparison based on the ownership of a single truck, ownership of an eight-truck fleet, and full-service leasing. The study was based on an operation of 15,000 miles per year for a gross-weight vehicle of 17,000 pounds and costing $5,720. The annual costs for the three types of operation were:

Single-truck ownership	$4,452.60
Eight-truck fleet operation	4,233.60
Full-service leasing	4,210.00

This would indicate that the decision of whether to own or lease would need to be made on factors other than cost. The number of miles driven per year, convenience, and flexibility of operation are factors that must be taken into consideration.

The Internal Revenue Service holds that automobile and truck rental payments under a lease arrangement are deductible only if they represent ordinary and necessary cost figures attributable directly to the operation of the vehicle for business purposes. No deductions are allowable when so-called lease expenses constitute payments toward the purchase price of the vehicle.

REGULATION OF TRANSPORTATION

Because transport companies operate in specific territories by government franchise, they are subject to special governmental regulations pertaining to routes, consolidation with other companies, rate structures, and curtailment of services. In many instances regulations are needed to protect the general public and the best interests of transport companies as well.

Most states have commissions that regulate *intrastate* transportation operations—those that occur entirely within the state. These commissions were first concerned with railroads, then later with motor carriers; now it is airport facilities.

Because most transport companies cross state lines, and state regulatory bodies have jurisdiction only within their own state, the federal government is responsible for the rules governing *interstate* transportation operations. The passage of the Interstate Commerce Act in 1887 was largely for the purpose of providing for railroad regulation. This law created the Interstate Commerce Commission, which dealt with rate discrimination. The law required that the tariffs or rates to be charged were to be reasonable and just. It further provided that railroads could not charge a higher rate for a short haul than for a long haul under similar circumstances.

As both transportation traffic and the number of types of transport companies have continuously increased since 1887, there have been several laws passed pertaining to the jurisdiction and responsibilities of the Interstate Commerce Commission. Not only has it jurisdiction over the tariff schedules of railroads, but it is concerned with the appraisal of the value of properties, and with methods of accounting, curtailment of services, financing, and consolidations.

The Interstate Commerce Commission was given jurisdiction over interstate pipeline shipments in 1906. It gained jurisdiction over water transportation in 1940.

The Motor Carrier Act

In 1935, with the passage of the Motor Carrier Act, the federal government officially recognized its responsibility to regulate motor transport companies that send their trucks across state lines. This act provided that the regulation of interstate motor transport lines should be under the jurisdiction of the Interstate Commerce Commission. Its supervision and control of interstate motor transport carriers is very similar to its overseeing of interstate railroad carriers. This commission is concerned with both common carriers (those that operate on regular schedules, offering their services to the general public) and contract carriers (those that contract for specific services, such as moving vans that transport household goods across state lines).

Regulation of Air Transportation

Although the construction and operation of airfields and terminals is largely up to municipal and state governments, the federal government is concerned with these to the point of making available funds for construction, and of establishing and enforcing safety regulations for airports and landing fields. The Federal Aviation Agency is the watchdog of airline safety, and the Civil Aeronautics Board is concerned with rate structures, routes, consolidations, air traffic, and the investigation of accidents. The Civil Aeronautics Board has jurisdiction over both domestic and international carriers; it is an independent agency reporting directly to Congress, as does the Interstate Commerce Commission.

TRAFFIC MANAGEMENT

Every manufacturer, wholesaler, and retailer has his own traffic problems. A major problem, shared by all three, is how to select the most advantageous shipping routes. This task is usually assigned, in a company large enough to employ one, to the traffic department.

The Traffic Manager

The person who heads the traffic department is called the *traffic manager.* Most of his routine work consists of collecting accurate, up-to-date information about tariff rates, selecting common carriers to be used in transporting foods, preparing claims of overcharge, damage, or loss, and auditing freight bills. He is also expected to trace lost shipments, supervise the actual handling of freight, and maintain control over back orders.

In addition to these routine duties, the traffic manager helps consolidate small orders into carload shipments, arranges systematic warehouse distribution points for less-than-carload lots, studies and perfects ways of reducing losses in shipments caused by improper packaging and handling of merchandise, and selects the most advantageous or strategic destination points for shipments. The traffic manager must know when to use rail, water, truck, or air to transport goods to customers. It is also his job to seek adjustments on overcharges caused by discriminatory rates; he actually prepares cases and presents them before commissions and government bodies. And he helps to select plant and warehouse sites that will ensure desirable transportation service.

In a large oil company, for example, transportation functions may be combined with supply functions. The person in charge, who is called the Manager of Supply and Transportation, advises the company president and furnishes functional guidance to department heads regarding supply coordination, transportation, traffic, buying and warehousing, and purchasing activities.

The Use of Electronic Computers

Railroads. One way to please a customer is to tell him when he may expect his shipments to arrive. The railroads, through the use of electronic computers and modern communications systems, help shippers to do just this. A railway can advise a shipper of the location of any shipment within a matter of minutes.

Many large railway companies own tens of thousands of freight cars, and operate in a dozen or more states over thousands of miles of track. Since a shipment may originate at almost any point along the line, supplying data to the computer is as important as processing it. A teletype network is used for this purpose. Details regarding freight shipments are sent by teletype from the yard offices directly to the computing center as trains are made up. Computers sort the information according to the code numbers of the cars in which each shipment is loaded.

Airways. In a similar manner, by linking an electronic computer to a high-speed communications network, airline traffic management can ascertain information on seat availability in a hundred different cities within a few seconds. Also, reservation agents can be supplied with up-to-the-minute flight arrival and departure information almost as soon as the data come into existence. Computers help perform these airline operations:

1. Check on seat availability on as many as eight to ten separate flights simultaneously.
2. Sell or cancel seats on any flight up to six months in advance.
3. Determine the number of seats already booked out of any particular city for a specific flight.
4. Examine any flight schedule for delays and cancellations.

Pipelines. Automatic equipment is also used to manage traffic through pipelines. Today, most new pipeline installations are being equipped to electronically guide products most of the way from the well or refinery to the market. Valves are opened and closed, pressure and temperature gauges are read, and engines turned on and off by a remote-control system combining electronic computing equipment and a modern telemetering communications system. An example of this operation is the Transwestern Pipeline Company's Texas-to-California line, which uses five large compressor stations along 1,800 miles of pipe. Whereas nonautomated stations require an operating crew of from five to 75, these stations operate without the aid of a single crewman.

SUMMARY

An efficient transportation system is essential to a mass production-mass distribution economy. It helps widen markets, makes possible specialization in agriculture and manufacturing, and increases working capital by reducing stock inventories. Approximately half the cost of marketing is accounted for by physical distribution.

The systems concept of physical distribution enables the marketing manager to see his work from the view of the user of goods as well as that of the seller. This concept includes the whole process of merchandise movement: of materials into and within the plant, as well as of finished goods from the plant and to the customer.

One of the most important means of transportation is the railroad, which is best suited to the overland movement of large, heavy freight shipments. Since railroads charge various rates for moving freight, the businessman must be familiar with the rates most appropriate to his type of shipment. Railroads offer the shipper many special services, including reconsignment and diversion service, pooling facilities, special cars, in-transit privileges, terminal services, and pick up, loading, and delivery service.

Trucks have added great flexibility to our distribution system, simplifying the handling of goods and making possible efficient, speedy deliveries in local areas.

Water transportation, especially suited to large, bulky shipments, is inexpensive, but waterway routes are inflexible.

Pipelines are increasing in number and size because of improved methods of piping coal, and because they are especially adaptable to automatic control devices.

The airways are transporting ever-increasing quantities of valuable, relatively lightweight goods. Quick flights are helping to take care of emergency needs in the fields of medicine and merchandising, as well as in many other fields.

Containerization is developing rapidly and is being used by all types of transport carriers. The use of containers reduces handling costs and cuts delivery schedules significantly. It has been estimated that within this decade more than half of all transatlantic cargo will be carried in containers.

Warehousing plays a significant role in physical distribution. Almost all goods spend some time in a warehouse. Ingress and egress must be done efficiently, and storage and materials handling within the warehouse must be done systematically and effectively.

Because transport companies have exclusive rights to certain routes and territories, they must be regulated and their tariff schedules approved by the government.

In large business organizations, transportation problems are handled by a traffic department under the direction of a traffic manager.

VOCABULARY REVIEW QUIZ

Match the following vocabulary terms with the statements below.

a. Common carrier
b. Consignee
c. Containerization
d. Contract carrier
e. Demurrage charge
f. Diversion
g. Feeder lines
h. Interstate
i. Intrastate
j. Place-utility
k. Private carrier
l. Time-utility
m. Transport diversification
n. Warehousing

1. Moving goods from a place of surplus to a location of demand or need
2. A carrier which offers its services to the general public
3. Scheduling the distribution of goods so they will be where they are needed at the time they are needed.
4. A carrier which markets its services through specific agreements with individual companies
5. Changing the delivery terminal of a shipment before it arrives at its original destination city
6. A carrier which transports its own goods
7. The person to whom a shipment is being sent
8. A charge made for failure to have railroad cars unloaded on schedule
9. The transporting of merchandise in sealed containers which are loaded on trucks, rail cars, or ships
10. Small shipping companies that connect small communities with major shipping terminals
11. Common ownership of different modes of transport companies
12. The storing, handling, and servicing of raw materials and finished goods
13. Transporting goods within a single state
14. Commerce that is carried on across state lines

QUESTIONS FOR REVIEW STUDY

1. What is included in the term *physical distribution*?
2. Explain how the use of air transportation might help a producer or wholesaler to cut his physical distribution costs.
3. Give an illustration to show how transportation gives time-utility to a particular good.
4. How does transportation aid specialization in production?
5. What changes are taking place in the makeup of that part of the labor force which is employed in the area of transportation?
6. What is the distinction between a common carrier and a private carrier?
7. What shifts are occurring in the way in which intercity freight shipments are distributed among the major types of carriers?
8. What advantages do railroads have over other types of carriers?
9. Which of the special service features of railroads do you feel is of the greatest value to most shippers?
10. In what areas do you think air freight will make its greatest contribution to our future business activities?
11. Why is containerization growing so rapidly in the freight transport business?
12. What are the advantages to a business enterprise in owning its own fleet of trucks?
13. How do you account for the fact that such a large percentage of freight shipments use water transportation?
14. Why does the fraction of the total freight shipment carried by water transportation remain fairly constant?

15. Why do we not have more integration of ownership among the different types of transport carriers in this country?
16. Why is warehousing so important in physical distribution?
17. What are the advantages of truck leasing over truck ownership?

PROBLEMS AND PROJECTS

1. We now have a Department of Transportation in the United States President's Cabinet.
   a. What do you see as the chief advantages of having such a department?
   b. What will probably determine how effective and how helpful this department will be?
2. Name the leading transportation centers within a 500-mile radius of your home community.
3. Write a brief report on the value and significance of the St. Lawrence Seaway.
4. An automobile manufacturer is contemplating building an assembly plant in Cincinnati, Ohio. What are the principal market areas to which shipments may be made from Cincinnati by using water transportation?
5. Name the factors you consider to be of greatest importance in determining the most desirable location of a public warehouse.

A BUSINESS CASE

Case 23-1 Transportation as a Location Factor

A producer of stoves and refrigerators is considering Cleveland, Ohio, as a location for a new fabrication and assembly plant. The company management has already discovered that this would be a good location as far as raw materials, cheap fuel and power, and labor are concerned.

You have been asked for a recommendation in relation to materials handling and physical distribution and marketing aspects of the operation. What are the various factors that enter into the solution of this problem?

International Trade

24

Although the era of the Yankee trader is past, the importance of trade between the United States and other nations continues to grow. Modern business relationships are now worldwide. It is not unusual to find a General Electric executive working on a project in Johannesburg, or a du Pont chemist conferring with his Japanese counterpart in Tokyo. In fact, American businesses and the fast-stepping executives who manage them cover the globe in search of trade opportunities. The value of international markets to manufacturers, merchants, financial agencies, and other business enterprises involved in international commerce is easily understood. Stated simply, international trade is a rich source of sales and profits.

Trade with other nations is more than stepping across a geographical line. It is a venture involving different politics and different economic, social, and managerial environments. It often requires great skill and knowledge to operate a business using another language and involving a different culture from your own. Differences in laws and customs present a challenge to the

American businessman who must live in a foreign environment. Then, there is the gnawing element of suspicion, on the part of business managers who go abroad, based on the fact that in the past some foreign governments have expropriated the property of American companies.

In this chapter we shall conduct a rather comprehensive analysis of international trade, starting with certain basic economic issues. This includes exploring the ways that domestic trade differs from international trade. Then, we shall discuss such topics as tariffs, trade policies, international payments, international markets, world economic communities, foreign exchange, financing international business, and career opportunities in international trade open to college graduates. Throughout this chapter the terms international trade, world trade, and international business transactions are used interchangeably.

THE DIMENSIONS AND IMPORTANCE OF WORLD TRADE

Considered in its broadest sense, world trade covers not only merchandise, but services, and also financial investments and monetary transactions between residents of different countries. However, the bulk of international economic transactions involve merchandise exports and imports.

Since there is an unequal world distribution of resources, food, wealth, population, and technology, the need for international trade is crucial. Fortunately, there is good reason to believe that, as the nations of the world continue to develop economically, world trade *will* increase, not only because of the growing demands of peoples achieving a higher standard of living, but also because of the expansion of productive activity, and the tendency for nations to achieve specialization.

What is *world trade?* It may be described as *business transactions between citizens, companies, and governments, conducted on an international scale.* Just as some persons possess skills not held by others, some nations have resources not found in abundance elsewhere. For instance, if one country has tin and another coal, it becomes mutually advantageous for them to exchange these materials with each other as long as an economic need exists in both countries. Domestic producers often stand to gain from international trade by way of importing, in that imports can do much to satisfy their constant need for low-priced raw materials. Oftentimes, imported raw materials are cheaper and more readily available than the same items supplied by domestic sources, whose prices reflect higher all-around costs, and whose deliveries may be erratic, time- or content-wise (due perhaps to dwindling natural resources). Domestic producers often stand to gain also from international trade by way of exporting. Exporting affords them a profit on sales, and often a larger production-scale that results in lower unit-costs. Export markets thus make possible means of additional economic growth which can enable domestic producers to compete more effectively with home competition. So we see that international trade is a two-way street.

Composition of International Trade

As you have no doubt already surmised, raw materials and manufactured goods entering a country are called *imports*, and when shipped out, they are known as *exports*. Importing and exporting are not restricted to the transfer of goods for profit: capital, business services, technical know-how, patents, trade-marks (and so on and on) are imported and exported. Once again it is clear that international trade is so important and permeating that few nations could become self-sufficient or maintain a high economic level without becoming involved in it.

The accompanying chart shows the value of United States exports and imports from 1955 through 1966. During the middle 1950's, exports grew more rapidly than imports, then tapered off until 1960. Since then, the trend in United States exports has been more upward than has that of imports. The dependence of this country on both imports and exports is much greater than is recognized by most people.

The United States, the United Kingdom, West Germany, and Japan are dominant in world trade. During the past several years these four nations alone have accounted for as much as 42 percent of the free world's exports,

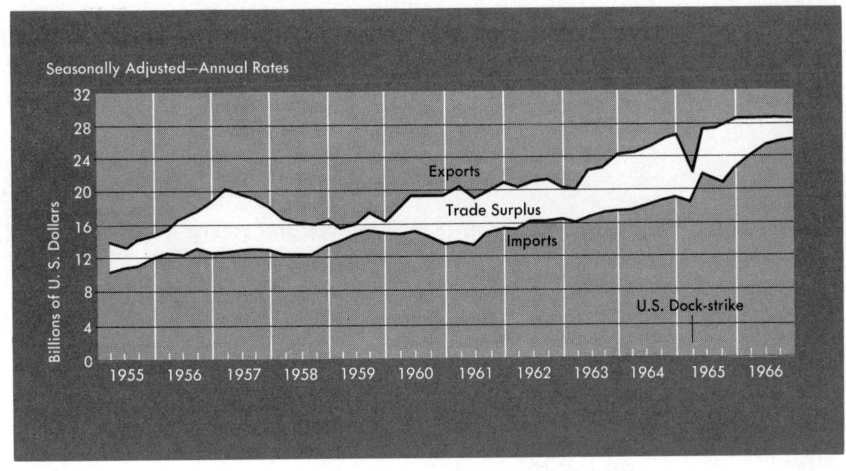

Source: United States Department of Commerce

and 39 percent of its imports. Europe continues to be the most important source of United States imports. The most dynamic markets for American exports during the present decade have been Western Europe and Japan (which since 1960 has been our largest market in Asia). During the same period, Canada and Latin America have bought slightly more than one-third of this nation's exports. Wheat and cotton have been our leading export products, while coffee and crude petroleum are top-ranking import products. Semimanufactured and crude materials represent a higher share of United States imports today than even in the period from 1900 to World War I, but manufactured food imports have been on the decline.

The Role of the United States in World Trade. With only slightly over 6 percent of the world's population and about 7 percent of the total land area, the United States produces and consumes about one-third of the world's supply of goods and services. This nation exports from 4 to 6 percent of its total production, and imports about 4 percent of the goods it consumes. (These percentages fluctuate somewhat from year to year, depending on economic conditions both here and in the countries shipping to us.) Our exports are generally highest when there is general worldwide prosperity, and lowest during an economic recession or depression.

International trade is particularly important to certain segments of our economy. We depend on foreign markets to absorb 38 percent of our milled rice and its byproducts, 53 percent of our grease and tallow, 33 percent of our cotton-farm products, and 34 percent of our mining, construction, and tractor parts.

TABLE 24.1

SOME IMPORTS OF BASIC COMMODITIES TO THE UNITED STATES FROM OTHER COUNTRIES

Commodity	Purpose	Net imports as a percentage of U.S. domestic consumption
Bananas	Food	100
Tea	Beverage	100
Diamonds (industrial)	Industrial cutting	100
Crude rubber	Tires, insulation	100
Coffee	Beverage	100
Cacao	Food and beverage	100
Spices	Flavoring	100
Tung oil	Varnish	100
Asbestos	Insulation, brakes, buildings	95
Cobalt	Cutting tools	95
Tin	Bearings and plate	81
Jute	Textile goods	78
Lapidary work	Jewelry	65

This country imports a large quantity of raw materials and agricultural commodities which either are not available here in ample quantities or are not produced here at all. A list of these items, though by no means a complete one, is given in Table 24.1. Notice that several of these are basic to our industrial needs, and many are important to use as food. Some items, such as coffee, tea, and cacao, are so common to us that they are taken for granted. It is only when our supply is cut off, such as during a war period, that we become acutely aware of their importance.

Changing Sources of Imports. A look at Table 24.2 shows how greatly the sources of the major imports of the United States (commodity- and raw-material imports) changed between 1940 and 1966. For example, in 1940, what with the war-enforced absence of many European nations from world trade, Asian and Oceanic countries dominated the list. In 1966, however, European and Latin American countries outnumbered all other countries as sources of United States imports. The East Indies, India, and the Philippines have fallen from the list because of our relatively reduced need for their products. Cuba and Mainland China have become political casualties. Meanwhile, the European share of the market has almost doubled. Likewise, Latin American countries are now among the leading supplying countries.

When we analyze how dependent the burgeoning American economy is on both importing and exporting, it becomes clear why this nation must continue to promote international business relations with other countries. Because the needs to our constantly growing population require evermore materials, many of which are not available here, it becomes necessary to seek foreign sources. If as a nation we were unable to obtain many imports

TABLE 24.2

CHANGING TRENDS IN SOURCES OF U.S. IMPORTS

Leading Supplying Countries in 1940	Leading Supplying Countries in 1966
1. British Malaya	1. Belgium and Luxembourg
2. Brazil	2. Brazil
3. Canada	3. Canada
4. China	4. France
5. Cuba	5. Italy
6. India	6. Japan
7. Japan	7. Mexico
8. Netherlands Indies	8. United Kingdom
9. Philippines	9. Venezuela
10. United Kingdom	10. West Germany

Note: Countries listed alphabetically, not in order of standing as importers.

we now receive, it would be necessary to substitute inferior goods, which could easily result in higher costs of production. And in the area of exporting, foreign markets often represent the difference between profit and loss for many American manufacturers. Indeed, it can be said that our export trade is equally essential to the stability of our economic welfare. For instance, we export about 20 percent of our total production of mining and construction equipment, textiles, and sewing machines. We also export between 2 and 3 percent of all automobiles made in this country, and roughly 40 percent of our annual cotton crop.

Actually, about 4.5 million jobs (in the U.S. alone) depend directly on import and export trade; millions more depend indirectly on our economic relations abroad. Railroads, steamship lines, banks, insurance companies, and trading concerns are among the many firms that derive direct benefits from foreign trade. Our agricultural economy also relies heavily on international trade, for we export large quantities of wheat, cotton, rice, tobacco, and dried fruits.

Major Exports from the United States

Canned sardines	Pens and pen points
Synthetic rubber	Oil-drilling equipment
Turpentine	Cigarettes
Newsprint	Cotton cloth
Fine paper	Chemicals
Automobiles	Soft coal
Textile machinery	Phosphate rock
Leaf tobacco	Inedible tallow
Milled rice	Agricultural equipment

THE THEORIES OF INTERNATIONAL TRADE

Since many textbooks have been devoted exclusively to the economic theories of international trade, or "international business" as it is sometimes called, and new books on the subject are appearing periodically, it is not our purpose here to discuss these theories in great detail. Rather, we shall deal only with the essential aspects of certain basic theories pertaining directly to our analysis of why international trade takes place.

Why Nations Trade

Through international trade a nation is able to obtain, more cheaply than if it were to produce them at home, certain goods that are needed to satisfy the desires of its population. International trade also enables each nation to combine its factors of production more efficiently by specializing in the production of those goods which it can make so economically and so well that, all factors (including tariffs) considered, they will outsell similar foreign goods in their own country of manufacture. Under this concept, nations export their specialties and import the specialties of other nations. World trade thus enables each nation to achieve a high degree of specialization by allowing it to make full use of its peculiar advantages (low labor-costs, favorable climate, mass-production techniques, deposits of scarce minerals, high educational level, etc.)

Advantages of Specialization. If all nations suddenly discontinued foreign trade, their own production would naturally be limited by their own resources. But by engaging in world trade, they can, as we have seen, specialize in those products they are best qualified to produce. Part of their total production can then be traded to other nations for those goods *they* are best able to make. By virtue of this exchange, each country can have a larger national income than would be possible without the trade and, at the same time, individuals in each country can attain a higher standard of living than if they tried to supply their own needs themselves.

What determines the products a country will decide to specialize in? One answer may be found in the *principle of comparative advantage.* In general, this principle implies what we have been stressing thus far in this

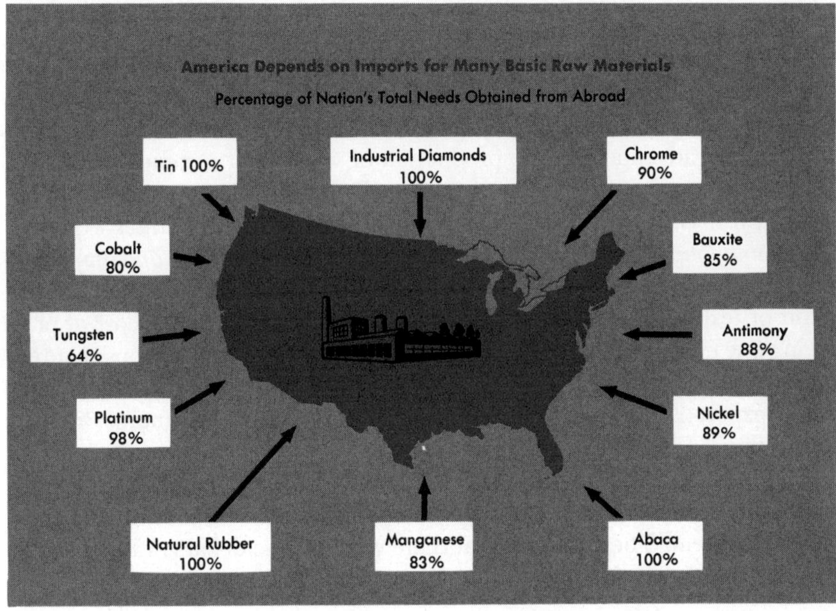

chapter: that it is to the economic advantage of a country to specialize in producing goods it can produce cheaper than other countries; that nations should refrain from producing those items they can buy more cheaply elsewhere. Comparative advantage may be due to such factors as a well-trained labor force, an abundance of raw materials, modern and efficient plants, and favorable climatic conditions. David Ricardo, one of the great classical economists, explained the principle of comparative advantage like this:

Two men can both make shoes and hats, and one is superior to the other in both employments. Now in making hats he can only exceed his competitor by one-fifth, or 20 percent, and in making shoes he can excel him by one-third, or 33⅓ percent. Will it not be for the interest of both that the superior man should employ himself exclusively in making shoes, and the inferior man in making hats?[1]

The principle of comparative advantage may be explained further by a hypothetical example. Suppose there were but two countries (the United States and Russia), and that, in isolation, each country produced but two commodities of mutual interest (wheat and textiles). Assume further that the cost ratios between wheat and textiles *differed* between the two countries as follows:

	United States (Dollars)	Russia (USSR) (Rubles)
Unit cost (price) of wheat	1.00	5.00
Unit cost (price) of textiles	2.00	1.00

Disregarding the exchange rate between the two currencies, in the United States the cost ratio of wheat to textiles is shown to be 1:2, and for Russia, 5:1. These ratios indicate that the United States would have a comparative cost advantage in the production of wheat and a comparative cost disadvantage in the production of textiles. In Russia, the converse situation would exist. *Gainful trade would occur when the United States exported wheat and imported textiles while Russia exported textiles and imported wheat.* The real cost of one unit of wheat in the United States would be half a unit of textiles. In Russia, on the other hand, the opportunity cost of producing one unit of wheat would be five units of textiles. It is obvious that the United States would have a lower opportunity-cost of producing wheat and would export it because it would have a comparative advantage in that commodity.

At this point you might ask: Why shouldn't the United States sell both wheat and textiles to Russia, bringing the dollars home without buying anything from them? The answer is that there would be no dollars in Russia with

[1] David Ricardo, *Political Economy* (London: Everyman's Library, 1911), p. 83.

which to pay for American wheat and textiles and, therefore, no dollars to bring home unless Russians could obtain dollars by selling something different to the United States. In other words, we cannot be paid for our goods and services unless we take payment in the form of foreign goods and services—all of which tends to reemphasize the fact that foreign trade travels on a two-way street.

Specialization in foreign trade is also encouraged under the *principle of absolute advantage,* which recognizes that the costs of producing commodities differ from country to country. According to this principle, a nation should specialize in an article when it enjoys the advantages of low costs due to a natural monopoly or some unusual technical development. As an illustration, let us assume that Brazil can produce coffee more cheaply than the United States. As a coffee producer, Brazil has an absolute advantage over this country. On the other hand, we have an absolute advantage over Brazil in making automobiles. Both countries will gain from the exchange of American automobiles for Brazilian coffee.

To compare the absolute advantage with the comparative advantage: It often pays a nation to import goods even though that nation can make them for lower labor costs than another—that is, even though it enjoys an *absolute advantage* over the other country. Whereas a nation may have a greater absolute advantage, its *comparative advantage* may dictate that it should specialize in the production of a second goods, using the income from this production to pay for the first goods bought from another country. In other words, unless we buy from other countries, they cannot buy from us. (Although these economic laws make sense to most economists, some governments sometimes ignore them by erecting trade barriers in the form of tariffs and import quotas, making it possible to increase prices of imports so they cannot undersell goods produced in those countries, and thereby eliminating any advantages a foreign country may have.)

Advantages of International Trade

Aside from these broad aspects of international trade, a high level of commerce with other countries provides individual businessmen with several specific advantages, which we shall discuss now.

Advantages to Importing. Business firms in this country import goods because: (1) foreign prices may be lower than domestic prices on similar goods; (2) certain goods are not available in this country—or, if available, the supply is not sufficient to meet the demand; and (3) ordering goods from foreign firms may encourage them to buy goods from more American firms. Moreover, some lines of foreign mechandise are considered to offer more style and prestige than are domestic products, and consequently will command higher prices in the United States.

Advantages to Exporting. Equally significant are the advantages that accrue to exporting. Many American firms engage in exporting because: (1) selling to foreign customers often is less expensive than expanding a new home-market; (2) foreign markets are a means of absorbing surpluses that would otherwise have to be sold at a loss in the home market; (3) some mass-production industries cannot earn satisfactory profits without foreign markets to maintain their volume at a high level—even a 5 percent increase in foreign sales may enable a company to reduce its unit cost; (4) industries with high fixed costs can by exporting spread these costs over a larger total volume, and thus reduce the average cost per unit, even on items produced for the domestic market; and (5) in some businesses, exporting is the one remaining source of new business that the company has not attempted to develop. (A large American integrated oil company just recently made the decision to "go international" because that appeared to be the only way to achieve continued growth in earnings.)

Difficulties in International Trade

Selling to foreign countries often proves more complicated and difficult for a manufacturer or producer than selling in the domestic market. Aside from the problems arising out of tariffs and reciprocal-trade agreements, which will be discussed later in this chapter, there are several other barriers to foreign-trade transactions.

The Language Barrier. One rather common barrier springs from differences in language—from the inability to communicate effectively and easily by conversation, correspondence, and even by advertising. Many exporters employ interpreters or take advantage of translation services that are generally available in most countries. Some persons find it useful to study the language of the country with which they plan to do business. Fortunately, more and more countries are encouraging the teaching of English in their schools, and in these places the language barrier is gradually disappearing—in our favor.

The Distance Barrier. The great distances over which goods must be shipped to foreign markets constitute another barrier to international trade. Perishable merchandise may spoil before it arrives, and livestock transported over long distances may lose so much weight that the shipper will suffer a loss. Finally, long distances increase the cost of transporting commodities.

Differences in Social Customs. One of the more interesting aspects of being involved in international trade is the contact one makes with cultures different from one's own. Sometimes this contact imposes obstacles of sorts. For example, the Latin American *siesta*—the long lunch and rest which make the working-day longer—is extremely bothersome to the average newly-arrived American businessman (though usually not to the long-since-arrived one). And in certain foreign countries, the custom of driving an automobile on the left-hand side of the road is confusing, especially when foreign cars have the steering-wheel on the right. And in India the cow is sacred and cannot be moved by force, even though it may be obstructing traffic. And familiarizing oneself with strange foods can be a strain on nerves and stomach alike. But then, the American businessman, like the American soldier, is highly adaptable, and soon overcomes such trifles. (Most do, anyway. Concerning those who don't, a 10-year study conducted by the International General Electric Co. to find out why overseas personnel fail in their work has revealed that 60 percent of the failures are due to inability to adapt to the existing culture.)[2]

William F. Whyte contends that cultural preparation for foreign assignments tends to be overlooked by companies in preparing their personnel to go overseas because it is difficult to measure cultural concepts and the impacts they have on people.[3] It is evident that a familiarity with social customs and cultures is important in the preparation of those going abroad to work.

Differences in Laws. Another barrier to foreign trade is the variety of laws that prevail in the world. Consider for instance the numerous patents that protect many products exported, or manufactured abroad but owned by an American company. Whether the patent protection by the home country is valid abroad depends upon both international agreements and host-country laws. For another example, in a code-law country the general power of attorney is not acceptable; instead, it must be drawn specifically and notarized.

And there are other differences in laws. The laws of some countries prohibit banking, insurance, or public-service industries from being carried on by any but enterprises owned and operated by natives. Many countries also require that a certain number of resident stockholders be maintained by foreign companies. And in some countries the laws governing ownership of trade-marks are different from those we are used to in the United States. In Latin American countries, for example, the ownership of a trade-mark goes to the man who registers it first, regardless of whether or not he originated the trade-mark or has ever used it. Clearly, it is important that you know what laws are in force when you market trade-marked goods abroad.

[2] Richard B. Blomfield, "The Importance of Foreign Language to a Career in Business," *Journal of American Society of Training Directors*, 1961, p. 35.

[3] William F. Whyte, "Culture, Industrial Relations, and Economic Development: The Case of Peru," *Industrial and Labor Relations Review*, July, 1963, p. 583.

Differences in Monetary Systems. Currencies differ throughout the world, both in value and in denomination. The United States and its possessions, of course, use the dollar. In England the unit is the pound sterling, while in France it is the franc, and in several other countries it is the peso. Imagine trying to conduct business in these countries without an intimate knowledge of their monetary systems!

A retailer in Argentina who buys a shipment of American-made typewriters sells them to his customers for pesos. But the American typewriter manufacturer cannot pay his employees in pesos, and insists that he be paid in American dollars. Consequently, the pesos must first be converted into dollars. There may be, however, a dollar shortage in Argentina, if that country has already imported more from the United States than it has sold to us. In that case, it must find some way other than in dollars to pay for its imports. To conserve dollars, therefore, foreign governments sometimes restrict the amount of currency their businessmen can convert into dollars. This has the effect of reducing the volume of export trade we carry on with that country, and in turn the amount of goods we can import from that nation. Another way to conserve dollars is to set import quotas (a subject we will discuss later in this chapter).

Why International Trade Is Important to the United States

People sometimes ask why as a nation we should bother to trade with other nations, especially when we can produce almost everything we need and can use substitutes for most of what we cannot produce. The truth is that this country is by no means a self-sufficient nation. There are many vital materials we either do not have, or else have only in small quantities. Even if we were able to provide substitutes in every case, it still would not be sensible to do so. For one thing, we would be isolating our country from the rest of the world, discouraging our producers from selling to others outside the country, and discouraging others from buying from us.

There are other reasons why international trade is necessary to the economy of the United States. It provides both our own nation and other nations with a higher standard of living. If American manufacturers were to cut off commercial relations with other countries, their output per man would be lowered and their unit cost per article increased. Then fewer persons at home would be able to afford manufactured goods, and purchasers in other countries might not be able to get any at all. By promoting world commerce, this nation is in an excellent position to maintain full employment, which is important to our own living standard.

From a political viewpoint, many people in the United States believe that encouraging world commerce is a desirable and important factor in promoting world peace. Countries that have extensive business dealings with

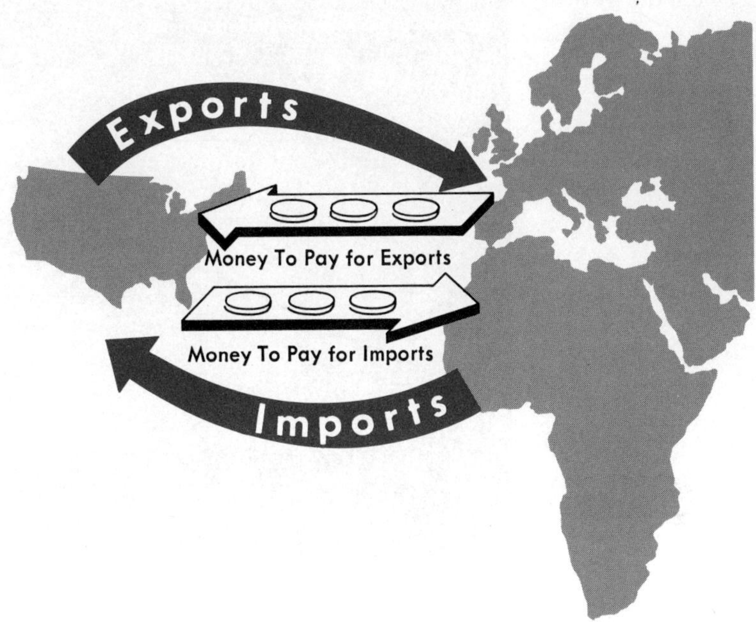

The United States is not self-sufficient. Importing goods from other nations encourages them to import goods from us.

the United States are presumed to be more friendly to us than those with which we do not deal.

The Impact Abroad of American Direct Investments

For several decades, the United States' direct investments abroad were concentrated mainly in the extractive industries—mining and petroleum. But during the past decade, manufacturing has become the most dynamic sector for American investments. A large proportion of these investments have occurred in Canada, Great Britain, France, Germany, Italy, and Mexico. More recently Spain, Japan, South Africa, and Australia have recorded substantial gains in foreign capital investments by Americans. The accompanying chart shows a continuous upward trend in total direct business investments in foreign countries by American companies. For the most part, the benefits from these direct foreign investments outweigh the disadvantages.

Benefits From Foreign Investments. Substantial benefits accrue to host countries as a result of American investments. One of the important

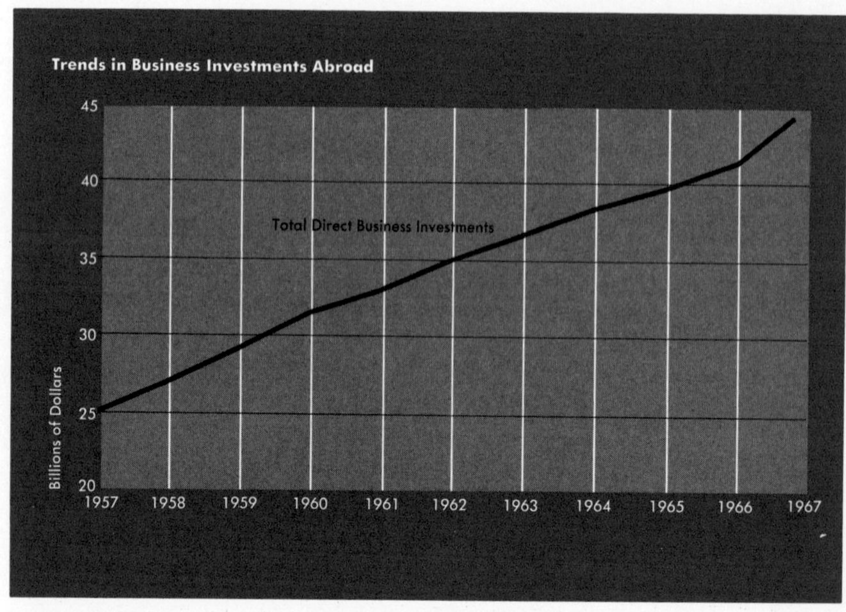

Source: U.S. Dept. of Commerce.

economic benefits is the inflow of new capital used to increase production quotas and improve marketing techniques. And for the base country, these foreign investments tend to multiply export opportunities which produce a beneficial effect on its balance of international payments.

The presence of more foreign capital in host countries has raised local standards of living, increased tax revenues, and expanded local employment. In addition, competition from American firms often encourages local companies to create better products. On the other hand, the higher wage paid by U.S. firms abroad, particularly in countries where skilled labor is scarce, has been cited as a cause of wage inflation in the host country.

American firms tend to provide vigorous competition with domestic firms, especially in those industries wherein their advanced technology, developed through years of research, gives them an edge. Finally, the expansion of U.S. investments abroad has had a markedly beneficial impact on less developed countries because of the new industries established.

TARIFFS AND NATIONAL TRADE POLICIES

Within this country, goods can be shipped from one state to another with little or no governmental interference. In international trade, however, the shipment of goods is subject to various kinds of controls established by governments of the trading nations. Tariffs, quantitative restrictions, and exchange controls are artificial impediments to the free movement of goods and services among nations; as such they interfere with the free play of economic forces.

Definition of Tariff

A *tariff* is *a tax or custom duty levied by a nation on goods imported from other countries.* The authority for levying import duties is derived from Article I, Section 8, Paragraph 1 of the Constitution of the United States.

Historically, depending upon which political party was in power, this nation has had high or low tariffs. From the early days of our Republic until the early 1930's the trend of tariff rates was steadily upward. The Smoot-Hawley Tariff Act of 1930 achieved the highest tariff on record. Then, in an attempt to combat the economic depression of the 1930's, Congress in 1934 passed the Reciprocal Trade Agreements Act, which reversed this more than century-old trend. This Act, and its numerous amendments since then (providing for further reductions of tariff restrictions) are discussed later in this chapter under the subject of the Trade Expansion Act of 1962, and subsequent negotiations resulting in the General Agreement on Tariffs and Trade (GATT).

KINDS OF TARIFFS

There are two broad kinds of tariffs: the *revenue,* and the *protective.* Each is designed for a specific purpose. A *revenue tariff* is a tax on imports to produce revenue. A *protective tariff* is a tax on imports to protect domestic producers against competition from foreign producers.

The *specific duty tariff,* usually designed to produce revenue, is levied on imports at so much per pound, ton, unit, or gallon. For example, the specific duty on imported champagne is $1.50 per gallon, and on chestnuts it is 6½¢ per pound.

The *ad valorem* ("according to value") type of duty is a protective tariff based on the *value* of the imported goods rather than on some quantity or unit of measure. Examples of ad valorem duties are the 15 percent tax on imported gold bags, the 25 percent duty on imported leather gloves, and the 9 percent duty on foreign automobiles imported into the United States.

Compound duties are a combination of specific and ad valorem duties. For example, the chemical compound ethylene glycol, used as an antifreeze in automobiles, has for years carried both a 15 percent ad valorem duty and a 3¢-per-pound specific duty.

Arguments for and against Tariffs

Almost every nation has at one time or another imposed some form of tariff duty, and in the United States no single domestic issue has provoked more prolonged political controversy than "the tariff." The very first Congress debated this issue in 1789, and since then almost every subsequent Congress has taken it up at one time or another. Some observers advocate "free trade," and would eliminate virtually all tariffs. Others argue for "protective tariffs." What are the arguments for and against tariffs?

The Infant-Industry Argument. This is one of the oldest pro-tariff arguments of all, and was voiced in the early days of the Republic. It holds that a new and struggling industry should be protected from foreign competition by a high protective tariff until the industry has had time to become well established. True, it is sometimes difficult for a new industry to get started in the face of foreign competitors operating in countries with lower labor costs and depressed living standards. Too often, however, even after the infant industry has grown up, new arguments are advanced to keep the protective tariff as high as before. History provides few examples of the lifting of tariffs that were first imposed to protect infant industries.

The Home-Industry Argument. This argument, also an old one, holds that a high duty shuts foreign goods out of the domestic market and insures that home industries will enjoy a maximum share of domestic business. A high tariff, however, means that domestic manufacturers can demand higher prices for their products than they could under a low tariff. In effect, the tariff serves as a subsidy to domestic producers—a subsidy that is financed by the consumers who must pay higher prices.

The Favorable-Balance-of-Trade Argument. The oldest of all arguments for tariffs is the one in support of a favorable balance of trade. The proponents of this argument contend that when we import goods, our money is being spent outside the country, whereas when we sell to other nations this is a means of building up the wealth of this country. In reality, a favorable-balance-of-trade policy is substantially impossible as a continuing matter. The truth is, foreigners can't buy from us unless they get dollars to pay for our products. And the way they obtain dollars is by selling us their goods and services.

Arguments for Free Trade. Free-traders argue that the elimination of tariff barriers would promote a free flow of goods between countries. They rest their case on the benefits from world-wide specialization of production which free trade would promote; all nations, they say, would be able to raise their standard of living.

The Reciprocal Trade Agreements Program. Although the present tariff policies of the United States are based on the Reciprocal Trade Agreements Act of 1934 (RTA) and its 11 amendments passed by Congress since, it was not until 1947 in Geneva that the United States and 22 other nations agreed upon a system of procedures and rules for studying tariffs. This was the aforementioned *General Agreement on Tariffs and Trade* (GATT). Despite its technical complexity, with tariff schedules listing thousands of negotiated tariff concessions, the basic elements of GATT are to provide the rules of nondiscrimination in trade relations, to agree on commitments to observe negotiated trade concessions, and to approve prohibitions against the use of quantitative restrictions on exports and imports. The member countries of GATT meet annually to review recommendations, to settle disputes, and to study ways to reduce tariffs.

Despite the progress made under GATT, Congress in 1962 passed the Trade Expansion Act, which the late President Kennedy signed into law on October 11, 1962. Unlike the previous 11 amendments of the original RTA of 1934, the TEA of 1962 provided for a complete and new approach unprecedented for the United States. This legislation gave President Kennedy the power to cut tariffs by 50 percent in negotiating new trade pacts during the five years following its inception. The purposes of TEA as expressed in the language of the Act are:[4]

1. To stimulate the economic growth of the United States and maintain and enlarge foreign markets for the products of United States agriculture, industry, mining, and commerce
2. To strengthen economic relations with foreign countries through the development of open and nondiscriminatory trading in the free world
3. To prevent Communist economic penetration

Some individuals are critical of the reciprocal-trade laws because, they say, tariff-making has been removed from the direct control of Congress in favor of Presidential control. The fact remains, however, that Congress has the power to modify or abolish the program if it is not satisfactory. The full impact of the law really depends upon the extent of cooperation between or among nations involved.

The Kennedy Round of Tariff Negotiations. The most sweeping reductions in the history of tariff negotiations were concluded in June, 1967, involving over 50 member-nations of GATT. These negotiations, called the *Kennedy Round* because they were initiated by President Kennedy under the 1962 Trade Expansion Act, cut duties on some 60,000 items, valued in

[4] Public Law 87-794, 87th Congress, H. R. 11970.

excess of $40 billion. Only a few items (including petroleum products, zinc, lead, watches, and rugs), which are either exempt from cuts under the 1962 Trade Expansion Act or are covered by special quotas or other controls, are not affected by the new agreements.

These cuts will, of course, stimulate U.S. exports as well as tend to intensify existing import competition confronting some producers. For instance, tariffs on most industrial items will be cut an average of 33 to 35 percent (the original goal of the United States was a maximum 50 percent reduction). The following lines would seem likely, on balance, to benefit from easier access to foreign markets or from lower costs on imports: air-conditioning units; aircraft (private); automobiles and parts; business machines including computers; coal; electrical machinery; farm equipment; home appliances; mining machinery; paper and paper products; rail equipment; rubber products; tobacco products; and trucks, including buses. On the whole, these are industries that have labor costs which are a relatively small part of the total product value, that benefit from the mass domestic U.S. markets, that make use of automation, and that face higher tariffs abroad than in the United States.

American goods that are likely to be relatively vulnerable to these tariff cuts are the following: bicycles and motorcycles; photographic equipment; chemicals; ceramics and cement; drugs; home furnishings; radios; television; musical instruments; shoes; silverware; sporting goods; steel products; textiles and apparel; and toys. These are industries that have a high proportion of labor costs, represent items cheaply transportable, and are lines currently enjoying high tariff protection.

There is every reason to believe that these tariff reductions will set the stage for further significant growth in international trade. And, the higher the level of economic consumption and activity in the highly industrialized countries, the more effective will be the help that can be given to developing nations, for the stronger will be the demand for the exports of those nations.

Quantitative Controls Other than Tariffs

Governments have come up with several devices other than the tariff to apply quantitative measures of restriction to international commerce. Notable among these devices are import quotas, embargoes, subsidies, and legislation against cartels. Quantitative trade restrictions are used mainly to regulate trade in commodities in order to give protection to domestic producers. Since these restrictions also affect the balance of international payments, both the commercial and industrial segment of a country, as well as its international economic relations, may be disturbed.

Import Quotas. An *import quota* is a quantitative restriction imposed upon both dutiable and duty-free commodities entering the country during a given period of time, such as "until further notice." A quota may be expressed in terms (of physical quantities or value) which restrict the limits of the total volume of trade regardless of the economic forces of supply and demand. As a nation we have not imposed import quotas as widely as other nations, but on occasions we have subjected such items as fox furs, molasses, sugar, cotton, cattle, oil, and certain dairy products to quota restrictions. In administering quotas, a license is usually issued to each importer, allowing him to bring in a specific quantity of items over a specified time. Under a *tariff quota* a specified quantity of a product may enter the country either at a given duty rate, or duty-free. If an additional quota is imported, it is at a higher duty. A tariff quota may combine the features of a quota and a tariff, and quotas may also be subject to exports.

Embargoes. An *embargo* is a government order prohibiting the shipment of goods either into or out of the nation for sanitary, moral, military, or economic reasons.[5] For moral reasons, the United States maintains an export embargo on certain drugs, gambling devices, and lottery tickets. For military reasons, there is an embargo on the export of helium gas. And on the economic front, President Kennedy in 1962 ordered an embargo on all imports from Cuba to the United States, to stop the Castro regime from getting U.S. dollars with which to promote Communism in the Western Hemisphere. (The President, however, left unchanged the policy allowing limited exports of foods, medicines, and medical supplies to Cuba for humanitarian reasons.)

Subsidies. A *subsidy* is a payment to a domestic company by the government, ostensibly to stimulate the expansion of the business or to encourage exporting. Goods produced under a subsidy that move in international trade tend to nullify the protective aspect of a tariff in the importing country. To correct this situation, the importing country may impose a regular tariff duty or a special surtax. This raises the cost to the domestic importer by the amount of the subsidy. Direct subsidies have been proposed as a substitute for tariff protection by those in opposition to tariffs. Under such reasoning, a subsidy would enable the domestic producer to lower his selling price to the amount needed to be competitive with the lower-priced foreign product. The United States government has granted subsidies from time to time to shipbuilders, airplane manufacturers, and producers of minerals, to help carry some of the costs of operation.

Legislation Against Cartels. A *cartel* is an association of individual companies for the purpose of controlling prices or the conditions of sale. Although American corporations have entered into cartel arrangements with

[5] The term "embargo" also refers to the refusal of transportation companies to accept or move freight in case of a strike or because of tariff congestion.

foreign corporations, there are no purely American cartels. Since they foster monopolistic practices, domestic cartels would be in violation of our antitrust laws. Cartels have been very common in international trade, however, and several have enjoyed government sponsorship.

Price-fixing by cartels sometimes leads to critical situations in international commerce. Suppose an American firm, which is prohibited by law from joining a cartel, suddenly finds itself competing with foreign companies that are members of a cartel. The American company is likely to be undersold, because a cartel can charge higher prices in noncompetitive marketing areas and lower prices in competitive areas. When this happens, the American company simply endeavors to conclude an agreement with the cartel not to reduce prices within a given market; this the American company can do without violating American antitrust laws. In return for this consideration, the cartel will likewise agree to do certain things favorable to the American company.

Under the Webb-Pomerene Act of 1918, American producers are permitted to organize export associations to operate like export cartels in foreign countries, provided the associations do not restrain trade or unduly affect prices and competition in the United States. This enables one or more American business firms to operate competitively with cartels outside the United States.

ORGANIZING FOR INTERNATIONAL MARKETING

When a domestic firm decides to sell abroad, it may do so by choosing one of two methods. One method of marketing is to sell directly through the company's own export department or division. The other is to sell indirectly by using the services of middlemen specializing in export selling and located in the United States. Among these latter middlemen are export merchants, export brokers, export commission houses, and resident buyers.

Using Direct-Export Marketing Channels

Companies that engage in a substantial amount of foreign commerce usually find that it pays to establish their own marketing outlets. In such a case the manufacturer may also have one of more factories abroad, and the marketing outlet is a part of the factory organization. A closer look at several of these direct outlets provides a more detailed analysis.

Foreign Branches. These are divisions of the domestic company that are located in a foreign country. They function very much like a foreign wholesaler where a company manufactures products that require servicing and parts. This type of operation allows the company to exercise unlimited control over the branch.

Foreign Subsidiaries. Foreign subsidiaries may resemble foreign branches, but actually they are separate companies owned and controlled by parent American corporations. These companies are chartered under the laws of the host country. One advantage of the foreign subsidiary over the foreign branch is the ability of management to control both cost and profit because all revenues and expenses are separated from the domestic organization. Moreover, the subsidiary is a separate corporation and, often, financing is less difficult. There is also an advantage in that the subsidiary can handle a complete line of products rather than one single line. In recent years many foreign subsidiaries have grown to the point where their operation is global and the multinational corporation evolves. As the name implies, the *multinational corporation* is an integrated operation covering a global perspective with its foreign and domestic interests interwoven into an international company. This type of structure is probably the most advanced organization in international business. Among the large American multinational companies are such firms as John Deere, a farm-machinery maker with subsidiaries in nine countries; Procter & Gamble, with four international divisions; Ford Motors, with plants in 20 countries; and International Business Machines with its IBM World Trade Corp. Firm figures are lacking, but it is probable that of the 20,000 American firms engaged in international business, about 3,500 have establishments abroad, including subsidiaries and branches. Probably 2,000 of these may be classed as multinational companies.

The Built-In Export Department. Aside from the aforementioned two marketing and operating channels is the *built-in export department*, in which export activities are assigned to certain personnel in the company. These persons may also have particular responsibilities in domestic operations. Usually, the built-in export department consists of an export manager and one or two clerks. The manager actually does the selling or directs it. The traffic department handles documents and transportation. The credit department determines credit risks. And the general accounting department handles the accounting function. This type of export organization is well adapted to the manufacturer whose export business is only a small part of his total volume.

Using Indirect Exporting Channels

The second category of exporting methods, *indirect exporting*, involves the use of outside organizations located in the home market. These organizations are export "middlemen" willing to assume the major portion of details involved in foreign trade. Some of these "middlemen" take title to goods, which involves assuming all the risks inherent in reselling the goods in the foreign country. These indirect exporting agencies will be discussed under the immediately following titles.

The Export Merchant. By definition, a merchant is a middleman who purchases at one price and hopes to resell at a higher price, thus making a profit. The *export merchant* is a marketing middleman, engaged in foreign trade, who buys and sells on his own account. Usually, he does both exporting and importing. Export merchants are used principally in marketing staple commodities—open-market goods not subject to a high degree of identification with the producer. In foreign countries, it is not uncommon for the export merchant's firm to be known as a trading company because it buys and sells a variety of products from a large number of companies.

The Export Agent. The *export agent* may represent several noncompeting American firms on a commission basis. Sales are made by the export agent for the manufacturer, who finances and ships the product.

Buyers for Export. *Buyers for export* are independent middlemen who canvass American markets in search of goods needed by foreign consumers. These buyers take orders from foreign clients and are paid a commission. American producers generally assume responsibility for shipping. The main advantage in selling to export buyers is that there is little marketing expense. The disadvantage is that this system is an irregular method of selling which does not provide a stable outlet. Using buyers is more complicated than selling through export merchants.

Organization for Importing

In some ways, importing products into the United States is more complex than buying on the home market. The methods a company uses to import goods are classified in the same manner as they are in exporting: direct and indirect. *Direct importing* is the purchase of foreign goods by American businesses directly from foreign sources. *Indirect importing* is the purchase of foreign goods by American businessmen from domestic middlemen who are specialists in locating goods from foreign companies.

Direct Importing. American companies that engage in direct importing usually maintain an import department staffed by foreign buyers—that is, persons who are familiar with foreign goods and markets. For example, resident buying offices buy for one or more firms, who share the expenses of maintaining an overseas office. Direct importing has two advantages: (1) it may be less expensive, since there is no commission paid to import middlemen; and (2) it enables the American firm to select from a wider assortment of goods, and often to become the exclusive distributor of certain items.

Indirect Importing. Rather than maintain a staff of foreign buyers, or even an import department, many concerns prefer to import through an import merchant, an import broker, or an import commission house. Any one of these methods of buying can be as convenient as buying goods from home markets. (The services performed by these indirect-importing middlemen will be described in the section of this chapter dealing with career opportunities in international trade.)

THE BALANCE OF INTERNATIONAL PAYMENTS

Perhaps the most useful tool for explaining the interrelations created by international transactions between residents of one country (including individuals, businesses, and government agencies) and the residents of all other nations is a statistical statement, prepared by the Department of Commerce, called *the balance of international payments*—often referred to simply as "the balance of payments." This statement is a summary of all economic transactions between domestic and foreign residents. Despite its name, this statement more closely resembles a business firm's profit-and-loss statement than it does a balance sheet because it reflects a nation's sales and purchases together with other forms of receipts and expenditures. For example, it includes such items as: total exports and imports; loans and investments in foreign countries by individual citizens, companies, and government agencies; the tourist expenditures in foreign countries as well as in the United States; interest payments; military expenditures abroad; dividend payments; and a host of smaller items. All modern nations prepare such statements, which are published monthly in *International Financial Statistics* (Washington, D.C.: The International Monetary Fund).

The Structure of the Balance-of-Payments Statement

Transactions between domestic and foreign residents are entered in the balance of payments as either debits or credits. *Debit transactions* are those that involve payments by domestic residents to foreign residents. In other words, the debit items involve payments by Americans to foreigners, and actually are imports. *Credit transactions* involve dollar receipts by domestic residents from foreign residents. In the main, these involve exports. This distinction is perhaps most clearly seen when we analyze Table 24.3, a balance-of-payments statement for this nation in 1965.

As a statistical summary, the balance of payments affords an over-all

TABLE 24.3

UNITED STATES BALANCE OF INTERNATIONAL PAYMENTS, 1965 (IN MILLIONS OF DOLLARS)

Items	Credits (Exports)	Debits (Imports)	Net Credits (+) or Debits (−)	
I *Current account*				
1 Merchandise (Adjusted)	$26.2	$21.5	+$4.7	
Invisible Items:				
2 Transportation	2.4	2.6	−.2	
3 Travel Expenditures	1.2	2.4	−1.2	
4 Income on Investments (Interest, Dividends, etc.)	6.4	1.1	+5.3	
5 Private Remittances		.6	−.6	
6 Miscellaneous Services	1.0	.3	+.7	
7 Current Balance, Private				+$8.7
United States Government:				
8 Exports of Military Goods and Services (+)	1.6			
Military Aid Payments (−) to allies		1.6	0	
9 Other Military Transactions	.8	2.8	−2.0	
10 Other Grants and Payments		2.2	−2.2	
11 Miscellaneous Government Transactions	.7	1.0	−0.2	
12 Current Government Transactions				−$4.4
13 Net Balance on Current Account				+$4.3
II *Capital account* (Long-Term Loans (−) or Borrowing (+) Items)				
14 Private Transactions			−4.4	
15 Government Transactions			−1.8	
16 Net Long-Term Foreign Investment				−$6.2
17 Net Balance on Current Account				−$1.9
18 Private Short-Term Loans (−) or Borrowing (+)			+.9	
19 Government			+.001	
20 Net Investment in Short-Term Debt				+.9
III *Gold Exports* (+) or Imports (−)				+1.6
21 Errors and Omissions				−.6
22 Offset to Deficit				++1.9

Source: Dept. of Commerce. Data presented in slightly revised form. Totals rounded off. Items that lead to an inflow of dollars are indicated by a plus sign; those that lead to an outflow of dollars are indicated by a minus sign.

view of a nation's international economic and trade position. For this reason, the statement is especially useful to government agencies, including central banks and the Treasury and Commerce Departments, and to many officials who are responsible for maintaining our external economic policy. Moreover, international trade is of such importance to many nations that the balance of international payments must be carefully watched in formulating domestic and foreign economic policies concerning tariffs, foreign aid, and the movement of capital abroad.

In analyzing Table 24.3, you will observe that the statement is divided into three sections. The first is the current-account items (lines 1–13). The balance of payments on current account includes all payments made because of current purchases of goods and services. The current account tells us how much the nation is receiving from the export of goods and services to other countries, and how much it is spending through the import of goods and services. When the nation is receiving more than it spends internationally, then the net balance on the current account is a credit. When current payments exceed receipts, the net balance on the current account is a debit.

The second section is the capital-account transactions (lines 14–20), which includes everything other than what is recorded in the current account. The main items are capital transfers which show whether domestic residents are investing abroad more or less than foreign residents are investing in the domestic country. Furthermore, the capital account indicates whether there is an export or import of monetary gold.

When residents of this country invest abroad either for long or short periods, the United States experiences a *capital outflow.* This may involve both loans and equity capital. Conversely, when foreign residents invest in the United States, this nation is said to experience a *capital inflow.* Whereas a capital outflow is a debit in the balance of payments, a capital inflow is a credit in the balance of payments because it involves dollar receipts for America. In return, foreign investors hold financial claims against American residents.

The third section of the balance-of-payments statement is gold movements (lines 21–22), representing gold exports and imports. The special treatment of gold in the balance-of-payments statement is due to the unique role of gold in international payments. Unlike other commodities, gold is accepted by all nations at a fixed price as a means of international payments. In Table 24.3, line 22, which is the offset to U.S. deficit in the balance of international payments, the movement of gold occurred to offset this deficit. In recent years gold has functioned chiefly as a means of providing international liquidity. It represents the means for making payments when other credits in the balance of payments are insufficient to offset debits; and it serves as a means for receiving payments when credits exceed debits.

Favorable Balance of Trade. If a nation sells (exports) more merchandise to other countries than it buys (imports) from them (line 1), it is said to enjoy a *favorable balance of trade.* Conversely, if it buys more than it sells, it is said to be burdened with an *unfavorable balance of trade.* The eighteenth-century classical economists used to thrill at having a favorable balance of trade. They regarded it as good fortune to have a surplus of exports (visible items) over imports (also visible items) because payments were made in gold. But the fact is that today these terms do not necessarily indicate an advantage or a disadvantage because there are many other transactions that take place, besides the movement of goods and services, that have a bearing on the balance of international payments.

By referring again to Table 24.3, you can readily see that our exports, as shown on line 1, exceeded our imports by $4.7 billion. When we include the invisible items (lines 2–6), this gives us a current total balance of $8.7 billion. However, if we examine the transactions (lines 8–11), it will be noted that these items are enough to wipe out much of the positive private balance and produce a net balance on current account (line 13) equal to $4.3 billion.

At this point let us turn to capital movements, shown in lines 14–19. These are transactions that record the transfer of long- and short-term government loans, credits, and private investments. For example, if an American businessman invests abroad, he must use American dollars, which must be converted into a foreign currency. Such transactions give rise to debit transactions because they result in importing IOU's. Conversely, when a foreign investor makes an investment in the United States, this contributes to a surplus on capital. Line 16 shows that in 1965 America was a net long-term foreign lender, which proved that we were doing more long-term investing or lending, by firms or through the purchase of foreign stocks and bonds, than foreigners were in either lending to or investing in the United States. Thus, by subtracting line 13 from line 16, it was possible to determine the net balance on current account.

Line 17 represents the total of all our then-current transactions and long-term capital movements. So large were current government debits and long-term private investment debits that America had a deficit in its balance of international payments amounting to $1.9 billion. The deficit was offset in part by the shipment of American gold abroad from our reserves, plus $1.9 billion in short-term dollar assets. After paying this gold and dollar asset, we achieved a balance.

By this time you must be aware that the balance of international payments, taken as a whole, is a double-entry bookkeeping system, which will always show a formal balance. For years this nation has had a chronic deficit in the current and long-term capital balance (which has been matched by an outflow of gold), as well as in short-term dollar obligations owned by foreigners who have not demanded gold.

Gold Movements in International Payments

The flow of gold from the United States since the early 1950's—caused by chronic deficits (17 out of 18 years) in our balance of international payments—has seriously reduced this nation's gold reserves. For example, the $22.9 billion in gold reserves, which the United States held a decade ago, dropped by mid-March, 1968 to less than $11.9 billion as nations with large dollar balances lost faith in our currency and demanded payment in gold. Since 1945 the United States has been required by law to maintain a gold reserve in Federal Reserve Banks equivalent in value to 25 percent of the total dollars in circulation. This gold reserve cover was intended to limit the issuance of currency by Federal Reserve Banks.

In the United States it is unlawful for a citizen to demand gold in lieu of dollars in exchange transactions. Gold can be bought only for industrial uses. With the United States off the gold standard, other countries can do business among themselves using gold for payments. By agreement they can also demand gold in lieu of dollars in international payments.

By mid-March, 1968 the movement of gold from the United States reached a peak. This precipitated (in the London and Paris markets) an historic international gold-buying rush by speculators and hoarders. The dollar was under assault because foreigners feared our gold reserve would be depleted. Speculators anticipated that the United States would immediately raise the price of gold well above the current rate of $35 per ounce in order to increase the value of American gold reserves. Thus, speculators abroad expected to realize substantial profits from gold purchases at $35. But raising the price of gold was stoutly resisted by the United States government.

Instead, on March 14, 1968, Congress quickly passed and sent to the President—in response to his request—a bill to repeal the 1945 law requiring the 25 percent gold reserve cover in Federal Reserve Banks. The immediate effect was to make gold available to the United States reserve.

What has caused this nation to have continued international payments deficits? Some basic reasons are immediately evident. For years, the United States has spent large sums for overseas military activities. In addition, substantial gifts and grants have been made to aid developing countries. Finally, there has been a capital flow created by the investments each year by American companies in enterprises abroad.

Cures for a Balance-of-International-Payments Deficit

No nation can continue indefinitely to carry a deficit in its balance of payments without damaging its economy. Though determining and implementing solutions will not be an easy matter, the need to achieve international solvency appears inevitable. Where do we start?

Those opposed to the present level of government spending abroad point out that our private accounts show a large surplus and that, consequently, it is the size of federal spending abroad that must be cut. The Federal spending under question would include all forms of aid (military and economic) to other nations.

A second cure involves improving our export position by reducing costs and prices so that more of our goods will be sold abroad. It should be noted, however, that during periods of inflation, it is virtually impossible to stem the upward spiralling of costs and prices without resorting to strong government controls.

A third measure involves reducing American business investments in capital expenditures abroad. One method of accomplishing this is by increasing corporation taxes on profits derived from American firms operating abroad.

A fourth cure is to reduce the dollar spending by American tourists abroad through a program of voluntary travel restrictions. As a rule, voluntary restrictions are ineffective. Some authorities suggest that Congress impose a tax on foreign travel. Such a tax would have to be high to prove effective.

INTERNATIONAL COOPERATION

In recent years, new developments in international trade relations have brought about greater economic cooperation among the major nations and the developing countries. One effective way to bring about trade cooperation is for several countries to remove trade impediments by forming a customs union. A *customs union* is a geographical region embracing more than one nation within which the parties to the union agree to commit themselves to free trade and a common tariff policy.

World Economic Communities

Two noticeable customs unions in Western Europe are the European Economic Community (EEC), better known as the "Common Market" and the European Free Trade Association (EFTA), sometimes called the "Outer Seven." In addition to various organizations established in Europe, similar customs unions have been organized in Latin America.

The European Economic Community. Adopting the Common Market scheme spelled out in the Treaty of Rome, signed March 25, 1957, six countries—France, Italy, Belgium, Germany, Luxembourg, and the Netherlands—formed the EEC on January 1, 1958.

The six nations that constitute the EEC have been striving to produce a full integration of their economies by 1970. Beyond this, their ultimate goal is political unity. The EEC has attempted much more than the formation of a *customs union,* which is a geographical region embracing several countries within which goods may move freely without being subjected to customs duties. Actually, it has set itself the difficult task of harmonizing technical standards and national laws. For example, the EEC has proposed regulation of the marketing of drugs and pharmaceuticals. The EEC is also working toward the elimination of restrictions in areas of insurance, banking, labor laws, and even the recognition of diplomas (such as those of professional people like lawyers and physicians).

The EEC is not necessarily barred to other European countries. Instead, there is envisioned an eventual political union of European nations—except the Soviet Union, which has bitterly opposed the EEC. In 1961 Great Britain, Denmark, and Ireland asked to be admitted. Early in 1963, President de Gaulle blocked Britain's admission. Since that time no action has been taken on Denmark or Ireland. Again, late in 1967, five Common Market countries bowed to the will of President de Gaulle and decided not to open negotiations for British entry. The reason given was that the British were not in a position to carry out the obligations of membership.

The success of the Common Market is reflected in the rate of production and economic growth of the member countries. The EEC's share of total world trade climbed steadily to 16 percent during the 1950's, and in the 1960's reached 26 percent. Tariffs on commodities among the Six are now only at 20 percent of their 1958 levels. Complete removal of all tariffs by 1970 has been anticipated.

The European Free Trade Association. In 1959, seven nations of Europe, not members of the EEC, met in Stockholm and drew up a charter that formed the first industrial free trade area in Europe. The charter was signed on January 4, 1960, by Great Britain, Sweden, Norway, Denmark, Switzerland, Austria, and Portugal. Finland was accepted as an associate member in July, 1961. EFTA has often been referred to as the "Outer Seven."

Unlike the EEC (which is a customs union), EFTA maintains no common tariff system with third countries. Instead, each member country maintains its own tariff and pursues its own trade policies with other nations outside of EFTA. The main reason behind the formation of EFTA was to set the stage for future negotiations with EEC to create regional trading arrangements that would take in the whole of Western Europe. This objective came to a halt when France opposed the admission of Great Britain.

Since the United States participates in a substantial amount of trade with both EEC and EFTA countries, one of the questions often asked is whether or not it has received any benefits from them. Most authorities feel that indeed the United States has thus far benefited greatly because both EEC and EFTA, as evidenced by the Kennedy Round negotiations, have cooperated with this nation's efforts to reduce tariffs. In fact, it was President Kennedy who took the position that a successful economic integration of Europe will in the long run be of benefit to all capitalistic countries. Perhaps the greatest benefit is cooperation between the United States and the Com-

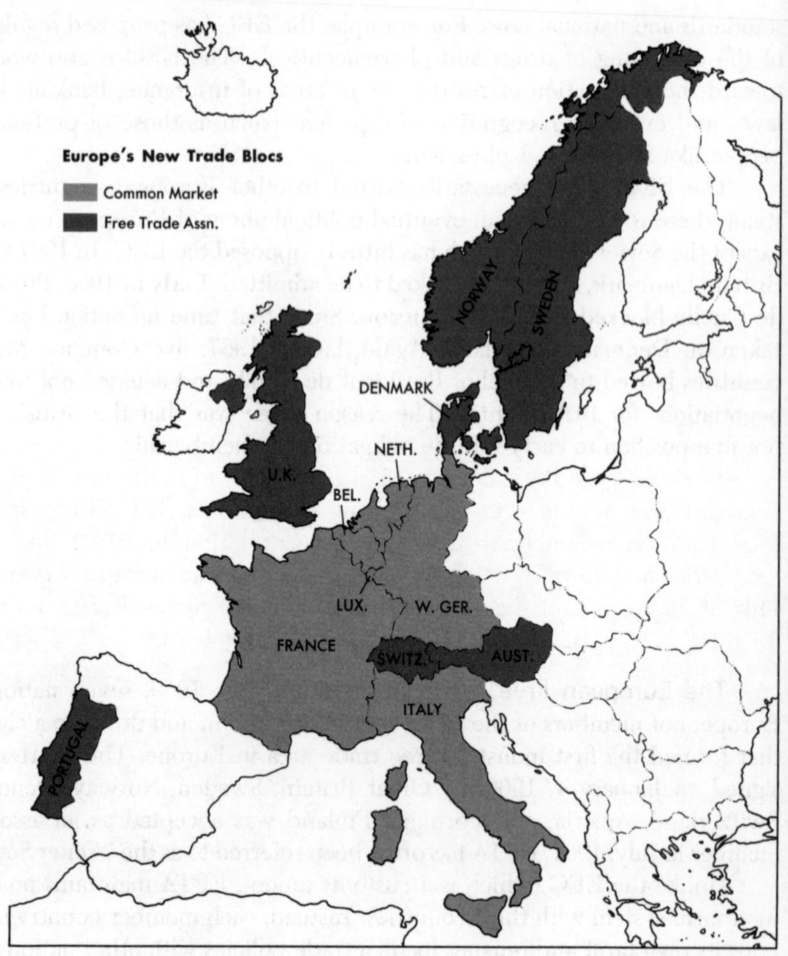

International trade organizations such as the Common Market and the Free Trade Association cut tariffs for members, but maintain duties on products from nonmember countries.

mon Market in working out solutions on such problems as how to increase exports, ways to check monetary inflation, deficits in the balance of international payments, and deliberate devaluation of a nation's currency.

Economic Intergration in Latin America. **In the Western Hemisphere two trading blocs have been established. The nine member countries of the Latin American Free Trade Association (LAFTA) are engaged in developing a free-trade area to serve Mexico, Argentina, Brazil, Chile, Columbia, Ecuador, Paraguay, Peru, and Uruguay. This association hopes to create a broad market that will encourage new industries. Unlike EFTA, which has** established automatic tariff reductions, LAFTA follows the procedure that each round of tariff concessions depends on negotiations, and members may select the products they are willing to bargain on. Until LAFTA adopts automatic tariff reductions over several years, it is doubtful that the organization will contribute much to Latin American trade.

Five countries in Central America—Honduras, El Salvador, Nicaragua, Guatemala, and Costa Rica—have organized the Central American Common Market (CACM). This association is also engaged in eliminating trade restrictions and in promoting common finance with a common monetary system. Latin America's trade with the United States has been essentially an exchange of their agricultural and mineral products for our manufactured goods. Increased trade here, as elsewhere, depends upon the removal of trade barriers.

FINANCING INTERNATIONAL TRADE

As has already been mentioned, one of the complications of international trade is the fact that although the seller of goods or services expects to be paid in the same kind of money which he can use in paying his debts, not all nations have the same currency system. English currency, for instance, being different from ours, must be converted into dollars before an English buyer can pay his American business associate.

Fortunately, buyers and sellers do not need to meet to complete transactions. In this and other countries are banks that buy foreign currencies (or claims to them) for sale by exporters, and also sell foreign currencies to importers who want to make payments in foreign money. These banks charge a commission for buying and selling the currencies or handling the negotiable instruments used in foreign exchange. Later in this chapter, when we discuss the use of various negotiable instruments, we shall see how the services of a bank are used in carrying out the details of a foreign trade transaction.

The Foreign-Exchange Market

The term *foreign exchange* may be defined in two different ways. In one sense it is a financial asset involving a cash claim held by a resident of one country against a resident of another country. As used in this sense, foreign exchange is represented by a variety of credit instruments, the most common of which is the bill of exchange, or bank draft (previously discussed in Chapter 17). As a negotiable instrument, the bill of exchange has three parties: (1) the *drawer,* who orders payment and initiates the draft; (2) the *drawee,* who is ordered to pay; and (3) the *payee,* to whom payment is to be made. When a bill of exchange is drawn against a commercial debtor (usually an importer), it is called a *trade bill.* When it is drawn against a bank it is a *bank bill.* As a rule, trade bills are drawn by exporters and other trade creditors, whereas bank bills may be drawn by banks or commercial creditors. Thus, a bill of exchange becomes foreign exchange when it is a claim held by a domestic resident against a foreign resident.

In another sense, foreign exchange is the process by which balances resulting from foreign transactions are settled. Under either definition a rate of exchange is established—and consequently, any nation's exports should (theoretically, at least) pay for its imports. By selling to foreign nations a country earns the necessary foreign exchange to buy from those nations.

You have already observed that the balance-of-trade status of the United States is reflected in the amount of its foreign exchange, or in other words, in the value of deposits that American banks, business firms, and individuals have in foreign banks, as compared with the value of deposits on the part of foreign countries in American banks. Our supply of foreign exchange in the market is increased when we sell goods and services to foreign customers, and corporate securities to foreign investors, and when we ship gold and currency out of the country. It is decreased when other nations obtain American dollars by selling us goods or services, and when we buy foreign securities or receive gold or currency from abroad.

Foreign-Exchange Rates. Market values for most of the world's currencies fluctuate almost daily. It is the function of foreign-exchange dealers located in large commercial banks in the major financial centers to buy and sell foreign exchange, based on the prevailing rate for a given day. An American importer, for example, who expects to buy a foreign article, must keep in mind not only the price he must pay for his item abroad, but also the price of whatever foreign currency he must buy to pay for his import. This price is called the *foreign-exchange rate,* and it may be defined as *the price of one currency in terms of another.* For example, assume that the exchange rate for Mexican pesos is one peso to the dime. An American wishing to obtain a foreign-exchange credit of 1,000 pesos for use in Mexico City would pay $100 for these pesos.

Suppose that American wheat is selling for $2 a bushel in the United States. With the exchange rate of £1 (one pound) = $3 (that is, a dollar costing £.33), the cost of 6,000 bushels to a British importer would be £4,000. Should the exchange rate change to £1 = $4 (that is, the dollar costing £.25), without any change in the American price of wheat, the same 6,000 bushels would cost £3,000. Thus, a drop in the exchange rate on the dollar reduces the export prices of American goods.

In all the great financial centers of the world—New York, London, Paris, Tokyo, and Hong Kong—the daily rates are quoted by commercial banks and listed in the major metropolitan newspapers. The accompanying illustration (see next page) lists the daily quotation rates for foreign exchange.

Foreign Exchange

Wednesday, April 17, 1968

Selling prices for bank transfers in the U.S. for payment abroad, as quoted at 4 p.m. (in dollars):

Country and Par Value	Wednesday	Prev. Day
Canada (Dollar, .925)	.9264	.9263
Great Britain (Pound, 2.40)	2.4037	2.4032
30-Day Futures	2.3965	2.3959
90-Day Futures	2.3807	2.3802
Australia (Dollar)	1.1218	1.1218
New Zealand (Dollar)	1.1250	1.1250
South Africa (Rand)	1.4021	1.4021
Austria (Schilling, .0384615)	.0388	.0388
Belgium (Franc, .02)	.020105	.020110
Denmark (Krone)	.1342½	.1342½
France (Franc, .20255)	.2031	.2030
Holland (Guilder, .267243)	.2762½	.2761
Italy (Lira, .0016)	.001604	.001604
Norway (Krone)	.1400½	.1400½
Portugal (Escudo, .0347826)	.0352	.0352
Sweden (Krona, .193304)	.1934	.1934
Switzerland (Franc, .228675)	.2305	.2304
West Germany (Deutschemark, .25)	.2510	.2510¼
LATIN AMERICA:		
Argentina (Peso)	.00288	.00288
Brazil (Cruzeiro)	.3135	.3135
Chile (Escudo)	.1350	.1350
Colombia (Peso)	.0617	.0617
Ecuador (Sucre, .0555)	.0470	.0470
Mexico (Peso, .08)	.0801	.0801
Peru (Sol)	.0248	.0248
Uruguay (Peso)	.0051	.0051
Venezuela (Bolivar, .298507)	.2230	.2230
NEAR EAST:		
Israel (Pound)	.2875	.2875
Iraq (Dinar)	2.83	2.83
Lebanon (Pound, .456313)	.3185	.3190
FAR EAST:		
Hong Kong (H.K. Dollar)	.1655	.1655
India (Rupee)	.1336	.1336
Japan (Yen, .00277778)	.002764	.002764
Pakistan (Rupee)	.2105½	.2105½
Philippines (Peso)	.2557	.2557

Prices for foreign banknotes, as quoted at 4 p.m. (in dollars):

	Buying	Selling
Argentina (Peso)	.00260	.00300
Australia (Dollar)	1.07	1.11
Austria (Schilling)	.0375	.0400
Belgium (Franc)	.0190	.0210
Brazil (Old Cruzeiros)	.00025	.00035
Canada (Dollar)	.9200	.9300
Chile (Escudo)	.0900	.1200
Colombia (Peso)	.0475	.0625
Denmark (Krone)	.1300	.1350
Egypt (Pound)	1.10	1.35
France (Franc)	.2015	.2050
Great Britain (Pound)	2.35	2.45
Holland (Guilder)	.2750	.2800
Hong Kong (H.K. Dollar)	.1550	.1650
India (Rupee)	.0800	.1100
Italy (Lira)	.00157	.00163
Japan (Yen)	.00255	.00270
Mexico (Peso)	.0785	.0812
Norway (Krone)	.1350	.1425
Pakistan (Rupee)	.1000	.1200
Philippines (Peso)	.2200	.2500
Portugal (Escudo)	.0330	.0365

Courtesy The Wall Street Journal, Dow Jones & Co., Inc.

Rates of exchange fluctuate in response to the supply and demand of international money transfers. If our total foreign sales are greater than our total foreign purchases, the foreign demand for dollars to make payments rises. This is because dollars would sell at a premium in terms of foreign currencies. But if our imports exceed our exports, the dollar will be at a discount in terms of foreign currencies. This illustrates the effect of our balance of trade. Actually, money is rarely shipped to another country to settle a debt. Instead, drafts or bills of exchange are used. These are provided through a bank as part of its service to its customers.

In addition to the trade demand and supply of foreign exchange, there is a speculative side to the exchange market. Professional speculators follow the exchange market closely and try to anticipate shifts in exchange rates. If they can buy a particular currency at one rate, and sell it at a higher rate, they realize a speculative profit. This activity is known as *arbitrage.* As an example, if the price of the pound sterling is quoted at $2.80½ in London and $2.80 in New York, a speculator would buy pounds in New York and sell them in London at a profit.

Financing Exports

Financing is more complicated in international trade than in domestic trade because there is greater risk in extending credit to buyers abroad. The parties may be unknown to each other. Or the seller may wish to be paid immediately. A variation of cash terms is the requirement of part payment with the order, and the balance payable on receipt of the shipment.

As a rule, when an exporter sells goods abroad, he takes the initiative in obtaining payment by drawing a draft for the amount of his invoice. This instrument is drawn directly on the buyer (importer) who is the debtor. It may be drawn to become due at sight, on arrival of goods, or at a designated future time. It is customary in such a case to use the services of a commercial bank that offers exporting services.

Export documents. The export documents that generally accompany drafts are of the following types:

1. Ocean bill of lading (usually indorsed in blank) (The bill of lading lists the goods shipped. It also contains the terms of the contract under which goods are shipped by the transportation agency.)
2. Commercial invoice (shows quantities, terms, and prices)
3. Marine insurance certificate
4. Special customs invoice (shows weight, value, destination, and class of goods)

5. Inspection certificate
6. Certificate of origin

On receipt of an order from a foreign customer, the American exporter draws a draft (either in dollars or in the foreign currency) against the importer and, together with the documents listed above, takes them to the bank for further handling.

Customer's Draft. The following illustration is an example of the steps involved in financing a foreign sale by the use of a draft. (The use of drafts in domestic trade was discussed in an earlier chapter.)

The Tejas Manufacturing & Equipment Co. of Houston, Tex., sells certain items of equipment to the Colombiana Importadora, S.A., Bogotá, Colombia.[6] On receipt of an order, the Houston firm (the seller) draws a customer's draft (shown below) made payable to itself, in the amount of $3,500, on Colombiana Importadora. This instrument instructs Colombiana Importadora (drawee and buyer) to pay the amount of the draft to the holder at a specified future date—that is, 30 days from the date of the draft.

The draft is presented to the buyer (drawee) for his acceptance. If the drawee chooses to accept it, he writes across the draft the word "accepted," followed by the date and his signature, and returns it to the drawer. This actually transforms the draft into a trade acceptance. It is customary for American exporters to draw drafts similar to this illustration, in dollars. Such a draft is often referred to as a *dollar draft.*

The buyer (drawee) cannot obtain physical possession of the goods that have been shipped to him until certain documents, such as the bill of lading, commercial invoice, and any others required to be attached to the draft, are

[6] The abbreviation S.A. used as part of the company title is derived from the Spanish term Sociedad Anonima, which means "stock company."

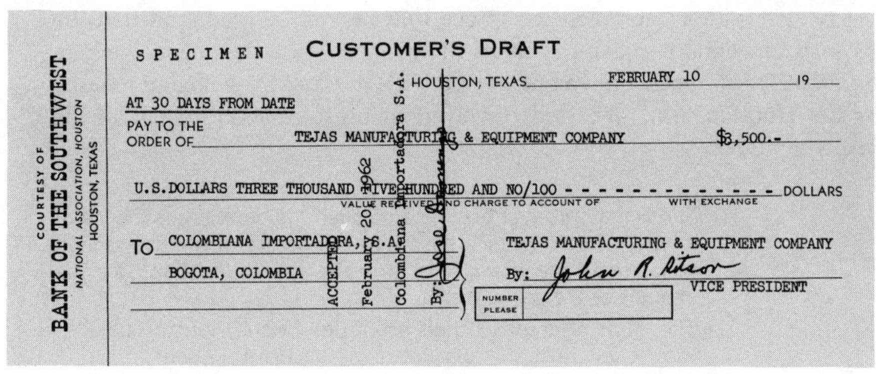
COURTESY OF
BANK OF THE SOUTHWEST
NATIONAL ASSOCIATION, HOUSTON
HOUSTON, TEXAS

SPECIMEN CUSTOMER'S DRAFT

HOUSTON, TEXAS FEBRUARY 10 19

AT 30 DAYS FROM DATE

PAY TO THE ORDER OF TEJAS MANUFACTURING & EQUIPMENT COMPANY $3,500.-

U.S.DOLLARS THREE THOUSAND FIVE HUNDRED AND NO/100 - - - - - - - - - - - - - - DOLLARS

VALUE RECEIVED AND CHARGE TO ACCOUNT OF WITH EXCHANGE

TO COLOMBIANA IMPORTADORA, S.A.
BOGOTA, COLOMBIA

ACCEPTED
February 20 1962
Colombiana Importadora S.A.
By:

TEJAS MANUFACTURING & EQUIPMENT COMPANY
By: John R. Ritson
VICE PRESIDENT

NUMBER PLEASE

Courtesy The Bank of the Southwest, Houston, Tex.

A customer's draft used in foreign trade transactions.

released to him by the bank. Actually, these documents are released to the buyer when he accepts the draft for payment. If the Tejas Co. decides not to keep this draft the full 30 days for payment, but sells it to its Houston bank, it must take a discount on the $3,500 face value in order to receive the cash immediately. This discount rate, which the bank charges for paying the draft before it is due, is normally the amount that would be charged for a 30-day, $3,500 loan to the Tejas Co.

Letters of Credit. Another term of payment used in international business is by means of letters of credit. The rather common use of the letter of credit stems from the weakness of the bill of exchange, or draft, under which the exporter (seller) must bear the entire risk of collecting from the importer (buyer). However, letters of credit have one disadvantage, and that is that they are not standardized, and each document must be carefully read. The money to be paid under a letter of credit is obtained by a bill of exchange drawn on a bank.

Letters of credit may be classified as either *irrevocable* or *revocable*. If the letter of credit contains an express waiver of the right to revoke or cancel the credit prior to a specified date, the document is regarded as irrevocable. On the other hand, if the opening bank reserves the right to withdraw from the transaction by stating that the credit is "good until canceled" or "unless sooner revoked," it is regarded as a revocable letter of credit. In addition to their use in commercial transactions, letters of credit may also be used by travelers going abroad.

The illustration opposite is an irrevocable letter of credit issued by The Bank of the Southwest, Houston, Tex., authorizing payment to the firm of Cafetero Manizales, Colombia, not to exceed $160,000 U.S. dollars. This amount is to be charged to the account of the Houston Coffee Importing Co., Houston, Tex., for the purchase of coffee by the Houston company.

This letter of credit is used on the assumption that the seller is not willing to ship without complete assurance that he will be paid, and that the buyer is unwilling to make payments in advance. It assures the Colombian firm that it will receive payment from the Texas bank for coffee purchased by the Houston firm. The steps involved in the transaction occur in the following order:

1. The Houston buyer arranges through his bank the issuance of a letter of credit which describes the nature of the transaction and directs the drawing of a draft against the bank for the amount of the purchase.
2. The letter of credit is then forwarded by the Houston bank to the seller in Colombia through a correspondent bank in Manizales, Colombia. The Colombia firm ships the coffee to Houston according to the conditions of the credit and presents

CABLE ADDRESS "SOWESTBANK"
CODES
PETERSON'S 3RD
BENTLEY'S-ACME

BANK OF THE SOUTHWEST

NATIONAL ASSOCIATION, HOUSTON

IRREVOCABLE
COMMERCIAL CREDIT

NO. 9600
UP TO US$160,000.-

SPECIMEN

HOUSTON, TEXAS

CAFETERO MANIZALES
Manizales, Colombia

February 25, 19

GENTLEMEN:

WE HEREBY AUTHORIZE YOU TO DRAW ON - - - - - - - O U R S E L V E S - - - - - - - -

FOR ACCOUNT OF - - - - - - - HOUSTON COFFEE IMPORTING COMPANY, Houston, Texas - - - - -
UP TO AN AGGREGATE AMOUNT OF - U.S. DOLLARS ONE HUNDRED SIXTY THOUSAND AND NO/100 - - -

AVAILABLE BY YOUR DRAFTS AT - - - - - - - - - - - SIGHT - - - - - - - - - - - - - - - -
ACCOMPANIED BY - Commercial Invoices
- Special Customs Invoices
- Full Set Clean On-board Ocean Bills of Lading issued to the order of BANK OF THE SOUTHWEST, N.A. HOUSTON, Houston, Texas notify HOUSTON COFFEE IMPORTING COMPANY, Houston, Texas - - - - - - - - -

Evidencing Shipment: - - - - - - - - not later than April 25, 196* - - - - - - - - - -

From: - - - - - - - - Colombia - - - - - - To: - - - - - - - - - Houston, Texas - - - - -

Of Merchandise Invoiced as: - 2,500 bags "WASHED COLOMBIAN COFFEE" - - - - - - - - - -

Special Stipulations: - Partial shipments are permitted. - - - - - - - - - - - - - -
- Insurance is covered by buyers. - - - - - - - - - - - - - -

DRAFTS MUST BE DRAWN AND NEGOTIATED NOT LATER THAN - - - - - May 5, 196* - - - - -
EACH DRAFT MUST BE MARKED "DRAWN UNDER LETTER OF CREDIT NO. - 9600 - OF THE BANK OF THE SOUTHWEST, N. A., HOUSTON, DATED February 25, 196* AND THE AMOUNT OF EACH DRAFT SO DRAWN ENDORSED BY THE NEGOTIATING BANK ON THE REVERSE SIDE HEREOF. WHEN PRESENTED BY THE MAKER DIRECT TO THE DRAWEE BANK, THE DRAFTS MUST BE ACCOMPANIED BY THIS LETTER OF CREDIT FOR THE PURPOSE OF SUCH ENDORSEMENTS BEING MADE THEREON.

WE HEREBY AGREE WITH THE DRAWERS, ENDORSERS AND BONA FIDE HOLDERS OF DRAFTS DRAWN UNDER AND IN COMPLIANCE WITH THIS CREDIT THAT SAME SHALL BE DULY HONORED UPON PRESENTATION TO THE DRAWEE BANK AS SPECIFIED ABOVE.

YOURS VERY TRULY

SPECIMEN John H. Doe — AUTHORIZED SIGNATURE A.V.P.   SPECIMEN Joseph P. Doaks — AUTHORIZED SIGNATURE V.P.

FORM 22506

Courtesy The Bank of the Southwest, Houston, Tex.

A commercial letter of credit.

to the Colombia bank the draft supported by the documents specified in the letter of credit.[7]

3. The bank in Colombia forwards the draft, along with the supporting documents, to the Houston bank.
4. Based on the terms of the commitment with its client, the Houston bank pays the Colombia bank, which in turn credits the Colombian exporter's bank account.
5. As per the contractual obligation between the buyer and his Houston bank, the buyer becomes legally obligated to reimburse the Houston bank for the amount of the credit used.

You will notice that the letter of credit also indicates that partial shipments are not permitted and that insurance is carried by the buyer.

Government and International Banks

Our present high volume of import-export trade could not be maintained without the indirect support of certain government and international banks. A general discussion of several of these organizations follows.

The Export-Import Bank. In 1934 the Export-Import Bank of Washington (D.C.) was established as an agency of the U.S. government. It provided help in the financing of American exports to ease the domestic unemployment problem common during the 1930's. The bank tries to supplement, rather than compete with, commercial banks, by restricting its loans to those ventures in which the ordinary commercial bank is not interested. It tends to restrict its loans to productive capital equipment for export, such as special machinery used in mining, industry, and agriculture. The capital stock is subscribed to by the U.S. Treasury.

The World Bank. More properly named the International Bank for Reconstruction and Development (IBRD), this bank finances exactly what its title says it does. Conceived in July, 1944, at the wartime Bretton Woods (New Hampshire) Conference, at the same time that the International Monetary Fund (IMF) was created, the bank began operating early in 1946 with slightly more than $9 billion of subscribed capital. Since then, the number of countries supporting the bank has grown from 43 to 105, with $21 billion in capital stock subscribed to (but only $2.2 billion paid in; the remainder is due only if needed to cover guarantees the bank has granted on

[7] Notice that among the specific documents to accompany the letter of credit in this illustration is a "Full set clean on-board ocean bills of lading." This term means all the original copies of the bills of lading that are issued. Having them protects the buyer because he knows that no one else has a full set who might present one of the copies and claim the goods. The term "clean" means there are no restrictions to the condition of the goods and that nothing has been lost or damaged due to a broken bag. (The possibility of loss or damage from *any* method of shipping *always* exists.)

loans). To date the bank has encountered no defaults on its loans, and is not likely to call on its members for additional payments of capital.

Actually, the bank was organized to solve the problem of long-term capital movements. This can be done in three ways: (1) by lending its own funds to needy countries for development purposes; (2) by underwriting loans to developing countries from other sources; and (3) by borrowing money itself from member-bank countries in order to finance loans. The fine reputation of the bank for screening its projects has made it possible for it to sell part of its loans to private banks and insurance companies. Initially, IBRD guaranteed the repayment of the loan to the purchasers, but that practice is no longer followed in all instances.

The International Finance Corporation. In 1956 a group of 55 nations (by 1967 the number had reached 81), all members of the World Bank, subscribed capital to form the International Finance Corp. (IFC). In association with other investors, IFC provides risk capital, though without government guarantee, for productive private enterprises. The corporation makes direct investments, usually on a mixed loan and equity basis. As you might have suspected, IFC is an affiliate of the World Bank.

The International Development Association. This organization was started in 1960 by several member countries of (once again) the World Bank, with which it is also closely allied. The association's aim is to make long-term loans, with or without interest, to underdeveloped countries, on terms more flexible and bearing less heavily on the balance-of-payments of recipient countries. Funds are used to build sanitation and water-supply systems, pilot housing developments, and other community projects. The loans have been largely for 50 years, with repayments generally beginning after 10 years. A service charge of ¾ of 1 percent per annum is made, but no interest is charged.

The International Monetary Fund. With over $20 billion in gold and national currencies, the International Monetary Fund (IMF) is the world's largest source of quickly available international credit. The purposes of the fund are to promote international monetary cooperation, to help eliminate restrictions on foreign trade, and to provide funds to meet temporarily unfavorable trade balances between nations. If country *A* desires to buy goods from country *B*, but lacks the currency to make the purchases, it can borrow the money from the fund in the currency of country *B*. Country *A* pays back its debt to the fund in gold or currency received through transactions with other nations. IMF was established, effective December 27, 1945, at the aforementioned Bretton Woods Conference.

The United States Tariff Commission. In 1916, Congress created the Tariff Commission, a nonpolitical agency of the government consisting of six members appointed by the President of the United States. The main function of the commission is to investigate, study, and submit to the President recommendations on tariffs and other matters pertaining to the foreign trade of the United States.

Before entering into negotiations with a foreign nation about tariff changes the President must, under the terms of the 1962 Trade Expansion Act, furnish to the commission, for study and recommendation, a list of contemplated tariff concessions. Prior to such negotiations by the President, to lower the tariff, the commission investigates to determine a "peril point" for each tariff item. The *peril point* is the tariff level below which, in the commission's opinion, the tariff cannot be cut without threatened or actual damage to a domestic producer. If the President exceeds this point in reducing a rate (he has the power to), he must explain his reason to Congress. Congress may then reverse him by a two-thirds majority vote of both Houses. Hence, this provision provides an escape clause by which the commission can recommend an increase in restrictions on imports if it finds that threatened or actual damage to a domestic producer would occur.

Under the Trade Expansion Act of 1962, Congress modified the use of both the peril point and the escape clause by offering tax relief, technical assistance, and loans to industries adversely affected by a tariff reduction. Employees may also receive a readjustment allowance for partial or complete unemployment caused by the tariff, or else they may receive training for new types of work, and in addition a relocation allowance to help defray their moving costs to new regions where employment may be available.

CAREER OPPORTUNITIES IN INTERNATIONAL TRADE

International trade has for many years played an important role in the success of our domestic companies. Today, an increasing number of American corporations are electing to engage in international business, and as a result career opportunities in this field are on the increase for interested and qualified college-trained persons. On the other hand, if you want to work for yourself, you may choose to become an independent importer, exporter, broker, commission merchant, or import merchant. For instance, career opportunities exist with domestic companies engaged in foreign-freight forwarding. And another developing field of employment is that of the foreign departments of domestic commercial banks. These banks, as you will recall from our previous discussion, provide a variety of financial services to the businessman or corporation engaged in exporting.

Generally speaking, there are probably more positions open to the beginner in international business who works in a domestic company than there are direct openings for immediate employment abroad. Usually, it is only the accumulation of experience that qualifies an individual for a foreign assignment—and also, many countries have laws that regulate the number of foreign citizens that international firms can bring into the country.

General Requirements

Like any other business occupation, a career in international commerce demands certain skills and personal qualifications. One of these skills is the ability to speak at least one foreign language. Another is the ability to adapt to a foreign culture, including its ways of doing business that are different from those used in the United States.

From the standpoint of education, one prerequisite is a degree in business administration, with a major in international business or in a related field such as finance, marketing, management, or accounting. Other important personal qualifications include a lively imagination, adaptability, stability, and a high degree of responsibility. (Of course, before assigning a person to a foreign post, his company almost invariably provides him with an orientation of its overseas operations, because a thorough knowledge of company policies is essential to an employee's comfort and composure as well as to his success.)

Fields of Employment in Exporting

Employment opportunities are available in both direct and indirect exporting, though the same jobs are not always found in both fields. Among the opportunities are the following:

The Foreign-Operations Director. Companies engaging in direct exporting through their own branches assign only topflight personnel to this post. The director of foreign operations must have a combination of administrative, selling, and diplomatic abilities. One of his responsibilities is to select personnel for foreign operations. He may be given the corporate title of president of one of the company's subsidiaries; often it is "vice-president in charge of foreign sales." He may live either in the United States or abroad, depending on the size of the operation.

The Export Manager. Another position is that of export manager, a post often one step below that of foreign-operations director. The export manager exercises direct supervision over company agents, salesmen, and clerks, and also over traffic operations. He must have experience in handling trade documents such as those previously mentioned in this chapter, and it is helpful if he also has a background in business administration, and a speaking knowledge of the foreign language of the country with which he is dealing.

The Export Agent. This is characteristically an indirect exporting position. The agent is similar to the manufacturer's agent in domestic trade—that is, he sells goods in the name of the manufacturer, who finances and ships them. The export agent is usually paid a commission by the manufacturer he represents. The more successful export agents are those who have lived in a foreign country long enough to know a great deal about its business operations and the people involved in them.

The Freight Forwarder. There are two types of freight forwarders. One is the domestic-freight forwarder engaged in consolidating and combining domestic shipments in order to take advantage of lower freight-rates. The foreign-freight forwarder is engaged in preparing shipments for foreign countries. A large volume of business is booked by both types. However, our concern in this discussion is chiefly with the work of the foreign-freight forwarder, because he performs a number of vital functions which his counterpart does not.

A manufacturer desiring to concentrate his energies on selling abroad will find the foreign-freight forwarder invaluable because of his knowledge of shipping routine. One important service this agent renders is the preparation of the documents to accompany overseas shipments. (These were discussed in this chapter under the topic of financing exports.) Both loading and unloading of shipments can be delayed if the documents are not properly prepared and executed. This type of forwarder is also helpful in determining things like proper routes, and which ports will have the necessary equipment to unload heavy cargo. If you want to gain wide experience, employment with a foreign-freight forwarder can give you a broad background in exporting.

Fields of Employment in Importing

It is more-or-less traditional for American importers to work through middlemen in foreign countries instead of dealing directly with producers. Among these middlemen are the *import broker*, the *import commission-house operator*, and the *import merchant*.

The Import Broker. The import broker's main function is to bring foreign sellers and American buyers together. This he does in much the same way as the domestic broker, who finds a buyer and then locates someone with the desired product to sell. Hence, the import broker rarely takes title to the goods or has anything to do with handling them. He is paid a commission, out of which he pays his expenses. Much of the Brazilian coffee trade is carried on by import brokers in the United States who deal with export merchants in Brazil.

The Import Commission-House Operator. This specialist, who also works on a commission, receives goods on consignment (transfer) from foreign producers and sells them on their behalf. He does not take title while the goods are in his custody. An understanding of foreign markets and the ability to search out the best sources of supply are essential for this type of employment.

The Import Merchant. Buying goods abroad and holding them either in a foreign or American warehouse until he can find a buyer is this person's specialty. This requires that he take title to the goods, which eventually are passed on to an American buyer. He renders other services as well, including the sorting, grading, mixing, or blending of goods where this must be done. Import merchants travel widely in foreign countries to locate goods they think will sell for a profit in another country. These merchants may specialize in one or a few products, or may import a great variety. Diamonds, rugs, china, liquor, seeds, bulbs, and leather goods are among the many items imported into this country through import merchants.

Opportunities in Foreign-Trade Banking

As we have seen, commercial banks play an important role in promoting trade overseas. Many large commercial banks located in harbor cities maintain fully-staffed international trade departments to handle all the details involved in preparing, processing, and collecting negotiable instruments used in foreign trade. These departments engage in currency exchange, prepare letters of credit, handle the negotiable instruments—drafts, checks, promissory notes—used by banks, and advise clients on specific problems.

If you are interested in a career in this phase of banking, you will need a broad background in general banking, including a working knowledge of procedures and documents, an understanding of the various credit instruments, such as those discussed in Chapter 17, and a familiarity with banking laws. Bank representatives sent abroad to solicit business must be fluent in the language of the country in which they are to work.

SUMMARY

Although the United States produces a major portion of the world's goods, it depends heavily on other countries for many raw materials, goods, and services. In the past, many American exporters have been able to promote new markets abroad with less difficulty than at home, because at home there is tremendous competition, whereas some foreign countries offer little competition. Exporting appears also to be a profitable way to sell our surpluses, which sometimes we cannot sell so easily here. We import partly because it is possible to buy foreign articles at lower prices than American producers must charge for them. In theory, our exports should balance our imports, but in practice this rarely happens.

A nation having more exports than imports has a favorable balance of trade. When imports exceed exports it has what is known as a unfavorable balance of trade. For more than a decade the United States has maintained a favorable balance of trade, but this so-called favorable situation is really not regarded as having produced a completely favorable condition. From an economic viewpoint, our policy of paying out annually in grants and loans to other countries, which turns out to be more than we collect from exports, is beginning to create an imbalance in our international balance of payments. To correct this situation, the government has embarked on a policy of lower tariffs, which will involve more cooperation and trade with the European Common Market nations. A second line of attack is for American producers to increase productivity as a means of making American goods more competitive from the standpoint of price. This involves the elimination of obsolete practices and the introduction of more automation. Thirdly, the federal government needs to adopt fiscal controls to slow down inflation. Thus, though the use of monetary restraints in periods of prosperity, booms can be kept from getting out of hand. Like the preacher who wants to spread virtue by discussing sin, an economist can illustrate the need for economic stability by identifying the evils of instability.

International trade problems are crucial for many countries. Nations importing large quantities of food, for instance, must sell their own goods abroad to pay for food imported. Nations importing large amounts of manufactured products must sell food and raw materials abroad. Many nations need export trade to pay for imports. Some nations need imports in order to allow other nations to purchase the goods they export.

Foreign exchange refers either to the process by which trade balances are produced from transactions between countries, or to the kinds of credit instruments used in foreign-trade transactions. Exchange rates for currencies of the various countries vary daily, and are quoted by certain large banks engaged in supplying foreign exchange.

Bills of exchange, either time- or sight-drafts, are used in international commerce to facilitate payment for goods. These instruments, together with trade documents such as bills of lading, commercial invoices, consular certificates, shippers' export declarations, and others, constitute the variety of international trade documents. Preparing and processing these documents is a function of commercial banks' international business departments.

Career opportunities in international trade are numerous and interesting. Many of the same kinds of positions are found in the international field as exist in domestic business. All of these positions require a high level of competency.

VOCABULARY REVIEW QUIZ

Match the following vocabulary terms with the statements below.

a. Ad valorem duty
b. Cartel
c. Customs union
d. Direct importing
e. Embargo
f. Export merchant
g. Foreign exchange
h. Foreign-exchange rate
i. Multinational corporation
j. Peril point
k. Protective tariff
l. Principle of absolute advantage
m. Revenue tariff
n. Subsidy
o. Specific duty

1. A nation which can produce an item better and cheaper than another because it enjoys a low cost due to a natural monopoly or some technical development is said to enjoy the
2. A tax or duty levied on imports expressed in terms of an amount of money per quantity of goods
3. A tax or duty levied on imports for the purpose of producing revenue
4. A tax on imports designed to protect domestic producers against competition from foreign importers
5. A tariff levied on the value of the goods
6. A government order prohibiting the shipment of goods in or out of the nation for sanitary, moral, or military reasons
7. Payment to a business by the government to stimulate the expansion of the business or to encourage exporting
8. An integrated operation with a global perspective having its foreign and domestic interests interwoven into an international business
9. A marketing middleman in foreign trade who buys and sells on his own account
10. The purchase of foreign goods directly from foreign sources by American businesses
11. The location of a geographical region within which goods may move freely without being subject to customs duties
12. Financial assets involving a cash claim held by a resident of one country against a resident of another country
13. The price of one currency used in terms of another
14. The level below which a tariff may not be lowered without damage to a domestic producer
15. An association of individual companies acting together for the purpose of controlling price, supply, and conditions of sale

QUESTIONS FOR REVIEW

1. What are the reasons why trade with other nations is so essential to the economy of this nation?
2. Explain the meaning of the *principle of comparative advantage* and the *principle of absolute advantage.*
3. Contrast the advantages to international trade with the difficulties involved in world trade.
4. What are the main obstacles to international trade? What is being done on a worldwide scale to remove them?
5. What, in your opinion, is the most valid argument for and against tariffs?
6. Has the reciprocal trade agreements program helped or damaged the economy of the United States?
7. Discuss some of the advantages and disadvantages of direct and indirect exporting.
8. Describe the difference between direct and indirect importing.
9. Explain the difference between a favorable and an unfavorable balance of trade. When does a dollar shortage take place?
10. Why is it important for the United States to cooperate with those nations belonging to the EEC and EFTA?
11. Discuss the two definitions given in the textbook for the term "foreign exchange."
12. Explain the main services that an international banking department of a commercial bank renders to business.

PROBLEMS AND PROJECTS

1. Using the most recent library materials, prepare a 2,000-word summary of the merits and disadvantages of the European Common Market, and show how this organization has helped to promote trade with the United States.
2. Beginning with the year 1900, trace the history of tariff legislation in the United States to the present. Include in your discussion reference to the Kennedy Round, explaining why the United States pressed so hard for a successful outcome of this project.
3. Referring to your library resources, prepare a written or oral report on any one of the following subjects:

    European Free Trade Association
    International Monetary Fund
    Central American Common Market
    Agency for International Development

A BUSINESS CASE

Case 24-1 The Decker Company

The Decker Co., a 25-year-old central Illinois firm, manufactures a line of home appliances consisting of portable dishwashers, electric stoves, and garbage-disposal units. The firm has a reputation for producing quality products. Almost half of the firm's annual business has been from new residential contractors, and the remainder from replacement sales. Last year the company earned 8 percent on its investment; annual sales amounted to $29 million.

For several months now the company's officials have been discussing ways to increase sales. The president and general salesmanager have in fact looked rather deeply into the possibility of going to a foreign market. Specifically, the idea has been suggested that the company consider the possibilities of establishing a subsidiary in one of the Central American countries to sell and service the product line.

A few weeks ago J. B. George, the general salesmanager, attended a luncheon in Chicago and heard a certain Prof. Allbright from Chicago speak on "Trade Opportunities for American Firms in Central America." The speaker presented a glowing report of the growth and stability of the Central American Common Market. According to his statistics, Guatemala had made the most progress of the Central American countries in constructing new public and private housing, and its general economy was strong. Also, employment there was high, and the country seemed to have a stable central government.

Upon returning to the company headquarters, George prepared a rather comprehensive report on the speaker's topic, which he submitted to the company president, and Frank Lee, director of research and advertising.

A meeting was called by the president, and it was agreed that the company should investigate the matter further. One month later, George and Prof. Allbright flew to Guatemala City, where they inspected local market conditions with an eye toward evaluating existing competition, and marketing channels. They discovered that business conditions were very favorable, but that only a few merchants spoke English, and so any permanent officials sent there would have to speak Spanish. Both the government and the economy seemed strong, and the exchange rate had not fluctuated during the previous six months.

Upon Lee's return to his office, the president directed him to conduct a marketing and economic study of Guatemala—especially of the possibility of locating in Guatemala City. This would involve setting up a branch office and warehouse, transferring a Spanish-speaking company man to be the manager, and hiring local clerks, salesman, and service representatives. The president approved a budget of $18,000 to cover the cost of the marketing study.

1. Where should the market research department look for facts for this study?
2. List all the factors that you consider to be necessary in making the analysis. Remember that George had already surveyed available marketing channels and the cost of renting a warehouse and office space.

PART 7
LOOKING TOWARD THE FUTURE

Business in the Future

25

Throughout this book we have dealt with a wide variety of subjects. For example, we have explored some of the economic laws which help to govern the environment in which business operates. We have analyzed how various forms of business ownership operate. And we have seen that although most businesses are staffed by a variety of specialists, each enterprise itself specializes in some type of activity, with the result that there is an interdependency among businesses both large and small.

A considerable part of this course has been devoted to the functional areas of business, such as finance, production, marketing, and management. We have observed, for instance, how management makes use of certain tools in the decision-making process. (You will recall that these tools include accounting, research methods, and quantitative analysis techniques; and that by using them properly, it is possible to make decisions that are more accurate.)

We have studied about the use of human resources employed in operating business at various levels of management and executive performance. And we know that the future economic progress of any organization depends largely on the collective effort of those individuals who make it up. Then, of course, we have also been concerned with such subjects as management and organized labor, marketing, advertising, and transportation; and finally with the subjects of business law and ethics, and the relationship of business to government at the state and federal levels in such areas as taxation and regulation.

Our understanding of current American business, then, has required a knowledge of how American capitalism works and of the basic environments in which modern businesses tend to flourish or fail. But what about our understanding of the future of American business? What does business have to look forward to? What are likely to be some of the key problems and opportunities of the business enterprise and the business community during the next few years? Our answers to these questions which will conclude this introduction to modern business, will be presented in the light of what we have been able to deduce from both past trends and present indications.

THE ECONOMIC OUTLOOK FOR BUSINESS

Space restrictions do not permit (nor does necessity warrant) making a detailed examination of all the prospective changes one might reasonably expect to take place in the economic outlook of the foreseeable future. Therefore, we shall restrict ourselves to just a few significant and representative forecasts.

Rising Per Capita Income

In the United States there is a definite trend toward higher per-capita incomes. Fewer American families live on a mere subsistence level than formerly. At the same time, the middle-income class continues to expand. These higher levels of income provide expanding markets for both domestic and international business. One of the most perplexing economic problems of the future will be how to keep markets growing as rapidly as production, without promoting inflation. What is going to happen in the decade ahead to per capita income if we have fewer people at work supporting a larger population? One conclusion might be that in order to achieve the Great Society program (or whatever you may wish to call it), it will be necessary in the future to accelerate the rate of production. Presently the labor force is about 75 million, and it is expected to be over 90 million by 1975—an increase of more than 20 percent. But how much of this total labor-force actually will be employed as income producers? Automation and increased mechanization could easily bring about a reduction in the number of skilled workers.

Increase in Business Ownerships

During the past several years the number of business ownerships has been on the rise. Today a higher percentage of individuals than ever before are going into business for themselves. They feel that there are more opportunities open to them if they "go it alone"—be their own boss—than if they work for someone else.

The records show there has also been an expanding public interest in owning stocks in (and thus "pieces of") more corporations. The Brookings Institution reported in 1952 that a total of 6.5 million people owned shares in American corporations. By 1962 the number of shareowners of securities listed on the New York Stock Exchange had grown to 11 million, and another 6 million investors owned shares not listed on the New York Stock Exchange but on the American and other stock exchanges. By 1967, the total number of shareowners of all publicly-held corporations reached 22 million. This rising trend in stock ownership is certain to continue during the 1970's.

The continued growth in the ranks of business owners, of both sole proprietorships and of corporations, is an indication of investors' confidence in our economic system. In the past it has been this venture capital that has supplied much of the money for research from which have been developed "miracle" drugs, modern plastics, better airplanes, new metals, more useful and attractive household appliances, and vastly improved communications methods and systems.

The Increased Need for Managers. As the number of enterprises increases, the need for more managers will rise sharply during the next decade. A part of this increase is bound to be due to the fact that productivity will continue to rise—probably by over 4 percent per year. The number of managers since 1900 has increased fourfold. By 1975 this number should double again. Consequently, many firms will continue to offer stock-option plans and other fringe benefits in order to retain these managers against the rising tide of competition from other firms to employ them at higher salaries.

Business Capital Expenditures

Although the increasing use of all types of machines will generate greater demands for capital, future *sources* of this capital will depend upon how favorably profits are expected to rise as a result of their purchase. The actual *amount* of funds to be made available to sustain the increasing capital expenditure pattern will depend mainly on how much income investors will be able and willing to set aside for investment purposes in new industries. In the past, even though taxes have been high, the volume of savings by individuals who have made private investments in insurance companies, savings accounts, corporate ownership, and mutual funds, plus the retention of profits by industry, has been adequate to sustain long-term capital requirements. Failure to make these investments would mean loss of both future income and export volume.

Population Growth

One of the most significant factors affecting the future of business is the population growth. Estimates prepared by the U.S. Bureau of the Census show a gain of over 25 million people between 1960 and 1970. The total population of the United States has been projected to reach 275 million by 1985.

Table 25.1 shows a projected population by 1975 as well as a projected personal income by that time. The table also shows the projected average annual rate of growth in population, projected employment, and individual income between 1962 and 1975. According to these projections, metropolitan areas in the Southeast, Southwest, Mountain States, and Far West will likely have higher average annual rates of growth than other parts of the

TABLE 25.1

MAJOR INDICATORS FOR U.S., BY REGIONS AND 224 METROPOLITAN AREAS

Area	1975 projections: Employment (000)	Population (000)	Personal Income in Millions 1960 Constant Dollars	Average annual growth rate 1962–75 (percent): Employment	Population	Personal Income	Per Capita Personal Income
UNITED STATES	85,987	225,284	$735,137	1.8	1.5	4.2	2.6
New England	5,214	12,997	44,464	1.3	1.5	3.6	2.1
23 metropolitan areas	4,183	9,932	37,722	2.0	1.9	4.3	2.4
Middle Atlantic	18,993	47,369	171,506	1.4	1.4	3.7	2.3
24 metropolitan areas	17,095	40,758	155,043	1.8	1.4	3.9	2.4
Great Lakes	17,093	44,278	149,146	1.6	1.4	3.9	2.4
44 metropolitan areas	13,071	33,750	119,273	2.2	2.0	4.4	2.4
Southeast	16,694	47,496	123,709	2.0	1.3	4.6	3.3
55 metropolitan areas	9,693	25,946	75,918	3.5	3.2	6.0	2.7
Plains	6,886	18,151	55,954	1.3	1.2	3.7	2.5
18 metropolitan areas	4,015	10,087	36,939	2.1	2.0	4.3	2.3
Southwest	6,754	18,720	53,521	2.6	1.7	4.7	2.9
28 metropolitan areas	5,000	13,026	40,693	3.4	2.7	5.6	2.9
Mountains	2,162	5,653	18,178	2.2	1.6	4.6	3.0
9 metropolitan areas	1,354	3,447	11,223	3.6	3.2	5.6	2.3
Far West	12,253	30,620	118,658	2.9	2.2	4.9	2.7
23 metropolitan areas	10,930	27,175	105,874	3.4	2.8	5.3	2.5

Source: *National Planning Association,* Center for Economic Projections, 1967.

country. The geographical region that is expected to have the highest personal income measured in 1960 constant dollars is expected to be the Middle Atlantic states.

These growth figures will, of course, have an economic impact of considerable magnitude on this country. More goods and services for the increasing population will be needed. The trend toward bigger families will mean a continued demand for roomier passenger-cars and station wagons, additional clothing and furniture, more spacious homes, and larger appliances. Far more educational facilities will be needed. Increased life insurance coverage and more property- and casualty-protection will be in order. The increasing number of senior citizens will have its impact on hospital and medical facilities. The Federal government will have the responsibility for maintaining a favorable climate for business firms by helping to sustain a stable economy with a high level of economic growth. Providing for all these needs will also place an added burden on local, regional, and state governments since more tax dollars will have to be collected in order to maintain the community services.

Some authorities question whether the total economic impact on the growth of prosperity caused by increasing population will not eventually create more social problems than the nation can solve. For instance, as we have already asked, will not a booming population need more housing, more medicine, and more hospitalization? If as a result of more automation we reduce the number of people working in industry, will it be possible to maintain a high employment-level? What is to happen to those likely to be displaced by automation, and those wanting to enter the labor market for the first time but unable to find employment?

The Outlook for Business Growth

As we learned in Chapter 1, the main factors affecting business growth are federal government spending, state and local government outlays, business capital expenditures, inventory buying, housing outlays, consumer spending, and international trade. When we add up these components, the end product represents the gross national product (GNP). We know that the GNP is a reasonably accurate and useful economic index as a measure of national economic well-being, but as an index it reflects only the size of our production output and does not tell us whether the goods are "right" for society.

The key to economic development lies in four fundamental factors: population, capital availability, natural resources, and technology. (Included in the general area of technology is the factor of education.) Without these, a nation lacks the necessary ingredients to produce a healthy economic climate.

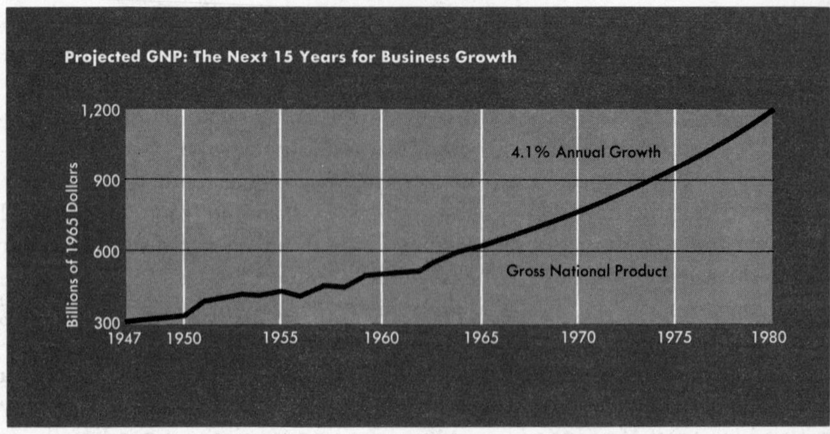

Source: U.S. Dept. of Commerce.

Economic analysts are in general agreement in predicting that between now and 1980 the GNP will, as indicated on the accompanying chart, continue to accelerate at the annual rate (4.1 percent) which has existed since about 1965. There should therefore be no major depression between now and 1980.

Inflation

The amount of progress this nation makes between now and 1980 may be vitally affected by several factors, one of which is our ability to grow without substantially increasing inflation. (Every rapidly developing country is tempted either to allow too much inflation or to use its resources in a manner that will not increase the standard of living.) Everyone agrees that inflation is a foe of economic growth because it dissipates the purchasing power of those depending upon wages, salaries, interest, and dividends. Moreover, as inflation increases, production has a tendency to drop because of the lack of consumer buying. And, at the same time, employees demand higher wages, since the prices of goods they buy are rising. In order to meet wage demands (and to offset their own higher costs), firms are then forced to charge higher prices for their products and services.

The ability of the federal government to control inflation without inhibiting economic growth is not very great. Therefore, inflation as an economic problem will no doubt continue to exist. In the last two years prices have been increasing an average of about 3 percent per annum, and there is little expectation that this inflationary rate will be reduced. Even the various controls exercised by the Federal Reserve Board are at best only temporary restraints on inflation.

No matter what may be considered the cause of inflation, we must conclude that the future will be bright or cloudy depending upon the ability of government, business, and labor to work cooperatively to curb expensive drains on our economic potential. The national interest should transcend those of individuals and groups. It must be maintained by the only authority powerful enough to guarantee its survival: the federal government.

THE RELATION OF BUSINESS TO GOVERNMENT

We have thus far discussed the future economic outlook for business in relation to business ownership, population growth, and business growth. Let us now turn to the relation of business to government.

Changing Patterns

Long after the Depression of 1929, businessmen persisted in their faith in the *laissez faire* philosophy. Many businessmen attacked the New Deal as symbolic of immorality and as highly impractical because government was "offering something for nothing." It was not until after World War II that business and government came closer together. At that time Washington, in quest of more competent government administrators, finally recognized the value of hiring top-ranking business executives. This was perhaps the most important step taken since the Depression to help bring business and government closer together, and fortunately the pattern of cooperation resulting from it has continued to prevail.

There is considerable evidence that the federal government is attempting to maintain a more favorable environment for business than ever before. Special committees composed of businessmen, educators, and professional leaders have from time to time studied national problems and submitted their recommendations to the President of the United States. Revisions in tax laws have helped to improve our economic climate. And there are fewer instances now where government is competing with business. It would appear that the trend is definitely toward less competition with the private business sector. Too, corporations are cooperating with the federal government to help reduce the deficit in the nation's balance of payments. And although businesses still fail, they do not usually do so because of an unfavorable economic climate.

In short, the future relationship of government to business should prove to be one of continued cooperation. One thing certain is that because businessmen will need to make their points of view heard more, yet at the same time will be expected to be more sensitive to the views of the government, they will come to participate in the government to a much greater extent.

Antitrust Legislation

Another area of relationship between government and business has been concerned with antitrust laws. A great deal has been written about antitrust laws in recent years. Yet there is probably no other area of legislation (unless it is labor legislation) that businessmen have experienced so much frustration from as in attempting to understand the laws as they are interpreted by court decisions. For one thing, these decisions because of their inconsistencies have made enforcement more uncertain. Furthermore, one may ask if present antitrust laws, as they are interpreted, really strengthen competition as they are supposed to.

Judging by the number of antitrust actions brought each year by the Justice Department and the Federal Trade Commission in an effort to convict alleged violators, it is obvious that antitrust legislation is not properly understood. Over half the cases the commission now encounters are complaints about product misrepresentation and corporate mergers. From 1948 to 1967 the number of suits initiated by the Justice Department more than doubled, and the FTC is currently preparing about 600 cases a year, as contrasted with about 100 a decade ago. As business prosperity continues during the next decade, it seems the number of antitrust actions is sure to be even greater as long as the current trend in antitrust policy is to maintain that corporate bigness is synonymous with monopolistic power.

In the area of business mergers (a closely related subject), Justice Department officials are having difficulty in administrating their antimerger policies. In rendering their decisions, it would seem the Department officials are considering social implications, as well as economic considerations, which many authorities consider to be outside existing laws. It is extremely difficult for a top company in a concentrated market to acquire other firms, either in its own field or a closely related one, without facing tangled and confusing legal problems from the federal government. (In one case, the Department even reversed itself on the ground that antitrust enforcement should consider dimensions other than the element of competition.[1]) To get the guidance they want in the future, businessmen obviously will have to exert more pressure on Congress to develop better-understood guidelines pertaining to the subject of mergers and consolidations.

LABOR-MANAGEMENT RELATIONS

Aside from problems arising out of strikes and featherbedding, a major post-World War II problem has been the relation of wage increases to infla-

[1] "Antitrusters Drop Fight on G. E. Deal as Senators Fear Closing of Plants," *Business Week*, April 17, 1965, p. 36.

tion and prices. For better or for worse, the power of the federal government has increasingly become a deciding factor in labor-management relations. This is because over the years (and more so recently) government has intervened in situations where disputes between management and labor have threatened the national interest. As we have seen, both the determination with which this interest is involved, and the choice of side to which government power will be thrown, are subject to many considerations, including the economic, the legal, and the political.

The Changing Labor-Management Environment

Judging by what has happened in the last few years, there is little doubt that the labor-management environment is changing. In view of the economic gains that unions have made for their members, it has been proposed that labor-movement officials now reevaluate their objectives in the light of contemporary social and economic problems. For one thing, population changes have created new problems. Half of the women over 35 now work, and this number will increase. Automation calls for new skills involving training rather than physical strength. Well-entrenched unions have the power to prolong uneconomical makeshifts; the railroads are an example of this. There are some critics who point to a deterioration of unions due to losses of union membership; and a few critics even argue that labor has outlived its usefulness. (We make no effort to justify or refute these observations in this discussion.)

Labor today finds itself in much the same predicament that business ownership was in four decades ago. For instance, labor still has certain responsibilities it did not ask for, and it still is guilty of the unwise use of power. Both of these factors have led to unfavorable public opinion at times, which in turn has caused restrictive legislation that labor seems unable to change in its favor.

Because jobs are being upgraded and automation is a reality, union leaders seem to fear that a reduction in the labor force is inevitable. They are aware that business is creating an economy which requires less and less labor, yet more and more production. In 1968 the labor force in the United States was only about 38 percent of the total population. It is conceivable that by 1980 it will be less than 35 percent. Should this drop occur, about one-third of our population will be working to support the other two-thirds.

Future Relationships With Management. It is very risky for anyone to try to predict future labor-management relations. As we have already pointed out in this chapter, the power of organized labor seems to be waning, and its general goals may be changing. One possible future action by unions might be to press for more social legislation in order to bring greater benefits to union members—for instance, to increase social security benefits (at the sole cost of business). At the state level, unions no doubt will continue to agitate for a higher minimum wage and for the broadening of pertinent laws to include more occupational groups. It is no secret that unions would like to have a stronger voice in business-management policies. (One way for the unions to gain this voice would be for them to invest more of their reserve funds in corporate enterprises—a move which would be especially effective in smaller and medium-size corporations.) But companies doubtless will continue to resist this. Finally, it is definitely predictable that unions will step up their campaign to reduce the normal work-day to about seven hours. If this campaign is successful—and it seems destined to be—every segment of the economy will be affected.

One recent trend in business that management may continue to promote is the "merger movement," whose purpose is the reduction of costs without the lessening of competition, and also the diversification of the investment resources of the business as a hedge against economic downturns in some segments of the economy. One of the more perplexing economic problems of the future will be how to maintain expanding product markets as rapidly as productive capacities, including labor, increase.

Although substantial progress has been made in labor-management relations over the past few years, there is still need for improvement. Whether they recognize them or not, both labor and business have inherited broad social responsibilities which they must accept with a greater degree of joint responsibility than they have heretofore shown.

FUTURE TRENDS IN FUNCTIONAL AREAS OF BUSINESS

Specific areas within the operation of any business are categorized as *functional areas* because they have to do with the functioning of the business: administrative, financial, organizational, and supervisory. The structure and relationship of these areas—incorporating such activities as marketing, production, management, and transportation—dictate the individual firm's internal organization. Although throughout this book we have analyzed from one point of view or another most, if not all, of the functions performed by business enterprises, we shall now, in our final discussion, consider what appear to be future trends in several of the more important functional fields.

The Next Decade in Management

The ranks of managerial, professional, and technical personnel are the fastest-growing in the business enterprise, and during the next decade may even double in number. It is expected that by the middle of the 1970's, one out of every two young men, and every third woman, entering the total labor force for the first time, will have attended college (although will not necessarily have graduated). It is from these two groups that the future managerial, professional, and technical workers will come. And these potential managers will need to have proficiency in every conceivable approach to problem-solving, and in understanding human behavior.

In the accompanying illustration, the projected increase in employment and in median years of school completed is highest for professional, technical, and kindred workers. Managers, officials, and proprietors, except farm, are

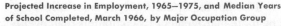

Projected Increase in Employment, 1965–1975, and Median Years of School Completed, March 1966, by Major Occupation Group

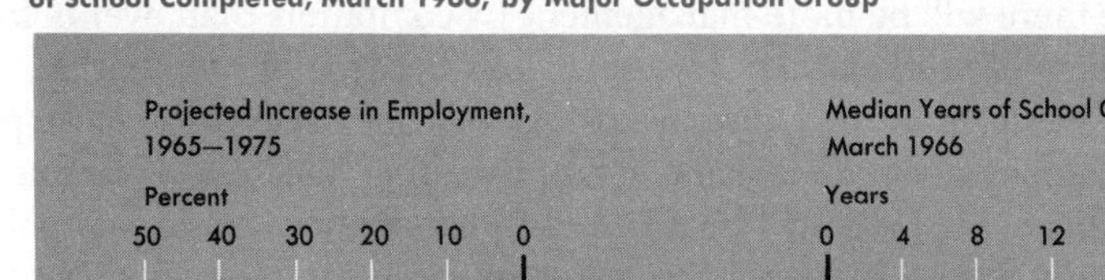

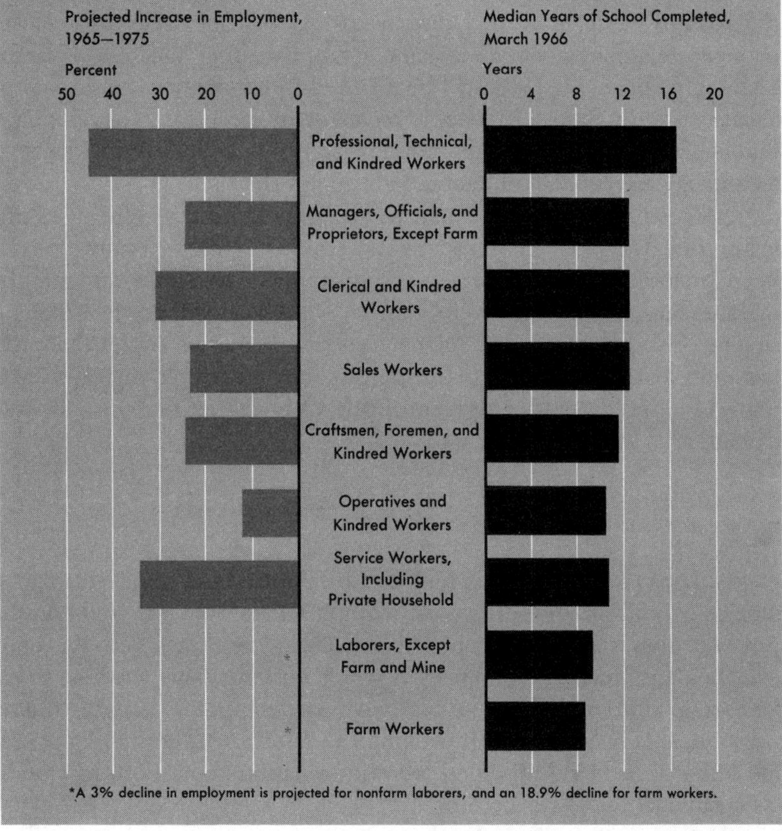

Source: Dept. of Labor.

predicted to rank second during the next decade in median years of school completed. In projected increase in employment, this latter group, as shown in the illustration, ranks fourth.

Most of the executives who will be retiring during the next decade began their business careers in the boom years of the 1920's and entered into executive jobs during the Depression years. Their successors, largely men whose first contacts with business were after World War II, will have to prove themselves worthy and capable of executive responsibility in a time of different circumstances but of equal, if not greater, challenge and opportunity.

Management's Tools of Tomorrow. The increasing use of the electronic computer as a tool used in decision-making almost inevitably raises questions about what will be the important tools of tomorrow. During the next decade there will be more management by computers than ever before. Large numbers of workers may lose their jobs because of automation, but (for reasons we have already discussed) this will not necessarily cause permanent unemployment. Electronic data-processing machines capable of seemingly impossible feats will be adapted to handle new kinds of problem situations in the future. Indeed, in recent years, progress in developing computers has been such that only those persons totally involved with computer technology are capable of keeping abreast of the times.

Meanwhile, top management will become less directly involved in making routine decisions but will spend more time in creating innovations. It has been predicted that the computer will reduce the status and number of middle managers, but this trend has not yet developed, nor is it likely to do so soon. Instead, today's middle manager's job is more complex than ever: he has more data to analyze, his responsibilities are increasing, and he is required to exercise more judgment. Little wonder that there is a shortage of managers!

Future Trends in Marketing

A new kind of partnership has developed between electronic data-processing and product designers, manufacturers, retailers, and consumers. Not only does it manage inventories in nationwide chains; but the computer tells the department-store managers which customers are the best prospects for certain kinds of goods. And not only is the computer changing the selling function; it is helping to better equip the salesman. Through its operation, the salesman is being provided more information about both his goods and his customers than ever before.

Just as clothes can make the man, packaging can go far in selling the product. The aerosol can, once confined to "bug-bombs," has exploded into a $150 million-a-year business for the hair-spray industry alone. We have witnessed only the beginning of an age of ingenious packaging which has introduced durable containers that have after-uses such as storage, display, and even cooking.

Future Trends in Banking

As we noted in Chapter 17, the commercial bank is an important source of short-term credit for both business firms and individuals. In recent years one form of consumer credit that has become popular is the charge account made instantly accessible through the use of credit cards. Cards issued by the Diners' Club, American Express, and a number of other organizations, allow one to purchase (among other things) train and plane tickets, gasoline and auto service, and restaurant and hotel service. Using computers to keep records, local banks reimburse local merchants, then forward their bills to the cardholders' own banks for collection.

Commercial banks all over the country have established credit-card programs, either through such organizations as American Express, or through other, larger commercial banks. The obvious goal of any ambitious bank or group of banks is to span the entire United States with a single credit-card system. The giant Bank of America, which created the Bank-Americard (a credit card), in 1966 began licensing banks outside of California to join the system. Five commercial banks in Chicago organized the Midwest Bank Card System, a credit-card system intended to meet the needs of individuals living in the greater Chicago area. Most of these bank-card systems cost consumers nothing—provided that within 30 days they pay their bills at the bank for their purchases. After that time the banks usually collect a 1½ per-cent-a-month interest on the balance. Thus, this becomes a new source of income for banks.

A revolution is occurring in the ways in which money is handled. The eventual outcome will be what may be described as "a cashless, checkless society," in which computers in banks will handle almost all financial transactions. Commercial banks already provide a service by which you can for a small monthly fee make arrangements with your bank to have checks drawn on your account to pay the monthly bills you incur. In the future you will not pay your bills by check, cash, or money order. Instead, by means of a telephone call, you will have your funds transferred from your account into the account of the individual, store, or institution you are paying. As a matter of fact, a good many payments made periodically, such as monthly mortgage payments, rent, utility bills, and insurance will be made automatically—without your even having to remind the bank. Furthermore, in the course of all this, should your bank account be exhausted, the computer will automatically lend you what is needed, up to a predetermined limit, and deduct the interest and repayments when due.

What is the reason for this revolution in banking? The main reason is that the amount of paperwork needed in the performance of today's transactions has almost become overwhelming. Take the area of checks, for instance: in 1966, Americans wrote 17 billion checks, with a value of nearly $4 trillion. And these figures are increasing annually at about 6 percent. Banks already refuse to accept any check, such as a counter check, that does not have account and transit numbers printed in magnetic ink. Another reason why bankers anticipate the inevitability of the paperless system is that it will enable them to concentrate in a highly profitable business: the mass-consumer installment- and small-loan market. Banks have in the past regarded small consumer-installment loans as too risky. Moreover, the high cost to the banks of credit investigation and of making such loans has been a matter of concern. Bankers are now finding that the computer may well be the long-awaited solution to the bothersome old problem of rapid and accurate credit investigation.

Commercial banks will in the future continue to perform a unique and important economic role by providing demand deposits and by serving as an important source of credit, especially for short-term financing for business. Few people today realize how much the services of our commercial and savings banks contribute to both domestic and international trade.

Transportation in the Future

As we observed in Chapter 23, economic progress depends largely on moving goods from one place to another at low cost. In fact, efficiency in transportation, including the task of physical distribution, can be the key that unlocks the door to greater economic resources. Transportation probably will undergo as much change during the next decade as any other business-related activity. Future historians most likely will regard the 1960's as the beginning of the second revolution in mass public transportation and physical distribution; the first one started with the airplane.

Several developments are projected for transportation. Improved methods of materials-handling used in warehouses will be introduced. Already, ramps have replaced stairs, and fork-lift trucks and conveyor belts have eliminated most hand labor. Much better inventory control systems will be introduced as part of warehousing.

Supersonic aircraft are on the horizon for use by commercial airlines—some of them capable of carrying up to 500 passengers at more than 1,800 miles per hour, and all offering rates cheaper than those of subsonic craft. Aircraft like these will also offer improved air cargo service at lower rates. And of course the versatile helicopter is bound to come into its own as an economical air-service craft.

Another projected development is the tube train which can travel above, on, or below the ground at speeds well over 100 miles per hour. Trains of this type could prove the salvation of the railroads, which have lost most of their passenger traffic and could lose out as the top carriers of long-distance freight if they do not keep up with the times. All things considered, whether the railroads will be able to recapture their lost passenger traffic and hold their leadership in freight handling depends largely upon the extent to which they are willing to invest in new ideas and equipment that will enable them to be more price competitive and to offer more efficient service.

Since World War II, railroads have gone through various changes. Profits from the heavy traffic burden placed on railroads during the war were high; their financial difficulties began in earnest only after the war, when equipment was worn out. The railroads tried a number of measures to restore profits. They cut passenger service, consolidated freight trains, introduced automation, modernized their rolling stock, succeeded in eliminating featherbedding, and—in some areas of the nation, at least—attemped to merge organizations in order to eliminate duplicate service and reduce property taxes. Today most of the railroads are enjoying higher earnings than a decade ago. The financial position of the railroads, especially those with transcontinental routes, should continue to improve during the next decade.

All things considered, truck lines are the leading freight competition of railroads. Although some truck lines are still relatively small-scale operations,

The artist's conception of metropolitan transportation in the future—the *PeopleMover*—designed to furnish faster and more convenient shopping trips from parking lots or bus stations to downtown areas. Other uses include travel at airports and on campuses of large universities. The *PeopleMover* cars have no motors but are propelled by power-driven wheels protruding from the ground.

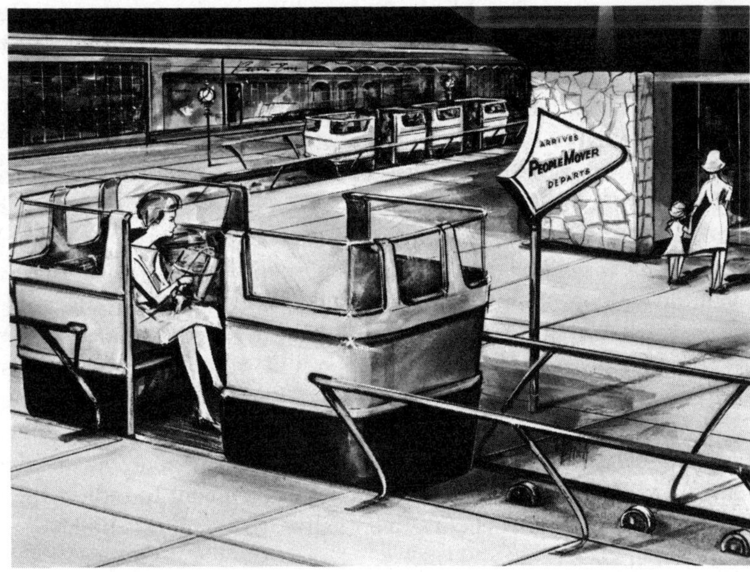

Courtesy, The Goodyear Tire and Rubber Co.

long-distance trucking has grown rapidly, and in the next few years will in fact be a serious threat to railroad freight traffic.

It is anticipated that inland water transportation, which has grown considerably since World War II, will continue its growth as more rivers are made navigable and new canals are cut from interior points to coastal towns and cities following the courses of the rivers. Shipping by water is cheaper than shipping by rail or truck, and likely will remain so for the next few years, but it has the disadvantage of being much slower.

SUMMARY

In this chapter we have attempted to take a broad look at the future of American business, with particular emphasis on certain areas of business. In short, the general future for American business in the decade ahead looks good. There is every reason to predict that the dynamic qualities of our business system will continue to stimulate economic growth. There will be, of course, cyclical changes. But one area of continued growth is likely to be in the number of new business establishments: statistics show a trend toward more business ownership. This is likely to be due in part to the growing number of small firms, to the rising number of individual investors in corporate stocks, and to the growth of mutual funds.

Another significant trend is the continuing population increase. This will pose a variety of problems. It should bring about an increased demand for new goods as large numbers of new family units are added to the total population. Too, booming population will require more housing. And workers are likely to have more leisure time. What is to happen to those who may be displaced by labor-saving devices?

Economists predict that the economic growth-rate as measured by the GNP will show an upward trend throughout the 1970's, but that at the same time there will be a corresponding increase in the rate of inflation. Indeed, many of them believe that inflation is certain during the next decade to remain the nation's most serious economic problem. It will, for example, cause increasing hardship for those who live on fixed incomes, such as retirees; it will produce periodic pressure from labor unions for higher wages (and therefore cause strikes); and it will continue to discourage personal saving.

Government and business are attempting to work more closely in planning a fiscal policy that will promote full employment. Businessmen and bankers are cooperating with the federal government to reduce the nation's balance-of-payments deficit. Eventually, the federal budget must be balanced.

Businessmen are constantly making demands for the clarification and rewriting of antitrust laws. They want more specific guidelines that apply to mergers, monopolistic practices, and restraint of trade.

The future of labor-management relations, particularly at the bargaining table, is likely to be stormy. As firms add more labor-saving equipment, more struggles will develop in which labor seeks to preserve the older methods of production. Labor finds itself in a position it did not seek. Traditionally, it has been an aggressive and even a militant force, demanding (and getting) better working conditions, fringe benefits, higher wages, and shorter hours. The future of the labor movement depends largely upon how well labor unions are able to play their role as a responsible social institution. If they are unable to act with responsibility, they may well lose some of their influence and be faced with new federal legislation requiring such governmental intervention as more compulsory arbitration.

The trend toward more mergers among business firms seems almost certain to continue, at its present rate, at least. Conglomerate mergers—those wherein a company in one industry takes over a company in a different industry—will go on, largely because of the benefits of size and diversification, despite the Justice Department's rather nervous vigil.

Transportation in the future will feature faster, quieter vehicles capable of greater payloads and giving off very little air-polluting exhaust. The railroads will make up for much lost ground as passenger carriers, and will continue to be the leading carrier of freight. Truck lines will be their major freight-shipping competition. And finally, the number of air travelers will increase very substantially as rates drop for certain kinds of flights, as business time during the shorter working-day becomes more valuable, and as the airlines continue to offer attractive and inexpensive opportunities to go now and pay later. (It has been estimated that slightly more than half the people in the U.S. still have not experienced a commercial flight.)

QUESTIONS FOR REVIEW STUDY

1. Why is it necessary to make predictions as to our economic future despite the fact that this is at best difficult?
2. What evidence do we have to show that there has been an increase in business ownership in the past and that this increase will continue in the future?
3. What are some of the factors that help to produce a rising per capita income?
4. Explain why there is likely to be an increasing need for more managers during the next decade.
5. What impact does population growth have on the economy?
6. Explain why inflation is an economic problem that affects business.
7. What are some of the changing patterns of relationship between business and government projected for the next decade?

8. Why has antitrust legislation been difficult for businessmen to understand?
9. What are some of the changing trends in labor-management relations that are predicted for the future?
10. Generally speaking, would you assume that labor is for or against corporate mergers of similar types of business? What are some of the reasons for labor's position?

Glossary

Absenteeism. Failure of workers to be present at their work stations.

Abstract of title. A summary record, tracing the title of real property, based on records in the Recorder's office in the county where the land is located.

Accountability. To hold a person liable for his conduct with respect to fulfilling his obligations.

Accounting. The recording, reporting, and interpreting of financial data resulting from business transactions. Its purpose is to assist management.

Ad valorem duty. A tariff duty levied on goods according to their value.

Adjective law. The rules of procedure or practice by which law is administered.

Administrative decisions. Decisions that formulate policy or relate to applying policies in the daily operation of a business enterprise.

Advertising. Any paid form of nonpersonal presentation of goods, ideas, or services, presented through the various media to induce the public to buy.

Advertising billings. Total dollar business done by an advertising agency as charged each client, including the client's media cost, production expenses, and agency charges.

Advertising medium. The means or channel through which the advertising message is carried to prospective consumers.

Advertising premiums. Sales promotion devices used to supplement advertising campaigns. Premiums generally fall into two classes: those given free, and those paid for by the consumer.

Agate line. A standard unit of measuring space one column wide and 1/14" deep.

Agency shop. A shop wherein nonunion employees as well as union members pay union dues.

Agent. A person authorized to act for another in transactions with third parties.

Alternate sponsor. A program sponsor who shares advertising time with another sponsor.

Analytical process. A manufacturing process in which raw material is separated into several components.

Apprenticeship training. Instruction given in connection with on-the-job experience.

Aptitude. The potential ability to perform satisfactorily a specific type of work.

Arbitration. Settlement of a dispute by a third party in a situation in which both sides agree in advance to abide by the decision rendered by that party.

Assets. Items of value owned by a business.

Authority. The power and right to command or to act in an official capacity in an organization.

Automation. The process of operating machinery which controls other machines without the aid of human effort.

Bailment. A legal relationship created when the owner delivers goods to another person who accepts them for an agreed purpose. Upon accomplishment of the stated purpose the goods are to be returned to the owner, as provided in the agreement.

Balance sheet. A statement of the financial condition of a business on a specified date.

Bankrupt. The financial condition of a person or corporation that indicates inability to pay debts. Often the term is used when a company's assets are being legally held to provide payment to creditors.

Beneficiary. A person for whose benefit a trust has been created, an insurance policy issued, or a will made, or who because of another's generosity is entitled to a certain income or the use of certain property.

Binary system. A number system, based on bits instead of decimals, which employs only two digits: zero (0) and one (1).

Bond. A written promise under seal, as evidence of a debt of a corporation, representing a specific sum with interest payable at a specified rate.

Bonus. A payment, usually in money, representing added commission for achieving a special goal or sales quota.

Boycott. An attempt by union members to curtail a company business through influencing the firm's customers to withhold their patronage.

Broker. One who has authority to act for or on behalf of either the buyer or seller in a marketing transaction.

Budget. A financial plan that shows the amounts of anticipated revenues and expenditures during a specified period of time.

Burglary. Forcible and unlawful entry into a business for the purpose of taking another's property.

Business. All the activities involving production, distribution, and services which are planned and carried out to meet economic needs of consumers.

Business unionism. Placing emphasis on economic rather than on social objectives of unions.

Capital goods. Products used in the manufacture of other goods.

Capital stock. Total aggregate equity ownership of a corporation as shown on the corporation's financial statement as the amount obtained from the sale of stock.

Capitalism. A system of economic organization based upon the right of private ownership and on the right to work for a profit.

Cartel. A contractual association of independent businesses in one or more countries, formed for the purpose of regulating production, prices, and marketing of goods by members.

Cash forecast. An estimate of the amount of cash expected to be received in a given period of time, the amount to be spent, and the anticipated balance on hand at the end of the period.

Cashier's check. A draft (bill of exchange) drawn by the cashier of the issuing bank and payable to the order of the person named as payee.

Centralized management. An organization plan that provides for the concentration of decision-making authority at the top level.

Certificate of deposit. An interest-bearing negotiable instrument, issued by a bank, stating that the person or corporation named has deposited a specified sum of money payable either to his order or to the bearer.

Classified advertising. A class of local advertising, familiarly known as "want-ads," which contains short statements of fact. It generally appears in a special section of a newspaper.

Close corporation. A corporation whose stock is not available for purchase by outsiders.

Coalition bargaining. A situation wherein several different unions within a given industry collaborate in their bargaining efforts.

Coding. Classifying and assigning identification numbers to various kinds of data.

Collateral. Property or securities pledged as security for a debt.

Collective bargaining. Negotiations between representatives of labor and representatives of management.

Commission merchant. A middleman who takes possession of, but not title to, the goods he markets. He arranges for the shipping, temporary storage, and delivery of the goods.

Commission plan. Compensation paid salesmen for performing a service or selling a product, which is based on a percentage of the total sales made.

Common carrier. One who offers transport services to the general public and charges uniform rates to all shippers.

Common stock. Shares of ownership in a corporation, usually carrying voting rights and without a fixed rate of return, but having a residual claim to the assets and profits of the company.

Competition. A state of rivalry existing among several persons or business firms seeking the same or similar goods (or whatever).

Composite estimate. The combining of a number of different judgments made by several persons in a business organization.

Computation. The performing of mathematical calculations.

Computer. An electronic calculator that operates at very high speeds.

Concentration. Locating a company's plants within a relatively small geographical area. (Also, centralization of authority in a few people.)

Conceptual skills. Personal skills involving the use of the power of the mind to see the whole enterprise as it functions, and not just one department.

Conciliation. A situation wherein a third party (a mediator) attempts to bring representatives of management and of a union together for the purpose of negotiation.

Consequential losses. Losses, suffered by the insured, caused by his inability to carry on his business in a normal way due to its destruction or damage by fire.

Consignee. The person to whom goods are being shipped.

Console. The instrument panel by means of which an operator controls computer equipment.

Consumer goods. Products bought by individuals for their personal use and satisfaction.

Consumer magazines. Magazines written and published especially to meet the interests of household consumers.

Consumer price index. An index, published by the federal government, that shows periodically the average price of a group of selected articles basic in determining the cost of living for a typical family in America.

Containerization. The shipping of goods in containers which permit them to be kept intact from origin to destination.

Continuous production. A manufacturing process that operates uninterrupted around the clock.

Contract. An agreement between two or more persons that is legally enforceable. It ordinarily provides for something to be given or done in return for compensation.

Contract carrier. One who sells transport services on the basis of individual agreements.

Control. Regulation of processes or procedures in order to attain or conform to uniform standards.

Controversy. A labor-management dispute that has not reached the stage of a threatened work-stoppage.

Convenience goods. Products which consumers buy at retail outlets near their homes.

Co-operative. A business organization owned and operated by the persons it serves.

Coordinating. A general function of management which may be defined as the process of reaching an agreement on plans and procedures through exchanging information.

Correlation. The establishment of a pattern in the relationships between or among two or more variables.

Copyright. An exclusive right to control and sell literary or artistic work. It is granted to the author or originator for a minimum initial period of 28 years.

Corporation. A group of persons, created by statute as a legal person, authorized with powers to contract, own, dispose of, and convey property in the name of the corporation, and to otherwise transact business within the limits of the powers granted in the charter.

Correspondent bank. A bank which acts as a representative bank for one or more banks in other cities.

Craft union. A union whose members are skilled workers, usually engaged in one of the trades.

Credit. The ability of an individual or business to secure goods or services in exchange for a promise to pay later. (Also, a promise to repay borrowed money.)

Credit insurance. A type of coverage that reimburses a seller for losses arising out of his inability to collect a debt.

Creditor. A person or business owning a debt owed by another person or business.

Current assets. Items of value, owned by a business, that will be converted into cash within a relatively short time.

Current ratio. A financial ratio, used by management, found by dividing the total of current assets by the amount of current liabilities.

Customs union. A geographical region composed of two or more countries within which goods may move freely without being subject to customs duties.

Data processing. That group of operations performed in handling units of business data from the original to the final entry.

Debenture bond. A bond, issued as a general claim against a corporation, for which no particular assets are pledged as security.

Decentralization. The location of new units of manufacturing or business over a wide geographical area.

Decentralized management. The assignment, both to and at lower executive levels, of decision-making authority and of freedom to act (as contrasted with the concentration of authority in a few individuals at high levels).

Deed. A written instrument, under seal, conveying ownership of real property to another.

Demand. The quantity of goods or services that will be purchased at a given price.

Demand forecast. Anticipation of future sales volume and trends.

Demurrage. A charge made for leaving a railroad car on a spur beyond the normal 48-hour unloading time.

Depreciation. A decrease in the economic value of capital goods due either to the passage of time or to use, if not to both.

Direct importing. The purchase of foreign goods obtained directly from foreign sources.

Discharge. Involuntary release from one's position by his employer; a "firing."

Dispatching. The preparation and issuance of work orders in manufacturing.

Dispersion. The scattering of factories and warehouses over a wide geographic area.

Disposable income. The income that one has essential freedom in spending: income remaining after taxes.

Distribution. The marketing and transporting of goods.

Distribution channel. The route which goods follow as they move from the producer to the consumer or from the seller to the buyer.

Diversification. The investment of materials and resources in a variety of ways in order to broaden the risk involved in production.

Diversion. Changing the terminal point of a shipment while it is en route but before it reaches its original destination.

Drawer. The person who executes or draws a bill of exchange or negotiable draft ordering the drawee to pay the instrument.

Economic freedom. The right to choose a way of earning a living, and the freedom to enter into contracts with others.

Economics. A study of the organization and utilization of the means of production in order to meet the economic needs of people.

Embargo. A federal government order prohibiting the shipment of goods in or out of the nation for sanitary, moral, or military reasons. (Also, the refusal by transportation companies to move freight in case of a strike or of undue traffic congestion.)

Endowment policy. A life insurance contract that combines life protection with an investment feature. The company will pay the face amount to the insured if he lives to a certain date, or the same amount to his beneficiary should the insured die before that date.

Entrepreneur. One who establishes a business, and assumes the risks involved in putting capital and labor to work, in the hope of economic gain.

Equity capital. The value of cash assets and of other assets of one's ownership in a business.

Estate tax. A tax imposed on the total value of real and personal property left by a deceased person.

Excise tax. A commodity tax imposed on the manufacture, sale, or consumption of goods or services within the country. It may be levied on wholesaler, retailer, or consumer.

Executive. A person in a business organization who occupies a position of authority over others and is responsible for their work.

Export merchant. A marketing middleman (merchant), engaged in foreign trade, who buys and sells on his own account rather than for a client.

Exports. Goods shipped out of a country to a foreign market through regular channels of trade.

Extractive process. A production method used in removing raw materiels from the earth, air, and oceans.

Fabrication. A manufacturing procedure involving reshaping the form of materials, and the assembling of parts into an integrated product.

Family income policy. A life insurance policy that combines straight life insurance with decreasing-term insurance.

Feeder lines. Small transport companies that connect small communities with main transportation lines.

Fidelity bond. Insurance coverage which protects an employer against loss due to acts of dishonest employees.

Fiscal period. A period of time used by a business as the length of its accounting cycle.

Fixed assets. Items that represent major capital investments. (Also, assets that will be used for a long time.)

Fixed capital. Long-term assets such as land, buildings, and equipment.

Formal organization. A system or arrangement of well-defined jobs to be performed at various levels and organized as part of a planned structure.

Franchise. A specific privilege, in the form of a contractual right, generally granted by government to an individual or company. In the case of an exclusive dealership, such right is granted by a business firm.

Franchisee. The party to a franchise agreement who accepts the responsibility to become an agent for the franchiser.

Free market. A name given to the locus of that competitive bidding which helps to maintain a balance between the supply and demand of a good.

Functional middlemen. Agents or brokers who serve as connecting links between manufacturers and wholesalers.

General partner. An owner of a general partnership who has unlimited personal liability for the operation and debts of the business.

General partnership. A form of business which, although owned by two or more persons known to have unlimited liability is not incorporated.

Grading. The sorting of goods into classes, or groups, according to size or quality.

Grievance. A worker's expressed complaint of dissatisfaction with his working conditions or with his relationship with his associates or superiors.

Grievance procedure. The method by which an employee registers complaints resulting from circumstances that develop in his working situation.

Gross national product (GNP). The total market value of all goods and services produced by the economy in one year.

Gross profit. The difference in the cost price and the sales price of a good; the profit on a sale before deducting expenses incurred in making the sale.

Growth stock. A stock whose market value is expected to increase rather rapidly.

Holding company. A corporation organized for the purpose of owning stock in one or more other corporations.

Import quota. A specified maximum amount of a commodity permitted to enter a country during a given period of time.

Imports. Goods of any kind entering a country through regular channels of trade.

Impulse buying. Consumer purchases based on sudden, unpremeditated urges to buy.

Income. The revenues or earnings resulting from business operations.

Income statement. A report of revenue received, the cost of goods purchased, and the expenses incurred in operation.

Incorporation tax. A tax levied by a state on a new corporation at the time its charter is granted.

Independent union. A union not affiliated with any labor federation.

Index number. A number that indicates changes that have occurred in groups of related data.

Industrial goods. Products used by businesses in the manufacturing of other products.

Industrial management. The application of the scientific approach to the problems of operating a factory.

Industrial union. A labor group organized according to the industry involved rather than to the specific type of work providing the immediate employment.

Informal organization. The absence of a planned network of personal and social relationships in the organization. Authority is earned or given permissively, rather than delegated.

Injunction. A court ruling preventing certain specified types of activity on the part of labor or management.

Input. The "feeding in" of information, material, and/or effort required by an operation. (Also, that which is "fed in.")

Insolvency. The financial condition of a debtor (the insolvent) whose real and personal property is insufficient in value to pay all his debts.

Insurable interest. An insurance principle that requires the policyholder to prove that he will suffer a financial loss if the insured property is lost, destroyed, or damaged.

Interstate. Between or among states.

Intrastate. Within a state.

Inventory. A physical count of goods or raw materials on hand at a given time.

Inventory control. The management of and accounting for all materials or goods purchased and on hand.

Investment banker. A banker who underwrites or handles the sale of investment securities for a business firm seeking additional capital.

Investment companies. Corporations that sell shares to individual investors and use the money received to buy securities in other companies.

Job analysis. A study of the functions carried on in a work position in order that a description and classification of the position may be prepared.

Job classification. The grouping together of work positions in a bracket or class.

Job description. A statement based on an analysis of the duties to be performed on a job, and of the qualifications needed by the worker who is to hold that position.

Joint-stock company. A form of business ownership that combines the unlimited liability of the general partnership with such features of the corporation as management by a board of directors, transferability of stock certificates, and the possibility of attracting a large number of share-owner investors.

Joint tenancy. An estate in real property held by two or more persons as a unit, and as one tenant. Upon the death of one joint tenant, his property passes to the survivor or survivors named in the joint tenancy.

Jurisdictional dispute. A controversy between unions as to which has the right over certain types of work activities or procedures.

Key-man insurance. Life insurance on an important or "key" executive, generally purchased by his company, with the company named the beneficiary.

Labor agreement. The contract between labor and management that contains the various provisions governing their working relationship.

Labor turnover. The rate at which employees fill and vacate positions within a firm's working force—that is, join and quit the company.

Larceny. A legal term used to describe the unlawful taking of property regardless of the method used.

Layoff. A situation (usually a slowdown in business) which causes employers to temporarily relieve at least some employees from their positions.

Layout. In the narrow sense, the arrangement of equipment and supplies in a factory or office. Broadly speaking, the entire physical arrangement of plant and material components. (Can also be applied to the sequential ordering of steps in a work process.)

Liabilities. The debts owed by a business; the equity of the creditors in the business.

Line relationship. A pattern of operation that recognizes a chain of command in which supervisors have direct control over, and responsibility for, those supervised.

Lockout. The act, on the part of management, of closing a plant and refusing to allow workers to enter it.

Low-pressure selling. Selling techniques based on the concept of service to the client rather than on the application of high-pressure tactics.

Management. Those at the executive level who plan, organize, and staff a business, and who coordinate and control activities, personnel, and resources.

Markdown. A reduction in the original selling price.

Market. A place where goods or services are exchanged at a mutually agreed-upon price.

Markup. The difference between the retailer's cost and his selling price.

Marketing. The process of selling and distributing goods or services.

Marketing functions. Activities or services performed in the process of distributing goods from the seller to the buyer.

Mean. An arithmetic average of certain given numerical data.

Mechanization. The preponderant use of machinery in manufacturing, hand labor playing only a supporting role.

Median. The middle number in a series of related numbers that are arranged in ascending or descending order.

Mediation. The offering of various suggestions by a third party assisting in labor-management negotiations.

Merchandising man. A person in a sales organization responsible for promoting his product line among jobbers, for product planning, and for the formulation of product policies.

Merger. Absorption of one business by another to form a single entity.

Middlemen. Those who buy and sell goods as an aid in distributing goods from the producer to the consumer.

Milline rate. An advertising rate used by advertisers to make comparisons of advertising costs based on the cost per line. The rate is computed by multiplying a publication's line rate by 1 million, then dividing by the circulation.

Mode. The point of greatest concentration; the number that appears most frequently in a series of numbers.

Monitor-type building. A building having a two-level roof whose upper level runs down the center of the structure.

Monopolistic market. A market controlled by one firm, or a small group of firms, for the purposes of eliminating competition and controlling the price and supply of a good.

Morale. The attitudes and feelings of employees toward their company and their working relationships.

Mortgage bond. A bondholder's claim which is secured by a mortgage against the corporation's assets. (Thus, a "first mortgage" bond means the bondholder's claim is secured by a first mortgage against the corporation's assets.)

Motion study. The breaking down of a worker's movements and procedures into all the basic motions he uses; and the analysis of this breakdown.

Multinational corporation. A corporation, conducting business in two or more countries, whose foreign and domestic interests are interwoven in an international operation.

Mutual insurance company. An insurance company owned by its policyholders. It has no stockholders, nor is there any capital stock.

Negotiable promissory note. A written contract containing the elements of negotiability, including a promise to pay a definite sum of money at a determinable future date.

Nominal damages. The awarding by a court of a small amount of money in damages to a person whose legal rights have been violated, but who has sustained no actual loss.

Nonparticipating insurance. An insurance contract on which no dividends are payable. The premium is calculated to cover as closely as possible the anticipated cost of the protection.

Observation method. A research-study way of watching and noting human behavior, such as that of people shopping or at work.

Oligopolistic market. A market in which only a few sellers or producers compete (but which none controls).

Open shop. A business enterprise wherein there is no organized union.

Organization. The structure for putting resources together into a total enterprise including facilities, materials, and people organized by positions based on levels of work.

Organizing. A function of the management process having to do with the way that business operations, personnel, and physical facilities are brought into proper relationship so that the major objectives of the business can be accomplished.

Output. That part of a computer system that prints out the reports after data have been processed. (Also, the productive measure realized by a work-performing entity.)

Par value. Originally, par value was supposed to represent the amount of capital first paid to the corporation for each share of stock. Today, par value is of little significance to investors because usually it is no more than an arbitrary value placed on the certificate as a minimum nominal value.

Payee. A party to a negotiable instrument to whose order the instrument is drawn.

Performance test. A test that indicates a worker's degree of skill in performing a specific type of work.

Peril point. A hypothetical limit beyond which reductions in tariff duties may not be lowered without injury to an industry.

Perpetual inventory. A record of materials or goods on hand that is kept up-to-date.

Personal property floater policy. An all-risk policy that covers household goods and other personal effects of the insured while he is at home or away, in transit or not.

Personal selling. Activities of both inside and outside salesmen, involving oral persuasion in direct contact with buyers.

Picketing. The stationing of union members (usually carrying placards) at store or plant entrances to influence customers not to patronize the firm, and to prevent other union members from reporting for work.

Piece wages. Wages paid on the basis of the number of units produced.

Place utility. The usefulness and value of a product due to its being in a place where there is a demand for it.

Planning. The initial step of any well-ordered operation. It involves the thinking through and setting up of all that is required in the execution of the chosen task.

Point-of-purchase advertising. Advertising appearing at or near the site of consumer purchase decisions—usually in show window's and at select locations within the store.

Police power. The limitation of private property rights by government for the purpose of protecting the property, life, and well-being of its citizens.

Policy. An oral or written statement used as a guide to action. (Also used to describe the terms of an insurance contract.)

Portfolio. The investment holdings, stocks, bonds, or other property, which the investor owns.

Poster. An outdoor signboard (standard size: 12′ × 25′) on which an advertisement is pasted or painted.

Pre-emptive rights. The rights of a stockholder to subscribe to additional shares of stock in advance of the time they are offered to the general public.

Preferential shop. A business wherein workers may choose not to be union members, but in which, because the union is the bargaining agent representing all the workers, union members enjoy certain preferences in employment over nonmembers.

Preferred stock. Corporation stock which has preference over common stock (e.g., preference in the payment of dividends). In case of bankruptcy, preferred stockholders have a preference over common shareholders.

Premium. The sum of money the policyholder agrees to pay to the insurance company for the protection being purchased.

Price-earnings ratio. The relation of market price to earnings. It is computed by dividing the price of a share by its earnings.

Primary data. Information gathered or reported for the first time.

Principle of insurable risk. An insurance principle that holds that if the requisites of insurability do not exist, then the risk is not economically insurable. One requisite of insurable risk is that the loss insured must be accidental and unintentional.

Private carrier. One who transports his own goods.

Private enterprise. A business system wherein individuals may hold legal title to property and are free to carry on business as they see fit in utilizing their property.

Procedure manual. A collection of written rules and procedures used as a guide for persons who work for an organization.

Processor. A unit of a computer that includes the control panel, the calculator, and the memory or storage element.

Product advertising. Advertising used to promote sales of a product, or a brand or family of related products.

Production. All activities involved in removing natural resources from the earth and processing them into finished goods.

Production sharing. Participation of workers in the distribution of profits which result from savings that accrue from a reduction in production costs.

Productivity. Efficiency of production: the amount of output in relation to input.

Profit sharing. Participation of workers in the distribution of profits earned by the business.

Program. A set of coded instructions that tell a computer which operations to perform.

Promotion. A position change that increases one's responsibility and pay.

Proportional tax. A tax which takes money from people in amounts directly proportional to their income. A tax is proportional when its rate remains the same, regardless of the size of the tax base.

Proprietorship. The right of ownership to capital goods. In accounting, it is the equity of the owners and is found by subtracting the amount of the debts from the value of the total assets owned. (Also, a single-owner type of business.)

Prospectus. A detailed analysis prepared to accompany the sale of a new issue of stock to the public and showing the financial condition, capitalization, record of earnings and profits, and dividends paid.

Protective tariff. A tariff on imports high enough to protect domestic producers against foreign competition.

Proxy. A person appointed to represent another and to act as his agent, particularly in a designated meeting or before a public body.

Public policy. A common code which decrees that conduct on the part of individuals, groups, or business firms shall not violate public morals or be injurious to the public at large.

Public relations. Any form of communication intended to promote good will or to create in the public mind a favorable image of the business or organization.

Public-liability insurance. An insurance policy which provides protection against claims arising out of bodily injuries or damage to property of the public.

Purchase order. The instrument, used when buying goods or materials, indicating the quantities and specifications desired.

Purchase requisition. A written request that certain materials or equipment be purchased. Usually the requisition suggests the desired specifications.

Purchasing agent. One who is responsible for buying raw materials, supplies, or equipment.

Pure risk. A type of risk that can result only in a loss should the peril occur. In pure risk, there is uncertainty as to whether the destruction of the object in question will occur.

Ratio. A relative number expressed as a fraction or percentage (in order to make a comparison or show a mathematical relationship).

Raw materials. Those basic commodities taken from or produced by the earth and including the natural resources it contains.

Real income. One's earnings, measured not in dollars but in terms of its purchasing power—the goods and services it will buy.

Real property. Land and anything permanently attached thereto (as distinguished from personal property, which includes all movable property).

Receiving report. A verification that the goods received are in the quantities and specifications as given on the purchase order.

Regressive tax. A tax whose rate takes a larger fraction of their pay from those with low incomes than from those in high income brackets. A sales tax is regressive because it bears most heavily on persons with low incomes.

Research. The process of discovering new information, interpreting it, and applying it to problem situations.

Responsibility. An individual's obligation to perform a certain task and to carry out duties assigned to him as part of his work.

Retailer. One who buys goods in quantity from wholesalers and sells them individually to consumers.

Revenue tariff. A tariff on imports, levied for the purpose of producing tax revenue.

Right-to-work law. State laws that prohibit union-shop contracts.

Risk. The possibility or uncertainty of loss arising from such hazards as fire, credit, life, health, or public liability risks.

Routing. Assigning a sequence to the various steps in a manufacturing or other process. (Also, sending something through such a sequence.)

Sales management. The performance of such functions as the planning, directing, and controlling of selling activities of a business.

Schedule bond. A type of fidelity bond which lists many employees of the firm by name and bonds them for specified amounts of coverage. Fidelity bonds are purchased by an employer for his own protection against the dishonesty of employees.

Scheduling. Setting time-tables for the arrival of materials, the operation of machinery in production, and the delivery of finished products.

Secret partner. A business partner who takes an active part in the management but who does not want to reveal his identity to the public.

Selling. A personal or impersonal process of persuading a buyer to react favorably to a sales appeal.

Separation. Voluntary or involuntary severance from one job.

Shopping goods. Articles, bought by consumers, whose price, fashion, and quality are of predominant importance.

Short-term financing. Obligations or debts that have a maturity of less than one year.

Sight draft. A bill of exchange constituting a written order issued by the drawer to the drawee to pay to a third party (the payee) a sum of money, certain in amount, either on sight or on demand.

Silent partner. A partner in a partnership who plays no active role in the business even though he may be known to the public as a partner.

Specialization. The regular performance of a limited part of an activity. (Also, the dividing of an activity into job-limited parts.)

Specialty goods. Articles preferred for some distinctive quality or special aspect they feature.

Specific duty. An import duty expressed in terms of an amount of money per weight or quantity of goods rather than by its dollar value.

Speculative risk. A situation, such as a wager in which there is both a chance of loss and a chance of gain.

Staff relationship. An organizational relationship which provides advisory or technical service to persons in line positions or performing operating functions.

Standard. A constant physical characteristic or quality that gives uniformity to a group of products.

Standardization. Using uniform methods and procedures in manufacturing.

Statistics. The science of working with numerical data in relationship to decision making and problem solving.

Statutory law. A law enacted by a legislative body.

Stock company. A corporation that issues stock certificates representing shares of ownership, and which provide a basis for distributing profits to the shareholders.

Stock dividend. The issue by a corporation, as dividends, of new shares to current stockholders.

Stock right. The legal right of a stockholder to buy additional shares within a stipulated time and at a designated price.

Stock turnover ratio. The number of times per given period of time in which a business sells its entire stock inventory.

Straight life insurance. A life insurance policy on which premiums are payable for the duration of the insured's life.

Straight-salary plan. A stated amount of wages paid per week, month, or year. In the case of a salesman it may be paid regardless of his sales volume.

Strike. The refusal of employees to report to work until management agrees to meet certain of their demands.

Subsidy. Financial assistance or its equivalent paid to a business by the government to induce, assist, or otherwise stimulate the business to help make an uneconomic operation profitable. (Also, a grant by a central government to a political subdivision for the support of specific public services.)

Substantive law. That part of the law that creates, defines, and regulates legal rights.

Supervisory training. Education pertaining to human relations; or instruction for persons being promoted to leadership positions.

Supply. The amount of a good or service that is available for purchase.

Supply forecast. An estimate of future availability of material, supplies, or products.

Surety bond. A written contract involving three parties—the principal (obligor), the one protected (obligee), and the insurer (surety—who agrees to make good on any default on the part of the principal in performing his duties toward the obligee). In surety bonds, the obligee is concerned not only with the obligor's honesty, but also with his capacity to act.

Survey method. Research that gathers data through the use of questionnaires, interviews, or an actual count of items or events.

Synthetic process. A production process whereby several raw materials are combined to form new products.

Tariff. A schedule or system of customs duties levied by the federal government on the importation of goods.

Tenancy in common. A form of real property ownership in which each owner has title to an undivided share of the real property. If one owner dies, his interest passes to the person named by him in his will, or to his heirs, but not to the surviving owner or owners of the estate.

Term insurance. A life insurance policy payable to a beneficiary at the death of the insured, provided death occurs within a specified period or before a specified age.

Term loan. Credit in the form of a loan ranging from one to 10 years.

Theft. The unlawful taking of property. The category includes larceny, burglary, and robbery.

Time draft. A bill of exchange, issued by the drawer to the drawee, constituting a written order to pay a third party (the payee), or his order, a sum of money certain in amount on a designated future date as shown in the instrument.

Time wages. Wages paid on the basis of the number of hours one has worked.

Time study. A formal method of determining the time needed by workers to perform the various elementary movements required by their jobs.

Time utility. The usefulness and value a good retains by being available at the time it is needed.

Title insurance. An insurance contract that provides protection against losses resulting from unknown defects in the title of real property.

Trade. The buying and selling of goods either between businesses or between businesses and individuals.

Trade credit. Credit granted for goods sold on an open-book account as accounts receivable, with the understanding that payment is due within a certain number of days after the date of invoice.

Transfer. A job change at the same level of employment, without changing one's degree of responsibility or rate of pay.

Transport diversification. Common ownership of various modes of transportation.

Transportation. Narrowly defined, the movement of goods from a place where they are not needed to a place where they are needed.

Trend analysis. The use of line graphs in studying a past historical sequence and applying it to the immediate future.

Trust. A combination of businesses operated under trust agreements by trustees for the benefit of the members. (Also, an organization for holding the property of one person for the benefit of another.)

Trustee. One who holds legal title to property but who uses it for the benefit of another.

Union shop. A shop wherein union membership is required of all employees.

Variable annuity. A retirement plan by which the saver accumulates funds in a life insurance company which are invested in units of common stocks so that the annuity will provide retirement income having a varying dollar value but a constant purchasing power. The theory of the variable annuity is that the prices of the stocks purchased by the annuity company will rise as fast as, and concurrently with, increases in the level of prices of consumer goods.

Vestibule training. Specialized instruction in a school situation that utilizes work processes and stations identical to those needed on the job.

Voluntary chain. A group of independent retailers who pool certain buying and distribution functions.

Warehouse receipt. A document, which may or may not be negotiable, used as evidence of the deposit of goods in a warehouse and for a contract for storage.

Warehousing. The storing of goods in large buildings until they are needed to meet consumer demand.

Wholesaler. One who buys and assembles goods in large lots from many producers and in turn sells goods in smaller quantities to many retailers.

Working capital. The amount of money available to a business to meet its daily operating costs; usually expressed as the excess dollar value of the current assets over the current liabilities.

Selected Readings

Part One

BUSINESS AND ITS ENVIRONMENT

Anderson, Ronald A., *Government and Business*, 3rd ed. (Cincinnati: South-Western Pub. Co., 1966).

Bunting, John R., *The Hidden Face of Free Enterprise* (N.Y.: McGraw-Hill Book Co., Inc., 1964).

Corley, Robert N., and Robert Black, *The Legal Environment of Business* (N.Y.: McGraw-Hill Book Co., Inc., 1963).

Davis, Keith, and Robert L. Blomstrom, *Business and Its Environment* (N.Y.: McGraw-Hill Book Co., Inc., 1966).

Dorfman, Robert, *Prices and Markets* (Englewood Cliffs, N.J.: Prentice-Hall, Inc., 1967).

Fox, Samuel, *Management and The Law* (N.Y.: Appleton-Century-Crofts, 1966).

Ganong, Carey K., and Richard W. Pearce, *Law and Society* (Homewood, Ill.: Richard D. Irwin, Inc., 1965).

Harriss, C. Lowell, *The American Economy—Principles, Practices, and Policies*, 5th ed. (Homewood, Ill.: Richard D. Irwin, Inc., 1965).

Lipsey, Richard G., and Peter O. Steiner, *Economics* (N.Y: Harper & Row, 1966).

MacGibbon, Elizabeth, *Fitting Yourself for Business,* 4th ed. (N.Y.: McGraw-Hill Book Co., Inc., 1961).

Mund, Vernon A., *Government and Business,* 4th ed. (N.Y.: Harper & Row, 1965).

Raphael, Jesse S., *Government Regulation of Business* (N.Y.: The Free Press, 1966).

Russon, Allen R., *Business Behavior,* 3rd ed. (Cincinnati: South-Western Pub. Co., 1964).

Smith, George Albert, and John B. Matthews, *Business, Society and the Individual,* rev. ed. (Homewood, Ill.: Richard D. Irwin, Inc., 1967).

Wilcox, Clair, *Public Policies toward Business,* 3rd ed. (Homewood, Ill.: Richard D. Irwin, Inc., 1966).

Wyatt, John W., and Madie B. Wyatt, *Business Law Principles and Cases,* 3rd ed. (N.Y.: McGraw-Hill Book Co., Inc., 1966).

Part Two
ORGANIZATION OF THE ENTERPRISE

Albert, Henry H., *Principles of Organization and Management,* 2nd ed. (N.Y.: John Wiley & Sons, Inc., 1966).

Alexis, Marcus, and Charles Z. Wilson, *Organizational Decision Making* (Englewood Cliffs, N.J.: Prentice-Hall, Inc., 1967).

Applewhite, Philip B., *Organizational Behavior* (Englewood Cliffs, N.J.: Prentice-Hall, Inc., 1965).

Ball, Gerald D., ed., *Organizations and Human Behavior* (Englewood Cliffs, N.J.: Prentice-Hall, Inc., 1967).

Broom, H. N., and Justin G. Longenecker, *Small Business Management,* 2nd ed. (Cincinnati: South-Western, Pub. Co., 1966).

Dale, Ernest, *Management: Theory and Practice* (N.Y.: McGraw-Hill Book Co., Inc., 1965).

Higginson, M. Valliant, *Management Policies, Vol. I: Their Development as Corporate Guides,* AMA Research Study 76. (N.Y.: American Management Assn., Inc., 1966).

Monsen, R. Joseph, and Mark W. Cannon, *The Makers of Public Policy: American Power Groups and Their Ideologies* (N.Y.: McGraw-Hill Book Co., Inc., 1965).

Monsen, R. Joseph, and Borje O. Saxberg, *Introduction to Business Readings* (N.Y.: Houghton Mifflin Co., 1967).

Wadia, M. S., *The Nature and Scope of Management,* 3rd ed. (Chicago: Scott, Foresman & Co., 1966).

Weimer, Arthur M., *Business Administration: An Introductory Management Approach* (Homewood, Ill.: Richard D. Irwin, Inc., 1966).

Wickesberg, Albert K., *Management Organization* (N.Y.: Appleton-Century-Crofts, 1966).

Part Three
TOOLS FOR MANAGERIAL CONTROL

Awad, Elias M., *Business Data Processing,* 2nd ed. (Englewood Cliffs, N.J.: Prentice-Hall, Inc., 1968).

Backer, Morton, *Modern Accounting Theory* (Englewood Cliffs, N.J.: Prentice-Hall, Inc., 1966).

Butler, William F., and Robert A. Kavesh, *How Business Economists Forecast* (Englewood Cliffs, N.J.: Prentice-Hall, Inc., 1966).

Dubois, Edward, *Essential Methods in Business Statistics* (N.Y.: McGraw-Hill Book Co., Inc., 1964).

Folsom, Marion B., *Executive Decision Making* (N.Y.: McGraw-Hill Book Co., Inc., 1962).

Guthrie, Harold W., *Statistical Methods in Economics* (Homewood, Ill.: Richard D. Irwin, Inc., 1966).

Jackson, Thomas W., and Jack M. Spurlock, *Research and Developmental Management* (Homewood, Ill.: Richard D. Irwin, Inc., 1966).

Kohler, Eric L., *Accounting for Management* (Englewood Cliffs, N.J.: Prentice-Hall, Inc., 1965).

Moore, Carl L., and Robert L. Jaedicke, *Managerial Accounting*, 2nd ed. (Cincinnati: South-Western Pub. Co., 1967).

Richards, Max D., and Paul S. Greenlow, *Management Decision Making* (Homewood, Ill.: Richard D. Irwin, Inc., 1966).

Stockton, John R., *Introduction to Business and Economic Statistics*, 3rd ed. (Cincinnati: South-Western Pub. Co., 1966).

Strong, Earl P., *Increasing Office Productivity* (N.Y.: McGraw-Hill Book Co., Inc., 1962).

Part Four

OPERATIONS OF THE ENTERPRISE

Cartter, Allan M., and F. Ray Marshall, *Labor Economics Wages, Employment and Trade Unionism* (Homewood, Ill.: Richard D. Irwin, Inc., 1967).

Chamberlain, Neil W., *Sourcebook on Labor* (N.Y.: McGraw-Hill Book Co., Inc., 1966).

Davis, Keith, *Human Relations at Work: The Dynamics of Organizational Behavior*, 3rd ed. (N.Y.: McGraw-Hill Book Co., Inc., 1967).

Gitlow, Abraham L., *Labor and Industrial Society*, rev. ed. (Homewood, Ill.: Richard D. Irwin, Inc., 1963).

Heckmann, I. L., *Human Relations in Management* (Cincinnati: South-Western Pub. Co., 1967).

Jucius, Michael J., *Personnel Management*, 6th ed. (Homewood, Ill.: Richard D. Irwin, Inc., 1967).

Moore, Harry D., and Donald R. Kibbey, *Manufacturing Materials and Processes* (Homewood, Ill.: Richard D. Irwin, Inc., 1965).

Owens, Richard N., *Management of Industrial Enterprises*, 5th ed. (Homewood, Ill.: Richard D. Irwin, Inc., 1965).

Pigors, Paul, and Charles A. Myers, *Personnel Administration*, 5th ed. (N.Y.: McGraw-Hill Book Co., Inc., 1965).

Sayles, Leonard R., and George Strauss, *Human Behavior in Organizations* (Englewood Cliffs, N.J.: Prentice-Hall, Inc., 1966).

Slone, Arthur, and Fred Whitney, *Labor Relations* (Englewood Cliffs, N.J.: Prentice-Hall, Inc., 1967).

Smith, Henry Clay, *Sensitivity to People* (N.Y.: McGraw-Hill Book Co., Inc., 1966).

Strauss, George, and Leonard R. Sayles, *Personnel: The Human Problems of Management*, 2nd ed. (Englewood Cliffs, N.J.: Prentice-Hall, Inc., 1967).

Timms, Howard L., *The Production Function in Business: Management Decision Systems*, rev. ed. (Homewood, Ill.: Richard D. Irwin, Inc., 1966).

Part Five

FINANCIAL MANAGEMENT

Athearn, James L., *Risk and Insurance* (N.Y.: Appleton-Century-Crofts, 1962).

Brands, L. K., *Business Finance* (Englewood Cliffs, N.J.: Prentice-Hall, Inc., 1965).

Eiteman, Wilford J., Charles A. Dice, and David K. Eiteman, *The Stock Market*, 4th ed. (N.Y.: McGraw-Hill Book Co., Inc., 1966).

Federal Reserve System, *The Federal Reserve System Purposes and Functions* (Washington D.C.: Board of Governors of the Federal Reserve System, 1963).

Huebner, S. S., and Kenneth Black, Jr., *Life Insurance* (N.Y.: Appleton-Century-Crofts, 1964).

Institute of Life Insurance, *Life Insurance Fact Book* (N.Y.: Institute of Life Insurance).

Loll, Leo M., and Julian G. Buckley, *The Over-the-Counter Securities Markets*, 2nd ed. (Englewood Cliffs, N.J.: Prentice-Hall, Inc., 1967).

National Consumer Finance Assn., *Finance Facts Yearbook* (Washington, D.C.: National Consumer Finance Assn.).

Osborn, R. C., *Business Finance* (N.Y.: Appleton-Century-Crofts, 1965).

Robbins, Sidney, *The Securities Markets* (N.Y.: The Free Press, 1966).

Walker, Ernest W., *Essentials of Financial Management* (Englewood Cliffs, N.J.: Prentice-Hall, Inc., 1965).

Part Six
MARKET MANAGEMENT

Adams, Charles F., *Common Sense in Advertising* (N.Y.: McGraw-Hill Book Co., Inc., 1965).

Alderson, Wroe, and Michael H. Halbert, *Marketing and Society* (Englewood Cliffs, N.J.: Prentice-Hall, Inc., 1967).

Buell, Victor P., *Marketing Management in Action* (N.Y.: McGraw-Hill Book Co., Inc., 1966).

Dowd, Laurence P., *Principles of World Business* (Boston: Allyn & Bacon, Inc., 1965).

Duncan, Delbert J., and Charles F. Phillips, *Retailing: Principles and Methods*, 7th ed. (Homewood, Ill.: Richard D. Irwin, Inc., 1967).

Hansen, Harry L., *Marketing: Text, Techniques, and Cases*, 3rd ed. (Homewood, Ill.: Richard D. Irwin, Inc., 1967).

King, Audrey Marsh, and Walton C. Marsh, *Adventures in Export* (Belleville, Ill.: Marsh Publishing Co., 1964).

Locklin, D. Philip, *Economics of Transportation*, 6th ed. (Homewood, Ill.: Richard D. Irwin, Inc., 1966).

Pederson, Carlton A., and Milburn D. Wright, *Salesmanship: Principles and Methods*, 4th ed. (Homewood, Ill.: Richard D. Irwin, Inc., 1966).

Root, Franklin R., Roland L. Kramer, and Maurice Y. d'Arlin, *International Trade and Finance*, 2nd ed. (Cincinnati: South-Western Publ. Co., 1966).

Stanton, William J., *Fundamentals of Marketing* (N.Y.: McGraw-Hill Book Co., Inc., 1964).

Still, Richard R., and Edward W. Cundiff, *Essentials of Marketing* (Englewood Cliffs, N.J.: Prentice-Hall, Inc., 1966).

Wirsig, Woodrow, ed., *Advertising—Today/Yesterday/Tomorrow* (N.Y.: McGraw-Hill Book Co., Inc., 1963).

Part Seven
LOOKING TOWARD THE FUTURE

Barach, Arnold R., *U.S.A. and Its Economic Future* (N.Y.: The Macmillan Co., 1964).

Calder, Nigel, ed., *The World in 1984*, Vols. I and II (Baltimore, Md.: Penguin Books, 1965).

Gabor, Dennis, *Inventing the Future* (N.Y.: Alfred A. Knopf, Inc., 1964).

McGuire, Joseph W., *Business and Society* (N.Y.: McGraw-Hill Book Co., Inc., 1963).

Tax Foundation, Inc., *Facts and Figures on Government Finance* (N.Y.: Tax Foundation Inc., 1967).

Walton, Scott D., *American Business and Its Environment* (N.Y.: The Macmillan Co., 1966).

Withers, William, *Business in Society* (N.Y.: Appleton-Century-Crofts, 1966).

Index

Trends of Stocks, Bonds, Profits, Business, and Commodities Since 1920

February 12, 1968

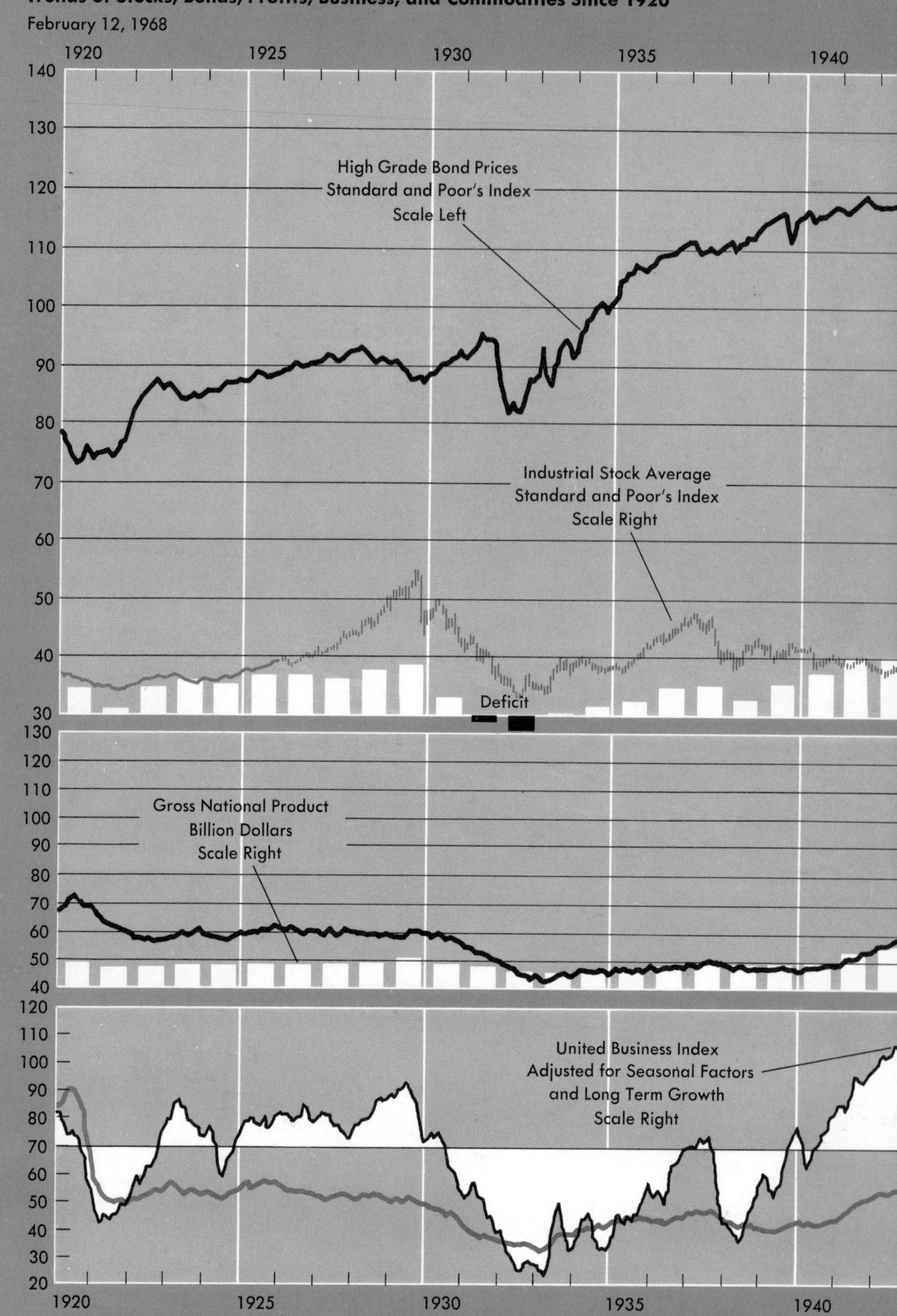